Lessons from a Successfully Export-Oriented, Resource-Rich Economy

"Morris Altman's text breathes new life into Canadian economic history by taking us back to big questions about the sources of successful development of small open economies. Altman demonstrates that plurality of economic theory is a richer approach to understanding the complexity of economic development, and variations in outcomes for economies and individuals in them, than a singular neoclassical economics focus that dominates most texts. Altman reminds us of the importance of investing time and energy into developing quality data suitable for answering the questions we have, rather than fitting our questions to whatever data we believe we have. Econometric methods are complementary inputs to quality data, rather than substitutes for salvaging the utility of flawed data. For students, theory, data and institutions combine, in this impressive book, to develop a provocative narrative that will allow them to recognize multidisciplinary linkages across courses in their studies."

—Herb Emery, *Professor of Economics and Vaughn Chair in Regional Economics, Department of Economics, University of New Brunswick, Canada*

"This worthy volume brings together much of Professor Altman's ground-breaking research into Canadian economic history. The diversity of topics reflects the controversies and complexity of the Canadian economy itself. The result is a well-written treatment of successful economic development in the face of unique challenges."

—Kris Inwood, *Professor of History and Economics, University of Guelph, Canada*

"There has been an absence in recent years of a comprehensive synthesis and overview of recent work in Canadian cliometrics providing a thematic narrative of Canadian economic history and this is a welcome addition that in the fullness of time shall go on to become a standard reference."

—Livio di Matteo, *Professor of Economics, Department of Economics, Lakehead University, and Adjunct Professor of History, Department of History, Lakehead University, Canada*

"Throughout his career, Morris Altman has addressed important questions in Canadian economic history with theory and data, a true cliometrician. The theory he favors has a greater social dimension than that used by many cliometricians; the data is carefully collected, often constructed, to meet the assumptions of the theory. The result, as this book demonstrates, is a cohesive, personal view of how the Canadian economy developed. This compilation of Altman's work covers two and a half centuries, from the late-seventeenth to the mid-twentieth. It tackles both macro- and micro-economic questions and demonstrates that Canada is indeed one of the world's success stories."

—Louis B. Cain, *Professor Emeritus, Economics, Quinlan School of Business, Loyola University of Chicago and Adjunct Professor Northwestern University, USA*

Morris Altman

Lessons from a Successfully Export-Oriented, Resource-Rich Economy

Quantitative Adventures into Canada's Past

palgrave
macmillan

Morris Altman
School of Business
University of Dundee
Dundee, Scotland, UK

ISBN 978-3-031-03886-0 ISBN 978-3-031-03887-7 (eBook)
https://doi.org/10.1007/978-3-031-03887-7

This Palgrave Macmillan imprint is published by the registered company Springer Nature Switzerland AG
The registered company address is: Gewerbestrasse 11, 6330 Cham, Switzerland

To my mentor and friend, the late Professor Harold (H.R.C.) Wright

Acknowledgments

This has been a long project constantly interrupted by other commitments. Chris Hajzler (now Dr.) was my first RA on this project, back in 2002–2003, when he was an undergrad at the University of Saskatchewan. He's now a Director with the Bank of Canada. He did a fantastic job! Many thanks. More recently, Ruth Bickerton was my RA at the University of Dundee. She was followed by Eric Brown. Many thanks to you both. I also must thank Louise Lamontagne (my wife and partner for over 40 years) and Hannah Altman (my daughter, now an economist) for their many comments and suggestions and support.

Contents

List of Figures

Chapter 5

Chapter 11

Chapter 12

List of Tables

Chapter 4

Chapter 5

Chapter 6

Chapter 7

Chapter 8

Chapter 9

Chapter 10

Chapter 11

Chapter 12

Chapter 13

Chapter 14

CHAPTER 1

Introduction: Quantitative Economics in a Canadian Context

1 Introduction: What's the Point?

This book is a product of my thinking and writing about some challenging questions in Canadian economic history which have implications for our understanding of important issues related to economic development, institutions, gender and power. This book is also a narrative about the implications of the careful and considered construction of data sets for a richer understanding of the past, especially when informed by an open-minded, more pluralistic, application of economic theory to the data and the challenging questions before us. I focus on issues, debates, controversies related to economic growth and development, the role of institutions and policy in the growth and development process, gender pay inequality, and the evolution of real wages in Canada. I pay special attention to the economic evolution of Early Canada (pre-Conquest), the economic development of Quebec in the later nineteenth century, the role of high wage in spurring economic growth, the gendered sectoral distribution of employment in the late nineteenth-early twentieth century and its impact on the gender pay gap, and the importance of staples to Canada's growth and development process, particularly in the 1870–1920 period.[1]

Underpinning the argument presented in this book and the hypotheses tested here is the construction new data sets designed to help address the questions and issues raised. This takes us back to late seventeenth century during which time a relative abundance of data is available to

M. Altman, *Lessons from a Successfully Export-Oriented, Resource-Rich Economy*, https://doi.org/10.1007/978-3-031-03887-7_1

piece together estimates for real gross national product and gross and net income per farm holding (held by the 'tenant' under the seigneurial system of land tenure.) Such data construction and re-construction forms the underbelly for the interpretive narrative presented in all of the chapters in this book.

Because the significance of all things empirical, this book sits somewhat in the tradition of the New Economic History which has been more formally named as Cliometrics.[2] For many practitioners, Cliometrics refers to the rigorous application of economic theory and econometrics to address and reassess fundamental questions in economic history. For many, theory and econometrics dominates a robust understanding of the past and of the data one inputs into one's econometric models. Moreover, there has been an undue reliance on 'neoclassical' theory as opposed to being more open to alternative theoretical perspectives to inform the analysis at hand. Amongst the early pioneers of the Cliometric 'revolution' are: Alfred H. Conrad, John R. Meyer, William Parker, Ken Fogel, Douglass North, Robert Gallman, Angus Maddison, and in Canada, M.A.C. Urquhart, K. A. H. Buckley, O.J. Firestone, Gordon Bertram, and Ed Safarian. As an historical footnote, I should add that Buckley and Safarian did much of their pioneering research at my old home base at the University of Saskatchewan. And, Marvin McInnis who also made significant contribution in this area, received his early training at this same university. I was fortunate enough to be mentored by Robert Gallman when he happened to come across my research on Early Canada and by Angus Maddison during my reworking of Canada real GDP estimates for the post-Confederation, pre-Great Depression period. I was also fortunate enough to discuss aspects of my research with M.A.C. Urquhart and Marvin McInnis, although we did not always see eye-to-eye on the questions at hand.

Where my research is situated in the domain of economic history was very much influenced by my primary PhD supervisor at McGill University the late Harold (H.R.C.) Wright, who emphasized the importance of the quality of the historical data one uses, its representativeness, the significance of being open to different and alternative economic models (methodological pluralism),and the importance of asking challenging questions that will help enrich our understanding of the past and the present through the lenses of the past, even if such questions might be upsetting to the power that be in the academic community. Wright, himself, was an economic historian, but one who had a very nuanced understanding of the history of his area of study as well as the source data that he used to construct his historical analytical narrative (see, for example, Wright 1955, 1961). I was also influenced by what was, in the 1970s and early 1980s, a very pluralistic economics department, where multiple theoretical perspectives were taught and debated and where economic history, history of economic thought, institutional economics, as well as different perspectives on economic theory, and even econometrics, held pride of place.

This book is very much an analytical one, informed by theory, based on constructing and reconstructing pertinent data sets. It is not a neoclassical-rooted econometric revision of Canadian economic history. My view is that economic historians are unique scholars; they are not econometricians who use historical data (without necessarily understanding these data) to test particular hypotheses. This would be especially the case where the focus of the statistical analysis is on tests of statistical significance as opposed to size effect, variance, the representativeness of the sample and, of course, the model that informs the statistical analysis.[3] An economic historian should be someone with a nuanced and deep understanding of the past and who is also well versed in economic theory and in the practice of historical data construction. Without properly constructed data sets, with assumptions clearly specified, any econometric analysis of the data, poorly constructed, is of little scientific value. In this sense, the chapters in this book are very in line with the contributions of Gallman, Maddison, Buckley, and Urquhart. Their approach remains a valid and necessary approach to economic history. But the additional value added of my book, which builds upon the pillars of data construction and reconstruction, is the economic analysis and reinterpretation of important questions in Canada's past which also has some relevance to our understanding of contemporary economic questions and issues, such as economic development, the importance of institutions to economic outcomes, and the role of gender equity in the labour maket.

2 Some Context

Before immersing ourselves more fully into some of the important details and debates regarding Canada's economic past, we need to orient ourselves by racing ahead and looking at the end of our story. Where does the Canadian economy stand today? I argue that Canada's past economic performance was largely a success. But has Canada's economic success faltered; has Canada's past experience acted as a break on its future efforts at economic development and growth? There are, needless to say, many conflicting interpretations as to the general direction of Canada's past as well as her future course of economic development. This book adds to this debate, focusing on the pre-1930 period and, hopefully, serves to clarify some pertinent issues and to re-orient some of the discussion.

Examples of clearly contrasting views on the Canadian economic development are expressed by Tom Naylor and Michael Bliss. Naylor (1972, 1975), in a highly influential and controversial work, argued that the particularities of Canada's economic evolution has meant that Canada entered the present century encumbered by a colonial and structurally flawed economy and, as a result, its economic performance to that date had been weak and our future prospects appeared dismal. Michael Bliss (1970, 1987), on the other hand, believed that Canada's development, while marked by many ups and downs, was on the whole a success story, one where the Canadian entrepreneur has been a vital force in the development process. The story told in this book is clearly supportive of Bliss' worldview, at least with regards to the relative success of Canada's early development performance.

It is useful to place this historical narrative in terms of where Canada is currently situated in terms of constant dollar or real total output per person. This measure provides us with some sense of the *potential* level of material wellbeing available, on average, in a country. This extends the narrative presented in Chapter 2, where revised historical real output estimates are presented and demonstrate the overall success of the Canadian economy post-Confederation up to the Great Depression period. Given the various debates on Canadian economic development, it would be useful to know if Canada has fallen from grace given the successes it achieved in the decades immediately following Confederation in 1867.

I also draw upon the United Nations' Human Development Report (2018) to position Canada globally in the context of a wider array of estimates. These estimates (the Human Development Index or HDI) incorporate total output as well as life expectancy and educational attainment. To get ahead of ourselves, both sets of estimates support the view that overall Canada has done rather well for itself, so that by the first part of the twenty-first century it ranks as one of the top countries in the world from various methodologically perspectives. There is, however, some evidence that Canada's position is heading in the wrong direction—albeit it is certainly not crashing downwards.

But as history clearly demonstrates, no path of economic and social development, once taken, is irreversible. Much depends on government policy. For this very reason, countries such as Canada, blessed with endowments of market valued natural resources, can achieve very high level of wellbeing, conditional on government policy and the institutional parameters within which decision are made. There is no such a thing as a staple trap (Sachs and warner 2001; see also Boyce and Herbert Emery). Being well endowed with staples does not mean that one is doomed to economic failure. Staples is a resource that can provide significant advantages to a country if well harvested. And institutional design, the quality of government, as well as the preferences of decision-makers are critical to determining the success or failure of a staple-related economy, just as these variables critically determine the future of economies not well endowed with staples.

In Table 1, data are presented on real or constant dollar output (in terms of Gross National Income) per capita in the of purchasing power parity (PPP) international dollars for the top ranked economies and their ranking. Also, presented is the HDI index for the top-ranked countries and their ranking. But in Table 1 countries that are top-ranked for HDI with these countries' rankings for real output per person is offered. Hence, top-ranking per capita GNI economies that fall below the top-28 HDI economies are not included. Amongst these are the oil and gas reliant economies: Qatar, Brunei Darussalam, Kuwait, and Saudi Arabia. We use data for 1990, 2000, 2010, and 2018. We also add relatively low ranked Argentina, a serious and successful 'staple' economy in the late nineteenth century (see Chapter 2). And we add rapidly growing China and India into the mix as a point of comparison especially given the fact that these two countries, combined, comprise almost 40% of the world's population of 7.6 billion. I've bolded those countries where staples are of some importance such as in Norway, Canada, New Zealand, and the United Arab Emirates.

Canada has dropped in its HDI ranking from 1 to 14 from 1990 to 2018. However, its HDI index in 2018 of 0.93 is almost identical to that of countries ranked 6th to 11th with 0.94. Switzerland and Norway are ranked 1 and 2 respectively with a rounded number HDI of 0.96. Therefore there is not much of a difference between Norway and Canada. So, at least in terms of the HDI, this more inclusive measure of well-being, Canada has continued to do pretty well, even though Canada's ranking has fallen. Inclusive of Canada and Norway, other staple related

Table 1 Human Development Index, Real Gross Nation Income (GNI) per capita (2017 PPP 2017 Dollars), and Rankings

	1990		*2000*		*2010*		*2018*		*1990*		*2000*		*2010*		*2018*		*2018*
	HDI	Rank	HDI	Rank	HDI	Rank	HDI	Rank	GNI/Pop	Rank	GNI/Pop	Rank	GNI/Pop	Rank	GNI/Pop	Rank	Pop millions
Switzerland	0.84	5	0.9	4	0.94	1	0.96	-	58,955	7	64,638	8	70,348	6	69,243	5	8.5
Norway	**0.85**	**4**	**0.92**	**1**	**0.94**	**2**	**0.96**	**1**	**40,544**	**13**	**55,613**	**10**	**61,156**	**9**	**66,180**	7	**5.3**
Ireland	0.77	23	0.87	14	0.9	18	0.95	2	24,384	36	41,963	21	44,852	21	65,762	8	4.8
Hong Kong, China (SAR)	0.78	19	0.83	25	0.9	16	0.95	3	27,931	30	36,633	29	52,435	13	63,984	9	7.4
Germany	0.81	11	0.88	9	0.93	4	0.95	4	37,232	16	42,616	19	47,860	19	55,155	17	83.1
Iceland	0.81	12	0.87	13	0.9	19	0.95	5	30,975	26	37,573	28	37,239	31	54,960	18	0.3
Singapore	0.72	42	0.82	27	0.91	12	0.94	6	37,076	17	55,809	9	77,505	5	88,099	3	5.8
Denmark	0.81	13	0.87	11	0.92	6	0.94	7	38,022	14	47,958	15	51,778	15	57,553	13	5.8
Netherlands	0.84	6	0.88	6	0.92	5	0.94	8	36,548	19	48,502	13	52,431	14	57,014	14	17.1
Sweden	0.82	8	0.9	3	0.91	10	0.94	9	33,934	23	41,236	22	49,800	16	54,020	19	10
Finland	0.79	17	0.86	15	0.92	8	0.94	10	32,063	25	39,633	25	46,463	20	48,360	21	5.5
Australia	**0.87**	**1**	**0.9**	**2**	**0.93**	**3**	**0.94**	**11**	**30,297**	**29**	**37,638**	**27**	**43,580**	**24**	**48,024**	**24**	**24.9**
United States	0.87	2	0.89	5	0.92	7	0.93	12	40,942	11	50,663	11	55,421	10	62,667	10	327.1
Belgium	0.81	10	0.88	7	0.91	11	0.93	13	35,737	21	44,239	17	48,791	18	51,619	20	11.5
Canada	**0.85**	**3**	**0.87**	**12**	**0.9**	**17**	**0.93**	14	**30,822**	**27**	**36,323**	**30**	**44,190**	**23**	**48,292**	**22**	**37.1**
United Kingdom	0.78	20	0.87	10	0.91	9	0.93	15	30,456	28	38,271	26	42,183	27	45,686	26	67.1
New Zealand	**0.83**	7	**0.88**	**8**	**0.91**	**13**	**0.93**	**16**	**26,183**	**33**	**30,182**	**34**	**34,780**	**34**	**40,559**	**31**	**4.7**

	1990		2000		2010		2018		1990		2000		2010		2018		2018
Liechtenstein	.	-	0.86	16	0.9	14	0.92	17	62,153	5	94,254	2	86,670	3	130,748	1	0.00004
Austria	0.8	14	0.85	21	0.9	15	0.92	18	37,994	15	46,309	16	52,564	12	55,533	15	8.9
Japan	0.82	9	0.86	19	0.89	24	0.92	19	32,323	24	36,045	31	38,455	29	42,564	29	127.2
Israel	0.8	15	0.86	17	0.9	21	0.92	20	23,668	38	29,644	37	34,306	36	39,568	33	8.4
Luxembourg	0.8	16	0.86	18	0.9	20	0.91	21	70,538	3	93,991	3	79,133	4	72,476	4	0.6
Korea (Republic)	0.73	37	0.82	26	0.89	23	0.91	22	12,655	63	22,825	42	34,480	35	42,002	30	51.2
Spain	0.76	26	0.83	24	0.87	27	0.91	23	27,327	31	34,583	32	36,844	32	40,419	32	46.7
Slovenia	0.77	22	0.83	23	0.89	22	0.91	24	22,042	40	26,249	40	33,058	39	37,423	36	2.1
France	0.79	18	0.85	20	0.88	25	0.9	25	33,981	22	40,512	23	43,282	25	46,537	25	65
Czechia	0.74	31	0.8	31	0.87	28	0.9	26	23,867	37	24,568	41	31,046	40	37,294	37	10.7
United Arab Emirates	**0.72**	**40**	**0.78**	**40**	**0.82**	**43**	**0.89**	**27**	**102,433**	**1**	**104,640**	**1**	**54,911**	**11**	**67,195**	**6**	**9.6**
Italy	0.78	21	0.84	22	0.88	26	0.89	28	36,282	20	43,098	18	42,782	26	42,657	28	60.6
Argentina	**0.72**	**43**	**0.78**	**41**	**0.83**	**40**	**0.84**	**47**	**13,597**	**59**	**18,179**	**46**	**22,727**	**52**	**21,918**	**61**	**44.4**
China	0.5	103	0.59	113	0.7	102	0.76	83	1469	169	3417	134	8847	110	15,187	78	1427.6
India	0.43	114	0.5	127	0.58	135	0.64	131	1787	159	2548	151	4182	139	6427	128	1352.6

Source Human development report, data center. Available at: http://hdr.undp.org/en/data

economies such as Australia, New Zealand also are highly ranked in terms of the HDI. In terms of real output per capita, Canada's ranking improved from 27 to 22 from 1990 to 2018. This places Canada ahead of Australia and the United Kingdom, its former colonial 'master. The United States remains well ahead of Canada, as it was in the early twentieth century (Chapter 2). But America's very high real per capita output has not driven its HDI above Canada's because of its relatively poor showing in education and life expectancy. This relates to the two countries different social infrastructure which falls in Canada's favour.

Argentina is introduced since it was once one of the formidable staple economies in the late nineteenth and early twentieth centuries, ranking amongst the top of the world in terms of real per capita output (Chapter 2). However, it's fortunes had fallen dramatically by the end of the twentieth century (it's fall began well before). Its performance is now relatively weak both in terms of the HDI and real per capita output, although it has been experiencing a turn-aroundin recent years. As mentioned above, being resource rich, in and of itself, is no golden nugget, and is no guarantee for sustained economic growth and development. Argentina experienced a series of dictatorships and corrupt regimes and this element of political economy no doubt negatively impacted Argentina's ability to positively exploit its staple endowment. And then we have India and China, certainly not staple type economies (but where exports of non-staples are important). Here the improvements in the real per capita output and the HDI have been dramatic, especially in China. Neither country suddenly discovered huge reserves of staples to facilitate rapid growth and economic development. Rather, in China, Deng Xiaoping led China's break with 'Maoist' extreme statist policies toward state direct market-oriented policy in 1978 and then again, more forcefully, in 1992. In the early 1990s, democratic India began to break with its statist (not very market sensitive) economic regime. Regime change, with no staples, to help things along, appears to have played a fundamentally important role in driving these two vast economies forward. To reiterate a point, staples aren't everything. It should be noted that both countries remain relatively poor even as they have experienced unprecedented economic growth. China's real per capita output was 32% of Canada's in 2018 and India's was 13% of Canada's at this time.

Canada's context can be visualized when looking at Fig. 1. Here I correlate the countries HDI's with their real per capita out (per capita GNI) for 2018 as presented in Table 1. We can now see from this diagram

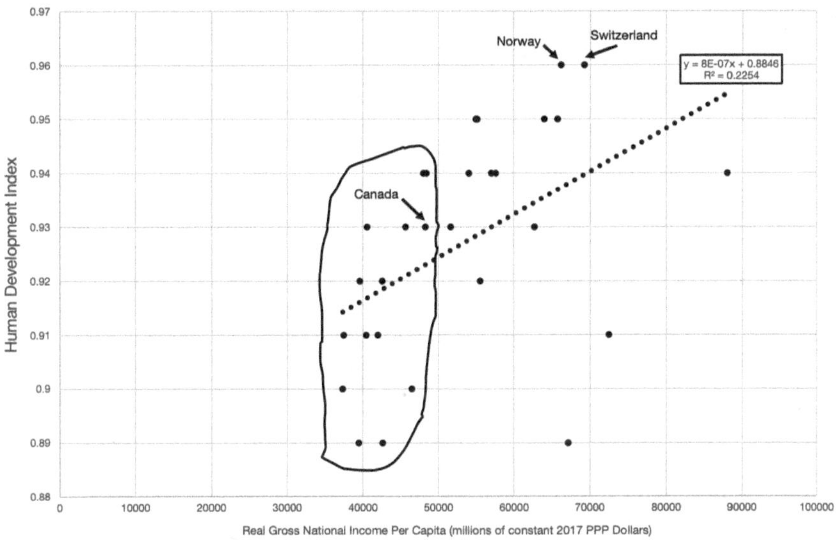

Fig. 1 The Human development Index and Real Gross Nation Income 2018

how Canada has performed, relatively speaking, in terms of both the HDI and real per capita output, at least amongst the top-27 ranked HDI countries.[4] For the 27 countries included here, it bears repeating that Canada did quite well. Perhaps, of even greater interest, is that when one highlights (circled in black) countries with a similar level of real per capita output, Canada has achieved amongst the highest level on the HDI amongst these countries. A particular level of per capita output does not guarantee a high HDI. Overall, there is a strong positive relationship (correlation) of 0.26 between real per capita output and the level of a country's HDI. Realizing the highest possible level of the HDI was not possible without a relatively high level of real per capita output.

Source Table 1

So, Canada, even now well into t he twenty-first century, continues to perform strongly in the world economy, affirming Bliss' more optimistic perspective on the Canada's economy and confirming what I've found to be the case from a more New Economic History perspective presented in this book. But this narrative is not about proving that Canada's economy did wonderfully well, it is about determining how well it actually did historically and trying to resolve some of the important questions raised with regards to Canada's overall economic performance.

3 About This Book

In Chapter 2, "Growth Theory and Economic History: A Staple Perspective," the staple theory in introduced. It is a subset of the export-led growth hypothesis, designed to explain the growth and economic development of resource rich economies. It is a misunderstood theory seen to be at odds with the stylized facts of economic growth and development as well as with mainstream neoclassical wisdom. This chapter presents a brief and critical historiography of the staple theory and its critiques from which a simple model of staple growth and development is developed. It should be noted that staple theory underscores how critically important it is for internal factors to be appropriately developed and fostered if staple exports afre to be a driving force in the growth process. Data, focusing in the 1870–1930 period, are presented here which suggest that the staple theory remains an important holistic analytical tool to help explain issues of economic development and growth. Moreover, the data show that Canada, very much of a staple economy, thrived particularly at a time when exports boomed.

In Chapter 3, "Economic Growth and Development in Early Canada," original estimates of real gross domestic product, per capita GDP, and growth rates for early Canada or New France are presented for the 1695–1739. This is made possible by the fairly comprehensive and accurate censuses that are available to the researcher, particularly from 1680 to I739 period. These estimates challenge the view that early Canada's economy was stagnant and relatively impoverished and instead present this colony as relatively well off compared to the British American colonies. Exports played an important role here. But fundamentally important was the ability of Early Canada to positively respond to the challenge of an increasing population and expanding export markets. Ultimately, it is this flexibility that underlies the relatively robust nature of early Canada's economy.

Chapter 4 relates to Chapter 3. Newly developed data sets reveal that the seigneurial system of land tenure modified the distribution of income in early Canada or New France. This changed the structure of demand, and thus the pattern of investment, probably reducing total output of the colony from what it otherwise might have been. This contravenes the romantic narrative that, prior to the conquest of New France in 1763, the state protected the peasant from excessive seigniorial exactions. I find that seigniorial institutions measurably reduced the favourable bargaining position of the peasant by imposing levies that restrained the economic development of the colony, even though the peasants retained a rising portion of their economic surplus. Without seigniorial dues, New France would probably have produced more artisan and agricultural goods generating increasing returns to scale and fostering further economic development.

Moving on to the mid-nineteenth century, a crucial finding of Chapter 5, "Quebec Agriculture in the Mid-Nineteenth Century: Comparing French Canadian and Non-French Farmers," is that French Canadian farmers typically earned a lower agricultural income than their non-French Canadian counterparts did, irrespective of the system of land tenure, in the mid-nineteenth century. This is actually consistent with the finding of Lewis and McInnis (1980) that there was a measured productivity differential of between 8–18% in favour of English farms. The income of French farmers was further reduced by the tax imposed on them by the seigneurial system of land tenure. They were characterized by a much poorer productivity performance for all key outputs and typically operated on a much smaller scale than non-French Canadian farmers. But to complicate matters, in the Montreal area, French Canadian farmers earned a higher agricultural income than did non-French Canadian farmers in spite of they being less productive and smaller, taking good advantage of market opportunities where and when available. Some of the failings of French Canadian farmers can be attributed to institutional factors such as lack of agricultural education and the seigneurial tax.

Chapter 6, "Economic Development with High Wages," takes us to the immediate post-Confederation (1867) period. Evidence is presented in this chapter which challenges the general applicability of the hypothesis that low wages are necessary or, in the very least, conducive to higher rates of manufacturing employment growth. An analysis of the Canadian censuses and other material for Quebec and Ontario for the period 1870–1910 shows that Ontario's manufacturing sector grew at a faster pace than Quebec's despite the higher labor income in Ontario. The more productive labor inputs in Ontario more than compensated for the possible supply-side constraints which its relatively high-priced labor might have caused. I also find that the most immediate economic cause for Quebec's lag in per capita manufacturing output growth was its relatively slow rate of manufacturing employment growth.

Chapter 7, "Labour Productivity in Nineteenth Century Quebec and Ontario: Explaining Ontario's Advantage," continues the analytical narrative presented in Chapter 6. Historical causes of interregional differentials in labour productivity are identified which played, and still continues to play, an important role in explaining interregional and international differences in the amount of goods and services available per person. Specifically, possible causes are presented for the persistent and substantial differential in labour productivity throughout the 1870–1910 period favouring Ontario over Quebec manufacturing. The interprovincial disparity in labour productivity between Quebec and Ontario coexisted with a disparity in literacy and schooling. However, there is no evidence that Quebec is still behind in terms of quality of education while still lagging in productivity. Another reason for Quebec's lower productivity could be that low wages have had a negative impact on Quebec's development process by negatively affecting labour productivity while high wages have had the opposite effect in Ontario. Continued low wages could be a possible impediment to Quebec's capacity in catching up with Ontario.

In Chapter 8 and 9, the focus shifts to a critical analysis of leading arguments as to why Quebec's post-Confederation economic performance was well below than what some experts argue it should have been. In Chapter 8, "Resource Endowments and Economic Development," the hypothesis that a region's or nation's laggard industrial development can be explained by its relatively more expensive supplies of coal and iron ore is examined and challenged. A simple model, based on location theory, is developed. Using this model, I demonstrate the conditions under which this hypothesis holds. A case study of Quebec and Ontario industry suggests that the differential resource cost hypothesis seriously lacks explanatory power. Quebec's relatively poor economic performance cannot be explained by location and natural resource endowments. In Chapter 9, "Railways as an Engine of Economic Growth?" it is argued, contrary to the received view, that railways played a significant role in Quebec's economic growth through their impact upon railway-related industry over the period 1870 to 1910. I also find that Quebec drew considerably more federal government subsidies for railway construction than Ontario did on a per capita basis. The importance of railways to Canadian manufacturing growth is also assessed. These findings provide further evidence that generalizations from Fogel's classic study on railway-related backward linkages in the United States can be misplaced and misleading. They also contravene scholarly arguments that Quebec held the short end of the stick, and was discriminated against, during Canada's railway building boom.

In Chapters 10 and 11, the focus shifts to critical issues related to Canadian economic growth. In Chapter 10, "Manufacturing Growth in Canada and the Canadian Wheat Boom," revised estimates of real gross manufacturing output and growth are presented. Original estimates are also presented for real total value added, per capita and per employee value added in manufacturing, and their corresponding growth rates. These estimates involve the use of sector specific price indexes as opposed to an unweighted aggregate price index. Details on the construction of these indexes and output estimates are also presented. These estimates refute the received view (at the time) that Canada's manufacturing sector sustained steady and relatively vigorous growth over the entire 1870–1010 period. This narrative of steady as it goes growth was based on the then dominant data set for Canadian manufacturing developed by Gordon Bertram. My findings suggest that the growth performance of Canada's manufacturing sector became substantive only at the turn of the twentieth century. This affirms the hypothesis that there is a strong positive relationship between the wheat boom and intensive Canadian economic growth.

Chapter 11, "New Historical Canadian Output Estimates: Implications for an Understanding of Canadian Economic Development," takes us from the manufacturing sector to the Canadian economy as a whole. Revised Canadian real GNP estimates for the 1870–1926 period, based on the nominal GNP estimates constructed by M.C. Urquhart and on a variety of sector-specific price indexes, are presented in this chapter. The construction of this revised real GNP series allows for the creation of more robust real output estimates for the major sectors of the Canadian economy, a new implicit price index series, and real output estimates for the Canadian economy as a whole. These revised estimates cast new light on our understanding of Canadian economic growth and reinforces the view, presented in Chapter 10, that the Canadian wheat boom probably played an important and positive role in the process of Canadian economic development. The revised estimates, presented here and in Chapter 10, underlie the importance of using sector-specific price indexes to construct real national output estimates as opposed to using a de facto *unweighted* price index for the whole economy to covert current to constant dollar output estimates.

In Chapter 12, "How Long Did Canadian Workers Actually Work? The Struggle For a Shorter Work Week and Workers' Standards of Living Before the Great Depression," the first set of hours of work estimates constructed for Canada and its regions for the 1880–1930 period is presented. These estimates suggest a trend decline in hours of work, especially following the First World War. In addition, these estimates suggest that the decline in hours of work came at no or little cost in terms of real weekly income. The trends uncovered for Canada are found to be similar to those revealed for the U.S. In effect, by the early twentieth century workers were realizing their long-expressed preferences for a shorter workweek at no loss in real income. Workers do not appear to have preferred less work if this came at the cost of a lower level of material wellbeing. It is quite likely that workers' increased bargaining facilitated workers' realizing their preference for a shorter work week at no loss in weekly real income.

In Chapter 13, "Gender Pay Inequality and Occupational Change in Canada, in the Early Twentieth Century," co-authored by Louise Lamontagne, we turn our attention to the gender pay in Canada. Using Canadian censuses data, we construct some of the most detailed historical estimates for the industrialized world for occupational structure and the gender pay gap from 1900 to 1930. Our findings suggest that pay inequality in Canada diminished over the period under study, although the rate of pay received by women remained substantially below that of men. This decline is found to be due, to a large extent, to the changing occupational structure between women and men over time which involved both the gradual dominance of women in clerical work and the absence of any change in labour market segmentation. We also find that, for each year examined in this study, the differential distribution of women and men between sectors did not play a large role in accounting for the pay gap.

Chapter 14, "On the Natural Intelligence of Women: How the Feminization of Clerical Work Contributed to Gender Pay Equality in Early Twentieth Century Canada," also co-authored by Louise Lamontagne, we zero in on the importance of the feminization of clericalization to the evolution of the gender pay gap. More specifically, the impact of labor market segmentation on gender pay inequality is investigated through the example of the feminization of clerical work in Canada in the 1900–1930 period. We find that female clerical workers were paid well above what they could earn in other sectors, although they were consistently paid less than male clerical workers, albeit they were catching-up. Given that women could seek market employment and had some freedom in realizing their occupational preferences, women flocked into clerical work. Nevertheless, the demand and skill requirements for female clerical workers sufficed to keep the female wage buoyant. Therefore, the feminization of clerical work had no negative impact the negative impact on the gender pay gap in the clerical occupation. Rather, it contributed towards reducing the overall gender pay gap in the pre-Depression period. Given the constraints which they faced, women were making smart occupational choices. Given the evidence presented, the sources of gender pay inequality must be situated outside the domain of labor market segmentation.

4 Conclusion

Although many scholars have argued that Canada's economic performance has been and continues to be dismal, we have shown that Canada's current economic record stands out as one of the most respectable in the world economy. This was already the case by the beginning of the twentieth century. Also, Canada, what was the French colony along the St. Lawrence River, pre-British conquest, (1860) also did exceptionally well, in spite of the constraints imposed on its population by the French colonial authorities. This book, by empirically reconstructing aspects of Canada's past, attempts to address important questions related to Canada's economic performance pre and post Confederation and pre and post conquest of New France, with one eye on how the past can inform the present. But just as significantly this book is about the importance of robust data construction and analyses and theory for our understanding of the past.

Some of the key points made in this book are:

- The penultimate importance of how data sets are constructed for one's analysis.
- The importance of the theories one uses to inform one's analysis, but also how one constructs pertinent data sets.

- The economic performance of Early Canada and Canada, post-Confederation, was quite strong relative to other economies.
- A revised and reconstructed staple theory of economic development helps explain when and why staple exports can facilitate the process of economic development. Key to success are the internal socio-economic and institutional conditions of a country and understanding how efficiency and technical are very endogenously determined.
- The Seigneurial system of land tenure negatively affected the economic development of Early Canada and, also, of Quebec post-conquest. This is one important example of Douglas North's 'institutions matter' argument (also put forth by the 'early' institutional economist, John Commons).
- French farms did less well than English farms, on average, in terms of income and surplus generation in mid-nineteenth century Quebec. However, French farms did quite well, given the constraints and opportunities which French-Canadian farmers faced. On the other hand, French farms, especially those on the margin with regards to surplus production were left in a relatively more precarious position given the institutionally based charged imposed on them by their Seigneurs.
- Contrary to conventional wisdom, 'low wages' did not provide a competitive advantage to the Quebec economy relative to that of Ontario's. Rather, it most probably contributed to lower levels of productivity.
- Quebec's economic development was not disadvantaged by Canada's post-Confederation railway boom, rather it was advantaged.
- Location, lack of coal and iron ore, did not disadvantage Quebec's economic development. This is evidenced by the data and best explained through the prism of location theory.
- Using the most robust deflators for measures of nominal manufacturing output and total output (gross domestic product) has important implications for our understanding of Canadian economic growth in the 1870-in1926 period. Revised estimates reveal that there was a surge in Canada's economic growth that coincided with Canada's wheat export boom.
- Hours worker per week diminished per week in Canada from 1900 to the Great Depression period. Hence, workers won their battle for

a shorter work week. But this occurred whilst workers maintained or increased their real weekly income.

- The gender pay gap in Canada diminished, from 1870 to 1926, largely due to the increased dominance of women in clerical work which was the highest paid occupation for women at the time. Women choosing clerical work was a sensible choice given the constraints they faced.

Appendix: Book Chapters' Sources

The chapters of this book (apart from this introduction) are based on the following published papers:

Chapter Two: Altman, Morris (2003). "Staple Theory and Export-Led Growth: Constructing Differential Growth," *Australian Economic History Review*, 43: 230–255; Chapter Three: Altman, Morris (1988). "Economic Growth, Economic Structure, and Real Gross Domestic Product in Early Canada, 1695–1739: Estimates and Analysis," *William and Mary Quarterly*, 3rd series, 45: 684–711; Chapter Four: Altman, Morris (1983). "Seigniorial Tenure in New France, 1688–1739: An Essay on Income Distribution and Retarded Economic Development," *Historical Reflections/Réflexions historiques*, 10: 335–375; Chapter Five: Altman, Morris (1998). "Land Tenure, Ethnicity and the Condition of Agricultural Income and Productivity in Mid-Nineteenth Century Quebec," *Agricultural History*, 72: 708–762; Chapter Six: Altman, Morris (1988). "Economic Development with High Wages: An Historical Perspective," *Explorations in Economic History*, 25: 198–224; Chapter Seven: Altman, Morris (1995). "Labour Productivity in Late Nineteenth Century Quebec and Ontario Manufacturing: Explaining Ontario's Advantage," *American Journal of Canadian Studies*, 25: 219–249; Chapter Eight: Altman, Morris (1986). "Resource Endowments and Location Theory in Economic History: A Case Study of Quebec and Ontario at the Turn of the Twentieth Century," *Journal of Economic History*, 46: 999–1009; Chapter Nine: Altman, Morris (1989). "Railways as an Engine of Economic Growth? Who Benefited from the Canadian Railway Boom, 1870–1910?," *Histoire sociale/Social History*, 21: 269–281; Chapter Ten: Altman, Morris (1987). "A Revision of Canadian Economic Growth, 1870–1910: A Critique of the Gradualist Approach," *Canadian Journal of Economics/Revue canadienne d'économique*, 20:

86–113; Chapter Eleven: Altman, Morris (1992). "Revised Real GNP Estimates and Canadian Economic Development." *Review of Income and Wealth*, Series 38: 455–473; Chapter Twelve: Altman, Morris (1999). "New Estimates of Hours of Work and Real Income from the 1880s to 1930: Long Run Trends and Workers' Preferences," *Review of Income and Wealth*, Series 45: 353–372; Chapter Thirteen: Altman, Morris and Lamontagne, Louise (1996). "Gender Pay Inequality and Occupational Change in Canada, 1900–1930," *Journal of Socio-Economics*, 25: 285–309; and Chapter Fourteen: Altman, Morris and Lamontagne, Louise (2003). "On the Natural Intelligence of Women in a World of Constrained Choice: How the Feminization of Clerical Work Contributed to Gender Pay Equality in Early Twentieth Century Canada," *Journal of Economic Issues*, 37: 1045–1074.

Notes

1. This book is designed to address very specific questions which are very academic in nature, and are inclusive of very detailed discussions and documentation of data construction and the analytical questions at hand. To garner a more complete and holistic picture of Canada's economic history the following textbooks would be most helpful: Easterbrooke and Aitken (1988; 1958); Norrie, Owram and Emery (2007); Patterson and Marr (1980); and Pomfret (1981). See Geloso (2017), for an overview of Quebec economic history.
2. Although he was not, by any means a New Economic Historian, my research has been influenced by the research of Harold Innis, who pioneered the staple approach to Canadian economic history by combining narrative style with reference to pertinent bits and pieces of data.
3. The latter perspective is heavily influenced by the contributions of Deirdre McCloskey (see for example, McCloskey and Ziliak 2001 and McCloskey 1973, 2006), whose research is informed by a deep and nuanced understanding of the past plus an appreciation of strengths and limitations of statistical analysis in general.
4. Liechtenstein is excluded from this sample as it is a significant outlier with a very small population of about 33,000. It's real per capita output was about two and half times of Canada's in 2018, with a much lower HDI.

References

Bliss, Michael. 1970. "Canadianizing American Business: The Roots of the Branch Plant." In *Close the 49th Parallel, etc: The Americanisation of Canada*, ed. Ian Lumsden, 26–42. Toronto: University of Toronto Press.

Bliss, Michael. 1987. *Northern Enterprise: Five Centuries of Canadian Business.* Toronto: McClelland and Stewart, Inc.

Boyce, J. R., and J. C. Herbert Emery. 2011. "Is a Negative Correlation Between Resource Abundance and Growth Sufficient Evidence that there is a "Resource Curse"?" *Resources Policy* 36: 1–13.

Easterbrook, W. T., and H. Aitken. 1988. *Canadian Economic History, 1st published, 1956*. Toronto: Toronto University Press.

Geloso, V. 2017. *Rethinking Canadian Economic Growth and Development since 1900: The Quebec Case*. Cham, Switzerland: Palgrave Macmillan.

Lewis, F., and M. McInnis. 1980. "The Efficiency of the French-Canadian Farmer in the Nineteenth Century." *Journal of Economic History* 40: 497–514.

McCloskey, D. N. 1973. *Economic Maturity and Entrepreneurial Decline: British Iron and Steel, 1870–1913.* Cambridge, MA: Harvard University Press.

McCloskey, D. N., and S. T. Ziliak. 2001. *The Cult of Statistical Significance: How the Standard Error Costs Us Jobs, Justice, and Lives*. Ann Arbor, MI: University of Michigan Press.

McCloskey, D. N. 2006. *The Bourgeois Virtues: Ethics for an Age of Commerce.*, vol. 1. Chicago: University of Chicago Press.

Naylor, R. T. 1972. "The Rise and Fall of the Third Commercial Empire of the St. Lawrence." In *Capitalism and the National Question in Canada*, ed. Gary Teeple, 1–41. Toronto: University of Toronto Press.

Naylor, R. T. (1975). *The History of Canadian Business, 1867–1914, Vol. II, Industrial Development*. (Toronto: James Lorimer & and Company).

Norrie, K., D. Owram, and J.C.H. Emery. 2007. *History of the Canadian Economy*. Toronto: Nelson College.

Patterson, D.G., and W.L. Marr. 1980. *Canada: An Economic History*. Toronto: Macmillan.

Pomfret, R. 1981. *The Economic Development of Canada*. Toronto: Methuen.

Sachs, J. D., and A. Warner. 2001. "The Curse of Natural Resources." *European Economic Review* 45: 827–838.

United Nations Development Programme (2021). *Human Development Reports*. Accessed August 26, 2021. http://hdr.undp.org/en/humandev.

Wright, H. R. C. 1955. *Free Trade and Protection in the Netherlands, 1816–1830: A Study of the First Benelux*. Cambridge, UK: Cambridge University Press.

Wright, H.R.C. 1961. *East-Indian Economic Problems of the Age of Cornwallis & Raffles*. London: Luzac and Co.

PART I

A Staple Modeling Perspective of Successful Economic Growth

CHAPTER 2

Growth Theory and Economic History: A Staple Perspective

1 Introduction

The central proposition of this paper is that the staple theory of economic growth, originally based on the *ouevres* of Canadian economic historians, remains an important contemporary model and framework for economic analysis in spite of the forceful critiques of the staple theory put forth from the 1950s. I argue that the staple theory helps explain the causes of different real per capita gross domestic product (GDP) growth rates through time in a particular region or country and patterns of differential per capita growth rates between regions and countries. This is achieved by identifying the necessary conditions for exports to increase real per capita GDP growth from what it would be in the absence of such exports. Staple theory, therefore, contributes towards an explanation of the lack of convergence of real per capita GDP between regions and nations (Altman 1999b; Baumol 1986; DeLong 1988; Pritchett 1997). This stylized fact is a question of fundamental importance that remains to be addressed by economic theory. The staple theory, therefore, serves to complement the recent research in growth economics, which aspires to explain the persistence of differentials in per capita growth rates, and in real per GDP (Abramovitz 1986; Altman 1996, 2000; Arthur 1990; Grossman and Helpman 1994; Lucas 1988; Parente and Prescott 2000; Romer 1986).

Although one side of the analytical equation related to economic growth is represented by the relevant stylized facts, the other side of the

M. Altman, *Lessons from a Successfully Export-Oriented, Resource-Rich Economy*, https://doi.org/10.1007/978-3-031-03887-7_2

equation is represented by the theory that both purports to explain the stylized facts and plays a critical role in determining which stylized fact are of analytical importance. In a very importance sense, it is theory which determines whether or not a particular explanation is acceptable, not a particular set of facts and, moreover, it is theory which tends to guide and direct empirical analyses (Coase 1994, pp. 26–28). For this very reason, it is important to address the underlying causal assumptions of a staple theory of economic growth as well as those of the competing theoretical constructs used to critique the staple theory. Indeed, central aspects of the critiques of the staple theory, writ large, are theoretically based.

A fundamental underlying assumption of the staple theory is that in the absence of staple exports a region would be significantly poorer in terms of per capita GDP. In other words, all factor inputs are assumed not to be equally productive either in a static or dynamic sense. Following upon the various contributions to the development of the staple theory and related critiques, I construct a synthetic representation of this theory. This paper therefore represents a revision and refashioning of the classic exposition of the staple theory put forth by Watkins (1963). No attempt is made, however, to build a comprehensive and operational rendition of the staple theory by engaging in a textual account and discussion on what the original proponents of the staple thesis did or did not say. I argue that the staple theory is best viewed as an export-led growth theory, which incorporates both supply and demand sides into its modeling framework. The staple theory must articulate an understanding of the details of the supply-side as it relates to staple exports, which includes the question of technological change and technological transfer as they relate to the process of staple exports as well as an understanding of demand-side shifts, and both supply and demand elasticities. Also of fundamental importance are the possible linkages (and their determinants) which staple exports have upon the larger economy and, thereby, on the growth process. Moreover, the staple theory posits a positive causal relationship between the economic and social infrastructure of a region and the extent to which staple exports are realized and the extent to which they can positively affect real per capita GDP. In this sense, I argue that the path and pattern of per capita economic growth is, to an important extent a product of public policy and, therefore, fundamentally depends on the supply side of the economy providing the existence of a market for the export staple or staples.

2 The Legacy of Harold Innis

The staple theory was developed by Harold Innis, an economic historian cum institutional economist at the University of Toronto, to help explain the process of economic change in newly settled regions (such as Canada) with a relatively small base population and thus with a relative abundance of land and other natural resources. Innis believed that the economic evolution of Canada and like countries could not be satisfactorily explained by the theories of the time (1920s and 1930s). The staple theory was developed from a detailed and judicious analysis of the economic history of Canada; placing Canada in the context of economic, technological, informational, and institutional parameters of which it was part (see Innis, bibliography). His writings had an important influence both outside and inside Canada, affecting the writing of economic history and the development of economic theory internationally. (See, for example, Chambers and Gordon [1966], Caves [1965, 1971], Fogarty [1985], Galenson and Menard [1980], McCusker and Menard [1985], Pomfret [1981], Shedvin [1990], North [1955, 1959] and Watkins [1963].) The staple theory did not develop in a vacuum. In 1923, W. A. Mackintosh, incorporating, "...the basic facts of economic and historical geography," provided an important outline to the theory that Innis later developed and added much empirical weight to, in an era when Canadian history was being written largely in terms of individuals and politics (Mackintosh (1967, p. 15). See also Neill (1972, 1991) and Watkins (1963). Mackintosh argues that critical to the economic development of Canada and the United States was markets for staple products (with emphasis on raw materials) and the ability of people to overcome or take advantage of geographical factors to bring the staples to these markets competitively. Thus, staple exports serve to drive the development process, both in terms of intensive and extensive growth. Mackintosh acknowledges the influence of the work of Guy Callender (1902, 1903) on American economic development, where a clear connection between staples and economic development is articulated.

Innis argued that since the beginnings of European settlement the Canadian economy and society has been deeply affected by the production of staples, from cod, to fur, to timber, to wheat, to nickel, and hydroelectricity because of the economic advantages to be had from such exports. Initially staples were sought after since only by exporting staples to the home country in Europe at a profit could the new migrants realize a standard of material well being obtainable in Europe. In exchange for staples European goods could be purchased that contributed to a high level of material welfare in the colonies.[1] What Innis implicitly assumes is that if factors of production had been reallocated to non-staple production, real output per capita would have been lower than it actually was. Moreover, it was the potential profitability of staple products that attracted immigrants and, therefore, staple exports were strongly related to the process of extensive economic growth or the growth in total output.

In pursuit of profitable staples the settlers were constantly on the look out for new products, but just as keenly they were at work to reduce their production costs. In particular, they sought to modify and improve the transportation systems through which staples were exported and European goods imported. For this reason, the importance of transportation to the evolution of the Canadian economy should not be underestimated. Efforts to reduce production costs involved efforts by economic agents at the level of both the firm or farm and government. The staple theory is, therefore, very much a supply-side theory of economic development whereby a country's capacity to grow is determined by the ability of its people to competitively produce staple products for markets over which they have little control. Demand is exogenously determined. But staple producers can affect the costs of production (such as the cost of transportation), and thereby shift the supply curve of the staple product(s) to a competitive position. Once staples can be sold it is assumed that they yield a higher level of per capita output than could otherwise be achieved.

The importance of the supply-side to the staple theory is illustrated in Fig. 1. Whatever the price elasticity of demand, be it perfectly elastic (D_0) or somewhat inelastic (D_1), the staple producers can affect the course of economic development by affecting the supply curve. At (S_0) and (D_0) the staple product cannot be sold. But by reducing transportation costs, for example, the supply curve is shifted to (S_1) and the staple becomes marketable. Given the demand curve, further shifts in the supply curve yield further increases in staple exports. The demand-side is also of importance of course. The elasticity of demand affects the quantity that can be sold as prices fall (compare the quantity sold under (D_0) to that sold under (D_1)). And shifts in the demand curve as markets expand through increases in population or in disposable income per capita or through changes in tastes, improve the position of the staple producers irrespective of their supply curves. Given that the non-Canadian component of

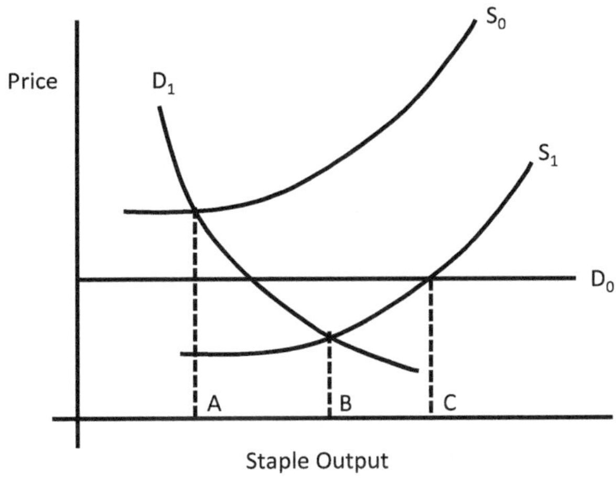

Fig. 1 Supply and demand and staple production

demand is exogenously determined, staple-led economic growth can only be driven domestically by shifts in the supply curve. In other words, shifts in the demand curve are not a necessary condition for export-led growth. On the other hand, given the demand curve, shifts in the supply curve are necessary to motivate the process of export-led growth.

This emphasis on the supply-side is consistent with Kravis' important critique of export-led growth theories, where he underlines the overriding importance of domestic supply-side variables to export-led growth. He argues: "The mainsprings of economic growth were internal; they must be sought in the land and the people and in the system of social and economic organization." Therefore, trade expansion should be viewed: "...as a handmaiden of growth rather than as an autonomous engine of growth" (Kravis 1970a, pp. 850, 859). Related to this, Rodriguez and Rodrik (1999, p. 39) find, "... that firms derive technological or other benefits from exporting per se; the more common pattern is that efficient producers tend to self-select into export markets. In other words, causality seems to go from productivity to exports [supply side changes], not vice versa." As North reiterates, growth can be export-led even if the mainsprings of trade expansion are found on the supply-side. For this reason, ignoring the supply side in investigating and identifying sources of export-led growth tends to paint an incomplete and misleading picture of the growth process.[2] What is of fundamental importance is whether or not staple exports, be they gotten by shifts in the demand or supply curve, underlie the process of per capita economic growth. In light of this discussion, it is important to note that there is strong evidence to support the proposition that staple exports have played an important role in driving the growth process in many countries in the twentieth century.[3]

Innis argues that a region's attachment to staple production tends to become cumulative. The production of staples results in staple producers becoming more efficient in their tasks and attracting more of a region's resources to the relatively and increasingly efficient staple industries. The economic evolution of the staple producing region becomes subordinate to staple production. This is true for the industry, trade, finance, and agriculture sectors as well for government activities. And the type of staple found in a country (its production function) plays a large role in determining the particular connection(s) between staples and the growth process. The continued dependence on staples also results in a country's dependence on export markets and on foreign supplies of manufactured goods. This can possibly result in a highly volatile economy, although characterized with a relatively high level of average per capita output.

3 The Staple Theory Refined

The staple theory has undergone many developments over the years, resulting in a richer and analytically more rigorous analytical framework. Of particular importance is the explicit introduction of the concept of economic linkages, which is related to input–output analysis pioneered by Wassily Leontief, (in this regard see Hirschman (1977), North (1955, 1959) and Watkins (1963). There are backward, forward, demand, and fiscal linkages. The backward and forward linkages refer to economic activities or industries related to the production and servicing of the staple and to the further processing of the staple respectively. Backward linkages refer not simply to activities related to the immediate production of the staple product, but also to the production of the infrastructure, such as transportation, necessary to make staple production economically viable. The more elaborate and substantial these linkages are, the greater the impact staple production can have upon the process of economic development. For many staple theorists these linkages are related to the production function of the staple product.

The demand linkage, which Innis paid little attention to, relates to the demand generated in the process of staple production. This demand can affect the development of new economic activities, in either the secondary or tertiary sectors of the economy, which serve to meet the needs of the staple producing population. When these economic activities serve local consumption needs, Douglass North refers to them as residentiary industries. The economies generated by these staple-linked industries can attract other industries to an area and some of these industries might even become export-oriented. If transportation costs were not important to their unit costs of production these industries would be footloose industries. Moreover, staple production and the economic linkages that they generate can also give rise to the growth of nodal centers that are home to staple and related industries (North, ibid.). Staple-linked demand, however, can always be used to import products instead of stimulating the growth of local industries. Watkins (1963, p. 144) summarizes the importance of linkages: "The central concept of a staple theory...is the spread effects of the export sector, that is, the impact of export activity on domestic economy and society. To construct a staple theory, then, it is necessary to classify these spread effects and indicate their determinants," Staple theorists at least implicitly assume that staple-related linkages generate a higher level of per capita output than would be produced in their absence. North (1955, 1959) is explicit in this point.

Directly related to the demand linkage of staple exports is the distribution of income. Baldwin (1956) makes the case that where income is relatively unequally distributed there are few market opportunities to develop local industry. The wealthy tend to import to meet their needs for luxuries as their per capita income increases with the rise of staple exports, whereas the poor stay poor in spite of increasing staple exports and spend their low income on the bare necessities of life. Moreover, it is argued that the wealthy do not devote the majority of their incremental income to investment-savings. Rather, a goodly portion of their savings are dissipated on luxuries. Moreover, actual savings represents only a portion of potential savings, where the latter consist of income above and beyond what is required to meet the basic needs of individuals. This surplus income can be saved or consumed, often in terms of 'conspicuous consumption' (Harris 1959; Baran 1969a, b). If individuals or the state consume rather than save and invest surplus income, higher levels of surplus real income need not contribute to the process of capital accumulation and, thereby, to the process of economic growth (Baran, ibid.).

To Baldwin, a more equal distribution of income creates an economic environment conducive to the development of local industry, by generating a market for output that does not have immediate export potential. As per capita income increases, in a world with a more equitable income distribution, individual and household demand moves beyond the basic necessities of life, where there is a much greater income elasticity of demand—demand is non-homothetic. The larger market allows the production of these products to become economically viable, allowing them to take advantage of economies in larger scale production and multiplier-accelerator interactions.[4] On the supply-side, a highly skewed distribution of income that is predicated upon relatively low returns to labor either on the farm, in the fishery, or in the factory, serves to reduce the level of labor productivity and thereby per capita income by inducing lower levels of economic efficiency and relatively low rates of technical change. Low returns to labor reduce the incentives and the pressures for firms to become more productive.[5]

Baldwin argues that income distribution is determined by the production function of the staple product(s) which, in turn, determines the type of economic organization necessary to produce the staple (slavery versus the freehold system of land tenure, for example). But it is has become evident that the same output can be profitably produced under different systems of land tenure or economic organization, yielding different distributions of income and thus dramatically different demand linkages. Thus an identical staple can yield different paths of economic development.[6] In this case, the potential demand-side impact of staple production is affected by the institutional parameters within which staple production takes place. And, individuals and government can affect such parameters.

Fiscal linkages relate to the income that the state receives as a result of staple and staple-related production. These linkages can result in the investment in social overhead, such as in transportation, education, research and development. In this manner fiscal linkages can make the staple economy more efficient and more competitive than it would otherwise be (external economies are generated). In this sense the state can use staple-related income to improve an economy's 'social capabilities'. On the other hand, the state can use its staple-related stream of income unproductively. The direction of fiscal linkages can, therefore, influence the course of the staple producing country's development.

The introduction of the concept of linkages explicitly and clearly incorporates the proposition that although the staple sector may be a leading sector in the economy other sectors might develop as a consequence of staple production itself. Staple production can have a multiplier effect on the rest of the staple producing economy. In this case, a staple-based economy can be one that consists of many key sectors. Indeed, the staple sector(s) need not be quantitatively the most important one(s). As North points out, even if staple production does not dominate an economy in terms of employment or output, this does not mean that staple production is not the dominant force in the economy if, by way of linkages, many of the economy's industries are dependant on staple production (North 1955, 1959). What the revised staple theory suggests is that if staples are important to the growth process, staple exports will lead the process of economic change both through direct and indirect (linkages) effects on the economy, even if staple exports, themselves, constitute a small percentage of GDP. Eventually staples might become of only marginal importance to the growth process as internal factors, largely independent of exports, take over the driver's seat in directing the process of economic change. It is, however, quite possible for country to fall into a 'staple trap'. Moreover, the staple economy need not develop the potential linkages associated with particular staple(s). For this reason, it is possible for a staple economy to evolve into a relative low per capita income economy.[7]

4 Isolating the Problematic

4.1 The Neoclassical Context

Any determination of the potential importance of the staple theory to either an analysis of past economic events or contemporary economic problems requires situating the staple theory in terms of growth theory and, moreover, identifying the key potential problems with the staple theory. One of the most serious criticism levied against the staple theory, one which remains a cornerstone of subsequent critiques, is vested in the theoretical modeling of the staple theory articulated by Chambers and Gordon which, in turn, is built upon a very simple neoclassical worldview. Their analysis is contextualized by an examination of the possible impact staple exports had on Canadian economic growth in the 1901–1911 period which was characterized by a boom in Canadian wheat exports;

a period that many Canadian scholars considered as having been critical to Canada's economic development.[8]

In terms of the mechanics of intensive economic growth, growth in real output per capita can be expressed as:

$$\frac{\dot{Y}}{P} = \dot{Y} - \dot{P}, \tag{1}$$

where a dot represents the average rate of growth of a variable per unit of time and Y and P represent real income or gross domestic product and population respectively. Since the level of real income equals the level of labor productivity times the number of workers employed (assuming that all workers are equal in terms of hours worked), the growth rate of real income can be expressed as:

$$\dot{Y} = \frac{\dot{Y}}{L} + \dot{L}, \tag{2}$$

where L is the number of workers employed and $\frac{Y}{L}$ is labor productivity. The rate of growth in real per capita output can, therefore, be rewritten as:

$$\frac{\dot{Y}}{P} = \frac{\dot{Y}}{L} + (\dot{L} - \dot{P}) \tag{3}$$

Per capita output growth is clearly a positive function of the growth in labor productivity, $\frac{\dot{Y}}{L}$, and whether or not employment grows at a faster pace than population or the percentage of the population that is employed increases. Staple theory implicitly assumes that an export boom in staples will at a minimum serve to increase the rate of growth in labor productivity.

What determines the latter is decomposed into key components in the basic neoclassical growth model developed by Robert Solow in 1956. In his analytical framework the long run equilibrium level of real output is given by factor inputs, reduced to capital and labor, and exogenously given technological change. Given the assumptions of constant returns to scale, diminishing returns to individual inputs, no production externalities, long run perfect competition, 'full employment', and the equality between employment and population growth, the level of per capita output is determined by an exogenously given propensity to save, which sets the capital per worker ratio, and by the rate of technical change (Solow 1956). It is further assumed that production is x-efficient and, therefore, all economic agents are working as hard and as well as they can (Altman (1996, 1998, 2001b; Leibenstein 1966).

A critical point that follows from the Solow model, is that there is a limit to which per capita output can be increased by way of increasing the capital to labor ratio and a limit to which the propensity to save can be increased. Only sustained increases in technological change can yield sustained increases in labor productivity and, thereby, in real per capita output.

The basic Solow growth model can be expressed as:

$$n + m = \frac{s}{\left(\frac{K}{Y}\right)} \tag{4}$$

where *m* is the rate of technical change, *n* is the employment growth rate, *s* is the average propensity to save and (K/Y) is the capital to labour ratio. Higher rates of technical change yield higher rates of economic growth and higher levels of per capita output. In Solow's basic model, technical change is exogenous and autonomous. It is independent of and not effected by movements in the model's other variables and is, in the Solow parable, a catch-all phrase for all variables other than capital which contribute towards increasing labor productivity or as Abramovitz refers to it, a measure of our ignorance. Technical change is like manna from heaven and is left unexplained in the model (Solow 1956, 1957; Abramovitz 1956). But clearly, differences in the rate of technical change, however explained, as well as differences in the propensity to save, yield differences in per capita income.

With respect to the staple hypothesis, it is implicitly assumed that a staple export boom will have a differential and positive effect on the propensity to save (assumed to be identically equal to investment) and on the rate of technical change and thereby on the level of per capita income. Exports are linked to per capita income levels and rates of growth through their positive affect on the rate of capital accumulation. Since technology is embodied in plant and equipment, best practice technology cannot easily be incorporated into the production process unless there is an increase in the rate of capital accumulation. Increasing the rate of capital accumulation increases the rate at which best practice technology is diffused throughout the economy, replacing the earlier vintages of capital stock with the more productive latest versions. In this sense, capital accumulation is the instrument that allows for the actualization of technical change, which remains the primary engine of economic growth (see Maddison [1991, pp. 65–66, 141–144], Nelson [1968], Salter [1960], and Solow [1960]). Therefore, to the extent that a staple export boom stimulates capital accumulation, staple exports can be said to contribute to increases in per capita output. However, technical change will take place only if the appropriate social capacity, inclusive of human capital, is present (Abramovitz 1986; Altman 1999b; Easterlin 1981; Kutznets 1965). In other words, as Ruttan concludes, "It should now be obvious that differences in productivity levels and rates of growth cannot be overcome by the simple transfer of capital and technology" (Ruttan 1997, p. 1523). Technical change appears to be a necessary but not sufficient condition for persistent per capita growth where, according to the staple theory, the export of staples accelerates the process of technical change given the existence of the necessary economic and social infrastructure, which is a supply-side rather than a demand-side phenomenon.

Staple exports can also affect the level of per capita output and growth through their potential impact on the structure of an economy. The basic Solow model pays no heed to this possibility since it abstracts from the effects of sectoral differences in productivity levels and growth rates and, in this context, the dynamic effects of structural change. Nevertheless, Simon Kuznets, in his classic empirical work on economic growth, stressed the importance of structural change in the economy, with labor shifting into the more productive sectors of the economy and into relatively more productive industries and product lines as being of fundamental importance to sustained per capita growth. Such structural change, itself, reflects the changing structure of demand (Kuznets 1965, also Rosenberg 1982a, p. 258). To the extent that a boom in staple exports contributes to shifting labor into more productive industries or sectors, it contributes towards increasing an economy's per capita output. This point can be illustrated as follows:

$$\frac{Y}{L} = L_a\left(\frac{Y}{L}\right)_a + L_b\left(\frac{Y}{L}\right)_b \tag{5}$$

where L_a and L_b are the shares of labor in sector a and b respectively. If increasing exports result in labor shifting into the higher productivity sector, total labor productivity increases and, ceteris paribus, so does per capita output (see Cornwall and Cornwall [1992] for details).

A long standing potential linkage between exports and per capita economic growth is related to the Smithian notion of increasing returns to scale and externalities which has been given much currency in the classic paper by Allyn Young. International trade, by widening the extent of the market, increases the scope of the division of labor, helps to overcome indivisibilities in production, and allows for increasing returns (Young 1928). See also Myint (1958). In Solow's basic model these possibilities are assumed away. To the extent that staple exports serve to expand market opportunities for other sectors, they contribute towards increasing productivity in the economy at large, thereby contributing to increasing the economy's per capita output. The relationship between trade and economic growth has been given very specific form in what is referred to as Verdoorn's Law, elaborated upon and popularized by Kaldor, which specifies a causal relationship between the growth rate of labor productivity in the economy at large and growth in industrial production (Kaldor 1966). This is expressed as:

$$\frac{\dot{Y}}{L} = m + a\dot{Y}_I, \tag{6}$$

where m is an exogenously given rate of technical change, Υ_I is the growth rate in industrial production, and a is the elasticity of labor productivity growth to industrial output growth. Here, both autonomous technical change and the growth in industrial output 'explain' the growth in labor productivity. The growth in aggregate industrial output is driven by both domestic demand and by exports, inclusive of staple exports. Underlying Verdoorn's Law is the notion that as per capita income increases, an increasing percentage of such increases are spent on non-agricultural products which, in turn, has the effect of increasing productivity and therefore real per capita income.

4.2 *The Chambers and Gordon Challenge*

Chambers and Gordon maintain that the claims of staple theorists as to the importance of staple exports to per capita growth have been ad hoc and literary, suffering from a nebulous theoretical framework and thereby failing to clearly identify the causal mechanism underlying staple theory.

They set out to correct this flaw by building a simple neoclassical model to test the proposition that Canada's wheat boom was responsible for most of the increase in Canada's per capita real income in the 1901–1911 period. They ask the counterfactual: what would have transpired, "if all the land that was brought under cultivation between 1901 and 1911 had been impenetrable rock", in other words, if there had been no wheat boom. Using their model, Chambers and Gordon estimate that the wheat boom contributed at most only 8.4% to the increase in Canada's per capita income and, more likely, only 5.2 or 1.5% of Canada's 1901 per capita gross domestic product. These results, they argue, suggest that a strong correlation between primary product export growth and increases in per capita income is spurious, with most of the per capita income increases attributable to variables other than increases in primary product exports (Chambers and Gordon 1966, pp. 316, 317, 320). Thus, policy-makers for presently underdeveloped countries have no good reason to expect much in the way of rising per capita income even with substantive increases in primary-product exports. It is important to realize that these rather strong conclusions are not fact based but are rather derived from the assumptions which underlie their model, a basic understanding of which helps identify the limits of both the staple theory and the neoclassical critique of this theory.

Chambers and Gordon assume two sector economy, with a staple (wheat) and a domestic manufacturing (gadgets) sector. Product prices are assumed to be given exogenously—Canada is too small a player in the world economy to affect prices. Individuals are assumed to behave in a manner consistent with profit maximization: labor is employed in each sector up to the point where the value of labor's marginal product equals her/his marginal cost (the wage rate). They further assume diminishing returns in agriculture and constant returns in manufacturing and, therefore, no scale economies. Finally, labor supply is assumed to be positively related to the real wage rate, which is set in the gadgets sector. Individuals who cannot find employment or self-employment in agriculture are employed in the gadget sector. Total labor supply is given by labour supply in the wheat and gadgets sectors.

The wheat boom is sparked by some exogenously determined technical change such as the introduction of Red Fife wheat. This shifts wheat's marginal product or the demand for labor curve outward, resulting in the staple sector employing more labor at the old real wage since the marginal product of labor in gadgets is unaffected by events in the wheat sector, yielding the constant real wage. Labor is simply drawn out of the gadget sector and the supply of labor in the wheat sector increases by the amount of the reduction of labor in the gadget sector. What happens to real output or income? Economic rents in the wheat sector increase as wheat's marginal product curve shifts outward and this serves to increase per capita income by the per capita increase in economic rents as it is assumed that population remains unchanged. But Chambers and Gordon argue that it would be incorrect to attribute this increase in income to staple production since, at the same time as Canada was experiencing a boom in staple exports, Canada's gadget industry was also experiencing exogenous shifts in marginal product, completely independent of the wheat boom, due to exogenous technical change (ibid., pp. 319, 327). The adoption of new technology, for reasons unrelated to the export wheat boom such as an appropriate level of human capital, shifts the marginal product curve in gadgets upward, yielding an increase in the 'equilibrium' real wage rate for the whole economy (ibid., pp. 327–328). Thus, income per capita would have increased through the increase in real wages whether or not there was a staple boom. For this reason, increases in economic rent exaggerates increases in per capita income due to the wheat boom once one nets out the exogenously determined independent effect of technological change on the wage rate.

The core attribute of Chambers and Gordon's critique of the staple hypothesis is simply to assume that those causal connections, which staple theorists deem to be of some importance, are non-existent, yielding their estimate of the overwhelming contribution of exogenous productivity increases in non-staple sectors to Canada increased per capita income in the 1901–1911 period. On the other hand, if one assumes that productivity improvements in the gadget sector were entirely due to incentives unleashed by the wheat boom—that they are endogenously determined—one would conclude that the wheat boom's contribution to the growth in per capita output was 100%. Of course, this is an extreme assumption that yields extreme results: a mirror image of the Chambers and Gordon parable. Such assumptions cannot result in a better understanding of the role played by staples in determining the path of intensive economic growth of any staple oriented economy. Rather, determining the veracity of the causal assumptions made by staple theorists, discussed above, is at the heart of any determination of role played by staple exports in intensive economic growth.

Caves finds, for example, that under alternative assumptions, the wheat boom contributed 21.4% to the 1901–1911 period's per capita income increase as opposed to Chambers and Gordon's 8.4%. Caves's revisions are largely attributable to his assumptions about the positive impact that the wheat boom had on labor force participation and employment. He maintains Chambers' and Gordon's assumptions no economies of scale and exogenous technological change.[9] Therefore, Cave's adjustments, represent only a lower-bound correction to the Chambers and Gordon estimates. With this said, Caves argues that Canada's growth performance should also be compared to economies with access to similar technological flows as Canada such as the United States. Canada's per capita growth exceeded that of the United States in the 1901–1911 period. The available estimates at that time indicate that real per capita income increased by 22% in Canada and by 15% in the United States during this decade whereas more recent estimates suggest a 45% increase in Canada compared to a 21% increase in the United States (Altman 1987, 1992). On the basis of the most contemporary growth estimates the wheat boom contributed, at a minimum, 59% Canada's per capita growth—the excess of Canadian over American growth.

5 The Staple Theory and Intensive Growth

In terms of one of the basic growth equations discussed above (Eq. 3) staple exports cause real output per capita to rise if they tend to cause, on average, an increase in the growth of labor productivity and/or in the growth of labor inputs relative population growth. More specifically, staple theory hypothesizes that staple exports positively and differentially affect the rate of technical change, in contrast to neoclassical theory and Chambers and Gordon's variant of it, inclusive of economies of scale, externalities, structural change, and embodied technical change (Eq. 4). In other words, it is hypothesized that in the absence of staple exports real per capita output would be lower than it would otherwise be. Staple exports could also affect per capita output by affecting the propensity to save in the economy. Staple theory, however, does not specify that staple exports must necessarily have strong effects on the above variables. Much depends on the production function, the degree of freedom available with respect to adopting different organization forms in producing a particular staple product (a more versus a less equal income distribution and extent of linkages), markets and the overall capacity of an economy to realize the full potential afforded by the production of a particular staple. Whether or not the potential of a staple export is fully tapped critically depends on the available social and economic infrastructure. Therefore, two regions producing identical staples may follow quite different paths of development simply as a result of different social and economic infrastructures, with one region evolving into a relatively low per capita income economy (Schedvin 1990). In this sense, the potential intensive growth afforded by staple exports is by no means automatic. The pre-conditions for realizing this potential must be constructed by society's economic agents and private and public organizations. For this very reason, supply side variables are of vital importance to the staple analytical framework.[10]

The most direct means by which a staple economy can achieve a relatively high level of per capita income is when the staple sector is characterized by a higher level of and/or rate of growth in labor productivity than in the non-staple sectors and when staple exports increase the extent to which factor inputs are employed. In this case, staple exports constitute a case of venting for surplus—the staple production simply yields higher returns than do non-staple production (Caves 1965; Myint 1958). Staple theory, even in its original form, emanating from the pen of Harold Innis, suggests that for this very direct effect to be realized supply-side changes to the economy are required. The economic and social infrastructure must be constructed for the staple to become economically viable. Therefore, staple theory implicitly predicts that this potential direct effect need not be realized if the appropriate supply-side conditions are not met.

Staple theory pays great heed to the potential indirect effects of staple production. It hypothesizes linkages between staple exports and non-staple output which result in higher levels of productivity and higher rates of factor employment. Of particular importance, staple theory hypothesizes linkages whereby currently employed and new labor is reallocated into relatively more productive and higher productivity growth non-staple sectors of the economy, reflected in structural change. Also of importance is the potential significance of increasing returns to scale and externalities made possible by the increasing markets generated by staple exports. Market size grows with both staple-induced increases in immigration and per capita income. Such increase in demand positively feed back into the process of intensive growth.

Staple exports can also increase the rate of growth of per capita income by increasing the rate of technical change through its affect upon the rate of capital accumulation and, therefore, upon the rate at which best practice technology is embodied in plant and equipment in both staple and non-staple sectors. One cannot simply assume, as do Chambers and Gordon, that technical change occurs independently from the production process. Moreover, because the impact of staples on growth can be an indirect one, simply focusing on the direct impact of staples can yield fundamentally misleading results on the relationship between staples and intensive economic growth. In addition, fiscal linkages emanating from staple production, if productive, improve the efficiency of all sectors, thereby increasing the level of labor productivity and the level of per capita output.

Finally, for staples to positively impact on the development process requires, as a necessary condition, foreign markets be relatively open to staple exports or that staple producers are capable of penetrating such markets through cost-cutting measures. In this sense, trade expansion is a necessary condition for the success of a staple-based economy. But this is not the same thing as free trade. The theoretical case favoring staple exports as either a handmaiden or engine of growth does necessarily depend on the openness of a staple economy to non-staple imports. This is important to note, given the ongoing theoretical and empirical debate attempting to causally link export and related economic success with the extent of an economy's overall. Moreover, for twentieth century, the evidence on a positive relationship between free trade and economic growth is mixed at best and, where positive, the relationship is a weak one.[11] In addition, as Bairoch points out in some detail, few economies developed outside of what were often significant tariff barriers in the nineteenth and early twentieth centuries including the rapidly growing United States, Canada, and England. The United States was a leading protectionist nations until the end of World War Two and England dropped its protectionist barriers only after becoming the leading industrial powerhouse in the mid-nineteenth century. Historically, in general, eras of high tariffs tend to coincide with relatively high rates of per capita GDP growth and eras of low tariffs often coincide with low rates of economic growth, albeit this does not demonstrate a causal relationship (Bairoch 1993, see also O'Rourke 2000). With regards to economic theory, various forms of protection, of a *transitional* nature, are consistent with high rates of economic growth. Such is especially the case for infant industries, where learning-by-doing can be critically important—that is where it takes time for individuals to learn how to produce efficiently and competitively relative to those economies where industries have established a first mover advantage.[12] Temporary protection can, thereby, facilitate the development of linkages derived from staple exports which, in turn, can serve to increase a staple economy's level of per capita output. On the other hand, protection which hinders staple exports will impede the capacity of staple exports to fuel the growth process. But this constraint can be overcome, on the supply side, if the staple producing economy has constructed the capacity to reduce production costs sufficiently to meet the challenge of high barriers to staple trade.

6 A Statistical Interlude

As the Chambers and Gordon intervention underlines, an important point of focus for empirical debates surrounding the staple theory is the Canadian export wheat boom that commenced in the mid-1890s.[13] For this reason it is important to appreciate the extent to which Canada's export wheat boom was actually correlated with its intensive growth performance and how Canada's growth performance compared with other relatively high income economies, including those countries identified as staple economies by the protagonists in the staple theory debate. Moreover, it is of importance to examine the statistical relationship between the wheat boom and Canada's regional per capita output growth.

I employ Maddison's current dollar per capita Gross Domestic Product estimates to produce annual growth rate estimates for a number of comparable countries including the so-called staple economies for the 1870–1929 period (Table 1). For Canada, I supplement Maddison's Canadian estimates which are based on Urquhart, with Altman's estimates which correct Urquhart's estimates for the deflation problems underlying his numbers (Altman 1992; Maddison 1995; Urquhart 1986, 1993). According to the revised estimates, the Canadian and Argentinean (another wheat exporting nation) growth rates for the 1870–1929 period, 2.2 and 2.0% per annum respectively, were the fastest of all countries, easily bettering the second best American growth rate. But the low growth rates of the other staple countries, Australia and New Zealand, only compare to the laggard growth performance of the United Kingdom. Growth in both Germany and France stood behind the American. During this period, Canadian and Argentinean per capita GDP more than tripled while the Australian per capita GDP increased by less than 50% while New Zealand fared only somewhat better than Australia. In contrast, American per capita GDP increased by 150%.

Table 1 International comparisons of per capita GDP

	Argentina	*Australia*	*Revised Canada*	*New Zealand*	*France*	*Germany*	*UK*	*USA*
Levels of Per Capita GDP in 1990 Geary-Khamis Dollars								
1870	1,311	3,801	1,438	3,115	1,858	1,913	3,263	2,457
1880	na	4,590	1,662	3,765	2,100	2,078	3,556	3,193
1890	2,152	4,775	2,226	3,774	2,354	2,539	4,099	3,396
1896	na	3,947	2,068	4,008	2,660	2,872	4,345	3,509
1900	2,756	4,299	2,756	4,320	2,849	3,134	4,593	4,096
1910	3,822	5,581	3,992	5,343	2,937	3,527	4,715	4,970
1913	3,797	5,505	4,551	5,178	3,452	3,833	5,032	5,307
1925	3,919	5,712	4,396	5,318	4,127	3,772	4,912	6,290
1929	4,367	5,095	5,255	5,289	4,666	4,335	5,255	6,907
Per Capita GDP Growth Rates								
1870–1880	na	1.90%	1.45%	1.91%	1.23%	0.83%	0.86%	2.65%
1880–1890	na	0.40%	2.96%	0.02%	1.15%	2.02%	1.43%	0.62%
1890–1900	2.50%	−1.04%	2.16%	1.36%	1.93%	2.13%	1.14%	1.89%
1900–1910	3.32%	2.64%	3.78%	2.15%	0.30%	1.19%	0.26%	1.95%
1896–1913	na	1.98%	4.75%	1.52%	1.54%	1.71%	0.87%	2.46%
1913–1929	0.88%	−0.48%	0.90%	0.13%	1.90%	0.77%	0.27%	1.66%
	–	–	–	–	–	–	–	–
1870–1900	2.51%	0.41%	2.19%	1.10%	1.44%	1.66%	1.15%	1.72%
1870–1896	na	0.15%	1.41%	0.97%	1.39%	1.58%	1.11%	1.38%
	–	–	–	–	–	–	–	–
1900–1929	2.47%	0.22%	3.01%	1.17%	2.39%	1.86%	0.86%	2.48%
1896–1929	na	0.78%	2.87%	0.84%	1.72%	1.26%	0.58%	2.07%
	–	–	–	–	–	–	–	–
1870–1929	2.06%	0.50%	2.22%	0.90%	1.57%	1.40%	0.81%	1.77%
Per Capita GDP Index Numbers; 1870 = 100								
1870	100	100	100	100	100	100	100	100
1880	na	121	116	121	113	109	109	130
1890	164	126	155	121	127	133	126	138
1896	na	104	144	129	143	150	133	143
1900	210	113	192	139	153	164	141	167
1910	292	147	278	172	158	184	144	202
1913	290	145	316	166	186	200	154	216
1925	299	150	306	171	222	197	151	256
1929	333	134	365	170	251	227	161	281
Per Capita GDP Index Numbers; Canada = 100								
1870	91	264	100	217	129	133	227	171

(continued)

Table 1 (continued)

	Argentina	*Australia*	*Revised Canada*	*New Zealand*	*France*	*Germany*	*UK*	*USA*
1880	na	276	100	227	126	125	214	192
1890	97	215	100	170	106	114	184	153
1896	na	191	100	194	129	139	210	170
1900	100	156	100	157	103	114	167	149
1910	96	140	100	134	74	88	118	125
1913	83	121	100	114	76	84	111	117
1925	89	130	100	121	94	86	112	143
1929	83	97	100	101	89	82	100	131

Sources All output estimates, except for the new Canada and the Firestone estimates, are from Angus Maddison, *Monitoring the World Economy, 1820–1992* (OECD: Paris, 1995), Tables D1-a and D1-d. The new Canada output estimates are derived from Morris Altman, "Revised Real GNP Estimates and Canadian Economic Development," *Review of Income and Wealth*, Series 38, no. 4 (1992), Table 1. Maddison's Canadian estimates are derived from M. C. Urquhart, *Gross National Product, Canada, 1870–1926: the Derivation of the Estimates* (Montreal: McGill-Queen's University Press, 1993). Firestone's estimates are from, O.J. Firestone, Canada's Economic Development, 1876–1953, With Special Reference to Changes in the Country's National Product and National Wealth, Income and Wealth Series VII (London: Bowes and Bowes, London, 1958)

Canada's most forceful growth performance took place in the 1896–1913 period, at the height of the wheat boom, with per capita GDP increasing by almost 5% per year, during which time wheat exports grew by 15% per year.[14] Only Argentina's growth performance came close to the Canadian. The American per capita growth rate, Cave's point of reference, was only 2.5%. Before 1896, prior to the wheat boom, Canada's growth record was certainly no better than the Argentinean, American, French, and German. It was especially during the 1896–1913 period that Canada was able to either significantly catch-up with other countries or pass them by. By 1929, only the United States remained ahead of Canada in terms of per capita GDP, and this by 31% as compared to 70% in 1896 (Tables 1 and 2). Staple producing Australia and New Zealand lost the large lead that they held over Canada in 1870, as did the well-established European economies. A key question for the staple theory to address is the great dispersion in economic performance amongst staple producing regions and between staple and non-staple regions.

Canada's regional growth record sheds some insight on the direct and indirect effects of staple production real per capita GDP growth (Table 2). However you cut it, compared to the Canadian average, only the

Table 2 The Canadian provinces in an international context: Per capita GDP and ranking

Capita GDP and ranking						
	1891	*Ranking*	*1991*	*Ranking*	*1929*	*Ranking*
British Columbia	3,616	4	5,951	1	7,091	1
USA	3,396	5	4,970	4	6,907	2
Ontario	2,483	8	4,691	6	6,208	3
Canada (revised)	2,226	11	4,394	7	6,122	4
New Zealand	3,774	3	5,343	3	5,289	5
UK	4,099	2	4,715	5	5,255	6
Alberta	n.a	n.a	3,730	10	5,133	7
Australia	4,775	1	5,581	2	5,095	8
Quebec	1,882	15	3,320	13	4,940	9
Manitoba	2,764	6	4,069	8	4,820	10
France	2,354	10	2,937	16	4,666	11
Argentina	2,152	12	3,822	9	4,367	12
Germany	2,539	7	3,527	11	4,335	13
Saskatchewan	2,420	9	3,482	12	4,015	14
Nova Scotia	1,907	14	3,244	14	3,567	15
New Brunswick	2,046	13	3,009	15	2,961	16
Prince Edward Island	1,737	16	2,353	17	2,488	17
GDP per Capita Index Numbers; Canada = 100						
British Columbia	162		135		116	
USA	153		113		113	
Ontario	112		107		101	
Canada (revised)	100		100		100	
New Zealand	170		122		86	
UK	184		107		86	
Alberta	n.a		85		84	
Australia	215		127		83	
Quebec	85		76		81	
Manitoba	124		93		79	
France	106		67		76	
Argentina	97		87		71	
Germany	114		80		71	
Saskatchewan	109		79		66	
Nova Scotia	86		74		58	
New Brunswick	92		68		48	
Prince Edward Island	78		54		41	

Sources and *notes* The provincial estimates are derived from Alan G.Green, Regional Aspects of Canada's Economic Growth (Toronto: University of Toronto Press, 1971), Appendices. See Table 1, for a discussion of national estimates

non-staple producing provinces of Quebec and Ontario, with the bulk of Canada's population (about 60% in the 1920s), witnessed an improvement in their relative positions. In terms of per capita GDP, British Columbia, whose share of Canada's population increased to 7% by 1931, remained Canada's lead province, although its relative position deteriorated sharply from 1891. The Atlantic Provinces witnessed a relative decline, as did Canada's two leading wheat producing regions, Manitoba and Saskatchewan. However, all of Canada's provinces saw some growth, with Manitoba's and Saskatchewan's per capita output increasing by about 80% from 1891 to 1929, while Quebec's and Ontario's almost tripled.

One can discern these regional patterns from a different vantage point when provincial per capita GDP is ranked along side of that of the already discussed national economies. It is clear how well the economies of British Columbia, Ontario, and Alberta fared, with British Columbia moved ahead of the United States by 1911, while Ontario and Canada as whole improved their ranking moving in behind the United States. Further behind, both Quebec and Alberta (another wheat producing region) improved their rankings. By 1929, Saskatchewan and Canada's Atlantic Provinces found themselves at the bottom of our sample of countries, while Manitoba was steadily moving towards the bottom tier of countries and provinces. To the extent that the wheat export boom positively affected Canada's growth performance, its impact was seemingly biased heavily in favor of the non-staple producing regions of the country. In this case, the indirect effects of staple exports must have been pervasive.

The notion that staple exports was the handmaiden of Canadian growth through its direct and indirect supply and demand side effects on Canadian development is provided by W. A. Mackintosh, in his classic study of Canadian economic development originally published in 1939. His interpretive rendering of the staple theory is at the core of what I have argued is central to any revised and refurbished general staple theory of economic growth and development. Mackintosh (1978, p. 47) writes: "The most fundamental single characteristic of the period [1895–1920] was a high rate of investment induced by improved expectations of profit from the exploitation of natural resources, which had been newly discovered, newly tapped by the extending railways, subjected to new productive techniques, or converted into profit possibilities by favorable shifts in costs and prices. Overwhelmingly most important were the wheat lands of the Prairie Provinces. Prospective profitableness in the exploiting industries created markets for other industries and for a time investment fed on itself….the investments of the great expansion had built up a greatly magnified exporting economy in which exporting regions were more specialized than formerly and provided larger markets for imports or the products of other regions…Wheat was not merely the largest export and the product of a new region, it was the central dynamic and unifying force of the expansion. The fortunes of regions with declining exports depended on their ability to share in the home market, to integrate themselves with the expanding export region."

7 Conclusions

In the ideal staple scenario, staple exports generate all of the direct and indirect benefits, in terms of higher per capita output, that can possibly be derived from a particular staple. But this ideal need not be realized. Proof of the usefulness of the staple theory is not contained, however, in a successful staple experience. Nor should divergent economic performances by erstwhile staple economies be taken as proof of failure of the staple theory. Rather, the staple theory provides a framework for analyzing the impact staple exports have on the economic evolution of a country by locating potential causal relationships on *both the demand and supply side* between exports and intensive growth. This impact might very well be of a differential nature either because a staple-producing region fails to realize its potential or because of the differential nature of the staples produced. Moreover, staple theory emphasizes the importance of supply-side changes, over which economic agents have some control, in affecting the growth process, given that the demand for staple products is often exogenously determined. Thus staple theory points to the capacity of individuals and society to significantly affect the course of economic development.

The potential causal relationships between exports and economic growth are soundly grounded in economic theory. Nor are they ruled out of order by the basic Solow growth model which simply serves to identify the likely sources of sustained economic growth, leaving key variables, such as technical change unexplained by the model itself. However, in their application of this model, Chambers and Gordon assume away such causal relationships a priori. Any correlation between staple exports and intensive economic growth is assumed to be of a spurious nature and the long term path of intensive growth is therefore simply assumed to be unaffected by trend movements in staple exports. Staple theory, on the other hand, demands that we determine the direct and indirect sources of technical change and other sources of productivity growth. Overall, the staple theory provides a useful framework for analyzing the growth process in countries, such as Canada, the United States, Australia, Argentina, and New Zealand, where traditional staple exports have played a prominent part in their history. Moreover, as North (1955) suggests, the staple framework can also be exploited, as a more general theory of export-led growth, to determine the importance of non-agricultural or raw material-based exports to the process of intensive economic growth.

Notes

1. Innis writes (1967, p. 16): "Goods were produced as rapidly as possible to be sold at the most advantageous price in the home market in order to purchase other goods essential to the maintenance and improvement of the current standard of living. In other words these goods supplied by the home country enabled migrants to maintain their standard of living and to make adjustments to the new environment without serious loss."
2. Rodriguez and Rodrik (1999, p. 39) and North (1955, p. 248). McInnis (1992), argues, on the contrary, that staple theory is defined in large part by whether or not staple exports are demand-side driven thereby shifting attention away from the critical issue of the importance of exports to economic growth.
3. Reynolds (1986, pp. 43–48), finds that primary product exports served as an engine of growth in many twentieth century less developed provided the existence of appropriate government policy, such as maintaining law and order, solid administration, provision of adequate human and physical infrastructure, and tax policy which is not strongly biased against imports. In an econometrically oriented paper focusing on the 1971–1989 period, Sachs and Warner (1995), find that primary export oriented economies tend on average—there is much variation about mean growth rates—to experience slower growth than economies which are not so oriented, attributable, in part, to poor government policy. This finding suggests that countries well endowed in staples might have realized their true growth potential under a more conducive institutional framework.
4. Baldwin (1956), p. 176. See Murphy et al. (1989), for a contemporary statement of the positive role which a more equal distribution of income plays in industrialization, focusing on diversification away from agriculture where the non-agricultural sectors are characterized by increasing returns to scale. See Aghion et al. (1999), on how a more equal distribution

of income can overcome market failures in human capital formation in a world of imperfect information.

5. Altman (1996, ch. 4, 1998, 2000, 2001b) and Habbakkuk (1962).
6. See, Altman (2000, 2001a, b), Blum (1957), North (1959), and Schedvin (1990). See also, Domar (1970), on the importance of institutional variables in determining the system of land tenure and labor organization irrespective of what is produced. See Ommer (1981, 1985), on the role of property rights in determining the course of staple development as exemplified in Canadian east coast fishing industry and Gordon (1954), for the landmark theoretical statement of the same. Rodrik (1997), argues that increasing trade, per se, need not generate development in the absence of institutional reform, especially related to the governance and judicial process, social safety nets, and education.
7. See, Caves (1965), North (1959), and Schedvin (1990). There is some evidence that many staple economies have fallen into a 'staple trap' (Sachs and Warner 1995).
8. It is important to note that Chambers and Gordon's (1966), theoretically embedded empirical test of the staple theory followed upon earlier detailed empirical work of Firestone (1958), on Canadian GNP and Bertram (1963) on Canadian manufacturing which challenged the traditional view that the wheat boom era was characterized by a major break with the past or the future. This challenge has, itself, been seriously questioned, if not refuted, by more recent empirical work on Canadian economic growth (Altman 1987, 1992, 1994, 2001a; Urquhart 1986; Green and Urquhart 1994).
9. Caves (1971, pp. 417–419). Caves assumes that the wheat boom induced immigration into Canada was characterized by a higher than average labor force participation rate, yielding more output and income than would be otherwise possible, contributing 77% to his estimate of the additional contribution of wheat boom. Scale economies comprise 6.5% of this total.
10. North (1990) emphasizes that the market does not and cannot guarantee the development of the necessary infrastructure so that an economy might not realize its maximum economic potential in terms of real per capita output (ibid., p. 9). Indeed, he argues that many Third World countries' institutions are designed to promote redistributive rather than productive activities and such perverse incentives become entrenched over time for transaction cost reasons.
11. On the free trade debate see, for example, Edwards (1998), Rodriguez and Rodrik (1999), and Rodrik (1997). Rodrik (2001, p. 4) concludes: "The available studies reveal no systematic relationship between a country's average level of tariff and nontariff barriers and its subsequent economic growth rate. If anything, the evidence for the 1990s indicates a positive relationship between import tariffs and economic growth. The only clear

pattern is that countries dismantle their trade restrictions as they grow richer." Studies which support the positive relationship between openness and growth, such as Edwards (1998), find only a very weak positive relationship in the 1980s for an array of countries with a tremendous variation about the mean.

12. See Altman (1999a), on infant industries and Arrow (1962), on learning-by-doing.
13. In the classic wheat export boom period, 1896 to 1913, the per annum growth rate of wheat exports in 1900 Canadian dollars was 15.5%. In the preceding 26 years, which followed the creation of Canada in 1867, the growth rate was only 2.8%. From 1913 to 1929 it was 8.2%. Within the 1896–1913 time-frame there was some variation in growth, but not much, 14% from 1896 to 1907 and 16% from 1907 to 1913 (derived from *Historical Statistics of Canada*, series L98, L139, L145). On the underlying causes of the wheat boom see, for example, Buckley (1974), Dick (1980), Emery and McKenzie (1996), Fowke (1957), Harley (1980), Lewis (1981), Mackintosh (1978), Meier (1953), Norrie (1975), and Ward (1995). On some important empirical issues surrounding the Canadian boom and its impact on the Canadian economy see Altman (1987, 1992, 2001a) and Green and Urquhart (1994), Inwood and Stengos (1991), Sparks and Green (1999), and Urquhart (1986, 1993).
14. McInnis (1999) argues against the hypothesis that the wheat boom played an important role driving Canadian growth because he concludes that the bulk of intensive Canadian economic growth took place in the 1896–1907 period, just prior to what he refers to the "real wheat boom" of 1907–1913. However, there was little difference in the growth of wheat exports in the 1896–1907 and 1907–1913 periods (note 46).

References

Abramovitz, M. 1956. Resource and Output Trends in the United States Since 1870. *American Economic Review* 46: 5–23.

Abramovitz, M. 1986. Catching Up, Forging Ahead, and Falling Behind. *Journal of Economic History* 46: 385–406.

Aghion, P., E. Caroli, and C. García-Peñalosa. 1999. Inequality and Economic Growth: The Perspective of the New Growth Theories. *Journal of Economic Literature* 37: 1615–1660.

Altman, M. 1987. A Revision of Canadian Economic Growth: 1870–1910 (a Challenge to the Gradualist Interpretation). *Canadian Journal of Economics* 20: 86–113.

Altman, M. 1992. Revised Real Canadian GNP Estimates and Canadian Economic Growth, 1870–1926. *Review of Income and Wealth*, Series 38: 455–473.

Altman, M. 1994. The Evolution of Plant Size in Canadian Manufacturing, 1870–1910. *Canadian Historical Review* 75: 557–585.

Altman, M. 1996. *Human Agency and Material Welfare: Revisions in Microeconomics and their Implications for Public Policy*. Boston: Kluwer Academic Publishers.

Altman, M. 1998. A High Wage Path to Economic Growth and Development. *Challenge: The Magazine of Economic Affairs* 41: 91–104.

Altman, M. 1999a. Free Trade and Protectionism. In *Encyclopedia of Political Economy*, vol. 1, ed. P. O'Hara, 372–375. London: Routledge.

Altman, M. 1999b. Social Capacity and Convergence. In *Encyclopedia of Political Economy*, vol. 2, ed. P. O'Hara, 1033–1035. London: Routledge.

Altman, M. 2000. A Behavioral Model of Path Dependency: The Economics of Profitable Inefficiency and Market Failure. *Journal of Socio-Economics* 29: 127–145.

Altman, M. 2001a. Quantitative Aspects of Canadian Growth and Development, 1850–1926. In *Canada: Confederation to Present*, ed. R. Macleod. Edmonton: Chinook Multimedia.

Altman, M. 2001b. *Worker Satisfaction and Economic Performance*. Armonk, NY: M.E. Sharpe Publishers.

Arrow, K.J. 1962. The Economic Implications of Learning by Doing. *Review of Economic Studies* 29: 155–173.

Arthur, B.W. 1990. Positive Feedbacks in the Economy. *Scientific American* 204: 92–99.

Bairoch. 1993. *Economics and World History: Myths and Paradoxes*. Chicago: Chicago University Press.

Baldwin, R.E. 1956. Patterns of Development in Newly Settled Regions. *Manchester School* 24: 161–179.

Baran, P.A. 1969a. On the Political Economy of Backwardness. In *P.A. Baran, The Longer View: Essay Toward a Critique of Political Economy*, ed. J. O'Neill, 249–270. New York and London: Monthly Review.

Baran, P.A. 1969b. Economic Progress and Economic Surplus. In *P.A. Baran, The Longer View: Essay Toward a Critique of Political Economy*, ed. J. O'Neill, 271–307. New York and London: Monthly Review.

Baumol, W.J. 1986. Productivity Growth, Convergence, and Welfare: What the Long-Run Data Show. *American Economic Review* 76: 1072–1085.

Bertram, G.W. 1963. Economic Growth in Canadian Industry: The Staple Model and the Take-off Hypothesis. *Canadian Journal of Economics and Political Science* 24: 159–184.

Blum, J. 1957. The Rise of Serfdom in Eastern Europe. *American Historical Review* 62: 807–836.
Buckley, K. 1974. *Capital Formation in Canada*, 1890–1930, first published in 1955. Toronto: McClelland and Stewart.
Callender, G. 1902–1903. The Early Transportation and Banking Enterprises of the States in Relation to the Growth of Corporations. *Quarterly Journal of Economics* 17: 111–162.
Caves, R.E. 1971. Export-Led Growth and the New Economic History. In *Trade, Balance of Payments, and Growth*, ed. J.N. Bhagwati, et al., 403–442. Amsterdam: North-Holland Publishing.
Caves, R.E. 1965. 'Vent for Surplus' Models of Trade and Growth. In *Trade, Growth and the Balance of Payments: Essays in Honor of Gottfried Haberler*, ed. R.E. Baldwin et al., 95–115. Chicago: Rand McNally and Company.
Chambers, E.J., and D.F. Gordon. 1966. Primary Products and Economic Growth. *Journal of Political Economy* 74: 315–332.
Coase, R.H. 1994. How Should Economists Choose? In *Essays on Economics and Economists*, ed. R.H. Coase, 15–33. Chicago: University of Chicago Press.
Cornwall, J., and W. Cornwall. 1992. Export-Led Growth: A New Interpretation. In *The Megacorp and Macrodynamics: Essays in Memory of Alfred Eichner*, ed. J. Milberg, 209–223. Armonk, NY: M.E. Sharpe.
DeLong, B.J. 1988. Productivity Growth, Convergence, and Welfare: Comment. *American Economic Review* 78: 1138–1154.
Dick, T.J.O. 1980. Canadian Wheat Production and Trade 1896–1930. *Explorations in Economic History* 17: 275–302.
Domar, E.D. 1970. The Causes of Slavery or Serfdom: A Hypothesis. *Journal of Economic History* 30: 18–32.
Easterlin, R.E. 1981. Why Isn't the Whole World Developed? *Journal of Economic History* 41: 1–19.
Edwards, S. 1998. Openness, Productivity and Growth: What Do We Really Know? *Economic Journal* 108: 383–398.
Emery, H.J.C. Herbert., and K.J. McKenzie. 1996. Damned If You Do, Damned If You Don't: An Option Value Approach to Evaluating the Subsidy of the CPR Mainline. *Canadian Journal of Economics* 24: 255–270.
Firestone, O.J. 1958. *Canada's Economic Development, 1867–1953, With Special Reference to Changes in the Country's National Product and National Wealth, Income and Wealth Series VII*. London: Bowes and Bowes.
Fogarty, J. 1985. Staples, Super-Staples and the Limits of the Staple Theory: The Experiences of Argentina, Australia and Canada Compared. In *Argentina, Australia and Canada: Studies in Comparative Development, 1870–1965*, ed. D.C.M. Platt and G. di Tella, 1–36. New York: St. Martin's Press.
Fowke, V.C. 1957. *The National Policy and the Wheat Economy*. Toronto: University of Toronto Press.

Galenson, D.W., and R.R. Menard. 1980. Approaches to the Analysis of Economic Growth in Colonial British America. *Historical Methods* 13: 3–18.

Gordon, H.S. 1954. The Economic Theory of the Common-Property Resource: The Fishery. *Journal of Political Economy* 62: 124–142.

Green, A.G., and M.C. Urquhart. 1994. New Estimates of Output Growth in Canada: Measurement and Interpretation. In *New Canadian Reading: Perspectives on Canadian Economic History*, ed. D. McCalla, 182–199. Toronto: Copp Clark Pitman.

Grossman, G.M., and E. Helpman. 1994. Endogenous Innovation in the Theory of Growth. *Journal of Economic Perspectives* 8: 23–44.

Habbakkuk, H.J. 1962. *American and British Technology in the Nineteenth Century: The Search for Labour-Saving Inventions*. Cambridge, UK: Cambridge University Press.

Hagemann, H., and S. Seiter. 1999. Verdoorn's Law. In*Encyclopedia of Political Economy, Volume 2: L-Z*, ed. P.A. O'Hara, 1229–1231. London and New York: Routledge.

Harley, K.C. 1980. Transportation, the World Wheat Trade, and the Kuznets Cycle, 1850–1913. *Explorations in Economic History* 17: 218–250.

Harris, M. 1959. The Economy Has No Surplus? *American Anthropologist* 61: 185–199.

Hirschman, A.O. 1977. A Generalized Linkage Approach to Development, with Special Reference to Staples. *Economic Development and Cultural Change* 25: S67–S98.

Innis, H.A., and W.T. Easterbrook. 1965. Fundamental and Historic Elements. In *The Canadian Economy: Selected Readings*, Revised, ed. J.J. Deutsch, B.S. Keirstead, K. Levitt, and R.M. Will, 440–448. Toronto: Macmillan Company of Canada.

Innis, H.A. 1967. The Importance of Staple Products, first published in 1930. In *Approaches to Canadian Economic History*, ed. W.T. Easterbrook and M.H. Watkins, 16–19. Toronto: McClelland and Stewart Limited.

Innis, H.A. 1973a. Significant Factors in Canadian Economic Development, first published in 1937. In *Essays in Canadian Economic History: Harold A. Innis*, ed. M.Q. Innis, 200–210. Toronto: University of Toronto Press.

Innis, H.A. 1973b. Unused Capacity as a Factor in Canadian Economic History, first published in 1936. In *Essays in Canadian Economic History: Harold A. Innis*, ed. M.Q. Innis, 141–155. Toronto: University of Toronto Press.

Innis, H.A. 1973c. Transportation as a Factor in Canadian Economic History, first published in 1931. In *Essays in Canadian Economic History: Harold A. Innis*, ed. M.Q. Innis, 62–77. Toronto: University of Toronto Press.

Innis, H.A. 1940. *The Cod Fisheries: The History of an International Economy*. Toronto: University of Toronto Press.

Innis, H.A. 1956. *The Fur Trade in Canada: An Introduction to Canadian Economic History*, first published in 1930. Toronto: University of Toronto Press.

Inwood, K., and T. Stengos. 1991. Discontinuities in Canadian Economic Growth, 1870–1985. *Explorations in Economic History* 28: 274–286.

Kaldor, N. 1966. *Causes of the Slow Rate of Growth in the United Kingdom*. Cambridge, UK: Cambridge University Press.

Kravis, I.B. 1970a. External and Internal Supply Factors in LDC Export Performance. *Banca Nationale del Lavoro Quarterly Review* 23: 157–179.

Kravis, I.B. 1970b. Trade as a Handmaiden of Growth: Similarities Between the Nineteenth and Twentieth Centuries. *Economic Journal* 80: 850–872.

Kravis, I.B. 1971. The Role of Exports in Nineteenth-Century United States Growth. *Economic Development and Cultural Change* 20: 387–405.

Kuznets, S. 1965. *Towards a Theory of Economic Growth*. New York: W. W. Norton.

Leibenstein, H. 1966. Allocative Efficiency vs. 'X-Efficiency. *American Economic Review* 56: 392–415.

Lewis, F.D. 1981. Farm Settlement on the Western Prairies, 1898 to 1911. *Journal of Economic History* 41: 517–535.

Lucas, R.E. 1988. On the Mechanics of Economic Development. *Journal of Monetary Economics* 22: 3–42.

Mackintosh, W.A. 1967. "Economic Factors in Canadian Economic History, first published in 1923. In *Approaches to Canadian Economic History*, ed. W.T. Easterbrook and M.H. Watkins, 1–15. Toronto: McClelland and Stewart Limited.

Mackintosh, W.A. 1978. *The Economic Background of Dominion-Provincial Relations*, first published in 1939. Toronto: Macmillan.

Maddison, A. 1991. *Dynamic Forces in Capitalist Development: A Long-run Comparative View*. Oxford and New York: Oxford University Press.

Maddison, A. 1995. *Monitoring the World Economy, 1820–1992*. Paris: OECD.

McCalla, D. 1993. *Planting the Province: The Economic History of Upper Canada, 1784–1870*. Toronto: University of Toronto Press.

McCusker, J.J., and R.R. Menard. 1985. *The Economy of British North America*. Chapel Hill, NC: University of North Carolina Press.

McInnis, R.M. 1992. The Early Ontario Wheat Staple Reconsidered. In *Canadian Papers in Rural History*, Vol. 8, ed. D.H. Akenson, 17–48. Gananoque, ON: Langdale Press.

McInnis, R.M. 1999. *Canadian Economic Development in the Wheat Boom Era: A Reassessment*. Paper Presented to the Canadian Economics Association Annual Meeting, May 28. Toronto.

Meier, G.M. 1953. Economic Development and the Transfer Mechanism: Canada, 1895–1913. *Canadian Journal of Economics and Political Science* 19: 1–19.

Murphy, K.M., A. Shleifer, and R. Vishny. 1989. Income Distribution, Market Size, and Industrialization. *Quarterly Journal of Economics* 104: 537–564.

Myint, H. 1958. The Classical Theory of International Trade and the Underdeveloped Countries. *Economic Journal* 68: 317–337.

Neill, R.F. 1972. *A New Theory of Value: The Canadian Economics of H.A. Innis.* Toronto: University of Toronto Press.

Neill, R.F. 1991. *A History of Economic Thought in Canada.* London: Routledge.

Nelson, R.R. 1968. A 'Diffusion' Model of International Productivity Differences in Manufacturing Industry. *American Economic Review* 58: 1219–1248.

Norrie, K.H. 1975. The Rate of Settlement on the Canadian Prairies 1870–1911. *Journal of Economic History* 35: 410–427.

North, D.C. 1955. Location Theory and Regional Economic Growth. *Journal of Political Economy* 63: 243–258.

North, D.C. 1959. Agriculture in Regional Economic Growth. *Journal of Farm Economics* 41: 943–951.

North, D.C. 1990. *Institutions, Institutional Change and Economic Performance.* Cambridge, UK: Cambridge University Press.

Ommer, R.E. 1981. 'All the Fish of the Post': Resource Property Rights and Development in a Nineteenth-Century Inshore Fishery. *Acadiensis* 10: 107–123.

Ommer, R.E. 1985. What's Wrong with Canadian Fish. *Journal of Canadian Studies* 20: 122–142.

O'Rourke, K. 2000. Tariffs and Growth in the Late Nineteenth Century. *Economic Journal* 110: 456–543.

Parente, L., and E.C. Prescott. 2000. *Barriers to Riches.* Cambridge, MA and London: MIT Press.

Pomfret, R. 1981. The Staple Theory as an Approach to Canadian and Australian Economic Development. *Australian Economic History Review* 21: 133–146.

Pritchett, L. 1997. Divergence, Big Time. *Journal of Economic Perspectives* 11: 3–17.

Reynolds, L.G. 1986. *Economic Growth in the Third World: An Introduction.* New Haven and London: Yale University Press.

Rodriguez, F., and D. Rodrik. 1999. Trade Policy and Economic Growth: A Skeptics Guide to the Cross-National Evidence. NBER Working Paper 7081. Cambridge, MA: National Bureau of Economic Research.

Rodrik, D. 1997. Globalization, Social Conflict and Economic Growth. Working Paper. Cambridge, MA: John F. Kennedy School of Government, Harvard University.

Rodrik, D. 2001. Trading in Illusion. *Foreign Policy: The Magazine of Global Politics, Economics, and Ideas*, March–April.

Romer, P.M. 1986. Increasing Returns and Long-Run Growth. *Journal of Political Economy* 94: 1002–1037.

Romer, P.M. 1990. Endogenous Technical Change. *Journal of Political Economy* 98: S71–S102.

Rosenberg, N. 1982a. The Historiography of Technical Progress. In *Inside the Black Box: Technology and Economics*, ed. N. Rosenberg, 3–33. Cambridge, UK: Cambridge University Press.

Rosenberg, N. 1982b. The International Transfer of Technology: Implications for Industrialized Countries. In *Inside the Black Box: Technology and Economics*, ed. N. Rosenberg, 245–279. Cambridge, UK: Cambridge University Press.

Ruttan, V.W. 1997. Induced Innovation, Evolutionary Theory and Path Dependence: Sources of Technical Change. *Economic Journal* 107: 1520–1529.

Sachs, J.D., and A.M. Warner. 1995. Natural Resource Abundance and Economic Growth. NBER Working paper Series # 5398. Cambridge, MA: National Bureau of Economic Research.

Salter, W.E.G. 1960. *Productivity and Technical Change*. Cambridge, UK: Cambridge University Press.

Schedvin, C.B. 1990. Staples and Regions of Pax Britannica. *Economic History Review* 43: 533–559.

Sen, A. 1970. Introduction. In *Growth Economics*, ed. A.K. Sen, 9–40. Harmondsworth, UK: Penguin Books.

Solow, R.M. 1956. A Contribution to the Theory of Economic Growth. *Quarterly Journal of Economics* 70: 65–94.

Solow, R.M. 1957. Technical Progress and the Aggregate Production Function. *Review of Economics and Statistics* 39: 312–320.

Solow, R.M. 1960. Investment and Technical Progress. In *Mathematical Methods in the Social Sciences*, ed. K.J. Arrow, S. Karlin, and P. Suppes, 89–194. Stanford, CA: Stanford University Press.

Sparks, G.R., and A.G. Green. 1999. Population Growth and the Dynamics of Canadian Development: A Multivariate Time Series Approach. *Explorations in Economic History* 36: 56–71.

Thirwall, A.P. 1983. A Plain Man's Guide to Kaldor's Growth Laws. *Journal of Post Keynesian Economics* 5: 345–358.

Urquhart, M.C., and K.A.H. Buckley, eds. 1965. *Historical Statistics of Canada*. Toronto: Macmillan.

Urquhart, M.C. 1986. New Estimates of Gross National Product, Canada, 1870–1926: Some Implications for Canadian Development. In *Long-Term Factors in American Economic Growth, Studies in Income and Wealth*, Vol. 51, ed. S.L.

Engerman and R. E. Gallman, 9–94. NBER. Chicago: University of Chicago Press.

Urquhart, M.C. 1993. *Gross National Product, Canada, 1870–1926: The Derivation of the Estimates*. Montreal: McGill-Queen's University Press.

Ward, T. 1995. Farming Technology and Crop Area on Early Prairie Farms. *Prairie Forum* 20: 19–36.

Watkins, M.H. 1963. A Staple Theory of Economic Growth. *The Canadian Journal of Economics and Political Science* 24: 141–158.

Young, A.A. 1928. Increasing Returns and Economic Progress. *Economic Journal* 38: 527–542.

PART II

Economic Growth and Development in Early Canada

CHAPTER 3

Economic Growth and Development in Early Canada

1 Introduction

By constructing rough approximations of constant dollar or real gross domestic product (RGDP) for early Canada (specifically the French colony in and about the St. Lawrence River Valley), I hope to provide a more solid foundation for an understanding of this colony's economic structure and evolution. At present, incoherent statistical and literary sources serve as the basis for most economic commentaries on early Canada. My constant dollar GDP series for 1695–1739 enables the computation of a per capita output series and of growth rates for that output. It also facilitates estimating the relative significance of different sectors. Furthermore, these GDP estimates permit an empirically grounded comparison of early Canada with British America, thus placing the economy of the French colony in a North American context. The construction of an RGDP series is made possible by the fairly comprehensive and accurate censuses, particularly from 1680 to 1739, prepared for Canada by the colonial authorities.[1] Although these censuses were not designed to account for all output, we can use them to extend and deepen our knowledge of early Canada's economy.

No consensus exists on Canada's economic condition during the period under scrutiny. Rather, two general points of view can be described. The dominant interpretation holds that the economic system

M. Altman, *Lessons from a Successfully Export-Oriented, Resource-Rich Economy*, https://doi.org/10.1007/978-3-031-03887-7_3

remained weak and stagnant, principally owing to exaggerated concentration on the fur trade and to insufficiency of internal or external markets; leading proponents of this view include Harold A. Innis, Jean Hamelin, and Louise Dechêne.[2] This reading is disputed by experts who, relying upon evidence of movements in wheat output, contend that the economy was becoming diversified and strong by the 1730s.[3] Cameron Nish, by comparing wage and foreign trade data, has ranked early Canada economically on a par with British America in the second quarter of the eighteenth century (Nish 1968). Although these lines of argument cannot be reconciled, the conflict need not result in stalemate; the evidence offered by both sides is too fragmentary to justify a firm conclusion. The situation requires a body of data sufficiently large and weighty to break the impasse.

The RGDP and related estimates presented here challenge the view that early Canada's economy was stagnant, that it was dominated by the fur trade, and that the fur trade caused the colony's economic malaise. Rather, I find that Canada was economically dynamic and prosperous, even when compared to British North America. My estimates thus substantiate and expand upon the positive interpretations of the colony's economic condition. The following pages discuss results stemming from the estimates. Details on their construction are largely found in Tables 5, 7, and 10, and the Appendix.

2 The Basis of the Real Gross Domestic Product Estimates

The RGDP estimates, presented in Table 1, are in terms of 1749 prices (*livres tournois*, New France). That year, Peter Kalm, the Swedish naturalist, passed through Canada and recorded unit output prices for key commodities. I have supplemented his data with other price data. Output data are multiplied by their corresponding 1749 prices to yield the constant dollar GDP estimates. These are divided into three parts: agricultural output, nonagricultural output, and the fur trade. The fur trade is the only series that does not reflect the output of an independent group of producers. It was dominated, the evidence suggests, by farmers working in the off-season, prospective farmers earning start-up capital, and urban craftsmen and their sons (Dechêne 1974, pp. 222–225). The fur trade estimates therefore indicate not simply this sector's contribution to total

Table 1 Total and per capita real (1749 *livres*) gross domestic product in Canada, 1695–1739

	Total				*Per capita*			
	Agricultural sector	*Non-agricultural sector*	*Fur sector*	*Total*	*Agricultural sector*	*Non-agricultural sector*	*Fur sector*	*Total*
1695	975,885	196,000	260,400	1,432,285	76	15	24	115
1698	1,097,984	212,000	195,920	1,505,904	79	15	14	108
1706	1,432,179	255,600	198,400	1,886,179	86	15	12	113
1707	1,417,325	269,200	198,400	1,884,925	81	15	11	107
	–	–	–	–	–	–	–	–
1712	1,826,761	287,600	198,400	2,312,761	97	15	11	123
1713	1,573,906	283,200	198,400	2,055,506	85	15	11	111
1714	1,885,783	295,200	248,000	2,428,983	98	15	13	126
1716	2,019,078	369,700	218,240	2,607,018	97	18	10	125
1718	1,907,854	357,600	301,795	2,567,249	82	15	13	110
	–	–	–	–	–	–	–	–
1719	2,028,965	345,600	909,237	3,283,802	90	15	40	146
1720	2,713,822	375,200	411,241	3,500,263	111	15	17	143
	–	–	–	–	–	–	–	–
1721	2,217,177	396,400	331,683	2,945,260	86	15	13	114
1722	2,372,442	400,400	441,130	3,213,972	91	15	17	123
1723	2,265,284	398,800	475,297	3,139,381	87	15	18	120
1724	2,352,287	488,100	400,720	3,241,107	87	18	15	120
1726	3,157,906	457,600	145,199	3,760,705	106	15	5	126
1727	3,198,486	499,682	987,580	4,685,748	103	16	32	150
	–	–	–	–	–	–	–	–
1730	3,279,876	644,660	643,469	4,568,005	96	19	19	134
1732	3,225,902	680,970	570,283	4,477,155	91	19	16	126
1734	4,231,703	710,739	578,861	5,521,303	112	19	15	146
1736	4,089,015	812,490	371,590	5,273,095	104	21	9	133
1737	2,698,357	683,537	436,003	3,295,908	67	17	11	95

(continued)

Table 1 (continued)

	Total				*Per capita*			
	Agricultural sector	*Non-agricultural sector*	*Fur sector*	*Total*	*Agricultural sector*	*Non-agricultural sector*	*Fur sector*	*Total*
1739	4,560,905	858,077	562,852	5,981,834	105	20	13	138

Sources Tables 5, 7, and 10

output but also its importance as a generator of supplementary income by farmers and craftsmen.

The most reliable of the output estimates are agricultural components taken directly from the censuses with only slight adjustments. Crop production data, for which we have good evidence, are adjusted only for seed requirements. The net result composes between 35 and 40% of agricultural output. Changes in animal inventory are based upon census data on numbers of livestock. The values of slaughtered cattle and swine, as well as of dairy output, wool production, on-farm construction, and land improvement, also have a firm basis in the census material. But, unlike the crop estimates, these require the use of a variety of coefficients that prove to be much more tentative than the census data. Finally, estimates of the production of firewood are based upon United States data for 1840 on the consumption of firewood as well as on estimates of early Canadian household consumption.

Estimates for nonagricultural output are even more tentative. I use wage data and estimates of the nonagricultural share of the total population to generate the largest segment of the nonagricultural output series. This is only a very rough approximation of what was produced in early Canada and is supplemented with estimates of shipbuilding and lumber exports. Finally, the fur trade estimates are based upon those of French imports of fur from Canada and are biased downward because they do not include the value of the illegal trade in furs. This bias does not appear to be significant.

Because I am attempting to measure the gross domestic product, my estimates incorporate the value of final output alone or, when necessary, approximations of it. This, of course, is to avoid double counting. For example, I exclude the value of fodder since this is included in my estimates of meat and dairy output. On the other hand, I present the value of wheat rather than bread. The value added to wheat in milling and baking is captured in my estimates of nonagricultural output. The RGDP estimates are biased downward because they exclude fishing, hunting, and the production of fruits, vegetables, and maple syrup, as well as the illegal fur trade. Discounting the last, such output might add as much as 20 *livres* to the RGDP estimates for all census years.[4] My results are therefore inherently biased in favor of the negative reading of the economic development of early Canada.[5] Even so, they support the more positive interpretation. Furthermore, upward revisions of these estimates, it should be stressed, only marginally reduce my per capita growth rates. This downward bias of the per capita output estimates thus yields upper-bound rates of growth.[6]

3 Real Gross Domestic Product Estimates and Their Analytical Implications

For analytical purposes my estimates are divided into four time frames for which averages are computed. The first is 1695–1707, before the Treaty of Utrecht. The 1712–1718 period includes the first years of *sustained* peace in the colony's history. The years 1719 and 1720 are deleted from the averages because they were years of exceptionally high output and would therefore give the average for the 1710s a considerable upward bias. An exceptionally high fur trade output dominated 1719 production, and an exceptionally high agricultural output characterized 1720 production (see Table 1). If the average for the period 1712–1720 is computed, the RGDP is 126 *livres* compared to 119 *livres* for the period 1712–1718 (see Table 2). Next are the 1721–1728 and 1730–1739 periods, plus a 1734–1739 subperiod. For the 1730s two sets of averages are given—one that includes and one that excludes the 1737 census year. I place greater confidence in the latter set of estimates because the exceptionally poor economic performance in 1737 reduces the averages for this period well below what they would otherwise have been (see Lunn 1943, pp. 96–99; Salone 1970, p. 376; See also Tables 1, 5 and 7).

An important point brought out by the estimates is that real per capita output in early Canada and British North America was similar. Robert Gallman calculates that the latter's constant per capita net national product ranged between $45 and $60 in 1840 prices in the period 1710–1720.[7] Claudia D. Goldin and Frank D. Lewis (1980) adjust Gallman's result to generate gross national product estimates of $46–61. These are more consistent with my estimates for Canada than are Gallman's, but they are also quite similar to Gallman's estimates. More recent estimates of British American output made by Alice Hanson Jones and by John J. McCusker and Russell R. Menard are consistent with Gallman's.[8]

To compare the constant dollar per capita output of Canada and British America I do not attempt to convert Canadian output, given in *livres tournois*, to its U.S. dollar equivalent using exchange rates. Gallman generates a U.S. dollar value for 1720 output by applying a growth rate to his 1840 dollar estimate of 1840 output and extrapolating backwards. He also provides a tentative and tenuous conversion of his 1720 U.S. dollar

Table 2 Period averages real (1749 *livres*) per capita gross domestic product and economic structure

	Period averages				*Percentage distribution of output*		
	Agricultural sector	*Non-agricultural sector*	*Fur sector*	*Total*	*Agricultural sector*	*Non-agricultural sector*	*Fur sector*
1 1695–1707	81	15	15	111	73	13.5	13.5
2 1712–1718	92	16	11	119	77.3	13.4	9.2
3 1721–1727	93	16	17	126	73.8	12.7	13.5
4 1734–1739a	97	19	12	128	75.8	14.8	9.4
5 1734–1739b	107	20	13	140	76.4	14.3	9.3
6 1730–1739a	96	19	14	129	74.4	14.7	10.8
7 1730–1739b	102	19	15	136	75.0	14.0	11.0
8 1712–1720	94	16.4	16	126	74.6	12.7	12.7

Notes All period averages are simple arithmetic averages derived from Table 1. The percentage distribution of output is derived from the period averages. Lines 4 and 6 include the output data for all census years. Lines 5 and 7 omit the output data for the 1737 census so as to compute the period averages in the absence of this exceptionally poor year

Sources Table 1 and Text

value of output to pounds sterling. This, in turn, can be converted into *livres tournois*, but only in an indirect and approximate manner yielding questionable results.[9] Even under the best of circumstances, at any point in time, one country's exchange rate relative to another country's does not typically reflect the relative purchasing power of these countries' currencies (for example, see Gallman 1966, pp. 4–6; Kravis 1984). Thus using exchange rates to convert the output of one country into its equivalent in another's currency can have misleading outcomes. Other means of comparison are needed.

One that is most appropriate converts early Canada's output to its British American equivalent using U.S. price data for wheat, pork, beef, and dairy produce for 1840. Such output represents about 66% of early Canada's net of firewood measured in *livres tournois* in the period 1712–1718 and is equivalent to $31.54 U.S. This is inflated to incorporate the remaining 34% of output for which U.S. price data are not readily available, yielding $47.51. To this figure is added the estimated value of firewood, giving a total of $53.40 U.S.[10] This very rough and lower-bound estimate for early Canadian real output per capita falls within the range of the modified GaLlman estimate for British America. I also compare the real output of Canada and British America in terms of the quantity of wheat that Canada's or British America's output could have purchased. The 119 livres of real per capita output in Canada for 1712–1718 could have purchased about 47 bushels of wheat at a 1749 price of 2.5 *livres* per *minot* (1 minot = 1.05 bushels). The $46.61 of British American constant dollar per capita output could have purchased between 37 and 49 bushels.[11] Thus early Canada also compares well to British America in the purchasing power of its constant dollar GDP relative to a major component of that GDP.

The growth rates of real per capita output in early Canada and British America also appear to have been similar. Both Gallman and Marc Egnal argue that its rate of growth in British America, 1712–1800, was between 0.3 and 0.5% per annum, an argument recently reiterated by McCusker and Menard.[12] I find that annual per capita growth in early Canada ranged from 0.5 to 0.6% during the period 1695–1739.[13] More compatible with the time frame of the British American growth estimates are my calculations for the 1712–1739 period: between 0.4 and 0.7% annually (see Table 3).[14] These growth rates would have generated an increase in per capita output of between 4 and 10% every ten years and between 22 and 42% every fifty years. One might argue, however, that Canada's growth performance for 1695–1739 should be compared with that of British America only for the 1650–1700 period; these were the formative years of Canada's and British America's economic development when, some would say, one would expect a higher growth rate.[15] In this case, my growth estimates appear less impressive only when compared to Anderson's 1.6% annual growth rate estimate for New England for the 1650–1680 period. However, Alice Hanson Jones estimates that growth in British America, from 1650 to 1700, was about 0.3% per annum.[16] Whatever standard for comparison one chooses, Canada's growth performance appears formidable, particularly in the context of the relatively high level of real per capita output realized there by the early eighteenth century.

My growth estimates also suggest that Canada's relatively high rate of growth did not result from a few exceptionally good years. From 1695 to 1718 Canada sustained a quite healthy 0.5% rate of growth, with a robust rate of 0.6% from 1712 to 1727. From 1721 to 1739 the growth rate was

Table 3 Percent rates of growth per annum

		Agricultural sector	*Non-agricultural sector*	*Fur sector*	*Total*
1	1695–1707 to 1734–1739a	0.5	0.7	−0.6	0.4
2	1695–1707 to 1734–1739b	0.8	0.8	−0.4	0.7
3	1695–1707 to 1730–1739a	0.5	0.7	−0.2	0.45
4	1695–1707 to 1730–1739a	0.7	0.7	−0.1	0.6
5	1695–1707 to 1712–1718	0.9	0.5	−2.2	0.5
6	1712–1718 to 1721–1727	0.1	0.0	4.9	0.6
7	1721–1727 to 1730–1739a	0.3	1.6	−1.8	0.2
8	1721–1727 to 1730–1739b	0.8	1.6	−1.1	0.7
9	1712–1718 to 1730–1739a	0.2	0.9	1.2	0.4
10	1712–1718 to 1730–1739b	0.5	0.9	1.6	0.7

Sources Period averages in Table 2

0.7% if the 1737 census year is excluded, but only 0.2% if it is included (see Table 3). If one places greater confidence in the former estimate, which the evidence suggests one should, then the growth rate improved clearly, albeit marginally, from one decade to the next.

4 Sectoral Growth Rates

We can also use the RGDP estimates to examine the roles of the different sectors in economic growth. First, one must ascertain the significance of each sector for total constant dollar per capita GDP and, thereby, the weight of each sector's growth rate in determining the overall rate (see Table 2). The agricultural sector was dominant for the entire 1695–1739 period, rising slightly in importance over time from 73 to about 75% of total per capita RGDP. The nonagricultural sector accounted for about 14% throughout the whole period, while the fur trade diminished from about 14 to 11%. One should note, however, significant fluctuations in the importance of the fur trade, which fell from 13.5% of the total in 1695–1707 to about 9% in 1712–1718, returned to about 13.5% in the 1720s, and fell again in the 1730s. These estimates confirm and extend Louise Dechêne's view that the fur trade was not dominant in the Canadian economy from 1708 to 1717—years of depression for the trade when the beaver fur monopoly refused to purchase any *castor gras*.[17] The economy of early Canada appears to have been fairly diversified, with the fur trade and other nonagricultural pursuits contributing a large, although not major, share of output. The predominance of the agricultural sector meant that its growth was the leading determinant of total per capita RGDP growth.

Over the 1695–1739 period the agricultural and nonagricultural sectors both experienced a phenomenal growth rate of 0.7% per annum, while the fur trade experienced an annual negative rate of 0.1% (see Table 3). The heavy weight of the agricultural sector in total output resulted in an overall rate of growth of 0.6% a year.[18] Indeed, even had the nonagricultural sector not increased, the agricultural sector would have yielded a 0.5% rate of growth in spite of the fur trade's negative growth (see Table 4).

While the fur trade did not always play a negative role in the growth process, it did so in the 1695–1718 period, with a −2.2% growth rate, and in the 1721–1739 period, with a −1.1% rate (see Table 3). Only in the 1712–1727 period did the fur trade experience vigorous growth: 4.9% per annum. At this time the agricultural sector grew by only 0.1% annually while the nonagricultural sector failed to grow at all, yielding an overall rate of 0.6% per annum. The growth rate in the fur trade alone would have permitted the economy to have grown at 0.55% annually. By itself, the agricultural sector could have generated only a meager annual growth rate of 0.08% (see Table 4). Thus, in the 1712–1727 period, the fur trade prevented the economy from stagnating: slow growth in the agricultural sector was compensated for by spectacular growth in the fur trade.[19]

From 1695 to 1718 the agricultural sector sustained the highest rate of growth it experienced in the entire 1695–1739 period: 0.9% per annum. This rate more than compensated for the very high negative growth rate of the fur trade and the negligible rate of only 0.2% of the nonagricultural sector, generating an overall annual growth rate of 0.5%. In the last period examined, 1721–1739, the agricultural sector returned to a prominent position, recovering from its low in the 1712–1727 period, with a rate

Table 4 A partition of the percentage per annum growth rates

		The partition				*Arithmetic means*		
		Agricultural sector	*Non-agricultural sector*	*Fur sector*	*Total*	*Agricultural sector*	*Non-agricultural sector*	*Fur sector*
1	1695–1707 to 1734–1739a	0.37	0.10	−0.07	0.04	74.4%	14.1%	11.4%
2	1695–1707 to 1734–1739b	0.60	0.11	−0.04	0.67	74.7	13.9	11.4
3	1695–1707 to 1730–1739a	0.37	0.20	−0.02	0.45	73.7	28.2	12.1
4	1695–1707 to 1730–1739b	0.52	0.10	−0.01	0.61	74.0	13.7	12.3
5	1695–1707 to 1712–1718	0.67	0.07	−0.25	0.49	75.2	13.4	11.3
6	1712–1718 to 1721–1727	0.08	0.00	0.55	0.63	75.5	13.1	11.3
7	1721–1727 to 1730–1739a	0.22	0.22	−0.22	0.22	74.1	13.7	12.1
8	1721–1727 to 1730–1739b	0.59	0.21	−0.13	0.67	74.4	13.3	12.2
9	1712–1718 to 1730–1739a	0.15	0.13	0.12	0.40	75.8	14.0	10.1
10	1712–1718 to 1730–1739b	0.38	0.12	0.16	0.66	76.1	13.7	10.1

Note The partitioning of growth rates involves attributing to each sector its share of the total growth rate consistent with its share in total output. Each sector's growth rate (Table 3) is multiplied by the arithmetic mean of its percentage share in total output over the period to which the growth rate pertains. This arithmetic mean (this table) is derived from the sectoral distribution of output estimates found in Table 2

Sources Tables 2 and 3

of 0.8%. Center stage was shared with the nonagricultural sector, which was experiencing a 1.6% annual rate of growth.

These high rates yielded an overall growth of 0.7% per annum in spite of the substantial rate of decline of the fur trade (see Table 3). However, the nonagricultural sector alone, in spite of its hardy growth, could have generated a growth rate of per capita RGDP of only 0.1% (inclusive of the negative growth performance of the fur trade), because of its relatively small share in per capita RGDP. The agricultural sector, on the other hand, because of its relatively large share, could have generated, by itself, an overall rate of growth of 0.5% (see Table 4).

The nonagricultural sector made its only significant contribution to the economic growth of Canada in this last period. Although not overwhelming, its contribution was of some importance. In absolute terms the economy grew by 10 *livres* per capita from 1721 to 1739, with the nonagricultural sector contributing 3 *livres* to this sum (see Table 2, rows 3 and 7). A spurt in shipbuilding and lumber exports (two components of the nonagricultural sector) was responsible for this lively performance (see Tables 9 and 10), and the growth of shipbuilding can be related to growth in the export of flour, fish, and timber (Lunn 1943, pp. 230, 240; Mathieu 1981, pp. 157, 218). It is fairly certain, therefore, that a good part of the last period's growth attributable to the nonagricultural sector was due to the impact of non-fur exports.

The relatively strong economic performance of early Canada stands out even more sharply when placed in the context of the colony's rapid population growth. Population increased at an annual rate of 2.8% over the entire 1695–1739 period and by 3.4% annually over the 1721–1739 period.[20] The economy responded to the challenge of a rapidly growing population, and its per capita RGDP continued to rise. The experience in British North America was parallel, with similar real per capita output growth rates and a population growing by 3.4% annually from 1710 to 1740 and by 3.2% annually from 1710 to 1770.[21]

5 Surplus Production in Early Canada

It is also evident from my series on wheat output that the Canadian economy was producing an increasing surplus of wheat beyond what was necessary for home consumption, which I assume to have been 8 *minots* per capita.[22] The surplus increased from 1.8 *minots* per capita in the 1695–1707 period to 4.5 *minots* per capita for 1730–1739—if one excludes the 1737 census year, when no surplus of wheat was available (see Table 5). The surplus stood at 2.7 *minots* and 3.0 *minots* in the 1712–1718 and 1721–1727 periods respectively. Only very rarely was too little wheat produced to feed the populations.[23] This increasing surplus

Table 5 Wheat output in early Canada, 1688–1739

	Surplus no. of people fed at 8 minots per capita	*Minots of wheat net of seed and consumption requirements at 8 minots per capita*	*Value of per capita wheat output net of seed*	*Value of wheat output net of seed (1749* livres*)*	*Wheat output per capita net of seeds (minots)*	*Gross wheat output per arpents (minots)*	*Minots of wheat net of seeds*	*Seed requirements (minots)*	*Arpents under wheat*
1688	10,686	21,373	100,974	9.5	9.8	252,435	24.5	18,550	2,318
1695	10,538	21,076	108,078	12.3	8.5	270,195	21.1	5,790	724
1698	12,193	24,386	136,592	13.2	9.9	341,480	24.7	26,072	3,259
1706	16,377	32,754	178,881	12.9	10.7	447,202	26.7	45,233	5,654
1707	16,313	32,624	147,231	11.0	8.4	368,077	21.0	6,839	855
1712	19,862	39,722	252,693	14.7	13.5	631,732	33.7	102,605	12,856
1713	20,598	41,196	210,267	12.2	11.4	525,667	28.5	62,531	7,816
1714	19,935	39,870	196,179	11.8	10.2	490,447	25.4	41,659	5,207
1716	21,465	42,930	209,374	9.8	10.0	523,435	25.1	42,254	5,282
1718	26,691	53,382	196,167	9.4	8.4	490,417	21.0	9,567	1,594
1719	23,637	47,274	187,292	9.9	8.3	468,230	20.8	7,052	881
1720	23,009	40,018	224,419	11.5	9.2	561,047	22.9	28,627	3,578
1721	23,308	46,614	236,086	12.1	9.1	590,215	22.8	29,270	3,659
1722	23,525	47,050	294,155	14.5	11.3	735,387	28.2	85,307	10,663
1723	30,842	61,684	233,838	9.6	9.0	584,595	22.5	25,846	3,231
1724	31,282	62,564	237,460	9.6	8.7	593,650	21.9	20,188	2,523
1726	36,076	72,152	338,918	11.4	11.4	847,295	28.4	100,046	12,506
1727	38,287	76,574	364,165	11.5	11.7	910,412	29.2	177,151	14,352
1730	49,047	98,047	360,628	9.4	10.6	901,570	26.4	87,684	10,960

(continued)

Table 5 (continued)

	Surplus no. of people fed at 8 minots per capita	*Minots of wheat net of seed and consumption requirements at 8 minots per capita*	*Value of per capita wheat output net of seed*	*Value of wheat output net of seed (1749* livres*)*	*Wheat output per capita net of seeds (minots)*	*Gross wheat output per arpents (minots)*	*Minots of wheat net of seeds*	*Seed requirements (minots)*	*Arpents under wheat*
1732	49,974	99,948	368,271	9.4	10.4	920,677	26.0	84,935	10,617
1734	61,167	122,334	615,558	12.1	16.3	1,538,895	40.8	313,830	39,229
1736	61,778	123,556	546,188	10.8	13.8	1,365,470	34.6	230,220	28,777
1737	58,989	117,978	223,710	5.8	5.6	559,275	13.9	−97,514	0
1739	70,539	141,078	493,527	9.0	11.4	1,233,817	28.5	146,471	18,309

Note To estimate the quantity of wheat entering the GDP (the value of per capita wheat output net of seed) seed requirements were estimated and netted from the census estimates of total wheat output. The censuses, however, provide no data on the number of arpents planted with wheat. I rely upon Harris for an estimate of three-quarters of land under cultivation planted with wheat and upon Dechêne for an estimate of two minots of wheat required to sow an arpent with wheat. This yields estimates of the number of arpents sown with wheat, seed requirements for wheat production, and net wheat output. I also assume, from Lunn, that the price of wheat in 1749 was 2.5 *livres* per minot

Sources For the census data see, in particular, Alfred Rowland Vanesse, "A Social History of the Seigniorial Regime in Canada, 1712–1739" (Ph.D., University of Montreal, 1958), 11. For other references see Louise Dechêne, Habitants et marchands de Montréal au xviie siécle (Paris, 1974), 327; Richard Colebrook Harris, ***The Seigneurial System in Early Canada*** (Madison, WI, 1966), 153; and AJ.E. Lunn, "The Economic Development of French Canada, 1740–1760" (M.A. thesis, McGill University, 1934), 120

permitted Canada to export enough wheat to feed about 2,600 individuals, who each consumed 8 *minots* annually in the first period examined. During the next period the surplus could have fed about 6,500; during the 1721–1727 period, about 10,200; and about 27,600 in the last period examined (see Table 5, col. 9).[24]

Jacques Mathieu suggests that such surpluses should have been easily absorbed by the growing markets in the French West Indies.[25] But it is well known that Canada was unable to supply the needs of the French sugar islands, which were forced to turn to mainland British America for supplies. This dependence on the British colonies, we can now say, was not the result of stagnation in the agricultural sector in Canada but, rather, of a small population base and thus a small farming community that limited the surplus of wheat and other produce.[26]

One hypothesis that remains to be rigorously tested is that this small population base was to a large extent due to a very effective French state policy designed to make Canada a Catholic colony.[27] This policy prevented Canada from attracting religious dissidents who fled from France in large numbers, particularly after the revocation of the Edict of Nantes, in contrast to English state practice that allowed New England, for example, to establish a relatively large initial population base with dissidents from England.[28]

My estimates also demonstrate that the increase in wheat output was not the result of "good luck" in yields, as the oft-quoted Elizabeth Lunn would have it (Lunn (1943), p.110). Yields per arpent declined continuously but gradually over the entire 1695–1739 period (see Table 5, col. 4). Increased wheat output was due entirely to a rise in the number of arpents being placed under cultivation, which rose from about nineteen in 1695–1707 to about twenty-two in 1712–1718. The next increase came in the 1730–1739 period, when about thirty-two arpents per farm were under cultivation.[29]

Farmers appear to have made an effort to compensate for declining yields, if not to increase output. And the significant increase in the amount of land under cultivation took place in the period when there was a great surge in exports of agricultural produce from Canada to the French West Indies (Lunn (1943), III, p.449, Mathieu (1981), p.153). Thus, as with the nonagricultural sector, one can relate at least part of the growth in the agricultural sector to the growth in exports. It is possible that the increase in wheat production was also due to a demand for more per capita wheat consumption on the farms as well as among the growing urban population.[30]

Other outputs also played an important role in raising agricultural production. Over the entire period an increase in the value of slaughtered swine contributed even more than the rise in the value of wheat output to the agricultural sector's overall performance. Growth in the per capita production of wool, in land improvement, and in livestock inventory was also important (see Table 6a). Broken down by period, the increase in slaughtered swine was significant only from 1695 to 1718, when it was more than double the growth in the value of wheat output in absolute terms. The 1712–1728 period brought only negligible growth in the agricultural sector, while from 1721 to 1739 the rise in agricultural production was dominated by wheat output, with an important contribution also made by livestock inventory and land improvement (Table 6b).

The growth in the value of slaughtered swine is directly related to the typical farm increasingly producing beyond subsistence requirements, not only to meet the demand for pork in the expanding urban markets but also, perhaps, to augment the consumption of the typical peasant family.[31]

Table 6a Period average of real (1749 *livres*) per capita gross product in the agricultural sector

	1695–1707	*1712–1718*	*1721–1728*	*1730–1739a*
Wheat	23.39	26.72	25.48	31.25
Peas	0.6	0.51	0.66	0.59
Tobacco	0.39	0.39	0.66	0.95
Hemp	0.05	0.07	0.12	0.17
Flax	0.18	0.48	0.64	0.61
Wool	0.37	1.29	1.17	1.69
Change in livestock inventory	1.95	0.27	0.29	2.92
Slaughter of swine	10.88	18.67	18.8	18.86
Slaughter of cattle	14.43	14.43	14.43	14.43
Dairy output	10.52	10.52	10.52	10.52
Land improvements	0.87	2.13	2.63	3.79
Construction	2.58	2.18	2.76	2.30
Total	80.24	91.69	92.19	102.11

Note The total includes my 1.03 *livres* per capita estimate for slaughtered fowl and my 13 *livres* estimate for firewood. The totals here differ slightly from those in Table 2 due to rounding
Sources Tables 5 and 7

Table 6b Period to period changes in agricultural output in terms of 1749 *livres*

	1695–1707 to 1712–1718	*1712–1718 to 1721–1727*	*1721–1728 to 1730–1739*	*1695–1707 to 1730–1739*
Wheat	3.33	1.24	5.77	7.86
Peas	−0.09	0.15	−0.07	−0.01
Tobacco	0.00	0.27	0.79	0.56
Hemp	0.02	0.05	0.05	0.12
Flax	0.30	0.16	−0.03	0.43
Wool	0.92	−0.12	0.52	1.32
Change in livestock inventory	−1.68	0.02	2.64	0.97
Slaughter of swine	7.79	0.13	0.06	7.98
Land improvement	1.26	0.50	1.16	2.92
Construction	−0.40	0.58	−0.36	−0.28
Total	11.45	0.50	9.92	21.87

Note The totals here differ slightly from those in Table 2 due to rounding and averaging
Sources Tables 5 and 7

Rises in the value of livestock inventory and land improvement are both related to the per capita growth in the output of wheat and other crops.[32] Increased production of wool and tobacco, on a per capita basis, has been attributed to farm families consuming homemade cloth and tobacco in place of more expensive imports from France.[33]

These advances in per capita agricultural output were made possible, my estimates suggest, by augmenting labor inputs into agricultural production. More individuals as a percentage of the total population may have become engaged in such production over time, or individuals may have contributed more time or effort to the process of production. No evidence currently exists to suggest that more land was placed under cultivation or that more swine were slaughtered as a result of increasing doses of capital or by reason of technological change.

6 Conclusion

The RGDP per capita estimates presented here seriously challenge the view that early Canada's economy was stagnant and relatively impoverished. The colony was able to overcome its geographical and climatic disadvantages to develop an economy that was as productive as the one constructed by its southern neighbors. Moreover, since the farmers, who were the mainstay of the economy, retained most of any increased output, my estimates suggest that the laboring folk of Canada were becoming increasingly well off.[34]

With respect to the causes of early Canadian economic growth it can be argued that exports played an important role. But it appears that the growing population, urban as well as rural, also served to drive the growth process. Critical to Canada, however, was the ability of its economic system to respond to the challenge of an increasing population and expanding export markets so that consistent economic growth was generated on a per capita basis; a similar scenario was unfolding in British America. Ultimately, it is this flexibility that indicates the relatively robust nature of early Canada's economy.

Appendix: The Construction of RGDP Estimates

The agricultural component of the RGDP estimates is based upon the calculations presented in Tables 5 and 8, which are, in turn, constructed largely from data in 24 censuses.[35] I give the output estimates in terms of 1749 livres only. The more detailed computations are presented elsewhere (Altman 1985). The methodology underlying the construction of specific output estimates is discussed in the notes to Tables 5 and 8. I use the census data for wheat, peas, tobacco, hemp, flax, wool, the number of livestock, and the number of arpents under cultivation for my final computations. All grain and related output estimates presented are net estimated seed requirements. Oats and barley are assumed to have been used as feed for livestock, as is a certain percentage of pea output, and are thus included in my livestock-related estimates.[36]

The output estimates for the nonagricultural sector consist of three segments: a series for basic nonagricultural income (Table 7, col. 18), one for shipbuilding (Table 8), and another for lumber exports (Table 9). The first series is derived by estimating the percentage of the total population engaged in nonagricultural pursuits. The 1681 census provides the data from which to construct such an estimate. In this year there existed a very diversified nonagricultural sector dominated by wheel-wrights, carpenters, shoemakers, masons, joiners, notaries, edge-tool makers, and tailors, who collectively constituted 373 of an estimated population of 9,677.[37] Evidence suggests that the typical family numbered 6 individuals. If this is correct, and if each of our 373 craftsmen was head of a household, the nonagricultural population composed 23.1% of the total in 1681.[38]

Table 7 Population data and per capita output estimates in terms of 1749 *livres*

	1	2	3	4	5	6	7 Changes in	8	9	10	11 Slaughter of	12	13	14	15	16	17	18
	Population	*Peas*	*Tobacco*	*Hemp*	*Flax*	*Wool*	*Swine*	*Cattle*	*Sheep*	*Horses*	*Swine*	*Cattle*	*Poultry*	*Dairy*	*Land improvement*	*Farm construction*	*Firewood*	*Basic non-agricultural output*
1695	12,786	0.64	0.39	0.00	0.00	0.28	0.32	0.88	0.003	0.24	10.97	14.43	1.03	10.52	0.00	2.48	13.00	15.3
1698	13,815	0.64	0.39	0.00	0.00	0.28	−0.07	1.28	0.01	0.10	9.26	14.43	1.03	10.52	1.80	2.06	13.00	15.3
1706	16,706	0.64	0.39	0.07	0.25	0.42	0.3	1.71	0.05	0.53	11.95	14.43	1.03	10.52	1.69	1.93	13.00	15.3
1707	17,549	0.50	0.39	0.13	0.47	0.52	0.08	2.21	0.16	0.01	11.36	14.43	1.03	10.52	0.00	3.86	13.00	15.3
1712	18,761	0.61	0.39	0.11	0.58	1.36	0.45	1.51	0.40	0.62	15.46	14.43	1.03	10.52	2.10	1.08	13.00	15.3
1713	18,467	0.61	0.39	0.13	0.41	1.24	2.19	−7.59	−0.23	−2.60	21.36	14.43	1.03	10.52	1.90	0.00	13.00	15.3
1714	19,315	0.50	0.39	0.07	0.45	1.34	0.78	2.67	0.21	2.60	21.90	14.43	1.03	10.52	0.00	2.33	13.00	15.3
1716	20,890	0.47	0.39	0.02	0.57	1.34	0.37	2.94	0.09	0.52	21.75	14.43	1.03	10.52	1.00	3.12	13.00	15.3
1718	23,325	0.41	0.39	0.03	0.37	1.16	−1.20	−1.74	−0.30	−0.55	12.87	14.43	1.03	10.52	5.64	4.35	13.00	15.3
1719	22,530	0.51	0.39	0.07	0.42	1.48	2.35	3.63	0.04	1.56	19.45	14.43	1.03	10.52	0.00	0.00	13.00	15.3
1720	24,474	0.56	0.39	0.02	0.58	1.98	2.16	13.53	0.92	2.04	22.97	14.43	1.03	10.52	0.00	3.83	13.00	15.3
1721	25,852	0.55	0.39	0.03	0.44	1.10	−0.98	−2.68	0.38	0.51	19.04	14.43	1.03	10.52	0.00	4.34	13.00	15.3
1722	26,106	0.77	0.39	0.02	0.44	1.16	0.37	−1.58	0.08	0.08	19.70	14.43	1.03	10.52	0.00	0.77	13.00	15.3
1723	25,999	0.62	0.39	0.10	0.75	1.12	−1.20	−2.25	0.02	−0.39	16.77	14.43	1.03	10.52	7.63	0.78	13.00	15.3
1724	27,159	0.60	0.68	0.14	0.73	1.10	1.34	1.68	0.06	0.34	19.20	14.43	1.03	10.52	0.80	3.48	13.00	15.3
1726	29,859	0.69	0.84	0.10	0.74	1.24	0.34	1.70	0.27	0.59	18.82	14.43	1.03	10.52	3.97	3.78	13.00	15.3
1727	31,169	0.74	0.96	0.35	0.76	1.30	0.61	1.86	0.26	0.49	19.26	14.43	1.03	10.52	3.40	3.42	13.00	15.3
1730	34,118	0.75	0.92	0.56	0.69	2.34	0.25	4.04	0.11	0.00	19.06	14.43	1.03	10.52	5.54	2.41	13.00	15.3
1732	35,417	0.78	0.92	0.15	0.75	2.58	0.61	−0.58	0.28	0.28	18.19	14.43	1.03	10.52	0.63	1.48	13.00	15.3
1734	37,716	0.42	0.92	0.02	0.51	1.06	−0.13	0.65	−0.28	−1.22	18.92	14.43	1.03	10.52	7.45	2.68	13.00	15.3
1736	39,496	0.45	0.95	0.08	0.49	1.06	0.25	2.39	0.06	1.89	19.12	14.43	1.03	10.52	0.37	1.86	13.00	15.3
1737	40,153	0.32	0.48	0.07	0.54	1.92	−0.86	−6.16	−0.17	0.33	16.85	14.43	1.03	10.52	0.00	1.33	13.00	15.3
1739	43,382	0.53	1.03	0.04	0.61	1.40	0.83	4.19	0.51	0.48	19.02	14.43	1.03	10.52	4.98	3.08	13.00	15.3

Table 7 (continued)

Notes and Sources For a detailed presentation of the above derivations see text and Morris Altman, 'Economic Growth, Economic Development and Real Gross Domestic Product in New France, 1695–1739: Estimates and Analysis' (Working Paper, Department of Economics, Concordia University, Montreal, 1985). Per capita estimates are derived by dividing total value estimates (not shown here) by census population estimates. Only one eight of the pea output is entered into the GDP computation, the rest is calculated in animal feed and seed. The 1749 price for peas of 2.5 *livres* per minot is taken from Peter Kalm, *The America of 1750: Peter Kalm's Travels in North America: The English Version of 1770*, ed. Adolph B. Benson (New York, 1937), II, 536, hereafter cited as *Kalm*, America. One-sixth of tobacco output is assumed to go toward seed. No data on tobacco output are available for the pre-1721 period: therefore it is assumed that the per capita output for this period was the same as 1721. The 1749 price for tobacco of 0.265 *livre* per pound is derived from Robert-Lionel Séguin's price of 4 to 5 *sols* per pound for 1728 (*La civilization traditionelle de l' "habitant" aux 17e et 18e siècles, fonds matériel* [Ottawa, 1967], 195), which I then adjust for possible price increases, assuming that the price of tobacco increased proportionally that that of wheat. For hemp production a seed requirement of one-sixth is assumed as well as a 1749 price of 0.40 *livre* or 8 *sols* per pound, taken from A. J. E. Lunn, "Economic Development in New France, 1713–1760" (Ph.D. diss., McGill University, 1943), 75–78. A one-sixth seed requirement for flax is also assumed and, since no price data for flax exist, a 1749 price of 0.25 *livre* per pound is assumed (the 1730 price of hemp) (*ibid*). This price is doubled to take into account the value added in the transformation of flax into linen. European sources in B.H. Slicher Van Bath's *The Agrarian History of Western Europe*, A.D. *500–1850*, trans. Olive Ordish (London, 1963), 287, assume that the typical sheep yielded 1.3 pounds of fleece annually (no data exist for early Canada). This is multiplied by the census estimate of the number of sheep to yield an estimate for total wool output. A 1749 price of 1.52 *livres* per pound is extrapolated using Arthur Harrison Cole's American price data from which the price ratio of wool to wheat is computed for the 1820s and applied to the Canadian 1729 price of wheat (*Wholesale Commodity Prices in the United States, 1700–1861: Statistical Supplement, Actual Wholesale Prices of Various Commodities* [Cambridge, MA, 1938]). The estimated price of wool is doubled to take into account the value added involved in transforming raw wool into cloth. Changes in livestock inventory assume a 1749 price of 15 *livres* per pig, 50 *livres* per head of cattle, 6 *livres* per sheep, and 40 *livres* per horse, as taken from Kalm, *America*, 536. These are similar to the prices quoted in Dechène, *Habitants et marchands*, 335. To estimate inventory changes for census years not immediately preceded by a census year the rate of interest formula is applied and data for the last census year are used as the base year. The value of slaughtered swine is estimated by assuming from Kalm, *America*, 536, that a fattened pig weighed

Table 7 (continued)

200 pounds with a slaughtered weight of 160 pounds as taken from Hugh Murray, *An Historical and Descriptive Account of British America... 2d ed. (Edinburgh, 1839). III, 115–116. A 1749 price of 4.7* sols *or 0.235 livre* per pound is extrapolated from Cameron Nish's Louisbourg price of 7 *sols* per pound deflated by a factor of 1.35 (Nish, ed., *The French Regime* [Scarborough, ON, 1965], 124), to account for the value added in shipping pork from Quebec City to Louisbourg (Jacques Mathieu, *Le commerce entre la Nouvelle-France et les Antilles au xviiie siècle* [Montreal, 1981], 198). This is then adjusted upward by a factor of 1.25 to account for any price increase, assuming that the price of pork rose proportionally to that of wheat. From the census data on the number of swine, one swine per farm family is deducted to account for breeding hogs. From Morris Altman, "Seigniorial Tenure in New France, 1688–1739: An Essay on Income Distribution and Retarded Economic Development," *Historical Reflections/Réflexions Historiques,* X (1983), 344–350, it is assumed that one head of cattle was slaughtered per farm family to meet family needs and the 1749 price of 50 *livres* per head, as taken from Kalm, *America,* 536, is doubled to take into account the value added in producing meat. To this is added a 12.5 *livres* per peasant family to account for the value of cattle sold to the nonagricultural sector. This follows from Dechêne's finding that cattle were sold infrequently (*Habitants et marchands,* 335). Moreover, this yields a per capita consumption of beef in the nonagricultural sector of 7 *livres,* just below the per capita consumption in the agricultural sector of about 8 *livres* – exclusive of the value added in the slaughtering process which is captured in my estimates of nonagricultural production. From Dechêne, *Habintants et marchands,* 320, and Séguin, *Civilisation,* 571, it is assumed that each peasant family kept 12 chickens and 1 cock and that 8 chickens were killed annually. A 1749 price of 10 *sols* per live chicken, taken from Kalm, *America,* 536, is doubled to account for the value added in the slaughtering process. Dairy output is in terms of butter for which a 1749 price of 0.75 *livre* per pound is taken from Séguin, *Civilisation,* 496. From Slicher Van Bath's European data, *Agrarian History,* trans. Ordish, 285, 335, it is estimated that one milch cow yielded 20 kg or 44 pounds of butter. From Dechêne, *Habitants et marchands,* 315–316, it is assumed that each peasant family kept three milch cows to meet subsistence needs. The value of land improvement is derived by estimating the increase in the number of arpents under cultivation from one year prior to a census year to a census year. This is multiplied by the value of labour required to clear an arpent. From Kalm, *America,* 411, and Cameron Nish, *Les bourgeois-gentilshommes de la Nouvelle-France, 1729–1748* (Ottawa, 1968), 39–41, it is assumed that an agricultural labourer earned 200 *livres* per annum in 1749 or 12.8 *sols* or 0.64 *livre* per day if employed 6 days per week. From Martin L. Primack's "Land Clearing under Nineteenth-Century Techniques: Some Preliminary Calculations," *Journal of Economic History,* XXII (1962), 491, American data for the 1850s, it is assumed that 33 "man days" were required to clear one acre of forested land including stumps or 28 "man days" per arpent. Dechêne, *Habitants et marchands,* 273, n.5, argues that land-clearing technology in New France was not very different from that in Primack's time frame. This yields a 1749 value per improved arpent of 17.92 *livres.* The value of constructions on new farms is derived from an estimate of the increase in the number of farms from one year prior to the census year. This is multiplied by the cost of constructing a barn and simple house. The cost of constructing a barn is assumed to be 317 *livres* and is derived from Robert-Lionel Séguin's 1704 cost estimate, *Les granges du Quèbec du xviie au xix siècle* (Ottawa, 1963), 13. This figure is doubled to account for the cost of building a house, based upon Murray, *Account of British America,* 116. The value of firewood is estimated from Gallman, "The Statistical Approach: Fundamental Concepts as Applied to History," in George Rogers Taylor and Lucius F. Ellsworth, eds., *Approaches to American Economic History* (Charlottesville, Va., 1971), 69, 78, who finds that firewood composed at least 18% of the per capita consumption of food in the United States over the eighteenth and nineteenth centuries. I apply this percentage to my estimate of per capita food consumption in early Canada of about 72 *livres* in 1749 prices composed of bread, 23 *livre*; peas, 0.075 *livre*; tobacco, 0.39 *livre;* hemp, *0.07 livre;* flax, 0.48 *livre*; wool, 1.20 *livres; swine, 12.5* livres; cattle, 16.7 *livres*; dairy, 165 *livres*; and poultry, 0.70 *livre.* Since Gallman's consumption estimate includes fruits, vegetables, sugar, and syrup, my estimate of firewood is lower-bound and could have been slightly higher at 16 *livres*

Table 8 Value of ship construction in early Canada (1749 *livres*)

	Total value	*Product total value per capita*	*Total value entering gross domestic product*	*Total value per capita entering gross domestic product*	*Hypothetical population*[b]
1704	8,750	0.55	0.0	0.00	15,931
1706	31,200	1.87	0.0	0.00	
1709	31,200	1.73	0.0	0.00	18,024
1711	15,750	0.85	0.0	0.00	18,512
1714	36,000	1.86	0.0	0.00	
1715	192,480	9.58	154,870	7.71	20,087
1716	88,375	4.23	49,300	2.36	
1717	84,000	3.8	42,603	1.93	22,074
1718	17,500	0.75	0.0	0.00	
1723	17,500	0.67	0.0	0.00	
1724[a]	122,500	4.51	71,700	2.64	
1729	65,100	1.97	3,310	0.10	33,105
1730	185,500	5.43	121,460	3.56	
1731	72,000	2.07	6,952	0.20	34,761
1732	128,450	3.63	62,334	1.76	
1733	52,325	1.43	0.0	0.00	36,548
1734	118,025	3.13	47,522	1.26	
1735	70,350	1.82	0.0	0.00	38,596
1736	212,000	5.37	138,236	3.50	
1737	30,450	0.76	0.0	0.00	
1738	167,625	4.02	89,732	2.15	41,736
1739	205,925	4.75	174,725	4.03	

[a]No tonnage data are available for this year. We know only that large boats were constructed. From other data presented by Lunn I infer that each vessel constructed averaged 100 tons
[b]Hypothetical population estimates are derived using the available census population estimates and the rate of interest formula
Sources See text

Unfortunately, no data exist from which to make similar deductions for later years. However, evidence presented by Alfred Rowland Vanesse on the urban/rural population breakdown, which excludes members of the religious community, allows one to approximate the size of the nonagricultural population for later years. The urban population is used as a proxy for the nonagricultural population. It constituted 23–26% of the population over the period 1695–1716 and 21–24% for 1723–1739 (Vanesse 1958, II, App. G). This allows me to assume that the nonagricultural population constituted about 23% of the total throughout

Table 9 Value of lumber exports (1749 *livres*)

	Total value of planks	*Total value of shingles*	*Total (1 + 2)*	*Total per capita*[b]
1727	18,557	3,125	21,682	0.7
1728	6,275	312	6,587	0.2
1732	63,077	12,359	75,436	2.12
1733	86,562	15,156	101,719	2.78
1734			84,817[a]	2.25
1735	58,469	12,255	70,724	1.83
1736	66,966	1,687	68,654	1.74
1737	101,829	18,096	119,915	2.99
1739	49,744	18,202	67,937	1.56

[a]No data are available for this year. I assume that exports for this year lie on a logarithmic growth path (in this case negative) from 1733 to 1735

[b]No census population estimates are available for 1728, 1733, and 1735. To generate per capita output estimates I construct hypothetical population estimates for these years of 32,122, 36,548, and 38,596 respectively using the census population estimates and the rate of interest formula

Sources See text

the whole period examined. I also assume that only one individual per average nonagricultural family of six was employed full time. Moreover, I assume that each such individual earned an average of 400 *livres* in 1749.[39] This income is believed to be indicative of the value added per worker in the nonagricultural sector. The 400 *livres* multiplied by the estimated number of workers generates a constant real per capita basic nonagricultural output series for the 1695–1739 period.

To the extent that individuals were typically not employed full time, my estimates are biased upward. But to the extent that more than one family member was fully employed, they are biased downward. These two biases could cancel each other. If the upward biases dominate, which I believe is most unlikely, the bias would be small. A reduction of my basic nonagricultural income estimates by 33%, for example, would increase my growth estimates and the significance of the agricultural and fur trade sectors, but only to a very negligible extent.[40]

I attempt to adjust the above estimates for any plausible downward biases by constructing an output series for ship construction and lumber exports in terms of 1749 *livres* (Tables 8 and 9). I add to the basic nonagricultural output series the value of ship construction exceeding 1.87 livres per capita, which appears to have been the maximum that could have been produced without increasing employment in the non-agricultural sector. By adding the total value of lumber exports to the basic output series I am once again assuming an increase in employment in this sector.

I conclude that employment increased because both industries were experiencing a surge of growth at a time when there is no evidence that other components of the nonagricultural sector were experiencing a decline, particularly as Canada's exports to the French West Indies were beginning to take off. This assumption increases my total nonagricultural output and, thereby, real GDP estimates as well as my per capita RGDP growth rates over what they might otherwise have been, particularly for the 1730–1739 period, but, again, only insignificantly.[41]

For the fur trade sector the most comprehensive data available on output and prices are presented by Elizabeth Lunn for 1714 onward. For the pre-1714 period other sources are used (see Table 10 notes). My estimates are least reliable for the pre-1704 period, for which I calculate only the 1749 *livre* value of beaver produced in Canada. Other furs were trapped at the time, although beaver was dominant. Nevertheless, my series on fur output for the pre-1704 period is biased downward (ibid.). The results are presented in Table 10.

Lunn's data are for fur exports from Canada to the French port of La Rochelle, which received almost all the furs sent from the colony. And almost all of the fur acquired by the French colonists was exported (Lunn 1943, pp. 130, 459–465; Innis 1970, p. 73). These data, given in terms of La Rochelle prices, are converted into a series on the poundage of beaver fur produced in early Canada, using Lunn's La Rochelle price series for *castor gras* and *castor sec* (the two key beaver furs). This is then converted into 1749 *livres* value estimates using Lunn's price data for Canada. The 1749 price of *castor gras* is given as 4 *livres* per pound and as 3.5–4.0 *livres* per pound for *castor sec*. I use 2 *livres* per pound as the price of *castor sec* because a price ratio of about 2 prevailed with respect to *castor gras* and *castor sec* for most of the period examined. A price of 3 or 4 *livres* would have exaggerated considerably the weight of *castor sec* in my computation of the value of total fur output. I estimate the 1749 *livre* value of the now significant "other furs" category using Lunn's La Rochelle fur import data by computing the significance of other furs relative to beaver in terms of their current La Rochelle values. These proportions are applied to my 1749 *livres* estimates of beaver output to yield a 1749 *livre* estimate of other furs. This series, plus my series for *castor gras* and *castor sec*, yields a series for total fur output for the 1718–1749 period in terms of 1749 *livres*.[42]

Table 10 Weight and value (1749 *livres*) of fur production in early Canada

	Beaver					*Beaver plus other furs*			
	Castor gras		*Castor sec*		*Other furs*				
	Poundage	*Value*	*Poundage*	*Value*	*Value*	*Total value (unadjusted)*	*Total value (adjusted)*	*Total value (adjusted)* ***per capita***	
1686–1695[a]	140,000	420,000				420,000	260,400	23.51	
1696[b]	80,000	320,000	70,000	140,000		460,000	285,200	21.57	
1697	107,000	428,000	97,000	194,000		622,000	385,640	28.64	
1698	55,000	220,000	48,000	98,000		316,000	195,920	14.18	
1699	158,000	632,000	138,000	276,000		908,000	562,960	39.79	
1700–1704[c]	80,827	723,308				723,308	448,451	29.52	(1702)
1706–1716[d]			70,000	140,000	140,000	280,000	173,600	10.36	(1706)
								9.89	(1707)
								9.25	(1712)
								9.37	(1713)
1714	15,000	60,000			200,000	400,000	248,000	12.84	(1714)
1716	9,000	36,000			176,000	352,000	218,240	10.45	(1716)
1718	1,920	7,680	109,420	218,840	120,371	346,891	301,795	12.93	
1719	98,260	393,040	90,360	180,720	471,340	1,045,100	909,237	40.36	
1720	13,260	53,040	93,780	187,560	232,361	472,691	411,241	16.81	
1721	11,000	44,000	82,080	164,160	173,085	381,245	331,683	12.83	
1722	39,260	157,040	37,340	74,680	275,326	507,046	441,130	16.89	
1723	56,820	227,280	95,600	191,200	127,838	546,318	475,297	18.28	
1724	21,740	68,960	25,840	51,580	321,958	460,598	400,720	14.75	
1725	38,080	152,320	39,340	78,680	176,407	407,407	354,444	12.45	
1726	21,840	87,360	7,140	14,280	65,256	166,896	145,199	4.86	

(continued)

Table 10 (continued)

	Beaver					*Beaver plus other furs*		
	Castor gras		*Castor sec*		*Other furs*			
	Poundage	*Value*	*Poundage*	*Value*	*Value*	*Total value (unadjusted)*	*Total value (adjusted)*	*Total value (adjusted)* ***per capita***
1727	53,800	215,200	213,080	246,160	493,790	1,135,150	987,580	31.68
1728	35,980	143,920	115,240	230,480	328,039	702,439	611,122	19.02
1729	31,780	127,120	96,860	193,720	236,174	557,014	484,602	14.63
1730	46,120	184,480	141,480	282,960	272,180	739,620	643,469	18.86
1731	43,020	172,080	100,880	201,760	244,077	617,917	537,588	15.46
1732	36,680	146,720	130,500	261,000	247,778	655,498	570,283	16.10
1733	42,040	164,160	156,240	312,480	336,739	813,379	707,640	19.36
1734	20,400	81,600	84,620	169,240	414,518	665,358	578,861	15.35
1735	14,120	56,480	109,520	219,040	84,051	1,124,571	978,377	15.58
1736	11,640	46,560	52,960	105,920	274,635	427,115	371,590	9.41
1737	14,260	57,040	28,440	56,880	387,233	501,153	436,003	10.86
1738	33,720	134,880	114,320	228,640	435,425	798,945	695,082	16.65
1739	8,880	35,520	56,640	113,280	498,156	646,956	562,852	12.97

[a]This is the annual average poundage of all beaver fur delivered to the fur trade monopoly, inferred from Innis and Eccles. A price of 3 *livres* per pound is used here—the average of the price of *castor gras* and *castor sec* used in this study. The per capita figure is derived using the 1692 census population estimate as this best represents the average population over the 1686–1695 period

[b]The poundage data and the division between *castor gras* and *castor sec* are derived from Innis for the 1696–1699 period. The per capita output estimates for 1696, 1697, and 1699 are based upon hypothetical population figures of 13,220, 13,463, and 14,147 respectively. These are derived using the census population estimates for 1695, 1698, and 1706 and the rate of interest formula

[c]This is an annual average which is derived from Innis, who finds that 1,356,208 *livres* of beaver were delivered over the 1700–1704 period or an average of 271,242 *livres* per annum. This is converted to 180,827 pounds using Eccles's average current price per pound of beaver of 1.5 *livres*. The per capita output estimate is based upon a hypothetical 1702 population Of 15,192 derived from the census population estimates for 1688 and 1706 and the rate of interest formula

Table 10 (continued)

[d]The poundage data for beaver are based upon Lunn. An average of 70,000 pounds per annum of *castor sec* was received by the beaver fur monopoly from 1706 to 1714. No data for 1716 exist, thus I assume the same figure for this year. From 1714 *castor gras* was again accepted by the monopoly. For my estimates of "Other Furs" I assume, along with Eccles, that by this period furs other than beaver constituted about one-half of the furs produced for sale in the colony along the St. Lawrence

Sources See text and W. J. Eccles, *The Canadian Frontier, 1534–1760* (New York, 1969), 125, 135; Harold A. Innis, *The Fur Trade in Canada; An Introduction to Canadian Economic History*, Rev. ed. (Toronto, 1970), 70–73; and Lunn, "Economic Development in New France," 456, 462

The fur output estimates from 1695 are adjusted downward to account for a 25% tax on beaver that lasted until 1717 and was embedded in the price of fur. The tax revenue was spent by the government largely on commodities produced in Canada. The value of these commodities should be captured in my estimates of agricultural and nonagricultural production. The fur trade output estimates are further adjusted downward by 13% for the entire 1695–1739 period to account for the value of trade goods imported or produced within the colony (items used to purchase fur from the Indians), which was also embedded in the price paid for furs by the trading companies. These adjustments should avoid any double counting and the inclusion of imports in my measure of RGDP.[43]

Unavoidably, the fur trade estimates, particularly for the post-1700 period, do not incorporate the illegal trade in furs.[44] Although it has been argued that this trade was very important, no concrete corroborating evidence has been produced.[45] Certainly, incentives to smuggle beaver existed from 1706 to 1714, when no *castor gras* was accepted by the beaver fur trade monopoly in Canada (Innis 1970, p. 80). A constant, but not necessarily important, incentive to smuggle furs to Albany resulted from the availability there of a commodity in demand by the Indians—a woollen cloth known as stroud.[46] The claim that the price of beaver was usually higher in Albany than in Montreal has been disputed.[47] Offsetting these incentives, to the extent that they existed, were the risk that smugglers ran of being caught and the investment required to carry furs to Albany from New France. Moreover, we do not know whether most of the illegal trade was conducted by members of the Indian nations. To the extent that it was, the output generated by the illegal fur trade was not part of the output produced by European settlers of Canada. Nevertheless, it should be noted that my fur trade output estimates are on the conservative side. This further contributes to making my RGDP estimates lower-bound.

Notes

1. Pelletier (1930) finds that the censuses of the second half of the seventeenth century were taken systematically on a fixed date using specified questions with enumerators going house to house. See also Salone (1970). This appears to have remained the standard procedure of census taking into the eighteenth century.

2. Innis (1970) focuses on an assumed concentration upon the fur trade, Hamelin (1968) discusses poor monetary policy and labor shortages as possible causes of economic stagnation in Canada, Dechêne (1974) emphasizes inadequate markets, and Delage (1970) emphasizes the concentration on fur production and a stagnant agricultural sector.
3. See, for example, Lunn (1943), Fregault (1969), and Salone (1970), all arguing that substantial economic progress was taking place by the 1730s. See also the more recent work by Miquelon (1987).
4. No estimates exist for such output in early Canada. However, Robert E. Gallman's estimates for the United States (Gallman 1972b) suggest that fruit, vegetables, sugar, and syrups composed 17% of the consumption of free men and household servants in 1840. If this percentage is applied to my estimate for per capita consumption in Canada, 1695–1739, one arrives at an estimate of 17 livres (1749 prices) for the consumption and production of the four products. My consumption estimate, derived from Altman (1983), and estimates presented in this article, is composed of firewood, 13 *livres*.- bread, 23; peas, 0.075; tobacco, 0.39; hemp, 0.07; flax, 0.48; Wool, 1.20; swine, 12.5; cattle, 16.7; dairy, 16.5; and poultry, 0.7. My original 20 *livres* for wheat consumption is increased by 3 *livres* to incorporate the value added by grinding the grain and transforming the flour into bread.
5. However, no attempt is made to measure the output produced by government. Such output should be captured in my RGDP estimates. And although estimates are available on government expenditures in New France (as distinguished from the smaller colony of early Canada), in Frégault (1969, pp. 347–348), I do not include these in my RGDP estimates since they should already be incorporated in my output estimates. One should note, however, that on a per capita basis government expenditures fell dramatically over the 1711–1740 period from about 17 *livres* in the 1710s to about 12.5 in the 1720s and about 10 in the 1730s. Also, using Frégault's current dollar government expenditure estimates and my real per capita GDP estimates, I find that government expenditures declined as a percentage of per capita GDP, from 17% in 1712–1718 to 8% in 1730–1739.
6. For example, a 20% increase in per capita output for the periods 1695–1707 and **1734–1739b** reduces the growth rate from one period average to another from 0.7 to 0.6% per annum.
7. Gallman (1972a, pp. 20–21). Gallman's output estimates are for 1710 in terms of 1839–1840 prices, but he applies them to the 1710–1720 period, perhaps due to the very approximate nature of his computations.
8. The most recent of these are by McCusker and Menard (1985, pp. 55–56) and are presented in 1980 prices. Their estimates are derived from the 1774 per capita income estimates presented by Jones (1980, pp. 63).

McCusker and Menard apply annual growth rates of 0.3% and 0.6% to Jones's 1774 per capita income estimate to generate their 1720 per capita income estimate (pp. 55–56). If one assumes, with Jones (p. 371), that her per capita income estimates for 1774 fall within those of Gallman (1972a) for 1774 of $60 to $70 (1840 prices), and applies annual growth rates of 0.3% and 0.6% to them, one generates per capita income estimates of between $41 and $59 for 1710 and 1720 (1840 prices). This compares to the $45–$60 figures suggested by Gallman for the period 1710–1720. Jones's own per capita income estimates for 1710 and 1720 would be equivalent to between $46 and $55 (1840 prices). For a more detailed discussion see Altman (1987a).

9. Apart from the general problems involved in using exchange rates to convert one nation's output into another's currency equivalent (discussed in more detail below), we lack price data for Canada for 1720 except for wheat. These data are required to convert my 1749 *livres* output into its 1720 price equivalent. Alternatively, one might convert the 1710–1720 British American output estimate to 1749 prices. But this could be done only by using a general price index, not, as one should, by deflating each sector by its own price index since estimates on the sectoral distribution of output in 1720 are not available. And the 1749 estimate would be in terms of only hypothetical U.S. dollars since no U.S. dollar existed at the time. This hypothetical figure would then be converted to its pound sterling equivalent, which can then be converted into its *livres tournois* equivalent. And keep in mind that *livres tournois* in New France and France were equivalent by law rather than as a result of the working of the "free market." This is a very roundabout procedure indeed, with each conversion being very problematic.
10. The U.S. price data used are averages for the years 1839–1840: wheat, $1.29 per *minot*; swine, $0.09 per pound slaughtered; beef, $0.075 per pound slaughtered; and butter, $0.19 per pound. These figures are derived from Cole (1938), and are for Philadelphia, except for butter, which is the arithmetic average for all cities listed, given the wide variation in the price of this commodity. These prices are multiplied by the average quantity of wheat, swine, and butter produced in the 1712–1718 period to yield per capita U.S. dollar values for these Outputs: $13.76, $7.06, and $3.22 respectively. See Tables 5 and 7 for details. To derive output estimates for beef production I assume slaughter weights for cattle ranging from 500 to 900 pounds per head. The 500-pound estimate is from Gallman (1970), and is a lower-bound estimate for 1860. The 900-pound estimate is from Lewis and McInnis (1981), A-4. We know that 1.125 cattle per farm were slaughtered (see Table 8). This yields lower- and upper-bound estimates for slaughtered poundage per capita and, thereby, the U.S. dollar value

of poundage per capita. I take the arithmetic average of the lower- and upper-bound estimates: $7.06.

11. The 2.5 *livres per minot* of wheat is from Lunn (1934, p. 120). Hamelin (1968, p. 61) cites a similar price. I use a U.S. price of $1.23 per bushel taken from Cole (1938).
12. See Gallman (1972a, pp. 20–21), for the 1712–1784 period, and Egnal (1975, p. 200), Table II, for the 1720–1795 period. The McCusker and Menard (1985, p. 268) estimates of 0.3%-0.6% per annum are for the 1720–1774 period.
13. The period averages for 1695–1707 and 1730–1739 are used to compute these growth rates.
14. These growth rates are computed using the period averages for 1712–1718 and 1730–1739.
15. This suggestion was made to the author by Allan Kulikoff.
16. Terry L. Anderson (1979, p. 246) and Jones (1980, p. 78). McCusker and Menard (1985, p. 59) suggest a growth rate of 0.52% annually for British North America's white population during the 1650–1720 period.
17. Dechêne (1974) estimates that 668 men or 12% of the adult male French population in Canada was engaged in the fur trade during the entire 1708–1717 period. On an annual basis it is probable that even fewer individuals earned their keep from the fur trade. See Allaire (1980), for data similar to, but much less comprehensive than, Dechêne's for the 1701–1745 period. These data also suggest a relatively small contribution of the fur trade to total employment.
18. The argument does not change if one includes the 1737 census year in the calculation (Table 3, line 3).
19. The fur trade was only just recovering from a period when not all beaver fur was accepted by the beaver fur trade monopoly in New France. See, for example, Lunn (1943, Chap. 2).
20. These growth rates are computed from the period averages of 15,214 for 1695–1707, 20,152 for 1712–1718, and 38,026 for 1730–1739, which, in turn, are derived from the census population estimates presented in Table 7. These numbers are for French settlers, ie excluding indigenous population.
21. These growth rates are derived from data in United States Bureau of the Census (1975), pt. II, Set. Z-19, 1168.
22. From Dechêne (1974, p. 342), whose data suggest a wheat requirement of 7.7 *minots* where one *minot* equals 60 pounds. However, Harris (1966), 160, assumes that the average peasant consumed only 6 *minots* of wheat annually during the pre-1760 period. A similar assumption is made by Reid (1947, p. 275), and by Meiklejohn (1823–1824). According to Clark and Haswell (1970, p. 58), a kg. of unmilled wheat yields 3,150 calories. They also conclude that somewhat fewer than 2,500 calories per day

are required to sustain the average individual working an eight-hour day (ibid., chap. I). Thus 10.6 *minots* would be required annually to supply 2,500 calories every day for one year (one *minot* = 27.18 kg). Eight *minots* for early Canada is therefore probably an upper-bound estimate of what was actually consumed, given the extent of the production of other agricultural produce.

23. This refutes Dechêne (1974, p. 345), and Hamelin (1968, p. 71).
24. This surplus would be 33% greater if one assumes that the average individual required only 6 *minots* of wheat annually.
25. Mathieu (1981, pp. 23–25, 156, 177). Also note the large populations of three of France's sugar islands. Martinique's population was 24,000 in 1700 and 74,000 in 1738 (Librarie Larousse 1902, p. 344). The population of Guadeloupe was 10,456 in 1699 and 35,496 in 1730 (Satineau 1928, pp. 380–385). That of St. Dominique was 37,000 in 1712 (Mathieu 1981, p. 18). Much of the foodstuffs of these islands had to be imported. If one assumes that wheat was imported to feed the entire population of the islands, the wheat surplus in Canada could not even have approached their wheat requirements for the 1730s. See also May (1930, p. 93).
26. Burton (1936, Sect. 2, pp. 139, 141, 149), makes strong claims for the relatively stagnant nature of agriculture in Canada as cause of its poor export performance with respect to wheat.
27. Salone (1970, pp. 44–45, 291,410, 451) argues that Canada's smaller population was a product of edicts instituted in 1627–1628 that forbade Protestants from settling there. With the revocation of the Edict of Nantes in 1685, Protestants were even forbidden to engage in commercial activities in New France. By 1750 only 12 Protestants resided in the colony. A similar point is made by Parry (1961, pp. 123–124) and most recently by Bardet and Charbonneau (1986, p. 77).
28. There was a ready supply of Protestant immigrants, particularly after 1685. During the 1685–1688 period, 40,000 Protestants left France annually; over the 1681–1720 period 200,000 Protestants left (Scoville 1960, pp. 118–121). A large percentage of these refugees, perhaps as much as 50%, were of urban origin (Butler 1983, pp. 24, 77). This bears a striking resemblance to the strong nonagricultural character of French Catholic immigrants to Canada, of whom between 40 and 75% were skilled in nonagrarian pursuits (Trudel 1971, pp. 147–150; Harris, 1972, pp. 320–323). Most of these individuals, however, eventually engaged in agriculture, as did many of their French Protestant counterparts. British America attracted 9,000–15,000 Huguenots by 1700 (Barck and Lefler 1958, p. 291); Thernstrom (1980, p. 318). This is considerably more than the estimated 4,894 Catholics who migrated to Canada by 1700. By 1760 this total had increased to about 10,000 (Trudel 1971, p. 143). It

is entirely possible that, had they been permitted, these Huguenots might have settled in Canada rather than in English-speaking British America. It should be noted, however, that Butler (1983, p. 49) estimates that no more than 2,000 Huguenots resided in British America by 1700. But this estimate appears to be unreasonably low given that about 66,797 individuals of French origin resided in the United States by 1790 (*Historical Statistics of the United States*, pt. 1, Ser. A1-5, 8, and pt. II, Ser. Z20-23, 1168). Since few French individuals migrated to America during the eighteenth century (Butler, 1983, p. 218), most of the increase in French population can be attributed to natural procreation. The natural rate of population growth in that century was about 2.5% per annum (Walton and Shepherd 1979, pp. 53–54). Using this growth rate to extrapolate from the 1790 population to 1700 yields an estimated population for 1700 of 7,238, a figure above Butler's estimate yet below the lowest of the traditional estimates for the Huguenot population in British America.

29. These period averages are derived from Altman (1983, pp. 351–353, Table 2). They are based on my assumption that the percentage of cultivated land under wheat remained constant throughout the period examined. Had this percentage fallen, yields might have risen. This seems unlikely, however, given the growing markets for wheat. See also Harris (1966, p. 153).
30. The urban population of early Canada was, in most years, more than 20% of the total. And since the total population was consistently increasing, so was the total urban population. See Vanesse (1958, II, App. G). In contrast with Canada, the urban population in British America was about 7–8% of the total by 1776, according to McCusker and Menard (1985, pp. 66, 250).
31. On average, in the 1695–1712 period, only enough swine were raised to meet the minimum requirements of the agricultural family and, perhaps, to sell one pig per family. See Altman (1983, pp. 345–346, 348).
32. This would be true except for sheep and swine. The increase in other livestock would just suffice to work the land. See ibid., 344–347.
33. For a discussion see ibid., 347–349.
34. Ibid., *passim*. I find that although the seigniorial system of land tenure shifted a considerable portion of farmers' income to landlords and the church, most income was retained by the farmers; their share of income increased over time. See also Altman (1987b, pp. 135–142) *passim*.
35. The census data used in this article can be found in Canada Department of Agriculture, *The Census of Canada, 1870–71* (Ottawa, 1873–1878),not yet referenced in this paper but included in int bibliography IV, hereafter cited as Census of Canada; Lunn (1943, pp. 443–444); and Vanesse (1958, II). Some of this material is reprinted in Altman (1983).

36. I find that oats and barley output did not even increase at a fast enough pace to keep up with the increase in livestock. See ibid., Table 8, and p. 37, n. 46. See also Lunn (1943, p. 59).
37. Census of Canada, IV. Moogk (1971, pp. 74–75), suggests that Canada retained a similarly diversified nonagricultural sector throughout the period under scrutiny.
38. For a detailed discussion of the derivation of my estimate of family size see Altman (1983, p. 354, Table 2, n. 2).
39. From Nish (1968, pp. 39–41). The highest annual wage was 600 *livres*. Most of these data are from the late 1730s and early 1740s. By 1749 labor income was, if anything, higher.
40. The nonagricultural income would be reduced by 5.11 *livres*.
41. Total per capita GDP is increased by 3 *livres* or by 2.2% for 1730–1739.
42. The 1714–1717 output estimates are constructed in a slightly different fashion. See Table 10, noted.
43. Hamelin (1968, pp. 54–55) presents 1685 data from which I make the 13% estimate. This percentage may have changed over time, but at this stage of research we have no way of knowing to what extent and in what direction.
44. Eccles (1969, pp. 121–125) finds that warfare impeded the flow of furs to Albany before 1702.
45. See Lunn (1939, p. 65) and Lunn (1943, pp. 134–135). Lunn's educated guesses remain the basis for understanding the significance of the illegal trade in furs.
46. Lunn (1939, p. 65) and Lunn (1943, pp. 134–135).
47. Lunn (1943, pp. 171–172) and Innis (1970, pp. 84–85). Eccles (1979, pp. 425, 429–435) argues that no evidence exists to support the view that prices in Albany were higher than those in New France, particularly once exchange rates are taken into account.

References

Allaire, G. 1980. Les engagements pour la traite des fourrures, évaluation de la documentation. *Révue d'histoire de l'amérique française* 34: 3–26.

Altman, M. 1983. Seignorial Tenure in New France, 1688–1739: An Essay on Income Distribution and retarded Economic Development. *Historical Reflections/Reflexions Historiques* 10: 343–350.

Altman, M. 1985. *Economic Growth, Economic Development and Real Gross Domestic Product in New France, 1695–1739: Estimates and Analysis*. Working Paper, Department of Economics, Concordia University, Montreal.

Altman, M. 1987a. *The Economy of Colonial America: A Critical Note on Real Per Capita Income Estimates, Histoire Sociale-Social History* 20: 337–342.

Altman, M. 1987b. Note on the Economic Burden of the Seigniorial System in New France, 1688–1739. *Historical Reflections* 14: 135–142.

Anderson, T.L. 1979. Economic Growth in Colonial New England: 'Statistical Renaissance.' *Journal of Economic History* 69: 44–57.

Barck, O.T., Jr., and H.T. Lefler. 1958. *Colonial America*. New York: Macmillan.

Bardet, J.P.,and H. Charbonneau. 1986. Culture et milieux en France et en Nouvelle-France. In *Evolution et éclatement du monde rural: structures, fonctionnement et évolution différentielle des sociétés rurales français et québécoises, xviie-xxe siècles*, ed. J. Goy and J.-P. Wallot. Paris: Editions de l'Ecole des hautes études en sciences sociales.

Burton, F.W. 1936. The Wheat Supply of New France, Royal Society of Canada. *Transactions*, 3d Ser., 30, sect. 2: 137–150.

Butler, J. 1983. *The Huguenots in America: A Refugee People in New World Society*. Cambridge, MA: Harvard University Press.

Clark, C., and M. Haswell. 1970. *The Economics of Subsistence Agriculture*. London: Macmillan.

Cole, A.H. 1938. *Wholesale Commodity Prices in the United States, 1700–1861: Statistical Supplement, Actual Wholesale Prices of Various Commodities*. Cambridge, MA: Harvard University Press.

Dechêne, L. 1974. *Habitants et marchands de Montreal au XVII siècle*. Paris: Plon.

Delage, D. 1970. Les structures economiques de la Nouvelle-France et de la Nouvelle-York. *L'actualite Economique* 46: 67–118.

Eccles, W.J. 1969. *The Canadian Frontier, 1534–1760*. New York: Holt, Rinehart and Winston.

Eccles, W.J. 1979. A Belated Review of Harold Adams Innis, the Fur Trade in Canada. *Canadian Historial Review* 60: 429–435.

Egnal, M. 1975. The Economic Development of the Thirteen Continental Colonies, 1720 to 1775. *William and Mary Quarterly* 32 (2): 191–122.

Fregault, G. 1969. *La civilization de la Nouvelle-France, 1713–1744*. Montreal: Fides.

Fregault, G. 1970. *Le XVIIIe siècle canadien: Etudes*. Montreal: Éditions HMH.

Gallman, R.E. 1966. Gross National Product in the United States 1834–1909. In *Output, Employment, and Productivity in the United States After 1800*, Studies in Income and Wealth, XXX, 3–90. New York: NBER.

Gallman, R.E. 1970. Self-Sufficiency in the Cotton Economy of the Antebellum South. *Agricultural History* 44: 5–24.

Gallman, R.E. 1972. The Pace and Pattern of American Economic Growth. In *American Economic Growth: An Economist's History of the United States*, ed. L.E. Davis, et al., 15–60. New York: Harper and Row.

Gallman, R.E. 1972b. The Statistical Approach: Fundamental Concepts as Applied to History. In *Approaches to American Economic History*, ed. G.R. Taylor and L.F. Ellsworth, 63–86. Charlottesville, VA: University Press of Virginia Press.

Goldin, C.D., and F.D. Lewis. 1980. The Role of Exports in American Economic Growth during the Napoleonic Wars, 1793 to 1807. *Explorations in Economic History* 17: 6–25.

Hamelin, J. 1968. *Economie et Societe en Nouvelle-France*. Quebec: Les Presses de l'Universite Laval.

Harris, R.C. 1966. *The Seigneurial System in Early Canada*. Montreal: McGill-Queen's University Press.

Harris, R.C. 1972. The French Background of Immigrants to Canada before 1700. *Cahiers de Géographie de Québec* 41: 320–323.

Innis, H.A. 1970. *The Fur Trade in Canada: An Introduction to Canadian Economic History*. Rev. ed. Toronto: University of Toronto Press.

Jones, A.H. 1980. *Wealth of a Nation to Be: The American Colonies on the Eve of the Revolution*. New York: Columbia University Press.

Kravis, I.B. 1984. Comparative Studies of National Incomes and Prices. *Journal of Economic Literature* 22: 1–39.

Lewis, F.D., and M. McInnis. 1981. *Agricultural Output and Efficiency in Lower Canada, 1851*. Discussion Paper, Institute for Economic Research, Queen's University, Kingston.

Larousse, Librarie. 1902. *La grande encyclopédie, inventaire raisonné des sciences, des lettres et des arts, XXIII*. Paris: H. Lamirault et cie.

Lunn, A.J.E. 1943. *Economic Development in New France, 1713–1760*. Ph.D. diss., McGill University.

Lunn, A.J.E. 1934. *The Economic Development of French Canada, 1740–1760*. M.A. thesis, McGill University, Montreal.

Lunn, A.J.E. 1939. The Illegal Fur Trade Out of New France, 1713–1760. Canadian Historical Association, *Reports*: 61–76.

Mathieu, J. 1981. *Le commerce entre la Nouvelle-France et les Antilles au xviiie siècle*. Montreal: Fides.

McCusker, J.J., and R.R. Menard. 1985. *The Economy of British North America*, 55–56. Chapel Hill, NC: University of North Carolina Press).

May, L.P. 1930. *Histoire économique de la Martinique (1635–1763)*. Paris: Rivière.

Moogk, P. 1971. Apprenticeship Indentures: A Key to Artisan Life in New France. *Canadian Historical Association, Historical Papers* 6: 65–83.

Meiklejohn, W. 1823–1824, (Testimony). *Report to the Legislative Assembly of Lower Canada*, Appendix of the Journals of the Legislative Assembly of Lower Canada, XXXIII (Montreal), App. T.

Miquelon, D. 1987. *New France: A Supplement to Europe*. Toronto: McClelland and Stewart.

Nish, C. 1968. *Les bourgeois-gentilshommes de la Nouvelle-France, 1729–1748*. Ottowa: Fides.

Parry, J.H. 1961. *The Establishment of the European Hegemony, 1415–1715: Trade and Exploration in the Age of the Renaissance*. New York: Harper & Row.

Pelletier, A.J. 1930. Canadian Censuses of the 17th Century. *Canadian Political Science Association, Papers and Proceedings* 2: 20–29.

Reid, S.W. 1947. The Habitant's Standard of Living on the Seigneurie des Mille Isles, 1820–50. *Canadian Historical Review* 28: 266–278.

Salone, E. 1970. *La Colonisation de la Nouvelle-France: Etudes sur les origins de la nation canadienne francaise*. Trois Rivieres, Canada: Boréal Express.

Scoville, W.C. 1960. *The Persecution of Huguenots and French Economic Development, 1680–1720*. Berkeley, CA: University of California Press.

Satineau, M. 1928. *Histoire de la Guadeloupe sous l'ancien régime, 1635–1789*. Paris: Payot.

Thernstrom, S., ed. 1980. *Harvard Encyclopedia of American Ethnic Groups*. Cambridge, MA: Harvard University Press.

Trudel, M. 1971. *Initiation á la Nouvelle-France*. Montreal: Editions HRW.

United States Bureau of the Census. 1975. *Historical Statistics of the United States, Colonial Times to 1970, part 2*. Washington, DC: Bureau of the Census, Set. Z-19, 1168.

Vanesse, A.R. 1958. *A Social History of the Seigniorial Regime in Canada, 1712-1739, vol. 2*. Ph.D. diss., University of Montreal.

Walton, G.M., and J.F. Shepherd. 1979. *The Economic Rise of Early America*. Cambridge: Cambridge University Press.

CHAPTER 4

The Economic Impact of the Seigniorial Tenure in Early Canada

1 Introduction

Publications about the economic and social history of New France are legion; yet few scholars have studied the reasons for the colony's relatively retarded economic development. Jean Hamelin attributes economic stagnation in New France to a shortage of capital and labour—a view found to be seriously deficient.[1] Louise Dechêne thinks the failure to integrate agriculture into the international trade sector—a core/periphery dichotomy mirrored in New France itself—helped maintain a generally autarkic, stagnant agricultural sector (Dechêne 1974, pp. 344–347, 482–486). Delage (1970, p. 117) argues that a dependence upon staple exports retarded economic development. W.J. Eccles argues that money to live in the style of Molière's monsieur Jourdain diverted capital to the detriment of economic developments.[2] But no one discusses the impact of the seigniorial régime on the economy of New France. This paper shows that it modified the distribution of income, thereby changing the structure of effective demand, and thus the pattern of investment, probably reducing total output of the colony from what it otherwise might have been.

But, based on first ever estimates of real gross domestic product of Early Canada (the French colony in what makes up part of the contemporary province of Quebec, Canada), I argue that this colony's economy performed *relatively* well (Chapter 3 above). The main finding of this

M. Altman, *Lessons from a Successfully Export-Oriented, Resource-Rich Economy*, https://doi.org/10.1007/978-3-031-03887-7_4

chapter is that the seigneurial regime held back the economic performance of this colony.

2 The Seigniorial Régime

Specialists argue[3] that before the conquest of New France in 1763 the state, protecting the peasant from excessive seigniorial exactions,[4] made it possible for farmers to live largely free of economic constraints. The issue is specious, for the peasant needed no protection since he enjoyed a favourable bargaining position because of the colony's sparse population.[5] I argue that seigniorial institutions measurably reduced the favourable bargaining position of the peasant by imposing levies that retarded the economic development of the colony, even though—as an analysis of the census data from 1688 to 1739[6] reveals—the peasants retained a rising portion of their economic surplus.[7]

In 1968 R.C. Harris argued that payments to the seignior were trivial, amounting to 5 to 10% of the peasant family's annual income—a cheap price to pay for land, he insists.[8] Although Harris omitted the tithe from his calculation—3.8% of the peasant's total grain production—some historians nevertheless use Harris as an authority to claim that the payments to the seignior and/or the church were trivial, amounting together to about 10% of the peasant family's yearly income (eg. Eccles 1969, p. 67; Eccles 1971, p. 15; Wallot 1969, p. 373).

Louise Dechêne (1971, p. 180) maintains, however, that the charges were burdensome. This may well have been the case. But the issue remains to be clarified for Dechêne does not argue from a factual basis. She resorts to a hypothetical computation by Harris in order to revise the estimate of the payments of the censitaire—the peasant farmer of New France—to the seignior, arriving at a figure of 10 to 14%. She goes on to argue that these charges consumed most of the peasant family's disposable income unless it produced more than fifty minots of wheat per annum.[9] Dechêne nowhere shows that the typical peasant family produced this or that quantity of wheat. The fifty minots of wheat is an imaginary figure, for Dechêne, like Harris, failed to consult the census material—the most reliable source from which to compute the level of wheat output.

Beyond the issue of computation and the reliability of sources lies the further problem of how much the state protected the censitaire against seigniorial exactions. Trudel, Harris, and Wallot maintain that the state exercised a stringent surveillance (Trudel 1971a, b, pp. 12, 17, 20; Harris

1968, pp. 194, 197; Wallot 1969, pp. 371, 379–380), Wallot going on to explain that the abundance of land and the desire to attract immigrants induced colonial authorities to take special care to oversee seigniorial charges (Ibid., pp. 369, 373). Dechêne insists the state never defended the censitaire's economic interests, allowing therefore the seignior to absorb a significant portion of the peasant family's disposable savings (Dechêne 1971, p. 148). My analysis of the census records reveals that although the state did little to protect the censitaire, he was able to capture an increasing portion of the economic surplus over the period 1688–1739—probably as a result of the favorable bargaining position of the peasant family. The portion of peasant economic surplus absorbed by the seignior and the church proceeded partly from the seigniorial régime itself and partly from the services rendered to the peasant family by the seignior and the church.

3 Seigniorial Charges in New France: 1688–1793

Seigniorial charges must be described, however briefly, before discussing census material to measure their economic influence. The levies in New France included: the cens et rentes, the grist-mill banalité, minor charges, the lods et ventes, and the tithe. They are discussed in light of the method of land concession. To obtain land a settler (the censitaire or the habitant) had to negotiate for the terms of a title-deed from a seignior - who received the land from the crown—paying a yearly rental to the seignior (cens et rentes), (Munro 1907, p. 76). The crown rarely granted wild land directly or freely to settlers; instead it granted *en seigneurie* territories conquered from the Indian nations helping, thereby, a select group (the seigniors) to live from the labour of an agricultural population. The crown could have introduced other forms of land tenure in New France; for example, settlers in some British North American colonies paid only a negligible fee for the land.[10] Since seigniorial dues helped to pay neither for the colony's administration nor for its military protection[11] and since its establishment in New France was unnecessary—for much of British North America flourished without it—it follows that fiscal and economic considerations do not explain why the crown imposed seigniorial tenure on its colonists.

The seigniors were under little pressure to make sub-grants. Therefore they could hoard land until they found censitaires with whom they could agree on terms for a title-deed. Only four seigniorial title-deeds—all issued after 1711—obliged seigniors to sub-grant land to potential settlers (Munro 1907, p. 59). In general, colonial officials and even the crown defied its own decrees directed against land hoarding. Although the crown repeatedly passed ordinances to have uncleared and unsettled seigniorial land reunited to the royal domain—the arrêts of Marly of 6 July 1711 are the most well-known—the colonial authorities refused to enforce these decrees even when, in 1700, only 4 to 5% of seigniorial land was cleared.[12] Indeed, the crown went on to approve decisions of the colonial authorities to increase the size of seigniories,[13] reuniting to the royal domain no more than one seigniory until 1741 (Harris 1968, p. 36). A similar inconsistency prevailed with respect to the number of seigniories created.

Conferring no grants from 1714 to 1732, Versailles then went on to make fifty seigniorial concessions by 1760, the standard size of these grants being forty square miles—the largest made in the history of New France.[14] Meanwhile the crown issued legislation-like the *arrêt de Versailles* (1732)—decrying the illegal refusal of colonial authorities to reunite uncleared and unsettled seigniorial lands to the royal domaine (Munro 1908, pp. 76–82). By 1763 the seigniors controlled 11,113,868 arpents (1 acre = 1.17869 arpents) of uncleared land, of which 9,313,888 were relatively fertile.[15] By 1739, I estimate that censitaires held only 802,530 arpents or 8.6% of the available fertile seigniorial land.[16] In sum, the seigniors presided over access to most of the colony's habitable land.[17]

The settler negotiated with the landlord, the seignior, who received in rent an amount that the two parties, bargaining freely, stipulated in the title-deed (Harris 1968, p. 66). Since government rarely interfered in these negotiations, market and social forces largely determined the rental terms.[18] Payments consisted of a token homage, the cens-an acknowledgement that land held in tenancy, *en censive*, could not be granted *en seigneurie*—and the rente, a genuine source of seigniorial revenue (Harris 1968, pp. 63–69, Munro 1907, pp. 54, 76, 85–96). Throughout the French régime the cens et rentes together remained—with few exceptions after 1732—at one sol eight deniers per arpent (twelve deniers [d] = one sol [s]; twenty sols = one livre tournois [L]). Only in the Montreal region did the rate differ significantly, 2 s ld per arpent, twenty percent higher than elsewhere.[19] People paid in cash or in kind. Payments varied from cash plus one or more capons in the seventeenth century to cash plus wheat in the early eighteenth; by the end of the French régime most payments were in cash (Harris 1968, p. 64).

The crown established another important seigniorial charge—the grist-mill banalité—when, in response to a petition from the seigniors in 1667, it decreed that censitaires must grind their grain at a seigniorial grist-mill, paying the fee of one-fourteenth of the grain ground. Prior to this date only a clause in a freely negotiated title-deed could compel a censitaire to grind the grain at the seigniorial Mill (Munro 1907, pp. 104, 108). But some confusion prevailed in this matter also. For almost twenty years later, in 1686, a royal arrêt ordered all seigniors in New France to construct banal-mills within one year of the arrêt. But this arrêt was published only in 1706 by the intendant Raudot who was somewhat mindful of the welfare of the censitaire (Ibid., p. 67; Munro 1908, pp. 61, 106). The delay in publication may have resulted from an unwillingness of a colonial administration, staffed mainly by seigniors, (Munro 1907, p. 106) to impose the high cost of mill construction upon their brethren.[20]

The censitaire had to take to the banal-mill only the grain required for subsistence.[21] Were he to take it elsewhere, the seignior could seize both the grain and the vehicle used to transport it.[22] Moreover, a seignior who operated a mill could demolish all other grist-mills in his seigniory.[23] If the seigniorial mill produced a defective product, the censitaire could grind his wheat elsewhere (Munro 1907, p. 112). He could also mill surplus grain anywhere, but the fee remained the same—one-fourteenth of the grain milled—within or outside his seigniory.

According to Article LXXI of the Custom of Paris, a cornerstone of the legal framework of New France since 1664, only a clause in the title-deed permitted a seignior to demand unpaid labour, the corvée, from his censitaire (Ibid., p. 127). Since free bargaining determined the incidence of the corvée, it proved to be a minor and unusual charge in New France (Ibid. Also Harris 1968, p. 70), rarely exceeding six days per annum and even this service could be commuted for two livres by an arrêt of 1714 (Munro 1907, pp. 129, 132). In some cases the seignior could demand labour service, a species of paid corvée, whereby in exchange the censitaire enjoyed the use of the seigniorial commons and forest. Similarly a seignior occasionally compelled his censitaire to clear land for pasturage. The censitaire then would receive in return the right to the future use of that pasturage. But these paid corvée, like payment for the right to fish in seigniorial waters, appear to have been infrequent (Harris 1968, pp. 70, 128; Munro 1908, p. 78).

For every mutation in land ownership—a sale, gift or inheritance other than in the line of direct succession—the censitaire had to pay a fine to the seignior within forty days. This fine, called lods et ventes, was fixed by the Custom of Paris at one-twelfth or 8.25% of the mutation price. On failure to pay, the seignior could obtain a judgment from the intendant to seize the offending censitaire's property, including the *en censive* holding. The seignior could remit one-third of the lods et ventes to the censitaire, but he had no legal obligation to do so (Munro 1907, pp. 96–100).

The censitaire could conceal the de facto sale price from the seignior, trying to sell the land for a price higher than the seignior knew. But the seignior enjoyed a *droit de retrait*, the option to purchase land sold by the censitaire at the official sale price (Munro 1907, p. 74, notes 1 and 2). Thus, if the landlord believed that the censitaire declared a price below the actual sale price, he could buy the land at the price declared by the censitaire, cancelling thereby the censitaire's contract with a third party to sell the land for more money. Under these circumstances, the censitaire was predisposed to declare the actual sale price. Although the intendant Jacques Raudot complained in a dispatch to France in 1707 that the *droit de retrait* appears nowhere in the Custom of Paris, the intendant in 1714, Bégon, authorized seigniors to resort to this procedure (Munro 1907, p. 99). In conjunction with the *droit de retrait* the lods et ventes imposed a burden on either the vendor or purchaser of a censive, depending upon whether the vendor could mark-up the price sufficiently to cover the costs of the lods et ventes. R.C. Harris estimates that land sold and bought by censitaires out of the line of direct succession brought to the seignior an average of L200 to L300 per annum for every 100 *en cens*ive holdings,[24] causing the censitaire to pay out, on average, two to three livres per annum in lods et ventes.

The church received one twenty-sixth or 3.8% of the grain produced by the censitaire annually. In 1663, Bishop Laval had ordered a tithe of 7.7% on all output produced, but censitaire protest prompted the bishop to agree to a tithe of 3.8% of all output—a tithe approved by the crown in 1679. And by 1705 the colonial authorities ruled that the tithe could be levied only with respect to grain output, a decision approved by the crown in 1707. These laws remained unchanged for the balance of the French régime (Munro 1907, pp. 183–184).

4 A Tabulation and Analysis of the Economic Burden of the Seigniorial Régime

An abundance of census material for New France, hitherto little used for economic analysis, helps to determine how deeply seigniorial dues and the tithe cut into the economic surplus of the censitaire. Without reference to the census records, the estimates made thus far, including those by R.C. Harris, must remain largely hypothetical.[25] I use the census material for 1688–1739—this includes the twenty-four years for which there was a census—to estimate the percentage of economic surplus consumed by seigniorial dues and the tithe. The same source also permits me to estimate the gross and net economic surplus per peasant family, as well as the number of arpents under crop, the wheat output per farm and the wheat output per arpent. The figures are presented in Tables 1, 2, and 3.The documentation permits consistent lower-bound estimates of the gross economic surplus per peasant family based upon wheat output, as the censuses for the period 1688–1739 provide a reliable data series for wheat output.

The computations presume that the peasant family consumed all but an insignificant portion of the non-wheat output from its farm. The wheat output net of seed requirements and the consumption needs of the peasant family give us the gross economic surplus while the net economic surplus or disposable savings may be computed by deducting the total seigniorial dues plus the tithe from the gross economic surplus. Specialists assume that the peasant family consumed most of the non-wheat output it produced, selling some dairy produce, beef and/or pork from time to time.[26] Presently, the data permit only very tentative, rough estimates of how much non-wheat output supplemented the gross economic surplus obtained from the sale of wheat. Information contained in the censuses and in the literature provides the bases for my upper-bound estimates of the gross economic surplus; they must be viewed, however, with healthy scepticism.

The censuses furnish a consistent data series for the number of horses, cattle, swine and sheep as well as for the minots of wheat harvested. Data are also available on the amount of corn, oats, flax, hemp and tobacco harvested, but only for few of the twenty-four census years under study. Computations for output per family farm for each of the twenty-four census years as well as the average output per family farm for the periods 1688–1714, 1716–1724 and 1726–1739 are presented in Table

Table 1 Non-grain output per family farm in New France: 1688–1739 (1)

Panel A

	Horses	*Cattle (number)*	*Pigs*	*Sheep*	*Peas*	*Corn (minots)*	*Oats*	*Other Grains*	*Flax*	*Hemp (lbs)*	*Tobacco*
1688	0.16	5.84	2.80	0.80	n.a	n.a	n.a	21.6	n.a	n.a	n.a
1695	0.35	5.59	3.25	0.56	n.a	4	8.5	12.6	n.a	n.a	n.a
1698	0.39	5.76	2.90	0.56	n.a	5.8	12.3	13.1	n.a	n.a	n.a
1706	0.87	6.62	3.45	0.85	19.9	n.a	n.a	44.2(2)	n.a	n.a	n.a
1707	0.89	6.65	3.33	1.02	15.5	n.a	n.a	34.4	n.a	n.a	n.a
1712	1.33	7.32	4.17	2.73	19.1	n.a	n.a	42.4	n.a	n.a	n.a
1713	0.85	6.25	5.38	2.75	n.a	n.a	n.a	n.a	n.a	n.a	n.a
1714	1.32	6.40	5.49	2.63	15.5	n.a	n.a	34.4	n.a	n.a	n.a
1716	1.41	6.80	5.46	2.67	14.6	n.a	n.a	32.4	n.a	n.a	n.a
1718	1.05	5.55	3.64	2.31	12.9	n.a	n.a	28.7	n.a	n.a	n.a
1719	1.39	6.31	4.99	2.92	16.0	2.24	17.4	35.7	15.9	1.76	n.a
1720	1.68	7.92	5.71	3.88	17.6	1.32	19.7	38.6	21.4	0.45	n.a
1721	1.69	7.05	4.90	4.17	17.3	2.70	19.3	39.3	16.5	0.63	14.5
1722	1.69	6.73	5.04	4.24	24.1	n.a	n.a	53.5	n.a	n.a	n.a
1723	1.62	6.41	4.44	4.22	19.2	n.a	n.a	42.7	n.a	n.a	n.a
1724	1.62	6.40	4.94	4.12	18.6	n.a	n.a	41.3	n.a	n.a	n.a
1726	1.69	6.34	4.86	4.42	21.6	n.a	n.a	48.0	n.a	n.a	n.a
1727	1.72	6.36	4.95	4.57	23.1	n.a	n.a	51.3	n.a	n.a	n.a
1730	1.57	7.55	4.91	4.60	23.5	n.a	n.a	52.2	n.a	n.a	n.a
1732	1.62	7.27	4.73	4.43	24.4	n.a	n.a	54.2	n.a	n.a	n.a
1734	1.04	6.86	4.88	4.09	13.1	1.08	33.9	48.1	19	0.46	34.3
1736	1.65	7.27	4.92	4.06	14.0	n.a	n.a	51.8	n.a	n.a	n.a
1737	1.69	6.19	4.40	3.77	10.1	n.a	n.a	37.4	n.a	n.a	n.a
1739	1.74	6.97	4.90	4.72	16.5	n.a	n.a	61.1	n.a	n.a	n.a

Panel B (3)

		1688–1714	1716–1724	1726–1739
Horses	x:(4)	0.77	1.52	1.59
	S.D.:(5)	0.44	0.22	0.23
	C. V.: (6)	57.1	14.8	14.4
Cattle	x:	6.30	6.65	6.85
	S. D.:	0.57	0.68	0.51
	C. V.:	9.05	10.2	7.39
Pigs	x:	3.85	4.89	4.82
	S. D.:	1.06	0.63	0.18
	C. V.:	27.6	12.9	3.76
Sheep	x:	1.49	3.57	4.33
	S. D.:	1.02	0.78	0.33
	C. V.:	68.3	22.3	7.53
Peas	x:	17.5(7)	17.5	18.3
	S. D.:	2.33	3.37	5.53
	C. V.:	13.3	19.3	30.2

Notes:
1. I estimated by dividing the census data for total output, found in Lunn (1943, p. 443) and in The Census of Canada (1876), by my estimates for the number of agricultural families in line 3 of Table 2. Where data are not available in the censuses, n.a. is used
2. For all but 1688 through 1698, 1719 through 1721, and 1734 data for 'other grains' are estimates made by applying the ratio of peas to all grain output during the 1719–1721 period to the 1706–1718 and 1722–1732 periods, while applying the ratio of peas to all grain output during 1734 to the 1736–1739 period
3. Calculated from the data in Panel A
4. The mean
5. The standard deviation
6. The coefficient of variation is derived by dividing the standard deviation by the mean. As opposed to the standard deviation the coefficient of variation is independent of the units used
7. Computations for peas pertain to the 1706–1714 period only.
Source Refer to Table 2

Table 2 Census data and estimates for New France: 1688–1739

		1688	*1695*	*1698*	*1706*	*1707*	*1712*	*1713*	*1714*
Panel A									
1	Population:	10,303	12,786	13,815	16,706	17,549	18,761	18,467	19,315
2	No. of families (2)	1717	2131	2302	2784	2925	3127	3078	3217
3	No. of agri. families:(3)	1322	1641	1772	2145	2252	2408	2370	2479
4	Arpents under crop:	28,497	28,102	32,515	43,671	43,501	52,965	54,927	53,161
5	Arpents under crop per agri. family (4/3)	21.5	17.1	18.4	20.3	19.3	23.0	23.2	21.4
6	Arpents under wheat(4)	21,373	21,076	24,386	32,753	32,626	39,724	41,195	39,871
7	Minots of wheat:	100,974	129,154	160,978	211,634	179,855	292,415	251,463	236,049
8	Minots of wheat per agri. family (7/3):	76.4	78.7	90.8	98.7	79.9	121.1	106.1	95.2
9	Minors of wheat per arpent (7/6)	4.7	6.1	6.6	6.5	5.5	7.4	6.1	5.9
10	Wheat seed; yield ratio:(5)	2.35	3.05	3.30	3.25	2.75	3.70	3.05	2.95
11	Seed requirements (minots):(6)	42,746	42,152	48,772	65,506	65,252	79,448	82,390	79,742
12	Seed per agri. family (11/3):	32.3	25.7	27.5	30.5	29.0	33.0	34.8	32.0
13	Agri. pop. wheat consumptions	47,592	59,076	63,792	77,220	81,072	86,688	85,320	89,244
14	11 + 13:	90,338	101,228	112,564	142,726	146,324	166,336	167,710	168,986
15	Gross surplus of wheat (7 − 4):	10,636	27,926	48,414	68,910	33,531	126,079	83,573	67,063
Panel B									
16	Gross surplus of wheat per agri. family (15/3):	8.0	17.0	27.3	32.1	14.9	52.3	35.3	27.0
17	Cens et rentes per agri. family (minots of wheat):(8)	5.5	5.8	3.2	7.7	7.7	5.8	5.8	3.7
18	Tithe per agri family (minots of wheat):(9)	2.9	3.0	3.4	3.7	3.0	4.6	4.0	3.6
19	Mill banalité per agri. family (minots of wheat): (10)	2.6	2.6	2.6	2.6	2.6	2.6	2.6	2.6

		1688	*1695*	*1698*	*1706*	*1707*	*1712*	*1713*	*1714*
20	Lods et ventes per agri. family (minots of wheat):(11)	1.0	1.0	1.0	1.0	1.0	1.0	1.0	1.0
21	17 + 18 + 19 + 20:	12.0	12.4	10.2	15.0	14.3	14.0	13.4	10.9
22	Net surplus of wheat per agri. family (16–21):	−4.0	4.6	17.1	17.1	0.6	38.3	21.9	16.1
23	Seign. dues + tithe as % of gross surplus of wheat (21/16):	150.1	72.9	37.4	46.7	96.0	26.8	38.0	40.4

		1716	*1718*	*1719*	*1720*	*1721*	*1722*	*1723*	*1724*
Panel A									
1	Population:	20,890	23,325	22,530	24,474	25,852	26,106	25,999	27,159
2	No. of families (2)	3482	3887	3755	4079	4309	4351	4333	4526
3	No. of agri. families:(3)	2681	2993	2891	3141	3318	3350	3336	3485
4	Arpents under crop:	57,240	71,176	63,032	61,357	62,154	62,734	82,246	83,419
5	Arpents under crop per agri. family (4/3)	21.3	23.8	21.8	19.5	18.7	18.7	24.6	23.9
6	Arpents under wheat(4)	42,930	53,382	47,274	46,018	46,609	47,050	61,684	62,564
7	Minots of wheat:	252,304	249,549	234,566	134,439	282,700	341,205	295,522	300,024
8	Minots of wheat per agri. family (7/3):	94.1	83.4	81.1	42.8	85.2	101.8	88.6	86.1
9	Minors of wheat per arpent (7/6)	5.9	4.7	5.0	2.9	6.1	7.2	4.8	4.8
10	Wheat seed; yield ratio:(5)	2.95	2.35	2.25	1.45	3.50	3.60	2.40	2.40
11	Seed requirements (minots):(6)	79,742	85,860	106,764	94,548	92,036	93,218	94,100	123,368
12	Seed per agri. family (11/3):	32.0	35.7	32.7	29.3	28.1	28.1	37.0	35.9
13	Agri. pop. wheat consumptions	95,516	107,748	104,076	113,076	119,448	120,600	120,096	125,460
14	11 + 13:	182,376	214,512	198,624	205,112	212,666	214,700	243,464	250,588
15	Gross surplus of wheat (7–14):	69,928	35,037	35,942	−70,693	70,034	126,505	52,058	49,436

(continued)

Table 2 (continued)

		1716	1718	1719	1720	1721	1722	1723	1724
Panel B									
16	Gross surplus of wheat per agri. family (15/3):	26.1	11.7	12.4	−22.5	21.1	37.8	15.6	14.2
17	Cens et rentes per agri. family (minots of wheat):(8)	1.6	1.3	1.9	5.0	5.8	5.0	3.9	3.9
18	Tithe per agri family (minots of wheat):(9)	3.6	3.2	3.1	1.6	3.2	3.9	3.4	3.3
19	Mill banalité per agri. family (minots of wheat): (10)	2.6	2.6	2.6	2.6	2.6	2.6	2.6	2.0.6
20	Lods et ventes per agri. family (minots of wheat):(11)	1.0	1.0	1.0	1.0	1.0	1.0	1.0	1.0
21	17 + 18 + 19 + 20:	8.8	8.1	8.6	10.2	12.6	12.5	10.9	10.8
22	Net surplus of wheat per agri. family (16–21):	17.3	3.6	3.8	−32.7	8.5	25.3	4.7	3.4
23	Seign. dues + tithe as % of gross surplus of wheat (21/16):	33.7	69.2	69.3	–	59.7	33.1	69.9	76.0

		1726	1727	1730	1732	1734	1736	1737	1739
Panel A									
1	Population:	29,859	31,169	34,118	35,417	37,716	39,496	40,153	43,382
2	No. of families (2)	4976	5195	5686	5903	6286	6583	6692	7230
3	No. of agri. families:(3)	3832	4000	4378	4545	4840	5069	5153	5567
4	Arpents under crop:	96,202	102,100	130,791	133,263	163,111	164,741	157,305	188,105
5	Arpents under crop per agri. family (4/3)	25.1	25.5	29.9	29.3	33.7	32.5	30.5	33.8
6	Arpents under wheat(4)	72,151	76,575	98,093	99,947	122,333	123,556	117,979	141,079

		1726	1727	1730	1732	1734	1736	1737	1739
7	Minots of wheat:	411,070	440,739	458,722	468,219	737,892	669,744	341,688	634,605
8	Minots of wheat per agri. family (7/3):	107.3	110.2	104.8	103.0	152.4	132.1	66.3	114.0
9	Minors of wheat per arpent (7/6)	5.7	5.7	4.7	4.7	6.0	5.4	2.9	4.5
10	Wheat seed; yield ratio:(5)	2.85	2.85	2.35	2.35	3.00	2.70	1.45	2.25
11	Seed requirements (minots):(6)	144,302	153,150	196,186	199,894	244,666	247,132	235,958	282,158
12	Seed per agri. family (11/3):	37.6	38.3	44.8	44.0	50.5	48.7	45.8	50.7
13	Agri. pop. wheat consumptions	137,952	144,000	157,608	163,620	174,240	182,484	185,508	200,412
14	11 + 13:	282,254	297,150	353,794	363,514	418,906	429,616	421,466	482,570
15	Gross surplus of wheat (7 - 14):	128,816	143,589	104,928	104,705	318,986	240,128	−79,778	152,035
Panel B									
16	Gross surplus of wheat per agri. family (15/3):	33.6	35.9	24.0	23.0	65.9	47.4	−15.5	27.3
17	Cens et rentes per agri. family (minots of wheat):(8)	5.8	5.0	4.6	5.0	4.6	5.8	3.9	3.9
18	Tithe per agri family (minots of wheat):(9)	4.1	4.2	4.0	3.8	5.8	5.0	2.5	4.3
19	Mill banalité per agri. family (minots of wheat): (10)	2.6	2.6	2.6	2.6	2.6	2.6	2.6	2.6
20	Lods et ventes per agri. family (minots of wheat):(11)	1.0	1.0	1.0	1.0	1.0	1.0	1.0	1.0
21	17 + 18 + 19 + 20:	13.5	12.8	12.2	12.4	14.0	14.4	10.0	11.8
22	Net surplus of wheat per agri. family (16–21):	20.1	23.1	11.8	10.8	51.9	33.0	−25.5	15.5

(continued)

Table 2 (continued)

		1726	1727	1730	1732	1734	1736	1737	1739
23	Seign. dues + tithe as % of gross surplus of wheat (21/16):	40.2	35.6	50.8	53.9	21.2	30.4	-	43.2

Notes

1. Unless otherwise indicated the data in this table are taken from material provided by the censuses of New France. The data can be found in The Canadian Census, 1870–1871; in Lunn (1943, p. 443, 444), as well as in M. Allard, L'histoire canadienne á travers le document, p. 114

2. The number of families is estimated by dividing the average number of individuals per family into the population. The number of individuals per family is estimated by using the information provided in the censuses of 1667 and 1681, where the number of families is recorded. If the number of families is divided into the population, I am left with a maximum estimate for the number of individuals per family: 5.8 for 1667 and 6.2 for 1681. For later years the census provides information on the number of married individuals only. By dividing this figure by two I estimate the number of couples. By dividing the population by the number of couples I obtain a maximum estimate for the number of individuals per family which consistently falls just below six. For the calculations I assume that the number of individuals per family is six throughout the period examined

3. The number of families engaged in agriculture is estimated through the use of 1681 census where data are given for the number of individuals engaged in non-agricultural pursuits. Assuming that each family consisted of six individuals, I estimate the non-agricultural population at 23% of the total. No such estimate is possible for the other census years. For this reason, I use the 23% figure for the estimate of the non-agricultural population for all census years. I must stress, however, that this figure is only an estimate

4. For all census years there is no information as to the amount of land under wheat. The estimate of the amount of land planted with wheat is, thus, taken from Harris (1968, p. 153), who found evidence suggesting that about 75% of the land under crop was planted with wheat in New France

5. The wheat seed: yield ratio is estimated by dividing the output per arpent by the amount of seed typically sown per arpent. This, in turn, has been estimated to have been typically two minots per arpent from thirty variegated examples by Dechêne (1974, p. 327)

6. The seed requirements are estimated by multiplying the number of arpents planted with wheat by the amount of seed sown per arpent

Table 2 (continued)

7. I assume that the typical censitaire consumed six minots of wheat per annum. Harris (1968, p. 160) makes the same assumption for the pre-1760 period in New France. Both Reid (1947, p. 275) and Meiklejohn (1823–1824) provide the historical underpinning for this assumption. The consumption of six minots of wheat per capita per annum constituted only a portion, albeit the major portion, of the possible diet of the typical censitaire. Clark and Haswell (1970, p. 58), find that a kg. of unmilled wheat yields 3150 calories. They also conclude that the typical individual working eight hours a day requires somewhat less than 2500 calories per day (Ibid., Chapter 1). It would take 10.6 minots of wheat to supply the 2500 calories every day for one year (each minot weighing approximately 27.18 kilograms). The six minots consumed by the censitaire would constitute only 60% of his/her minimum annual diet. This is a plausible figure given that in other communities a greater proportion of the peasant's diet was and is composed of wheat (Clark and Haswell 1970, ch. 4)

8 The cens et rentes is estimated using the data provided in The Report of the Commissioners (1844). The estimates made in this report are derived from an analysis of title deeds listed in item no. 128 of the appendix to the report. Prior to 1663 the cens et rentes was one sol and eight deniers per arpent, where twelve deniers = one sol and twenty sols = one livre. From 1663 to 1760 the highest rate of cens et rentes stood at two sols and one denier per arpent. This was for the Montreal region. Throughout the period under examination, however, the rate of cens et rentes generally charged throughout New France was one sol and eight denier per arpent. I converted the estimates of the cens et rentes from nominal terms into terms of minots of wheat using the price data in Hamelin (1970, p. 61). Use is also made of the price data in The Report of the Commissioners (1844), item no. 126 of appendix F. Similar price estimates are found in Lunn (1934, p. 120). The cens et rentes is estimated for the total land held per peasant family. No such data, however, is available for the census years. I estimate the land held per peasant family to have been 111 arpents during the period under study from data on the en roture concessions made during the French regime. This data is found in The Report of the Commissioners of 1843, item no. 128, Appendix F

9 The tithe consisted of one twenty-sixth of the total grain production of the peasant family. My estimates refer to the wheat production

10 The gristmill banalité, instituted in New France on June 4, 1686, constituted one-fourteenth of the grain used for the peasant family's domestic consumption

11 From the data in Harris (1968, p. 76), I estimate that the typical peasant family paid an average of two to three livres per annum in lods et ventes, or one to one and one-half minots of wheat depending upon the price of wheat

Sources Allard et al. (1976), Census of Canada (1876), Clark and Haswell (1970), Dechêne (1974), Hamelin (1970), Harris (1968), Levière and Angers (1856), Lunn (1934, 1943), Meiklejohn (1823–1824), Munro (1907, 1908), Reid (1947), The Report of the Commissioners (1844)

Table 3 Derivations from the census material

			1688–1714	*1716–1724*	*1726–1739*
1	No. of agri families	x:(1)	2049	3149	4673
		S.D.:(2)	421	274	595
		C.V.:(3)	20.5	8.7	12.7
2	Land under crop per agri. family (arpents)	x:	20.5	21.5	29.5
		S. D.:	2.2	2.4	3.2
		C. V.:	10.7	11.2	11.0
3	Output per arpent (minots of wheat)	x:	6.1	5.2	4.9
		S. D.:	0.8	0.8	1.0
		C.V.:	13.1	13.1	20.1
4	Wheat seed: yield ratio	x:	3.05	2.61	2.47
		S.D.:	0.4	0.7	0.5
		C.V.:	13.1	14.9	20.2
5	Wheat output per agri. family (minots of wheat)	x:	93.4	82.9	111.3
		S. D.:	15.3	17.5	24.7
		C.V.:	16.4	21.1	22.2
6	Seed requirements per agri. family (minots of wheat)	x:	30.6	32.3	45
		S. D.:	3.0	3.6	5.0
		C. V.:	9.8	11.2	11.1
7	Seigniorial dues + tithe per agri. family (minots ofwheat)	x:	12.8	10.3	12.6
		S. D.:	1.7	1.7	1.4
		C.V.:	13.2	16.7	11.1
8	Cens et rentes per agri. family (minots of wheat)	x:	5.8	3.5	4.8
		S. D.:	1.70	1.74	0.73
		C.V.:	27.9	48.9	15.2
9	Tithe per agri. Family (minots of wheat):	x:	3.5	3.2	4.2
		S. D.:	0.60	0.68	0.95
		C.V.:	16.6	21.3	22.6
10	Non-wheat output sold per agri. family (minots of wheat)	x:	6.5	8.3	14.3
11	Gross economic surplus per agri. family (minots of wheat) lower-bound estimate	X:(4)	27.7	20.2	34.1
		S. D.:	13.8	9.3	16.3
		C. V.:	49.8	46.0	48.0
12	Gross economic surplus per agri. family (minots of wheat) upper-bound estimate	x:(5)	34.2	28.5	48.4
13	Net economic surplus per agri. family (minots of wheat) lower-bound estimate	X:(6)	14.0	12.4	23.9
		S. D.:	12.5	11.8	13.8
		C. V.:	89.6	95.1	57.9
14	Net economic surplus per agri. family (minots of wheat) upper-bound estimate	x:(7)	20.5	20.7	38.2

(continued)

Table 3 (continued)

			1688–1714	*1716–1724*	*1726–1739*
		S. D.:			
		C. V.:			
15	% of gross ec. Surplus absorbed by seign. dues + tithe (lower-bound estimate)	x:(8)	46.2	51.0	36.9
16	% of gross ec. Surplus absorbed by seign. dues + tithe (upper-bound estimate)	x:(9)	37.4	36.1	26.0

Notes
1. The mean
2. The standard deviation
3. The coefficient of variation which is derived by dividing the standard deviation by the mean. As opposed to the standard deviation, the coefficient of variation is independent of the units used
4. Based upon the gross surplus in the production of wheat, Table 2 line 16
5. Derived by adding the mean in line 10 to the mean in line 11
6. Based upon the net surplus in the production of wheat, Table 2 line 22
7. Derived by subtracting the mean in line 7 from the mean in line 12
8. Derived by dividing the mean in line 7 by the mean in line 11
9. Derived by dividing the mean in line 7 by the mean in line 12

Source Refer to Table 2 and section entitled "Tabulation and Analysis of the Economic Burden of the Seigniorial Régime"

1. I group the years so as to make each of the three periods contain eight census years.

The number of horses rose dramatically from 1688 to 1714 from 0.16 per farm to 1.32, for an average of 0.77 for the period 1688–1714, a time when many farms probably had no horses while others possessed only one. The average number of horses for the period 1716–1724 was 1.52 while from 1726 to 1739 it was 1.29 per peasant family. Once established in New France, from at least 1716, the number of horses per farm remained relatively stable. There were barely enough horses for the family farm, above all for transportation, a task they performed more efficiently than other live-stock (Dechêne 1974, p. 319).

The number of cattle per farm rose from about six in 1688 to about seven in 1739. The average number of cattle increased from 6.30 during the period 1688–1714 to 6.65 during the period 1716–1724 to 6.85 in the years 1726–1739. Evidently, the number of cattle per farm increased most from 1688 to 1714. Dechêne (1974, pp. 335–316) found that the average habitant in the Montreal region in the late sixteenth and early seventeenth century kept two pairs of oxen for ploughing and two to three milch cows. Prior to 1850 in New France (known as Lower Canada and later as Quebec) approximately three milch cows proved sufficient to meet the annual dairy requirements of a peasant family of six.[27] Assuming the same to be true a century earlier, the number of cattle kept, per peasant family, would have been just sufficient to meet its overall needs.[28] The number of cattle rose slightly from 1688 to 1739 probably because more land was put under crop during this time (line 5, Table 2). Of course, people occasionally sold a bull or a cow to pay debts or because the animals were too old to be of further economic use, earning thereby some extra income to supplement the gross economic surplus earned from the sale of wheat or simply to cover a previous deficit (Dechêne 1974, pp. 316, 318; Harris 1968, p. 155). Sales of butter and cheese, however, remained negligible.

The number of sheep per farm rose steadily from about one during 1688 to about five during 1739. But the peasant family probably produced wool for its own needs, replacing thereby, at a lower cost, the woollens previously imported from France.[29] The little wool that was sold originated mainly on seigniorial estates.[30] The number of swine per farm also increased from about three in 1688 to about five pigs in 1739. From 1688 to 1714 the average number of swine per farm was 3.85, rising to an average of 4.89 during the period 1716–1724 and falling to 4.82 in the period 1726–1739. Little change is recorded, therefore, during the last two periods. Louise Dechêne finds that two pigs satisfied the annual needs of a peasant family of six.[31] She explains that the typical farm kept four to five swine, two were fattened for the market (Dechêne 1974, p. 320). R. C. Harris observes that when the peasant family kept three to four swine, one might be sold annually.[32]

If Dechêne and Harris are correct, Table 1 shows that after 1712 a typical peasant family sold one to two pigs annually. Pea production increased only slightly from 1688 to 1739, rising from an average of 17.5 minots per farm during both the periods 1688–1714 and 1716–1724 to 18.3 minots during the period 1726–1739. Dechêne maintains that peasants grew peas largely for pig feed and to make porridge (Dechêne 1974, p. 302)—an argument consistent with the fact that 17 to 18 minots of peas net of seed requirements had to accommodate the needs of four to five pigs per annum plus those of the peasant family. Some peas, however, were sold every year, at least beginning in the 1720s.[33] But only in 1727 did the export of peas exceed I minot per peasant family; after that date it only approached I minot (Lunn 1943, p. 449). The value of peas sold probably never exceeded two livres per annum.[34]

Oats were the most important grain in New France outside of wheat, therefore, they are the most important component of the "other grains" of Table 1. Although oat production rose steadily from 1688 to 1739, it fed a growing number of livestock. Oats or corn (an insignificant output) probably provided no marketable surplus (Harris 1968, p. 154). Also hemp production proved equally insignificant (see Table 1 and also Lunn 1943, pp. 76–78). But people did produce larger amounts of flax to provide the family with the linen necessary to make the materials previously available only at a much higher cost from France (Lunn 1943, p. 82).

The habitants were heavy smokers, Lunn (1943, p. 82). Some tobacco was, no doubt, sold in the urban markets, although for most of the years 1688 to 1739 the producers probably consumed most of their own crop (Lunn 1943; Séguin 1973, p. 195). The census provides data for tobacco production only for 1721 and 1734 (Table 1). If the difference in the amount of tobacco produced between these two years indicates a trend, it reveals a tendency to commercialize tobacco production. In 1721, 14.5 pounds and in 1734 over 34 pounds of tobacco were harvested. Extrapolating from this information one might suppose that from 1726 to 1739 a peasant family sold 20 pounds of tobacco annually, earning approximately four livres per annum.[35]

The highest income from non-wheat output sold in New France from 1688 to 1739 would have been earned from 1716 to 1739. From 1688 to 1714 only the sale of some beef and cattle earned a significant income for the farm. In the period 1716–1724 people sold more peas, swine, beef and cattle, and finally, from 1726 to 1739 tobacco sales probably assumed some significance. The price data we possess indicate that people may have sold an ox, a cow or a bull for twenty to sixty livres, depending upon the age of the animal, its quality and the year and season it was sold (See Harris 1968, p. 9; Dechêne 1974, p. 335). Assume that the sale of an ox, a cow or a bull brought in forty livres, and since people sold cattle infrequently, assume also that they sold one animal every three years. The peasant family would then earn thirteen livres per annum from the sale of cattle, a hypothesis permitting one to suppose thirteen livres per annum to be the value of non-wheat output sold from 1688 to 1714.

Swine were sold every year for about ten livres per pig from at least 1716 to 1730 (Dechêne 1974, p. 335). Since one to two pigs were sold annually, probably fifteen livres was the average value of swine sold per peasant family per annum. During the period 1716–1724, people probably sold one livre of peas annually as well. This would be in addition to the thirteen livres earned from the sale of cattle and the fifteen livres from the sale of swine. This yields twenty-nine livres as a tentative value of the non-wheat output sold per annum per farm from 1716 to 1724. To determine the tentative value of the non-wheat output sold annually per farm in the years 1726 to 1739, the sum of four livres—from the annual sale of tobacco—must be added to the non-wheat output for 1716 to 1724, making a total of thirty-three livres for the period 1726–1739.

The upper-bound estimates of the gross economic surplus are made by adding to the lower-bound estimates the estimated values of the non-wheat output sold. The upper-bound estimates of the net economic surplus are computed in the same fashion. All estimates are formulated in terms of minots of wheat. The computations are presented in Tables 2 and 3. Table 2 presents the results for the twenty-four census years of the period 1688–1739. These computations are related to the determinants of the lower-bound estimates for the gross and net economic surplus. The data in Table 3 are divided into three time-spans of eight years each: 1688–1714, 1716–1724, and 1726–1739. After calculating the mean for the relevant categories, I compute the standard deviation to indicate the variations about the mean. The coefficient of variation is calculated to make the standard deviation independent of the units used, permitting one to discern movements over time in averages and variability. The upper-bound estimates of the gross and net economic surplus are also presented in Table 3.

Estimates of the seigniorial dues are inclusive of the cens et rentes, the lods et ventes, and the grist-mill banalité. Those of the cens et rentes in terms of wheat are derived from the data on the nominal cens et rentes, the land held per peasant family and the price of wheat from 1688 to 1739. Since the nominal cens et rentes per arpent was relatively constant throughout the period 1688–1739 and since the average size of the typical censitaire's holding was 111 arpents throughout this period, it follows that the cens et rentes per peasant farm was relatively constant in nominal terms until 1739.[36] Finally, the nominal cens et rentes is converted into cens et rentes in terms of minots of wheat using the available price data (Hamelin 1970, p. 61).

I assume the lods et ventes to be constant in terms of minots of wheat throughout the years 1688 to 1739. However, the lods et ventes averaged two to three livres annually per peasant family in the same period. Since the lods et ventes are assumed to be constant in terms of wheat and since there were wide fluctuations in the price of wheat, the lods et ventes fluctuate, in nominal terms, between two and three livres throughout the years 1688–1739. The other seigniorial charge, the banalité, is assumed to be a constant at 2.6 minots of wheat. Finally, the tithe is simply proportional to the output of wheat.

Seigniorial dues plus the tithe as a percentage of the lower-bound gross economic surplus (henceforth referred to as the L.B.G.) declined considerably from 1688 to 1739. In the period 1688–1714, 46.2% of the L.B.G. went toward seigniorial dues and tithe, while from 1716 to 1724, 51% of the L.B.G. was directed toward these levies, while 36.9% of the L.B.G. was so directed from 1726 to 1739.

The increase in the percentage of the L.B.G. going toward seigniorial dues and tithe over the periods 1688–1714 and 1716–1724 was a product of the L.B.G. declining by 27.6% whereas the seigniorial dues and tithe declined by only 19.5%, this being conditioned by the 39.6% fall in the cens et rentes. During the periods 1716–1724 and 1726–1739, the percentage of the L.B.G. absorbed by seigniorial dues and tithe declined, in spite of the cens et rentes increasing by 37.1% and the total levies rising 22.3%. These increases could not negate the massive increase in the L.B.G. of 68.8%.[37]

An increase of 37.3% in the amount of land under crop per family explains why the L.B.G. rose to the extent it did over the last two periods. Although wheat output per arpent fell from 1716–1724 to 1726–1739 by 6.1%, from 5.2 minots to 4.9 minots, the greater amount of land planted with wheat produced a substantial increase of 34.2% in the amount of wheat produced per farm, from 82.9 minots for the years 1716–1724 to 111.3 minots for the period 1726–1739. From 1688–1714 to 1716–1724, on the other hand, the L.B.G. fell largely because of a decline in wheat output per arpent of 14.7% when the arpents under crop grew by only 4.9%. The amount of wheat produced per farm dropped 11.2% from 93.4 minots for the years 1688–1714 to 82.9 minots for the period 1716–1724.

Adding to the gross economic surplus of wheat (the L.B.G.) the value of the non-wheat output sold in terms of minots of wheat (Table 3) reduces the percentage of the gross economic surplus going to seigniorial dues and tithe. This upper-bound estimate of the percentage of gross economic surplus absorbed by seigniorial dues and tithe was 37.4% during the period 1688–1714, 36.1% during the period 1716–1724, and 26.0% from 1726 to 1739. This differs considerably from the lower-bound estimate of the percentage of gross economic surplus captured by the seigniorial dues and tithe, which, as we saw, was 46.2% for the period 1688–1714, 51.0% for the period 1716–1724, and 36.9% from 1726 to 1739. For both the lower and upper-bound estimates of the gross economic surplus, the percentage going to the economic levies declined from 1688 to 1739, albeit, the addition of the non-wheat output sold to the L.B.G. makes the economic burden of the seigniorial dues and tithe much less significant than it would otherwise be.

The quantity of economic surplus retained by the typical peasant family (the net economic surplus) increased substantially from 1716–1724 to 1726–1739 with respect to both the lower and upper-bound estimates for the gross economic surplus (the latter to be henceforth referred to as the U.B.G.), from an average of 12.4 minots of wheat (L.B.G.) and 20.7 minots of wheat (U.B.G.) to an average of 23.9 minots (L.B.G.) and 38.2 minots (U.B.G.), after having declined from an average of 14.0 minots (L.B.G.) and 20.5 minots (U.B.G.) during the years 1688–1714. Thus, the typical peasant family benefited considerably from increases in wheat output in spite of the seigniorial dues and the tithe. Clearly, the typical peasant family enjoyed an increase in real income, reflected in the rise of both the lower and upper-bound estimates of the net economic surplus from 1688 to 1739.

In only two of the census years was the censitaire unable to produce a surplus of wheat: 1720 and 1737 (Table 2, line 16). In 1720 there was a deficit of 22.5 minots and in 1737, 15.5 minots—in this regard, recall that an individual consumed 6 minots of wheat annually and that a typical peasant family counted six individuals. Nevertheless, these years were exceptions; disastrous harvests never became a permanent feature of the censitaire's life. Moreover, when harvests failed, the state provided farmers with seed for next year's planting (Lunn 1943, pp. 92–93).

The large variability in the wheat output per family—as measured by the coefficient of variation—and the negligible variability in the seigniorial dues and tithe combine to produce a substantial variability in the net economic surplus per family (L.B.G.) which declines from 89.6% in the period 1688–1714 to 57.9% during the period 1726–1739, after rising to 95.1% in the period 1716–1724. This variability would probably be reduced when non-wheat output is included in our calculations. Its contribution to the economic surplus, I would suspect, was much more stable than that of the wheat output. In spite of the net variability of the economic surplus, the economic position of the typical peasant family appears to have improved significantly over the last two periods examined.

The analysis of the census material demonstrates that the seigniorial dues and the tithe were not high enough to absorb the gross economic surplus of the typical peasant family at any time from 1688 to 1739, even in the context of the variability in the gross economic surplus. Nevertheless, since the lower and upper bound estimates reveal that seigniorial dues did absorb a large portion of the gross economic surplus, the task remains to establish what proportion of the economic levies imposed on the peasant family proceeded directly from the seigniorial regime.

5 An Analysis of the Data

In New France no economic relationship compelled the censitaires to pay an economic rent to the seigniors. Only because the seigniors controlled the supply of habitable land was any economic rent paid to them. If peasants had controlled the land they held, they themselves would have captured any rent; but control of the land was not determined by economic factors. Moreover, economic factors cannot explain the stable level of cens et rentes prevailing uniformly throughout New France from 1688 to 1739, for by 1739 habitable land was still so abundant that had the seigniors competed for tenants they would have driven the economic rent toward zero throughout the colony. Yet the censitaire continued to pay the cens et rentes at the same rate. Economic factors explain only the differential rent (only one type of economic rent) in the Montreal region—2s ld as opposed to Is 8d elsewhere in the colony—where land was both more fertile and more advantageously located.

Perhaps the stability of the cens et rentes in New France—apart from the differential rent in the Montreal region—may be related to the fact that the state charged the same rate as the seigniors (Is 8d) when it granted land directly to the censitaire (prior to 1711) except for the Montreal region where 5d were added to total rent (*Report of the Commissioners*, p. 4). The state acted as a "price leader" and, typically, the seigniors did not deviate from the level of cens et rentes set by the "price leader." Perhaps the seigniors realized that to try to compete for tenants by leasing land for less than the cens et rentes charged by the state would eventually result in a zero rent for all. Finally, economic factors prevented the seigniors from raising the level of rent.

Thus, the state intervened to transfer income from the peasant family to a third party, and it also, albeit indirectly, set the level of cens et rentes. Only the 20% differential rent in the Montreal region is attributable to economic factors. Outside of New France, in Georgia in 1750 one could rent for the equivalent of 2d per arpent. In New York, in 1767 people paid a sum equivalent to 5d per arpent (Harris 1953, pp. 214, 233). Thus in British North America land rents remained 10 to 20% of that found in New France. Since the seignior invested neither in the land granted to the censitaire nor in the process necessary to grant the land, the cens et rentes represented no payment for service rendered.[38] State intervention to establish and to protect the seigniors, therefore, certainly reduced the income of the peasant family from what it otherwise could have been.

The lods et ventes, a tax upon the sale of land by the censitaire, and the tithe, a proportional tax upon his grain production, were economic levies imposed by the state; but they were collected and retained by the seignior and the church respectively. Without the lods et ventes, the peasant family would probably have retained more of its income. In contrast, the tithe contributed toward paying the costs to establish and to maintain the church in New France. Since the clergy participated at births, marriages, deaths and in most other solemn occasions, the tithe, unlike seigniorial dues, could not have been eliminated without providing for some equivalent charges to pay for religious services.

The crown established the grist-mill banalité in New France which, like the tithe, was a fee for services rendered. Without a law establishing a fixed charge for the milling of grain, people would have had to pay the grist-mill owner to grind their grain. Even grain ground on the family farm required investment of labour and income. All grain destined for family consumption had to be ground at the seigniorial mill, if one existed. Surplus grain potentially available for milling (of which wheat is our proxy)[39] represented 43% of the total grain potentially available for milling during the period 1688–1714, 29% from 1716 to 1724, and 46% during the years 1726 to 1739.[40]

The extent to which the income accrued per banal-mill exceeded the cost of grinding the grain measures the degree to which the banalité represented an avoidable economic cost to the typical peasant family. In a free market, without a banalité, any revenue above the cost of milling would have exercised a downward competitive pressure on the price of milling, bringing the revenue of the grist-mill in line with the costs of production. Assume that all wheat that could be ground was brought to a banal-mill which received in revenue one-fourteenth of the wheat ground (the banalité). To operate a grist-mill cost L500 per annum, inclusive of depreciation (Harris 1968, p. 73); and by converting this cost estimate into minots of wheat-using available price data (Hamelin 1970, p. 61)—I calculate the income per banal-mill by dividing its revenue by the total number of grist-mills—a figure obtained from the censuses. The results appear in Table 4.

I assume that all wheat potentially available for milling was brought to a banal-mill because the peasant family had to grind the wheat necessary for its subsistence at the mill and the surplus was most marketable when sold as flour (Lunn 1943, p. 86). People could not get along without grinding their grain, but it remains to be seen whether the price peasants paid at the banal-mill corresponded to the cost of its operation. There are good reasons to think that the banal-mill offered the most economical means for the peasant family to grind its wheat.[41] For we shall see that, except for the period 1716–1724, the banalité never generated an income sufficient for the banal-mill owner to cover his costs.

From 1688 to 1714 there were about 50 grist-mills in 180 seigniories, and the average mill ran a deficit of 61.3 minots of wheat. From 1716 to 1724 the average mill realized a surplus of 19.8 minots of wheat—an improvement following a 43% reduction in the cost of operation—in terms of minots of wheat—at a time when the average revenue per mill fell only marginally. The decrease in the average revenue per mill remained negligible from 1688–1714 to 1716–1724 because the wheat available for milling increased by 21% when the number of mills grew by 29%, from 50 to 70. Finally, from 1726 to 1739 the typical grist-mill suffered a deficit of 30.9 minots of wheat—a loss attributable to a 52% rise in the cost of operation at the same time that the average revenue per mill rose only 14%; for the number of grist-mills grew by 68%, from 70 to 118, over the periods 1716–1724 to 1726–1739, while the wheat available for milling increased by 92%. Profitable operations from 1716 to 1724 probably spurred mill construction, expanding total capacity beyond the point of profitability.

Only in the years from 1716 to 1724 did the typical grist-mill realize an accounting profit (revenue in excess of operating costs)—and even this short-lived "prosperity" followed from the fact that unusually high

Table 4 Revenue and cost in the Banal Grist-Mill

		1688–1714	*1716–1724*	*1726–1739*
1	Number of seigniories:(1)	180	180	210
2	Number of seigniories with banal grist-mills:(2)	50	70	118
3	Number seigniories with no banal grist-mills:	130	110	92
4	Income per banal grist-mill (minots of wheat):(3)	189	163	186
5	Operating costs per banal grist-mill (minots of wheat):(4)	250	143	217
6	Net income per banal grist-mill (minots of wheat) 4–5:	-61.3	19.8	-30.9

Notes

1. Data for the number of seigniories are taken from Harris (1968, pp. 35–36) and the back inner cover. By 1714 there were 180 seigniories open for settlement. No seigniories were granted from 1714 to 1732. Thereafter about 50 seigniories were granted, while 17 seigniories were reunited to the royal domain
2. The censuses provide data only for the number of grist-mills in 1685, 1688, 1692, 1695, 1698, 1719, 1720 and 1734 when there were 41, 46, 43, 39, 43, 76, 70 and 118 grist-mills respectively. The figures are hypothetical averages based upon the above data
3. This is derived by dividing the amount of wheat available for milling, multiplied by the grist-mill banalité of one-fourteenth, by the number of grist-mills. The amount of wheat available for milling is derived by subtracting the total seed requirements from the total output of wheat, lines 11 and 7 respectively of Table 2
4. The operating cost per grist-mill, inclusive of depreciation charges, was L500 per annum (Harris 1968, p. 78). I convert this nominal cost estimate into cost in terms of minots of wheat using the price data in Hamelin (1970, p. 61)

Sources Tables 2 and 3

wheat prices reduced the real cost of operation.[42] The typical grist-mill ran a deficit from 1688 to 1714 and again from 1726 to 1739 which—subsidized from the seigniors' other sources of income—accounted for 79.1% of the income from the cens et rentes and the lods et ventes for the typical seigniory with a mill during the period 1688–1714 and 23.5% in the period 1726–1739. From a more general perspective, the deficit equalled 22.0% of all income realized by all seigniories through the cens et rentes and the lods et ventes from 1688 to 1714 and 13.2% in the years 1726 to 1739 (Table 5). Therefore the banalité probably represented no avoidable economic cost to the typical peasant family before 1739. For without the banalité farmers would have had to pay a similar, probably a higher, fee to grind their grain.

Table 5 Table seigniorial income

		1688–1714	*1716–1724*	*1726–1739*
1	Net income per seigniory with no banal-mill (minots of wheat):(1)	77	75	131
2	Net income per seigniory with no banal-mill (livres tournois):(2)	154	262	303
3	Net income per seigniory with a banal-mill (minots of wheat):(3)	16	95	101
4	Net income per seigniory with a banal-mill (livres tournois):(4)	31	331	232
5	Economic losses as a % of cens et rentes + lods et ventes per seigniory with a banal-mill:(5)	79.1	0.0	23.5
6	Economic losses as a % of cens et rentes + lods et ventes of all seigniories:(6)	22.0	0.0	13.2

Notes

1. This is estimated by multiplying the proportion of seigniories with no banal-mills (refer to lines 1 and 3 of Table 4), by the total income generated through the cens et rentes and lods et ventes (refer to line 20 of 4 Table 2 and line 8 of Table 3) and dividing this by the number of 5 seigniories with no banal-mills (refer to line 3 of Table 4)

2. The price data in Hamelin (1970, p. 61), is used to convert income estimates in terms of minots of wheat into nominal terms

3. This is estimated multiplying the proportion of seigniories with banal-mills (refer to lines 1 and 2 of Table 4), by the total income generated through the cens et rentes and lods et ventes (refer to line 20 of Table 2 and line 8 of Table 3) and dividing this by the number of seigniories in line 6 of Table 4

4. Refer to note 2 above

5. The net income of the banal-mill, when negative, is the only assumed loss sustained by the typical seigniory. The estimate is therefore obtained by dividing the loss sustained by the typical banal-mill (line 6 of Table 4) by the information contained in line 1 of this table

6. I estimated by dividing the losses sustained by all seigniories (net loss per banal-mill multiplied by the number of banal-mills, refer to Table 4) by the total income generated through the cens et rentes and lods et ventes (refer to line 20 of table 2 and line 8 of Table 3)

Sources Tables 2 through 4

In contrast to the cens et rentes and to the lods et ventes—all charges peculiar to the seigniorial tenure in New France—the banalité and to some extent the tithe were levies against the censitaire's income that represented a fee determined by economic factors. The banalité amounted to only 20.3% of the total levies on peasant income from 1688 to 1714; 25.2% from 1716 to 1724; and 20.0% in the period 1726–1739. The tithe accounted for 27.1%, 31.1% and 34.1% of the total exactions on peasant income for each of these periods respectively (Table 6). After eliminating the banalité and after deleting the tithe plus the losses sustained by the banal-mill (for they provided a subsidy to the peasant family) from the calculation of the percentage of the gross economic surplus absorbed by the seigniorial dues and the tithe, institutional factors account for 18.8% of the L.B.G. and 15.2% of the U.B.G. from 1688 to 1714; 22.3% of the L.B.G. and 15.8% of the U.B.G. during the years 1716 to 1724; and 14.8% of the L.B.G. and 10.3% of the U.B.G. in the period 1726–1739. This is opposed to 46.2% of the L.B.G. and 37.4% of the U.B.G. from 1688 to 1714; 51% of the L.B.G. and 36.1% of the U.B.G. in the period 1716–1724; and 36.9% of the L.B.G. and 26.0% of the U.B.G. from 1726 to 1739 absorbed by seigniorial dues and the tithe when the calculations include the banalité and the losses sustained by the banal-mill plus the tithe (Table 6).

Estimates of the net revenue per grist-mill help to assess how much the institutionalized levies on peasant income added to seigniorial revenues. Seigniories with no banal-mill realized an income of 77 minots of wheat from 1688 to 1714; 75 minots in the period 1716–1724; and 131 minots from 1726 to 1739 or, expressed in Iivres tournois: L154, L262 and L303 respectively (Table 5).[43] Losses sustained by seigniories with a banal-mill explain why they realized an income of only 16 minots of wheat from 1688 to 1714. In the period 1716–1724, however, they earned an income of 95 minots, and in the years 1726 to 1739—when banal-mills again sustained substantial losses—the average mill realized an income of 101 minots. Expressed in nominal terms, seigniories with a mill received an income of L31, L331 and L232 respectively.

The seigniorial income that was a product of the seigniorial levies, inclusive or exclusive of the banalité, appears meager in comparison to the L600 per year that a skilled worker could earn in New France. Government officials could earn from L1800 to L2400 yearly (Nish 1968, pp. 39–41). From 1720 to 1740 almost half (49%) of the lay seigniories had more than one seignior. The seigniorial dues therefore provided most seigniors with revenues less than the earnings of a baker in New France, as low as L120 per annum Nish (1968, pp. 39–41) and Harris (1968, p. 55). The relatively low level of income from seigniorial dues, however, provides no warrant to trivialize the fact that these revenues came from the seigniorial system and from the efforts of the colonial authorities who acted on its behalf. In contrast, peasant families realized their income through the labour-time and capital that they invested in agriculture.

Table 6 The relative significance of the economic levies

			1688–1714	*1716–1724*	*1726–1739*
1	The banalité as a % of the total seigniorial dues plus the tithe:(1)		20.5	25.2	20.0
2	The tithe as a % of the total seigniorial dues:		27.1	31.1	34.1
3	The total seigniorial dues (exclusive of the banalité plus the tithe) as a % of the gross economic surplus:	L.B.G.(3) U.B.G.(4)	24.2 19.6	22.2 15.8	17.0 12.0
4	The total seigniorial dues (exclusive of the banalité and the % of the cens et rentes and lods et ventes equivalent to the losses sustained by the seigniories plus the tithe) as a % of the gross economic surplus:(2)	L.B.G U.B.G	18.8 15.2	22.3 15.8	14.8 10.3
5	The total seigniorial dues plus the tithe as a % of the gross economic surplus:	L.B.G U.B.G	46.2 37.4	51.0 36.1	36.9 26.0

Notes
1. By the total seigniorial dues I am referring to the cens et rentes, the tods et ventes, and the grist-mill banalité. All estimates in this table are made in terms of the typical peasant family
2. The percentage of the cens et rentes and lods et ventes equivalent to the losses sustained by the seigniories is calculated with the data of line 20 of Table 2, line 8 of Table 3, and line 6 of Table 5
3. The lower-bound estimate of the gross economic surplus
4. The upper-bound estimate of the gross economic surplus
Sources Tables 2, 3 and 5

6 The Allocation of Resources and Economic Development

The cens et rentes, the lods et ventes and the tithe constituted three different types of taxes that—to the extent they diminished the censitaire's disposable income and/or altered the structure of market prices or the opportunity cost of agricultural production—may have directly affected the allocation of resources in New France. Also by arbitrarily shifting income from the peasant farmer to the seignior, and to some extent the church, these economic levies may have altered the structure of effective demand—expanding and in some cases creating a market for a range of products—and thereby, indirectly, altered the allocation of resources, with consequences for the economic development of the colony.[44] Perhaps the censitaire could pass the burden of seigniorial dues on to the consumers of his commodities. But the ability to do so would be determined by the measure of elasticity in both demand and supply. Only if the demand for the censitaire's marketable output can be plausibly assumed to be perfectly elastic can it be argued that the peasant family absorbed the entire cost of seigniorial charges. In this case these dues would have modified the allocation of resources through their impact on the supply of output.

Assume the price of the most marketable peasant output, wheat, to be governed by the price of imported grain. In "equilibrium" the price of wheat in New France would not rise above that of imported wheat, for if it did, people would buy imported wheat. War and inclement weather at times delayed wheat imports, permitting the price of domestic wheat to rise above that imported from France—a situation prevailing when wheat was in short supply in New France.[45] Conversely, a surplus over domestic demand would encourage the export of wheat at the export price.[46] Since the export and import price are assumed to be beyond the control of the peasant farmer—a reasonable assumption—it follows that the demand for wheat was perfectly elastic from 1688 to 1739. Under these conditions economic levies would reduce the income of the peasant family, and, conversely, removal of these charges could only increase its revenue.

Ideally, the introduction of a tax can reduce output in three ways. It could force marginal producers out of business. In a multi-sector economy the tax may alter the opportunity cost of agricultural production and, thus, encourage a shift of resources to the non-taxed sectors. Finally, a tax can reduce savings; in this case, it would diminish the potential investment fund of a unit of production, the family farm, and thereby diminish investment and output, where *ex ante* investment and savings are equal.

The typical peasant family of New France realized a healthy net economic surplus throughout the 1688–1739 period. Since most settled land was equal in productive value (only the Montreal region produced a differential rent), probably even the marginal producers could cover their costs and remain in business. With respect to altering the opportunity cost, in agricultural production, with no feasible alternative to the taxed sector, producers will be immobile so long as their average revenue remains at least equal to the post-tax average cost of production. New France offered few alternatives to employment in agriculture—the fur trade and the fledgeling handicraft sectors provided no substantial alternatives.[47] Agriculture continued to be the most feasible and accessible avenue of employment from 1688 to 1739. The economic levies, therefore, probably prompted few individuals on the farm to seek employment in another economic sector.

The peasant family retained a net economic surplus from 1688 to 1739. Since it failed to invest even this money,[48] elimination of seigniorial levies probably would not have increased farm investment. The abundance of land encouraged a rational indifference to investment in agriculture because the output per farm worker could remain relatively high without any additional input of labour-time and/or capital per unit of land.[49] Since the economic charges probably did not diminish the peasant family's output, the seigniorial dues and the tithe had no direct influence on the allocation of resources. But the charges did alter the distribution of income. This might have altered the structure of effective demand if the seignior or the church—both beneficiaries of the economic levies—allocated their marginal expenditures in ways significantly different from those of the typical peasant family, modifying, in turn, the allocation of resources.

The peasant family spent its surplus for clothing, leather goods, household appliances, agricultural implements as well as for luxury commodities (Harris 1968, pp. 165–166; Séguin 1973, pp. 470–475, 484–487). Most of these items were "necessities," produced largely in New France.[50] The seignior, with a high income, most likely allocated any marginal increase or marginal income toward the purchase of luxury commodities, mostly imported from France.[51]

In New France, seigniorial income far exceeded the revenue from seigniorial dues. Typically, seigniors held a high military or administrative position and/or were engaged in a business venture while residing in Montreal or Quebec—a fact demonstrated by Cameron Nish (Nish 1968, pp. 113–115, 134–135). These non-agricultural pursuits might have generated an income in excess of L1800 annually, and possibly as much as L3000 to L4000.[52] Revenue from the typical seigniory ranged from about L200 to L300 annually from 1716 to 1739 (Table 5 above and the price data from Hamelin 1970)—only a marginal proportion of the seigniors' total income, ranging from a low of 5 to a high of 15%. The seignior's total income exceeded the median annual income of a labourer, L300 (Nish 1968, pp. 40–41)—a sum necessary for subsistence-by 6.6 to as much as 14.3 times.

A peasant family probably earned from L300 to L350 annually in the period 1716–1739 net of the seigniorial dues and the tithe—without these levies the family would have earned an additional L30 per annum.[53] The seigniorial charges represented 8 to 10% of the peasant family income[54]; therefore, receiving earnings comparable to those of a labourer, the family probably would have allocated a marginal increase in income to purchase more necessities: clothing, cloth, boots, shoes, some utensils, farm equipment and no doubt some luxuries—all items most likely to be produced in New France, with the exception of luxuries.[55] Conversely, a marginal fall in the high income of seigniors would probably diminish their purchase of imported luxury products.

Abolition of the seigniorial dues (the cens et rentes and the lods et ventes) would have augmented the economic surplus retained by the peasant family and, therefore, also increased the market for the non-farm output of New France by approximately 27.3% from 1688–1714, by 21.7% in the period 1716–1724, and by 15.2% during the years 1726–1739. Removal of the tithe might have also increased the market for artisan production. But revenues for the church supported the clergy, most of whom lived modestly, and paid the cost of constructing and maintaining churches, educational and medical facilities. The church spent much of what it received through the tithe in New France, stimulating indirectly the agricultural and artisanal sectors of the economy. Therefore removal of the tithe probably would not have altered the structure of effective demand sufficiently to effect the allocation of resources.

7 Conclusion

All the evidence suggests—though it is not certain—that a mere rescission of seigniorial dues would have stimulated the consumption of goods either produced or producible in New France in the context of an expanded market and altered aggregate demand structure. Additional expenditures from the agricultural sector would have raised the output of the handicrafts sector and, in turn, the expanded handicrafts sector would have allocated its new income largely to purchase goods produced in the agricultural and handicraft sectors—contributing, thereby, to diversify the entire economy. The resulting increase in specialization and the division of labour might have generated increasing returns—at least in the handicraft sector and perhaps in agriculture—augmenting output per capita.[56] Luxury imports would have probably declined in the wake of the abrogation of seigniorial levies and the marginal diminution of seigniorial income.

In sum, there are good reasons to think that seigniorial dues effected the allocation of resources in New France by changing the distribution of income from what it otherwise would have been. The dues biased spending patterns toward the purchase of imported luxury goods; consequently, output and productivity in the handicraft and agricultural sectors were, most probably, less than they would have been without seigniorial dues. To be sure this argument is counter-factual. But if true, it provides an explanation as to why New France failed to develop an economy commensurate with its human and natural resources and the state of foreign markets.

Contrary to prevailing professional opinion, the seigniorial system of land tenure in New France did nothing to reduce the transfer of income from the peasant family to the seignior and the church. The crown and the colonial authorities intervened in the economy to transfer income from the peasant family to the seignior—levies that are otherwise inconceivable where labour was scarce and land abundant. Since seigniories enjoyed high income from sources outside agriculture, their appropriation of a portion of the gross surplus produced by the peasant family served only to increase their own purchase of imported luxury goods.

At the same time, of course, the money taken from the peasant family's disposable savings significantly narrowed the market for the output from the handicraft sector of the economy. In fine, without seigniorial dues, peasant families probably would have spent more; therefore, New France would probably have produced more artisan and agricultural goods and, thus, generated increasing returns to scale and fostered economic development.

The colonial authorities may be considered a firm that produced coercion: a product that it distributed at no charge to the seigniors and the church.[57] For coercion resided at the center of the laws and regulations that permitted seigniors and the church to appropriate a portion of peasant produce. However substantial the proportion of the gross economic surplus retained by the peasant family, the state, nevertheless, intervened in the process of income distribution in favour of the seignior. Without this intervention, the distribution of income certainly would have been different and probably sufficiently altered to influence the structure of effective demand and, thereby, the pattern of economic development in New France.

Early Canada-New France experienced a relatively health rate of economic growth in spite of its land tenure system. Given this institution, the power of the peasant population derived from the scarcity of labour and availability of alternatives to agriculture at this time, prevented the seigniors from extracted additional income from the peasant family. This, in turn, was made possible by the unwillingness (or inability) of the state invest any further in coercion.

Notes

1. Hamelin, (1970, p. 123). Contrary to Hamelin, Delage (1970) finds that labour scarcity posed no problem to the economic development of New France (p. 108). Nish (1968) shows the economic elite to have had ready access to disposable savings, that is, potential capital. Meanwhile, even among the peasantry I find considerable potential savings. Finally, Hamelin's notions about the crucial role of merchant capital find little scholarly acceptance. Authorities agree that not even in Europe was merchant capital a condition necessary for economic development. For example, see Kindleberger (1978, pp. 135–166), and Bairoch (1974, pp. 45–70).
2. Eccles (1969, especially pp. 70, 98) and Eccles (1971). Eccles (1969, p. 96) also argues that reluctance to work hard made peasants less prosperous. Meanwhile merchants dissipated savings in conspicuous consumption (Eccles 1971, p. 14).
3. Discussed generally by Ouellet (1981).
4. This essay does not discuss how fiscal and monetary policies effected the economic standing of the peasant family; rather it measures the seigniorial régime's impact—within the framework of established fiscal and monetary policies—on the censitaire's retained earnings. See Frégault (1958–1959, 1959–1960), for the fiscal and monetary aspects of state policy.
5. Domar (1970) explains: When the scarce factor of production is not land but labour "...in the absence of specific governmental action to the contrary ... the country will consist of family-size farms because hired labour, in any form, will be either unavailable or unprofitable: the wage of a hired man or the income of a tenant will have to be at least equal to what he can make on his own farm; if he receives that much, no surplus [rent] will be left to his employer. A non-working class of servitors or others could be supported by the government out of taxes levied [directly or indirectly] on the peasants, but it could not support itself from land rents.".
6. The last reliable census year for the pre-conquest period is 1739.

7. Economic surplus is defined as the output in excess of that required for consumption and the renewal of the cycle of production; it encompasses the "normal" profit, the economic rent plus any "disequilibrium" profit earned by the peasant family—its potential investment fund. Harris (1959) discusses the concept of economic surplus.
8. Harris (1968, p. 81). Harris' method of calculation is not made explicit. More details are given on pp. 160–161. See note 12, below.
9. Ibid. Dechêne cites Harris (1968, pp. 160–161), who argues that if a farm produced fifty minots of wheat, almost all of the economic surplus, or 16% of wheat output, would be captured by the economic levies, the cens et rentes, the grist-mill banalité and the tithe.
10. Davis (1977, pp. 276–278) discusses land acquisition in British North America. For more details see Harris (1953) especially pp. 116, 288 on New England.
11. For government subsidies to New France see Guy Frégault (1958–1959, pp. 460–461; 1959–1960, pp. 175–177). See Davis (1977, pp. 286–287), and North (1966, p. 54), for English subsidies to the North American colonies.
12. On the arrêts of Marly see Munro (1908, pp. 91–93). Colonial authorities failed to enforce royal decrees published in 1672 and 1697 to annex unsettled seigniorial lands to the royal domain. See W.B. Munro (1907, pp. 35, 36, 38), Munro (1908, p. 38), Harris (1968, p. 31).
13. Harris (1968, p. 31). Many members of council in New France were seigniors - a fact explaining why colonial authorities showed special favour to the seigniors. See Munro (1907, p. 38).
14. Ibid. Although, in 1741, the crown forced the colonial authorities to reunite to the royal domain twenty largely unsettled seigniories in the Lake Champlain-Richelieu River areas, these lands were nevertheless eventually reconceded to their original grantees. See Munro (1908, p. 82). In contrast seigniories annexed 460 censive holdings to their domain by 1732 for alleged violations of the arrêts of Marly, Ibid., p. 176.
15. Minutes of evidence taken before the Assistant Commissioner of Crown Lands and Emigration, the testimony of Davidson (1839, p. 41).
16. An estimate made by multiplying the average amount of land held by censitaires by the number of agricultural families. See Table 2, notes 2 and 8.
17. This land was the most accessible to river transportation, the only reliable mode of transportation at the time, unlike the Canadian Shield to the north and the Appalachian Highlands south of the St. Lawrence and east of Lake Champlain.
18. *The Report of the Commissioners Appointed to Inquire into the State of Laws and Other Circumstances Connected with the Seigniorial Tenure in Lower Canada and Appendix* (1844), 3:3, appendix F; Harris (1968,

p. 64), concludes that there was no rent control in New France. Only the title-deed issued by the colonial authorities to the Seminary of Montreal in 1717 specified the rent to be paid to the seignior. See *The Report of the Commissioners* (1844, p. 13). If the seignior refused to sub-grant at a rental payment only and the prospective tenant complained to the governor, the lieutenant-governor or the intendant, the government would sub-grant the seigniorial land at the rate prevailing for the seigniory in question, collecting the rental payments itself (Munro 1907, p. 59).

19. *The Report of the Commissioners* (1844, p. 4), Harris (1968, p. 67), confirms the Commissioner's findings that rents tended toward no increase in New France.
20. Harris (1968, pp. 72–73), finds that to construct a small commercial grist-mill costs at least L2000.
21. Ibid., p. 117. Munro refers to Article LXX I of the Parlement of Paris.
22. Ibid., p. 110. According to a royal order of July 1675.
23. Ibid., p. 120; Lelièvre and Angers (1856, pp. 76a–79a).
24. Harris (1968, pp. 76, 140–146) shows that the sale and purchase of land was a crucial part of the peasant farm economy during the French régime. See also, Munro (1907, p. 97), Dechêne (1971, p. 157).
25. The most frequent references are to estimates in Harris (1968, pp. 77–81). See also note 9 of this article.
26. Ibid., pp. 154–155; Dechêne (1974, pp. 301–302, 316, 318–319, 320, 344), Lunn (1943, pp. 80–112), who also argues that New France was gradually developing into "...the level of an exporting country, when it was overtaken by the catastrophe of war" (p. 111).
27. From the evidence presented by Evans (1836, p. 156) and The Report of the Special Committee on the State of Agriculture in Lower Canada and Appendix (1850), Appendix TT of the Appendix, vol. 9, I estimate the potential output per milch cow: the quantity of milk produced and the quantity of cheese and butter produced therefrom plus the amount of dairy produce consumed per individual on the typical peasant farm. Handyside finds that a milch cow produced 600 gallons of milk per annum, furnishing 240 pounds of cheese and 120 pounds of butter, equivalent to eight pounds fifteen shillings. Evans finds that with 12 milch cows per farm, there remains five pounds currency in excess of family consumption. Thus in a six person family—typical of the period—3024 gallons of milk were consumed annually or 514 gallons per individual. My calculations are based on this information.
28. Also Dechêne (1974, pp. 315–316) finds that even as late as 1739, there was no tendency to commercialize meat and butter production.
29. Dechêne (1974, p. 320), explains that sheep were introduced by the peasant family in the eighteenth century to satisfy its needs. Lunn (1943)

finds that enough sheep were kept to fulfill family wool requirements by the 1820s, while Séguin (1973, p. 567), quotes Peter Kalm who discovered that the habitant raised only enough sheep to provide for 'his' wool requirements in 1749.

30. Dechêne (1974, p. 320). Séguin (1973, p. 566), lists the large herds of sheep found on ecclesiastical estates during 1681.
31. Dechêne (1974, p. 345); more generally, Van Bath (1966, p. 295), finds that Western European peasantry raised one or two pigs for their own use prior to the commercialization of agriculture in the eighteenth and nineteenth centuries.
32. Harris (1968, p. 161), argues that when a peasant family possessed three to four pigs, one or two oxen and five or six cows, a pig or cow was sold annually whereas if at least six swine were kept, one would be sold annually.
33. Harris (1968, p. 154), thinks peas were exported almost every year during the eighteenth century. But Table 1 in this article shows that pea production rose only in the period 1726–1739 and only by about 1 minot per family annually-coinciding with the export of peas approaching 1 minot per family annually. Therefore pea sales probably provided no significant income for the peasant family from 1688 to 1714.
34. The data in, "Summary Statement of Merchandise from Canada to Louisbourg, 1740," reprinted in Nish (1965), permit me to estimate the price per minot of peas to be 2 livres 14 sols.
35. The price per pound of tobacco in 1728 and in the 1830s was four sols according to Séguin (1973, p. 195) and Lunn (1943, p. 84) respectively.
36. I estimate 111 arpents from examining the title-deeds contained in *The Report of the Commissioners*, document no. 28. Harris (1968) finds, through an examination of title-deeds, 95% of the rotures were 40 to 200 square arpents, while 80% were 120 arpents or less.
37. Fluctuations in the cens et rentes and wheat output per farm were positively related over the period 1688–1739. For example, when wheat output per farm declined by 11.2 percent from 1688–1714 to 1716–1724, the cens et rentes fell by 39.4 percent and when wheat output per farm rose by 34.2 percent from 1716 to 1726–1739, the cens et rentes increased by 37.1 percent. This positive correlation is, in a round-about way, tied to the positive nexus between fluctuations in the price of wheat and wheat output per farm and the negative relation between variations in the cens et rentes and the price of wheat.
38. I am aware of no evidence that seigniorial investment in the seigniories justified the payment of the cens et rentes and the lods et ventes as indirect compensation. On the duties of the seignior see Trudel (1971a, b, pp. 187–190).

39. According to Harris (1968, p. 153), a view confirmed by inspecting the census records, see Tables 1 and 2.
40. I make this calculation by deducting the seed and consumption requirements from total wheat output, dividing this by total wheat output net of seed requirements. Refer to Table 3, lines 5 and 6; and Table 2, note 7.
41. In his classic text, Duby (1968, p. 17) explains that farmer payments for the use of the banal-mill "...underlies the success of mechanical innovations and shows that, in spite of taxes and the preemption on their own harvest, peasants found it to their own advantage to make use of the manorial mills. A mill wheel turned by a jet of water could release throughout the neighbourhood, in the peasant hut as well as in the lordly mansion, a great deal of manpower. Time freed in this way could be occupied in productive work on the land and was a far from negligible factor in economic growth." With respect to New France, Harris (1968, p. 72), observes, "...if the mill turned out acceptable flour, and if the service was reasonably rapid, most censitaires probably did take their surplus to the seigneurial mill.".
42. Since we convert the L500 cost figure into real terms—minots of wheat—the rise in the average price of wheat from 1688–1714 to 1716–1724 reduced the real cost of milling from 1716 to 1724. For price data see Hamelin (1970, p. 61).
43. The nominal figures are calculated by multiplying the minots of wheat computation by the average price of wheat for the relevant period. For the price data refer to Hamelin (1970, p. 61).
44. Fishlow (1973, p. 78), argues with respect to the nexus between supply and demand: "Some discussions have dismissed demand as a significant variable because there are few countries so small as not to permit the establishment of at least a single plant of optimum size throughout a broad spectrum of industrial activity. There the market is not a limiting factor in instituting industrialization. This is an entirely static view of the matter and lacks the support of history. It ignores the reciprocal influence of demand in shaping present supply, as well as the effects of potential sales in determining the introduction of new productive techniques and products. Not least of all, it ignores the conditions under which an effectively competitive structure of production can evolve." Baldwin (1956, p. 176), makes a similar point: "The more equitable distribution of income ... is more favourable for the induced development of domestic industry. A smaller proportion of the national budget is devoted to food expenditures.... Furthermore, there is a relatively larger market demand for services and durable consumer goods. Profit opportunities arise in these lines of production." Both Fishlow and Baldwin were foreshadowed by Malthus (1974 (reprint of the 1836 edition), p. 375), who argues: "Practically it has always been found that the excessive wealth of the few is in no

respect equivalent, with regard to effectual demand, to the more moderate wealth of the many. A large body of manufacturers and merchants can only find a market for their commodities among a numerous class of consumers below the rank of the great proprietors of the land. And experience shows us that manufacturing wealth is at once a consequence of a better distribution of property, and a cause of further improvements in such distribution, by the increase in the proportion of the middle classes of society, which the growth of manufacturing and mercantile capital cannot fail to create." See also pp. 349, 373.

45. The price data in Hamelin (1970, p. 61). Table 2, lines 15 and 16, above, show that the price of wheat rose with a shortfall in the wheat surplus of New France; prices rise to relatively high levels because of the difficulty to import wheat when required. See Lunn (1943, pp. 93–100).
46. Ibid., pp. 94–100, finds that a surplus of wheat in excess of that consumed in the country and in town was always exported-also the price tended to fall as surpluses increased.
47. Dechêne (1974, pp. 220–224, 486–487), also argues that the fur trade provided no important alternative source of employment to agriculture.
48. Lunn (1943, pp. 55–57); Séguin (1973, pp. 642–661) describes in detail the equipment used by the peasant family in New France.
49. Harris (1968, p. 151), Boserup (1965, p. 117), finds: "As long as the population of a given area is very sparse, food can be produced with little input labour per unit of output and with virtually no capital investment, since a very long fallow period helps to preserve soil fertility. As the density of the population of the area increases, the fertility of the soil can no longer be preserved by means of long fallow and it becomes necessary to introduce other systems which require a much larger agricultural labour force." See also pp. 30, 37–38, 43, 71, 95, 104.
50. A traditional view holds that the economic structure of New France was bereft of either heavy or handicraft industry. For example, Fauteux (1927, pp. 193, 195, 198, 214, 408, 435–436), finds that the only successful industries were lumber and tanning operations. Hamelin (1970, p. 35), also writes: "Les succès dans le domains agricole ne compensent pas les déficiences de l'industrie canadienne: la colonie n'a ni savonnerie, ni briquerie, ni tuiterie, ni manufacture de drap ou le toile, ni fonderie capable de la ravitailler en ustensiles et en outils. La colonie dépend de la métropole pour tout ce qui a trait aux objets manufacturés." This view has been strongly challenged by Moogk (1971, pp. 73–77), after a study of apprenticeship contracts of New France. He finds Quebec and Montreal to be manufacturing centers responding to the needs of the rural community and the export sector. In Quebec, an important export centre requiring barrels for shipping, for example, coopers represented about 20% of all apprenticeships for the period 1648–1760, while

composing only 1.5% of the total in Montreal (p. 74). By contrast, in Montreal, a more important service centre for the rural population, 14.4% of the apprenticeships during the years 1648–1760 were in blacksmithing, whereas in Quebec these represented only 1.9% of the total (p. 74). Since the wealthy resided in Quebec, the city specialized in luxury production (p. 75). Both cities manufactured important quantities of clothing and leather goods (pp. 74–75). In Montreal, 32.6% of apprenticeships were in the clothing and leather goods trades, whereas in Quebec they represented 19.8% of the total. The other crafts found in Montreal and Quebec include bakers, butchers, barber-wigmakers, braziers, carpenter-cartwrights, farriers, goldsmith-jewellers, joiner-sculptors, joiner-turners, locksmiths, nailsmiths, navigator-pilots, millers, roofers, roofers-chimney sweeps, saddlers, sculptors, shipwrights, tinsmiths, turners, weavers and wooden shoe makers.

51. Reid (1953, p. 24), finds that New France imported from Europe wines and brandies, grain, military and naval supplies, manufactures from Paris, salt meat, iron, English cloth, copper, olives, soap, candles and string, guns and bolts of cloth, pipes and window-glass, while Reid (1951, pp. 245–246), finds that New France imported from the French West Indies "...large quantities of sugar, molasses syrup, and rum as well as various delicacies to titillate the palates of Quebec gourmands .... Coffee, rice, olive oil and soaps came too from the French colonial trade during the French Regime." On imports from the French West Indies see also Mathieu (1972, p. 484).
52. According to Nish (1968, pp. 46–49), a highly paid administrator received L1800 annually, while a business venture might earn a minimum of L1000 to L1200. A seignior was often an administrator and/or engaged in business. The typical fortune of New France consisted of savings ranging from L50,000 to L60,000.
53. Derived from Table 2 above and the price data in Hamelin (1970, p. 61). I use my upper-bound estimate of the net economic surplus to which a rough estimate of farm consumption, inclusive of 36 minots of wheat, 2 pigs, a cow and clothing are added.
54. Harris (1968, p. 81), insists that the seigniorial dues absorbed about 5 to 10% of the peasant family's total revenue.
55. It is possible that the peasant family might have reacted to a decline in seigniorial dues by investing in leisure. This presumes, however, that leisure was a "superior good": that the family was satisfied with the prevailing standard of living. This does not appear to have been the case in light of the relatively low standard of living of the typical peasant family who were, moreover, readily exposed to the more affluent lifestyles of labourers and seigniors. See Trudel (1971a, b, p. 223) on the low standard of living of the typical peasant family. He writes: "...l'examen des

inventaires après décès démontre que l'habitant moyen est pauvre: ses habitudes somptuaires ne correspondent pas à I'état de sa fortune.".

56. Young (1928) argues that as the market expands and with it production, increasing returns on an industry-wide basis are realized through specialization and the division of labour generating increased productivity and economic development. Kaldor (1967, pp. 55–56), revising Young's argument adds that the most important determinant of market size in a backward region is the agricultural surplus. Both Young and Kaldor pay little heed to the influence of the distribution of income upon the size of the market. Integrating the arguments of Malthus and others (see footnote 95 above) and those of Young and Kaldor, I argue that the distribution of the agricultural surplus was critical to the size and, in some cases, existence of a market for handicraft production wherein lay much potential for increasing returns. Given the size of the agricultural surplus, the extent of the market was determined by the distribution of that surplus. More generally, the distribution of income limits the extent of the market, and in turn, the extent of the market sets limits to increasing returns and, ultimately, economic development.
57. Lane (1958, pp. 401, 405, 413), and Lane (1975, pp. 9, 12, 13), argue that government produced protection and sold it at a price greater than cost, having a monopoly in the production of protection.

References

Allard, M. et al. 1976. *L'histoire canadienne à traivers le document, La Nouvelle-France 1713–1760*. Montreal: Guérin.

Bairoch, P. 1974. *Revolution industrielle et sous-developpement*. Paris: Mouton.

Baldwin, R.E. 1956. Patterns of Development in Newly Settled Regions. *Manchester School of Economic and Social Studies* 24: 161–179.

Boserup, E. (1965). The Conditions of Agricultural Growth: The Economics of Agrarian Growth Under Population Pressure. London: Aldins.

Census of Canada, 1870–71. 1876. Ottawa. Vol. 3.

Clark, C., and M. Haswell. 1970. *The Economics of Subsistence Agriculture*. Glasgow: Macmillan-St. Martin's Press.

Davis, R. 1977. *The Rise of the Atlantic Economies*. London: Weidenfeld and Nicolson.

Davidson, J. 1839. (testimony), *Report on the Affairs of British North America from the Earl of Durham, with Appendices, The Colonies, Canada*, published in 1839 in *The British Parliamentary Papers*. Irish University Press, 1968.

Dechêne, L. 1971. L'évolution du régime seigneurial, le cas de Montréal aux XVIIe et XVIIIe siècles. *Recherches Sociographiques* 12: 143–252.

Dechêne, L. 1974. *Habitants et marchands de Montreal au XVII siècle*. Paris: Plon.
Delage, D. 1970. Les structures economiques de la Nouvelle-France et de la Nouvelle-York. *L'actualite Economique* 46: 67–118.
Domar, E.D. 1970. The Causes of Slavery or Serfdom: A Hypothesis. *Journal of Economic History* 30: 18–32.
Duby, G. 1968. *Rural Economy and Country Life in the Medieval West*. Columbia: University of South Carolina Press.
Eccles, W.J. 1969. *The Canadian Frontier, 1574–1760*. Hinsdale, Illinois.
Eccles, W.J. 1971. The Social, Economic and Political Significance of the Military Establishment in New France. *Canadian Historical Review* 52: 1–22.
Evans, W. 1836. *Supplementary Volume to a Treatise on the Theory and Practice Adopted to the Cultivation and Economy of Animal and Vegetable Productions of Agriculture*. Montreal: L. Perrault.
Fauteux, J.-N. 1927. *Essai sur l'industrie au Canada sous le regime français*. Quebec: Ls.-A. Proulx.
Fishlow, A. 1973. Comparative Consumption Patterns. The Extent of the Market, and Alternative Development Strategies. In *Micro Aspects of Development*, ed. E.B. Ayal. New York: Praeger.
Fregault, G. 1958–1959. Essai sur les finances canadiennes, *Revue d'histoire de l'amérique francaise*, 12: 459–484.
Fregault, G. 1959–1960. Essai sur les finances canadiennes. *Revue d'histoire de l'amérique francaise*, 13: 157–182.
Hamelin, J. 1970. *Economie et Societe en Nouvelle-France*. Quebec: Les Presses de l'Universite Laval.
Harris, M. 1953. *The Origin of the Land Tenure System in the United States*. Ames: Iowa State College Press.
Harris, M. 1959. The Economy Has No Surplus? *American Anthropologist* 61: 186–199.
Harris, R.C. 1968. *The Seigneurial System in Early Canada: A Geographical Study*. Montreal: McGill-Queen's University Press.
Kaldor, N. 1967. *Strategic Factors in Economic Development*. Geneva, New York: W.F. Humphrey Press.
Kindleberger, C. 1978. *Economic Response: Comparative Studies in Trade, Finance and Growth*. Cambridge, Mass.: Harvard University Press.
Lane, F.C. 1958. Economic Consequences of Organized Violence. *Journal of Economic History*, 18: 401–417.
Lane, F.C. 1975. The Role of Governments in Economic Growth in Early Modern Times. *Journal of Economic History* 35: 8–17.
Lelievre, M., and M. Angers, eds. 1856. *Lower Canada Reports: Seigniorial Questions*, vol. A. Montreal.

Lunn, A.J.E. 1934. *The Economic Development of French Canada, 1740–1760.* M.A. thesis, McGill University, Montreal.

Lunn, A.J.E. 1943. *Economic Development in New France, 1713–1760.* Ph.D. diss., McGill University.

Malthus, Thomas. 1974. *Principles of Political Economy.* Clifton: Augustus M. Kelley; reprint of the 1836 edition.

Mathieu, J. 1972. La Balance Commerciale: Nouvelle-France-Antilles au xviiie siécle. *Revue D'histoire De l'amerique Française* 25: 465–497.

Meiklejohn, W. 1823–1824. *Report to the Legislative Assembly of Lower Canada.* Appendix of the Journals of the Legislative Assembly of Lower Canada, vol. 33, Montreal.

Moogk, P. 1971. Apprenticeship Indentures: A Key to Artisan Life in New France. *Historical Papers, Canadian Historical Association*: 65–83.

Munro, W.B. 1907. *The Seigniorial System in Canada: A Study of French Colonial Policy.* New York: Longmans, Green.

Munro, W.B. 1908. *Documents Related to the Seigniorial Tenure in Canada.* Toronto: The Champlain Society,

Nish, C. ed. 1965. *The French Régime.* Scarborough, Ontario: Prentice-Hall.

Nish, C. 1968. *Les bourgeois-gentilshommes de la Nouvelle-France, 1729–1748.* Montreal: Fides.

North, D.C. 1966. *Growth and Welfare in the American Past: A New Economic History.* Englewood Cliffs, N.J.: Prentice-Hall.

Ouellet, F. 1981. La formation d'une société dans la vallée du Saint-Laurent: d'une société sans classe à une société de classes. *Canadian Historical Review* 62: 407–450.

Reid, S.W. 1947. The Habitant's Standard of Living on the Seigneurie des Mille Isles, 1820–1850. *Canadian Historical Review* 28: 266–278.

Reid, A.G. 1951. Intercolonial Trade during the French Regime. *Canadian Historical Review* 32: 236–251.

Reid, A.G. 1953. General Trade Between Quebec and France during the French Regime. *Canadian Historical Review* 34: 18–32.

Report of the Commissioners Appointed to Inquire into the State of Laws and Other Circumstances Connected with the Seigniorial Tenure in Lower Canada and Appendix (1844), (Kingston: Journals of the Legislative Assembly of the Province of Canada).

Report of the Special Committee on the State of Agriculture in Lower Canada and Appendix (1850), report of David Handyside (Kingston: Journals of the Legislative Assembly of the Province of Canada), Appendix TT of the Appendix, vol. 9.

Séguin, R.L. 1973. *La civilisation traditionnelle de l'habitant aux xviie et xviiie siècles.* Montréal: Fides.

Trudel, M. 1971a. The Seigneurial Regime. *Canadian Historical Association Booklets* 6

Trudel, M. 1971b. *Initiation à la Nouvelle-France, histoire et institutions*. Montréal: Holt, Rinehart et Winston.

Van Bath, S. 1966. *The Agrarian History of Western Europe, 500–1850*. London: Edward Arnold.

Wallot, J.P. 1969. Le régime seigneurial et son abolition au Canada. *Canadian Historical Review* 50: 343–371.

Young, A.A. 1928. Increasing Returns and Economic Progress. *Economic Journal* 38: 527–542.

PART III

Explaining Quebec's Relative Laggard Economic Development

CHAPTER 5

The State of Quebec Agriculture in the Mid-Nineteenth Century: Comparing French Canadian and Non-French Farmers

1 Introduction

There appears to be no end to the debate and research on the possible economic, social, cultural, and institutional factors that underlie the differences, or lack thereof, in the economic well-being between French Canadian and non-French Canadian farms or between farms under the seigniorial versus the freehold system of land tenure in Quebec (Lower Canada) during the first half of the nineteenth century. With the freehold system of land tenure, land could be purchased by prospective settlers outright or over time. Apart from the cost of purchase, this land was not subject to the various annual and special charges associated with the seigniorial tenure. The seigniorial tenure, on the other hand, did not require the farm family to advance any funds to secure seigniorial land. However, various seigniorial governing principles applied. The seigniorial system of land tenure, an institutional import from France, arrived on shores of Quebec with the establishment of the Company of New France in 1627, receiving legal sanction from the British in 1766, shortly after its conquest of Quebec in 1760. It was only abolished in 1854.

Under this system of land tenure land was technically held in trust by the seigniors from the Crown and by the censitaires from the seignior (peasant farmers granted land in this fashion). Although rules of obligations and rights were established by the Crown between the seignior and censitaire, in practice the seignior was more akin to a landlord and

M. Altman, *Lessons from a Successfully Export-Oriented, Resource-Rich Economy*, https://doi.org/10.1007/978-3-031-03887-7_5

the censitaire to a tenant. The seignior was obliged to try to settle land which he or she was subgranted by the Crown and, in turn, was entitled to specified fees and services from the censitaires. In point of fact, in Quebec and later in Lower Canada, the levels of some of the more significant seignoral charges were determined by the relative bargaining power of the seignior and censitaire. This was true of the highly significant annual rent (*cens et rents*) and the less important obligation of the censitaire to work on the domain land of the seignior (*corvée*). The seignior was also entitled to a mutation fine of 8.3% (*lods et ventes*) of the purchase price of the land when the censitaire sold land out of the direct line of inheritance. In addition, the censitaires were obliged to grind their grain at a seigniorial grist-mill at a fixed price of one-fourteenth of the grain milled (the grist-mill *banalité*). Seigniorial charges against the censitaire increased dramatically in the nineteenth century as population pressure on seigniorial lands mounted, thereby increasing the relative bargaining power of the seignior, and increasing numbers of seigniors found ways of levying additional charges on the censitaire.

Indeed, a central hypothesis driving much of Canadian economic and social history is that French Canadian farmers, who dominated the economic landscape of Quebec and laboured largely under the seigniorial tenure, were less productive and poorer than their non-French counterparts, be they of American or British origin, most of whom held their land freehold in the townships. It is further held that the relative poverty of the French Canadian farm population heavily weighted the demand for manufacturing goods as well as the wages in the nonagricultural sector. This, in turn, impeded the further economic development of the province as compared to others, for example Ontario.[1] However, in spite of the protracted and prolific nature of this debate, we still have little rigorous empirical evidence as to the actual state of French Canadian, non-French Canadian, seigniorial, and freehold farms during this period. The purpose of this study is to provide estimates for net agricultural output or surplus per farm, partial factor productivity, and land use in Quebec using the published 1851–1852 agricultural census. These estimates, constructed for French Canadian and non-French Canadian farms in general as well as for French Canadian and non-French Canadian farms operating within the framework of the seigniorial and freehold systems of land tenure, help us address a basic question, yet unanswered, which is central to all current debates that seek to compare farms occupied by different linguistic or ethnic groups or subject to different systems of land tenure: How do these farms actually fare when compared one to the other?[2]

The 1851–1852 census is the most detailed agricultural census for Lower Canada for the 1800–1851 period and provides us with a relatively clear snapshot of Lower Canada's agriculture just prior to the abolition of the seigniorial system of land tenure in 1854.[3] But, of course, results stemming from the study of a one-year data set must, as always, be regarded with healthy degree of scepticism.[4] The published 1851–1852 census has already been used to good effect by Frank Lewis and Marvin McInnis to address the question of whether French Canadian farms were less efficient than non-French Canadian farms and the possible determinants of the variations in total factor productivity (a measure of output divided by inputs) between regions in Lower Canada (Lewis and McInnis 1980, p. 501, n. 14; 1984, pp. 49, 87). Since much empirical groundwork on the 1851–1852 census has already been laid by Lewis and McInnis, our computation of net farm revenue follows theirs closely, with some critical exceptions.

A crucial finding of this article is that French Canadian farmers typically earned a lower agricultural income than did their non-French Canadian counterparts. They were also characterized by a much poorer productivity performance for all key outputs, especially for dairy products, and they typically operated on a much smaller scale than the non-French Canadian farmers. In addition, under both the seigniorial and freehold systems of land tenure, French Canadian farmers typically realized a lower agricultural income than non-French Canadian farmers—land tenure does not appear to have affected the relative standing of French Canadian farmers. We also find that farms operated under the seigniorial system of land tenure earned a much higher agricultural income than those operated under the freehold system.

This casts some doubt on the hypothesis that problems in Quebec agriculture can be attributed largely to the seigniorial system of land tenure. But French Canadian farming and agriculture was by no means homogeneous across the province. Indeed, in the Montreal area, French Canadian farmers earned a higher agricultural income than did non-French Canadian farmers in spite of their being less productive and smaller. The French Canadian farmers more than compensated for their lower productivity by placing a much larger percentage of their smaller acreage under cultivation, ultimately earning a relatively large income from wheat production, the traditional mainstay of French Canadian agriculture.

The estimates presented here, therefore, suggest that in Lower Canada differences in agricultural income per farm are most closely associated with ethnicity, for which language is a proxy, as opposed to a particular system of land tenure. Why, exactly, this is the case is a critical question, the detailed response to which is beyond the scope of this study. On the other hand, some support is provided to the argument presented by scholars such as Fernand Ouellet that, on average, French Canadian farmers did not fare as well as their non-French counterparts. Nevertheless, since a large minority of French Canadian farms actually outperformed the non-French Canadian farms, one cannot easily attribute to ethnicity and ethnicity alone all of the successes or failings of Lower Canadian agriculture.

2 Language, Land Tenure, and the State of Quebec Agriculture

Fernand Ouellet is the leading proponent of the view that historically and well into the nineteenth century French Canadian farmers persistently used less advanced farming technologies than those employed by non-French Canadian farmers. This had the effect of causing a crisis in Lower Canadian agriculture from 1802 on, during which time yields per unit of land and per unit of livestock fell. As a result, the level of material well-being obtainable by the French Canadian farm family fell throughout the first half of the nineteenth century. Ouellet attributes this persistent use of relatively less advanced technology primarily to the *mentalité* or collective psychology of the French Canadian farmer; specifically, to his reluctance to use more advanced technology regardless of the increased prosperity such technology could yield.[5]

An alternative explanation for the French Canadian farmer's hypothesized poor performance in agriculture was first articulated by experts contemporary with the seigniorial system who argued that this system of land tenure reduced the incentive and the means of adopting more productive technologies. For example, the 1843 government report contended that the various exactions imposed by the seignior on the peasant farmer were such that "all the generous emotions of [the peasant farmer] nature are stifled. Thus he gradually becomes impoverished; he toils through existence with-out the hope of relief, and transmits to his posterity a worthless inheritance" (*Report of the Commissioners* 1843).

A contemporary restatement of this report's analysis has been expressed by Paul Phillips (1974, pp. 35–45).

If French Canadian farms were using less advanced technology when compared to non-French Canadian farms in Lower Canada, one would expect yields per unit of land and per unit of livestock on French Canadian farms of comparable size to be less. Moreover, one would also expect that French Canadian farmers would produce a smaller income unless they could compensate for their lower yields by placing more of their land under cultivation. It is important to note that those who have argued that French Canadian farms were relatively less technologically advanced consider that the employment of comparably modern farming practices demanded the application of more manure on the land, more frequent and careful ploughing and weeding of the land, better care, feeding, and breeding of livestock, increased use of artificial meadows, and the use of better equipment such as heavier ploughs and warmer and cleaner barns (see, for example, Ouellet 1971, pp. 222, 256, 258, 338, 455, 458; 1972, pp. 189–190; Harris 1971, p. 34; Harris and Warkentin 1984, pp. 81–86; Jones 1942, p. 115; Parker 1957, p. 190).

Fundamentally, these practices involved the application of more inputs into the production process. Thus, implicit in the proposition that French Canadian farms were technologically less advanced is the argument that, for one reason or another—the reasons themselves also form the subject of much heated debate—these farms did not invest as much labour and capital as did their non-French Canadian counterparts (Paquet and Wallot 1986). In contrast to the non-French Canadian farmers, it is assumed that French Canadian farmers chose not to invest the income and capital necessary to generate higher levels of agricultural income. Such increases in inputs were consistent with the types of agricultural change possible at this time. As Ester Boserup writes: "In this period [1800–1850], peasant families obtained higher real incomes mainly by working many more hours in agriculture, while real output per work hour probably declined, due to the intensification of agriculture, especially fodder production" (Boserup 1983, p. 398). A similar argument could be made when comparing seigniorial and freehold or township farms.

Given that Lewis and McInnis have already found that French Canadian farmers were less efficient than non-French Canadian farmers, by between 8 and 16%, it is of considerable importance to understand that the Ouellet perspective on Lower Canadian agricultural history does not address the issue of the relative efficiency of French Canadian and non-French Canadian farms (Lewis and McInnis 1980, pp. 510–511). Rather, estimates which suggest even insignificant differences in the efficiency of French Canadian and non-French Canadian farmers tell us little about the relative agricultural income produced by the different farms in Lower Canada, and it is this issue which is one of the main bones of contention in Quebec economic history. As Theodore Schultz points out in his classic analysis of agricultural development, relative allocative efficiency amongst farmers is quite consistent with one group of farmers employing relatively traditional farming practices and thus earning a relatively poor agricultural income (Schultz 1983). Even the relatively efficient farmer can be poor as a product of inadequate human capital, inadequate infrastructure, distorted market prices and, possibly, a culturally or socially determined preference for leisure.

The contention that Lower Canadian agriculture was in a state of crisis during the first half of the nineteenth century and that this was reflected in a deterioration in the standard of material well-being of the French Canadian farmer has not been without its detractors. Gilles Paquet and Jean-Pierre Wallot, for example, have argued that Lower Canadian agriculture was not in crisis, but rather underwent a period of restructuring and modernization such that it is probable that the French Canadian population, both rural and urban, witnessed an improvement in their standard of material well-being from 1800 to 1850. They argue that French Canadian farmers shifted out of wheat into other products in response to changing market signals. By properly and rationally responding to these changing incentives, French Canadian farmers prospered. The movement out of wheat was not a sign of crisis and impoverishment but rather of modernization and economic advance (Paquet and Wallot 1975, p. 159).

Serge Courville and his associates have been on the cutting edge of the modernization hypothesis. They have argued from detailed research on the development of small urban centers and rural industry in Quebec that Quebec rural society was neither stagnant nor backward in the first half of the nineteenth century. The Montreal area apparently dominated these developments. However, the province of Quebec was characterized by different types of agriculture, some more advanced than others. Some regions and localities of Quebec might have been in crisis, while others fared well by any standard. Still, there was no generalized crisis in Quebec agriculture (Courville 1980, pp. 196, 201, 204–207, 212–213, 218–221). In addition, according to Courville, yields did not fall, and the French Canadian farm family did not, as a rule, suffer any decline in its standard of material well-being, at least not as a direct result of a reduction in the farm family's productive capacity.[6]

But critical to the crisis hypothesis is whether or not the majority of the farming population had become gradually impoverished or suffered a significant drop in their standard of living over the course of the first half of the nineteenth century. However, to date, no direct evidence has been presented that calls into question the view that French Canadian farmers were worse off than their non-French Canadian counterparts. Finally, we remain completely ignorant as to the differences in the agricultural income produced by seigniorial and freehold farms. In a word, if the debate is to be advanced, we must get our factual house in order.

3 Organizing and Adjusting the Census Material

The 1851–1852 census data for 458 districts in the thirty-six listed counties are organized into seigniorial and township districts.[7] These data are then further organized into French Canadian, non-French Canadian, and mixed categories. A French Canadian district is defined as one where at least 80% of the population is of French Canadian origin. A non-French Canadian district is one where at least 80% of the population is of non-French Canadian origin. The non-French Canadian districts include individuals who are largely of U.S. origin together with many individuals from Britain and from what is today Atlantic Canada. A mixed district is one where neither the French Canadian nor the non-French Canadian population constitute 80% or more of the population. On average, French Canadians comprised 95, 11, and 51% of the French Canadian, non-French Canadian, and mixed districts respectively.[8] Such a categorization of the census material is necessary for an examination of the various hypotheses discussed above, regarding the relative performance of French Canadian and non-French farms and seigniorial and free-hold (township) farms. Obviously, given the limitations of the data, we are not actually comparing specific farms. We can only compare census districts that embody these farms.

To facilitate our analysis, the thirty-six counties listed in the census are grouped into four regions (see map, Image 1).[9] Moving from west to east, three of these regions, thereafter designated as Region A (the Montreal-Ottawa Region), Region B (Central Lower Canada), and Region C (Eastern Lower Canada), contain twenty-eight counties and

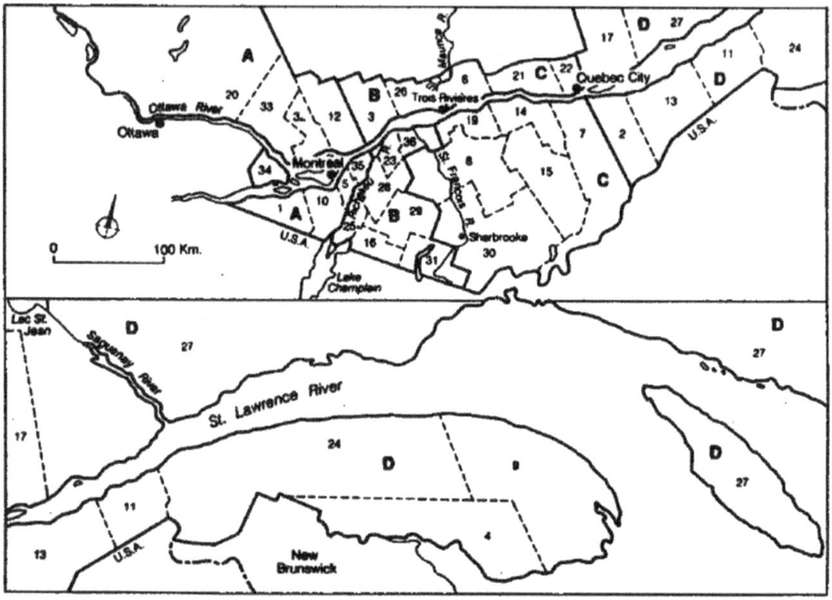

Image 1 Map of the 1851–1852 Census Districts of lower Canada (*Notes and Sources* The numbers on the map are those assigned by the census authorities to the various census districts of Lower Canada. Region A [the Montreal-Ottawa Region] consists: 1. Beauharnois; 5. Chambly; 10. Huntington; 12. Leinster; 18. Montreal; 20. Ottawa; 32. Terrebonne; 33. Two Mountains; 34. Vaudreuil; and 35. Vercheres. Region B [Central Lower Canada] consists of: 3. Berthier; 6. Champlain; 8. Drummond; 16. Missisquoi; 19. Nicolet; 23. Richelieu; 25. Rouville; 26. St. Maurice; 28. Shefford; 29. Sherbrooke; 31. St. Hyacinthe; and 36. Yamaska. Region C [Eastern Lower Canada] consists of: 7. Dorchester; 14. Lotbiniere; 15. Megantic; 21. Portneuf; 22. Quebec; and 30. Stanstead. Region D [the Gulf Region] consists of: 2. Bellechasse; 4. Bonaventure; 9. Gaspe; 11. Kamouraska; 13. L'lslet; 17. Montmorency; 24. Rimouski; and 27. Saguenay. This map is a revised and more detailed rendering of an unpublished base map found in R.L. Gentilcore, ed., *Census Districts in Eastern Canada. 1851–1891: A Folio of Base* [Hamilton, ON: McMaster University, August 1980]. This folio of maps was produced for R.L. Gentilcore, ed., *Historical Atlas of Canada: the Land Transformed*, vol. 2 [Toronto: University of Toronto Press, 1993]. I would like to thank Andy Hubbertz, Head Librarian, Government Publications, University of Saskatchewan, for helping me locate this folio and Keith Bigelow, Cartographic Technician, Department of Geography, University of Saskatchewan, for his fine work in generating the final product)

incorporate all of the thirteen counties included in Lewis's and McInnis's study of the efficiency of the French Canadian farmer.[10] Moving past Quebec City to the east, we have Region D (the Gulf Region), which incorporates the remaining eight counties.

Region A consists of those counties to the west of the Richelieu River, including the island of Montreal. It incorporates 27% of the French Canadian, 30% of the non-French Canadian, and 46% of the mixed farms listed in the census. Moreover, 28% of French Canadian seigniorial farms as well as 38% of non-French Canadian and 52% of mixed seigniorial farms are found located in Region A. This Montreal-Ottawa region also contains about 30% each of the French and non-French township farms and 40% of the mixed township farms (Table 1). Region B largely consists of those counties bounded by the Richelieu and St. François Rivers together with those counties lying on the north shore of the St. Lawrence River to the west of the St. Maurice River, facing the town of Sorel and inclusive of the town of Trois Rivières. This region contains 27% of the French Canadian, 37% of the non-French Canadian, and 16% of the mixed farms. Also, about 30% of both the French Canadian and non-French Canadian seigniorial farms are found here as well as 13% of the French Canadian township farms and almost 40% of the non-French Canadian township farms. Region C embraces those counties that lie largely between the St. François and St. Maurice Rivers to the west and Quebec City to the east. This region embraces 25% of the French Canadian and the mixed farms as well as 30% of the non-French Canadian. In addition, almost 25% of the French Canadian and 32% of the non-French Canadian seigniorial farms are situated in eastern Lower Canada, while almost 40% of the mixed seigniorial farms are found here. This region also contains almost 40% of the French Canadian and about 30% of the non-French Canadian township farms. Finally Region D, embracing those counties to the east of Quebec City, is home to more than 20% of the French Canadian farms, but to only 2% of the non-French Canadian farms. Thirteen percent of the mixed farms are found here as well. Although the Gulf Region incorporates 21% of the French Canadian seigniorial farms, there are no non-French Canadian seigniorial farms in this region and only 3% of the mixed seigniorial farms are to be found here. In addition, about 20% each of the French Canadian and mixed township farms lie in this region, while only 4% of the non-French Canadian township farms are located here. Of all regions defined for this study, Region D is of least importance to the non-French Canadian population.

Table 1 The distribution of farms by region and language group

	Larger farms	*Larger/all farms (%)*	*Distribution of larger farms within regions (%)*	*Distribution of larger farms across regions by language and tenure (%)*	*Distribution of larger farms across regions by language (%)*
Region A					
Seigniories					
French	13,866	77	82	28	24
Non-French	371	96	2	38	3
Mixed	2,754	80	16	52	23
Fr and NF	14,237	77	84		
Total	16,991	78	100		
Townships					
French	1,831	79	23	26	3
Non-French	3,232	90	41	30	27
Mixed	2,787	92	36	40	23
Fr and NF	5,063	86	64		
Total	7,850	88	100		
Region B					
Seigniories					
French	14,444	83	96	29	25
Non-French	301	93	2	31	3
Mixed	364	91	2	7	3
Fr and NF	14,745	83	98		
Total	15,109	83	100		
Townships					
French	896	91	14	13	2
Non-French	4,045	92	63	37	34
Mixed	1,507	92	23	22	12
Fr and NF	4,941	91	77		
Total	6,448	92	100		
Region C					
Seigniories					
French	11,543	91	83	23	20
Non-French	311	88	2	32	3
Mixed	1,996	96	14	38	16
Fr and NF	11,854	91	86		
Total	13,850	92	100		

(continued)

Table 1 (continued)

	Larger farms	*Larger/all farms (%)*	*Distribution of larger farms within regions (%)*	*Distribution of larger farms across regions by language and tenure (%)*	*Distribution of larger farms across regions by language (%)*
Townships					
French	2,643	99	38	38	5
Non-French	3,176	92	46	29	27
Mixed	1,154	99	17	17	9
Fr and NF	5,819	95	83		
Total	13,850	92	1000		
Region D					
Seigniories					
French	10,530	79	98	21	18
Non-French					
Mixed	162	99	2	3	1
Fr and NF	10,530	79	98		
Total	10,692	79	100		
Townships					
French	1,624	91	47	23	3
Non-French	383	90	11	4	3
Mixed	1,435	89	42	21	12
Fr and NF	2,007	91	58		
Total	3,442	90	100		
All regions					
Seigniories					
French	50,383	82	89	100	88
Non-French	983	92	2	100	8
Mixed	5,276	87	9	100	43
Fr and NF	51,366	82	91		
Total	56,642	82	100		
Townships					
French	6,994	90	28	100	12
Non-French	10,836	91	44	100	92
Mixed	6,883	93	28	100	57
Fr and NF	17,830	91	72		
Total	24,713	91	100		

Source See text

Overall, the French Canadian districts incorporate about 70% of all farms as compared to about 15% each for the non-French Canadian and mixed districts respectively. The French Canadian farms also make up almost 90% of all seigniorial farms as compared to only 2% of the non-French Canadian farms, and 9% of the mixed farms. On the other hand, the French Canadian farms contributed only 28% to the township farms, while the non-French Canadian and mixed farms contributed 44 and 28% respectively. Finally, about 8% of the non-French Canadian farms were located on the seigniories as compared to 88% of the French Canadian farms. On the other hand, the townships encompassed 92% of the non-French Canadian farms and only 12% of the French Canadian farms (see Table 1).

Prior to constructing net output and productivity estimates, the census data must be adjusted to correct for what Marvin McInnis refers to as the pitfalls of the 1851–1852 census (McInnis 1981). The published census reports all land in terms of acres and all grain output in terms or bushels when, in fact, farmers operating under the seigniorial system of land tenure, who were mostly French Canadian, typically reported their land in terms of arpents, where one arpent equals 0.845 acres. In addition, French Canadian farmers, whether in a seigniory or a township, typically reported their crop output in terms of minots, where one minot equals 1.1073 bushels (Evans 1835, p. 11). Since most farmers were French Canadian, the census nomenclature poses a serious problem. The census enumerators apparently did not convert arpents into acres and minots to bushels. Using the raw census to estimate yields and output would only generate artificially low numbers for the French-Canadian farms. To avoid this problem, we convert the arpent measure into their acre equivalent by multiplying what the census reports as acres for the seigniorial areas by 0.845. Minots are converted into bushels by multiplying what the census reports as bushels of output by 1.1073, weighted by the percentage of the districts that are French Canadian.[11]

The census also fails to distinguish between occupiers of the land who were farmers and those who, for residential purposes, simply occupied small plots of land. The census, however, does distinguish between individuals who occupied less than eleven acres of land from those who occupied more than ten acres. McInnis finds that it is highly probable that a large proportion of holdings of less than eleven acres were actually comprised of garden plots of about one acre. If one assumes that all of the occupiers of less than eleven acres of land simply held garden plots and were not true farmers, then one can simply eliminate these small occupants together with the amount of land they are assumed to have occupied from one's computations. This, in fact, is the procedure Lewis and McInnis follow and the one adopted in this article.[12] However, by assuming that the smaller occupants are not farmers, one differentially affects the per farm income estimates in favour of French Canadian farms since the smaller occupants are more important in most French Canadian districts, especially in the seigniories. In total, the smaller occupants comprise about 18% of the total in the French Canadian districts, about 9% in the non-French Canadian districts, and about 10% in the mixed districts (Table 1). Although, there is little difference in the importance of the smaller occupants to the French Canadian and non-French Canadian districts in the townships, the smaller occupants were much more important among the French Canadian districts in the seigniories in Regions A and B.

4 Partial Factor Productivity and Land Use

Apart from the odd partial productivity estimates constructed for some districts or farms, no such estimates have been constructed on a systematic basis for Lower Canada.[13] The 1851–1852 census provides us with the information needed to construct distinct productivity estimates for many key farm outputs including wheat, oats, and milk cows. However, apart from oats, which were grown for the most part as a fodder crop, inadequate data are available to produce such estimates for the various fodder crops that were so important for feeding livestock: hay, clover, timothy, and other grass seed, mangel wurtzel, and beans, with hay generally being the most important of these. With the exception of Region A, and regardless of the system of land tenure, fodder crops dominated the land under crop in the non-French Canadian districts whereas on both the French Canadian and mixed districts other crops were of far greater consequence, wheat and oats being the most important of these. This is clear from Table 2. In every single region, non-French Canadian districts devote a much larger percentage of land under crop to fodder crops than the French Canadian districts. (Here I employ the definition used in the Canadian census, that is, land under crop plus land under pasture equals land under cultivation.) This is especially true of the townships. On average, almost 80% of the land under crop in non-French Canadian

Table 2 Selected land characteristics

	Acreage per larger occupant								*% of land under crop with*						
	1 Total	*2 Wheat*	*3 Under crop*	*4 Under pasture*	*5 Under cultivation*	*5/1 (%)*	*3/5 (%)*	*4/5 (%)*	*Wheat*	*Barley*	*Rye*	*Peas*	*Oats*	*Potatoes*	*Fodder crops*
Region A															
Seigniories															
French	79	8	33	20	53	67	62	38	24	1	1	11	28	2.77	56
Non-French	106	3	19	19	38	36	49	51	16	0	1	4	35	9.27	65
Mixed	77	5	26	14	40	53	64	35	20	1	0	7	22	4.44	64
Fr and NF	79	8	32	20	53	66	61	38	24	1	1	11	28	2.87	56
Total	79	7	31	19	51	64	62	38	23	1	1	11	27	3.08	57
Townships															
French	81	7	26	15	41	51	63	36	25	1	0	10	26	3.50	55
Non-French	111	3	20	16	36	32	55	44	15	0	1	6	30	6.59	68
Mixed	103	4	19	12	30	29	62	39	22	1	1	10	26	5.13	57
Fr and NF	100	4	22	16	38	38	58	41	19	1	0	8	28	5.27	62
Total	101	4	21	14	35	35	59	40	20	1	0	9	27	5.23	61
Region B															
Seigniories															
French	75	6	24	15	39	52	61	38	25	1	2	11	34	1.97	54
Non-French	78	5	33	15	49	62	67	31	14	0	2	3	16	4.15	71
Mixed	93	3	12	6	18	19	67	31	24	0	0	7	18	4.06	60
Fr and NF	75	6	24	15	39	52	61	38	25	1	2	10	34	2.03	54
Total	75	6	24	15	39	51	61	38	25	1	2	10	34	2.05	54
Townships															
French	93	2	13	7	20	22	67	33	17	1	2	7	26	4.00	63

	Acreage per larger occupant								% of land under crop with						
	1 Total	2 Wheat	3 Under crop	4 Under pasture	5 Under cultivation	5/1 (%)	3/5 (%)	4/5 (%)	Wheat	Barley	Rye	Peas	Oats	Potatoes	Fodder crops
Non-French	104	2	27	17	44	43	60	39	7	1	1	1	10	2.87	81
Mixed	92	1	18	10	28	30	65	34	8	1	1	2	13	3.84	75
Fr and NF	102	2	24	15	40	39	61	38	8	1	1	1	12	2.98	79
Total	100	2	23	14	37	37	62	37	8	1	1	1	12	3.14	79
Region C															
Seigniories															
French	87	2	19	17	36	41	52	46	13	1	1	5	39	2.89	73
Non-French	98	1	23	9	32	33	71	28	2	0	0	0	22	13.78	82
Mixed	89	1	12	16	29	32	43	57	8	1	3	4	48	9.73	71
Fr and NF	87	2	19	16	36	41	53	46	13	1	1	5	38	3.24	73
Total	87	2	18	16	35	40	52	47	12	1	1	5	39	3.89	73
Townships															
French	67	2	10	6	16	24	60	39	18	5	9	7	21	7.41	46
Non-French	122	2	26	20	46	38	56	44	9	1	1	1	13	4.15	79
Mixed	105	2	17	11	29	27	60	40	13	2	1	4	21	5.93	68
Fr and NF	97	2	19	14	33	34	57	43	11	2	3	2	15	4.93	71
Total	98	2	18	14	32	33	57	42	11	2	3	3	16	5.08	71
Region D															
Seigniories															
French	99	5	21	22	42	42	50	51	22	6	9	6	27	3.98	53

(continued)

Table 2 (continued)

	Acreage per larger occupant								*% of land under crop with*						
	1 *Total*	*2* *Wheat*	*3* *Under crop*	*4* *Under pasture*	*5* *Under cultivation*	*5/1 (%)*	*3/5 (%)*	*4/5 (%)*	*Wheat*	*Barley*	*Rye*	*Peas*	*Oats*	*Potatoes*	*Fodder crops*
Non-French															
Mixed	143	3	18	16	34	24	51	48	18	20	3	6	19	6.82	43
Fr and NF	99	5	21	22	42	42	50	51	22	6	9	6	27	3.98	53
Total	100	5	21	22	42	42	50	51	22	6	9	6	27	4.02	53
Townships															
French	103	3	12	9	21	20	56	43	23	18	7	12	14	8.09	32
Non-French	136	1	9	7	16	12	57	43	6	5	0	1	20	11.20	74
Mixed	93	1	8	6	15	16	57	42	15	8	0	3	48	12.64	59
Fr and NF	109	2	11	8	20	18	56	43	20	16	6	10	15	8.57	38
Total	102	2	10	7	18	17	57	43	18	14	4	7	27	10.00	46
All regions															
Seigniories															
French	84	5	24	18	43	51	57	42	22	2	3	9	31	2.79	58
Non-French	95	3	24	15	39	42	61	38	11	0	1	3	23	8.51	72
Mixed	84	3	20	14	34	41	57	42	17	2	1	7	28	5.76	65
Fr and NF	84	5	24	18	43	51	57	42	22	2	3	9	31	2.89	58
Total	84	5	24	18	42	50	57	42	21	2	2	9	31	3.11	59
Townships															
French	82	3	15	9	24	30	61	38	22	5	4	9	23	5.35	50
Non-French	112	2	24	17	41	37	57	42	10	1	1	2	16	4.31	77

	Acreage per larger occupant								*% of land under crop with*						
	1 *Total*	*2* *Wheat*	*3* *Under crop*	*4* *Under pasture*	*5* *Under cultivation*	*5/1 (%)*	*3/5 (%)*	*4/5 (%)*	*Wheat*	*Barley*	*Rye*	*Peas*	*Oats*	*Potatoes*	*Fodder crops*
Mixed	99	3	16	10	26	26	62	38	16	2	1	6	24	5.77	64
Fr and NF	101	3	20	14	35	35	59	41	13	2	2	4	18	4.61	69
Total	100	3	19	13	32	32	59	40	14	2	1	5	19	4.88	68
Seigniories and townships															
French	84	5	23	17	40	48	58	42	22	2	3	9	31	2.99	57
Non-French	111	2	24	17	41	37	58	41	10	1	1	2	17	4.67	77
Mixed	93	3	18	12	30	32	59	40	17	2	1	6	26	5.77	64
Fr and NF	88	5	23	17	41	46	58	42	20	2	2	8	28	3.28	61
Total	89	4	23	16	39	44	58	42	20	2	2	8	28	3.57	61

Sources and notes Arpents are adjusted to their acres equivalents. These estimates are derived from, *The Census of Canada, 1851–52*, vol. II (1855). Only the major crops listed in the census are listed here. I exclude buckwheat, Indian corn and turnips which occupied only a small percentage of the land under crop. Fodder crops include oats

districts was planted with fodder crops as compared to less than 60% in the French Canadian districts.

It is also clear from Table 2 that the two leading crops in Lower Canada, regardless of language classification, were wheat and oats. On average, in the seigniories, French Canadian districts devoted 22 and 31% of their land under crop to wheat and oats respectively as compared to the 11 and 23% devoted to these crops in the non-French Canadian seigniorial districts. The percentage of land under crop devoted to wheat in the French Canadian township districts was also 22% while oats fell to 23%. In comparison, in the non-French Canadian townships, the share of land under crop allocated to wheat and oats fell to 10 and 16% respectively.

The estimates presented in Table 2 also show that patterns of land holding and cultivation had little to do with land tenure. In all regions and under both systems of land tenure farms in the non-French Canadian districts were larger than farms in the French Canadian districts. However, farmers in French Canadian districts, apart from those in Region B and the townships of Region C, had more land under cultivation than did the non-French Canadian farmers since they compensated for their relatively small holdings by placing a greater percentage of their land under cultivation. This is especially true of Region A (the Montreal-Ottawa region). In Region B, on the other hand, particularly in the townships, and also in the townships of Region C, not only were farmers in the non-French Canadian districts operating on a much larger scale than those in the French Canadian districts, but they also placed a much larger percentage of their land under cultivation.

Turning to Tables 3 and 4, the partial productivity estimates reveal that with the notable exception of Region A, especially in the seigniories and regardless of the system of land tenure, crop yields were consistently much greater in non-French Canadian districts. In the seigniories of Region A, farmers in the French Canadian districts bettered their non-French Canadian counterparts' productivity performance in all listed crops with the exception of wheat, buckwheat, and turnips. The latter two crops were only of marginal importance and wheat was, next to oats, the most important crop (Table 2). Farmers in the mixed districts fared even better than those in French Canadian districts in Region A. As for the other regions, farmers in non-French Canadian districts dominated partial factor productivity for all crops, almost without exception. For example, for wheat and oats, the two dominant crops, output per unit of land was much greater

Table 3 Total factor productivity

	Bushels per acre						*Butter per Milch Cows (lbs.)*		
	Wheat	*Barley*	*Rye*	*Peas*	*Oats*	*Potatoes*	*Census*	*Total*	*Wool/sheep*
Region A									
Seigniories									
French	9	18	10	12	19	67	31	48	1.8
Non-French	11	11	8	11	16	61	49	65	2.7
Mixed	14	21	11	14	22	75	46	62	2.1
Fr and NF	9	18	10	12	19	67	32	49	1.9
Total	10	18	10	12	20	68	34	51	1.9
Townships									
French	10	15	10	10	18	57	32	55	2.4
Non-French	11	14	10	11	16	58	88	112	2.5
Mixed	8	12	10	8	18	63	38	64	2.3
Fr and NF	11	15	10	11	17	58	68	91	2.4
Total	10	14	10	10	17	59	58	82	2.4
Region B									
Seigniories									
French	9	13	9	9	18	54	19	40	2.0
Non-French	13	26	18	16	25	84	66	82	2.3
Mixed	11	11	8	8	19	54	41	77	2.4
Fr and NF	9	13	9	9	18	55	20	41	2.0
Total	9	13	9	9	18	55	20	41	2.0
Townships									
French	9	10	7	8	17	64	29	68	2.0
Non-French	12	16	12	13	29	62	70	90	2.6
Mixed	9	11	10	9	22	51	54	85	2.4
Fr and NF	11	15	11	11	26	62	66	88	2.5
Total	11	14	11	10	26	59	63	87	2.5
Region C									
Seigniories									
French	10	13	10	10	19	94	29	53	2.3
Non-French	13	38	16	92	22	95	26	45	2.7
Mixed	10	12	12	8	19	96	35	63	2.2
Fr and NF	10	13	10	10	19	94	29	53	2.3
Total	10	13	10	10	19	95	30	54	2.3
Townships									
French	10	12	12	9	17	60	19	73	2.0

(continued)

Table 3 (continued)

	Bushels per acre						*Butter per Milch Cows (lbs.)*		
	Wheat	*Barley*	*Rye*	*Peas*	*Oats*	*Potatoes*	*Census*	*Total*	*Wool/sheep*
Non-French	12	15	13	10	26	76	67	90	2.6
Mixed	10	11	14	8	17	63	41	76	2.3
Fr and NF	12	13	12	9	23	70	55	85	2.5
Total	11	13	13	9	21	69	53	84	2.5
Region D									
Seigniories									
French	8	14	9	9	17	88	43	64	1.9
Non-French									
Mixed	7	4	8	10	10	125	41	74	1.8
Fr and NF	8	14	9	9	17	88	43	64	1.9
Total	8	14	9	9	17	89	43	65	1.9
Townships									
French	7	12	7	8	14	62	21	62	1.9
Non-French	10	13	16	16	28	105	53	89	2.5
Mixed	10	11	12	4	18	81	30	73	2.1
Fr and NF	7	12	7	8	17	71	29	69	2.0
Total	8	12	7	8	17	75	29	71	2.1
All regions									
Seigniories									
French	9	15	9	11	19	75	29	50	2.0
Non-French	12	24	15	17	20	82	48	65	2.4
Mixed	13	18	12	13	21	84	42	63	2.1
Fr and NF	9	15	9	11	19	75	30	50	2.0
Total	9	15	9	11	19	77	31	51	2.0
Townships									
French	10	12	10	9	17	60	26	63	2.1
Non-French	12	15	12	11	22	66	74	96	2.6
Mixed	8	11	11	8	18	65	41	72	2.3
Fr and NF	11	13	11	10	20	64	61	87	2.5
Total	10	13	11	9	20	64	56	83	2.4
Seigniories and Townships									
French	9	14	9	10	19	73	29	51	2.0

(continued)

Table 3 (continued)

	Bushels per acre						*Butter per Milch Cows (lbs.)*		
	Wheat	*Barley*	*Rye*	*Peas*	*Oats*	*Potatoes*	*Census*	*Total*	*Wool/sheep*
Non-French	12	15	12	12	22	68	71	93	2.6
Mixed	11	14	12	10	20	74	42	67	2.2
Fr and NF	9	14	9	11	19	72	36	57	2.1
Total	9	14	9	11	19	72	37	59	2.1

Source and notes Arpents and minots are adjusted to their acres and bushels equivalents. See text and sources in Table 2 for further details

in the non-French Canadian districts. Outside of Region A, the productivity advantage in wheat production held by the non-French Canadian districts ranged from a high of 43% in Region B (Central Lower Canada) to a low of 24% in the township districts of Region C (Eastern Lower Canada). With respect to oats production, the advantage held by the non-French Canadian districts ranged from a high of over 100% in the township districts of Region D (the Gulf area) to a low of 15% in the seigniories of Region C (Table 4). Partial factor productivity on mixed farms was typically between that of the farms in the French Canadian and non-French Canadian districts.

Estimates or wool production per sheep are also presented in Tables 3 and 4 (see Table 5 for estimates on the number of sheep and other livestock per farm). With one exception, farms in non-French Canadian districts bettered those in French Canadian districts, ranging from 6% in the township districts of Region A to about 45% in the seigniorial districts of this same region. The performance on mixed farms was once again between that of non-French Canadian and French Canadian farmers. No estimates can be constructed from the censuses on meat output per animal. This problem will be discussed below when detailing the net output estimates.

One can, however, construct productivity estimates for milk cows (Tables 3 and 4). The census provides data on the number of milk cows and the amount of butter and cheese produced. No estimates for liquid milk production are available. One proxy for the productivity of milk cows is the amount of butter and cheese, converted to butter equivalents, per milk cow.[14] Irrespective of the system of land tenure, farms

Table 4 Relative partial productivity

	Wheat	*Barley*	*Rye*	*Peas*	*Oats*	*Potatoes*	*Census butter*	*Total butter*	*Wool*
Region A									
Seigniories									
NF/F	1.19	0.62	0.81	0.90	0.85	0.91	1.59	1.36	1.45
M/F	1.48	1.17	1.13	1.13	1.16	1.12	1.47	1.29	1.13
Townships									
NF/F	1.09	0.92	1.03	1.07	0.90	1.02	2.78	2.02	1.06
M/F	0.74	0.77	1.02	0.73	1.02	1.11	1.19	1.15	0.97
Region B									
Seigniories									
NF/F	1.44	2.09	2.12	1.76	1.37	1.57	3.50	2.08	1.12
M/F	1.22	0.89	0.87	0.90	1.04	1.01	2.21	1.95	1.20
Townships									
NF/F	1.33	1.59	1.73	1.53	1.72	0.97	2.44	1.31	1.29
M/F	0.24	0.28	0.25	0.25	0.58	1.33	1.42	2.23	0.06
Region C									
Seigniories									
NF/F	1.31	2.94	1.64	9.50	1.15	1.00	0.90	0.86	1.20
M/F	0.99	0.91	1.23	0.87	1.00	1.02	1.19	1.19	0.99
Townships									
NF/F	1.24	1.22	1.02	1.15	1.50	1.26	3.56	1.22	1.36
M/F	1.01	0.92	1.10	0.95	1.00	1.04	2.20	1.03	1.17
Region D									
Seigniories									
NF/F									
M/F	0.91	0.31	0.90	1.06	0.59	1.42	0.96	1.15	0.95
Townships									
NF/F	1.35	1.08	2.35	1.99	2.02	1.68	2.56	1.44	1.33
M/F	1.37	0.91	1.74	0.54	1.30	1.29	1.45	1.17	1.11
All regions									
Seigniories									
NF/F	1.35	1.65	1.62	1.62	1.09	1.09	1.62	1.30	1.22
M/F	1.47	1.21	1.32	1.20	1.11	1.12	1.44	1.27	1.07
Townships									
NF/F	0.88	0.90	1.11	0.83	1.08	1.08	1.57	1.14	1.08
M/F	0.88	0.90	1.11	0.83	1.08	1.08	1.57	1.14	1.08

(continued)

Table 4 (continued)

	Wheat	*Barley*	*Rye*	*Peas*	*Oats*	*Potatoes*	*Census butter*	*Total butter*	*Wool*
Seigniories and Townships									
NF/F	1.30	1.08	1.37	1.14	1.19	0.94	2.45	1.84	1.28
M/F	1.19	0.96	1.27	0.97	1.05	1.02	1.43	1.33	1.10

Source Table 3

in the non-French Canadian districts were far more productive than the farms in the French Canadian districts, exceeding their productivity from a low of 59% in the seigniorial districts of Region A to a high of 250% in those of Region B. Only in Region C did milk cow productivity of the French Canadian seigniorial districts better than in the non-French Canadian districts. However, milk cow productivity in these French Canadian districts was only twenty-nine pounds per head, far below that of the non-French Canadian districts in all other regions regardless of the system of land tenure. Moreover, the non-French Canadian districts of this region comprised only 3% of all non-French Canadian farms (Table 1). On average, the non-French Canadian farms in the townships were relatively much more productive than those in the seigniories. The productivity of the mixed farms exceeded that of French Canadian farms by a substantial margin in all regions.

These estimates appear to further support the Ouellet view that French Canadian farmers were employing relatively unproductive methods of production. However the census provides no data on liquid milk production. Therefore, for the dairy estimates to be of any use in comparing the relative productivity of farms in the non-French Canadian with the French Canadian districts, one must assume that liquid milk production per milk cow on the French Canadian farms (although this was not recorded in the census) could not have been high enough to compensate for the productivity gap in butter and cheese production between French Canadian and non-French Canadian districts. This is an important point since the dairy productivity differential, when incorporated into our net output estimates, plays a large role in determining per-farm differences in net output between farms in French Canadian and non-French Canadian districts (see Table 8).

Table 5 Livestock per larger occupant

	Bulls, oxen, steer	*Milch cows*	*Calves or heifers*	*Horses*	*Sheep*	*Pigs*
Region A						
Seigniories						
French	1.2	4.6	2.5	3.6	10.8	4.3
Non-French	0.6	4.9	2.9	2.4	6.6	4.1
Mixed	0.8	4.5	2.5	3.3	7.3	4.2
Fr and NF	1.2	4.6	2.5	3.6	10.7	4.3
Total	1.1	4.6	2.5	3.5	10.1	4.2
Townships						
French	0.7	3.4	2.4	3.0	7.0	3.8
Non-French	1.1	3.4	2.5	2.0	6.7	3.2
Mixed	0.9	3.1	2.1	1.9	5.3	2.7
Fr and NF	0.9	3.4	2.5	2.4	6.8	3.4
Total	0.9	3.3	2.3	2.2	6.3	3.2
Region B						
Seigniories						
French	1.1	3.8	2.2	2.6	8.9	3.5
Non-French	2.4	3.9	3.2	3.2	15.3	2.3
Mixed	0.5	2.2	1.2	1.3	4.0	1.6
Fr and NF	1.1	3.8	2.3	2.6	9.1	3.5
Total	1.1	3.8	2.2	2.6	9.0	3.5
Townships						
French	0.7	1.9	1.1	1.3	3.7	1.9
Non-French	3.0	3.8	3.4	1.9	9.8	1.5
Mixed	1.8	2.6	1.8	1.3	5.1	1.6
Fr and NF	2.6	3.4	3.0	1.8	8.7	1.6
Total	2.4	3.2	2.7	1.7	7.9	1.6
Region C						
Seigniories						
French	1.6	3.6	2.2	1.6	7.8	2.9
Non-French	0.6	3.7	1.5	1.6	1.6	2.4
Mixed	1.1	2.7	1.6	1.3	3.9	2.6
Fr and NF	1.6	3.6	2.2	1.6	7.7	2.9
Total	1.5	3.5	2.1	1.6	7.2	2.9
Townships						
French	0.7	1.4	0.8	0.8	3.3	1.8
Non-French	3.1	3.3	3.0	1.8	9.4	2.1
Mixed	1.4	2.2	1.8	1.1	5.4	2.0

(continued)

Table 5 (continued)

	Bulls, oxen, steer	*Milch cows*	*Calves or heifers*	*Horses*	*Sheep*	*Pigs*
Fr and NF	2.0	2.4	2.0	1.3	6.6	2.0
Total	1.9	2.4	2.0	1.3	6.4	2.0
Region D						
Seigniories						
French	1.5	4.0	2.3	2.0	11.1	3.2
Non-French						
Mixed	0.7	2.3	1.0	1.0	4.6	2.0
Fr and NF	1.5	4.0	2.3	2.0	11.1	3.2
Total	1.5	4.0	2.2	2.0	11.0	3.2
Townships						
French	0.6	1.6	1.0	1.0	4.5	2.2
Non-French	1.4	2.3	1.6	0.7	5.4	1.9
Mixed	1.3	1.8	1.2	0.8	5.2	2.4
Fr and NF	0.8	1.7	1.1	0.9	4.7	2.1
Total	1.0	1.8	1.1	0.9	4.9	2.2
All regions						
Seigniories						
French	1.3	4.0	2.3	2.5	9.5	3.5
Non-French	1.1	4.2	2.5	2.4	7.7	3.0
Mixed	0.9	3.6	2.0	2.3	5.7	3.3
Fr and NF	1.3	4.0	2.3	2.5	9.5	3.5
Total	1.3	4.0	2.3	2.5	9.1	3.5
Townships						
French	0.7	2.0	1.3	1.5	4.6	2.4
Non-French	2.4	3.5	3.0	1.8	8.6	2.2
Mixed	1.3	2.6	1.8	1.4	5.2	2.3
Fr and NF	1.7	2.9	2.3	1.7	7.0	2.3
Total	1.6	2.8	2.2	1.6	6.5	2.3
Seigniories and Townships						
French	1.2	3.7	2.2	2.4	8.9	3.4
Non-French	2.3	3.5	2.9	1.9	8.5	2.3
Mixed	1.1	3.0	1.9	1.8	5.4	2.7
Fr and NF	1.4	3.7	2.3	2.3	8.9	3.2
Total	1.4	3.6	2.2	2.2	8.3	3.1

Source Table 2

In the course of constructing estimates for the relative efficiency of French Canadian and non-French Canadian farms in Lower Canada, Lewis and McInnis assume that milk cow productivity was the same on French Canadian and non-French Canadian farms in 1851. They reject the census report on milk cow production for the French Canadian districts as being impossibly low, reflecting the fact that the census authorities took no account of liquid milk production. Their assumption of equal productivity stems from their belief that French Canadians consumed much more liquid milk than did their "English" (non-French Canadian) counterparts (Lewis and McInnis 1980, pp. 50, 51, 74). But this claim has not been well documented. Moreover, we find that if the productivity gap between milk cows on French and non-French Canadian farms approached equality, the French Canadian farm family would have had to consume, on average, 185 imperial gallons (222 gallons) of liquid milk in the seigniories and in the townships, and this is only if one assumes that the non-French farm families consumed no liquid milk whatsoever.[15] Lewis and McInnis assume that output per milk cow was ninety-two pounds in butter equivalents in contrast to my census-based estimate of twenty-nine and seventy-one pounds in the French and non-French Canadian districts respectively (Table 3) (Lewis and McInnis 1980, p. 74). This implies that, on average, the French Canadian farm family must have consumed 559 imperial gallons (671 gallons) of liquid milk compared to 166 imperial gallons (199 gallons) consumed by the non-French Canadian farm family regardless of the system of land tenure.[16] However, various estimates for liquid milk consumption for this period suggest that per annum consumption for a family of six was only 175 imperial gallons (210 gallons).[17] The majority of French Canadian families would have had to consume more than three times the liquid milk known to have been consumed by a typical family at that time. This suggests that the assumption of equal productivity in dairy production in French Canadian and non-French Canadian farms is highly implausible. Therefore, although the census record no doubt underestimates the amount of dairy production in Lower Canada for both French Canadian and non-French Canadian farms, this does not mean that the census record does not provide the basis with which to construct a fair representation of the differences in dairy production between French Canadian and other farms.

To compensate for the presumed under-reporting of milk production by census authorities, this paper adjusts milk cow productivity to what many experts agree were typical levels of milk consumption for the period. Each adult consumed at most about 42 imperial gallons (50 gallons) of liquid milk, each child about 17 gallons (20.4 gallons) (Shammas 1982). These assumptions of milk consumption per adult and child are applied to our estimates of family size and the age distribution of the family for 1851–1852 to generate estimates for liquid milk consumption per family by region and ethnic-language group for seigniories and townships.[18] These estimates, in turn, are used to construct estimates of liquid milk production per milk cow, which are then employed to inflate the census-based estimates of dairy production per milk cow (Table 3). Since the French Canadian family was somewhat larger than the non-French Canadian family, this increases French Canadian dairy production relative to non-French Canadian production from what it would otherwise be, but not by much. Moreover, the adjusted estimates also affect the relative dairy productivity estimates, somewhat reducing the advantage of non-French Canadian over French Canadian regions (Table 4).

5 Net Agricultural Output Per Farm

The next set of estimates is for the value of net output per farm in 1851–1852 prices converted to American dollars (Table 6). In constructing these estimates the procedures developed by Lewis and McInnis in their construction of total factor productivity estimates are followed with some notable exceptions. The prices used to value the different outputs are drawn largely from Lewis and McInnis, as are the assumptions for seed requirements per acre. In addition, their slaughter ratios and livestock weight assumptions are applied to our livestock estimates (Table 5).[19] The latter assumes that French Canadian and non-French Canadian farms produced livestock of identical weight and meat of identical quality. This biases our net output estimates against the Ouellet hypothesis since they stand in stark contrast with the Ouellet view of French Canadian agriculture, which holds that French Canadian farms produced lower quality and less weighty livestock than did their non-French Canadian counterparts (see Armstrong 1984, p. 156). The dairy production estimates used in this study are the adjusted census-based estimates that take into account the failure of census takers to record liquid milk production. However, unlike Lewis and McInnis, it is not assumed here that census-based differences in dairy production between French and non-French

Table 6 Value of surplus per large occupant

	Variant 1	*Variant 2 (smaller occups possess 1 horse)*	*Variant 3 (excludes horse surplus)*	*Variant 4 (all occups are farmers)*
Region A				
Seigniories				
French	201	187	145	155
Non-French	156	154	133	150
Mixed	202	191	150	162
Fr and NF	200	186	144	155
Total	200	187	145	156
Townships				
French	169	156	117	133
Non-French	151	146	127	136
Mixed	108	104	92	100
Fr and NF	158	150	123	135
Total	140	134	112	123
Region B				
Seigniories				
French	135	126	113	111
Non-French	204	200	172	189
Mixed	73	73	73	67
Fr and NF	136	128	114	113
Total	135	126	113	112
Townships				
French	76	73	67	69
Non-French	137	136	135	126
Mixed	87	86	86	80
Fr and NF	126	124	122	115
Total	117	115	114	107
Region C				
Seigniories				
French	119	117	115	109
Non-French	152	150	150	133
Mixed	106	105	102	102
Fr and NF	120	118	116	110
Total	118	116	114	109
Townships				
French	72	72	72	71
Non-French	157	154	146	145

(continued)

Table 6 (continued)

	Variant 1	*Variant 2 (smaller occups possess 1 horse)*	*Variant 3 (excludes horse surplus)*	*Variant 4 (all occups are farmers)*
Mixed	99	99	99	98
Fr and NF	119	117	112	113
Total	115	114	110	111
Region D				
Seigniories				
French	168	162	157	128
Non-French				
Mixed	170	170	169	74
Fr and NF	168	162	157	128
Total	168	162	158	127
Townships				
French	108	108	107	99
Non-French	177	175	175	160
Mixed	137	135	135	122
Fr and NF	121	120	119	111
Total	128	126	125	115
All regions				
Seigniories				
French	156	148	130	127
Non-French	169	167	150	156
Mixed	156	149	126	133
Fr and NF	156	148	131	128
Total	156	148	130	128
Townships				
French	106	103	91	96
Non-French	149	146	137	136
Mixed	108	106	100	99
Fr and NF	132	129	119	120
Total	125	122	114	114
Seigniories and Townships				
French	150	142	126	124
Non-French	150	147	138	138
Mixed	128	124	112	115
Fr and NF	150	143	128	126
Total	147	140	125	124

Source and notes See text. The output-specific value estimates are detailed in Morris Altman, "Land Tenure, Ethnicity and the State of Agricultural Income and Productivity in Mid-Nineteenth Century Quebec." Paper presented to the Nineteenth Conference on the Use of Quantitative Methods in Canadian Economic History, Montreal, 1994

Canadian farms are necessarily compensated by relatively large quantities of liquid milk consumption by French Canadians.

A procedure similar to that of Lewis and McInnis is used to estimate the percentage of horses and the percentage of bulls, oxen, and steer used as draft animals (Lewis and McInnis 1984, pp. 70–74 and n. 34). This allows for rough estimates of the number of horses sold on the market as well as the number of cattle raised for beef. Estimated differences in the number of horses for sale or of cattle raised for beef per farm between farms in the French Canadian, non-French Canadian, and mixed districts are, to a large extent, a product of differences in the amount of land under crop and land under pasture as well as in the number of cattle and horses maintained by these farms (Tables 2 and 5).[20] Nevertheless, an important fraction of the difference in horses for sale on French Canadian and non-French Canadian farms is due to the assumption, initially forwarded by Lewis and McInnis, that individuals occupying less than eleven acres of land did not own any horses. If, on the other hand, one assumes some ownership of horses among the smaller-scale occupiers—who it must be remembered were more important in the French Canadian regions, as a percentage of all occupiers (Table 1)—in order to meet their transportation needs for example, the relative differences in surplus horses on French Canadian and non-French Canadian farms diminishes.[21] Therefore, by adopting the assumption that only the larger-scale occupants owned horses, it is clear that the net output results are biased against the hypothesis that French Canadian farmers realized a relatively low level of farm output. This is evident from Table 6, where the net output or surplus estimates are presented.

The net value of grain production is estimated by first netting out all estimated seed requirements together with all the grain estimated to have been used for feed. To achieve the latter, following the example of Lewis and McInnis, feeding standards (dry matter required per animal) presented in Bailey's *Cyclopedia of American Agriculture* are used.[22] The result of this procedure is that only wheat and barley remain after animal feed is netted out of total grain production.

Once all inputs into the production process are netted out, one is left with the net value of output inclusive of the output required by the farm family to meet its basic needs. Since these estimates of net output or surplus are contingent upon assumptions which mostly bias our results against the non-French Canadian farm, a set of alternative net output estimates are constructed by adjusting our assumptions on surplus horses, dairy output, and the holders of the relatively small plots of land (Table 6). Variant 1 of our four net output estimates is the most biased against the non-French Canadian farm. Of course, all of these net output estimates are lower-bound for all linguistic-ethnic groups since they exclude the value of garden crops, firewood, and poultry for which the census provides no information. There is, nevertheless, no reason to believe that the production of these items was biased in favour of one linguistic group or another.

At first glance our findings suggest that the value of net agricultural output produced by farms in the non-French Canadian districts exceeded what was produced by farms in the French Canadian districts by, at most, 11%—this assumes that all occupants large and small are farmers (Table 6). These average differences in net output in favour of the non-French farms are consistent with the finding of Lewis and McInnis that French Canadian farmers were probably between 8 and 16% less efficient than their non-French Canadian counterparts.[23] Our results change little even if one only examines those counties encompassing both French Canadian and non-French Canadian farms (Table 7). The latter results are for districts situated in similar geographic and climatic zones and, therefore, attempt to account for the effect such differences might otherwise

Table 7 Average agricultural surplus with counties with both French and non-French occupants

	Occupants	*Surplus*
French	9,615	133
Non-French	6,777	145
Mixed	5,309	112
Seigniories	11,085	161
Townships	5,307	127
FR Seigniories	4,324	160
NF Seigniories	983	167
FR Townships	5,291	110
NF Townships	5,794	142

Source and notes Table 6 and Morris Altman, "Land Tenure, Ethnicity and the State of Agricultural Income and Productivity in Mid-Nineteenth Century Quebec." Paper presented to the Nineteenth Conference on the Use of Quantitative Methods in Canadian Economic History, Montreal, 1994. The counties with both French and non-French occupants are: Leinster, Two Mountains, Beauharnois, Rouville, Shefford, Megantic, Drummond, Quebec, Sherbrooke, Bonaventure, Gaspe

have on the net output produced on French Canadian and non-French Canadian farms. In this case, farms in non-French districts were 9% more productive than their counterparts in the French Canadian districts. Our net output estimates are also consistent with the fact that, on average, the lower factor productivity that characterized the farms in the French Canadian districts was not compensated for by larger holdings. Although, on average, farms in these districts placed a much larger proportion of their smaller holdings under cultivation and under crop, this only partially compensated for their lower factor productivity (Table 2).

A further decomposition of these net output estimates suggests that the non-French Canadian farms generated a greater output than the French Canadian farms in both the seigniories and the townships (Table 6). No matter which variant of net output one examines, the difference in net output was much greater in the townships than in the seigniories—with respect to Variant I, by over 40% in the townships and by only 8% in the seigniories. However, both French Canadian and non-French Canadian farms fared better in the seigniorial districts. Indeed, the output produced by the farms in the French Canadian seigniorial districts bettered that produced by the farms in the non-French Canadian township districts. Once again, these results change but little if one examines only those districts incorporating both French Canadian and non-French Canadian farms (Table 7). These results are reinforced once the net output estimates are examined by region (Table 6).

Apart from Region A, farms in the non-French Canadian districts produced a much greater net output than did those in the French Canadian districts, regardless of the system of land tenure. Net output in the non-French Canadian districts exceeded that in French Canadian districts ranging from a low of 28% in the seigniorial districts of Region C to a high of 118% in the township districts of the same region. Overall, the ratio of net output of the farms in the non-French Canadian to the French Canadian districts is greatest in the townships. However, in Regions B, C, and D, farms in both non-French Canadian and French Canadian districts generated a greater—typically much greater—output in the seigniories than in the townships (Lewis and McInnis 1980, pp. 510–511). These observations are all based on Variant I, the net output estimates most biased against the non-French Canadian farm. Changing our assumptions about smaller-scale occupants and surplus horses only serves to increase the advantage of the non-French Canadian farm (Variants 2, 3, and 4).

Standing in clear contrast to the other three regions to the east, the farms in the French Canadian districts of Region A (the Montreal-Ottawa region), incorporating the districts around and including the Island of Montreal and containing about 30% of French Canadian and non-French Canadian farms, plainly outperformed those in the non-French Canadian districts in both the seigniories and townships. This is true for all variants of surplus or net output in the seigniories, although the net output gap between farms in French Canadian and non-French Canadian districts diminishes as one changes the assumptions underlying the construction of net output. Moreover, the difference in output between the two is greatest in the seigniorial districts. In the townships, however, the French Canadian advantage disappears once we assume that no horse surplus exists or that all occupants, large and small, were farmers.

In other words, the horse surplus was critical to the superiority of farms in the French Canadian districts in the townships. And, assuming that all of the smaller occupants were not farmers—the truth probably leans towards this assumption—biases our results in favour of the French Canadian farms. Apart from the advantage held by the French Canadian farms in the seigniories and in the townships, the net output produced by farms in the French Canadian and non-French Canadian districts was much greater in the seigniories than in the townships. This is especially true of the farms in the French Canadian districts. The superior performance of French Canadian farms took place in spite of the fact that, even in Region A, partial factor productivity in the French Canadian districts was inferior to that in the non-French Canadian districts for most key outputs, including wheat and dairy products. The net output produced on the farms in the French Canadian seigniorial districts in the Montreal-Ottawa region was also greater than what was produced in all other regions regardless of ethnicity or system of land tenure, except for the farms in the non-French Canadian seigniorial districts of Region B. But these represented only 2.5% of non-French Canadian farms in Lower Canada.

The high value of output produced by farms in the French Canadian seigniorial districts of Region A served to significantly reduce the average ratio of non-French Canadian to French Canadian net output in Lower Canada as a whole from what it would otherwise be. Also, in the seigniories of Region D, which were home to 21% of all French Canadian seigniorial farms, the net output produced by the French Canadian farms was only bested by the performance of farms in the French Canadian seigniorial districts of Region A and that of the non-French Canadian seigniorial districts of Region B. There were no non-French Canadian farms in the seigniories of Region D. However, the net output produced by the farms in the non-French Canadian districts of Region D, all of which were in the townships, was also quite high, exceeded only by the net output produced by the farms in the non-French Canadian seigniorial districts of Region B and by the farms in the French Canadian seigniorial districts Region A. The non-French Canadian farms of Region D, however, incorporated only 4% of all non-French Canadian farms.

6 Decomposing Net Output

One can identify those factors which are directly responsible for the differential in the value of net output between farms in the French Canadian and non-French Canadian districts by subtracting the value of each component of net output per farm in the French Canadian districts of each region from that in the non-French Canadian districts. A positive difference represents a particular output's positive contribution to the net output differential in favour of French Canadian farms. A negative difference represents a particular output's positive contribution to the net output differential in favour of non-French Canadian farms. Where the sum of positive differences exceeds the sum of negative differences, as in Region A, the value of net output is greater on the French Canadian farms. These results, based on Variant 1 of our net output estimates, are presented in Table 8.

In Region A, the only region where farms in French Canadian districts produced a greater surplus than did farms in non-French Canadian districts, the difference in the value of net income per farm between French Canadian and non-French Canadian farms amounts to $46 (1851–1852 American dollars) in the seigniories and $18 in the townships.[24] The positive difference comes to $69 in the seigniories and $50 in the townships, whereas the negative difference equals $24 in the seigniories and $32 in the townships. The value of wheat output contributes 35% and the value of surplus horses 31% to the positive difference in net income in the seigniories and 42 and 41% respectively in the townships. In the seigniories about 12% of the positive difference consists of the value of slaughtered livestock and another 5% of the difference is related to the value of barley.

Table 8 Decomposition of the French/non-French differential in the value of net surplus

	Region A		*Region B*		*Region C*		*Region D*
	Seigniories F/NF	*Townships* F/NF	*Seigniories* F/NF	*Townships* F/NF	*Seigniories* F/NF	*Townships* F/NF	*Townships* F/NF
Positive sum	69	50	21	7	52	3	25
Negative sum	−24	−32	−91	−68	−84	−88	−94
Net sum	46	18	−69	−61	−32	−85	−69
Percentage share of positive sum							
Potatoes	0.0%	0.0%	0.0%	0.0%	0.0%	0.0%	0.0%
Wheat	35.4%	42.4%	0.0%	0.0%	20.6%	0.0%	31.1%
Barley	5.0%	4.3%	1.0%	0.0%	0.9%	27.4%	33.5%
Butter	0.0%	0.0%	0.0%	0.0%	3.4%	0.0%	0.0%
Tobacco	2.0%	1.1%	5.2%	3.3%	0.6%	5.7%	0.4%
Hops	0.6%	0.0%	0.0%	0.0%	0.0%	0.0%	0.0%
Maple sugar	3.7%	1.9%	21.7%	0.0%	15.2%	0.0%	6.8%
Wool	0.6%	0.0%	0.0%	0.0%	5.2%	0.0%	0.0%
Cider	0.0%	0.0%	0.0%	0.0%	0.0%	0.0%	0.0%
Flax and hemp	1.1%	0.4%	6.3%	3.3%	2.2%	11.1%	1.1%
Fulled cloth	2.9%	1.5%	12.1%	0.0%	4.6%	0.0%	0.9%
Linen	3.5%	1.7%	21.8%	8.5%	9.0%	55.8%	6.3%
Flannel	2.4%	0.0%	4.0%	0.0%	9.1%	0.0%	7.4%
Swine	1.1%	5.6%	28.0%	22.1%	4.6%	0.0%	6.6%
Sheep	3.0%	0.3%	0.0%	0.0%	5.9%	0.0%	0.0%
Milch cows	0.0%	0.0%	0.0%	0.0%	0.0%	0.0%	0.0%
Horses	31.2%	40.7%	0.0%	62.8%	3.8%	0.0%	5.9%
Cattle	7.5%	0.0%	0.0%	0.0%	14.2%	0.0%	0.0%
Calves or heifers	0.0%	0.0%	0.0%	0.0%	0.6%	0.0%	0.0%
Fish	0.0%	0.0%	0.0%	0.0%	0.0%	0.0%	0.0%
	100%	100%	100%	100%	100%	100%	100%

(continued)

Table 8 (continued)

	Region A		*Region B*		*Region C*		*Region D*
	Seigniories F/NF	*Townships F/NF*	*Seigniories F/NF*	*Townships F/NF*	*Seigniories F/NF*	*Townships F/NF*	*Townships F/NF*
Percentage share of negative sum							
Potatoes	56.1%	23.0%	33.4%	6.0%	99.5%	14.6%	19.1%
Wheat	0.0%	0.0%	8.1%	4.0%	0.0%	7.7%	0.0%
Barley	0.0%	0.0%	0.0%	0.7%	0.0%	0.0%	0.0%
Butter	40.6%	60.7%	19.0%	30.2%	0.0%	18.7%	9.4%
Tobacco	0.0%	0.0%	0.0%	0.0%	0.0%	0.0%	0.0%
Hops	0.0%	3.4%	2.4%	0.0%	0.0%	3.4%	0.1%
Maple suger	0.0%	0.0%	0.0%	9.5%	0.0%	1.1%	0.0%
Wool	0.0%	0.2%	3.7%	5.2%	0.0%	4.2%	1.1%
Cider	0.0%	0.0%	0.1%	0.1%	0.0%	0.1%	0.0%
Flax and hemp	0.0%	0.0%	0.0%	0.0%	0.0%	0.0%	0.0%
Fulled cloth	0.0%	0.0%	0.0%	0.9%	0.0%	1.5%	0.0%
Linen	0.0%	0.0%	0.0%	0.0%	0.0%	0.0%	0.0%
Flannel	0.0%	1.1%	0.0%	5.9%	0.0%	5.1%	0.0%
Swine	0.0%	0.0%	0.0%	0.0%	0.0%	1.5%	0.0%
Sheep	0.0%	0.0%	3.5%	4.5%	0.0%	3.4%	0.5%
Milch cows	2.5%	0.2%	0.3%	6.1%	0.5%	5.0%	1.6%
Horses	0.0%	0.0%	17.0%	0.0%	0.0%	9.3%	0.0%
Cattle	0.0%	11.8%	11.9%	28.6%	0.0%	24.0%	5.0%
Calves or heifers	0.8%	−0.3%	0.5%	1.2%	0.0%	0.3%	1.9%
Fish	0.0%	0.0%	0.0%	−2.9%	0.0%	0.0%	61.5%
	100%	100%	100%	100%	100%	100%	100%

Source Table 7

It is apparent that the value of wheat production on the farms of the French Canadian districts played a decisive role in pulling them ahead of their counterparts in the non-French Canadian districts of Region A. The clear advantage held by farmers in the French Canadian districts over the farmers in the non-French Canadian districts in the production of wheat, however, had nothing to do with French Canadian farmers being more productive in wheat because yields were 19% greater on non-French Canadian farms in the seigniories and 9% greater in the townships (Table 4). In spite of their relatively lower yields, farmers in the French Canadian districts produced much more wheat per farm because they placed many more acres of land under wheat than did their counterparts in the non-French Canadian districts—eight acres per farm as compared to three acres in the seigniories and seven acres per farm as compared to three acres in the townships (Table 2). This is in spite of the fact that the farms in the French Canadian districts were much smaller than the farms in the non-French Canadian districts. The French Canadian farms also placed significantly more land under cultivation and under crop in both the seigniories and townships. The final key advantage of farms in the French Canadian districts over the farms in the non-French Canadian districts of Region A is their superior holdings of livestock, which resulted in a higher value of slaughtered cattle, sheep, swine, livestock, wool, and fulled cloth. Most importantly, this resulted in a much higher surplus horse population available for sale in the marketplace.

In sum, French Canadian farmers achieved more than their non-French Canadian counterparts in Region A by working their smaller plots of land more intensively. As a result, more wheat was produced and much of the extra land placed under crop and pasture contributed toward feeding their relatively larger horse and general livestock population.

The negative difference in the value of net output in Region A can be accounted for by the value of dairy production and potatoes, which contributed 41 and 56% respectively to the total in the seigniories and 61 and 23% in the townships (Table 8). Even though there was little difference in the holdings of milk cows by farms in the French Canadian and non-French Canadian districts (Table 5), the dairy productivity differential in favour of farms in the non-French Canadian districts was so great that non-French Canadian dairy production overwhelmed French Canadian dairy production. The value of potatoes was greater on farms in the non-French Canadian districts where more land was devoted to its production.

The advantage held by farms in the non-French Canadian districts over farms in the French Canadian districts in Region B is estimated to have been about $69 per farm in the seigniories and $61 in the townships. In this region, however, farms in the French Canadian districts were superior to farms in the non-French Canadian districts in the value of swine slaughtered and linen produced and, to a lesser extent, in the value of flax and hemp and tobacco produced in both the seigniories and the townships. In the seigniories, French Canadian farms also produced more maple sugar and fulled cloth. But their inferior partial factor productivity combined with the relatively small size of their holdings, which were not exploited as intensively as they were in Region A, resulted in farms in the non-French Canadian districts overwhelming the farms in the French Canadian districts, particularly in the value of potatoes, wheat, dairy, and cattle produced in both the seigniories and the townships. In the seigniories, farms in the non-French Canadian districts even outdid their counterparts in the French Canadian districts in the value of surplus horses produced.

In Region C, the advantage of farms in the non-French Canadian districts over farms in the French Canadian districts amounted to \$32 per farm in the seigniories and \$85 in the townships. In Region D, the advantage of farms in the non-French Canadian districts over farms in the French Canadian districts was \$69 in the townships. There were no non-French Canadian farms present in the seigniories of Region D. In both these regions, for the most part, farms in the non-French Canadian districts were much more productive than farms in the French Canadian districts. Farms in the non-French Canadian districts were also larger than farms in the French Canadian districts. However, in both the seigniories of Region C and in the townships of Region D, farms in the French Canadian districts placed a much larger percentage of land under cultivation, resulting in more land being cultivated here than on the farms in the non-French Canadian districts. This did not, however, suffice to neutralize the lower productivity of the French Canadian farms. In the seigniories of Region C, the key advantage of farms in the non-French Canadian districts rested with their potato production. Farms in the French Canadian districts, on the other hand, held an advantage, although obviously not enough of one, in the value of a variety of outputs produced, such as wheat, butter, maple sugar, wool, flax and hemp, fulled cloth, linen, flannel, and slaughtered swine, sheep, and cattle. In the townships of Region D, fish production gave farms in the non-French Canadian districts their primary advantage over farms in the French Canadian districts. This advantage, however, is unrelated to any measures of partial factor productivity or land use. But even without their edge in fish output, farms in the non-French Canadian districts still would have bettered their counterparts in the French Canadian districts with their superior performance in the production of potatoes, butter, and cattle.

Finally, in Region C's townships, not only were farms in the French Canadian districts much smaller than farms in the non-French Canadian districts, but they also placed a much smaller percentage of land under cultivation. When combined with the much higher productivity of farms in the non-French Canadian districts, this produced the advantage of farms in the non-French Canadian districts in the important components of net output.

It was not impossible for farms in the French Canadian districts to compensate for their relatively small size and for low yields for most of the outputs recorded in the 1851–1852 census. Our estimates for Region A suggest that an important ingredient for success was the more intensive use of land. By placing more land under cultivation not only could more crops be grown but more livestock, including surplus horses, could be raised. But more often than not, however, this did not occur. As a result, many French Canadian districts, regardless of the system of land tenure, generated a lowers level of surplus than did their non-French Canadian counterparts.

7 The Ranking of Counties by Net Output, Language and System of Land Tenure

Ranking all of the census counties contained in our four regions, which embody close to five hundred census districts, by net output or surplus per farm provides more information on the relative standing of farms in the French Canadian and non-French Canadian districts. It is evident from Table 9 that farms in the French Canadian districts were characterized by both the highest and the lowest levels of net output. The same can be said for the mixed farms. Of course, these relatively well-off farms are found in the counties included in Regions A and D. Moreover, farms in these counties are located largely in seigniories. On the other hand, farms in counties with the lowest levels of net output are in the townships. The farms in the non-French Canadian districts are found largely in the middle of the ranking. Upon closer inspection, all farms in the non-French Canadian districts generated a higher net output than the poorest 9% of farms in the French Canadian districts. At the other end of the net output spectrum, the top 10% of French Canadian farms produced a higher net output than all non-French Canadian farms. Moving away from extremes, about 90% of the farms in the non-French Canadian districts were characterized by

Table 9 Ranking of counties in lower Canada by surplus per larger occupant

Rank	*County*	*Language*	*Region*	*Tenure*	*Surplus*	*% of population by language group*
1	Montreal	M	A	S	409	3.6
2	Gaspe	F	D	S	328	0.2
3	Chambly	M	A	S	320	1.3
4	Montreal	F	A	S	299	1.5
5	Chambly	F	A	S	278	2.0
6	Vercheres	F	A	S	266	2.3
7	Two Mountains	F	A	S	243	2.4
8	Two Mountains	M	A	S	235	1.3
9	l'Islet	F	D	T	234	0.1
10	Rimouski	M	D	S	234	0.8
11	Montmorency	F	D	S	206	1.5
12	Gaspe	NF	D	T	206	1.9
13	Rouville	NF	B	S	204	2.5
14	Huntington	F	A	S	198	3.6
15	Beauharnois	F	A	T	198	2.6
16	Gaspe	F	D	T	193	0.5
17	Leinster	F	A	S	191	4.4
18	l'Islet	F	D	S	191	2.7
19	Kamouraska	F	D	S	181	3.0
20	Stanstead	NF	C	T	180	15.5
21	Gaspe	M	D	T	175	3.6
22	Vaudreuil	M	A	S	172	4.9
23	Huntington	M	A	S	172	3.5
24	Beauharnois	NF	A	T	170	12.3
25	Bonaventure	F	D	T	161	0.4
26	Terre Bonne	F	A	S	159	3.6
27	Quebec	M	C	S	158	2.2
28	Two Mountains	NF	A	S	156	3.1
29	Saguenay	F	D	S	155	2.5
30	Vaudreuil	F	A	S	153	2.2
31	Rouville	F	B	S	153	3.9
32	Quebec	NF	C	S	152	2.6
33	St. Maurice	F	B	S	150	3.9
34	Missisquoi	NF	B	T	147	12.1
35	Ottawa	NF	A	T	141	10.8
36	Megantic	NF	C	T	138	4.9
37	Rimouski	F	D	S	138	5.1

(continued)

Table 9 (continued)

Rank	*County*	*Language*	*Region*	*Tenure*	*Surplus*	*% of population by language group*
38	Bonaventure	NF	D	T	137	1.4
39	Sherbrooke	NF	B	T	137	16.9
40	Leinster	NF	A	T	136	2.5
41	Bellechase	F	D	S	134	3.3
42	Richelieu	F	B	S	132	4.0
43	Beauharnois	M	A	S	132	5.9
44	Dorchester	M	C	S	131	2.7
45	Nicolet	F	C	S	131	3.7
46	Dorchester	F	C	S	131	6.8
47	Drummond	NF	C	T	128	4.0
48	St. Hyacinthe	F	B	S	126	5.2
49	Berthier	F	B	S	126	5.4
50	Montmorency	M	D	S	123	0.6
51	Yamaska	F	B	S	123	2.7
52	Beauharnois	M	A	T	122	7.1
53	Beauharnois	F	A	S	120	1.4
54	Bonaventure	M	D	T	119	7.6
55	Shefford	NF	B	T	113	5.2
56	Lotbiniere	F	C	S	112	2.4
57	Huntington	M	A	T	109	1.7
58	Berthier	F	B	T	107	0.5
59	Portneuf	F	C	S	106	2.9
60	Drummond	M	C	T	106	5.8
61	Two Mountains	M	A	T	106	5.2
62	Champlain	F	C	S	105	3.1
63	Dorchester	NF	C	T	104	2.5
64	Quebec	F	C	S	102	1.2
65	Two Mountains	NF	A	T	101	1.7
66	St. Hyacinthe	M	B	S	100	0.7
67	Lotbiniere	M	C	S	99	5.9
68	Ottawa	M	A	T	98	7.8
69	Leinster	M	A	S	96	0.7
70	Rimouski	M	D	T	93	0.2
71	Shefford	M	B	T	92	10.0
72	Megantic	M	C	T	92	2.8
73	Nicolet	F	C	T	85	0.1
74	Terrebonne	M	A	S	84	1.6

(continued)

Table 9 (continued)

Rank	*County*	*Language*	*Region*	*Tenure*	*Surplus*	*% of population by language group*
75	Sherbrooke	F	B	T	84	0.2
76	Portneuf	M	C	S	82	5.7
77	Megantic	F	C	T	81	2.0
78	Rimouski	F	D	T	79	0.5
79	St. Maurice	F	B	T	78	0.2
80	Dorchester	M	C	T	74	0.9
81	Saguenay	F	D	T	72	1.2
82	Leinster	M	A	T	69	0.2
83	Sherbrooke	M	B	T	68	1.2
84	Rouville	M	B	S	66	2.3
85	Drummond	F	C	T	65	2.5
86	Ottawa	F	A	S	62	0.8
87	Berthier	M	B	T	62	1.3
88	Terrebonne	F	A	T	58	0.2
89	Kamouraska	F	D	T	58	0.2
90	Shefford	F	B	T	51	0.7
91	Leinster	F	A	T	49	0.4
92	Bellechase	M	D	T	43	0.6
93	Terrebonne	M	A	T	36	1.0
94	Lotbiniere	F	C	T	25	0.02

Source See Table 7

a higher level of surplus than were about 60% of the farms in the French Canadian districts.

Table 9 reveals that if one were to group all counties by land tenure and then rank these by net output, farms in the non-French Canadian districts dominated the top of the net output hierarchy for the townships. With respect to the seigniories, however, farms in the French Canadian districts clearly dominated the top of the net output hierarchy. When the counties are grouped by ethnicity and then ranked by net output, it is clear that township farms in the non-French Canadian districts monopolized the bottom rungs of the net output hierarchy. They also dominated the lower segment of the net output hierarchy in the French Canadian districts. In contrast, seigniorial farms are found on top of the net output ranking for farms in both the non-French Canadian and French Canadian districts.

Some of these results are highlighted in Table 10, where the farm population is segmented into ten income groups. At one extreme, we have

Table 10 The distribution of surplus by income group

		Percentage distribution of population by language group		
Surplus	*Income group*	*French*	*Non-French*	*Mixed*
$409				
$390	1	0.0	0.0	3.6
$371				
$351	2	0.0	0.0	0.0
$332				
$313	3	1.7	0.0	1.3
$294				
$275	4	4.2	0.0	0.0
$255				
$236	5	2.5	0.0	2.1
$217				
$198	6	18.2	19.9	0.0
$179				
$159	7	12.7	41.0	14.1
$140				
$121	8	52.1	37.4	36.1
$102				
$83	9	6.6	1.7	40.1
$63				
$44	10	2.3	0.0	3.0
$25				
		100	100	100

Source Table 9

farms in the mixed districts (about 4% of all mixed farms), which monopolize the top 20% net output range. The vast majority of farms in the mixed districts, however, lie at the bottom 30% net income range. Farms in the French Canadian districts along with farms in the mixed districts monopolize the third, fourth, and fifth deciles at the top of the net output range. Just over 8% of the farms in the French Canadian districts are found in this high surplus group as well as about 3% of the mixed farms. All of these farms are in Regions A and B. The very next decile is home to 18% of the farms in the French Canadian districts and 20% of the farms in the non-French Canadian districts. It is only here, towards the middle of the net output range, that the non-French farms make an appearance. The next decile is dominated by farms in the non-French districts where 41%

of such farms are located compared to 13% of the farms in the French Canadian districts. In the following decile, moving down in net output, one finds close to 40% of the farms in the non-French districts, but over 50% of the farms in the French Canadian districts. The bottom two deciles are dominated by farms in the French Canadian and mixed districts. These results serve to underline the fact that French Canadian farms tended to dominate the extremes of the net output hierarchy whereas non-French Canadian farms were bunched in the middle. All told, the county-by-county analysis simply reaffirms my four-region findings on the relatively superior performance of farms in the non-French Canadian districts, on the one hand, and of the seigniorial farms, on the other. But this analysis also reveals those farms in the French Canadian districts that did well did better than their counterparts in the non-French Canadian districts.

8 Conclusion

More generally, the findings presented here provide a macro-framework within which to structure and locate micro-studies of French Canadian and non-French Canadian farms. The detailed estimates serve to locate where output and productivity differences were most pronounced and provide some of the basic statistical reasons for these differences. Where do all these partial factor productivity and net output estimates, albeit they are only for one year, leave us with respect to our understanding of the relative standing of French Canadian and non-French Canadian farms and of farms operating under the seigniorial and freehold systems of land tenure?

Clearly, in 1851–1852 the majority of French Canadian farmers were worse off than their non-French Canadian counterparts regardless of the system of land tenure under which they operated. Their situation was directly related to their inferior productivity performance and their inability to compensate for lower yields by increasing the proportion of their relatively smaller holdings of land under cultivation. These findings affirm important aspects of the Ouellet account of Lower Canadian agriculture. They also cast some doubt on the view that the seigniorial system of land tenure was responsible for the low levels of agricultural output in Lower Canada (this tends to support the findings of Percy and Szostak [1992]). Rather, for reasons that remain to be explained, relatively low levels of agricultural output were most closely associated with farms in the townships, especially with the farms in the French Canadian districts in the townships.

On the other hand, the estimates derived from the 1851–1852 census make it clear that French Canadian farms were not always less productive or less prosperous than non-French Canadian farms. For this reason, one cannot draw a simple line of causation running from ethnicity cum language to productivity and surplus production. Moreover, it is now evident that one cannot easily link the relatively poor performance of so many French Canadian farms with the seigniorial system of land tenure. However, one hypothesis is whether French Canadian farmers who established themselves on the townships—originating largely from the seigniories—were relatively cash poor due to mounting seigniorial dues. Such a constraint might have limited the capacity of French Canadian farmers to develop their farms to the level achieved by their non-French Canadian counterparts in the townships, most of whom were not burdened by a seigniorial past.

Why the farmers in the French Canadian districts in and around Montreal were so much more successful than farmers in other French Canadian districts throughout Lower Canada and more successful than farmers in the non-French Canadian districts in this same region as well remains unexplained. Approaching the problem from another perspective, one might ask what factors caused the majority of farms in the French Canadian districts, especially those outside of Montreal, to lag behind their counterparts in the non-French Canadian districts with respect to productivity and net output.

Our estimates suggest that analyses of the regional differences in markets for wheat and horses will play an important role in answering these questions, a point also raised by Courville (1986, pp. 141–145). More specifically, the results presented in this study are consistent with the finding of the *Report of the Special Committee on the State of Agriculture in Lower Canada* (1850) that French Canadian farmers were reluctant to improve their methods of production or to shift out of wheat, their traditional staple product, particularly given their inadequate stock of knowledge on the available more "advanced," albeit more labour and capital intensive, methods of agricultural production. Given these constraints, the French Canadian farmers did their best, choosing to place more land under wheat and raise more horses and livestock for the market when the opportunity arose. But, by 1851–1852 such opportunities were largely limited to the Montreal region. Elsewhere, French

Canadian farmers suffered the consequences of low productivity and small plots of land.

Under these circumstances, the choices made by French Canadian farmers would have differed from those made by non-French Canadian farmers as a result of the different objective constraints they faced, not necessarily as a result of different *mentalités*, as the Ouellet hypothesis would have it.

Although the majority of farms in the French Canadian districts were less productive and less prosperous than their counterparts in the non-French Canadian districts, it is far from clear that this addresses a generalized crisis of poverty amongst French Canadian farm families. We estimate that a family of six in Lower Canada required at least $70 of the net output produced per farm to subsist.[25] This does not, however, include those items not counted in the census and, therefore, in our estimate of net output, such as garden products, poultry, and firewood. If one assumes that even the poorest of farm families produced an adequate supply of these "missing" commodities, it is likely that only about 5% of the farm families in the French Canadian districts might have had some difficulty in making ends meet, and the same is true of approximately 7% of farms in the mixed districts (Table 9). In addition, most of these farms are to be found in the townships and were therefore not burdened with the economic charges facing farmers in the seigniories such as an annual rent (*cens et rentes*), a mutation fine of 8.3% (*lods et ventes*), a monopoly price for milling grain, and a *corvée*. Moreover, to the extent that these low output farms had their incomes supplemented by off-farm work or, for example, by the production of a surplus of logs for the forestry industry, the potential poverty that might otherwise have been generated on the low productivity farms would have been mitigated.[26]

On the other hand, farmers in the seigniories were subject to economic charges which cut into their economic surplus by as much as $30 on a farm of about 80 acres, just below the average farm size in the seigniories. Such farmers would have had to realize a surplus of at least $100 to subsist after deducting the seigniorial charges. About 15% of seigniorial farmers in the mixed districts generated a surplus of between $70 and $100. These farmers might have had some difficulty in making ends meet. In addition, close to 10% of farmers in the French Canadian districts produced a surplus of between $100 and $110 and, therefore, were not far removed from subsistence once seigniorial charges are netted out.[27] In spite of this, it is clear that as late as 1851–1852 supply-side problems were not necessarily driving the vast majority of the French Canadian landholding farm population into economic despair, although the majority lagged behind their non-French Canadian counterparts and many marginal French Canadian farms were hard hit by seigniorial charges. Nevertheless, it is important to consider that for marginal farms, institutional imposed charges against farmers living in the seigniories damaged the wellbeing of such farm families and reduced their net surplus, limiting their capacity to investment in their land and in their families. This does not address the dilemma faced by many of Quebec's increasing landless population, many of whom emigrated to the United States. But that is another story.

Notes

1. The link between low agricultural income, the market, and economic development has been forcefully made most recently by John McCallum (1980). The link between low agricultural income, wage rates, and economic development has been advanced by Altman (1988b, 1995).
2. This article is part of a larger project which seeks to reconstruct and analyze various economic facets of agricultural life in Quebec by making use of the available censuses. See Altman (1983, 1987, 1988a, 1992, 1994).
3. It should be noted that on the Island of Montreal and in its environs, an ordinance of 1840 allowed for the commutation of seigniorial tenure into freehold—the seignior, in this case the Sulpician Order, could not refuse a request by a censitaire for commutation. However, few peasants took advantage of the terms of this ordinance. Demands for commutation were dominated by the nonagricultural population outside of the domain of this study. In fact, the ordinance greatly facilitated the ability of the Sulpician Order to enforce the terms of the seigniorial tenure upon those who chose not to commute. See Young (1986).
4. It should be re-emphasized that in this study published census tables are used as opposed to the manuscript census, much of which has been destroyed. Since our estimates are constructed using the district level data, not the more aggregate county-level data, many of the errors in addition made in the published tables are corrected. Some of the manuscript censuses, however, were employed to check for apparent inconsistencies in published tables at the district level. The retabulation of the available manuscript censuses would be the best solution for correcting such

errors in the published tables. Cost constraints have thus far kept interested parties from engaging in such a venture, although I am now in the process of undertaking this task.

5. At one point, Ouellet (1971, p. 456), writes: "This inclination of the French-Canadian farmer for lavish spending and unproductive investments still constituted a characteristic of his mentality and a lasting element in his culture. despite the unfortunate circumstances which beset him. Too great a proportion of his income went to the fulfilment of his need for prestige, which took concrete form not only in his clothing, but also in his religious practices. This mental trait continued to operate even in times of crisis, to the detriment of his material progress" (translated by Morris Altman). See also Ouellet (1971, pp. 256, 282, 336, 338, 360, 361, 455; 1972, pp. 177–196), for an excellent summary of his position.
6. Courville (1980, pp. 422–423), argues that the state of the French Canadian farm family's standard of material well-being was related not to any failure in production but rather to the increasing payments for the use of the land. These payments were required under the terms of the seigniorial system of land tenure until its abolition in 1854.
7. The data contained in *Report on the Affairs of British North America* (1839) are used to identify the system of land tenure which prevailed in the relevant census district.
8. The categorization of districts by ethnic or national origin is based on the "Lower Canada Personal Census by Origin," *Census of Canada. 1851–52.* Lewis and McInnis (1980, p. 501), categorize districts into those which are English (non-French Canadian) and French (French Canadian) only. Further. they define an English district its one where no more than 10% of the population is French. By using the 20% cut off point, my results are more biased towards refuting the hypothesis that French Canadian farms were employing relatively inferior technology than if the 10% cut off point was used. It must be noted here that the census report defines French as one who is French Canadian. It should also be emphasized that the census does not distinguish individuals along purely linguistic lines. For this reason, the nomenclature of English is not used to refer to the non-French Canadian districts, since the census defines this population to include individuals whose origin is English, Welsh, Scottish, Irish, American, as well as from other parts of British North America and other parts of the world.
9. The regional mapping of Lower Canada into four distinct areas is one of convenience, not one based on a detailed study of common factors in economy, geography, and climate. This type of regional subdivision of a larger political zone is, of course, the norm in the literature. Another mapping of Lower Canada divides the province into the districts Montreal, Trois Rivières, and Quebec City. This is a political (arbitrary) subdivision

and is used to facilitate and simplify economic, social, and geographical analysis. The mapping presented in this article defines a fourth region, the Gulf area, where fishing played a more important role in the economy than in the interior of the province.

10. Lewis and McInnis (1980, pp. 501–502). Their Regions I and II are incorporated in Region A, their Region III in Region B, and their Region IV in Region C.
11. This procedure is similar to that used by McInnis (1981, pp. 224–226). Only land estimates in districts under the seigniorial system of land tenure are converted into acres, as only in such districts was land surveyed and measured in arpents. He also only converts output of districts under seigniorial tenure in bushels. But since French Canadian farmers resided in the townships as well, our conversion is along ethnic lines. This method of converting minots into bushels increases the output of the French Canadian category relative to the non-French Canadian and mixed categories as compared to the output estimates which would be generated by using the method McInnis adopts. This biases our results against the Ouellet hypothesis.
12. Lewis and McInnis (1984, p. 499, n. 7). According to McInnis (1981, pp. 221–222), the census category of occupiers of ten acres or under largely consists of plots of one acre or less. In this study it is assumed that the smaller occupants held an average of two acres of land. This estimated size of holding per smaller occupant and the census report on the number of smaller occupants are used to estimate the number of acres held by this group. The estimated acreage held by the smaller occupants is deducted from the census totals for the total acreage held, although this represents only a tiny fraction of all land held (Tables 2 and 3).
13. Courville (1980, pp. 212–215), calculated yields per unit of land from 1686 to 1861 by simply adding the minots of all types of output produced and dividing this by the land under cultivation. This doesn't tell us about partial factor productivity, in particular since different types of crops were characterized by different outputs per unit of land. Also, land under cultivation includes land under pasture as well as land under crop. Courville makes similar calculations for English (non-French Canadian) and French (French Canadian) farms for selected counties in widely dispersed areas, finding that there was no productivity differences between French Canadian and English Canadian farms in 1851. See Little (1985, pp. 428–430), for an inclusive critique of Courville's computations.
14. Since it takes approximately eleven pounds of liquid milk to produce one pound of solid cheese and 23.36 pounds of liquid milk to produce one pound of butter, 2.12 pounds of cheese equals one pound of butter. This procedure is identical to the one adopted in Bateman (1968, p. 256, n. 5), in estimating the productivity of milk cows in the United States. He,

too, relies solely on the census data for butter and cheese since no reliable data are available for liquid milk production.

15. These estimates are derived by multiplying the difference in the census-based milk cow output in French Canadian and non-French Canadian districts (Table 3) by their estimated holdings of milk cows (Table 5). These estimates are converted to their liquid milk equivalents where one pound of butter equals 23.36 pounds of liquid milk and an imperial gallon of milk equals 10.3 pounds of liquid milk.
16. These milk consumption estimates are derived by subtracting the census-based dairy output per milk cow in French Canadian and non-French Canadian districts from the ninety-two pounds assumed by Lewis and McInnis. These are multiplied by the number of milk cows per family and are converted into liquid milk equivalents, where one pound of butter equals 23.36 pounds of liquid milk and an imperial gallon of milk equals 10.3 pounds of liquid milk.
17. No direct estimates are available as to liquid milk consumption in Lower Canada by any ethnic or linguistic group. We have only very general pieces of information, such as that from 1791 when, according to Greer (1985, p. 35), a French Canadian couple kept one milk cow to meet their yearly needs. More generally, Shammas (1982, pp. 250–252), building on the work of Lemon (1976, pp. 152–153, 163), finds that in well-to-do Lancashire County, Pennsylvania, post-1760, a farm family of nine consumed about 300 gallons of milk (250 imperial gallons) per year. Shammas assumes that the adults consumed fifty gallons and children consumed twenty gallons. Lemon finds that two milk cows could have produced no more than 150 gallons of milk each which is equivalent to about fifty pounds of butter.
18. Using the data in *The Census of Canada, 1951–52*, vol. I (1853), I estimate that average family size was 5.8 in both the French Canadian and non-French Canadian seigniorial districts of Region A; 5.9 and 5.3 respectively in Region B; 6.2 and 5.1 respectively in Region C; and 6.2 in the French Canadian districts of Region D. With respect to the townships, average family size was 6 in Region B in both French Canadian and non-French Canadian districts; 5.4 in Region B; 5.6 in Region C; and 6 in Region D. In addition, in the seigniorial districts about 46% of both the French Canadian and non-French Canadian families was less than fifteen years of age in Region A; 45 and 55% respectively in Region B; 45 and 43% in Region C; and 43% in the French Canadian districts of Region D. In the French Canadian and non-French Canadian township districts, the percentage of the families less than fifteen years of age was about 48% in Region A; 44 and 43% respectively in Region B; 50 and 43% in Region C; and 44% in both French Canadian and non-French Canadian districts in Region D.

19. See especially Lewis and McInnis (1984, pp. 76–78). The prices of flannel and linen are from Taché (1855, pp. 133–134), which is also the source for some of Lewis and McInnis's prices. The price quoted for a barrel of fish is for 1854 and is taken from Innis (1940, p. 360). The slaughter rates for livestock are from Lewis and McInnis (1984, pp. 71–74). However, since they provide no information on calves and heifers, the 10% slaughter rate for the 1840–1860 period in the United States is used. This is from Towne and Rasmussen (1960, p. 283). Also, instead of using Lewis and McInnis's slaughter rate for cattle raised for beef of 40%, a slaughter rate of 30% is employed. This is more consistent with cattle being slaughtered at 3–4 years of age (Lewis and McInnis 1984, p. 83, n. 8). The 30% slaughter rate is also more in line with the 20% slaughter rate for the United States for the years 1840–1860 adopted by Towne and Rasmussen (1960, p. 283).
20. The census records the number of bulls, oxen, and steers under one heading and thus does not distinguish between those raised for beef and those used as draft animals. This must be estimated. Also, we accept Lewis and McInnis's (1984) assumption that the ratio of colts and fillies to mature horses was the same in 1851–1852 as it was in 1861 when such a ratio can be estimated from the censuses. Lewis and McInnis estimate it to be 0.33. Thus, colts and fillies represented 25% of all horses. To estimate draft animal requirements Lewis and McInnis's assumption that one yoke of oxen or a pair of horses was required to work each 50 acres of cultivated land is followed, where for the purposes of estimating draft animal requirements cultivated land is defined as the land under crop plus 50% of the land in pasture. We also accept their assumption that owners of the garden plots did not own horses. To estimate the number of horses each farm is assumed to require at least one horse since a horse serves a dual function of a draft animal and as a means of travel. It is further assumed that a farm required two horses only if more than twenty-five acres were under cultivation. And. four horses would be required if more than 105 acres were under cultivation. These assumptions are consistent with Evans's (1835, p. 156) yield estimates for horses used as draft animals and thereby horses available for sale.
21. For example, if one assumes that the smaller occupants possessed at least one horse, the number of surplus horses falls to 11,019 in the French Canadian districts and to 1,593 in the non-French Canadian districts.
22. Lewis and McInnis (1984, pp. 77–81). The feeding requirements stipulated in Bailey (1912, pp. 107–118), are best-practice requirements.
23. These estimates are not much affected if the averages are calculated as unweighted averages, giving the net output produced in each county or district equal weight. For all regions the unweighted average of net output for farms in French Canadian districts is $136 and $143 for farms in

non-French Canadian districts. For the townships and the seigniories the unweighted averages are $116 and $157 respectively. The unweighted average in the non-French Canadian districts in the township farms is $137 as compared to $98 for their counterparts in the French Canadian districts. The farms in the non-French Canadian seigniorial districts realized an unweighted average net output of $168 whereas farms in the French Canadian districts located in the seigniories produced an unweighted average net output of $156.

24. These estimates assume that the smaller occupants possessed one horse.
25. The lower level of net output or surplus for farms in the French Canadian districts must be seen in the context of what the French Canadian farm family required for consumption. We estimate that about $66 was required to meet the basic needs of a family of six. The consumption basket consists of $28.95 of wheat, $19.68 of pork, $2.60 of peas, $3.00 of tobacco, $1.88 of maple sugar, $7.50 of dairy products, and $2.70 of rum. We assume that an adult required 8.5 bushels of wheat to subsist and that two adults required 175 pounds of meat, typically pork, to subsist (Reid 1947, p. 275; Greer 1985, p. 35). We also assume that two adults consumed 2.1 bushels of peas per year as well as thirty pounds of tobacco and twenty-five pounds of maple sugar (Greer 1985, p. 35). The assumption is made that dairy consumption comes to about 170 gallons of milk or seventy-five pounds of butter (see text). The rum consumption estimate is from Reid (1947, p. 275). Following Gallman (1972, p. 75, n. 20), we assume that children consumed at half the adult rate. Prices are from Lewis and McInnis (1984, p. 76).
26. See Little (1989, ch. 1), on the potential importance which farm family participation in the lumber industry had on the income of township farms in the eastern townships, which are largely incorporated in my Regions B and C. See Séguin (1977) for a discussion of the importance of the forestry sector to the farm population of the Saguenay area (contained in Region D).
27. Courville (1980, pp. 411–414), argues that in the nineteenth century seigniorial charges for a seventy-six acre farm in the county of Two Mountains probably amounted to about $27. These charges do not include the tithe, which Catholics hold to pay to the Church, of one-twenty-sixth of grain output. See also *The Report of the Commissioners*... (1843).

References

Altman, M. 1983. Seignorial Tenure in New France, 1688–1739: An Essay on Income Distribution and retarded Economic Development. *Historical Reflections/Reflexions Historiques* 10: 343–350.

Altman, M. 1987. Note on the Economic Burden of the Seigniorial System in New France, 1688–1739. *Historical Reflections/Reflexions Historiques* 14: 135–142.

Altman, M. 1988a. Economic Growth in Canada, 1695–1739: Estimates and Analysis. *William and Mary Quarterly* 45: 684–711.

Altman, M. 1988b. Economic Development with High Wages: An Historical Perspective. *Explorations of Economic History* 25: 198–224.

Altman, M. 1992. The Relative Prosperity of French Canadian and Non-French Canadian Farms in Lower Canada, 1851–1852: A Cross-Sectional Analysis of the 'Backwardness' Hypothesis. Discussion Paper 92-2, Department of Economics, University of Saskatchewan.

Altman, M. 1994. Land Tenure, Ethnicity and the State of Agricultural Income and Productivity in Mid-Nineteenth Century Quebec. Paper presented to the Nineteenth Conference on the Use of Quantitative Methods in Canadian Economic History, Montreal.

Altman, M. 1995. Labour Productivity in Late Nineteenth Century Quebec and Ontario Manufacturing: Explaining Ontario's Advantage. *American Journal of Canadian Studies* 25: 219–249.

Armstrong, R. 1984. The Efficiency of Quebec Farmers in 1851. *Histoire Sociale/Social History* 17: 149–163.

Bailey, L.H., ed. 1912. *Cyclopedia of American Agriculture: A Popular Survey of Agricultural Conditions, Practices and Ideals in the United States and Canada*, vol. 3. London: Macmillan.

Bateman, F. 1968. Improvement in American Dairy Farming, 1850–1910: A Qualitative Analysis. *Journal Economic History* 28: 255–273.

Boserup, E. 1983. The Impact of Scarcity and Plenty on Development. *Journal of Interdisciplinary History* 14: 283–407.

Courville, S. 1980. La crise agricole du Bas-Canada, élements d'une réflexion géographique (deuxieme partie). *Cahiers de Géographie du Québec* 24: 385–428.

Courville, S. 1986. Villages and Agriculture in the Seigneuries of Lower Canada: Conditions of a Comprehensive Study of Rural Quebec in the First Half of the Nineteenth Century. In *Canadian Papers in Rural History*, vol. 5, ed. D.H. Akenson, 121–149. Gananoque, ON: Langdale Press.

Evans, W. 1835. *A Treatise on the Theory and Practice of Agriculture Adopted to the Cultivation and Economy of the Animal and Vegetable Productions of Agriculture in Canada*. Montreal.

Gallman, R.E. 1972. The Statistical Approach, Fundamental Concepts as Applied to History. In *Approaches to American Economic History*, ed. G.R. Taylor and L.F. Ellsworth, 63–86. Charlottesville: University Press of Virginia.

Greer, A. 1985. *Peasant, Lord, and Merchant: Rural Society in Three Quebec Parishes, 1740–1840*. Toronto: University of Toronto Press.

Harris, R.C. 1971. Of Poverty and Helplessness in La Petite-Nation. *Canadian Historical Review* 52: 23–50.

Harris, R.C., and J. Warkentin. 1984. *Canada Before Confederation: A Study in Historical Geography*. Toronto: Oxford University Press.

Innis, H.A. 1940. *The Cod Fisheries: The History of an International Economy*. Toronto: University of Toronto Press.

Jones, R.L. 1942. French Canadian Agriculture in the St. Lawrence Valley, 1815–1850. In *Approaches to Canadian Economic History*, ed. W.T. Easterbrook and M.H. Watkins (reprint 1967). Toronto: McClelland and Stewart.

Jones, R.L. 1946. French Canadian Agriculture, 1792–1815. *Canadian Historical Review* 27: 33–51.

Lemon, J.T. 1976. *The Best Poor Man's Country*. Baltimore: W. W. Norton.

Lewis, F., and M. McInnis. 1980. The Efficiency of the French Canadian Farmer in the Nineteenth Century. *Journal of Economic History* 40: 497–514.

Lewis, F., and M. McInnis. 1984. Agricultural Output and Efficiency in Lower Canada, 1851. *Research in Economic History* 9: 45–87.

Little, J.I. 1985. Agricultural Progress in Canada East/Quebec: Problems in Measuring Relative Productivity during the Grain-Dairy Transition Period. *Histoire Sociale/Social History* 18: 425–431.

Little, J.I. 1989. *Nationalism, Capitalism and Colonization in Nineteenth Century Quebec: The Upper St. Francis District*. Montreal and Kingston: McGill-Queen's University Press.

McCallum, J. 1980. *Unequal Beginnings, Agriculture and Economic Development in Quebec and Ontario Until 1870*. Toronto: University of Toronto Press.

McInnis, M. 1981. Some Pitfalls in the 1851–1852 Census of Agriculture of Lower Canada. *Histoire Sociale/Social History* 14: 219–231.

Ouellet, F. 1971. *Histoire économique et sociale du Québec, 1760–1850*. Montreal: Fides.

Ouellet, F. 1972. *Le Bas Canada, 1791–1840, changements structuraux et crise*. Ottawa: University of Ottawa Press.

Paquet, G., and J.-P. Wallot. 1975. The Agricultural Crisis in Lower Canada. 1802–12: mise au point. A Response to T. J. A. Le Goff. *Canadian Historical Review* 66: 133–161.

Paquet, G., and J.-P. Wallot. 1986. Stratégie foncière de l'habitant: Québec 1790–1835. *Révue d'Histoire de l'Amérique Française* 19: 551–581.

Parker, W.H. 1957. A Revolution of the Agricultural Geography of Lower Canada, 1833–38. *Revue Canadienne de Géographie* 2: 189–194.

Percy, M.B., and R. Szostak. 1992. The Political Economy of the Abolition of Seigneurial Tenure in Canada East. *Explorations in Economic History* 29: 51–68.

Phillips, Paul. 1974. Land Tenure and Economic Development: A Comparison of Upper and Lower Canada. *Journal in Canadian Studies* 9: 35–45.

Reid, S.W. 1947. The Habitant's Standard of Living on the Seigneurie Des Mille Isles, 1820–50. *Canadian Historical Review* 28: 266–278.

Report of the Commissioners Appointed to Inquire into the State of the Laws and Other Circumstances Connected with the Seigniorial Tenure in Lower Canada (1843), Appendix F. Journals of Legislative Assembly of the Province of Canada (Montreal).

Report on the Affairs of British North America from the Earl of Durham with Appendices (1839), document nos. 3, 8, 9, and 10, British Parliament, House of Commons, Reports and Papers, London

Séguin, N. 1977. *La conquête du sol au 19e siècle*. Quebec: Boréal express.

Schultz, T.W. 1983. *Transforming Traditional Agriculture*. Chicago: University of Chicago Press.

Shammas, C. 1982. How Self-Sufficient Was Early America? *Journal of Interdisciplinary History* 8: 247–272.

Tache, J.C. 1855. *Esquise sur le Canada considéré sous le point do vue économiste*. Paris.

Towne, M.W. and W.D. Rasmussen. 1960. Farm Gross Product and Gross Investment in the Nineteenth Century. In Conference on Research in Income and Wealth, *Trends* in *the American Economy in the Nineteenth Century*, Studies in Income and Wealth, vol. 24, ed. William N. Parker. Princeton: Princeton University Press.

Young, B. 1986. *In Its Corporate Capacity: The Seminary of Montreal as a Business Institution, 1816–1876*. Montreal and Kingston: McGill-Queen's University Press.

CHAPTER 6

Economic Development with High Wages: An Historical Perspective

1 Introduction

This paper argues that per capita manufacturing output was greater in Ontario than in Quebec by 1910 and that this differential increased from 1870 to 1910. Furthermore, this paper challenges the view that Ontario's advantage in per capita output was a product of its population growing at a slower pace than Quebec's. This is the now classic interpretation of events put forth by André Raynauld (1961).[1] More generally, I test the hypothesis that a relatively high-wage region should industrialize at a slower pace than a relatively low-wage region. Such a hypothesis is eloquently expressed by Joel Mokyr (1976a, 1976b, 1977). However, it was first given theoretical bearing by Arthur Lewis in his classic "Economic Development with Unlimited Supplies of Labour" (1954).[2] This case study provides some evidence which challenges what I refer to as the high-wage/slow-growth (HWSG) hypothesis.

I find that from 1870 to 1910 income per employee in Ontario manufacturing was significantly greater than in Quebec; yet this did not prevent per capita manufacturing output in Ontario from growing at a faster pace than that in Quebec and, more significant for the HWSG hypothesis, higher income per employee did not prevent manufacturing employment from growing at a faster pace in Ontario. These developments took place in the context of both Quebec and Ontario manufacturing possessing

M. Altman, *Lessons from a Successfully Export-Oriented, Resource-Rich Economy*, https://doi.org/10.1007/978-3-031-03887-7_6

similar capital to labour ratios throughout the period under examination. Ontario's relatively high labour income did not hinder its industrial growth since labour productivity there was consistently greater than in Quebec. Consequently, labour cost per unit of output was similar in both regions over the period 1870–1910. Moreover, the higher labour productivity in Ontario prevented its more highly priced labour from constraining the supply of potential savings and, thereby, potential investment. What my findings suggest, therefore, is that the HWSG hypothesis is not valid for the Quebec/Ontario comparison and that for this hypothesis to be of general validity it must be shown that what I find for Quebec and Ontario is not generally true: that relatively high labour income is associated with relatively high output per employee.

In this sense, the recent cross-country study of cotton textiles in the early twentieth century by Gregory Clark (1987) weakens the general applicability of the HWSG hypothesis. Clark finds that relatively high wages are associated with relatively high levels of labour productivity and vice versa, with the high levels of labour productivity being a product of a greater input of labour effort as opposed to greater doses of capital per unit of labour time. High wages characterized the more developed countries, while low wages characterized the less developed parts of the world. My finding against the HWSG hypothesis is also consistent with Jeffrey Williamson's (1985, pp. 177, 188) recent critique of Arthur Lewis' (1954) labour surplus model. Williamson finds that increasing real wages and an increasing standard of living for English workers coincided with England's spurt of industrialization in the 1820s. He also finds that increasing income inequality away from the labouring classes did not correspond to an increasing investment share of gross domestic product.[3]

It must be noted that although this paper focuses largely on the supply-side aspects of the HWSG hypothesis, a critical demand-side assumption also warrants examination. For the HWSG hypothesis assumes that low wages do not result in any significant demand-side constraints to economic growth.[4] However, with this point in mind, the purpose of this paper is to ascertain whether supply-side components of the HWSG hypothesis can be validated in the Quebec/Ontario comparison since it is only with respect to the supply-side criteria for economic growth that the HWSG hypothesis suggests that an economy benefits from low wages.

2 The High-Wage/Slow-Growth Hypothesis

The HWSG hypothesis assumes that the real wage rate does not affect the marginal product of labour and that different real wage rates in different regions are not associated with different levels of labour productivity which are, in turn, positively related to that region's wage rate. Thus, if the wage rate is at a subsistence level, entrepreneurs have more potential savings than when the wage rate is above the subsistence level. Since the classic HWSG hypothesis assumes that *ex ante* savings and investment are equal, minimizing the real wage rate serves to maximize investment—investment is assumed to be a positive and direct function of savings (Lewis, 1954, pp. 151–152; Mokyr, 1976a, pp. 146–155, 214). Once invested, the savings absorb more labour into the industrial sector given the capital/labour ratio. And, given this ratio, and given technology and efficiency, the growth of industrial employment is directly proportional to the potential savings available to firms per employee: the firms' share in the manufacturing value added per employee. For simplicity it is assumed that all non-labour income is saved.[5]

Should the marginal product of labour not be independent of the wage rate and, indeed, if it is positively related to it, then the HWSG hypothesis loses much of its predictive power. If labour productivity changes in the direction of, and in proportion to, changes in the wage rate, a higher wage rate results in the maintenance of the previous ratio of saving to total output. Moreover, more potential savings per worker are available to firms. Given the capital/labour ratio, this generates a higher rate of employment growth, assuming *ex ante* savings and investments are equal.[6] Thus, if two regions possess different wage rates and these correspond to positively related different levels of labour productivity, the potential growth rate of labour employment is greater in the high-wage region since more potential savings per worker is available to the firms in this region.

The literature on efficiency wage suggests reasons for this positive relationship between wages and labour productivity.[7] Elsewhere, building upon Harvey Leibenstein's pioneering work on "*x*-efficiency" (for example, 1978, 1980) I provide an alternative explanation for the existence for such a causal nexus, one which best explains my findings for Quebec and Ontario (Altman, 1986b). A model is developed which attempts to explain interregional differences in labour productivity as a result of interregional differences in wage rates. Firms in the low-wage region produce below potential (above their production isoquant) and thus "*x*-inefficiently" given the existing capital to labour ratios, firm sizes, and level of labour force education. The low wages, therefore, result in the low-wage firms generating unit labour costs similar to those of the high-wage firms. Ultimately, increasing wages in the low-wage region relative to the high-wage region, with which it competes, forces the low-wage firms to increase their labour productivity, thus reducing *x*-efficiency so as to prevent unit labour costs from rising.[8] A detailed examination of the evidence suggests that the reduction of the labour productivity gap between Quebec and Ontario manufacturing (discussed below), which remained in Ontario's favour, was a result of the reduction of *x*-inefficient production in Quebec. This increasing efficiency of Quebec manufacturing was driven by labour income in Quebec manufacturing rising relative to that in Ontario (Altman, 1986b).

3 The Evidence

My empirical analysis is drawn largely from a reconstruction of the available census material on manufacturing production. The evidence is presented at a general level and is based upon more detailed work found elsewhere on manufacturing output, employment, labour income, fixed and working capital, and output deflators for Quebec and Ontario manufacturing (Altman, 1984, 1986a, 1987).[9] My estimates are presented in both current and constant dollars. I focus on the latter estimates which are constructed with sector specific input and output deflators (Altman, 1986a, 1987). The existing statistical work on Quebec and Ontario economic development indicates that Quebec lagged behind Ontario over the period 1870–1910 in both gross domestic product (GDP) and manufacturing output per capita. And, until now, no systematic attempt has been made to analyze the economic reason(s) for this gap.[10] Raynauld's already mentioned work dealt mainly with the post-1910 period.

Data on GDP for Quebec and Ontario for 1890 and 1910 are available in a study by Alan Green (1971). With some minor adjustments his estimates indicate that Quebec produced 75.7% of the nominal per capita GDP which Ontario generated in 1890 and 70.6% in 1910 (see Table 1). Quebec, in other words, produced \$48 (Canadian) less per capita GDP than Ontario in 1890 and \$101 less in 1910. The per capita GDP gap constituted 32.1% of Quebec's per capita GDP in 1890 and 41.5% in 1910. And the manufacturing sector increasingly contributed to this

Table 1 Gross domestic product and output ggaps

	Quebec				Ontario			
Year	*Agri*	*Mfg*	*Other*	*Total*	*Agri*	*Mfg*	*Other*	*Total*
Panel A: Gross domestic product per capita (current $)								
1890	38.7	41.8	69.1	149.6	63.3	50.4	84.0	197.7
1910	48.6	80.7	113.5	242.8	85.5	107.4	150.8	343.7
Panel B: Percentage of total (from panel A)								
1890	26.0	27.9	46.1	100.0	32.0	25.5	42.5	100.0
1910	20.0	33.3	46.7	100.0	24.9	31.2	43.9	100.0
Panel C: Quebec panel A/Ontario panel A (percentage)								
1890	61.1	82.9	82.3	75.7				
1910	56.8	75.1	75.3	70.6				
Panel D: Output gaps (Quebec panel A)–(Ontario panel A); current $								
1890	−25	−8.6	−14.9	−48.1				
1910	−37	−27	−37.3	−101				
Panel E: Sectoral output gaps as a % of the total (from panel D)								
1890	51.1	17.9	31.0	100.0				
1910	36.5	26.5	37.0	100.0				

Source Except for agricultural (Table 12, below) and manufacturing output data (Table 2, below) all value added estimates are from Green (1971, Appendix B). These estimates are divided by the census population estimates presented in Table 3, below

GDP gap. Quebec produced $9 less manufacturing output per capita than Ontario in 1890 and $27 less in 1910. This constituted 18 and 26% of the per capita GDP gap in 1890 and 1910, respectively. The agricultural sector contributed 51% to this gap in 1890 and only 37% in 1910. Since the manufacturing sector was of similar and increasing importance to both Quebec's and Ontario's per capita GDP, by focusing on this sector one gains important insights into the evolution of both provinces' per capita GDP as well as improving upon ones' understanding of their industrial development.

Quebec fell increasingly behind Ontario with respect to both constant and current dollars per capita manufacturing output—I use value added as my measure of output—from 1870, when the per capita manufacturing output gap was $6 in constant dollars. In 1880 this gap rose to $8.5, jumping to $10.6 in 1890, and to $31 by 1910. This gap represented 15.0, 19.5, 19.4, and 35.7% of Quebec's real per capita manufacturing output in 1870, 1880, 1890, and 1910, respectively. Also, the ratio of Quebec's to Ontario's real per capita manufacturing output fell from 0.87

Table 2 Constant dollar manufacturing value added

Year	*Quebec*	*Ontario*	*Quebec/Ontario (percentage)*
Panel A: Total manufacturing value added ($000)			
1870	47,515	74,348	
1880	59,164	100,308	
1890	81,221	137,857	
1910	164,130	285,153	
Panel B: Manufacturing value added per capita			
1870	39.86	45.86	86.9
1880	43.53	52.05	83.6
1890	54.56	65.20	83.7
1910	81.83	112.84	72.5
Panel C: Output gaps (Quebec panel B)–(Ontario panel B); current $			
1870	−6.0		
1880	−8.5		
1890	−10.6		
1910	−31.0		
Panel D: Output gap as a % of Quebec manufacturing value added per capita			
1870	15.0		
1880	19.5		
1890	19.4		
1910	35.7		

Source See Altman (1986a, Table Al) on the total value added estimates. These are divided by the census population estimates presented in Table 3, below. Refer also to the Appendix, below

in 1870 to 0.72 in 1910, with the most significant decline in this ratio commencing in 1890 (Table 2). The scenario is similar for the current dollar estimates.[11]

The deterioration in Quebec's position relative to Ontario's can be directly related to the interprovincial differentials in the growth of per capita manufacturing output which can, in turn, be broken down into interprovincial differentials in the growth of manufacturing value added and population:

$$\hat{y}_Q - \hat{y}_O = (\hat{Y}_Q - \hat{Y}_O) - (\hat{P}_Q - \hat{P}_O) \tag{1}$$

where $\hat{y}$ is the annual growth rate of per capita output; $\hat{Y}$ is the annual growth rate of output; $\hat{P}$ is the annual growth rate of the population; and the subscripts Q and O represent Quebec and Ontario.

Table 3 Value added and population annual growth rates

Period	*Quebec*	*Ontario*
Panel A: Total constant dollar manufacturing value added growth		
1870–1880	2.22	3.04
1880–1890	3.22	3.23
1890–1910	3.58	3.70
1870–1910	3.14	3.42
Panel B: Per capita constant dollar manufacturing value added growth		
1870–1880	0.88	1.27
1880–1890	2.28	2.28
1890–1910	2.05	2.78
1870–1910	1.80	2.28
Panel C: Population growth		
1870–1880	1.32	1.74
1880–1890	0.92	0.93
1890–1910	1.50	0.90
1870–1910	1.31	1.11

Source For panels A and B see Table 2. The population growth rates are derived from the census population estimates for 1870, 1880, 1890, and 1910 for Quebec of 1,191,516; 1,359,027; 1,488,535; and 2,005,776, respectively, and for Ontario of 1,620,851; 1,926,922; 2,114,321; and 2,527,291, respectively. See *The Census of Canada, 1930–1931* (1932, Vol.1, Table 17a)

The per capita growth rate of real manufacturing output was greater in Ontario in all periods examined except for the 1880s when both provinces experienced a growth rate of 2.28% per annum. From 1870 to 1910 the annual growth rate in Quebec was 1.8% compared to 2.28% in Ontario. In the 1870s the growth rates were 0.88 and 1.27%, respectively, while in the period 1890–1910 the growth rates were 2.05 and 2.78%, respectively. Ontario experienced these higher rates of growth even when its population grew at a faster pace than Quebec's. In the 1870s Ontario's population increased at a rate of 1.74% per annum compared to a growth rate of 1.32% in Quebec. In the following decade these provinces' population growth rates were similar at about 1.9%. Only from 1890 to 1910 did Quebec's population rise at a faster pace than Ontario's: 1.5 compared to only 0.90% (Table 3).

In the first period examined Ontario's higher population growth rate was accompanied by a significantly higher growth rate in real output than that experienced in Quebec: 3.04 compared to 2.22%. In the 1880s both provinces' similar population growth rates were accompanied by a similar growth rate in total real output of about 3.2%. And, in the period 1890–1910, Quebec's output growth rate was marginally less than Ontario's: 3.6 and 3.7%, respectively, even though Quebec's population growth rate was so much higher than Ontario's. In contrast, no matter how high Ontario's rate of population growth was, it's output growth rate was consistently high enough to generate greater growth rates of per capita output than those experienced in Quebec (Table 3).

The interprovincial differentials in the growth rates of output can be further broken down into interprovincial differentials in labour productivity and manufacturing employment growth rates

$$\hat{Y}_Q - \hat{Y}_O = \left[(Y/L^\rho)_Q - (Y/L^\rho)_O \right] + \left[L^\rho_Q - L^\rho_O \right] \quad (2)$$

where the new symbols are (Y/L^ρ), the rate of growth of manufacturing output per employee in manufacturing and L^ρ, the rate of growth in manufacturing employment. Constant dollar labour productivity growth in Quebec marginally exceeded that in Ontario from 1870 to 1910: 0.88 compared to 0.82%. But in the 1870s the growth rates were −0.39 and 0.11% in Quebec and Ontario, respectively. In the following decade the growth rates were 0.18 and −0.01%, respectively. Finally, in the period 1890–1910 the growth rate of labour productivity in Quebec was 1.89 compared to 1.76% in Ontario (Table 5).

In terms of my current dollar estimates of labour productivity, Quebec's advantage in labour productivity growth is much more evident.[12] In contrast to labour productivity growth in manufacturing, Ontario held a clear advantage over Quebec in the growth of manufacturing employment from 1870 to 1910: 2.57 compared to 2.24%. In the 1870s the annual growth rates were 3.16 and 2.61%, respectively, and, 3.32 and 3.04%, respectively from 1880 to 1890. In the period 1890–1910 the growth rates for manufacturing employment were 1.90% in Ontario and 1.65% in Quebec (Table 5).

Ontario's advantage in employment growth resulted in its constant dollar output growing at a faster pace than Quebec's over the period 1870–1910. If Quebec had been characterized by the same higher rate of employment growth, its manufacturing output growth rate would have just exceeded Ontario's in this period: 3.45 compared to 3.42% (Table 6).[13] The hypothetical growth estimate assumes that Quebec's actual real manufacturing value added per employee growth remains unchanged.

Table 4
Manufacturing income and value added per employee

Year	*Quebec*	*Ontario*	*Quebec/Ontario*
Panel A: Constant dollar income per employee			
1870	262	342	0.766
1880	296	360	0.822
1890	320	375	0.853
1910	482	528	0.913
Panel B: Current dollar income per employee			
1870	183	242	0.756
1880	213	258	0.825
1890	257	297	0.865
1910	443	487	0.910
Panel C: Constant dollar value added per employee			
1870	753	883	0.853
1880	724	873	0.827
1890	737	865	0.852
1910	1,072	1,227	0.874
Panel D: Current dollar value added per employee			
1870	492	573	0.858
1880	499	565	0.883
1890	569	671	0.848
1910	1,058	1,168	0.907
Panel E: Manufacturing employment			
1870	63,111	84,220	
1880	81,702	114,952	
1890	110,228	159,296	
1910	153,033	232,345	

Source For the value added and employee income estimates see Altman (1986a), Tables Al through A3. The manufacturing employment estimates are derived from the censuses. See the Appendix of this paper for further details

This presumes that the actual trend capital to labour ratio in Quebec manufacturing remained unchanged as well and that adequate savings existed in Quebec for the additional capital stock to be generated. This is a reasonable assumption given the small size of the manufacturing sector in the Quebec economy.[14] Also assumed are constant returns to scale and, therefore, a Cobb-Douglas-type production function. Keeping these assumptions in mind, the economic significance of this counterfactual proposition can be evaluated by estimating Quebec's hypothetical constant dollar manufacturing output for 1880, 1890, and 1910 (see Table 7.6 for details).

Table 5 Manufacturing income and value added per employee: Annual growth rates

Period	*Quebec*	*Ontario*
Panel A: Constant Dollar Income Per Employee Growth		
1870–1880	1.23	0.51
1880–1890	0.78	0.41
1890–1910	2.06	1.72
1870–1910	1.53	1.09
Panel B: Current dollar income per employee growth		
1870–1880	1.53	0.64
1880–1890	1.89	1.42
1890–1910	2.76	2.50
1870–1910	2.23	1.76
Panel C: Constant dollar value added per employee growth		
1870–1880	−0.39	−0.11
1880–1890	0.18	−0.01
1890–1910	1.89	1.76
1870–1910	0.88	0.82
Panel D: Current dollar value added per employee growth		
1870–1880	0.14	−0.14
1880–1890	1.25	1.73
1890–1910	3.20	2.81
1870–1910	1.94	1.80
Panel E: Manufacturing employment growth		
1870–1880	2.61	3.16
1880–1890	3.04	3.32
1890–1910	1.65	1.90
1870–1910	2.24	2.57

Source Table 4

These hypothetical output estimates generate hypothetical per capita output estimates for Quebec. The ratio of these to Ontario's corresponding actual per capita output estimates are: 0.88 in 1880, 0.91 in 1890, and 0.82 in 1910 compared to 0.84, 0.84, and 0.72, respectively, when Quebec's actual per capita output estimates are used in the calculation (Tables 2 and 6). The hypothetical per capita output estimates also generate much smaller per capita output gaps (the interprovincial differences in per capita output) for these years than do the actual values. The hypothetical per capita output gap for 1880 constitutes only 13.2% of Quebec's hypothetical per capita output compared to the 19.5% derived

Table 6 Hypothetical constant dollar value added estimates

Panel A: Total value added annual growth rates				
Period	Quebec (hyp.)	Quebec (actual)	Ontario (actual)	
1870–1880	2.77	2.22	3.04	
1880–1890	3.50	3.22	3.23	
1890–1910	3.79	3.58	3.70	
1870–1910	3.45	3.14	3.42	
Panel B: Manufacturing value added				
	1	2	3	4
Year	Quebec hyp. total value added ($000)	Quebec hyp. per capita value added	Ontario acutal per capita value added	(2/3)
1880	62,444	$45.9	$52.0	0.883
1890	88,083	$59.2	$65.2	0.908
1910	185,354	$92.4	$112.8	0.819
Panel C: Hypothetical per capita manufacturing value added gap				
	1	2		
	Quebec hyp. value added gap	(1)/Quebec hyp. per capita value added		
1880	−6.1	0.132		
1890	−6.0	0.101		
1910	−20.4	0.221		

Notes The hypothetical growth rate is derived by adding the actual employment growth rate in Ontario to the actual Constant dollar value added per employee growth rate in Quebec. In panel B, column 1 is derived by applying the hypothetical 1870–1880 total value added growth rate to Quebec's actual total constant dollar value added estimate for 1870. The hypothetical total value added growth rates for the 1880–1890 and 1890–1910 periods are applied to the hypothetical total constant dollar value added estimates for 1880 and 1890, respectively, generating the 1880, 1890, and 1910 hypothetical total constant dollar value added estimates. Column 2 is derived by dividing the total hypothetical value added estimates by the census estimates for Quebec's population. Finally, in panel C, column 1 is derived by subtracting column 2 from column 3 in panel B
Source Tables 2, 3, and 5

from the actual output figures. The corresponding estimates for 1890 are 10.1 compared to 19.4% and, finally, 22.1 compared to 35.7% in 1910 (Tables 2 and 6). Thus, if firms in Quebec had increased their labour employment in pace with firms in Ontario, Quebec's manufacturing sector would not have fallen behind Ontario's as dramatically as it actually did. And, if Quebec's manufacturing employment growth had exceeded Ontario's, Quebec's manufacturing sector need not have fallen behind Ontario's at all. However, if one accepts Ontario's employment growth rate as the maximum obtainable—although it should be more realistically considered as only a lower bound maximum—some relative fall of Quebec's manufacturing sector was inevitable given Quebec's more rapid population growth rate from 1890 to 1910.[15]

Quebec's rapid population growth coincided with a population age structure which differed significantly from Ontario's from at least 1880. Although a larger proportion of Quebec's population was becoming active (between 15 and 65 years of age), this proportion diminished relative to that in Ontario. This resulted in a relatively larger percentage of Quebec's population becoming peripheral to the labour market. From 1870 to 1880 Quebec's active population rose from 52.1 to 55.9% of the total. And in comparison, this percentage increased from 52.6 to 58.2% in Ontario. By 1910, Quebec's active population constituted 57.1% of the total whereas, in Ontario, it comprised 65.1% of the total population (Table 7). If, however, the same percentage of population had been active in Quebec as in Ontario, there would have been fewer dependents in Quebec—basically fewer children—and, correspondingly a smaller population and rate of population growth (Table 8). This would have generated a greater per capita manufacturing output in Quebec. Combined with the hypothetical output estimates, the more favourable age structure in Quebec yields a per capita manufacturing output in Quebec which is 88% of Ontario's in 1870, 92.0% in 1880, 99.0% in 1890, and 93% by 1910 (Table 7.8). Still, the key economic variable responsible for Quebec's laggard manufacturing performance was Quebec's relatively slow rate of manufacturing employment growth.

Table 7 Population age structure

Year	*Active population*		
	Ages 1–14	*Ages 65–100*	*Ages 15–64*
Quebec			
1870	44.2	3.7	52.1
1880	39.9	4.2	55.9
1890	39.5	4.5	56.0
1910	38.4	4.5	57.1
Ontario			
1870	44.4	3.0	52.6
1880	37.9	3.9	58.2
1890	34.5	4.5	61.0
1910	29.3	5.6	65.1

Source From *The Census of Canada, 1930–1931* (1932, Vol. 1, Table 17a)

Table 8 Hypothetical population and related

Year	1 Quebec hyp. Population (000)	2 Quebec hyp. Constant dollar value added per capita (hyp. population)	3 (2)/Ontario actual constant dollar value added per capita
1870	1178	40.3	0.879
1880	1304	47.9	0.920
1890	1368	64.4	0.988
1910	1757	105.5	0.935

Period	4 Quebec hyp. Population annual growth rates	5 Quebec actual population annual growth rates
1870–1880	1.02	1.32
1880–1890	0.48	0.92
1890–1910	1.26	1.50
1870–1910	1.00	1.31

Source Column 1 is derived by dividing Quebec's active population (Tables 3 and 7) by the percentage of the total population in Ontario which is active (Table 7). This generates a hypothetical population for Quebec with the same active/inactive population ratio as in Ontario. Column 2 is derived by dividing Quebec's actual constant dollar total value added estimate for 1870 (Table 2) and Quebec's hypothetical constant dollar total value added estimates for 1880, 1890, and 1910 (Table 6) by Quebec's hypothetical population estimates (this table)

Critical to the HWSG hypothesis is the context in which Ontario's superior rate of manufacturing employment growth took place. The available data suffice only to compute the income per employee in manufacturing which then becomes my proxy for wages per hour of work. For each of the relevant census years real income per employee was significantly lower in Quebec although the ratio of Quebec to Ontario income per employee increased over the period 1870–1910, a result of Quebec's income per employee growing at a faster pace than Ontario's.[16] This ratio rose from 0.77 in 1870 to 0.82 in 1880, and, to 0.85 in 1890, rising finally, to 0.91 in 1910 (Table 4). Thus, Quebec's manufacturing employment was growing at a slower pace than was Ontario's despite Quebec's clear, although diminishing, advantage in the immediate cost of labour.

As mentioned, labour productivity, as measured by output per employee, rose at a faster pace in Quebec than in Ontario. Nevertheless, labour productivity in Ontario was higher than in Quebec in the 4 census years examined in this paper. The ratio of Quebec to Ontario real manufacturing output per employee was 0.85 in 1870, 0.83 in 1880, 0.85 in 1890, and 0.87 in 1910 (Table 7.4). Ontario's advantage in labour productivity more or less neutralized its disadvantages in income per employee. This can be seen through my estimates of labour cost per unit of output (income per employee divided by output per employee). In 1870 the unit labour cost in Quebec was $0.35 and, in Ontario, $0.39. This cost rose to $0.41 in both provinces by 1880. By 1890 the unit labour cost increased to $0.44 in Quebec and to $0.43 in Ontario. By 1910 the unit labour cost was $0.45 in Quebec and $0.43 in Ontario (Table 9). It is evident that Quebec held no actual advantage in terms of "cheap labour"—except for in 1870. And Ontario's high labour income did not generate "high cost" labour inputs.[17]

Low wages are critical to the process of industrial development in the HWSG hypothesis. For low wages result in more potential savings per employee being made available to the firms (the firms' share of the manufacturing value added) and, thereby, allow for a higher rate of growth in manufacturing employment given the capital to labour ratio. However, it

Table 9 The efficiency wage and potential firm savings

Year	Quebec	Ontario	Quebec/Ontario	(1)–(2)
Panel A: Manufacturing per unit labor cost: The "efficiency wage"				
1870	$0.35	$0.39	0.897	
1880	0.41	0.41	1.000	
1890	0.44	0.43	1.023	
1910	0.45	0.43	1.046	
	1	2	3	4
Panel B: Potential constant dollar savings available to firms in manufacturing per employee				
1870	$491	$541	0.907	−$50
1880	428	513	0.834	−85
1890	417	490	0.851	−73
1910	590	699	0.844	−109

Notes and Source The ":efficiency wage" is derived by dividing constant dollar labour income per employee by constant dollar value added per employee (Table 4). The savings per employee estimates are derived by subtracting the income per employee estimates from the value added per employee estimates (Table 4)

is clear from Table 7.9 that constant dollar potential savings per manufacturing employee available to firms in Ontario exceeded that in Quebec for all years examined. In 1870 the firms' share of the manufacturing value added per worker in Quebec was 91% of Ontario's. In 1880, it was 83% of Ontario's, 85% in 1890, and 84% in 1910. The gap between potential savings per employee available to firms in Quebec and Ontario rose from $50 in 1870 to $109 in 1910. Potential savings per employee available to the firm are computed by subtracting my estimates of income per employee from my estimates of value added per employee. The lower cost of labour in Quebec did not result in more potential savings per employee being made available to firms in Quebec as compared to firms in Ontario, given the more productive labour inputs in Ontario. More productive labour coinciding with higher wage rates makes the requisite of cheap labour unnecessary for industrial development. Potentially, at least, the greater potential savings per worker available to firms in Ontario allowed for the growth of manufacturing employment in this high-wage region to be greater than in Quebec for the entire period 1870–1910 (given that both provinces possessed a similar capital/labour ratio).[18]

Since no adequate deflators for fixed capital are readily available, only nominal capital/labour ratios are computed (Table 10). The

Table 10 Current dollar fixed capital per employee estimates in manufacturing

Year	*Quebec*	*Ontario*	*Quebec/Ontario*
1870	209	221	0.946
1880	337	306	1.101
1890	510	485	1.051
1910	978	1006	0.972

Source These estimates were constructed from data in the censuses. Detailed estimates are found in Altman (1984), Vol. 2, Appendix C. As defined in the censuses fixed capital includes the value of buildings, land, machinery, tools, implements, and motive power. Only the 1890, 1900, 1906, and 1910 censuses provide information on the value of fixed capital. The 1870 and 1880 censuses provide data on the value of all capital employed, inclusive of working capital. One can estimate the value of fixed capital for 1870 and 1880 by multiplying the ratio of fixed to total capital in 1890 by the value of total capital in 1870 and 1880. The assumption of a constant ratio of fixed to total capital from 1870 to 1890 appears plausible given that this ratio changed only marginally from 1890 to 1910. For a further discussion see Altman (1984), Vol. 2, pp. 50–51

capital/labour ratios in Quebec and Ontario were similar for all years examined, with Ontario's exceeding Quebec's in 1870 and 1910 by 6 and 3%, respectively, and, Quebec's exceeding Ontario's in 1880 and 1890 by 9 and 5%, respectively. Since both Quebec and Ontario were characterized by relatively greater capital/labour ratios in the different census years both regions faced relative disadvantages with respect to generating a given rate of manufacturing employment growth. A higher capital to labour ratio demands more savings per worker to sustain a given rate of employment growth. Yet, Ontario was able to overcome this constraint, generating systematically high employment growth rates in the manufacturing sector, and thus taking advantage of the relatively greater pool of potential savings per employee available to its firms.

The similar capital to labour ratios in both provinces and the smaller pool of potential savings per employee available to firms in the manufacturing sector in Quebec compared to Ontario is evidence against a derivative of the HWSG hypothesis. Such a derivative argues that a lesser rate of manufacturing employment growth was achieved in Quebec due to a trend increase in its manufacturing capital to labour ratio, made possible by its relatively cheap labour which should have yielded additional potential savings per worker. Employment growth would then be sacrificed for higher productivity growth which would be driven by the relative trend increase in the capital to labour ratio. But, of course, the cheap labour in Quebec did not generate the additional savings, due to the relatively low labour productivity of these workers. And, although manufacturing labour productivity in Quebec relative to Ontario did in fact increase as we have shown; this was not driven by a trend increase in Quebec's manufacturing capital to labour ratio relative to Ontario's. In fact, when this ratio increased in Quebec's favour, Quebec's manufacturing labour productivity fell relative to Ontario's and vice versa (Tables 4 and 10). As already argued, the closing of the Quebec/Ontario labour productivity gap was due to other factors, notably the reduction in x-inefficient production in Quebec (Altman, 1986b).

Quebec's relatively poor growth performance must also be placed in the context of its relatively impoverished agricultural sector. I estimate the current dollar value of output per farm net of farm expenses from the censuses and data presented by M. C. Urquhart (1985). Although my estimates are very rough and are only simple averages, they indicate that the farms in Quebec were considerably worse off than their Ontario counterparts.[19] These estimates also suggest that the relative position of the Quebec farm deteriorated from 1870 to 1910 (Table 11). The 1870 ratio of net farm output in Quebec relative to that in Ontario was 0.73, dropping to 0.59 in 1880. But this ratio jumped to 0.80 in 1890 due to a sharp fall in net farm output in both provinces which struck Ontario more severely.[20] Quebec's situation appears even less favourable once the likely possibility that the average farm family in Quebec was larger than that in Ontario is taken into consideration.[21] Since net farm output is what remains to the farm family for consumption, savings, and/or investment, my findings suggest that Quebec farms had a considerably smaller reserve of potential savings to make available to industry than did farms in Ontario. Apart from this, Quebec farms could only sustain a demand for a smaller array and amount of commodities than could farms in Ontario. This might have resulted in demand-side blockages to manufacturing investment by reducing the market opportunities in Quebec relative to Ontario, adding to Quebec's supply-side problems.[22]

The fact that the net output per farm was much lower in Quebec also suggests that the opportunity cost of engaging in nonagrarian pursuits to an individual in Quebec was much lower than to an individual in Ontario. This low-opportunity cost constituted just one more economic pressure keeping manufacturing income per employee in Quebec lower than that in Ontario. Obviously such economic pressure was becoming increasingly inoperative as one approached 1910 since the income per employee in Quebec was in the process of catching-up to its Ontario counterpart. Further research is required to determine other possible causes for the low labour income in Quebec, among which might be the role played by the Catholic Church in pacifying labour.[23]

The massive emigration of French Canadians to the United States which took place from 1860 to 1910 is probably one reason why labour income in Quebec's manufacturing sector was rising relative to that in Ontario. There was also some emigration to other parts of Canada. Emigration per decade to the United States amounted to over 10% of the population in Quebec in 1870, 1880, and 1890, while emigration from 1900 to 1910 constituted about 4% of Quebec's 1910 population. These percentages increase only slightly when one includes net emigration to other parts of Canada in the calculation.[24] Thus, this flood of emigrants probably resulted in the opportunity cost of industrial employment in Quebec to increasingly include the cost of foregoing the perceived employment opportunities existing in the United States

Table 11 Current dollar agricultural output

		Quebec				*Ontario*			*Quebec/Ontario*
	1	*2*	*3*	*4*	*5*	*6*	*7*	*8*	*9*
Year	*No. of farms (000)*	*Gross output ($000)*	*Net output ($000)*	*(3/1)*	*No. of farms (000)*	*Gross output ($000)*	*Net output ($000)*	*(7/5)*	*(4/8)*
1870	118.0	47,547	37,657	319	172.1	94,466	74,817	435	0.73
1880	138.2	57,754	44,933	325	207.0	147,615	114,844	555	0.59
1890	203.1	67,362	57,577	283	378.5	177,526	133,855	354	0.80
1900	129.9	86,404	64,284	495	185.1	221,514	164,806	890	0.56
1910	160.0	133,337	97,469	609	227.1	296,594	216,810	955	0.64

Source The number of farms is estimated from the census data on the number of farm owners and tenants. For the first 3 census years, census data are available on output only. The value estimates for these years are estimated using the price data in Altman (1984), Vol. 2, Appendix A and the price series in Coats (1910) for the 1890–1909 period which are projected backward using my commodity price indexes (Altman (1984), Vol. 2, Appendix A). The value of field crops for the first three census years, however, are from the *Monthly Bulletin of Agricultural Statistics* (1921). For 1900 and 1910 the value estimates are taken from the censuses. This generates gross value estimates. Net value estimates are derived using Urquhart's (1985), pp. 35–41 estimates for farm expenses and the value of gross farm output in Canada. From this, I estimate that the former as a percentage of the latter was 20.8% in 1870, 22.2% in 1880, 24.6% in 1890, 25.6% in 1900 and 26.9% by 1910. These percentages are applied to my estimates of the value of Quebec and Ontario gross agricultural output to derive my net agricultural value estimates. For more details see Altman (1984), Vol. 1, pp. 143–144

Table 12 Family size and current dollar income estimates for families engaged in manufacturing

	Quebec			*Ontario*			*Quebec/Ontario*	
	1	*2*	*3*	*4*	*5*	*6*	*7*	*8*
Year	*Family size*	*Income per family*	*Income per family member*	*Family size*	*Income per family*	*Income per family member*	*(2/5)*	*(3/6)*
1870	6.4	434	67.8	6.4	539	84.2	80.5	80.5
1880	6.2	512	82.6	6.2	609	98.2	84.0	84.0
1890	6.1	620	101.6	6.0	766	127.7	80.9	79.6
1910	5.9	1023	173.4	5.2	1140	219.2	89.7	79.1

Source Upper-bound estimates of family size are derived by dividing the census estimate for the total population by the census estimate for the number of married males. Thus, those individuals who are single and outside of the family unit are included in my estimate of family size. Estimates of income per family are derived from census data on the age distribution of employees given for all relevant census years and the census data given only for 1910 on the relative earnings of employees in different age groups. The 1910 data are applied to the earlier census years. For further details refer to Altman (1984), Vol. 1, pp. 135–144

and other parts of Canada. And this, no doubt, put some upward pressure on labour income in Quebec. Clearly one cannot attribute the relative rise of labour income in Quebec's manufacturing sector to the demand for manufacturing labour in Quebec rising to a greater extent than in Ontario; which is what the HWSG hypothesis suggests should have occurred. For in the Quebec/ Ontario comparison, low income in Quebec relative to Ontario did not generate a relatively higher rate of labour employment growth in Quebec. Indeed, manufacturing labour income in Quebec rose relative to Ontario's despite labour employment growth in Quebec manufacturing being consistently less than in relatively high income Ontario for the entire 1870 to 1910 period (Table 5).

4 Conclusion

Relatively high labour income in its manufacturing sector did not prevent Ontario from increasing its lead over Quebec with respect to manufacturing output per capita and the growth of manufacturing employment. Indeed, the higher labour income in Ontario is found to be consistent with higher savings per employee which in turn created opportunities on the supply-side for generating high manufacturing growth in Ontario as compared to Quebec. As was the case in Ontario, relatively high manufacturing labour income does not pose a supply-side problem when accompanied by relatively high labour productivity. Thus the HWSG hypothesis is not valid for the Ontario/Quebec comparison.

The argument presented here has important welfare implications. Apart from Ontario's relatively higher average farm incomes, Ontario was characterized by a relatively high average income per family engaged in manufacturing; a direct result of the higher incomes earned by its workers compared to those in Quebec (Table 12). Income per family member in Quebec was consistently about 80% of that in Ontario. At least in the Quebec and Ontario comparison, relative poverty was not the handmaiden of relative success in manufacturing growth. And, of course, relative poverty was not a necessary supply-side condition for such success. From the demand-side, it can be argued, as I do elsewhere, that the higher incomes in Ontario contributed to its relatively strong growth performance by facilitating the purchase of a greater variety and a greater quantity of manufacturing commodities thereby increasing the incentive to entrepreneurs to invest (Altman, 1984, Vol. 1, Chap. 5).

Appendix

Only 4 census years are used in this study (Census of Canada, 1875; Census of Canada, 1883; Census of Canada, 1894; Census of Canada, 1913; Census of Canada, 1932; see also, Dominion Bureau of Statistics, 1948). The 1900 census is excluded as it covers only firms engaging five workers or more. No data exist to adjust the provincial estimates for this deficiency unless one assumes that both Quebec and Ontario were characterized by the same percentage of output being produced by firms with five or more workers, an untenable assumption in a study dealing with differences in interprovincial manufacturing development. The 4 census years used in this study are located in cycle-peaks and thus allow for the census estimates to be used as indicative of time trends (Bertram, 1964, pp. 129–136). I exclude from estimates census data on gas lighting and heating, carpenters and joiners, painters and glaziers, photo galleries, dentistry, plumbers and gasfitters, electric light and power, and house building since these were not included in the Dominion Bureau of Statistics' *Standard Industrial Classification Manual's* (1948) manufacturing classification. Also, I do not adjust upward the 1910 estimates although they do not encompass all firms with less than five workers. All told, the 1910 estimates for Canada embody 97.3% of the estimated "actual" value added (Altman, 1984, Vol. 1, p. 53), and, probably a similar proportion of Quebec and Ontario output. No data exist to make adjustments on a provincial basis. Thus my growth rates which include the 1910 data are marginally underestimated. The nominal value added estimates in this paper are derived by subtracting from the gross output estimates found in the censuses estimates for nonlabour inputs. These are constructed by taking the census estimates for the cost of raw materials and adding to these the estimated cost of fuel, lighting, power, and heating. The census provides data on these costs for 1900 only. I assume that these costs constituted the same proportion of the value of gross output for all relevant census years as in 1900 so as to derive estimates for the value of fuel, lighting, power, and heating for 1870, 1880, 1890, and 1910. These costs were negligible, amounting to only 1.4% of the value of gross output in both Quebec and Ontario. It should be noted that my output estimates are upper-bound, as they incorporate miscellaneous expenses which consist mainly of rent of works and office (Urquhart, 1986b, p. 83).

Data are available to estimate these expenses for 1900 on a provincial basis—a problematic census year particularly for interprovincial comparisons. Moreover, the 1900 census data provides information on explicit rents alone. No data are available for implicit rents. Thus, if one uses the census data to estimate miscellaneous expenses for Quebec and Ontario one runs the risk of biasing downward the value added in that province where, during 1900, there was a predisposition to rent as opposed to own one's facilities. I find that explicit rents constitute about 5% of Quebec's 1900 gross manufacturing output and only less than 3% of Ontario's. Given the available data, incorporating miscellaneous expenses in my estimates would bias downward Quebec's value added *relative* to Ontario's. Urquhart (1986b, pp. 83, 84; 1986c) uses the available census material to estimate the value of miscellaneous expenses for Canada as a whole from 1870 to 1910. If one applies Urquhart's estimate of miscellaneous expenses to gross output ratio to Quebec and Ontario, my real value added estimates would be reduced by 10.6, 11.3, 14.5, and 16.8% in Quebec and by 6.5, 6.4, 7.5, and 15.8% in Ontario for the 1870, 1880, 1890, and 1910 census years, respectively.[25] These lower-bound estimates are, of course, tentative since they are based upon the Canadian totals and are also exclusive of implicit rents.

My constant dollar estimates for manufacturing value added are constructed by deflating the current dollar gross output and input estimates on a sectoral basis using appropriate sectoral gross output and input deflators detailed in Altman (1987), for each of the 17 manufacturing sectors into which my provincial output and input estimates are categorized. The sectoral price index numbers used are identical for Quebec and Ontario. The constant dollar estimates for inputs are then subtracted from the constant dollar estimates for gross output. See Altman (1986a, Table Al) for further details. One should note that since each sector represents a different percentage of total manufacturing output and input in Quebec and Ontario for each census year examined, the general price index numbers for manufacturing output for Quebec and Ontario, which are the weighted average of the sector-specific price index numbers, need not be the same despite using the same sector-specific deflators for both provinces. And there are negligible differences in Quebec's and Ontario's general price index numbers for each of the census years examined. These general index numbers can be derived by dividing panel D of Table 4 by panel C.

The current dollar estimates for labour income are drawn from the census data on salaries and wages. The constant dollar value of labour income are derived by deflating the current dollar values, sectorally, by the appropriate sectoral gross output deflators detailed in Altman (1987). This yields estimates of real labour income in terms of the cost of labour to the firm with respect to the real output produced by labour. See Altman (1986a, Table A2) for further details.

Notes

1. Raynauld (1961, pp. 29, 43–48, 55–57) finds that the annual growth rate for the current dollar gross output in the manufacturing, mining, and agricultural sectors in Quebec and Ontario was similar from the 1870s to the 1950s. Quebec's higher population growth rate however, resulted in the interprovincial disparity in per capita output. In contrast to Raynauld's output estimates, those presented in this paper are in terms of real value added to minimize any possible double counting.
2. Lewis (1954, pp. 172–173, 175; 1958, pp. 19–20) argues that an increase in the wage rate in the industrial sector, ceteris paribus, causes a decline in the rate of industrial growth. Even with technological change resulting in

an increase in output per worker, any increases in the wage rate reduces the rate of growth from what it would otherwise be. Mokyr (1976a, pp. 165–166; 1976b, pp. 392–393) makes a similar argument for a two region comparison.

3. See also Kelley el al. (1972, pp. 171–172), who suggest that real wages rose dramatically in Japan's early period of vigorous economic growth. And refer to Fei and Ranis (1975, p. 46) who find that real wages in industry increased during both Taiwan's and Korea's process of industrial development. The note by Ranis (1977–1978, pp. 55–56) is also relevant to the discussion.
4. This is implicit in Lewis (1954, pp. 153–155) and explicit in Mokyr (1976a, pp. 136, 155, 148, 214–215). However, Fei and Ranis (1964, pp. 114–118) argue in their presentation of a Lewis-type model of economic development, that low wages and low agricultural incomes are compatible with industrial development if these low incomes are supplemented by exogenous demand such as government spending. This would create demand-side incentives for investment of potential savings. Gerschenkron (1966, pp. 19, 79, 123, 126) argues along similar lines when analyzing Russian economic development in the late nineteenth century. It is important to note that Mokyr (1976a), in his study of the Low Countries, presents evidence which suggests that economic development with low wages might face severe demand-side problems if foreign markets and/or government demand are not readily forthcoming. Low-wage Belgium's main market for linen was Spain (p. 15). Most wool and nails were exported (pp. 19–20). Output of cottage industries were also largely exported (p. 22). Napoleon's continental system created a market for Belgium's cotton industry while the loss of this market created a crisis for this industry (p. 31). This market, however, was replaced by another market in the Dutch East Indies, with the temporary economic union of Holland and Belgium. The break-up of this union generated another crisis in Belgium's cotton industry (p. 32). Then, in the 1830s and 1840s, demand was created by government-induced railroad construction (p. 35), although foreign markets remained dominant (p. 78). It is important to note that the assumption made by Lewis and Mokyr that low industrial wages and even low agricultural incomes do not result in demand-side constraints to rapid industrial growth has been critically scrutinized, at a general level, in other contexts by Fishlow (1973), Gilboy (1932, 1934), and Myrdal (1957). Mokyr (1977) is, in part, a response to Gilboy's type of argument. For an interesting account of how low wages can

constrain industrial investment see Brenner (1979, pp. 5–78) and also Altman (1986a).

5. Hirschman (1958, pp. 34–37) argues that not all nonlabour income is saved for investment in plant and equipment. Much potential savings can be alternatively spent on luxury commodities including gold and foreign currency if the incentive to invest is inappropriate. See also Nurske (1962, p. 26) and Gould (1972, p. 154).
6. If the annual rate of growth in the number of employed workers is given by n (assuming for simplicity a homogeneous work force of identical skills) and the required capital/labour ratio is given by k^*, the amount of capital per worker (assuming constant prices) required to maintain k^*, given n, is nk^*. Since it is assumed that ex ante savings equals investments which equal the increase in total capital stock (assuming zero depreciation), nk^* is equal to the required savings per worker to maintain k^* when employment is growing by n. Given a propensity to save of s^* out of total income (only entrepreneurs save and they save all of their income) the required savings per worker can be written as $s^*(YIL)$ where Y/L is real income per worker. Given these assumptions, more workers could be employed only if Y/L and/or s^* increases. See Jones (1975, pp. 75–78) for a simple theoretical discussion. If the propensity to save (s) is given by the real wage rate (w), and given technology, Y/L is independent of w, any increase in the wage rate would, *ceteris paribus*, reduce s^* and, thereby, reduce the growth rate of employment. However, if the Y/L is a positive function of w, an increase in w can result in such a rise in Y/L that savings per worker increases (even s^* might rise) thereby generating an increase in the rate of employment growth.
7. Leibenstein (1962, pp. 62–76) develops the argument that higher real wages can result in greater output per labour-hour if this wage increase is used to augment a worker's critically low level of consumption and this, in turn, generates more effort per hour worked. He later argues that the increased labour productivity need not be readily forthcoming and must more often than not be induced (Leibenstein, 1978, pp. 60–64). The former argument has been developed further by, for example, Bliss and Stern (1978a, 1978b) and Stiglitz (1976) under the "efficiency wage" hypothesis. More recently Yellen (1984) and Akerlof (1984) have suggested that changes in real wages can effect labour productivity even if one is analyzing workers who are living above the level of physiological subsistence. Akerlof (1984, pp. 80–82) argues that higher wages induce increased labour productivity if workers become more satisfied with their job and if employers become increasingly loyal to their employees.

8. See also Kaldor (1970, pp. 342, 343), who finds that relatively high-wage regions are able to compensate for their higher labourcosts by being more productive; effecting a lower unit labour cost or efficiency wage. This permits a high-wage economy to effectively compete with low-wage economies. This argument was dramatically evidenced in the past in the rise of 17th-century Holland (Cipolla, 1976, pp. 253–254).
9. Bertram (1964) provides an important reclassification of the Quebec and Ontario census material on manufacturing. But his work relates only to current dollar gross manufacturing output and value added. Moreover, he categorized the census material into only 17 major sectors of the Dominion Bureau of Statistics', *Standard Industrial Classification Manual*. Altman (1984), on the other hand, develops a statistical package for current and constant dollar manufacturing gross output and value added estimates which are categorized into the 17 major sectors and their respective sub sectors. A similar approach is taken for the census data on labour employment, wages and salaries, and working and fixed capital (see also Altman, 1986a, 1987).
10. Green (1971, pp. 44, 68), discussing this gap, calls for a search for causal explanations. Isbister (1976–1977) attempts to explain why Quebec was so close to Ontario in terms of per capita manufacturing output while my findings suggest that Quebec was failing increasingly behind Ontario—this development being what I set out to explain.
11. Current Dollar Manufacturing Value Added Per Capita.

	1 *Quebec*	*2* *Ontario*	*3* *Que/Ont*	*4* *(1)–(2)*	*5* *(4)/(1)*
1870	26.1	29.8	0.875	3.72	0.144
1880	30.0	33.7	0.890	3.70	0.123
1890	41.9	50.4	0.830	8.56	0.204
1910	80.7	107.4	0.753	26.67	0.330

Source Altman (1986a), Table Al

12. Is the closing of the interprovincial real labour productivity gap evidence supportive of the HWSG hypothesis? According to this hypothesis the lower income per employee in Quebec provides the savings to increase the capital to labour ratio in Quebec relative to that found in Ontario thus causing the fall in labour productivity gap between the two provinces. However, since the lower income in Quebec compared to Ontario is

accompanied by a relatively lower labour productivity, the lower income does not yield higher savings per worker in Quebec relative to Ontario (see text below and tables 7.4 and 7.9). Also, the capital to labour ratio in both provinces' manufacturing sectors is similar from 1870 to 1910 and there is no positive relationship between the capital to labour ratio and output per worker in manufacturing (see Table 7.10 and Altman (1986b) for details).

13. The hypothetical employment growth rate generates 21,115 more employed workers in manufacturing in 1910 than were actually recorded. This is equivalent to only 1.89% of Quebec's active population in 1910 of 1,115,327 (see Tables 7.2 and 7.7) or 13.7% of those actually employed in manufacturing in 1910. Given the relatively small size of manufacturing employment and the massive emigration from Quebec in the period under study (see footnote 20 below), such an increase in employment could have probably been sustained without creating any significant bottlenecks in the labour market.
14. Ibid.
15. One should note, however, that historically nations with very rapid population growth rates have been characterized by relatively higher per capita manufacturing output growth rates than nations with lower population growth rates (Easterlin, 1967, pp. 106–107; Simon, 1977, pp. 45, 140). Given Quebec's population growth rate its problems remain situated in its relatively low manufacturing growth rates.
16. Labour income is deflated using price indices for the commodities produced by the workers in question and thus serves to indicate the cost of labour in terms of the output produced by the firms employing the labour (see Appendix for details). This is also the approach suggested by Kelley et al., (1972, pp. 169, 171).
17. The data presented in this paper are for mean labour cost and mean value added per employee. Elsewhere (Altman, 1984, Vol. 1, pp. 68–72), I demonstrate that lower labour costs and lower labour productivity characterized most of Quebec's manufacturing sectors. I also show that even had Quebec been endowed with a manufacturing structure which was identical to Ontario's in terms of the percentage distribution of employment among its manufacturing sectors, Quebec's mean labour costs and mean labour productivity would not have altered significantly.
18. For the current employment growth to be maintained given the capital/labour ratio k^*, $s^*Y/L = nk^*$ (see footnote 6), from which $n = (s^*Y/L)/k^*$ is derived. Since s^* is the propensity to save, s^*Y/L equals S/L, where S/L is total savings per worker. Thus $n = (S/L)/k^*$. Any increase in savings per worker yields a higher rate of employment growth.

19. Most of the output generated by the average farm was retained by the farm family in both provinces since most farmers owned their land. But the percentage of farms owned by their occupiers was greater in Quebec over the period 1870–1910 except for 1910. See Altman (1984, Vol. 1, p. 143).
20. This was a result of the number of farms increasing in Quebec by 47% and in Ontario, by 83% from 1880. This, in turn, coincided with the farm size decreasing in Ontario (it rose slightly in Quebec). The census year 1880 was also the only one in the period 1870–1910 where the farm size, in terms of acres per farm, significantly differed in Quebec and Ontario, being 24% larger in Quebec. See Altman (1984, Vol. 1, p. 143).
21. Isbister (1976–1977, p. 697) finds, from an analysis of samples taken from the 1850, 1860, and 1870 censuses, that the average size of the agricultural family was 7.1 individuals in Quebec and 6.2 in Ontario. Isbister also finds that, in terms of calories produced, the average Quebec farm was much less productive than that in Ontario over the period 1850–1910.
22. See Bairoch (1974, p. 474), Baldwin (1956, p. 176), and Nicholls (1963, pp. 23–25) on the significance of higher per capita agricultural incomes on regions' ability to industrialize.
23. Ryan (1966, pp. 66, 80, 108–110, 158, 163, 200, 208, 272, 280) finds that the Catholic Church played an important role creating a relatively passive labour force.
24. There are various estimates for the net emigration of French Canadians from Quebec to the United States. The most recent, by Paquet and Smith (1983, pp. 145–147) suggests that in the 1870s, 120,000 French Canadians emigrated, 165,000 in the 1880s, 195,000 in the 1890s, and 75,000 from 1900 to 1910. These estimates do not differ significantly from the series previously developed by Lavoie (1973, p. 78). From Urquhart and Buckley (1965, Series A 200–220, p. 21), I derive the number of net emigrants (irrespective of linguistic group) from Quebec to other provinces of Canada: 15,400 in the 1870s, 16,400 in the 1880s, 10,400 in the 1890s, and 27,600 from 1900 to 1910. These two series yield a rough approximation of total net emigration from Quebec: 135,400 in the 1870s, 181,400 in the 1880s, 205,400 in the 1890s, and 102,600 in the period 1900–1910.
25. These computations are based upon the estimates contained in the worksheets (Urquhart, 1986c) to Urquhart's (1986b) study on Canadian gross national product so kindly provided to me by Professor Urquhart. The miscellaneous expenses deflators used are from Altman (1987, pp. 90–91). And the very tentative lower-bound real value added estimates are $47,515, $59,164, $72,475, $164,130 for Quebec and $74,348, $100,308, $132,748, and $285,153 for Ontario for the 1870, 1880, 1890, and 1910 census years, respectively.

References

Akerlof, G.A. 1984. Gift Exchange and Efficiency-Wage Theory: Four Views. *American Economic Review, Papers and Proceedings* 74: 79–83.

Altman, M. 1984. *A Comparative Economic History of Quebec and Ontario, 1870–1910*, Ph.D. dissertation. McGill University, Montreal, Vols. 1 and 2.

Altman, M. 1986a. *Economic Development With High Wages: An Historical Perspective*, Working Paper. Department of Economics, Concordia University, Montreal.

Altman, M. 1986b. *'X-Efficiency' and Differential Labour Productivity Growth: Case Study of Quebec and Ontario, 1870–1910*. Paper presented at the Eastern Economics Association Meetings, (Philadelphia, 1986b).

Altman, M. 1987. A Revision of Canadian Economic Growth: 1870-1910 (a challenge to the gradualist interpretation). *Canadian Journal of Economics* 20: 86–113.

Bairoch, P. 1974. *Révolution industrielle et sous-développement*. Paris/la Haye: Mouton éditeur.

Baldwin, R.E. 1956. Pattern of Development in Settled Regions. *The Manchester School of Economic and Social Studies* 24: 161–171.

Bertram, G.W. 1964. Historical Statistics on Growth and Structure of Manufacturing in Canada, 1870–1957. In *Conference on Statistics, 1962 and 1963, Papers*, eds. J. Henripin and A. Asimakopulos, 93–146. Toronto: Toronto University Press.

Bliss, C., and N. Stern. 1978a. Productivity, Wages and Nutrition, Part I: The Theory. *Journal of Development Economics* 5: 331–362.

Bliss, C., and N. Stern. 1978b. Productivity, Wages and Nutrition, Part II: Some Observations 5: 363–398.

Brenner, Y.S. 1979. *Looking into the Seeds of Time: Social Mechanisms in Economic Development*. The Netherlands: Van Gorcum.

Census of Canada, 1870–1871. 1875. Ottawa. Vol. 3.

Census of Canada, 1880–1881. 1883. Ottawa. Vol. 3.

Census of Canada, 1890–1891. 1894. Ottawa. Vol. 3.

Census of Canada, 1911. 1913. Ottawa. Vol. 3.

Census of Canada, 1930–1931. 1932. Ottawa. Vol. 1.

Cipolia, C.M. 1976. *Before the Industrial Revolution, European Society and Economy, 1000–1700*. London: Methuen.

Clark, G. 1987. Why Isn't the Whole World Developed? Lessons From the Cotton Mills. *Journal of Economic History* 47: 141–173.

Dominion Bureau of Statistics. 1921, May. *Monthly Bulletin of Agricultural Statistics*, Vol. 14, Ottawa.

Dominion Bureau of Statistics. 1948. *Standard Industrial Classification Manual*, Ottawa.

Easterlin, R.A. 1967. Effects of Population Growth in the Economic Development of Developing Countries. *The Annals of the American Academy of Political and Social Science* 369: 98–108.

Fei, J.C.H., and G. Ranis. 1964. *Development of the Labor Surplus Economy, Theory and Policy*, Homewood, IL: Irwin.

Fei, J.C.H., and G. Ranis. 1975. A Model of Growth and Employment in the Open Dualistic Economy: The Cases of Korea and Taiwan. *Journal of Development Studies* 11: 32–63.

Fishlow, A. 1973. Comparative Consumption Patterns. The Extent of the Market, and Alternative Development Strategies. In *Micro Aspects of Development*, ed. E. B. Ayal. New York: Praeger.

Gerschenkron, A. 1966. *Economic-Backwardness in Historical Perspective*. Cambridge, MA: Belknap, Harvard University Press.

Gilboy, E. 1932. Demand as a Factor in the Industrial Revolution. In *Facts and Factors in Economic History*, ed. A. H. Cole. Great Britain: Russell and Russell.

Gilboy, E. 1934. *Wages in Eighteenth Century England*, Harvard Economic Studies, Vol. 45. Cambridge, MA: Harvard University Press.

Gould, J.D. 1972. *Economic Growth in History: Survey and Analysis*. London: Methuen.

Green, A.G. 1971. *Regional Aspects of Canada's Economic Growth*. Toronto: Toronto University Press.

Hirschman, A.D. 1958. *The Strategy of Economic Development*. New Haven, CT: Yale University Press.

Isbister, J. 1976–1977. Agriculture, Balanced Growth, and Social Change in Central Canada Since 1850: An Interpretation. *Economic Development and Cultural Change* 25: 673–696.

Jones, H. 1975. *An Introduction to Modern Theories of Economic Growth*. Surrey, England: Nelson.

Kaldor, N. 1970. The Case for Regional Policies. *Scottish Journal of Political Economy* 82: 339–348.

Kelley, A.C., J.G. Williamson, and R.J. Cheetham, (Eds.). 1972. *Dualistic Economic Development, Theory and History*. Chicago/London: University of Chicago Press.

Lavoie, Y. 1973. Les mouvements migratoires des canadiens entre leur pays et les États-Unis au XIX6 au XX6 siécies: étude quantitative. In *La population du Québec: études rétrospective*, ed. H. Charbonneau. Montreal: Les éditions du boréal express.

Leibenstein, H. 1962. *Economic Backwardness and Economic Growth: Studies in the Theory of Economic Development*. New York: Wiley.

Leibenstein, H. 1978. *General X-Efficiency Theory and Economic Development*. New York: Oxford University Press.

Leibenstein, H. 1980. *Beyond Economic Man: A New Foundation for Microeconomics*. Cambridge, MA: Harvard University Press.
Lewis, A.W. 1954. Economic Development With Unlimited Supplies of Labour. *The Manchester School of Economic and Social Studies* 26: 139–191.
Lewis, A.W. 1958. Unlimited Labour: Further Notes. *The Manchester School of Economic and Social Studies* 30: 1–32.
Mokyr, J. 1976a. *Industrialization in the Low Countries, 1795–1850*. New Haven, CT: Yale University Press.
Mokyr, J. 1976b. Growing-Up and the Industrial Revolution in Europe. *Explorations in Economic History* 13: 371–396.
Mokyr, J. 1977. Demand vs. Supply in the Industrial Revolution. *Journal of Economic History* 37: 981–1008.
Myrdal, G. 1957. *Economic Theory and Underdeveloped Regions*. London: Duckworth.
Nicholls, W.H. 1963. An 'Agricultural Surplus' as a Factor in Economic Development. *Journal of Political Economy* 71: 1–29.
Nurske, R. 1962. *Problems of Capital Formation in Underdeveloped Countries*. Oxford: Blackwell.
Paquet, G., and W.R. Smith. 1983. L'émigration des canadiens français vers les États-Unis, 1790–1940: problématique et coups de sonde. *L'Actualité économique. Revue d'analyse économique* 59: 423–453.
Ranis, G. 1977–1978. Development and the Distribution of Income: Some Counterevidence. *Challenge* 20: 55–56.
Raynauld, A. 1961. *Croissance et structure économique de la province du Québec*. Quebec: Government of Quebec.
Ryan, W. 1966. *The Clergy and Economic Growth in Quebec (1896–1914)*. Quebec: Les presses de l'Université Laval.
Simon, J. 1977. *The Economics of Population Growth*. Princeton, NJ: Princeton University Press.
Stiglitz, J.E. 1976. The Efficiency Wage Hypothesis, Surplus Labour, and the Distribution of Income in the L.D.C.s. *Oxford Economic Papers* 28: 185–207.
Urquhart, M.C. 1985a. *New Estimates of Gross National Product, Canada, 1870 to 1926: Some Implications for Canadian Development*, Discussion Paper, No. 586. Department of Economics, Queen's University, Kingston, Canada.
Urquhart, M.C. 1986b. New Estimates of Gross National Product, Canada, 1870–1926: Some Implications for Canadian Development. In *Long-Term Factors in American Economic Growth*, eds. S. L. Engerman and R. E. Gallman. Chicago: Chicago University Press.
Urquhart, M.C. 1986c. Worksheets: Manufacturing Summary Charts, Mimeo, Department of Economics, Queen's University, Kingston, Canada.
Urquhart, M.C., and K.A.H. Buckley (Eds.). 1965. *Historical Statistics of Canada*. Toronto: Toronto University Press.

Williamson, J.G. 1985. The Historical Context of the Classical Labour Surplus Model. *Population and Development Review* 11: 171–191.

Yellen, J.L. 1984. Efficiency Wage Models of Unemployment. *American Economic Review, Papers and Proceedings* 74: 200–205.

CHAPTER 7

Labour Productivity in Nineteenth Century Quebec and Ontario: Explaining Ontario's Advantage

1 Introduction

This article presents a case study of the historical causes of interregional differentials in labour productivity which played, and still continue to play, an important role in explaining interregional and international differences in the amount of goods and services available per person. I attempt here to spell out the possible causes for a persistent and substantial differential in labour productivity throughout the period 1870–1910, favouring Ontario over Quebec manufacturing; this sector represented about 30% of the total output of these provinces (Altman, 1988a, p. 204). This was a critical period in Canadian history, since it was at this time that the economic and political foundations of Confederation were being laid.

These years proved, moreover, to be formidable ones in both provinces' development, just as they were for the Canadian economy as a whole; it experienced the fastest growth rate of all western economies at this time. Particularly during the 1896–1913 period—which encompassed Canada's "wheat boom,"—Canada's economic growth was most pronounced in terms of total output, per capita output, and labour productivity. The same holds true for the manufacturing sector (Altman, 1987b, 1992a, 1992b, 1994). It has been long established that, throughout these four formative decades, manufacturing output per capita as well as total commodity output per capita was greater in Ontario

M. Altman, *Lessons from a Successfully Export-Oriented, Resource-Rich Economy*, https://doi.org/10.1007/978-3-031-03887-7_7

than in Quebec. Moreover, Ontario's advantage actually increased, particularly from 1890 to 1910, and its greater per capita manufacturing output is attributable, in large measure, to its edge in labour productivity.[1] To date, the reasons for this productivity differential remain to be explained, although much effort has been spent attempting to explain, more generally, Quebec's laggard economic performance relative to Ontario's.

2 The Quandary Over Quebec's Comparative Economic Development

André Raynauld (1962) was the first to compare Quebec and Ontario economic development based on a careful assessment of the available statistical sources. He found that there was little difference in the provinces' current dollar growth rates of total output and, more specifically, in manufacturing output, over the 1870–1954 period. He attributes the different levels of per capita manufacturing output in 1870 largely to interprovincial differences in labour productivity and further increases in the per capita differential in manufacturing output to Quebec's more rapid rate of population growth. More recently, some of Raynauld's general findings, in particular the importance of the interprovincial differential of labour productivity, have been corroborated by Altman (1988a) for the manufacturing sector for the 1870–1910 period using real or constant dollar output estimates.

In an effort to refute a longstanding view that Quebec's laggard economic performance was a product of the mentality of French-Canadians, Albert Faucher and Maurice Lamontagne (1953) advanced an alternative and influential hypothesis to explain Quebec's lag in industrial development from the 1860 to 1911. They argue that, compared to Ontario, Quebec was both distant from and poorly endowed with coal and iron ore in an age when these resources were critical to industrial development, resulting in a cost disadvantage to Quebec producers of iron and steel products. Quebec's industrial development, such that it was, became dependent on its relatively abundant supply of low-priced labour, joining the "sweating-system industry belt" as opposed to the "tool-producing and steel industry belt" of North America. Thus material, not cultural, factors were responsible for Quebec's relatively poor economic performance in the late-nineteenth century. However, available statistical evidence strongly suggests that Quebec's deficiencies in resource endowments were not responsible for its development problems. Its fuel costs were similar to Ontario's and, like Ontario, Quebec experienced the development of a significant iron and steel products sector based on imported inputs. Moreover, Quebec and Ontario industries were protected by the transportation costs incurred by firms exporting manufacturing iron and steel products to these regions (Altman, 1986a).

Other scholars attribute the Quebec economy's inability to catch up with Ontario's to the economic policies adopted by the Federal government from the time of Confederation. In particular, Canada's focus on the construction of a transcontinental railroad is said to have been detrimental to Quebec's economic development (Anger, 1976). However, most recent estimates speak against this particular hypothesis (Altman, 1988b). Although much more track was laid in Ontario than in Quebec by 1910 (over 8,000 miles compared to less than 4,000 miles), Quebec received more Federal government subsidies both per capita and per mile of track than Ontario did. Moreover, the subsidized track in Ontario and in Western Canada served the economies of both Quebec and Ontario. In addition the indirect benefits accruing to the Quebec economy from the construction and maintenance of the railroads greatly exceeded the gains to the Ontario economy. This differential advantage in Quebec's favour only mounted over the course of the 1870–1910 period.

The persistence of poor markets—based on relatively low productivity in the agricultural sector—underlines another important attempt at explaining Ontario's persistent economic advantage over Quebec. This argument has been forcefully made for the pre-Confederation period by John McCallum (1980). He concludes that a successful and productive agriculture sector was the engine of Ontario's industrial development, whereas Quebec's unproductive counterpart forced its industrial development to be reliant on foreign markets and cheap labour. The poor performance of Quebec's agricultural sector persisted into this century, as income per farm in Quebec relative to Ontario fell from 1870 to 1910 from 73–64%. A relatively weak domestic market, therefore, remained a potential problem in Quebec (Altman, 1988a).[2] John Isbister (), who also finds that Quebec's agriculture sector was far behind Ontario's, argues instead that Quebec's industrial growth was not unduly hampered by poor domestic markets. Rather, it developed as a "quasi-enclave," seeking markets in Ontario and in the United States. Nevertheless, Quebec's persistent lag in labour productivity remains unexplained.

In an attempt to determine which variables were responsible for the Quebec-Ontario productivity differential in the manufacturing sector, a series of estimates, largely based on the Canadian censuses and on price indexes developed elsewhere, have been constructed (see Appendix). The evidence presented here suggests that some of the explanatory variables economic historians traditionally employ, such as the structure of manufacturing, capital per worker, and plant size, do not, upon closer scrutiny, satisfactorily explain why workers in Quebec were less productive than their Ontario counterparts over the 1870–1910 period. Another variable often used in the economic literature to explain inter-regional productivity differentials, however, does find resonance in the evidence. Important differences in both the quantity and quality of human capital formation or education that favoured Ontario between 1870 to 1910 appear to account for at least some of this differential. Yet the problem remains that Quebec's population achieved a level of education commensurate with that realized in more industrialized parts of the world during this time. This begs the question as to whether or not Quebec's lag in education was primarily responsible for its lag in manufacturing productivity.

Another possible explanation for Quebec's lag in labour productivity is that the labour productivity differential between Quebec and Ontario coincides with Quebec's income per employee being consistently lower than Ontario's. This differential posits that Quebec's relatively low manufacturing wage rates protected its firms—as would transportation costs, tariffs, and a lax competitive environment—from more productive and cost efficient, although relatively high-wage, firms in Ontario. On the other hand, relatively high rates of pay to Ontario workers pressured firms in that province into becoming more productive so that they could remain cost competitive despite the higher rates of pay their workers received. For this reason, although Ontario labourers were more costly than their Quebec counterparts, they were not necessarily more expensive because of their higher productivity. In this case, contrary to conventional wisdom, Quebec's relatively low-priced labour did not play a positive role in fostering industrial development there. Rather, by negatively affecting manufacturing productivity, low-wage rates contributed to Quebec's persistent lag in per capita manufacturing.

Given the significance of interprovincial differences in wage rates to this paper, it is important to cast some light on the potential causes of the established differences in labour compensation in Quebec and Ontario. Discussing the pre-1870 period, McCallum concludes that, "the opportunity cost of accepting wage employment was much greater for the agricultural population of Ontario than for that of Quebec... the very much higher productivity of Ontario agriculture, together with the greater capacity of that province to absorb increased population, were the major factors behind the wage differential" (1980, pp. 97–98). This situation did not change much towards the turn of the century. The opportunity cost of accepting wage employment in Quebec, relative to Ontario and as determined by agricultural productivity and income, in fact deteriorated from 1870 to 1910. Moreover, the Catholic Church played an important role in pacifying labour in Quebec, trusting that this would help generate jobs in the province and thereby stem the flood of French-Canadians out of Quebec (Altman, 1988a, p. 216). In spite of this, Quebec's manufacturing wage gradually moved towards Ontario's from 1870 to 1910 without ever actually catching up, reaching 91% of Ontario's (Table 1, Panel 1). In part, this can be attributed to the fact that Quebec lost over 10% of its population to the United States in each of the last three decades of the nineteenth century and about 4% from 1900 to 1910, totalling well over one-half million people. In addition, thousands of French Canadians moved to other parts of Canada. Increasingly, the opportunity cost of engaging in wage labour in Quebec was no doubt determined by the expected opportunities available outside of the province (Altman, 1988a).

Assigning a positive role to relatively high wage rates is foreign neither to the historical or the economics literature. It was central to Sir John Habakkuk's (1962) classic reinterpretation of nineteenth-century American economic history, where he argues that the relatively high industrial wages in the United States compared to Britain created appropriate incentives for American firms to become relatively more productive so as to remain competitive and profitable. In part, a rise in labour productivity was reflected in the increasing mechanization of industry. However, shifting resources away from the relatively expensive input would not suffice to keep costs from rising. If costs were to be contained, the firms' increasing capital-to-labour ratio had to embody technical change. Ways and means could also be devised for making labour more productive even without increasing the level of mechanization. Habakkuk argues that high wages in the United States forced American firms to become increasingly mechanized and innovative as well as more efficient in their use of labour. In the economics literature, x-efficiency theory argues that firms need not be operating at maximum productivity. Specifically, relatively low wage

Table 1 General constant dollar estimates for Quebec and Ontario manufacturing (1913 = 100)

I. Labor Income Per Employee				II. Value Added Per Employee		
	Quebec	Ontario	Quebec/Ontario	Quebec	Ontario	Quebec/Ontario
1870	262	340	0.77	757	883	0.86
1880	296	360	0.82	724	872	0.83
1890	320	385	0.83	723	852	0.85
1910	482	528	0.91	1,079	1,224	0.88
III. Non-Labor Costs Per Employee				IV. Labor Income Plus Non-Labor Costs Per Employee		
	Quebec	Ontario	Quebec/Ontario	Quebec	Ontario	Quebec/Ontario
1870	825	853	0.97	1,087	1,193	0.91
1880	880	926	0.95	1,176	1,286	0.91
1890	932	957	0.97	1,252	1,342	0.93
1910	1,310	1,374	0.95	1,792	1,902	0.94
V. Efficiency Wage (labor income/value added)				VI. Non-Labor Costs/Value Added		
	Quebec	Ontario	Quebec/Ontario	Quebec	Ontario	Quebec/Ontario
1870	0.35	0.39	0.9	1.09	0.97	1.13
1880	0.41	0.41	0.99	1.22	1.06	1.14
1890	0.44	0.45	0.98	1.29	1.12	1.15
1910	0.45	0.43	1.04	1.21	1.12	1.08

VII. Non-Labor Costs Plus Labor Income/Value Added				VIII. Non-Labor Costs Plus Labor Income/Gross Output		
	Quebec	Ontario	Quebec/Ontario	Quebec	Ontario	Quebec/Ontario
1870	1.44	1.35	1.06	0.69	0.68	1.01
1880	1.62	1.48	1.1	0.73	0.71	1.03
1890	1.73	1.58	1.1	0.79	0.75	1.05
1910	1.66	1.55	1.07	0.75	0.74	1.02
IX. Fixed Capital Per Employee						
	Quebec	Ontario	Quebec/Ontario			
1870	191	178	1.07			
1880	330	297	1.11			
1890	573	539	1.06			
1910	1,080	1,114	0.97			
X. Hypothetical Costs						
	(Hyp Quebec Ontario Actual Efficiency Wage)	(Quebec Labor + Hyp Quebec VA)/(Ontario Actual Labour + Non-labour Costs)	Hyp Quebec Efficiency Wage/(Quebec Actual Efficiency Wage)	(Quebec Labor + Hyp Quebec VA)/(Quebec Actual Labour + Non-labour Costs)	Hyp Quebec (Ontario VA per Employee & the Quebec Distribution of Labour Across Sectors)	Hyp Quebec Efficiency Wage" (Actual Quebec Wage/ Hyp Quebec VA Per Employee)
1870	0.75	0.89	0.84	0.84	904	0.29
1880	0.81	0.9	0.82	0.82	882	0.34
1890	0.75	0.84	0.77	0.77	941	0.34
1910	0.91	0.94	0.88	0.88	1,226	0.39

Source See appendix

rates protect relatively low productivity firms from their more productive competitors. On the other hand, relatively high wage firms are forced to become more productive if they are to survive in the market place. For this reason, high wages may contribute to high productivity and, thereby, to higher levels of per capita output.[3]

3 X Inefficiency, Labour Productivity, Labour Income and Production Costs

What is x-inefficiency? When output per unit of labour input in one set of firms is less than in another set of firms which is characterized by the same economic structure, applies the same technology, possesses the same capital-labour ratios, has the same plant size, and employs workers with the same level and quality of human capital, the less productive firms are said to be x-inefficient. In this study of Quebec and Ontario manufacturing, Ontario firms, since they are more productive, act as our proxy for the x-efficient firms. The less productive Quebec firms, on the other hand, can be seen to be x-inefficient. But first, their poorer productivity performance must be shown to be unrelated to the more traditional economic variables discussed above, the capital-labour ratio, plant size, and the quantity and quality of education. What follows is an attempt, therefore, to determine whether the differences in labour productivity in Quebec and Ontario manufacturing can be related to interprovincial differences in the structure of manufacturing, capital per employee, plant size, and/or education and literacy. To the extent that these variables cannot account for the inter-provincial labour productivity differentials, x-inefficiency becomes a plausible explanation for these differentials.

Estimates for this article are derived largely from data available for census years. I use data for only four (1870, 1880, 1890, and 1910) of the possible five decennial census years, since data for 1900 are incomplete and incompatible with what are available from the other censuses.[4] We can be fairly confident that the data for these years fall approximately on the peaks of Canada's economic upturns, making my inter-decennial comparisons appropriate. At present, however, there is no way of determining whether the timing of the Quebec or Ontario cycles deviated significantly from each other or from Canada's.[5]

I have categorized and refined the census data in order to generate current and constant dollar estimates for output, income, and fixed capital per employee in the manufacturing sector as a whole as well as in the manufacturing sub sectors. Constant dollar values, which are adjusted for movements in prices, are the more important estimates. I also construct estimates for plant size as well as for the level of education and literacy in Quebec and Ontario. Some of the more detailed computations are presented in Table 10, while a detailed account of the construction of these estimates is found in the Appendix.

Labour productivity or value added per employee in Quebec, in terms of constant dollars, was less than in Ontario for all the census years examined. In 1870, labour productivity in Quebec was 86% of what it was in Ontario; falling marginally to 83% in 1880; and rising to 85% by 1890. This percentage rose slightly to 88% by 1910. Quebec was also well behind Ontario in 1870 with respect to real income per employee. The Quebec total was only 77% of Ontario's. This percentage, however, rose steadily throughout the period, reaching 91% by 1910 (Table 1, Panels I and II). In terms of current dollars, over the entire 1870–1910 period, the Quebec/Ontario productivity ratio failed to rise while the Quebec/Ontario income per employee ratio increased from 74 to 91% (Table 2, Panels I and II). These results are similar for the manufacturing sub sectors as well (Table 10). The only major sub sectors where Quebec was consistently more productive than Ontario were textile products and clothing, and in both of these sub sectors Quebec's labour income was fast approaching Ontario's.

One important determinant of one region's potential competitive advantage over another is its labour cost per unit of output, or what is otherwise known as the efficiency wage. When the wage rate rises

Table 2 General current dollar estimates for Quebec and Ontario manufacturing

	Quebec	*Ontario*	*Quebec/Ontario*	*Quebec*	*Ontario*	*Quebec/Ontario*
1870	182	245	0.74	479	556	0.86
1880	214	258	0.83	474	547	0.87
1890	258	303	0.85	552	638	0.87
1910	443	488	0.91	969	1,137	0.85
1870	0.381	0.441	0.86	209	197	1.06
1880	0.450	0.472	0.95	337	306	1.1
1890	0.466	0.475	0.98	510	485	1.05
1910	0.457	0.429	1.07	975	1,006	0.97

Source See appendix

while labour productivity remains unchanged unit production costs will increase.[6] The efficiency wage is derived by dividing estimates for income per employee by those for labour productivity. For the more important constant dollar estimates, the efficiency wage in Quebec and Ontario was, with the exception of 1870, similar for all census years examined. In 1870, Quebec's efficiency wage was 90% of Ontario's. By 1910, Quebec's efficiency wage exceeded Ontario's by 4% in spite of labour compensation in Quebec labour being 91% of Ontario's. All the while, the constant dollar efficiency wage increased from $0.35 to $0.45 in Quebec from 1870 to 1910 and from $0.39 to $0.43 in Ontario. The current dollar estimates show an increase in Quebec's efficiency wage and fall in Ontario's such that by 1910, Quebec's efficiency wage bettered Ontario's by 7% (Tables 1, Panel V and Table 2, Panel III). Quebec's and Ontario's efficiency wage remained similar in spite of there being relatively higher income per worker in Ontario and in spite of income per worker in Quebec increasing at a faster pace than in Ontario. Otherwise, initially Ontario would have had a much higher efficiency wage than Quebec and, over time, Quebec's efficiency wage would have eventually surpassed Ontario's by a wide margin. Results for the manufacturing sub sectors are not much different from the average results (Table 10). The only major sub sector in which Quebec's efficiency wage was markedly greater than Ontario's was food and beverages. But much of the output produced here was for the local market and was, therefore, protected by transportation costs. On the other side of the coin, Ontario's efficiency wage was typically greater than Quebec's in most sub sectors, but Ontario's position improved, for the most part, over the course of the 1870–1910 period. And like Quebec's industries, Ontario's were protected by transportation costs. But unlike Quebec, Ontario afforded its producers a much larger market for its output.

A region's competitive advantage is also a product of the cost of non-labour inputs, here defined as the cost of raw materials and fuel. My estimates for constant dollar non-labour inputs (Table 1, Panel III) show that the cost of these inputs per unit of labour was somewhat lower in Quebec. But what is important to a region's competitive advantage is the cost of non-labour inputs per unit of output. Seen from this perspective, Quebec's non-labour costs were greater than Ontario's by 8% in 1910 (Table 1, Panel VI). Thus Quebec's relatively low labour productivity more than offset any competitive advantage which lower non-labour costs would have otherwise bestowed on Quebec's manufacturing. Together, labour and non-labour costs per unit of labour were lower in Quebec. However, more importantly, labour and non-labour costs combined per unit of output are greater in Quebec than in Ontario (Table 1, Panel VII). It is evident that Quebec's advantage in labour and non-labour costs was only able to partially offset its lower labour productivity. Quebec's per unit value added costs were greater than Ontario's by between 7 and 10% throughout the entire 1870–1910 period. Not much changes if one estimates these costs per unit of total or gross output (Table 1, Panel VIII).

To further highlight the importance of differences in labour productivity to Quebec's and Ontario's competitive position, I estimate what Quebec's relative labour costs per unit of output would have been had Quebec manufacturing been characterized by Ontario's value added per worker across its various manufacturing sectors (Table 1, Panel X). As expected, with Ontario's labour productivity, Quebec's efficiency wage as well as its total costs per unit of output would have been much less than its actual unit costs and would, therefore, have been consistently lower than Ontario's. As it was, Ontario's superior productivity performance gave it a competitive edge over Quebec, even in spite of its higher labour and non-labour costs.

Apart from low wages, further protection was afforded to Quebec's low productivity firms in the Quebec market and in markets to the east of Quebec by transportation costs.[7] This helps explain how Quebec's manufacturing could continue to grow in spite of Quebec's average relative per unit value added costs exceeding Ontario's over the entire 1870–1910 period. Thus, in sum, Quebec manufacturing remained viable over the 1870–1910 period, in spite of its poor labour productivity performance due, at least in part, to the protection provided to its firms by transportation costs.

4 Some Possible Causes of Quebec's Lag in Productivity

Quebec's shortfall in labour productivity could have been caused by concentrating its manufacturing in what are traditionally thought to be cheap labour industries, such as clothing and textiles. If this were true, Quebec's productivity problem would have been largely one of the structure of its manufacturing sector relative to Ontario's. However, estimates on the percentage distribution of manufacturing employment in

Quebec and Ontario suggest that, for the most part, there were no major differences in the structure of their manufacturing sectors. Nevertheless, a much larger percentage of Quebec's manufacturing workers were employed in leather products throughout the 1870–1910 period and, for most of this period, a much larger percentage of Ontario's manufacturing workers were employed in iron and steel products. Also, the textile products sub sector was consistently more important in Ontario whereas the manufacture of clothing became more important in Quebec by 1910 (Table 3).[8] Quebec's dominance in particular manufacturing sub sectors cannot easily be related to the availability of relatively cheap labour (Table 10). Apart from this, only an insignificant proportion of the Quebec/Ontario labour productivity differential can be attributed to the provinces possessing a different manufacturing structure. This conclusion becomes evident when estimating what labour productivity in Quebec's manufacturing sector would have been had Quebec's manufacturing sector been characterized by the same structure as Ontario's in terms of the percentage distribution of employees amongst the major manufacturing sub sectors. It is assumed here that Quebec retains its estimated actual sectoral labour productivities. In this case, constant dollar labour productivity would have been less than it actually was in 1870, 1880, and 1890, and somewhat greater, by 3%, in 1910 (Table 4). Thus a different structure of labour employment in Quebec would not have improved its real labour productivity performance except for in 1910. Quebec's manufacturing structure, therefore, only explains a diminutive portion of the labour productivity gap, and then only for 1910.

Economic theory suggests that the region characterized by lower capital-labour ratios should also be characterized by a lower level of labour productivity. This assumes that similar capital-labour ratios in the two regions are proxies for like technologies—a reasonable assumption for the Quebec-Ontario comparison. However, from Table 1 (Panel 9) it becomes clear that there is no association between constant dollar fixed capital to labour ratios in Quebec and Ontario and inter-provincial differences in labour productivity. Labour productivity in Quebec remained consistently below that in Ontario over the period examined, whether its average capital to labour ratio was above Ontario's—as in 1870 and 1890—or marginally below Ontario's, as was the case in 1910. This is also true when each manufacturing sub sector is examined individually (Table 10). Keeping in mind the tentative nature of my capital stock estimates (see Appendix), these results suggest that an unfavourable

Table 3 The structure of Quebec and Ontario manufacturing

		The percentage distribution of employees							
		Quebec				*Ontario*			
		1870	*1880*	*1890*	*1910*	*1870*	*1880*	*1890*	*1910*
1	Food & beverages	5.99	7.18	15.23	7.87	8.22	8.61	9.50	11.08
2	Tobacco & products	1.88	2.98	3.13	3.34	0.84	1.01	0.96	1.19
3	Rubber products	0.78	0.64	0.99	0.29	0.00	0.00	0.17	0.52
4	Leather products	19.36	18.02	12.99	9.56	11.53	8.30	5.25	4.17
5	Textile products	2.44	4.53	6.01	8.20	6.13	7.42	7.49	4.49
6	Clothing	9.01	15.58	12.49	11.91	10.89	13.66	17.53	12.61
7	Wood products	25.00	20–84	17.59	20.13	26.16	23.54	24.67	17.73
8	Paper	0.73	1.59	2.52	5.70	0.41	0.77	1.02	2.13
9	Printing & publishing	2.14	2.41	2.07	2.63	2.23	3.53	3.70	4.24
10	Iron & steel products	13.80	13.12	11.16	8.54	18.30	17.93	14.57	19.89
11	Transportation equip	7.28	5.47	5.62	9.68	6.56	6.71	5.27	7.53
12	Nonfer. metal products	1.55	0.51	0.95	0.79	0.53	0.47	0.82	1.09
13	Elec. apparatus & sup	none	none	0.47	1.71	none	none	0.28	1.57
14	Nonmet. mineral prod	3.95	3.60	4.55	2.38	5.10	4.98	4.91	4.16
15	Petroleum& coal prod	0.27	0.28	0.85	0.32	0.65	0.54	0.54	0.50
16	Chemical products	3.34	2.17	2.35	3.31	1.18	0.84	0.89	2.19
17	Miscellaneous industries	2.48	1.08	1.02	0.97	1.28	1.68	2.43	3.24
18	All other industries	none	none	none	2.68	none	none	none	1.67
Total: All manufacturing		100	100	100	100	100	100	100	100

Source See appendix

Table 4 The hypothetical Quebec value added per employee and the structure of manufacturing

	Quebec Hyp	*Quebec Hyp./Ontario Actual*	*Quebec Hyp./Quebec Actual*
1870	708	0.80	0.94
1880	686	0.79	0.95
1890	707	0.83	0.98
1910	1,109	0.91	1.03

Source See appendix and Table 3. The hypothetical constant dollar value added estimates for Quebec are constructed by taking Ontario's percentage distribution of labor employment in manufacturing across manufacturing subsectors and multiplying these percentages by their respective actual sectoral value added per employee estimates for Quebec

capital-to-labour ratio was not the cause of Quebec's relatively poor labour productivity performance and, therefore, that other variables, perhaps plant size, human capital, or x-efficiency, must have accounted for this situation. This is not to say that the amount of capital stock per worker did not affect labour productivity, but rather that the capital-to-labour ratio which characterized most of Quebec manufacturing sufficed to realize Ontario's level of labour productivity.

Plant size, measured in terms of the number of employees per plant, was small (about five) in both provinces from 1870 to 1890. One might expect labour productivity in Quebec to be less than in Ontario, *ceteris paribus*, if plant size in Quebec had been relatively smaller, assuming of course that economies of scale existed. But from 1870 to 1890 plant size in Quebec was marginally greater than in Ontario. Quebec's lag in labour productivity over these years, therefore, cannot be "explained" away by interprovincial differences in plant size. By 1910, however, plant size stood at twenty-three employees in Quebec and thirty-one employees in Ontario. Paradoxically, when plant size in Quebec fell substantially below that in Ontario, Quebec's labour productivity increased. A similar story unfolds when each manufacturing sub sector is individually examined (Table 5).[9]

Table 5 Plant size: Number of workers per plant

		Quebec				Ontario			
		1870	*1880*	*1890*	*1910*	*1870*	*1880*	*1890*	*1910*
1	Food & beverages	3	4	4	4	3	4	4	11
2	Tobacco & products	47	84	64	78	17	20	28	42
3	Rubber products	246	175	156	55	3	3	27	203
4	Leather products	6	7	5	81	3	3	2	48
5	Textile products	4	8	9	144	12	7	17	52
6	Clothing	7	8	4	49	7	7	9	79
7	Wood products	5	6	6	19	6	7	9	30
8	Paper	46	42	43	132	25	28	25	75
9	Printing & publishing	14	19	16	34	9	14	14	82
10	Iron & steel products	3	3	4	59	4	3	5	208
11	Transportation equip	5	4	5	124	4	4	5	54
12	Nonfer. metal products	13	4	6	42	5	3	3	33
13	Elec. apparatus & sup	none	none	37	164	none	none	7	135
14	Nonmet. mineral prod	5	6	9	27	4	5	5	20
15	Petroleum& coal prod	19	23	156	83	10	11	17	78
16	Chemical products	6	10	16	75	3	4	5	37
17	Miscellaneous industries	11	5	5	30	6	6	9	46
Total: All manufacturing		5.0	5.5	5.5	23	4.6	4.9	5.4	31

Source Censuses of Canada 1870–1871, 1880–1881, 1890–1891, 1910–1911

5 Education and Labour Productivity Differentials

Investment in education might serve to explain part of Quebec's labour productivity performance if it can be shown that Quebec's manufacturing workers were less productive than their Ontario counterparts as a result of their being less well-endowed with education-related human capital stock. Given the available evidence, a suitable proxy for such human capital formation is the literacy rate. Despite its limitations, this proxy is, of course, often used in studies examining the relationship between education and productivity or economic development, in particular in those studies focusing on the historical economic significance of education.

Presently, there exists an extensive literature on the relationship between literacy and economic development. For example, W.A. Lewis has argued that widespread literacy was not necessarily a prerequisite for industrialization and that, specifically, for the latter part of the nineteenth century, there is no clear causal relationship between more education and increases in labour productivity (1978, p. 138). In his work, L.G. Sandberg provides data which does not indicate that there is any significant positive association between the percentage of a population which is literate and a country's level of per capita income (1982, p. 687).[10] Data for less-developed countries from the 1960s and 1970s also fail to demonstrate any strong positive relationship between the literacy rates of an adult population and the growth of per capita gross national product. Taiwan, for example, fared as well as Hong Kong in terms of GNP growth, even though its literacy rate was 54% as compared to Hong Kong's 70%. In comparison, Thailand's growth rate was mediocre in spite of an impressive literacy rate of 68% (Psacharopoulos & Woodhall, 1978, p. 18).

These bits of evidence are consistent with the now classic findings of Bowman and Anderson, who argue that an adult literacy rate of 30 to 40% was probably a prerequisite to the realization of between \$200 and \$300 per capita in U.S. 1955 dollars in the early 1950s, and that increasing the literacy rate from 30–40 to 70% tended to have little effect on the level of per capita income realized in a country (1963, pp. 252–254).[11] Therefore, once a region had realized a 30 to 40% level of literacy, consistent with a relatively low level of output per capita, it was unlikely that further increases in literacy would affect per capita output except if the increases in literacy were substantial.

The best available census data from which to construct comparative estimates of literacy for Quebec and Ontario for the 1870–1910 period is for 1890, as this the only year for which relatively detailed estimates for literacy can be constructed (Table 6).[12] For both 1870 and 1880, no census data are available from which to construct even crude measures of literacy. For 1860, however, I am able to estimate the percentage of the greater than 19-year-old population who were capable of reading or

Table 6 Literacy: The percentage of the population who can read and/or write

	Those who can read and write			*Those who can read or write*		
	Quebec	*Ontario*	*Quebec/Ontario*	*Quebec*	*Ontario*	*Quebec/Ontario*
1860						
Greater than 19 yrs	na	na		64.6	92.8	0.7
1890						
Total Population	52.7	75.9	0.69	59	78.5	0.75
Greater than:						
9 yrs	68.2	91.6	0.74	74.3	93.8	0.79
19 yrs	63.9	90.5	0.71	70.4	93.1	0.76
Under 10 yrs	12.9	24.1	0.54	19.9	28.4	0.7
Oct-19	77.8	94.2	0.83	83.1	95.4	0.87
20–29	75.9	94.8	0.8	80.1	95.7	0.84
30–39	68.2	92.6	0.74	73.7	94.3	0.78
40–59	59.1	88.6	0.67	67.2	92	0.73
60 and over	37.9	79.6	0.48	48.4	86.3	0.56
1900						
Greater than 5 yrs	77.9	89.8	0.87	82.3	91.3	0.9
1910						
Greater than 5 yrs	85.6	93.2	0.92	87.3	93.5	0.93

Note The only detailed literacy breakdown is for the census of 1890
Source Censuses of Canada

writing: 65% in Quebec and 93% in Ontario. For 1890, the percentage of these provinces' greater than 19-year-old population who could read or write was 70 and 93% respectively. Also for 1890, I am able to estimate the percentage of this age cohort who could read and write: 64 and 91% in Quebec and Ontario respectively. The greater than 9-year-old age cohort able to read or write was 74% in Quebec and 94% in Ontario. Regarding the ability to read and write, these percentages fall to 68 and 92% respectively. In 1890, the percentage of the 10- to 29-year-old population with the capacity to read or write was over 80% in Quebec and over 95% in Ontario and, for the 30- to 39-year-old age cohort, over 70% could read or write in Quebec as compared to 94% in Ontario. As for the 40- to 59-year-old age cohort, the literacy rate approaches 70% in Quebec, but it exceeds 90% in Ontario. Although literacy was lower in Quebec than in Ontario for all age groups by 1890, it was still relatively high for those age cohorts most relevant to our discussion, the 10- to 40-year-old population, which contributed most to the potential work force.[13]

Given the available data for both 1900 and 1910, it is only possible to estimate literacy rates for the broader population, those greater than five years old. For 1900, the percentage of this age cohort able to read and write was 78 and 90% in Quebec and Ontario respectively and the percentage of this population capable of reading or writing was 82% in Quebec and 91% in Ontario. By 1910, 86% of Quebec's and 93% of Ontario's greater than five-year-old population could read and write while 87 and 94% respectively of this age cohort in Quebec and Ontario could read or write. It becomes clear from these estimates, that Quebec consistently lagged behind Ontario in literacy, although Quebec was rapidly catching up. Quebec's literacy rate was 70% of Ontario's in 1860 and rose to over 75% in 1890, and to over 90% by 1910 (Table 6).

While the literacy estimates give some indication of the quantity of human capital stock, it is also important to try to determine, where possible, the quality of the available human capital in Quebec and Ontario. A region's labour productivity is affected by both the quantity and quality of the human capital with which it is equipped. One proxy for the quality of human capital is years of schooling. It is clear from the evidence (Table 7) that a greater percentage of the five- to nineteen-year-old age cohort was enrolled in school in Ontario than in Quebec over the 1870–1910 period. But a much higher percentage of those enrolled in school attended class in Quebec, with Ontario catching up to Quebec only by 1910, at which time 42 to 43% of the five- to nineteen-year-old age cohort attended class in both provinces.

Of those enrolled in school, Quebec had a much larger percentage in the pre-first to fourth grades. Ontario, on the other hand, had a much greater percentage enrolled in grades five through eight (37 as compared to 7% in 1890 and 34 as compared to 9% in 1910 in Quebec and Ontario respectively). Ontario also had 7% of its enrolled population in grades nine to thirteen in 1890 and 9% in 1910. The percentage of Quebec's population in these grades in 1890 and 1910, on the other hand, was 0.0 and 0.2% respectively (Table 8). These estimates strongly suggest that a larger percentage of Ontario's educated population had more human capital per student invested in them than did Quebec's, even though in

Table 7 Enrolment and attendance in elementary and secondary schools

	I. Percentage of the 5–19 year age Cohort enrolled in school		*II. Percentage of the enrolled population attending class*		*III. Percentage of the 5–19 year age Co-hort attending class*	
	Quebec	*Ontario*	*Quebec*	*Ontario*	*Quebec*	*Ontario*
1870	47.4	71.9	na	42.5	37.3	29.5
1880	41.8	70.8	88.4	45.5	37.0	32.4
1890	46.5	71.5	89.7	52.2	38.5	36.4
1900	53.0	71.9	73.8	55.9	40.5	40.0
1910	55.1	71.2	77.5	58.9	43.1	41.8

Note In Panel (1), 1870 data can be obtained only for the 6 to 21 age cohort. In Panel (111), for Quebec, 1873 attendance data are used for 1870 since no such data are available for earlier years, and, 1899 and 1901 data are used to yield a 1900 estimate for which no actual data exist
Source Jackson (1965, pp. 567–589); Wisenthal (1983, p. 388); Censuses of Canada 1871 and 1931

Table 8 The percentage distribution of enrolment

	Grades:	*Pre-3 to 4*	*3 to 4*	*5 to 6*	*7 to 8*	*9 to 10*	*11 to 13*
1870	Quebec	na	na	na	na	na	na
	Ontario	27.8	19.8	20.5	16.9	14.8	0.2
1890	Quebec	63.8	28.9	5.7	1.6	0.0	
	Ontario	37.2	18.7	19.6	17.4	6.8	0.2
1900	Quebec	67.5	24.6	6.4	1.5	0.1	0.0
	Ontario	38.5	17.7	18.7	17.1	6.4	1.7
1910	Quebec	61.4	28.9	7.7	1.7	0.3	0.0
	Ontario	40.3	17.3	17.1	16.6	5.8	2.9

Note For Quebec there are no data for 1890. In its place, 1892 data are used. These data, however, are only for the Roman Catholic population
Source Jackson (1965, p. 593)

Quebec a larger percentage of the overall population attended class. For this reason and, perhaps also, for reasons of greater efficiency in Ontario's educational system, Ontario was able to produce a more literate populations.[14] And although Quebec was catching up with Ontario in terms of literacy from 1860 to 1910, Quebec was in no way approaching Ontario's distribution of enrolment towards more years of schooling—our proxy for human capital invested per student.

To be sure, this lag in both literacy and in the depth of human capital formation in Quebec affected Quebec's lag in labour productivity in the

1870–1910 period. However, if this deficiency in human capital is to account for Quebec's lag in labour productivity, it is necessary to demonstrate that a larger percentage of the population of Quebec had to be both literate and possess a grades five through thirteen education for its workforce to have achieved the level of labour productivity realized in Ontario. No direct evidence for such a proof exists. Indeed, it is more likely that in the late-nineteenth century Quebec's population was well enough endowed with human capital to realize Ontario's level of labour productivity. Richard Easterlin, for example, finds that typically no more than 8% of a population attending primary school is necessary for a country to industrialize in the twentieth century (1981, p. 6). In Quebec, 13 to 15% of the population was enrolled in school over the 1870–1910 period. In Ontario, this percentage increased from 7% in 1870 to 12% by 1910 (from Table 7). Clearly, Quebec met Easterlin's criterion for modern economic growth with respect to education.[15] Nevertheless, Quebec's clear and enduring lag in human capital formation might have had serious repercussions for future economic development as more education was required on the labour market over time.

Traditional economic variables, including education, do not offer a satisfactory explanation of the Quebec-Ontario labour productivity differential. In this light, the case for x-inefficiency as a cause of much of this differential appears strong. The interprovincial differential in labour productivity was, therefore, possibly due to the relatively low wages paid to Quebec workers, allowing Quebec manufacturing establishments to remain less productive than their Ontario counterparts and, thereby, relatively more x-inefficient. In this case, and in terms of constant dollars, x-inefficiency (which becomes the difference between labour productivity in Quebec and Ontario) would have constituted 17% of Quebec's actual manufacturing value added in 1870, 20% in 1880, 18% in 1890, and 13% in 1910. Once the impact of the structure of manufacturing on average manufacturing labour productivity is taken into account, x-inefficiency as a percent of Quebec's manufacturing value added falls, somewhat, to 11% in 1910 (Table 9). Accordingly, had Quebec firms been more x-efficient, the real wealth produced in Quebec manufacturing would have been much greater, yielding a lower efficiency wage or facilitating a higher income per worker.

Table 9 Upper-bound estimates for x-inefficiency per employee in Quebec manufacturing

	x-inefficiency	*x-inefficiency as a % Actual Quebec VA*	*x-inefficiency as a % Actual Ontario VA*
1870	126	16.7	14.3
1880	148	20.4	17.0
1890	129	17.9	15.2
1910A	145	13.4	11.8
1910B	115	10.6	9.4

Note The 1910B x-inefficiency and related estimates are net of the effect which the differential Quebec and Ontario manufacturing structure has upon Quebec's level of labour productivity
Source Tables 3 and 4

6 Conclusion: 'Cheap' Labour and Substandard Labour Productivity

It has been shown that in Quebec and Ontario an interprovincial disparity in labour productivity in manufacturing and a marginal reduction in that disparity coexisted with a literacy gap, a schooling differential, and changes therein, as well as with interprovincial differences in income per worker throughout the 1870–1910 period. If it can be shown that Quebec's lag in human capital formation did not preclude Quebec from realizing Ontario's level of labour productivity, then x-efficiency theory suggests that firms operating below their potential productivity were largely responsible for the labour productivity gap between Quebec and Ontario. Direct evidence with which to affirm or refute such a hypothesis is not yet available.

Our present state of knowledge, however, does not support the argument that Quebec society had not yet attained the level and quality of education necessary to achieve Ontario's higher levels of productivity. For this reason, and given the available evidence, it is reasonable to conclude that low wages had a negative impact on Quebec's development process by negatively affecting labour productivity. This resulted in the persistence of x-inefficiency in Quebec manufacturing. High wages probably had the opposite effect in Ontario. Given what we now know, relatively low wage rates can no longer be seen as the panacea to Quebec's historical problems in economic development but, rather, low wages should be viewed as a possible impediment to Quebec's capacity in catching up with Ontario.[16]

Table 10 Constant dollar labour income, value added and fixed capital per employee in Quebec relative to Ontario

		Labour income				*Value added*				*Fixed capital*				*Efficiency wage*			
		1870	*1880*	*1890*	*1910*	*1870*	*1880*	*1890*	*1910*	*1870*	*1880*	*1890*	*1910*	*1870*	*1880*	*1890*	*1910*
1	Food & beverages	0.66	0.72	0.51	0.93	0.31	0.17	0.39	0.61	1.33	1.08	0.57	1.10	2.16	4.18	1.32	1.52
2	Tobacco & products	0.76	0.7	0.94	1.14	1.71	0.52	0.91	1.06	2.00	1.18	1.30	2.29	0.45	1.36	1.04	1.07
3	Rubber products	0.33	0.48	1.16	0.72	0.18	0.53	0.51	0.94	1.80	1.06	2.14	0.21	1.85	0.91	2.26	0.77
4	Leather products	0.80	0.82	0.64	0.95	1.07	1.13	0.77	0.64	0.72	0.82	0.62	0.89	0.75	0.72	0.83	1.49
5	Textile products	0.81	0.86	0.95	1.02	1.17	1.13	1.04	1.40	1.52	2.39	2.11	1.39	0.69	0.76	0.91	0.73
6	Clothing	0.69	0.73	0.97	0.99	1.24	0.90	1.08	1.09	1.25	0.83	1.16	0.82	0.56	0.81	0.90	0.91
7	Wood products	0.67	0.81	0.79	0.74	0.89	0.90	0.79	0.79	1.09	1.22	1.17	1.08	0.75	0.90	1.00	0.94
8	Paper	0.77	0.83	0.98	0.94	0.91	0.95	0.98	0.96	0.56	1.02	0.84	0.73	0.84	0.88	1.01	0.98
9	Printing & publishing	0.82	1.05	1.03	0.94	0.84	1.09	1.99	0.92	1.13	1.19	1.12	1.07	0.98	0.97	0.52	1.02
10	Iron & steel products	0.73	0.81	0.90	0.98	0.86	0.83	0.90	1.17	1.39	1.27	1.21	1.02	0.85	0.97	0.99	0.83
11	Transportation equip	0.72	0.89	1.11	1.04	0.89	0.90	1.38	0.89	1.08	1.10	0.97	0.73	0.81	0.98	0.81	1.18
12	Nonfer. metal products	0.85	1.10	1.08	1.12	0.72	1.28	0.92	1.10	1.51	1.91	1.32	1.28	1.18	0.86	1.18	1.02

		Labour income				*Value added*				*Fixed capital*				*Efficiency wage*			
		1870	*1880*	*1890*	*1910*	*1870*	*1880*	*1890*	*1910*	*1870*	*1880*	*1890*	*1910*	*1870*	*1880*	*1890*	*1910*
13	Elec. apparatus & sup	none	none	0.47	1.00	none	none	0.29	1.34	none	none	0.24	0.89	none	none	1.63	0.74
14	Nonmet. mineral prod	0.94	1.00	1.05	0.97	1.23	1.02	1.08	1.09	1.25	1.81	1.12	0.85	0.77	0.98	0.97	0.89
15	Petroleum& coal prod	0.84	0.95	0.83	0.99	0.45	0.44	0.8	0.38	2.63	1.95	0.98	0.55	1.88	2.17	1.04	2.62
16	Chemical products	0.57	1.01	0.74	0.84	0.7	0.78	0.56	0.77	0.99	1.33	0.97	1.03	0.82	1.29	1.33	1.10
17	Miscellaneous industries	0.51	0.55	0.60	0.83	0.52	0.84	0.53	0.88	0.63	0.57	0.54	0.76	0.97	0.65	1.12	0.94
Total: All manufacturing		0.77	0.82	0.83	0.91	0.86	0.83	0.85	0.88	1.07	1.11	1.06	0.97	0.90	0.99	0.98	1.04

Source See appendix

Appendix

Most of the detailed computations upon which the tables in this article are derived are from two previously published papers of mine (Altman, 1986b, 1987a).[17] Final estimates are derived from a reorganization of the census data into major manufacturing sectors (see Table 10) in accordance with the 1948 *Standard Industrial Classification Manual* (Altman, 1989). In another paper, the derivation of real output, real input, and real labour income estimates is discussed. These estimates are all presented in terms of 1913 prices (Altman, 1988a). One should note that my output estimates are upper-bound since they incorporate miscellaneous expenses, consisting mainly of rent of works and offices. Data are available to estimate these expenses on a provincial basis for 1900 only. Moreover, the 1900 census data provides information on explicit rents alone. No data are available for implicit rents. If one uses the census data to estimate miscellaneous expenses for Quebec and Ontario, one runs the risk of biasing downward the value added in the province where, during 1900, there was a predisposition to rent as opposed to own one's facilities. I also find that explicit rents constitute about 5% of Quebec's 1900 gross manufacturing output and less than 3% of Ontario's. Given the available data, incorporating miscellaneous in my estimates would bias downward Quebec's value added thereby inflating my estimates of x-inefficiency for Quebec relative to Ontario. M.C. Urquhart (1986a, 1986b, pp. 83–84) uses the available census material to estimate the value of miscellaneous expenses for Canada as a whole from 1870 to 1910. If one applies Urquhart's miscellaneous expenses to gross output ratio to Quebec and Ontario, my real value added estimates would be reduced by 10.6, 11.3, 14.5, and 16.8% in Quebec and by 6.5, 6.4, 7.5, and 15.8% in Ontario for the 1870, 1880, 1890, and 1910 census years respectively.[18]

Census data are also used to construct estimates of real fixed capital which consists of the value of buildings, land, machinery, tools, implements, and motive power. Data on total fixed capital are contained only in the 1890, 1900, and 1910 censuses. The 1870 and 1880 censuses provide information on the total capital employed by firms, inclusive of working capital. Thus, the value of fixed capital for these two years is estimated using the fixed to total capital ratio drawn from the 1890 census of manufacturing. This ratio, estimated for each of the major manufacturing sectors, is applied to the value of total capital in 1870 and 1880 in order to generate nominal fixed capital estimates for these sectors. It is assumed, therefore, that the share of fixed capital in total capital was the same for the first three census years of this study. This assumption, it should be emphasized, is only a working hypothesis.

Nevertheless, one can draw comfort from the fact that the fixed capital to total capital ratio was similar in 1890 and 1910 in Quebec as well as in Ontario: 0.49 in Quebec and 0.45 in Ontario. The value of land and buildings to total fixed capital, derived from the 1890 census (the only year in our period for which such information is available), is assumed to be the same for the other three census years under study. The value of land and buildings is deflated by price index numbers for building construction (no appropriate price data for land values are available) whereas the value of machinery, tools, implements, and motive power are deflated by price index numbers for iron and steel products (Statistics Canada, 1978; Altman, 1987b, p. 90).[19] It goes without saying that my estimates for real fixed capital are of a very tentative nature.

Notes

1. For a detailed discussion of Quebec and Ontario economic development in the 1870–1910 period see Altman (1988a), pp. 198–224, 204, 208–211, or Ch. 6 of this book. As of 1910, Quebec's total current-dollar-commodity output per capita was 71% of Ontario's, whereas its manufacturing output per capita was 75% of Ontario's (73% in constant dollars [see Table 1, Panel C]). In 1870, real per capita manufacturing output in Quebec relative to Ontario was 87% (Table 2, Panel B). Throughout the 1870–1910 period, labour productivity in Quebec manufacturing was about 85% of Ontario's. Together, Quebec's lower productivity and lower labour employment growth in manufacturing were largely responsible for the province's lag in per capita manufacturing output.
2. Demand-side problems in Quebec may have been at least partially responsible for Quebec's manufacturing employment growth being consistently below Ontario's in the forty-odd years following Confederation. This lag in Quebec's employment growth was largely responsible for the increasing per capita manufacturing output gap between Quebec and Ontario in the latter's favour (Altman 1988a).
3. For an overview of the concept of x-efficiency, see Leibenstein (1966, 1979, 1981). For a methodological and theoretical discussion of the application of x-efficiency theory in this article, see Altman (1990, 1992b, 1992a). An underlying premise of much of the conventional (neoclassical) economic theory of the firm is that workers, managers, owners,

and owner/managers work as hard and as well as they can, given the constraints they face in terms of technology, information, education, and the law. Thus, according to conventional theory, all firms will be as productive as they can be given these constraints. X-efficiency theory, on the other hand, suggests that employees, employers, and managers are generally not ideal–typical, and do not work as hard or as diligently as they might potentially as long as their behaviour is consistent with the survival of the firm on the market place. In this case, output per worker would be less than it might potentially be. Generally, if firm managers and owners can keep unit prices competitive without working harder or better, x-efficiency theory holds that this less work-intensive option will be chosen. If, for example, wages can be kept low enough to keep prices competitive, this option will be chosen over one which involves increasing wage rates and investing more time and effort on the part of owners and managers into the process of production.

4. The 1900 census does not cover firms employing less than five employees with the exception of butter and cheese factories and brick and tile works. And there is no data with which to make adjustments for this deficiency on a provincial basis. The same holds true for the 1910 census. However, by 1910 the smaller firms were apparently of little consequence, contributing no more then 6% of total output (Bertram, 1964, p. 99, notes 5 and 6). Nevertheless, one should note that the 1910 estimates constructed for this article are not completely consistent with the estimates for 1870, 1880, and 1890. However, given the present state of knowledge, we simply do not know whether this biases our Quebec-Ontario comparative estimates in any meaningful way.
5. On Canadian business cycles see Bertram (1964) and Chambers (1964). See also Urquhart (1986b) and Altman (1992b, 1992a) for annual real Canadian GNP estimates for the 1870–1910 period. Both sets of estimates reinforce Bertram's and Chambers' conclusions.
6. Unit production costs can be written as: (total cost)/(total output). Total cost can be broken down into total wage cost and other costs such that unit production costs can be rewritten as: (W*L + OC)/(total output), where W is the wage rate and L is the labour time employed. As W increases so do unit production costs. Therefore, as the wage rate increases in one region relative to another, unit production costs increase in one region relative to another, *ceteris paribus*.
7. For a discussion of the importance of transfer costs with respect to the Quebec iron and steel products industry see Altman (1986a, 1986b).
8. One neat method of determining the extent to which the distribution of manufacturing employment differed in Quebec and Ontario is to estimate the Duncan Index of Dissimilarity. This index is constructed by

subtracting the percentage of labour employed in each of the manufacturing sub sectors in the two provinces, summing the absolute values of these differences and dividing the total by two. The index ranges from 0 to 1, with 0 indicating an identical distribution of employment across manufacturing sub sectors in Quebec and Ontario. The Duncan Index of Dissimilarity was 0.15, 0.16, 0.20, and 0.22 for 1870, 1880, 1890, and 1910 respectively, suggesting only small, albeit increasing, differences in the distribution of employment in the two provinces. It is important to note that increases in this index coincides with a small increase in Quebec labour productivity relative to Ontario's (Table 1, Panel 2).

9. My plant size estimates for 1910 are inflated since they exclude most plants employing less than five employees. However, we have no way of knowing whether my estimates are biased upward relatively more for Quebec or Ontario. For Canada, plant size in 1910 was 33 workers. Adjusting Canadian plant size to incorporate the excluded smaller plants yields an average plant size of 12 workers for 1910. Moreover, one cannot compare plant size in 1890 and 1910 on a provincial level since the 1890 estimates are based on data that include both the smaller and the larger firms. See Altman (1994) for further details.
10. Sandberg's conclusions, however, are different from my own. Also, Cipolla argues that around 1850 poorer countries such as Ireland, Sweden, and Scotland were more literate than either the more developed England or France (Cipolla 1969, pp. 75, 115). See also Sandberg, who points out that by 1850, relatively impoverished Sweden was Europe's most literate country (1979, p. 230). However, both Cipolla and Sandberg make the argument that high levels of human capital endowment facilitate future rapid rates of economic development when a higher level of education becomes necessary.
11. Bowman and Anderson conclude: "Taking into account the special characteristics of countries with literacy rates under 70% that managed nevertheless to attain incomes above $300, the data strongly suggest that rising literacy alone contributes very little to development over the range from 30 to 70% literate. Two-thirds of the fourteen countries with literacy rates between 70 and 90% do manage to exceed average incomes of $300 though not above $500. Moreover, the others, still under the $300 level, underline the fact that extending literacy to a majority of the population is no guarantee of even modestly high income; it may be necessary, but it is clearly not a sufficient condition" (1963, pp. 253–54).
12. Greer (1978) provides us with a rich array of estimates for Quebec literacy from the beginning of the nineteenth century. He also includes census-based estimates for Quebec from 1860 to 1890. Greer's work emphasizes an analysis of the differential in literacy between the French and English-speaking communities in Quebec.

13. In 1890, the ten- to thirty-nine year old age group contributed 78% to the 10 to 59 year old population (computed from data in the Census of Canada, 1890–1891 [1894]).
14. For an insightful analysis of the determinants of both quality and quantity aspects of educational attainment for French and non-French populations in Prescott County, Ontario, during the 1860–1890 period see Gaffield (1987, ch. 4). Although this chapter addresses problems related to human capital formation of only one county in Ontario, its focus on comparing formal education in the French and non-French communities is pertinent to an understanding of our Quebec-Ontario comparison where, of course, the French community dominated the Quebec population and non-French communities dominated Ontario.
15. Easterlin further argues that formal education is critical to modem economic growth, but he recognizes that countries industrialized prior to an abundance of formal education being realized (1981, pp. 9–11). Lewis argues, from an assessment of nineteenth century economic development: "it is highly doubtful whether workers with eight years of primary schooling will produce more industrial output than workers with six years of primary schooling. Some present-day economists assert that part of today's higher industrial output is due to additional hours of primary schooling per head of the industrial population. This case has not been proved. It is better to be educated than uneducated, but more schooling does not necessarily result in greater industrial output" (1978, p. 138).
16. The results presented here tend support to some of the results in Clark (1987, pp.169, 171), a recent study on cotton mills of the late nineteenth and early twentieth century. Clark also finds a positive relationship between labour productivity and income per worker. X-efficiency theory can, perhaps, better explain Clark's findings. Clark tentatively attributes to "local influences" international differences in labour productivity. See also Altman (1988a), for an application of my variation of x-efficiency theory to the question of the role of industrial wages in the process of economic development.
17. Both papers are available from the author on request. The censuses used in the article are: Census of Canada, 1870–1871, vols. 2 and 3 (1875–1876); Census of Canada, 1880–1881, Vol. 3 (1883); Census of Canada, 1890–1891, Vol. 2 (1893); Census of Canada, 1890–1891, Vol. 3 (1894); Census of Canada, 1900–1901, Vol. 3 (1905); Census of Canada, 1911, Vol. 3 (1913); Census of Canada, 1931, Vol. 1 (1931).
18. These computations are based upon the estimates contained in the worksheets (Urquhart, 1986a) which underlie his (Urquhart, 1986b) study on Canadian gross national product. A copy of the worksheets were kindly provided to me by Professor Urquhart. The miscellaneous expenses deflators used are from Altman (1987b, pp. 90–91).

19. The price index numbers used to deflate the components of fixed capital stock yield weighted general price index numbers with a 1913 base year. These index numbers are: 1.09, 1.02, 0.89, and 0.90 for Quebec and 1.09, 1.03, 0.90, and 0.90 for Ontario for 1870, 1880, 1890, and 1910 respectively. These index numbers are weighted for the share of land and buildings, and machinery, tools, implements, and motive power in total fixed capital. For further details see Altman (1987a).

References

Altman, M. 1986a. Resource Endowments and Location Theory in Economic History: A Case Study of Quebec and Ontario at the Turn of the Twentieth Century. *Journal of Economic History* 46: 999–1009.

Altman, M. 1986b. *'X-Efficiency' and Differential Labour Productivity Growth: A Case Study of Quebec and Ontario, 1870–1910*. Paper presented at the Eastern Economic Association Meetings, Philadelphia.

Altman, M. 1987a. *Interregional Labour Productivity and Wage Differences: The Case of Quebec and Ontario, 1870–1910 (Statistical Appendix)*. Mimeographed, Department of Economics, University of Ottawa, Ottawa.

Altman, M. 1987b. A Revision of Canadian Economic Growth, 1870–1910: A Critique of the Gradualist Approach. *Canadian Journal of Economics/Revue canadienne d'économique* 20: 86–113.

Altman, M. 1988a. Economic Development With High Wages: An Historical Perspective. *Explorations in Economic History* 25: 198–224.

Altman, M. 1988b. Railways as an Engine of Economic Growth? Who Benefited from the Canadian Railway Boom, 1870–1910?. *Histoire social/Social History* 21: 269–281.

Altman, M. 1989. *A Framework for Organizing the Canadian Manufacturing Census Material, 1870–1910*. Discussion paper, Department of Economics, University of Saskatchewan, Saskatoon.

Altman, M. 1990. Interfirm, Interregional, and International Differences in Labour Productivity: Variations in the Levels of 'X-Inefficiency' as a Function of Differential Labour Costs. In *Studies in Economic Rationality: X-Efficiency Examined and Extolled*, eds. Klaus Weiermair and Mark Perlman, 323–350. Ann Arbor: University of Michigan Press.

Altman, M. 1992a. The Economics of Exogenous Increases in Wage Rates in a Behavioural/X-Efficiency Model of the Firm. *Review of Social Economy* 50: 163–192.

Altman, M. 1992b. Canadian GNP Estimates and Canadian Economic Growth, 1870–1926. *The Review of Income and Wealth* 38: 455–473.

Altman, M. 1994. The Evolution of Plant Size in Canadian Manufacturing, 1870–1910. *Canadian Historical Review* 75: 557–585.

Angers, F,-A. 1976. L'évolution économique du Canada et du Québec en cent ans de Confédération. In *L'économie québécoise: histoire, développement, politiques*, ed. R. Tremblay, 241–254. Montreal: Presses de l'Université du Québec.

Bertram, G. 1964. Historical Statistics on Growth and Structure in Canada, 1870–1957. In *Conferences on Statistics, 1962–1963 Papers*, eds. J. Henripin and A. Asimakopulos, 93–146. Toronto: University of Toronto Press.

Bowman, M.J., and A.C. Anderson. 1963. Concerning the Role of Education in Development. In *Old Societies and New States: The Quest for Modernity in Asia and Africa*, ed. C. Geertz, 247–279. New York: Free Press of Glencoe.

Census of Canada, 1860–1861. (1863). *Personal Census*. Vol. 1. Quebec.

Census of Canada, 1870–1871. (1875). Vol. 2. Ottawa.

Census of Canada, 1870–1871. (1876). Vol. 3. Ottawa.

Census of Canada, 1880–1881. (1883). Vol. 3. Ottawa.

Census of Canada, 1890–1891. (1893). Vol. 2. Ottawa.

Census of Canada, 1890–1891. (1894). Vol. 3. Ottawa.

Census of Canada, 1901. (1905).Vol. 3. Ottawa.

Census of Canada, 1901. (1906). Vol. 4. Ottawa.

Census of Canada, 1911. (1913). Vol. 2. Ottawa.

Census of Canada, 1911. (1913). Vol. 3. Ottawa.

Census of Canada, 1931. (1931). Vol. 1. Ottawa.

Chambers, E. 1964. Late Nineteenth Century Business Cycles. *Canadian Journal of Economics and Political Science* 30: 191–212.

Cipolla, C.M. 1969. *Literacy and Development in the West*. Harmondsworth, England: Penguin.

Clark, G. 1987. Why Isn't the Whole World Developed? Lessons From the Cotton Mills. *Journal of Economic History* 47: 141–173.

Dominion Bureau of Statistics. 1948. *Standard Industrial Classification Manual*, Ottawa.

Easterlin, R.A. 1981. Why Isn't the Whole World Developed?. *Journal of Economic History* 41: 1–19.

Faucher, A., and M. Lamontagne. 1953. History of Industrial Development. In *Essays on Contemporary Quebec*, ed. J.C. Falardeau, 23–37 (Quebec).

Gaffield, C. 1987. *Language, Schooling, and Cultural Conflict: The Origins of the French-Language Controversy in Ontario*, Ottawa.

Greer, A. 1978. The Pattern of Literacy in Quebec, 1745–1899. *Histoire social/Social History* 11: 295–335.

Habakkuk, H.J. 1962. *American and British Technology in the Nineteenth Century: The Search for Labour-Saving Technology*, London: Cambridge University Press.

Isbister, J. 1976–1977. Agriculture, Balanced Growth, and Social Change in Central Canada since 1850: An Interpretation. *Economic Development and Cultural Change* 25: 673–697.

Jackson, W.R.B. 1965. Education. In *Historical Statistics of Canada*, eds. M.C. Urquhart and K.A.H. Buckley, 567–589. Toronto: Cambridge University Press.

Leibenstein, H. 1966. Allocative Efficiency vs. 'X-efficiency'. *American Economic Review* 56: 392–415.

Leibenstein, H. 1979. A Branch of Economics is Missing: Micro-Micro Theory. *Journal of Economic Literature* 17: 477–502.

Leibenstein, H. 1981. Microeconomics and X-Efficiency Theory. In *The Crisis in Economic Theory*, eds. D. Bell, and I. Kristol, 97–110. New York: Basic Books.

Lewis, A.W. 1978. *Growth and Fluctuations*, 1870–1913. New York: G. Allen and Unwin.

McCallum, John. 1980. *Unequal Beginnings, Agriculture and Economic Development in Quebec and Ontario until 1870*. Toronto: University of Toronto Press.

Psacharopoulos, G., and M. Woodhall. 1978. *Education for Development: An Analysis of Investment Choices*. New York: Oxford University Press.

Raynauld, A. 1962. *Croissance et structure économique de la province du Québec*, (Quebec).

Sandberg, L.G. 1979. The Case of the Impoverished Sophisticate: Human Capital and Swedish Economic Growth before World War I. *Journal of Economic History* 39: 225–241.

Sandberg, L.G. 1982. Ignorance, Poverty and Economic Backwardness in the Early Stages of Industrialization: Variations on Alexander Gerschenkron's Grand Theme. *Journal of European Economic History* 2: 675–697.

Statistics Canada. 1978. *Fixed Capital and Flows and Stocks, 1926–1978*, Ottawa.

Urquhart, M.C. 1986a. *Worksheets: Manufacturing Summary Charts*, Mimeographed. Department of Economics, Queen's University, Kingston, Ontario.

Urquhart, M.C. 1986b. New Estimates of Gross National Product, Canada, 1870–1926: Some Implications for Canadian Development. In *Long-Term Factors in American Economic Growth, National Bureau of Economic Research, Studies in Income and Wealth*, eds. S.L Engerman, and R.E. Gallman Vol. 51, 9–94. Chicago: University of Chicago Press.

Wisenthal, M. 1983. Education. In *Historical Statistics of Canada*, ed. F.H. Leacy. 2nd ed. Series W67–93, Ottawa.

CHAPTER 8

Resources Endowments and Economic Development: Why Location and the Bounties of Nature Can't Explain Quebec's Laggard Economic Performance in the Pre-World War One Period

1 Introduction

Albert Faucher and Maurice Lamontagne argued in their classic 1953 article, "History of Industrial Development," that Quebec's relative distance from sources of coal and iron ore retarded its industrial development from the 1860s to 1911 in comparison with that of Ontario. Quebec was able to acquire these resources only at a higher cost than was Ontario in an era when iron and steel production was critical to industrial development.[1] Clearly implied by Faucher and Lamontagne is the counterfactual that had Quebec and Ontario possessed similar resource and locational advantages their industrial development would have been similar.[2]

But can interregional differentials in material input costs influence a region's ability to industrialize? I present a model which incorporates material input cost variables into an analysis of interregional economic development.[3] Specifically, I ask whether higher costs in coal, iron ore, and iron and steel ingots in Quebec relative to Ontario could have been a cause of Quebec's relatively retarded industrial performance in the late nineteenth and early twentieth centuries.[4] I demonstrate the conditions

M. Altman, *Lessons from a Successfully Export-Oriented, Resource-Rich Economy*, https://doi.org/10.1007/978-3-031-03887-7_8

under which higher material input costs could have hindered Quebec's industrial development and the extent to which these conditions were present.

I find resource endowments and location problems could have hindered development under only very extreme circumstances, with coal costs constituting a significantly larger proportion of the value of total output in Quebec compared with Ontario while, at the same time, representing a large share of the value of total output. Furthermore, Quebec could not have produced iron and steel products with imported ingots. Quebec would have had to rely on imported iron ore. An analysis of the 1900 manufacturing census (the only year for which adequate data are available) reveals that these circumstances were not present in Quebec.

2 A Modeling Narrative

To isolate the significance of differential material input costs for industrial development, I focus on transfer costs as the determining factor in the interregional distribution of industry.[5] To this end I make the following simplifying assumptions for Quebec and Ontario: all firms identical; there is one center of production in each region which is also the market core; firms are price takers and the law of one price rules, distribution costs per unit of output produced in both regions for sale in Quebec are identical as are transportation costs per ton/mile for inputs and outputs, capital and labour costs per unit of output, and raw material costs per unit of output net of transfer costs. I also assume that firms are characterized by identical fixed coefficients of production. Under these conditions, had Quebec transported its raw materials from a greater distance than Ontario - assume for simplicity that the raw materials originate in Ontario - the cost of raw materials per unit of output in Quebec would have exceeded those in Ontario because of the resulting differential in transfer costs. Quebec could have produced this output only if transportation costs per unit of output from Ontario to Quebec were greater than or equal to the costs per unit of output of transporting the raw materials from Ontario to Quebec. Otherwise, firms in Quebec would have had to charge a higher price for the same output produced by Ontario firms for sale in Quebec or operate at an economic loss. Eventually Quebec firms would have lost their market to the lower unit cost Ontario firms.[6] One alternative, to be considered later, would have been for Quebec firms to reduce their material inputs per unit of output.

Given my assumptions, unit costs of producing the same output in Quebec and Ontario for the Quebec market is not greater in Quebec if the weight of raw materials transported to Quebec per unit of output does not exceed the weight of a unit of output delivered to Quebec. Also, if the value of inputs constitutes an insignificant proportion of the value of total output, their higher cost per unit of output in Quebec cannot be an important constraint on firm location.[7] However, even if the value of inputs is relatively significant, firms could still locate in Quebec if the output weighs as much as the inputs per unit of output. Transportation costs would protect Quebec firms from Ontario firms which hold an advantage in raw material costs per unit of output.[8]

3 The Faucher-Lamontagne Hypothesis

Faucher and Lamontagne identify coal and iron ore as key determinants of industrial location. These inputs are weight losing because most of their weight disappears in the process of producing the final output.[9] By locating closer to the source of the raw materials (again assumed for simplicity to be in Ontario) firms reduce transportation costs. It would be economical for firms to locate in Ontario rather than in Quebec when the unit weight of the final product to be shipped to Quebec is less than the unit weight of the coal (coal and iron ore when producing iron and steel ingots) that is shipped to Quebec for the production of the final product. Iron ore cannot determine the location of industry except for the production of iron and steel ingots. An iron and steel products industry could have developed in Quebec using imported ingots – a possibility ignored by Faucher and Lamontagne.[10] Because iron and steel ingots do not lose weight in the production of iron and steel products, firms would not reduce transportation costs by locating in Ontario as opposed to Quebec except for the costs of transporting weight-losing coal.[11] Thus, the weight of coal per unit of output shipped to Quebec for the production of iron and steel products must have exceeded the unit weight of the iron and steel products shipped to Quebec from Ontario for the unit costs in Quebec to have been prohibitive for iron and steel products production here.

Thus, to impede Quebec's industrial development the costs of coal per unit of output must have been significantly greater in Quebec than in Ontario. Moreover, coal costs must have constituted a significant portion of total costs. But if the underlying assumptions of my model are relaxed,

Quebec's competitive position is strengthened. Labour costs per unit of output were not the same in both provinces. They were lower in Quebec in almost all industries including the iron and steel products sector.[12] Transportation costs per ton/mile appear to have been higher for final products than for raw materials, (see Nourse (1968), p. 76 and Estall and Buchanan (1972), pp. 21–41). These two factors would help counteract any unit cost disadvantage in Quebec for coal.

4 Testing the Faucher-Lamontagne Hypothesis

To test the significance of resource endowments and location to Quebec industrial development, I rely on manufacturing data for the 1900 census year, the only one containing data on the cost of fuel, light, power and heat (FLPH costs) in Quebec and Ontario for the period 1870 to 1910. The FLPH measure includes the cost of coal and of alternative sources of fuel, light, power and heat. Therefore, it is a more meaningful indicator of coal-related costs than are coal costs per se. These data plus the census data on manufacturing output and employment are restructured and reclassified by major manufacturing sectors and subsectors (see Tables 1 and 8.2). One limitation is that these data are only for those firms employing five or more workers. Nevertheless, most of the manufacturing capacity in both provinces is covered.[13] With these data I approximate the proportion of FLPH costs to the gross manufacturing output in Quebec and Ontario (Table 1). This ratio is my proxy for FLPH costs per unit of output since I make the simplifying assumption that average output prices were the same in both provinces. Estimates of the value of gross manufacturing output are inclusive of accounting profits which are assumed to be part of the economic costs of production.

Data on transportation costs are not necessary if the reasonable assumption is made - biasing my results in favour of the Faucher-Lamontagne hypothesis—that transportation costs per ton/mile for inputs and outputs are the same. Data on the weight of inputs (coal and other fuels) and outputs are not readily available. Such a serious statistical gap would not be important if FLPH costs are only a negligible proportion of gross value of output or if FLPH costs per unit of output (FLPH costs as a percentage of gross value of output) are similar in both provinces.

I find that for all manufacturing, FLPH costs constitute an almost identical percentage of the value of gross manufacturing output in both

Table 1 Cost of Fuel, Lighting, Power, and Heat (FLPH) as a Percentage of Current Dollar Gross Output in Manufacturing in 1900 (in Thousands of Canadian Dollars)

	Ontario			*Quebec*		
	Gross Output	*FLPH*	*(2/1)*	*Gross Output*	*FLHP*	*(2/1)*
All Manufacturing[1]	$236,441	$3,352	1.42%	$153,135	$2,202	1.44%
Food & beverages	71,874	672	0.93	33,084	321	0.97
Tobacco & products	2,736	11.3	0.41	8,231	30.7	0.37
Rubber products	1,134	16.1	1.42	440	7.5	1.70
Leather products	11,971	81.8	0.68	20,549	168	0.82
Textile products	11,001	261	2.38	12,169	288	2.37
Clothing	18,872	202	1.07	13,495	78.8	0.58
Wood products	41,825	235	0.56	15,796	77.1	0.49
Paper products	4,267	138	3.22	6,542	165	2.53
Printing, publishing & allied industries	7,168	107	1.49	3,510	80.3	2.28
Iron & steel products[2]	30,188	917	3.04	14,565	448	3.07
Agricultural implements	8,295	105	2.30	1,162	24.2	2.08
Fabricated & structural steel	738	9.3	1.26	1,129	11.3	1.80
Hardware & boilers	1,977	41.1	2.08	371	10.4	2.19
Household, office & store machinery	554	5.4	0.97	56	1.3	2.37
Machinery & boilers	12,988	270	2.08	6629	124	1.88
Primary iron & steel	1,894	316	16.68	329	42.3	12.86
Wire & wire products	2,998	164	5.46	4,688	230	4.91
Transportation equipment	10,561	158	1.49	8,432	169	2.01

(continued)

Table 1 (continued)

	Ontario			*Quebec*		
	Gross Output	*FLPH*	*(2/1)*	*Gross Output*	*FLHP*	*(2/1)*
Nonferrous metal products	1,902	25.1	1.32	920	14.9	1.62
Electrical apparatus & supplies	1,171	21.6	1.84	1,815	114.6	6.32
Nonmetallic mineral products	4,716	290	6.16	1,716	21.1	1.32
Petroleum & coal products	3,221	4.9	0.15	495	5.5	1.11
Chemical products	5,231	53.4	1.02	7,449	32.4	0.43
Miscellaneous products	5,569	62.2	1.12	703	8.7	1.24
Unclassified industries[3]	2,989	94.3	3.15	3,625	177	4.88

Note All census data are reclassified in accordance with the Standard Industrial Classification Manual. [1]All industries reported in the 1900 census are encompassed in my major manufacturing sectors and subsectors except for gas lighting and heating; electric light and power; painters and glaziers; photography; and plumbing and tinsmithing. These are categorized as services by the Dominion Bureau of Statistics, Standard Industrial Classification Manual, used here to classify the census data. [2]All but three of this sector's subsectors are listed here. These are, blacksmithing, sheet-metal products, and miscellaneous iron and steel products, all of marginal importance in both provinces. [3]When an industry in a province encompasses less than three firms, data on these firms are listed in the "all other industry" category in the census. The unclassified industries category embodies the census data for this category minus industries which could be identified using census data for Canada and the other provinces. Data for the identified industries are included with that of the major sectors of which they are part. For example, the census lists only one firm in Quebec producing rubber and elastic goods. This industry's data are included by the census in the "all other industry" category. But census data for Ontario and Canada are available for this industry since there were six and seven industries respectively in these regions. From this I derive FLPH and output estimates for Quebec. Data for this industry are classified under the rubber products sector.

Sources The Census of Canada, 1900–1901 (Ottawa, 1901), vol. 3; and Dominion Bureau of Statistics, Standard Industrial Classification Manual (Ottawa, 1948)

Quebec and Ontario - approximately 1.4% (Table 1). Thus, no differential in FLPH costs per unit of output existed between the two provinces in 1900. These costs were also a trivial fraction of the total value of gross output, in spite of the price of coal being about 10% greater in Quebec.[14] This lends support to the argument that the Faucher-Lamontagne thesis is incorrect. It also suggests that Quebec firms were able to adjust their

Table 2 Manufacturing Value-Added and Employment

	Quebec				*Ontario*			
	Value-Added		*Number of Labourers*		*Value-Added*		*Number of Labourers*	
All Manufacturing	$95,217	100.0%	161,770	100.0%	$65,961	100.0%	107,297	100.0%
Food & beverages	15,888	16.7	19,827	12.2	7,612	11.5	10,584	9.9
Tobacco & products	1,750	1.8	1,219	0.7	5,702	8.6	3,981	3.7
Rubber products	376	0.4	536	0.3	202	0.3	217	0.2
Leather products	3,965	4.2	6,533	4.0	7,932	12.0	13,458	12.5
Textile products	4,956	5.2	9,711	6.0	5,094	7.7	10,171	9.5
Clothing	9,133	9.6	25,360	15.7	6,513	9.9	11,915	11.1
Wood products	19,855	20.8	38,629	23.9	8,176	12.4	19,167	17.9
Paper products	2,072	2.2	3,199	2.0	3,595	5.4	5,040	4.7
Printing, publishing & allied industries	4,804	5.0	7,037	4.3	2,462	3.7	3,346	3.1
Iron & steel products	16,154	17.0	22,560	13.9	7,218	10.9	9,785	9.1
Agricultural implements	4,558	28.2	5,691	25.2	662	9.2	990	10.1
Fabricated & structural steel	247	1.5	393	1.7	628	8.7	582	5.9
Hardware & tools	1,041	6.4	1,621	7.2	247	3.4	409	4.2
Household, office & store machinery	312	1.9	474	0.3	36	0.5	48	0.0
Machinery & boilers	8,148	50.4	11,323	50.2	4,030	55.8	4,840	49.5
Primary iron & steel	303	1.9	868	3.8	80	1.1	255	2.8

(continued)

Table 2 (continued)

	Quebec				*Ontario*			
	Value-Added		*Number of Labourers*		*Value-Added*		*Number of Labourers*	
Wire & wire products	1,189	7.4	1,843	8.2	1,584	21.9	2,493	25.5
Transportation equipment	5,062	5.3	8,593	5.3	3,324	5.0	7,054	6.6
Nonferrous metal products	1,082	1.1	1,327	0.8	553	0.8	721	0.7
Electrical apparatus & supplies	480	0.5	949	0.6	1,231	1.9	1,040	1.0
Nonmetallic mineral products	2,003	2.1	6,176	3.8	1,344	2.0	2,423	2.2
Petroleum & coal products	1,139	1.2	612	0.4	140	0.2	109	0.1
Chemical products	2,339	2.4	3,116	1.9	3,396	5.1	5,600	5.2
Miscellaneous products	3,178	3.3	4,844	3.0	463	0.7	739	0.7
Unclassified industries	983	1.0	1,542	0.9	1,004	1.5	1,947	1.8

Notes For a general discussion on the construction of the estimates refer to Table 1. The value added estimates are in thousands of Canadian dollars and are derived by subtracting from the census estimates of gross output, the census estimates of the value of raw material, FLPH costs, and taxation. The value added estimates, however, are inclusive of depreciation charges. Employment estimates are drawn from the census estimates of individuals employed on salary or wages.
Sources See Table 1

coal inputs so as to keep total FLPH costs per unit of output from becoming relatively excessive. Thus, Quebec firms probably did not face fixed coefficients of production in the components of FLPH costs.

Faucher and Lamontagne are most concerned with iron and steel production. Here, FLPH costs constitute only 3.04% of the gross value of iron and steel products in Ontario and 3.07% in Quebec (Table 1). The similarity of FLPH costs per unit of output and their small magnitude with respect to the value of total output suggest that Quebec's lag in the iron and steel products sector was not caused by its relatively high-priced sources of fuel, light, power, and heating, resulting in comparatively high

FLPH costs per unit of output. This sector contributed 17.0% to the 1900 manufacturing value added in Ontario and only 10.9% in Quebec, and in manufacturing employment it added 13.9% in Ontario and only 9.1% in Quebec (Table 2).

Within the iron and steel products sector, machinery production provided 50.4% of the value added in Ontario and 55.8% in Quebec. Machinery production also contributed 50.2 and 45.9% of Ontario's and Quebec's respective employment in this sector (Table 2). In this important subsector FLPH costs constituted only 2.08% of the value of gross output in Ontario and 1.88% in Quebec (Table 1). FLPH costs per unit of output were more favourable in Quebec than in Ontario. Nevertheless, these costs represented an insignificant portion of the value of gross output in the machinery subsector in both provinces and, hence, only a negligible proportion of total economic costs. In a subsector that was much more important to Ontario, the production of agricultural implements (Table 2), Quebec held a slight advantage over Ontario in FLPH costs per unit of output. These costs contributed 2.30% to this subsector's value of gross output in Ontario and 2.08% in Quebec. Ontario's slight disadvantage in FLPH costs per unit of output did not hinder its highly successful development of agricultural implements production. Even in the production of primary iron and steel or smelting, Quebec held an advantage over Ontario in FLPH costs per unit of output. These costs comprised 12.9 and 16.7% of their gross value of smelting output respectively. This subsector, however, was more important in Ontario and contributed only marginally to both provinces' iron and steel products' value added and employment. In this case, Quebec's advantage in FLPH costs per unit of output did not result in Quebec's smelting industry being more important than Ontario's. But in the wire and wire products subsector, marginally lower FLPH costs per unit of output in Quebec coincided with this subsector's greater importance to Quebec. Overall, FLPH costs were too small to determine the location of specific subsectors of iron and steel products. Additionally, there is no obvious relationship between an inter-provincial differential in FLPH costs per unit of output and the location of subsectors.

Wood products is a sector that was critical to the size of manufacturing in both provinces, representing 20.8% of the manufacturing value added in Ontario and 12.4% in Quebec, and 23.9 and 17.9% respectively of manufacturing employment. The FLPH costs constituted 0.56% of this sector's value of gross output in Ontario and 0.49% in Quebec—too insignificant to have any causal effect upon the relative size of this sector in either province. The same argument can be applied to almost all major manufacturing sectors in Quebec and Ontario (see Table 1). In many of these sectors there was also no positive relationship between a region's advantage in FLPH costs per unit of output in an industry and the relative importance of that industry. For example, in the transportation equipment sector, FLPH costs contributed 1.49 and 2.01% to the value of gross output in Ontario and Quebec. This sector was of similar importance in both provinces—between 5 and 6% of manufacturing value added and employment—in spite of the inter-provincial differential in FLPH costs per unit of output. In the leather products sector, a major sector in Quebec contributing about 12% to its manufacturing value added and employment but only 4% to Ontario's, FLPH costs encompassed 0.82 and 0.68% respectively of the value of gross output. Although Ontario held a clear advantage in FLPH costs per unit of output, these costs were too inconsequential to impede the more significant development of the leather industry in Quebec.

5 Conclusion

The evidence presented here - and it must be emphasized that it is only for one year—tends to refute the thesis that unit cost disadvantages in the supply of coal and iron ore impeded Quebec's process of industrial development. Other factors must be identified to explain the lag in industrial development in Quebec compared with Ontario, particularly the limited size of its iron and steel products sector. Elsewhere I argue that inter-provincial differences in market structure play an important role in such an explanation.[15]

If the comparison between Quebec and Ontario is any indication, the emphasis upon location and resource endowments for coal and iron ore in determining industrial development has been exaggerated. The absence of coal and iron ore cannot impede industrial and, in particular, manufacturing development if these inputs and iron and steel ingots can be imported unless their absence increases costs per unit of output relative to competing regions and if these costs are a significant component of total costs. Even so, firms in a region importing inputs are protected, up to a point, by the transportation costs incurred by firms exporting the final output to this region.

Notes

1. Faucher and Lamontagne (1953), vol. 1, pp. 259, 260, 264 They refer largely to manufacturing development as opposed to the broader concept of industrial development.
2. Ibid., (p. 264). Faucher and Lamontagne write: "Cultural factors had nothing to do with … the relative lethargy of Quebec's industry in comparison with that of Ontario: this difference is explained by the simple fact that Quebec, in the steel economy of that period, had no coal and no iron and was located too far from the Appalachian coal fields." They conclude: "In an economy of coal and steel, when the locational factors were not favourable, [Quebec] developed less rapidly than other regions in a more advantageous position. On the other hand, when these factors became favourable, progress was immediately felt" (p. 268). Thus, prior to the predominance of the iron and steel economy, Quebec experienced a prosperity related to wood and shipbuilding. And after 1911, with the increased development of and emphasis upon hydroelectricity, with which Quebec was so well endowed, Quebec's industrial development was able to resume a relatively healthy economic demeanour, pp. 260, 265, 267. They also mention the distance from markets as a factor which potentially hindered Quebec's industrial development, but only in passing, p. 260. For Faucher and Lamontagne, what determined the changes in Quebec's development process over the nineteenth and twentieth centuries was, largely, changes in the type of resources critical to the development process.
3. Pollard (1982), (p. 4), argues that economic historians tend to underrate the importance of natural resources to economic development, possibly as the result of the influence of theoretical economics. Pollard also argues that the locationn of coal in Britain was a necessary condition for its industrialization. But this last point remains to be demonstrated. My intention is to use a variant of location theory to establish the conditions where natural resources can be important to industrial development.
4. Faucher and Lamontagne (1953), p. 257 base their arguments for Quebec's relatively poor industrial performance almost entirely upon literary sources. They argue: "Due to the scarcity and, in many instances, the complete absence of statistical data, our approach has to be non-quantitative." Using census material, Raynauld (1961), pp. 29, 43–48, 55–57, finds that total manufacturing value added in Quebec and Ontario grew at a similar pace from 1870 to 1956 and that their manufacturing sectors developed similar structures. The difference in per capita manufacturing growth, in Ontario's favour, was the result of the faster rate of population growth in Quebec. Also using the censuses, I find that the manufacturing sector in Quebec lagged even further behind that of

Ontario than is suggested by Raynauld. See Altman (1984), vol. 1, p. 91; vol. 2, appendices D and I. Nominal manufacturing value added per capita in Quebec relative to Ontario fell from 87 to 75% from 1870 to 1910, while in real terms this ratio fell from 89 to 78%. I also find that the iron and steel products sector, so important to Faucher and Lamontagne, comprised 14.3% of the nominal manufacturing value added in 1870 and only 10.9% in 1910 in Quebec and 19.0 and 19.7% respectively in Ontario. This sector contributed 13.8 and 8.5% respectively to Quebec's manufacturing employment in 1870 and 1910 and 18.3 and 19.9% respectively to Ontario's, Ibid., vol. 2, appendix H.

5. One of the basic tenets of location theory is that, ceteris paribus, transfer costs play a determining role in the location of industry. The argument presented below flows from and is an attempt to extend the concepts in location theory eloquently illustrated in Hoover (1963), Chapter. 3; and Nourse (1978), pp. 74–85.
6. This is an extreme result following from my simplifying assumptions. More realistically, under these conditions, the most efficient firms in Quebec would survive. But these firms would be less profitable than firms of equal efficiency in Ontario.
7. Estall and Buchanan (1972), pp. 62–64, make this argument. The logic of this argument is to the extent that value is a rough proxy for weight when comparing inputs and outputs of a specific commodity, as the value of fuels diminishes relative to that of total output the weight of the fuels diminishes relative to that of total output. In this case, when the percentage of the value of fuels to the value of total output falls below 100, the cost of transporting fuels to Quebec falls below that of transporting the final output from Ontario to Quebec. Transfer costs protect Quebec firms from their higher fuel costs. However, if a dollar worth of fuel outweighs a dollar worth of final output, the critical point of 100 percent is too high. But it is likely that if this percentage falls as low as 10% the Estall and Buchanan argument would hold.
8. The argument can be expressed more precisely as $Q_a > 0$, if $[B_a + (I_a + W_{la}D_{la}) + W_{Qa}D_{Qa}]/Q_a \leq [B_b + (I_b + W_{lb}D_{lb}) + W_{Qb}D_{Qb}]/Q_b$. Total output in Quebec (Q_a) exceeds zero if the unit cost of production of Quebec output produced for the Quebec market is less than or equal to the unit cost of Ontario output delivered to Quebec. The bracketed term is total delivered cost. Q_b is total output in Ontario. B_a and B_b are the basic costs (largely labour) in Quebec and Ontario; I_a, and I_b are the material input costs prior to delivery; and W_a and W_b are the weight of these inputs. B, I, and W_l per unit of output are assumed equal in Quebec and Ontario. D_{la} and D_{lb} are the distances which the material inputs must be transported to reach Quebec and Ontario multiplied by some identical price per ton mile. D_{la} is assumed to be positive and D_{lb}, zero. W_{Qa}

and W_{Qb} are the weights of the final output produced in Quebec and Ontario for the Quebec market (assumed to be equal per unit of output), and D_{Qa} and D_{Qa} are the distances which the final output is transported to arrive in the Quebec market from Quebec and Ontario multiplied by some identical price per ton mile. This is assumed to be zero for Quebec and positive for Ontario. My assumptions allow the first equation to be reduced to: $Q_a > 0$, if $(W_{la}D_{la}/Q_a) \leq (W_{Qb}D_{Qb}/Q_b)$. Since D_{la} and D_{Qb} are assumed to be equal, this equation can be reduced to, $Q_a > 0$, if $(W_{la}/Q_a) \leq (W_{Qb}/Q_b)$. The per unit weights of inputs and output become the critical determinant of whether output in Quebec is positive.

9. By the late nineteenth century one ton of coke was required to produce one ton of pig iron, and one ton of coal yielded 70% coke. Thus, one ton of pig iron required 1.43 tons of coal for its production. No more than 3% of the weight of coal was absorbed into the pig iron. For production of steel and iron and steel products the entire weight of coal was lost. Depending on the type of ore used, from 40 to 70% of the weight of the iron ore used to produce a ton of pig was lost in the process of production. Using the poorest of ores, it required 4.7 tons of coal and iron ore to produce one ton of pig iron. Using a higher grade of ore might have necessitated 3.1 tons of these inputs to produce one ton of pig iron. These estimates are derived from Pounds (1963), pp. 15, 20, 33, 65.
10. Donald (1915), p. 60, states that in the 1850s and 1860s most of Canada's iron and products industry was based on imported pig iron. The same was true of the 1880s and 1890s (pp. 98, 100). From the statistical appendix provided by Donald, I compute that from 1884 to 1890 only 32.8% (on average) of the pig iron used in Canada was produced in Canada. In the 1891 to 1900 period the average increased to 52.4%, jumping to 79.7% during 1901 to 19 10, p. 328.
11. See Pounds (1963), p. 70. When iron and steel are processed into iron and steel products, 40 to 60% of the inputs become scrap metal which, however, does not result in weight loss. Scrap is melted down and used, in turn, as inputs in production of iron and steel products.
12. For all manufacturing, the constant dollar cost of labour per unit of output in Quebec divided by that in Ontario was 0.90 in 1870, 1.00 in 1880 and 1890, and 1.05 in 1910. In terms of current dollars these ratios are: 0.88 in 1870, 0.93 in 1880, 1.02 in 1890, and 1.00 in 1910. For iron and steel products these ratios are 0.85 in 1870, 1.00 in 1880, 0.98 in 1890 and, 0.83 in 1910 for my constant dollar estimates. A similar story arises for most of the major manufacturing sectors. See Altman (1986), appendix table 3.
13. It is impossible to determine the percentage of each province's output covered by the 1900 census. This census, however, provides data on

the percentage of Canadian manufacturing output produced by firms employing less than five workers in 1890. No such information is available on a provincial basis. The percentage of such output is 21.5% (The Census of Canada, 1900-1901, Ottawa, 1901, vol. 3). Using this information and data for firms employing less than five workers in 1915, Bertram (1964), p. 99, estimates that in 1900 firms employing more than four workers produced 87.8% of total manufacturing output in Canada. This assumes that the share of small firms in total output fell at a constant rate from 1890 to 1915. This percentage might be used as a very rough proxy for Quebec and Ontario.

14. From the 1900 census data, The Census of Canada, 1900-1901, vol. 3, I estimate a ton of coal in Quebec was $3.89 and $3.52 in Ontario or about 10% greater in Quebec. These estimates are derived by taking a weighted average of foreign and Canadian coal used in both provinces.
15. Altman (1984), vol. 1, Chapter. 5.

References

Altman, M. 1984. *"A Comparative Economic History of Quebec and Ontario, 1870–1910: An Analysis of the Statistical Sources", (two volumes*. PhD diss.: Department of Economics, McGill University).

Altman, M. 1986. *X-Efficiency' and Differential Labour Productivity Growth: Case Study of Quebec and Ontario, 1870–1910*. Philadelphia: Paper presented at the Eastern Economics Association Meetings.

Bertram, G.W. 1964. "Historical Statistics on Growth and Structure of Manufacturing in Canada, 1870–1957," In J. Henripin and A. Asimakopulos, eds., *Conferences on Statistics, 1962–1963, Papers* (Toronto), 93–146

Census of Canada, 1901 (1913). Ottawa. Vol. 3.

Donald, W.J.A. 1915. *The Canadian Iron and Steel Industry: A Study in the Economic History of a Protected Industry*. Boston: Houghton Mifflin Co.

Estell, R.C., and R.O. Buchanan. 1972. *Industrial Activity and Economic Geography*. London: Hutchinson and Co.

Faucher, A., and M. Lamontagne. 1953. History of Industrial Development. In *Essays on Contemporary Quebec*, ed. J.C. Falardeau, 23–37. Québec: Les Presses de l'Université Laval.

Hoover, E.G. 1963. *The Location of Economic Activity*. New York: McGraw-Hill Book Company.

Nourse, H.O. 1968. *Regional Economics: A Study in the Economic Structure, Stability, and Growth of Regions*. New York: McGraw Hill.

Pollard, S. 1982. *Peaceful Conquest: The Industrialization of Europe, 1760–1970* (Oxford)

Pounds, J.G. 1963. *The Geography of Iron and Steel*. London: Oxford University Press.

Raynauld, A. 1961. *Croissance et structure économique de la province du Québec*, (Quebec: Ministère de l'lndustrie et du commerce).w

CHAPTER 9

Railways as an Engine of Economic Growth? Who Benefited from the Canadian Railway Boom?

1 Introduction

It is generally argued that the Canadian railway construction boom of the late nineteenth and early twentieth centuries did little to benefit the Quebec economy.[1]

This construction boom was heavily subsidized by the dominion government of Canada. François-Albert Angers forcefully and eloquently argued that the dominion government discriminated against Quebec in terms of railway construction and aid for economic development. Dominion spending, he claimed, was biased in favour of Ontario and Canada's western provinces. In a word, the dominion government chose to allocate its available resources towards the development of Canada, west of Quebec, prior to providing Quebec with the government assistance thought necessary for Quebec to realize its maximum feasible level of economic development. This choice, which was against the best interests of Quebec, was made so as to insure the profitability of the western railways. Such an agenda restrained Quebec's economic development in the late nineteenth century.[2] Recently, Angers' line of argument has been reiterated by P.-A. Linteau, R. Durocher, and J.-C. Robert in *Histoire du Québec contemporain*. These authors emphasize that Quebec did not benefit nearly as much as did Ontario from investments in railways.[3] Brian Young, in his study of the construction of Quebec's north-shore railway, has forwarded a similar argument.[4]

M. Altman, *Lessons from a Successfully Export-Oriented, Resource-Rich Economy*, https://doi.org/10.1007/978-3-031-03887-7_9

Evidence in support of discrimination presently rests upon an implicit assumption that the economic benefits which might accrue to a region from railway construction can be inferred simply from data on total dominion government grants for railway construction and on the mileage of track constructed in each province. Such an assumption does not take into consideration whether Dominion subsidies were less on a per capita basis or, more importantly, as an inducement to private investment in railway construction, on a per mile of track basis. And, on a more general level, the discrimination thesis fails to consider the effects that railway construction (wherever it was carried out) might have had on Quebec's manufacturing, primarily through its impact upon railway-related manufacturing activities as well as in making markets in Ontario and the western provinces more accessible to Quebec's industry.

2 Estimates on Canada's Railway Boom: A Preliminary Analysis

In order to examine Angers' important thesis, I construct estimates of dominion government subsidies for railway construction in Quebec and Ontario. These estimates indicate that, in terms of subsidies granted per mile of track, Quebec benefited more from dominion government grants than did Ontario. In this respect, I find that the dominion government did not discriminate against Quebec. Estimates of municipal and provincial governments subsidies for railway construction in Quebec and Ontario are also produced. I find that while, according to all measures, municipalities in Ontario granted more for railway construction than their Quebec counterparts, Quebec is found to be far ahead of Ontario with respect to provincial government grants. Moreover, total subsidies per mile of track were far greater in Quebec than in Ontario, even after taking into consideration the subsidies granted by all levels of government.

I also present estimates which measure the importance of railway-related manufacturing activities to the growth and size of total manufacturing activities in Quebec, Ontario and Canada as a whole. In that way, I attempt to evaluate the indirect impact which railway construction had upon Quebec, Ontario and Canadian manufacturing growth from 1870 to 1910. For the discrimination thesis to be confirmed, I should find, at the very least, that Quebec derived little indirect benefit from railway construction. This thesis would be further reinforced if I find that most indirect benefits were captured by Ontario. My findings, however, are quite the contrary. Indeed, I find that railway-related industries played a critical role in Quebec's manufacturing growth while being relatively insignificant to Ontario's manufacturing growth.

These findings allow me to address some of the more general questions related to the importance of railways raised in the now classic works of Robert Fogel (1964) and Albert Fishlow (1971). Fogel argues that the indirect benefits with respect to backward linkages from railway construction were insignificant to American manufacturing growth.[5] My results, on the other hand, indicate that these indirect benefits were of greater importance in Canada, especially in Quebec, particularly from 1900 to 1910. These results caution against generalizing from the American experience. Moreover, they are consistent with some studies on the European experience.[6] Ultimately, my study suggests that significant growth in one industry can play a critical role in a region's or country's growth process.

Supporters of the discrimination thesis have provided little concrete evidence to support the view that Quebec was discriminated against by the dominion government. We know only that Quebec possessed consistently less railway mileage than Ontario from 1870 to 1910 (see Table 5). Also, Gaétan Gervais finds that total dominion government grants for railway construction to Ontario exceeded those going to Quebec over the 1867 to 1896 period.[7] The discrimination thesis implicitly assumes that if Quebec had received its "fair share" of dominion government aid, more track would have been laid in Quebec which, in turn, would have resulted in more economic growth. However, a careful examination of my estimates for government grants for railway construction and for the significance of railway-related industry suggests that this implicit assumption is incorrect.

3 Was Quebec Discriminated Against Duriong Canada's Railway Boom: Assessing the Evidence

At first glance (Table 1), it appears that my estimates tend to corroborate the discrimination thesis. By 1909, it would appear that Quebec received substantially less dominion government aid than did Ontario: $22.2 million for Quebec compared to about $36.7 million for Ontario. But this is a statistical illusion. Over 70% of dominion government subsidies to Ontario were for a mere 11% of the total mileage of track in Ontario by 1909. This heavily subsidized stretch of track (953 miles in all) constituted the portion of the Canadian Pacific main line running

Table 1 Government grants for railroad construction in Quebec and Ontario

		Quebec	*Ontario*
Total Grants:			
1	Dominion Government	$22,195,776 [a]	$10,568,081
1a	Dominion Government inclusive of grants for the Canadian Pacific main line [b]		36,691,792
2	Provincial Government	14,181,259	8,787,325
3	Municipal Government	983,291	9,815,257
4	Total	37,360,326	29,170,663
4a	Inclusive of 1a		55,294,374
Total grants per mile of track: [c]			
1	Dominion Government	6,059	1,434
1a	Dominion Government inclusive of grants for the Canadian Pacific main line [d]		4,978
2	Provincial Government	3,871	1,192
3	Municipal Government	268	1,332
4	Total	10,198	3,958
4a	Inclusive of 1a		7,502
Total grants per capita: [e]			
1	Dominion Government	11.07	4.18
1a	Dominion Government inclusive of grants for the Canadian Pacific main line [d]		14.51
2	Provincial Government	7.07	3.48
3	Municipal Government	0.49	3.88
4	Total	18.63	11.64
4a	Inclusive of 1a		21.87

Notes The estimates for grants are deduced from data in the "Report of the Department of Railways and Canals," 1910. For details, refer to Morris Altman, "Railroads as an 'Engine' of Growth?" statistical appendix.

[a] The Dominion government subsidies include $5,160,053 given to the Quebec government, "Report of the Department of Railroads and Canals", 1910, p. 15.

Table 1 (continued)

[b] According to the "Report of the Department of Railways and Canals," 1910, p. 84, Canadian Pacific received $29,416,346 in subsidies for its main line. This grant pertains only to that portion of the line running from Callander, Ontario to Vancouver, British Columbia: 2,560.9 miles. Of this track, 953 miles are in Ontario, of which 653 miles are front Callander to Fort Williams (now Thunderbay). The remainder, leading to the Ontario-Manitoba border was constructed at government expense and turned over to the Canadian Pacific. This approximately 300-mile stretch of track was not covered by the above bonuses. In total, the 722 miles of the main line constructed at government expense was not covered by the bonuses (see Glazenbrook, A History of Transportation, p. 72). Ontario's share of the main line covered by bonuses is 35.5 percent (653 of 1,839 miles). Therefore, Ontario's share of Dominion bonuses for the mainline amounted to $10,442,803. I estimate the value of the 300 miles of government-constructed track in Ontario to have been $15,680,908. This appears to be an upper-bound estimate which in turn biases my results in favour of the discrimination hypothesis (see Table 2, note b). Total government aid to Ontario for the construction of the Canadian Pacific main line was, therefore, $26,123,711.

[c] In 1909, Quebec possessed 3,663 miles of track compared to Ontario's 7,370 miles, exclusive of the Ontario section of the Canadian Pacific main line referred to in note a.

[d] Government subsidies are $26,123,711 and the mileage estimate used is 8,323.

[e] The population of Quebec in 1910 was 2,005,776 and in Ontario, 2,527,291.

Sources Morris Altman, "Railroads as an 'Engine' of Growth in Canada and its Central Provinces, 1870–1910", working paper, Department of Economics, University of Ottawa, 1987; Canadian Pacific Railway, ***Annual Report of the Year and Report of Proceedings at the Tenth Annual Meeting of Shareholders***, Montreal, 1891: *Census of Canada, 1930–1931*, Ottawa, 1932, on population data; G. P. de T. Glazenbrook, *A History of Transportation in Canada:National Economy, 1867–1936*, vol. 2, Toronto, 1964; "Report of the Department of Railways and Canals," ***Sessional Papers of the Parliament of Canada***, no 10, Ottawa, 1900; "Report of the Department of Railways and Canals," ***Sessional Papers of the Parliament of Canada***, no 20b, Ottawa, 1910; Table 2, notes. *Notes*: The estimates for grants are deduced from data in the "Report of the Department of Railways and Canals," 1910. For details, refer to Morris Altman, "Railroads as an 'Engine' of Growth?" statistical appendix

from Callander, Ontario to the Ontario-Manitoba border, a region whose hinterland was consistently isolated, sparsely populated and unexploited territory from 1870 to 1910. The dominion government's purpose in seeing this section of the main line built was to link Ontario and Quebec to the western part of the Canadian Confederation. Thus, one might argue that aid to this line constituted aid, not only to Ontario, but also to Quebec, since both provinces stood to benefit from access to the Canadian west. This, then, serves as a legitimate basis for excluding all dominion government subsidies for this portion of the Canadian Pacific main line from the Ontario total.

In this case, Ontario's share of dominion government railway subsidies falls to only $10.6 million (Table 1). On a per mile of track basis, Dominion aid amounts to $6,059 to Quebec and $1,434 to Ontario, excluding the Canadian Pacific main line, but still only $4,978 to Ontario, if one includes it. On a per capita basis, dominion government subsidies come to $11.07 to Quebec and $4.18 to Ontario, if one excludes the Canadian Pacific track, and to $14.51, if one includes it. However, the most important measure of government aid is grants per mile of track. This is what generates the incentive for private enterprise to invest in the construction of railways. Thus, on a per line of track basis, no matter whether or not one excludes the Canadian Pacific main line, Quebec attracted more than its fair share of dominion government grant money. On a per capita criterion, Quebec did not fare as well (however, only marginally so), but only if one includes subsidies for the Canadian Pacific main line in the Ontario total (Table 1). This argument changes little when one examines total subsidies for railway construction by 1897, which is closer to Gervais' end-year (Table 2). However, when one compares the estimates for 1897 and 1909, it is evident that, in terms of Dominion aid, the increase of aid going to Quebec exceeded that going to Ontario.

With respect to provincial government grants, Quebec governments provided considerably more money for railway construction than their Ontario counterparts, irrespective of which measure one chooses. This is in sharp contrast to the considerable difference in municipal subsidies to railway construction between both provinces. Urban centres in Quebec spent only $268 per mile of track by 1909 as compared to the $1,332 spent in Ontario (Table 1). Provincial government subsidies in Quebec, however, more than compensated for the unwillingness or, more probably, the inability of Quebec municipalities to raise more grant money.

Table 2 Government grants for railroad construction in Quebec and Ontario by 1897 (current Canadian dollars)

		Quebec	*Ontario*
Total grants:			
1	Dominion Government	$14,942,450 [a]	$5,203,799
1a	Dominion Government inclusive of grants for the Canadian Pacific main line [b]		29,759,707
2	Provincial Government	12,250,479	6,791,323
3	Municipal Government	506,074	9,433,349
4	Total	27,699,003	21,428,471
4a	Inclusive of 1a		45,984,379
Total grants per mile of track:[c]			
1	Dominion Government	4,538	891
1a	Dominion Government inclusive of grants for the Canadian Pacific main line [d]		4,297
2	Provincial Government	3,720	1,137
3	Municipal Government	154	1,579
4	Total	8,412	3,607
4a	Inclusive of 1a		7,013
Total grants per capita:[e]			
1	Dominion Government	9.44	2.41
1a	Dominion Government inclusive of grants for the Canadian Pacific main line		13.8
2	Provincial Government	7.74	3.15
3	Municipal Government	0.32	4.38
4	Total	17.5	9.94
4a	Inclusive of 1a		21.33

Notes The estimates for grants are deduced from data in the "Report of the Department of Railways and Canals," 1898. For details, refer to Morris Altman, "Railroads as an 'Engine' of Growth?" statistical appendix

[a] See Table 9.1, note a.

Table 2 (continued)

[b] According to the "Report of the Department of Railways and Canals," 1898, the Canadian Pacific received $56,093,888 in subsidies. This includes the $31,093,888 of government-constructed track turned over to the Canadian Pacific plus $25,000,000 of grants. The former sum is lower than the $37,785,319 referred to as the cost of the government-built track by the "Report of the Department of Railways and Canals," 1910, p. 15. The higher total is also quoted by Fowke, The National Policy, p. 49, and by Easterbrook and Aitken, Canadian Economic History, p. 429. It appears that the lower sum excludes the cost of surveys. I use the higher figure for my estimates. Ontario's share of the government-constructed track amounted to 300 miles or 41.6 percent of the total (see Table 1, note a). The value of Ontario's share of government track was, therefore, $15,680,908. And, since Ontario's possessed 35.5 percent of the Canadian Pacific main line which was covered by federal government bonuses (see Table 9.1, note a), Ontario captured $8,875,000 of the $25,000,000 of bonuses. Total grants for the Canadian Pacific main line located in Ontario, therefore, amounted to $24,555,908.

[c] In 1897, Quebec possessed 3,293 miles of track and Ontario, 5,973 miles, exclusive of its share of the Canadian Pacific main line.

[d] Government subsidies are $29,759,707 and the mileage estimate used is 6,926 miles.

[e] No census data for the 1897 population are available. The population figures which I use, 1,582,740 and 2,155,242 for Quebec and Ontario respectively, are hypothetical and are derived using the interest rate formula and the census estimates for these provinces' populations in 1890 and 1900.

Sources W.T. Easterbrook and Hugh G.T. Aitken, Canadian Economic History, Toronto, 1956; V.C. Fowke, The National Policy and the Wheat Economy, Toronto, 1957; "Report of the Department of Railways and Canals," Sessional Papers of the Parliament of Canada, no. 8, Ottawa, 1898; Table 1, sources.

When all government grants are taken together, grants per mile of track in Quebec are almost 40% more than in Ontario, even after one takes into account the Dominion funds granted for the Callander to Ontario-Manitoba segment of the Canadian Pacific main line. On a per capita basis, total government grants add up to $18.63 for Quebec and $21.87 for Ontario (Table 1).

Clearly, in Quebec, much more grant money was required to realize a mile of railway. In other words, railway construction in Quebec was much more inelastic to state subsidies than in Ontario. This suggests that the absence of railway track in Quebec was not a product of dominion government discrimination, but rather of underlying problems in the Quebec economy, which made rail construction in this province relatively less profitable than in Ontario (as hinted at by Gervais (1978), p. 359; see also Brian and Young (1978), pp. 7, 80, 113). One cause for this might have been the relative poverty of the Quebec economy which, apart from Montreal, generated a smaller need for railways than the more prosperous Ontario economy.[8]

4 Indirect Benefits from Railway Construction

I estimate the indirect benefits from railway construction by measuring the growth of value added and employment in railway-related manufacturing industries relative to the growth of total manufacturing value added and employment. The railway-related industries include the census classifications of car repairs, car and car works, and railway supplies. This measure indicates the percentage of overall manufacturing growth which can be attributed to railway construction and the use and maintenance of the railways. But this measure excludes the purchases made by these industries in other sectors of the economy, such as in iron products, and is, therefore, very much of a lower-bound estimate of the indirect benefits of railways.

My upper-bound estimate for such benefits is the growth of gross output in the railway-related industries relative to growth of the total manufacturing value added. Gross output incorporates inputs purchased from other industries by the railway-related industries. This latter estimate, however, includes imports and, thus, represents a biased measure of upper-bound benefits. I provide no upper-bound estimate for employment attributable to railway construction.[9] This upper-bound estimate still cannot do justice to the actual indirect benefits, which railways generated, since its focus is upon the manufacturing sector. Quebec, for example, gained considerably from the grain trade, much of which passed through the port of Montreal by way of Canada's transcontinental railway and feeder lines.[10]

Immediately, an objection may be raised by some experts that the methodology which I adopt to measure the indirect benefits of railways is incorrect. Those economic historians who use the general equilibrium-neoclassical theory framework to guide their analysis would argue that the indirect benefits of railways can only be measured by the extent to which the railway-related industries generated more value added and employment than other sectors. For it is assumed, by ahistorical definition, that had there been no railway-related manufacturing in Canada, other manufacturing activities would have taken its place. Therefore, the railway-related manufacturing activities which did take place only crowded out other potential manufacturing activities. It is assumed that full employment of all resources (human and nonhuman) is the rule, and that all potential savings are always invested, and that the potential level of savings is fixed. Therefore, the government-inspired railway boom could only affect the allocation of scarce and fixed economic resources as opposed to affecting an increase in such resources.[11]

However, such assumptions have little empirical bearing upon Canadian economy and, in particular, upon the economy of Quebec. Over 60,000 people left Quebec from 1870 to 1910 to other regions of Canada and to the United States (Altman (1988), p. 28). Canada, as a whole, generated 471,000 emigrants from 1870 to 1900. Only from 1900 to 1910, during Canada's wheat boom, was Canada's net migration positive: 716,000 individuals (Marr and Paterson (1980), table 6:7). Therefore, the supply of labour in Canada was flexible throughout the 1870–1910 period, responding to the ebb and flow of labour demand. Moreover, there is ample evidence that Canada was capable of attracting foreign capital (savings) when the need arose (see, for example, Hartland (1953), pp. 70–80). And, there is no evidence to suggest that Canadians were investing all or even most of their potential savings. For this reason, it is likely that the railway-related industries added to total production as opposed to crowding-out other economic activity. And, for this reason, my upper-bound estimates for the indirect contribution of railways to economic growth are unlikely to be an exaggerated measure.

My estimates indicate that, particularly from the 1880s onwards, Quebec's indirect benefits were considerable and substantially greater than Ontario's. From 1870 to 1880, between 3 and 9% of Quebec's increase in real manufacturing value added can be attributed to railway industries as compared to between 2 and 5% in Ontario (Table 3). Over the next decade, these industries accounted for between 12 to 24% of the growth of real manufacturing value added in Quebec and between only 0.6 to 0.7% in Ontario; and this was during the era of the construction of the Canadian Pacific's main line for which Ontario received so much Dominion grant money. From 1890 to 1910, Quebec's indirect benefits changed little from what they were in the 1880s, while Ontario's now ranged from 4 to 6%. With respect to employment growth, 6% of Quebec's and 5% of Ontario's manufacturing employment growth took place in the railway industries in the 1870s. In the 1880s, these industries

Table 3 Significance of the Growth in Railroad-Related Manufacturing Activities in the Growth of Total Manufacturing (for Constant Canadian Dollars, 1913 = 100)

Period	*Value Added (Railroads) / Value Added (Total Mfg)*	*Gross Output (Railroads) / Value Added (Total Mfg)*	*No. of Employees (Railroads) / No. of Manufacturing (Total Mfg)*
A. Quebec			
1870–1880	3.49%	8.72%	7.74%
1880–1890	12.45	24.06	6.17
1890–1910	9.49	24.41	20.94
B. Ontario			
1870–1880	2.11	5.38	5.15
1880–1890	0.58	0.72	0.13
1890–1910	4.12	6.06	7.41
C. Canada			
1870–1880	2.17	6.89	4.58
1880–1890	5.84	11.53	1.79
1890–1910	7.39	24.81	16.16
1890–1900	1.14	18.06	13.21
1900–1910	7.71	16.95	16.95

Sources These percentages are derived from the total real output and employment estimates for Quebec and Ontario in Morris Altman, "Economic Development with High Wages: An Historical Perspective," mimeo, Department of Economics, University of Ottawa, 1986, Tables 2 and 4. For the Canadian totals, I use Morris Altman, "A Revision of Canadian Economic Growth, 1870–1910: A Challenge to the Gradualist Interpretation," *Canadian Journal of Economics*, 20, 1987, Table 9. For the railroad-related manufacturing sector estimates, I construct output and employment estimates found in the appendix to this paper.

generated 6 and 0.13% of these provinces' employment growth respectively. From 1890 to 1910, however, the railway industries contributed over 21% to Quebec's manufacturing employment growth but only 7% to Ontario's.[12]

One can see that growth in Quebec's manufacturing sector was very dependent upon those manufacturing activities most directly spawned by railway construction in Canada as a whole. And, in the 1890–1910 period, that period which encompassed Canada's wheat boom, Quebec's indirect benefits from railway construction were even more substantial, even though railway construction in Quebec was negligible in this era (Table 5). Ontario's indirect benefits were also of significance, but fade in comparison to Quebec's. Quebec, it would appear, received more than its share of indirect benefits. The railway-related industries were significantly larger in Quebec than in Ontario for all census years, except 1880, in spite of Quebec's consistently smaller population (Table 6).[13] One can only hazard to guess what Quebec's manufacturing growth would have been without a dynamic railway-related manufacturing sector. My results suggest that Quebec's manufacturing growth would have been even further behind Ontario's in 1910 than it already was.[14] This, of course, assumes that, particularly in Quebec, all resources were not fully employed or otherwise fixed in supply.

Table 4 illustrates the share of railway industries in total manufacturing output and employment. Their share is negligible, albeit rising, in both provinces, in 1870 and 1880. From 1880 to 1890, and again by 1910, the share of railway industries in Quebec's manufacturing output increases substantially. The same holds true for Ontario. By 1910, the %age of total manufacturing output comprised of railway-related industries is between 7 and 10% in Quebec and between 2 and 4% in Ontario. The share of these industries in total manufacturing employment is 8% in Quebec and only 3% in Ontario. This static measure of indirect benefits from railway construction indicates a less dramatic, but nevertheless important, contribution to manufacturing output and employment.

The results for Canada as a whole are largely a reflection of what transpired in the two most populated provinces of the Dominion. In the 1870s, the railway industries' share in the growth of manufacturing output ranged between 2 and 7%, rising to between 6 and 11% in the 1880s (Table 3). This share increased to between 7 and 25% in the 1890–1910 period. With respect to the growth of manufacturing employment, the railway industries contributed 4.5% in the 1870s, only 2% in

Table 4 The share of the railroad-related manufacturing sector in total manufacturing activities (For Constant Canadian Dollars, 1913 = 100)

Year	*Value Added (Railroads) / Value Added (Total Mfg)*	*Gross Output (Railroads) / Value Added (Total Mfg)*	*No. of Employees (Railroads) / No. of Employees (Total Mfg)*
A. Quebec			
1870	0.31%	0.58%	0.21%
1880	0.94	2.18	1.76
1890	4.06	8.12	2.9
1910	6.8	16.53	7.95
B. Ontario			
1870	0.13	0.33	2.12
1880	0.64	1.64	1.53
1890	0.62	1.39	1.14
1910	2.43	3.8	3.11
C. Canada			
1870	0.16	0.44	0.2
1880	0.62	1.89	1.37
1890	1.78	4.04	1.49
1900	1.75	4.84	2.44
1910	4.87	11.19	5.81

Sources See Table 3, sources

Table 5 Mileage of railroad track

Year	*Quebec*	*Ontario*	*Canada*
1867	523	1,275	2,087
1870			2,617
1880			7,194
1890			13,627
1894	3,024	6,267	15,627
1900	3,414	6,818	17,657
1909	3,663	8,229	24,104

Sources Department of Agriculture, *The Statistical Yearbook of Canada for 1894*, Ottawa, 1895, p. 679; *The Statistical Yearbook of Canada for 1900*, Ottawa, 1901, p. 354; *The Statistical Yearbook of Canada for 1910*, Ottawa, 1911, pp. 361, 362

Table 6 Real output estimates and employment estimates for railroad-related manufacturing activities (thousands of Canadian dollars, 1913 = 100)

Year	*Value Added*		*Gross Output*	*Number of Employees*
A. Quebec				
1870	$147	($119)[a]	$276	138
1880	554	($442)	1,292	1,439
1890	3,300	($2,854)	6,598	3,200
1910	11,167	($9,391)	26,842	12,164
B. Ontario				
1870	95	($77)	247	179
1880	642	($512)	1,645	1,761
1890	860	($744)	1,915	1,819
1910	6,935	($5,832)	10,836	7,229
C. Canada				
1870	216		569	368
1880	1,035		3,170	3,391
1890	3,853		8,728	5,265
1900	4,002		11,083	9,363
1910	23,504		53,971	29,075

Notes These estimates are derived from the censuses of Canada and the Dominion Bureau of Statistics' Standard Industrial Classification Manual. The current dollar gross output and value added estimates yielded by the censuses (not shown here) are converted into constant dollar values using deflator for iron and its products provided by the Dominion Bureau of Statistics, found in Historical Statistics of Canada. No deflator for railroad-related manufacturing activity with respect to inputs or outputs are presently available. The current dollar gross output estimates are derived by summing the census figures for the gross output in railroad-related industries such as rolling stock, railway supplies, car repairs, car and car works, and spike and axle factories. To generate current dollar value added estimates, I deduct, from the gross output estimates, the census figures for the cost of raw materials, fuel and heating. For the Canadian estimates, I also deduct the value of miscellaneous expenses using M.C. Urquhart's estimates for the transportation sector, drawn from his worksheets, which he so kindly made available to me. This makes my railroad-related output estimates compatible with my total output estimates for Canada. No estimates on miscellaneous expenses are available for Quebec and Ontario. Thus, my value added estimates for these provinces and Canada are not compatible. To be made so requires that the provincial value added estimates be reduced by about 18 percent using the Canadian estimates for miscellaneous expenses. These tentative estimates are presented in brackets above. Changing my provincial value added estimates would not alter the results presented in Table 9.2. In Table 9.3, however, the results in column 2 are less than they would have been if the value added estimates were reduced by 18 percent.

[a] The bracketed-term is the value added estimate which incorporates M.C. Urquhart's estimates of the value of miscellaneous expenses for all of Canada. This reduces my original value added estimates by 19.0, 20.2, 13.5 and 15.9% for each of the above census years respectively.

Sources *Census of Canada, 1870–1871*, vol. 3, Ottawa, 1875; *Census of Canada, 1880–1881*, vol. 3, Ottawa, 1883; *Census of Canada, 1890–1891*, vol. 3, Ottawa, 1894; *Census of Canada, 1900–1901*, vol. 3, 1902; *Census of Canada, 1911*, vol. 3, Ottawa, 1913: Dominion Bureau of Statistics, *Standard Industrial Classification Manual*, Ottawa, 1948; M.C. Urquhart and K.A.H. Buckley, eds., *Historical Statistics of Canada*, Toronto, 1965; M.C. Urquhart, "Worksheets: Manufacturing Summary Charts," mimeo, Department of Economics, Queen's University, Kingston, Ontario, 1986

the 1880s, but over 16% from 1890 to 1910. The share of these industries in total manufacturing output and employment is less significant, but still, of some moment by 1910, comprising between 5 and 11% of the manufacturing value added, and about 6% of manufacturing employment (Table 4). And although the contribution of railways to Canadian manufacturing was never overwhelming, it was definitely more important than in the United States.[15] Growth in Canadian manufacturing might have been severely constrained had the railway industries not existed.

5 Conclusion

In conclusion, not only was Quebec not discriminated against by the dominion government with respect to its share of direct and indirect benefits emanating from railway construction, but it gained significantly from railway construction, both in absolute terms and in comparison to Ontario. Quebec's serious shortfall in the supply of railway mileage relative to Ontario should in no way detract from these benefits. Rather, this shortfall should direct further attention to the structural problems in the Quebec economy that precluded the construction of more rail by private enterprise or by any group hoping for profits as a result of its investment.

Ontario's and indeed all of Canada's gains from railway construction were of importance. But railway construction made its greatest contribution to Quebec which, when compared to Ontario, was a relatively backward economic entity.[16] Perhaps it is in relatively backward economies that a large investment project, such as Canada's railway construction boom of the late nineteenth and early twentieth centuries, can have its greatest impact through its backward and forward linkages in a region's economy. If, however, relatively backward regions are to benefit from a large investment project, like Quebec, they would have to be the heart of such an investment project, writ large, and possess economies capable of responding to the incentives generated by such an investment.

Appendix

Table 7 (Appendix): Constant dollar railroad industry output, 1890 = 100 (In thousands of Canadian dollars)

	Quebec			*Ontario*			*Canada*		
	Gross	Value Added		Gross	Value Added		Gross	Value Added	
1870	$312	$146	($173)	$279	$107	($87)	$640	$302	($244)
1880	1,459	626	(499)	1,858	726	(579)	3,580	1,464	(1,169)
1890	7,337	3,726	(3,223)	2,162	978	(848)	9,854	5,026	(4350)
1910	30,298	12,605	(10,601)	12,231	7,827	(6,583)	60,920	31,526	(26,530)

Notes and Sources The construction of the constant dollar estimates for the railroad-related manufacturing activity follows the procedure elaborated in Table 6. Only here, the deflator is to a base-year of 1890.

Table 8 (Appendix): Constant dollar total manufacturing output, 1890 = 100 (In thousands of Canadian dollars)

	Quebec		*Ontario*		*Canada*	
	Gross	Value Added	Gross	Value Added	Gross	Value Added
1870	$75,000	$33,628	$114,299	$53,562	$227,082	$93,381
1880	100,930	41,793	160,855	71,590	313,638	119,526
1890	145,094	60,872	231,415	103,495	453,000	171,782
1910	182,422	137,333	529,334	243,880	1,067,674	429,890

Notes and Sources The constant dollar estimates for total manufacturing activity are derived by deflating current dollar output estimates for Quebec and Ontario found in Morris Altman, "Economic Development with High Wages: An Historical Perspective," Explorations in Economic History, 25, 1988, with price index numbers to a base-year of 1890 found in Morris Altman, "A Revision of Canadian Economic Growth, 1870–1910: A Challenge to the Gradualist Interpretation," Canadian Journal of Economics, 20, 1987. This article also provides 1890 dollar estimates for Canadian manufacturing output.

Table 9 (Appendix): Significance of the growth of railroad industries to total manufacturing output

	Quebec		*Ontario*		*Canada*	
	(Value Added Railroads) / (Value Added Total Mfg)	(Gross Output Railways) / (Value Added Total Mfg)	(Value Added Railroads) / (Value Added Total Mfg)	(Gross Output Railways) / (Value Added Total Mfg)	(Value Added Railroads) / (Value Added Total Mfg)	(Gross Output Railways) / (Value Added Total Mfg)
1870–1880	5.88%	14.05%	3.43%	8.76%	4.44%	11.24%
1880–1890	16.25	30.81	0.79	0.95	6.82	121.01
1890–1910	11.61	30.03	4.88	7.17	10.27	19.78

Notes and Sources Same as for Table 8 (APPENDIX).

Notes

1. As the data in Table 9.5 make clear, each decade of the 1870–1910 period experienced significant railroad construction. See Green (1986): 779–778 1 0, for an empirical assessment of the growth of Canada's railroads.
2. Angers (1976): 245, argues that Canada's east-west railroad project was a product of British inspired military considerations rather than any economic imperative. Unlike the development policies adopted in other countries, which concentrated on developing those regions first settled, the Canadian government decided to open up new lands, "[...] condamnait formellement le Québec a être en quelque sorte abandonné pour une période indéterminée [...] développer d'abord tout le reste du Canada a l'ouest de Montréal, puis retour au Québec ensuite, seulement quand le développement du reste du Canada aura permis la réalisation d'un état normal de rentabilité des investissements déjà engagés dans l'Ouest." Montreal benefited from the western oriented railroad policy in so far as it was a port of entry to the Canadian west. See also pp. 246, 249.
3. Linteau, Durocher, and Robert (1979), p. 84. To substantiate their argument, the authors refer to Gervais (1978) who finds that between 1967 and 1896, Quebec received only 13.8% of Dominion railroad subsidies compared to Ontario's 28%.
4. Young (1978), p. 144, concludes: "in making the contribution to tying Canada by steel *a mari usque ad mare*, Quebec paid a high price.".
5. Fogel (1964), pp. 145, 2–34, finds that the manufacturing value added purchased directly or indirectly by railroads amounted to no more than

3.94% in 1859. Fishlow (1971), pp. 143–145, 149, 156, 160–161, is less pessimistic as to the indirect contribution of railways to American manufacturing. But it is not clear to what extent Fishlow would adjust upward Fogel's estimate.

6. Though many studies on railroads in Europe suggest that backward linkages were relatively insignificant to the manufacturing sector of most European nations (see O'Brien (1977),pp. 59–70, for a summary of the literature and refer to O'Brien (1983) for a selection of country studies: Rainer Fremdling, writing on Germany, and Michel Laffut, writing on Belgium, argue that the backward linkages from railways were important to Germany's and Belgium's industrial growth, pp. 125–127, 137, 209–212, though the significance of these linkages are never clearly specified. See also Fremdling (1977), pp. 584–593, 601.
7. Gervais (1978), p. 46, finds that the dominion government spent $14,667,000 on railroad construction in Quebec and $29,889,000 in Ontario from 1867 to 1896. My estimates, using the 1897 end-year, are similar. I find that Quebec received $14,942,450, while Ontario attracted $29,759,707 (see Table 9.2).
8. On the relative poverty of the Quebec economy, see Altman (1988).
9. Craven and Traves (1983), p. 264, argue that the Canadian census of 1870–1871 excludes railway company manufacturing activities from its aggregate tables "resulting in a grossly distorted picture of the scale and organization of the Canadian railway supply and heavy engineering industries." If this was indeed the case, my estimates of the relative growth of railway-related manufacturing activities might be exaggerated, while I would be underestimating the size of such output. However, the evidence presented by Craven and Traves, p. 266 (Table 3), does not indicate whether the omitted firms had their output classified under census classifications not identified by the authors. And this is a possibility which Craven and Traves admit to, p. 264, ln 17.
10. See Broillette (1943), pp. 167–174, on the significance of railroads to Montreal.
11. See Heim and Mirowski (1987) for a critique of the crowding-out approach to the analysis of economic growth.
12. These estimates are in terms of a 1913 base-year (*see* Table 9.6 for details). If a 1890 base-year is used, my findings would be similar; only now, railroads would be of even greater significance. This can be seen in Annex 1.
13. The population in 1870, 1880, 1890, 1910 for Quebec is 1,191,516, 1,359,027, 1,488,535, 2,005,776 respectively, and for Ontario, 1,620,851, 1,926,922, 2,114,321, 2,527,291 respectively. *See: The Census of Canada, 1930–1931*, Ottawa, 1932, vol. 1, Table 17a.

14. With respect to the growth of manufacturing value added, Quebec grew at a rate of 2.22% annually in the 1870s, 3.22% in the 1880s, 3.58% from 1890 to 1910 as compared to growth rates of 3.04, 3.23, 3.70 and 3.42% respectively for Ontario. Quebec is even further behind Ontario with respect to the growth of per capita output. In terms of manufacturing employment growth, Quebec experienced annual growth rates of 2.61, 3.04, 1.65 and 2.24% in the 1870s, 1880s and the 1890–1910 period respectively, while Ontario employment grew by 3.16, 3.32 and 1.90% respectively. See Altman (1988), Tables 3 and 5.
15. Recall that Fogel (1964), pp. 145, 234, finds that the manufacturing value added purchased directly or indirectly by railroads amounted to no more than 3.94% in 1859.
16. However, Coatsworth (1979) provides us with an example of a relatively backward economy which was unable to capture much of its railroads' backward linkages which, instead, added to the demand for foreign-produced railway components. For a variety of reasons, Mexico was unable to undergo a process of import substitution. Quebec, on the other hand, was able to develop a manufacturing sector to service Canada's railroads. And this sector was one engine driving Quebec's manufacturing growth. See Altman (1988) on the extent of Quebec's relative economic backwardness.

References

Altman, M. 1988. Economic Development With High Wages: An Historical Perspective. *Explorations in Economics History* 25: 198–224.

Angers, F.A. (1976). "L'évolution économique du Canada et du Québec en cent ans de Confédération, " In Tremblay R., ed., *L'économie québécoise: histoire, développement, politiques*, (Montreal: Presses de l'Université du Québec) 241–254

Brian, J., and B.J. Young. 1978. *Promoters and Politicians: The North-South Railways in the History of Quebec, 1854–1885.* Toronto: University of Toronto Press.

Broillette, B. (1943). "Le port et les transports," In Minville, E., ed., *Montréal économique*, (Montréal: Fides), pp. 167–174

Census of Canada, 1930–1931 (1932). Ottawa. Vol. 1.

Coatsworth, J.H. 1979. Indispensable Railroads in a Backward Economy: The Case of Mexico. *Journal of Economic History* 39: 955–966.

Craven, P., and T. Traves. 1983. Canadian Railroads as Manufacturers, 1850–1880. *Canadian Historical Association, Historical Papers* 18: 254–281.

Fishlow, A. (1971). *American Railroads and the Transformation of the Ante-Bellum Economy*, (Cambridge, Mass.: Harvard University Press)

Fogel, R.W. 1964. *Railroads and American Economic Growth: Essay in Econometric History*. Baltimore: John Hopkins Press.
Fremdling, R. 1977. Railroads and German Economic Growth: A Leading Sector Analysis with a Comparison to the United States and Great Britain. *Journal of Economic History* 37: 584–601.
Gervais, G. 1978. *L'expansion du réseau ferroviaire québcois, 1875–1895*. Ph.D. diss.: University of Ottawa.
Green, A.G. (1986). "Growth and Productivity Change in the Canadian Railway Sector, 1871–1926," In S.L. Engennan and R.E. Gallmann, eds., *Long-Term Factors in American Economic Growth*, (Chicago and London), pp. 779–810
Hartland, P. 1953. "Private Enterprise and International Capital", *Canadian Journal of Economics and Political. Science* 19: 70–80.
Heim, C., and P. Mirowski. 1987. Interest Rates and Crowding During Britain's Industrial Revolution. *Journal of Economic History* 47: 128–139.
Linteau, P.A., R. Durocher, and J.C. Robert. 1979. *Histoire du Québec contemporain: De la Confédération à la crime, 1867–1929*. Montréal: Boréal Express.
Marr, W.L., and D.G. Paterson. 1980. *Canada: An Economic History*. Toronto: Macmillan.
O'Brien, P. 1977. *The New Economic History of the Railways*. New York: Routledge.
O'Brien, P., ed. 1983. *Railways and the Economic Development of Western Europe, 1830–1914*. New York: Palgrave Macmillan.

PART IV

Staples Were Actually Importance to Canada's Early Post Confederation Economic Development

CHAPTER 10

A Revision of Canadian Economic Growth: 1870–1910 (A Challenge to the Gradualist Interpretation)

1 Introduction

The contemporary view of Canadian manufacturing growth and development during the post-Confederation/pre-First World War era has been shaped by the work of Gordon Bertram, who constructed estimates of constant dollar gross manufacturing output from which he derived annual growth rates. These growth rates suggest that Canadian manufacturing output increased impressively, and with some regularity, from 1870 to 1910 (Bertram (1964), pp. 96, 98; Bertram (1965), pp. 170–171). This increase challenged, and, some would argue, undermined the view of the old economic history, exemplified in the work of Skelton and Buckley (Bertram (1964), p. 96, table 1, p. 98; (1965), pp. 170–171), that Canadian manufacturing realized a sustained take-off only from 1896 following a rather dismal performance from the time of Confederation in 1867. Accordingly, Bertram's data questions any strong or significant relationship between a noteworthy and unique spurt in manufacturing growth and development and Canada's wheat boom which commenced in 1896.[1]

Although Bertram's work marked an important empirical milestone in an economic analysis of Canada's past, he seriously erred in his calculation of real manufacturing output and, therefore, of corresponding growth rates. Moreover, he did not examine the question of the growth of real manufacturing output per capita and abstracted from the question of the growth of employment in the manufacturing sector. All these factors are

M. Altman, *Lessons from a Successfully Export-Oriented, Resource-Rich Economy*, https://doi.org/10.1007/978-3-031-03887-7_10

relevant to an understanding of manufacturing growth and development; as it stands, the critique of the old economic history must be viewed as incomplete and problematic.

In response to Bertram's errors in deriving real gross manufacturing output I present new sets of real gross manufacturing output estimates for the 1870–1910 period, making use of his current dollar estimates for gross manufacturing output but applying different and more accurate deflation procedures. I also construct two sets of real manufacturing value added estimates by deflating the current dollar manufacturing value added estimates recently developed by M.C. Urquhart (1984, 1985). These real value added estimates are more accurate than can be derived from Bertram's current dollar value added estimates, since Urquhart nets out the cost of fuel, power and miscellaneous expenses from his gross output estimates.[2] Bertram does not provide us with any estimates for real manufacturing value added, although it is the more accurate proxy for total output as it avoids double-counting. The more accurate real output estimates are used to generate annual growth rates of manufacturing output per capita and per employee engaged in manufacturing. I also present estimates of manufacturing employment. A brief comparison is made with the American record to place Canada in its North American context. Moreover, the real manufacturing value added estimates are used to examine the changing structure of the Canadian manufacturing sector.

My aggregate real gross output growth rates differ significantly from Bertram's on a decadal basis, suggesting that the Canadian manufacturing sector grew at a much slower pace than he suggested. This is particularly true of the period 1870–1890 upon which Bertram ((1964), pp. 96, 139; (1965), pp. 170–171) placed so much emphasis. Also contrary to Bertram's views, I find that there was a definite and relative spurt of growth from 1900–1910.[3] A similar story unfolds from an analysis of my real value added growth rates. These same findings also suggest that stagnation in the growth of real output took place with respect to output per capita and per employee from 1870–1900. There is some evidence to suggest that 1880 to 1890 was a strong decade, at least when compared with the 1870s and 1890s. But I find that the growth of manufacturing employment was respectable in Canada throughout the 1870–1910 period when compared with the United States, except for the 1890s, when the Canadian growth rate fell for the first and only time below the American. I also find that the structure of Canadian manufacturing altered dramatically over the same period, but particularly from 1900 on, in terms of my real value added estimates. This paints a different picture of Canadian manufacturing development from the one drawn from current dollar value added estimates - the approach taken by Bertram (1965), pp. 176–177) and, more recently, by Urquhart (1985, 25, 114). My research suggests that Bertram's optimistic view of Canadian manufacturing growth in its first years should be rejected, while the more pessimistic view put forth by the old economic history should, once again, be given serious analytical consideration. Overall, my findings indicate that there was a clear break in Canadian manufacturing growth and development at the time of Canada's wheat boom; these are consistent with Urquhart's (1985, pp. 21, 27–28) recent conclusions based on his construction of current dollar Canadian gross national product statistics for the 1870–1926 period.

2 A Revision of Constant Manufacturing Output and Growth Estimates

Bertram constructed constant dollar estimates for gross manufacturing output by utilizing the general price index numbers provided by the Dominion Bureau of Statistics (DBS), for the five decennial years between 1870 and 1910 inclusive, to deflate his current dollar estimates for gross manufacturing output. For 1870 and 1880 these index numbers are unweighted and are derived mainly from agricultural commodity prices (Asimakopulos (1965), p. 282). The 1890, 1900, and 1910 index numbers are weighted, but only in accordance with the distribution of commodities sold wholesale in 1900 alone - not in accordance with the distribution of commodities produced in the manufacturing sector (see Table 1).

A distorted picture of real gross manufacturing output and growth would be generated if the price relatives of the commodities composing the general DBS price index numbers were, on average, significantly different from the price relatives of the commodities which actually constituted manufacturing output. Even in the absence of this possible problem, distortions might arise when the price relatives of the different commodities differ significantly, if the weight of each price relative in the general price index differ substantially from what they should be to reflect each price relative's commodity's contribution to manufacturing output. To

Table 1 Gross (G) output, input (I), and value added (VA) price indexes; base year = 1913

	Standard Industrial Classification Manual, Major manufacturing sectors or commodity categories	*1870*			*1880*			*1890*			*1900*			*1910*		
		G[a]	I[b]	VA[c]	G	I	VA	G	I	VA	G	I	VA	G	I	VA
1	Food & beverages	99.5	108.0	71.1	101.1	111.1	72.0	95.2	93.3	83.1	77.7	71.6	125.6	103.3	96.7	134.2
2	Tobacco & products	49.5	-	49.5	60.2	-	60.2	71.8	-	71.8	92.9	-	92.9	99.9	-	99.9
3	Rubber products	110.9	-	110.9	111.0	-	111.0	95.5	-	95.5	73.9	-	73.8	101.5	-	101.5
4	Leather products	59.8	70.9	49.2	72.5	95.5	50.2	62.6	41.6	200.8	70.9	63.5	97.5	83.2	82.0	84.9
5	Textile products	128.7	159.1	97.3	116.5	128.3	98.4	95.5	111.6	85.8	83.2	95.9	69.4	96.0	116.7	71.7
6	Clothing	128.7	-	128.7	116.5	-	116.5	92.5	-	92.5	93.2	-	83.2	96.0	-	96.0
7	Wood Products	40.2	53.0	29.4	39.1	44.1	33.5	60.2	72.7	48.3	63.5	74.2	51.1	91.5	93.4	88.7
8	Paper	40.2	53.0	29.1	39.1	44.1	32.2	60.2	72.7	45.2	63.5	74.2	52.0	91.5	93.4	88.5
9	Printing & publishing	40.2	-	40.2	39.1	-	39.1	60.2	-	60.2	63.5	-	63.5	91.5	-	91.5
10	Iron & steel products	146.3	116.2	194.5	137.1	112.5	186.3	112.9	111.3	114.7	108.8	108.8	108.8	90.3	91.4	89.3

	Standard Industrial Classification Manual, Major manufacturing sectors or commodity categories	*1870*			*1880*			*1890*			*1900*			*1910*		
11	Transportation equipment	146.3	-	146.3	137.1	-	137.1	112.9	-	112.9	108.8	-	108.8	90.3	-	90.3
12	Non-Ferrous Metal Products	151.7	118.6	216.3	115.7	98.2	145.9	111.2	89.8	150.6	104.0	93.3	118.7	89.2	91.0	86.7
13	Electrical Apparatus & Supplies	-	-	-	-	-	-	111.1	-	111.1	104.0	-	104.0	89.2	-	89.2
14	Non-metallic Mineral Products	119.2	-	119.2	85.6	-	85.6	88.0	-	88.0	85.5	-	85.5	95.2	-	95.2
15	Petroleum & Coal Products	105.1	-	105.1	88.4	-	88.4	77.3	-	77.3	79.7	-	79.7	92.1	-	92.1
16	Chemical Products	98.2	-	98.2	95.0	-	95.0	78.3	-	78.3	77.4	-	77.4	86.5	-	96.5
17	Miscellaneous Industries	40.2	-	40.2	39.1	-	39.1	60.2	-	60.2	63.5	-	63.5	91.5	-	91.5

(continued)

Table 1 (continued)

	Standard Industrial Classification Manual, Major manufacturing sectors or commodity categories	*1870*			*1880*			*1890*		*1900*				*1910*		
18	Weighted General Price Index [d]	72.6	86.0	59.1	74.4	83.2	61.7	81.7	83.1	79.5	78.3	76.6	81.0	93.9	94.1	93.7
19	Bertram's DBS General Price Index [e]		95.7			86.1			90.4			74.8			94.1	
20	Weighted General DBS Price Index [f]		79.5			75.5			81.2			79.2			93.2	

[a] All gross output price index numbers, with a few exceptions, are the wholesale price index numbers provided by the DBS (Asimakopulos, 1965), brought to a base of the year 1913. Rubber products is deflated by the vegetable products price index: textile products and clothing by the fibres, textiles, and textile products price index: wood products, paper, and, printing and publishing by the wood. wood products, paper price index: iron and steel products and transportation equipment by the iron and its products price index: nonferrous metal products and electrical apparatus and supplies by the nonferrous metals and their products (excluding gold) price index: nonmetallic mineral products by the nonmetallic minerals and their products price index: chemical products by the chemicals and allied products price index: and miscellaneous industries is deflated by the wood, wood products, paper price index since much of its output is wood based. Food and beverages is deflated by a price index weighted for the current dollar distribution of the components of the gross output in this sector - the weights are derived from the censuses. I construct this price index from price data in Bolton (1916) for bacon, ham, pork, butter, cheese, flour, ale, whiskey and sugar: in Michell (1931) for dressed beef and hogs, bacon, smoked ham, pork, butter, cheese, flour, bread, whiskey and sugar: and in Barnett (1963) for milk and bread. Tobacco products is deflated by a price index which I construct from data in Bolton (1916) and Michell (1931). Leather products is deflated by a price index which I develop from data in Bolton (1916) and Michell (1931). Petroleum and coal products is deflated by a price index based on data drawn front Bolton (I 916) and Michell (1931) on anthracite coal.

Table 1 (continued)

[b] All inputs are deflated by price indexes developed for this paper except for these relatively minor sectors (see text, fn. 6): rubber products: clothing: printing and publishing transportation equipment: electrical apparatus and supplies: non-metallic mineral products: chemical products: and miscellaneous industries. The outputs of these sectors are deflated by the same DBS wholesale price index numbers used to deflate these sectors' gross output. Tobacco and products and petroleum and coal products are deflated by my gross output price index. Inputs of the food and beverages sector are deflated by a price index weighted for the current dollar distribution of the components of this sector's inputs, the weights being derived front the censuses. The data for this price index are found in Bolton (1916) for cattle, hogs, milk (input for butter and cheese), wheat, flour (input for bread), and barley and rye (inputs for beverages); in Michell (1931) for cattle, hogs, wheat, flour, barley, and rye; in Barnett (1963) for milk: and in the Trade and Navigation Reports for data on the quantity and value of raw sugar imported. Data for the price index of leather products inputs are taken front Bolton (1916) and Michell (1931) on steers and cows and green calfskins. For textile products I am forced to rely upon price data on raw wool only taken from Bolton (1916) and Michell (1931). For wood products and paper I use data on the prices of oak, pine and spruce logs drawn from the Trade and Navigation Reports on the quantity and value of logs exported. The data for the price index of the inputs of the iron and steel products sector are taken from Bolton (1916) and Michell (1931) on pig and bar iron. Finally, I use data in Bolton (1916) on copper, lead, silver, tin and zinc prices, and, in Michell (1931) on copper, lead and tin prices to develop a price index for the inputs of the nonferrous metal products sector.

[c] Derived by dividing the current dollar value-added estimate taken from Urquhart (1985) into my constant dollar value-added estimates. See appendix.

[d] Derived by dividing the total current dollar estimates for gross output, inputs, value added respectively into their corresponding total constant dollar values. The constant dollar values referred to here are derived using the price indexes discussed in notes (1) and (2) above.

[e] This is simply the DBS's general wholesale price index (Asimakopulos 1965) brought to a base of the year 1913.

[f] Derived by dividing the current dollar value for total gross output into my estimate for total current dollar gross output. The latter estimate is derived by deflating the gross output of each commodity category by the appropriate price index number provided by the DBS. My index numbers for food and beverages, tobacco and products, leather products, and petroleum and coal products are replaced by appropriate DBS index numbers.

Sources The appendix, notes and table: Bolton (1916) for data on the 1890–1913 period: Michell (1931) for data on the 1870–89 period: Barnett (1963) for data on the 1870–1900 period, the Trade and Navigation Reports for quantity and value data, for the entire 1870–1913 period, from which unit price estimates can be derived: and the censuses for the data on gross output and raw materials from which my weights for the food and beverages sector are constructed. The derivation of the weights are not shown here but are available from the author upon request

reduce the probability of such distortions I deflated Bertram's estimates of the current dollar value of gross output for each major manufacturing sector by a deflator specific to that commodity category, as opposed to Bertram's use of a general price index number to deflate the current dollar value of total gross manufacturing output.[4] To this end, I used the DBS's wholesale price index numbers for vegetable products; wood, wood products, paper; fibres, textile products; iron and its products; and chemicals and their products. I also developed price index numbers for the five decennial years from 1870 to 1910 for food and beverages; tobacco and products; leather products; and petroleum and coal products, to supplement the DBS's numbers (Tables 1 to 3). These price index numbers were used to deflate the output estimates for the major manufacturing sectors. These constant dollar output estimates were then summed up, yielding estimates of total constant dollar gross manufacturing output (Table 4).[5]

I also used four base years for my output deflators: 1913, 1890, 1880, and 1900. The last two generated constant dollar estimates for the periods 1870–1890 and 1890–1910, respectively. The 1913 base year is consistent with the DBS's general wholesale price index numbers which Bertram used to deflate his current dollar gross manufacturing output estimates. The DBS general index numbers were originally to a 1935–1939 base. And the 1870–1910 segment of the general DBS wholesale price index was made up of two parts: an 1870–1889 segment to a base of 1890 and 1890–1912 segment to base of 1913. The general index numbers of these segments were then shifted by the DBS to a base of 1935–1939 (Asimakopulos (1965), p. 283). I shifted the base of the 1870–1910 DBS segment of the general price index to 1913, which changed the value of the index numbers by only a constant. Therefore, using Bertram's method resulted in identical growth rates, whether a base of 1913 or 1935–1939 is chosen.

A technical problem emerges, however, when using 1913 as a base year—or 1935–9 for that matter—and deflating current dollar estimates sectorally as I do. This can result in growth rates being underestimated, a typical problem that arises when an end-of-period base year is selected. Therefore, in addition to computing constant dollar values using deflators to a base of 1913 (Table 1), I also compute constant dollar values using deflators to a base of 1890 (Table 2). The latter would be recommended by Gallman ((1972), pp. 47, 49), since this base year is at the midpoint of the two limiting years of this study. But as a matter

Table 2 Gross (G) output, input (I), and value added (VA) price indexes; base year = 1890

		1870			*1880*			*1900*			*1910*		
	Standard Industrial Classification Manual, Major Manufacturing Sectors or Commodity Categories	G	I	VA	G	I	VA	G	I	VA	G	I	VA
1	Food & beverages	104.5	115.7	70.1	106.2	119.1	70.3	81.6	76.7	113.5	108.5	103.6	129.1
2	Tobacco & products	68.9	-	68.9	83.8	-	83.8	129.4	-	129.4	139.1	-	139.1
3	Rubber products	116.1	-	116.1	116.2	-	116.2	77.3	-	77.3	106.2	-	106.2
4	Leather products	95.4	170.4	59.4	115.8	229.6	60.5	113.2	152.6	70.5	132.9	197.1	91.4
5	Textile products	139.1	142.6	130.7	122.0	115.0	139.0	87.1	85.9	88.9	103.8	104.6	102.3
6	Clothing	139.1	-	139.1	122.0	-	122.0	87.1	-	87.1	103.8	-	103.8
7	Wood Products	66.8	72.9	58.6	64.9	60.7	72.2	105.5	102.1	111.7	152.0	128.5	211.4
8	Paper	66.8	72.9	59.0	64.9	60.7	74.2	105.5	102.1	111.1	152.0	128.5	218.5
9	Printing & publishing	66.8	-	66.8	64.9	-	64.9	105.5	-	105.5	152.0	-	152.0
10	Iron & steel products	129.6	104.6	167.4	121.4	101.1	160.2	96.4	97.7	95.4	80.0	92.1	78.2
11	Transportation equipment	129.6	-	129.6	121.4	-	121.4	96.4	-	96.4	80.0	-	80.0
12	Non-ferrous Metal products	136.4	132.1	141.3	104.0	109.3	98.4	93.5	103.9	84.4	80.2	101.3	61.3
13	Electrical Apparatus & Supplies	-	-	-	-	-	-	93.5	-	93.5	80.2	-	80.2
14	Non-metallic mineral products	135.4	-	135.4	97.3	-	97.3	97.5	-	97.5	108.2	-	108.2
15	Petroleum & coal products	136.0	-	136.0	114.3	-	114.3	103.1	-	103.1	119.1	-	119.1
16	Chemical products	125.4	-	125.4	121.3	-	121.3	98.8	-	98.8	110.5	-	110.5
17	Miscellaneous industries	66.8	-	66.8	64.9	-	64.9	105.5	-	105.5	152.0	-	152.0
18	Weighted General Price Index	97.5	108.0	82.4	96.8	167.2	86.7	93.2	91.1	97.3	107.4	106.9	108.2

Sources See Table 1 for details on the construction of Table 2. The only significant distinction between the two is that index numbers in Table 2 are to a base year of 1890.

of course, the growth rates generated here should be biased downward for the period 1870–1890 and inflated for the period 1890–10. I also generate further growth rates by deflating current dollar output estimates with deflators to base years of 1880 and 1900 (Table 3), and, typically, these should yield inflated growth rates for the 1880s and 1900 to 1910 and depressed growth rates for the 1870s and 1890s. Clearly there is no one absolute picture that can be painted of the growth rates of real manufacturing output due to inherent 'index number problems.' But the results presented here allow us to critique Bertram on his own grounds (using the 1913 base year) as well as to re-examine the structure of Canadian manufacturing growth from the added perspective of growth rates generated through the use of alternative base years.

Using the 1913 base year, my real gross output estimates for 1870 and 1880 are much greater than Bertram's, exceeding his by 31.7 and 15.8%, respectively (Table 4). For the remaining three census years the two real gross output series are very similar. The differences in output estimates are largely due to my deflating the output in each commodity category by its own deflator, unlike Bertram who simply uses the DBS's general price index numbers. My approach, in effect, is equivalent to deflating the current dollar gross manufacturing output by a price index number weighted for the distribution of output in the manufacturing sector. These weighted index numbers should be compared with those used by Bertram, which are to a base of 1913 (Table 1, rows 18, 19). The difference between the two, for 1870 and 1880, is significant, but it is important to note that this difference is not entirely due to the weighting procedure. It is also—but in 1870 to only a small extent—due to my replacement of the DBS's index numbers for vegetable and animal products as deflators of food and beverages, tobacco and products, and leather products with index numbers specific to these commodity categories developed for this study—a more accurate approach (for further details see Table 1, notes). Had I used the DBS's index numbers alone, the weighted average price index numbers would have differed significantly from my own only in 1870 (Table 1, row 20), and the weighted average index number for 1870 would still have been much lower than the one used by Bertram: 79.5 compared with 95.7.

The annual growth rates for real gross manufacturing output (to a base of 1913) generated through my deflation procedure differ considerably from those generated through Bertram's procedure for the period

Table 3 Gross (G) output, input (I), and value added (VA) price indexes: base years = 880 and 1900

		Base year = 1880						*Base year = 1900*					
		1870			*1890*			*1890*			*1910*		
	Standard Industrial Classification Manual, Major Manufacturing Sectors or Commodity Categories	G	I	VA	G	I	VA	G	I	VA	G	I	VA
1	Food & beverages	98.4	97.2	105.0	94.2	84.0	164.5	122.5	130.5	101.2	132.9	135.0	127.2
2	Tobacco & products	82.2	-	82.2	119.3	-	119.3	77.3	-	77.3	107.5	-	107.5
3	Rubber products	99.9	-	99.9	86.0	-	86.0	129.4	-	129.4	137.5	-	137.5
4	Leather products	82.5	74.2	97.6	86.3	43.6	92.4	88.3	65.5	168.0	117.3	129.1	103.5
5	Textile products	110.5	124.0	86.2	82.0	87.0	74.4	114.8	116.4	111.8	115.4	121.7	115.4
6	Clothing	110.5	-	110.5	82.0	-	82.0	114.8	-	114.8	115.4	-	115.4
7	Wood Products	102.8	120.2	84.2	154.0	164.8	140.8	94.8	97.8	90.8	144.1	125.9	185.2
8	Paper	102.8	120.2	84.2	154.0	164.8	140.8	94.8	97.8	90.8	144.1	125.9	185.2
9	Printing & publishing	102.8	-	102.8	154.0	-	154.0	94.8	-	94.8	144.1	-	144.1
10	Iron & steel products	106.7	103.2	110.2	82.3	98.9	69.4	103.8	102.3	105.5	83.0	84.0	82.1
11	Transportation equipment	106.7	-	106.7	82.3	-	82.3	103.8	-	103.8	83.0	-	83.0
12	Non-ferrous Metal products	131.1	120.8	144.2	96.1	91.4	101.9	106.9	96.2	121.8	85.8	97.5	72.8
13	Electrical Apparatus & Supplies	-	-	-	96.1	-	96.1	106.9	-	106.9	85.8	-	85.8
14	Non-metallic mineral products	139.2	-	139.2	102.8	-	102.8	102.9	-	102.9	113.4	-	113.4
15	Petroleum & coal products	118.9	-	118.9	87.4	-	87.4	97.0	-	97.0	115.5	-	115.5
16	Chemical products	103.4	-	103.4	82.4	-	82.4	101.2	-	101.2	111.7	-	111.7
17	Miscellaneous industries	102.8	-	102.8	154.0	-	154.0	94.9	-	94.8	144.1	-	144.1
18	Weighted General Price Index	100.2	100.5	99.6	98.0	96.9	99.7	105.3	105.8	104.5	112.9	115.1	109.9

Sources See Table 1 for details on the construction of table 3. The significant difference between the two tables is that in table 3 use a base year of 1880 for the price index numbers of 1870 and 1890 and a base year of 1900 for the price index numbers of 1890 and 1910.

Table 4 Gross Output and Value Added in Canadian Manufacturing in Constant $000

		1870	*1880*	*1890*	*1900*	*1910*
1	Gross output (general DBS price index): 1913 = 100	226,150	352,485	563,433	770,053	1,219,979
2	Gross output (DBS's price indexes): 1913 = 100	278,349	401,898	556,620	761,580 (707,131)	1,231,027
3	Gross output (DBS's and my price indexes):					
	a) 1913 = 100	297,917	408,155	554,622	738,038 (684,397)	1,220,883
	b) 1890 = 100	227,082	313,638	453,000	618,116 (570,906)	1,075,154
	c) 1880 = 100	220,991	303,490	462,330		
	d) 1900 = 100			430,116	576,000 (533,952)	1,015,689
4	Value added (value added price indexes):					
	a) 1913 = 100	130,160	167,932	216,317	247,198 (229,173)	482,131
	b) 1890 = 100	93,381	119,526	171,782	205,743 (189,889)	425,000
	c) 1880 = 100	77,249	103,490	172,164		
	d) 1900 = 100			164,348	200,146 (185,535)	409,530
5	Value added (gross output price indexes):					
	a) 1913 = 100	107,579	146,367	211,665	252,636 (234,215)	486,679
	b) 1890 = 100	79,551	109,673	171,691	209,984 (194,023)	429,890
	c) 1880 = 100	76,306	103,490	176,471		
	d) 1900 = 100			163,334	200,146 (185,535)	411,539

Notes Row (1) is derived by deflating the current dollar value of total gross output by the DBS's general wholesale price index. Row (2) is derived by deflating the current dollar value of gross output in each commodity category, as provided by Bertram (1964, table 3), by the appropriate DBS price index number. These values are then summed. Rows (3a) to (3d) are derived similarly to row (2), except that the appropriate DBS's and my price index numbers are used as deflators. Rows (4a) to (4d) are derived by subtracting from the constant dollar value of gross output the constant dollar value of inputs for each commodity category and summing the resulting values. Rows (5a) to (5d) are derived by deflating the current dollar values of value added for each commodity category by the gross output deflators and summing the resulting values. The bracketed terms refer to the output estimates arrived at using Bertram's estimation technique for 1900.
Sources See text

1870–1890: 3.2 versus 4.8%. In the 1870s the growth rates were 3.2 and 4.7%, respectively and in the 1880s, 3.1 and 4.8%, respectively. According to both sets of estimates, the 1890s was an era of slow growth of 2.1 and 2.4%, respectively. The 1890s marked a dramatic fall in the growth rate, according to Bertram's estimates, while according to my own, the decline in the growth rate was of much lesser portent. Both sets of estimates reveal a relatively high rate of growth for the period 1900–1910. According to Bertram's estimates this indicates only a return to the high growth rates of the first two decades following Confederation; according to mine, a radical break with the past is revealed (Table 5). My results, therefore, challenge Bertram's conclusion that growth in Canada's manufacturing sector was consistently strong over the period 1870–1910, with the exception of the 1890s. Changing the base year to 1890 or to 1880 and 1900 does not alter these conclusions significantly, except that the 1880s appear as relatively stronger, particularly when 1880 is used as the base year. However, growth in the 1880s still remains significantly below that of the period 1900–1910.

The story told using my real value added estimates is, obviously, of greater significance. I provide two sets of such estimates, all of which are in terms of the series of base years previously discussed with respect to my real gross output estimates (Table 4). One set of estimates is derived by deflating Bertram's current dollar gross output estimates using the above mentioned deflators and subtracting from the resulting constant dollar estimates my constant dollar estimates for inputs. The latter estimates are derived by first subtracting from Bertram's current dollar estimates of gross output Urquhart's current dollar estimates of value added. The current dollar estimates of inputs are deflated using price index numbers for inputs developed for this study (Table 1). I use price data in Bolton (1916), Michell (1931), and, to a lesser extent, Barnett (1963), to construct these index numbers. Sufficient data were found to develop deflators for inputs of the food and beverages; leather products; textiles; wood, wood products, paper; iron and steel; and non-ferrous metal products commodity categories only. But these categories encompass the major proportion of the manufacturing value added.[6] For the rest, inputs are deflated by the same index numbers used to deflate the current dollar estimates of gross output.

These constant dollar value added estimates incorporate differences between price index numbers of inputs and outputs. Dividing the current

Table 5 Per Annum growth rates of real output in manufacturing (Percentages)

		1870–1880	*1880–1890*	*1890–1900*	*1900–1910*	*1870–1880*	*1880–1890*	*1890–1900*	*1900–1910*
1	Gross output (general DBS price index): 1913 = 100	4.54	4.8	3.17 (2.39)	4.71 (5.50)	4.67	4.17 (3.91)	3.94	4.3
2	Gross output (DBS's and my price indexes):								
	a) 1913 = 100	3.2	3.11	2.90 (2.12)	5.16 (5.96)	3.16	3.07 (2.81)	4.02	3.59
	b) 1890 = 100	3.28	3.74	3.16 (2.34)	5.69 (6.53)	3.51	3.39 (3.12)	4.42	3.96
	c) 1880 = 100	3.22	4.3			3.76			
	d) 1900 = 100			2.96 (2.18)	5.84 (6.64)			4.39	
3	Value added (value added price indexes):								
	a) 1913 = 100	2.58	2.56	1.34 (0.58)	6.91 (7.72)	2.56	2.16 (1.90)	4.09	3.32
	b) 1890 = 100	2.49	3.72	1.82 (1.01)	7.52 (8.39)	3.09	2.67 (2.39)	4.63	3.86
	c) 1880 = 100	2.97	5.22			4.09			
	d) 1900 = 100			1.99 (1.22)	7.42 (8.24)			4.67	

		1870–1880	1880–1890	1890–1900	1900–1910	1870–1880	1880–1890	1890–1900	1900–1910
4	Value added (gross output price indexes):								
	a) 1913 = 100	3.12	3.76	1.78 (1.02)	6.78 (7.59)	3.44	2.89 (2.63)	4.25	3.84
	b) 1890 = 100	3.26	4.58	2.03 (1.23)	7.43 (8.28)	3.92	3.29 (3.02)	4.7	4.31
	c) 1990 = 100	3.09	5.48			4.28			
	d) 1900 = 100			2.05 (1.26)	7.47 (8.29)			4.73	
5	US value added	6.17	7.79	4.17	3.57	6.98	6.03	3.87	5.41

Notes The growth rates in rows (1) through (4) are derived from table 4. The bracketed terms refer to the growth rates which use the 1900 real output estimates derived through Bertram's estimation technique. Row (5) is derived from Gallman (1960, 56, table A-5) except for the growth estimates depending upon the 1909 real value added. This is obtained by deflating the 1909 current dollar value added estimate in *Historical Statistics of the United States* (1975, part two, 666) by the Bureau of Labor general wholesale price index (deleting farm products), brought to a base of 1879, making it compatible with Gallman's manufacturing value added deflators. The Bureau of Labor price index is found in part one, p. 200, of the above volume. As opposed to Gallman's deflators, what I use for 1909 is unweighted, making my estimate for the real manufacturing value added of 1909 of a more tentative nature than those of Gallman for the previous census years.

Sources Table 4; Gallman (1960); and *Historical Statistics of the United States* (1975).

by the constant dollar value added estimates yields my value added price index numbers (Table 1). This approach is taken by Robert Gallman to derive American real manufacturing value added estimates for the period 1839–1899 (1960, p. 56). Further research should make available a larger and more comprehensive sample of price data and, therefore, even more precise constant dollar value added estimates. But it must be noted that this approach has been criticized as laden with potential problems, both theoretical and empirical, which can result in the generation of negative value added estimates (see David, (1962), pp. 148–155). Such was not the case in this study.

The other set of constant dollar value added estimates is derived by deflating Urquhart's current dollar value added estimates with the price index numbers used to deflate the current dollar gross output estimates. It is not yet clear which of the two approaches used to derive real value added estimates is the more accurate.[7] In this study the growth rates yielded by both deflation techniques permit me to present two sets of growth rates, each of which might encompass the actual path and pattern of Canadian manufacturing value added growth.

For the census year 1900 I deflate two current dollar value added estimates. The one taken from Urquhart is consistent with the assumption that the percentage of value added produced by firms employing less than five workers was the same in 1890 and 1900—for 1900 the census provides data on only the larger firms. The other current dollar value added estimate assumes, along with Bertram ((1964), p. 99 no, 5), that the percentage of output produced by the smaller firms declined at a constant rate from 1890 to 1915. Urquhart's value added estimate inflates the current dollar value added and, therefore, constant dollar value added for 1900 by 7.7%, unless one assumes that the small firms collapsed in importance from 1900, perhaps as a result of Canada's wheat boom taking on greater force. For this reason, using Urquhart's 1900 current dollar value added estimate, unadjusted, to derive a constant dollar value added estimate for 1900 might result in inflation of the growth rate for the 1890s and underestimation for the period 1900–1910.

My two sets of real value added estimates are significantly different only for the first two census years when base years of 1913 or 1890 are chosen. The real value added estimates generated using the input–output deflation technique exceed those generated using the gross output deflators alone by between 21.0 and 7.4%, respectively, in 1870 and 14.7 and

9.0%, respectively, in 1880 (Table 4). These differences are due largely to the fact that the input deflator for wood products and paper is greater than the corresponding gross output deflators (Tables 1 and 10A.2). This difference is reinforced by a similar situation arising in the food and beverages and in the leather products commodity categories. However, the opposite arises in the iron and steel products commodity category, which acts to counter, in part, this reinforcing effect. When deflators to a base of 1880 and 1900 are used, both sets of real value added estimates are similar for all census years.[8]

The growth rates derived from both sets of real value added estimates tend to corroborate the results drawn from my real gross output estimates. The first set of estimates—derived using the input–output deflation technique—yields consistently lower rates of growth. Also, an inspection of Table 5 reveals that shifting the base year from 1913 through to 1880 and 1900 yields higher growth rates, particularly and most significantly for the 1880s. For a base year of 1913 (this being most consistent with Bertram's estimates) both sets of value added estimates suggest slow growth for the 1870s and 1880s, with even slower growth in the 1890s. The period 1900–1910 marks a radical break with the past with a growth rate of between 6.8 and 7.7%, depending on which set of real value added estimates one chooses.

If the 1890 base year is assumed, growth for the 1880s is between 3.7 and 4.6% annually compared with between 2.6 and 3.8% for a base year of 1913. The 1880 base year yields an even higher rate of growth of about 5.3% for this period. It is quite possible, therefore, that there was a spurt of growth in the 1880s which coincided with Canada's government-induced railroad construction boom. But using 1890 and the 1880 and 1900 base years also yields an even higher growth rate for the period 1900–1910 of about 8.0%. These estimates suggest that the 1880s were relatively strong years in the comparatively depressed three decades following Confederation; and that the 1900–1910 period was, once again, a period whose growth performance broke radically with the past. Bertram's view of gradual growth over the period 1870–1910 does not hold, whichever base year is chosen to estimate real value added.

More pertinent to an understanding of industrial development are my growth estimates of real value added per capita (Table 6). Using real output estimates with a 1913 base year reveals depressed growth in the period 1870–1900 with a spurt of growth between 1900 and 1910. The

Table 6 Per Annum growth rates of real output per capita and per employee in manufacturing (Percentages)

		1870–1880	*1880–1890*	*1890–1900*	*1900–1910*	*1870–1890*	*1870–1900*	*1890–1910*	*1870–1910*
	Per capita growth								
1	Value added (value added price indexes)								
	a) 1913 = 100	0.98	1.11	0.28 (-0.48)	3.93 (4.74)	1.04	0.90 (0.64)	2.07	1.63
	b) 1890 = 100	0.88	2.27	0.76 (-0.55)	4.54 (5.41)	1.57	1.41 (1.13)	2.61	2.17
	c) 1880 = 100	1.37	3.77			2.57			
	d) 1900 = 100			0.93 (0.16)	4.44 (5.27)			2.64	
2	Value added (gross output price indexes)								
	a) 1913 = 100	1.52	2.31	0.72 (-0.04)	3.80 (4.61)	1.92	1.63 (1.37)	2.23	2.15
	b) 1890 = 100	1.66	3.13	0.97 (0.17)	4.45 (5.30)	2.4	2.03 (1.76)	2.68	2.62
	c) 1880 = 100	1.49	4.05			2.76			
	d) 1900 = 100			0.99 (0.22)	4.49 (5.31)			2.71	
3	US Value added	3.83	5.49	2.24	1.65	4.66	3.84	1.94	3.29

		1870–1880	*1880–1890*	*1890–1900*	*1900–1910*	*1870–1890*	*1870–1900*	*1890–1910*	*1870–1910*
	Per employee growth								
1	Value added (value added price indexes)								
	a) 1913 = 100	-0.57	-1.02	-0.28	5.01	-0.8	-0.61	2.33	0.76
	b) 1890 = 100	-0.66	0.1	0.2	5.65	-0.27	-0.11	2.87	1.3
	c) 1880 = 100	-0.17	1.64			0.73			
	d) 1900 = 100			0.37	5.53			2.91	
2	Value added (gross output price indexes)								
	a) 1913 = 100	-0.03	0.18	0.16	4.88	0.98	0.12	2.49	1.28
	b) 1890 = 100	0.12	1	0.41	5.57	0.56	0.52	2.94	1.54
	c) 1880 = 100	-0.05	1.9			0.92			
	d) 1900 = 100			0.43	5.57			2.97	
3	US value added	3.26	4.86	1.18	0.05	4.06	3.09	0.62	2.32

Sources These growth rates are derived from the growth estimates in tables 5 and 7

1890s, once again, were the most depressed years by far. The 1880s were characterized by the healthiest growth performance of the period 1870–1900, with growth rates of between 1.1 and 2.3%. These growth rates were somewhat higher than had been experienced in the 1870s (between 1.0 and 1.5% annually). If one shifts to the 1890 base year, the growth rate for the 1880s increases to between 2.3 and 3.1 per cent compared with between 0.9 and 1.7% for the 1870s and between 4.5 and 5.4% for the period 1900–1910. The 1880 base year yields an even higher growth rate for the 1880s of between 3.8 and 4.1%. These growth rates must be seen in the context of the rate of population growth diminishing gradually between the 1870s and the 1890s, from 1.6 to 1.1%, and then increasing to about 3% in the period 1900–1910 (Table 7). This makes the high rate of per capita growth during this last period that much more impressive.

Clearly, two stories can be told from my growth estimates. In one, growth in the 1880s is lower than in the other. Both stories, however, are inconsistent with Bertram's; and, compared with the American rates of real per capita value added growth, the Canadian rates appear meagre for all decades except 1900–1910 (Table 6). This is in the light of the American population's growing at a significantly faster pace than that of Canada, except for the period 1900–1910 (Table 7).

My estimates for labour productivity growth, in terms of real manufacturing value added per employee, suggest that the period 1900–1910—that decade coloured by the Canadian wheat boom - marked an even more significant break with the past than my previous estimates would indicate (Table 6), true no matter which base year is used. If one refers to estimates generated using the 1913 base year, then my two sets of real value added estimates yield either negative or marginally positive growth rates for each of the three decades in the period 1870–1900. In the period 1900–10 the growth rate vaulted to a relatively spectacular 5.0% per annum. With the 1890 base year, real labour productivity growth based on my gross output deflators is 1.0 per cent for the 1880s, and about 5.6 per cent for the period 1900–1910. The former is still relatively low, but at least it is an improvement over the even poorer performance of the 1870s. The 1880 and 1900 base years generate growth rates of between 1.6 and 1.9% for the 1880s, about 5.5% for the period 1900–10, and little growth in the 1870s and the 1890s. Different base years still generate different stories, but not significantly so. It remains to be determined whether the significant increase in labour productivity growth in the first

Table 7 Per Annum population and employment growth rates (Percentages)

	Population		*Manufacturing employment*		*Total employment*	
	Canada	USA	Canada	USA	Canada	USA
1870–80	1.60	2.34	3.14	2.91	3.15	2.86
1880–90	1.45	2.3	3.58	2.93	1.55	2.51
1890–1900	1.06	1.93	1.62	2.99	1.04	2.12
			(0.84)			
1900–10	2.98	1.92	1.90	2.56	4.33	1.98
1870–90	1.52	2.32	(2.68)			
1870–1900	1.26	2.19	3.36	2.92		
			2.77	2.56		
1890–1910	2.02	1.93	(2.51)			
1870–1910	1.69	2.12	1.76	3.25		

Notes The Canadian population growth rates are derived from Urquhart and Buckley (1965, series A2-14, 14). The American population growth rates are derived from *Historical Statistics of the United States* (1975, part one, series A6-9, 9). The Canadian employment growth rates are computed from estimates of manufacturing employment derived from the Canadian censuses: 182,115 (1870); 248,042 (1880); 352,630 (1890); 413,996 or 383,654 for 1900; and 499,938 (1910). My 1900 employment estimates are constructed by inflating the original census based estimate by 22.8 and 13.8 per cent, respectively, to correct for the fact that the 1900 census only reports on firms employing more than four individuals. The first adjustment is consistent with Urquhart's adjustment technique for 1900 output while the second is consistent with Bertram's adjustment procedure. Both adjustments represent underestimates if labour productivity in the small firms was less than that in the larger firms. I make the rough assumption that employment need be adjusted in proportion to output. From the original census data I deduct the number of employees of those firms not considered to be part of the manufacturing sector by the DBS's Standard Industrial Classification Manual (Altman 1984a, vol. 2, 24). The American growth rates are drawn from Davis et al. (1972, 187). The total Canadian employment growth rates are derived from data in Urquhart and Buckley (1965, 59) for 1880 through to 1910. For total employment data for 1970 1 rely upon *The Census of Canada, 1870–71* (1873, vol. 2). The bracketed terms are the growth rates based upon the 1900 employment estimates constructed with Bertram's adjustment technique.

Sources Altman (1984a, vol. 2); The Census of Canada for decennial years: *Historical Statistics of the United States* (1975); Urquhart and Buckley (1965).

decade of the twentieth century was induced by the new and increased demands flowing from the wheat boom.[9] It would also be worthwhile to determine if the surge in railway construction of the 1880s was a significant cause for the increase in labour productivity growth in this decade, at least according to the estimates using the 1890 and the 1880 base years.

These findings on labour productivity growth make Canada's notable gains in total real manufacturing value added in the period 1870–1900 a product of reasonably high manufacturing employment growth rates.

These were 3.1% in the 1870s; 3.6% in the 1880s; and between 0.8 and 1.6% in the 1890s, depending on whether one uses Bertram's or Urquhart's adjustment techniques for 1900 output (Table 7). Of course, for the 1880s, if one uses the 1890 or the 1880 base years, more substantial total growth is also related to relatively higher labour productivity growth rates. In the period 1900–1910 the very high labour productivity growth rate is related to manufacturing employment growing at between 2.7 and 1.9% annually. But in this last period labour productivity growth contributed significantly to the growth of total output. At least with respect to the growth of manufacturing employment, the period 1900–1910 was not characterized by a positive surge in growth relative to the past. Manufacturing employment thus is one variable whose growth history conforms to Bertram's view of the past.

Canada's manufacturing employment growth rates were lower than those of the United States in the 1890s and, possibly, in the period 1900–1910 (if one assumes that the percentage of manufacturing output produced by small firms collapsed after 1900). In terms of manufacturing employment, growth was healthy even when compared with the American record. But America's real labour productivity growth was significantly higher than the Canadian throughout the period 1870–1900, particularly from 1870 to 1890 (Table 6). But when Canada's real labour productivity growth took off, its American counterpart collapsed. The timing of the changes in American labour productivity growth is the reverse of the Canadian and, statistically, is a product of the fact that real manufacturing value added growth in the United States was significantly less in the period 1900–1910 than in the three previous decades (Table 5).

These results affirm John Dales's ((1963), pp. 303, 308, 311) argument that Canada's decision to increase tariffs on manufactured commodities was a failure in its inability to cause Canada's performance in manufacturing to catch up to that of the United States. Where Canada's manufacturing performance was unambiguously strong, in its employment growth, it was so prior to the establishment of higher tariffs in 1878. To the extent that Canada's manufacturing performance improved in the 1880s, it might have been a product of the railroad boom, not the higher tariffs. A hypothesis to be examined is whether the manufacturing performance would have been even hardier without the introduction of across-the-board tariff increases.

3 The Changing Structure of Canadian Manufacturing

An examination of the changing structure of Canadian manufacturing from 1870 to 1910 in terms of real manufacturing value added using either the 1913 or 1890 base years (as opposed to the traditional use of current dollar value added estimates) adds further support to the view that the wheat boom marked a turning point in Canadian manufacturing growth and development (Table 8). The current dollar value added estimates suggest that the major manufacturing sectors retained a similar importance throughout the 1870–1910 period in their contribution to total manufacturing value added. It must be emphasized, however, that this finding is no substitute for that stemming from the current dollar estimates. It only sheds some light on a different side of the coin: dealing with the changing structure of the volume of output produced as opposed to that of value.

The nominal output estimates suggest that food and beverages were responsible for about 15 per cent of total manufacturing value added from 1870 to 1910. Constant dollar estimates suggest that this sector produced 12.1% of the manufacturing value added in 1870 if one uses the 1913 base year and 17.2% for the 1890 base year. This sector gradually diminishes in significance by 1910. Leather products experienced a gradual decline according to all estimates. Also, according to all estimates, textiles and clothing increased in importance but only over the period 1870–1900.

Wood products experienced a decline in importance according to all estimates. However, according to the constant dollar estimates, wood products contributed 42% to the total manufacturing value added in 1870 for a base year of 1913 and 29% for an 1890 base year, whereas the current dollar estimates suggest a contribution of only 21%. For 1900 the first two sets of estimates suggest a contribution of 27 and 15%, respectively for this sector, and about 17% for the current dollar estimates. By 1910 my constant dollar estimates suggest that wood products comprised 17 and 8%, respectively, of manufacturing value added, while the current dollar estimates indicate little change from 1900. My constant dollar estimates clearly suggest a dramatic fall in the importance of wood products from 1900 to 1910, contrary to what is implied by the current dollar estimates.

Table 8 Percentage distribution of current and constant dollar manufacturing value added

		1870			*1880*			*1890*			*1900*			*1910*		
		Curr	Con 1913	Con 1890	Curr	Con 1913	Con 1890	Curr	Con 1913	Con 1890	Curr	Con 1913	Con 1890	Curr	Con 1913	Con 1890
1	Food & beverages	14.6	12.1	17.2	13.9	12.1	17.1	15.3	14.6	15.3	16.6	10.8	14.2	14.3	9.9	11.9
2	Tobacco & products	1.3	1.6	1.6	1.2	1.2	1.2	1.6	1.7	1.6	2.0	1.8	1.5	1.9	1.8	1.5
3	Rubber products	0.2	0.1	0.1	0.2	0.1	0.2	0.3	0.2	0.3	0.8	0.9	0.9	1.0	0.9	1.0
4	Leather products	12.5	18.3	21.1	12.4	15.2	17.7	9.6	3.4	8.6	7.9	6.6	10.9	5.9	6.5	7.0
5	Textile products	3.5	2.1	2.2	4.9	3.1	3.1	5.5	5.0	5.5	6.4	7.5	7.0	4.0	5.2	4.2
6	Clothing	7.0	3.2	4.1	9.1	4.9	6.4	11.2	9.6	11.2	10.8	10.6	12.1	11.2	10.9	11.7
7	Wood products	21.0	42.2	29.2	21.4	39.5	25.7	20.4	33.5	20.4	17.0	27.1	14.8	16.0	16.9	8.2
8	Paper	0.9	1.8	1.2	1.0	1.9	1.2	1.4	2.4	1.4	2.4	3.7	2.1	2.7	2.9	1.3
9	Printing & publishing	3.0	4.4	3.6	3.5	5.4	4.6	3.4	4.5	3.4	4.5	5.7	4.1	3.5	3.6	2.5
10	Iron & steel products	16.6	5.0	8.2	14.9	4.9	8.1	15.8	10.9	15.8	14.5	10.9	14.8	16.8	17.6	23.2
11	Transportation equipment	7.7	3.1	4.9	6.9	6.0	4.9	6.9	4.8	6.9	5.4	3.1	5.4	6.9	7.2	9.4
12	Non-ferrous metal products	1.0	0.3	0.6	1.8	0.7	1.6	1.9	1.0	1.9	3.1	2.1	3.6	5.4	5.8	9.4
13	Electrical apparatus & supplies	0.0	0.0	0.0	0.0	0.0	0.0	0 2	0.2	0.2	0.8	0.6	0.8	1.6	1.7	0.4
14	Non-metallic mineral products	3.1	1.5	1.9	3.4	2.4	3.0	3.0	2.7	3.0	3.2	3.0	3.2	3.8	3.7	3.8
15	Petroleum & coal products	1.5	0.8	0.9	1.3	0.9	0.9	0.6	0.6	0.6	0.5	0.5	0.5	0.5	0.5	0.5
16	Chemical products	2.0	1.2	1.3	2.3	1.5	1.6	2.1	2.1	2.1	2.3	2.4	2.2	2.9	3.1	2.8
17	Miscellaneous industries	1.4	2.1	1.7	1.9	3.0	2.6	1.8	2.4	1.8	1.9	2.4	1.7	1.7	1.8	1.2

Sources. The first column, the current dollar distribution, is from Urquhart (1985, table 18). The second and third columns, the constant dollar distributions, are derived from the estimates in table 9 based on the value added price indexes

For both the iron and steel products and transportation equipment sectors the current dollar estimates imply that there was little change in their relative importance from 1870 to 1910, with these sectors producing about 15 and 7% respectively of the total manufacturing value added. But, according to the constant dollar estimates there was a marked increase in the importance of iron and steel products over the 1880s and, more particularly, over the period 1900–1910, from between 10.9 and 14.8% in 1900 to between 17.6 and 23.2% in 1910, of the total manufacturing value added. The transportation sector also experienced a dramatic increase in importance, but over the period 1900–1910 alone, from between 3.1 and 5.4% to between 7.2 and 9.4% of the total manufacturing value added.[10] The current dollar estimates also suggest that the share of chemical products in the total manufacturing value added changed little over the period 1870–1910, with the exception of an increase from 2.3 to 2.9% from 1900 to 1910. The constant dollar estimates, however, indicate that chemical products became increasingly significant from 1870 to 1910, seeing its share of total manufacturing value added increase from about 1.2 to about 3.0%. Both current and constant dollar estimates suggest that the share of non-ferrous metal products and electrical apparatus and supplies rose most significantly from 1900 to 1910.

During the first decade of the twentieth century a structural change took place in Canadian manufacturing. This cannot be clearly deduced from an examination of current dollar manufacturing output estimates. The high growth rates for real manufacturing output, which my deflation procedures reveal for the period 1900–10, encompass the rise to prominence of key sectors. This break with the past, coinciding with the wheat boom, lends support to the view of the old economic history as to the significance of that boom.

Nevertheless, my findings in no way demonstrate any causal relationship, but are merely suggestive. It is also clear that important changes were taking place during the 1890s, although these were not as sharp as those experienced in the period 1900–10.

4 Conclusion

My real output estimates paint two different pictures of Canadian manufacturing growth and development, both of which challenge the gradualist interpretation put forth by Gordon Bertram. Bertram's only finding which is supported by my estimates is that substantial extensive manufacturing growth took place prior to the wheat boom, beginning at least from Confederation. If a base year of 1913 is chosen for my price indexes, the extensive growth in the period 1870–1900 was in the context of slow or negative growth in per capita output and labour productivity. Using the 1890 and, particularly, the 1880 and 1900 base years yields higher growth rates for the 1880s, suggesting that the manufacturing performance in the period 1870–1900 was poor, with the exception of one decade. But this would be unambiguously true only for the growth in output per capita.

All my real output estimates clearly reveal a radical break with the past from 1900. What remains to be explained in a rigorous fashion is why the era of the wheat boom marked such an important period of change in the Canadian economy.

Appendix

See Tables 9a, 9b, 9c, 9d.

Table 9a Appendix: Derivations of real value added estimates ($000), 1913 = 100

	1870		*1880*		*1890*		*1900*		*1910*	
	1	2	*1*	2	*1*	2	*1*	2	*1*	2
Food & beverages	15,838	11,319	20,310	14,256	31,670	27,650	26,407	42,637	47,894	62,698
Tobacco & products	2,049	2,049	2,005	2,005	3,778	3,778	4,319	4,319	8,594	8,594
Rubber products	101	101	219	219	529	529	2,054	2,054	4,430	4,430
Leather products	23,833	19,594	25,540	17,690	7,377	23,658	16,210	22,374	31,491	32,147
Textile products	2,766	2,091	5,201	4,391	10,926	10,140	18,461	15,415	24,941	18,639
Clothing	4,184	4,184	8,046	8,046	20,811	20,811	26,044	26,044	52,711	52,711
Wood products	55,064	40,231	66,327	56,846	72,468	58,198	66,520	53,581	81,336	78,872
Paper	2,300	1,667	3,210	2,647	5,219	3,975	9,130	7,483	13,993	13,539
Printing & publishing	5,646	5,646	9,154	9,154	9,649	9,649	14,097	14,097	17,229	17,729
Iron & steel products	6,584	8,751	8,313	11,295	23,596	23,977	26,725	26,725	84,847	83,951
Transportation equipment	4,062	4,062	5,196	5,196	10,457	10,457	9,894	9,894	34,665	34,665
Non-ferrous metal products	356	507	1,247	1,478	2,216	3,001	5,273	6,016	27,889	27,095
Electrical apparatus & supplies	-	-	-	-	374	374	1,566	1,566	8,161	8,161
Non-metallic mineral products	2,002	2,002	4,121	4,121	5,919	5,919	7,402	7,402	17,937	17,937
Petroleum & coal products	1,065	1,065	1,479	1,479	1,319	1,319	1,349	1,349	2,557	2,557
Chemical products	1,589	1,589	2,454	2,454	4,592	4,592	5,844	5,844	14,902	14,902
Miscellaneous industries	2,721	2,721	5,090	5,090	5,165	5,165	5,837	5,837	8,554	8,554
Total	130,160	107,579	167,932	146,367	216,137	211,665	247,198 (229,173)	252,636 (234,215)[a]	482,131	486,679

Table 9b Appendix: Derivations of real value added estimates ($000), 1890 = 100

	1870		*1880*		*1890*		*1900*		*1910*	
	1	2	*1*	2	*1*	2	*1*	2	*1*	2
Food & beverages	16,069	10,778	20,507	13,571	26,323	26,323	29,234	40,652	49,794	59,693
Tobacco & products	1,472	1,472	1,440	1,440	2,713	2,713	3,100	3,100	6,172	6,172
Rubber products	96	96	209	209	505	505	1,961	1,961	4,234	4,234
Leather products	19,723	12,292	21,190	11,075	14,810	14,810	22,494	14,013	29,256	20,125
Textile products	2,059	1,934	3,681	4,193	9,390	9,390	14,417	14,724	17,490	17,239
Clothing	3,872	3,872	7,683	7,683	19,251	19,251	24,878	24,879	48,752	48,752
Wood products	27,304	24,211	30,762	34,248	35,035	35,035	30,452	32,250	34,144	47,479
Paper	1,135	1,003	1,387	1,595	2,393	2,393	4,275	4,504	5,670	8,150
Printing & publishing	3,399	3,399	5,514	5,514	5,809	5,909	8,485	8,485	10,372	10,372
Iron & steel products	7,646	9,979	9,663	12,755	27,070	27,070	30,482	30,163	96,909	94,760
Transportation equipment	4,585	4,585	5,953	5,853	11,800	11,806	11,167	11,167	39,128	39,128
Non-ferrous metal products	545	564	1,878	1,778	3,337	3,337	7,414	6,692	39,442	30,136
Electrical apparatus & supplies	-	-	-	-	416	416	1,741	1,741	9,077	9,077
Non-metallic mineral products	1,771	1,771	3,626	3,626	5,209	5,209	6,518	6,519	15,792	15,782
Petroleum & coal products	824	824	1,144	1,144	1,020	1,020	1,043	1,043	1,977	1,977
Chemical products	1,244	1,244	1,923	1,923	3,596	3,596	4,579	4,578	11,665	11,665
Miscellaneous industries	1,638	1,638	3,066	3,066	3,109	3,109	3,514	3,514	5,149	5,149
Total	93,391	79,551	119,526	109,673	171,782	171,691	205,743 (189,889)	209,984 (194,023)	417,521	429,890

Table 9c Appendix: Derivations of real value added estimates ($000), 1880 = 100

	1870		*1880*		*1890*	
	1	2	*1*	2	*1*	2
Food & beverages	10,730	11,446	14,413	14,413	15,997	27,944
Tobacco & products	1,233	1,233	1,207	1,207	2,274	2,274
Rubber products	111	111	243	243	587	587
Leather products	12,006	14,202	12,825	12,825	17,161[b]	17,161
Textile products	3,122	2,435	5,116	5,116	12,604	11,439
Clothing	4,875	4,875	9,373	9,373	23,476	23,476
Wood products	19,209	15,732	22,227	22,227	24,877	22,750
Paper	800	691	1,035	1,035	1,750	1,554
Printing & publishing	2,208	2,208	3,579	3,579	3,772	3,772
Iron & steel products	11,614	11,999	15,485	15,485	38,996	32,892
Transportation equipment	5,570	5,570	7,105	7,105	14,345	14,345
Non-ferrous metal products	534	587	1,849	1,849	3,276	3,472
Electrical apparatus & supplies	-	-	-	-	432	432
Non-metallic mineral products	1,723	1,723	3,528	3,528	5,067	5,067
Petroleum & coal products	941	941	1,308	1,308	1,167	1,167
Chemical products	1,509	1,509	2,332	2,332	4,364	4,364
Miscellaneous industries	1,064	1,064	1,990	1,990	2,019	2,019
Total	77,249	76,306	103,490	103,490	172,164	176,471

Table 9d Appendix: Derivations of real value sdded estimates ($000), 1900 = 100

	1890		*1900*		*1910*	
	1	2	*1*	2	*1*	2
Food & beverages	26,017	21,488	33,172	33,172	50,894	48,734
Tobacco & products	3,510	3,510	4,012	4,012	7,986	7,986
Rubber products	390	390	1,516	1,516	2,171	2,171
Leather products	8,813	16,772	15,863	15,863	25,844	22,801
Textile products	8,370	8,095	12,825	12,825	15,507	15,507
Clothing	16,769	16,769	21,669	21,669	43,852	43,852
Wood products	38,573	36,957	34,024	34,024	38,963	50,082
Paper	2,673	2,524	4,752	4,752	6,529	8,597
Printing & publishing	6,127	6,127	8,952	8,952	10,940	10,940
Iron & steel products	26,079	26,079	29,077	29,077	92,299	91,335
Transportation equipment	11,374	11,374	10,765	10,765	37,713	37,713
Non-ferrous metal products	2,740	3,122	6,257	6,257	33,180	28,169
Electrical apparatus & supplies	389	389	1,628	1,628	8,484	8,484
Non-metallic mineral products	5,063	5,063	6,329	6,329	15,058	15,058
Petroleum & coal products	1,052	1,052	1,075	1,075	2,039	2,039
Chemical products	3,553	3,553	4,523	4,523	11,540	11,540
Miscellaneous industries	3,280	3,280	3,707	3,707	5,431	5,431
Total	164,348	163,334	200,146	200,146	409,530	411,539
			(185,535)	(185,535)		

Table 9d (continued)

[a] All gross output price index numbers, with a few exceptions, are the wholesale price index numbers provided by the DBS (Asimakopulos, 1965), brought to a base of the year 1913. Rubber products is deflated by the vegetable products price index: textile products and clothing by the fibres, textiles, and textile products price index: wood products, paper, and, printing and publishing by the wood. wood products, paper price index: iron and steel products and transportation equipment by the iron and its products price index: nonferrous metal products and electrical apparatus and supplies by the nonferrous metals and their products (excluding gold) price index: nonmetallic mineral products by the nonmetallic minerals and their products price index: chemical products by the chemicals and allied products price index: and miscellaneous industries is deflated by the wood, wood products, paper price index since much of its output is wood based. Food and beverages is deflated by a price index weighted for the current dollar distribution of the components of the gross output in this sector - the weights are derived from the censuses. I construct this price index from price data in Bolton (1916) for bacon, ham, pork, butter, cheese, flour, ale, whiskey and sugar: in Michell (1931) for dressed beef and hogs, bacon, smoked ham, pork, butter, cheese, flour, bread, whiskey and sugar: and in Barnett (1963) for milk and bread. Tobacco products is deflated by a price index which I construct from data in Bolton (1916) and Michell (1931). Leather products is deflated by a price index which I develop from data in Bolton (1916) and Michell (1931). Petroleum and coal products is deflated by a price index based on data drawn front Bolton (I 916) and Michell (1931) on anthracite coal.

[b] All inputs are deflated by price indexes developed for this paper except for these relatively minor sectors (see text, fn. 6): rubber products: clothing: printing and publishing transportation equipment: electrical apparatus and supplies: non-metallic mineral products: chemical products: and miscellaneous industries. The outputs of these sectors are deflated by the same DBS wholesale price index numbers used to deflate these sectors' gross output. Tobacco and products and petroleum and coal products are deflated by my gross output price index. Inputs of the food and beverages sector are deflated by a price index weighted for the current dollar distribution of the components of this sector's inputs, the weights being derived front the censuses. The data for this price index are found in Bolton (1916) for cattle, hogs, milk (input for butter and cheese), wheat, flour (input for bread), and barley and rye (inputs for beverages); in Michell (1931) for cattle, hogs, wheat, flour, barley, and rye; in Barnett (1963) for milk: and in the Trade and Navigation Reports for data on the quantity and value of raw sugar imported. Data for the price index of leather products inputs are taken front Bolton (1916) and Michell (1931) on steers and cows and green calfskins. For textile products I am forced to rely upon price data on raw wool only taken from Bolton (1916) and Michell (1931). For wood products and paper I use data on the prices of oak, pine and spruce logs drawn from the Trade and Navigation Reports on the quantity and value of logs exported. The data for the price index of the inputs of the iron and steel products sector are taken from Bolton (1916) and Michell (1931) on pig and bar iron. Finally, I use data in Bolton (1916) on copper, lead, silver, tin and zinc prices, and, in Michell (1931) on copper, lead and tin prices to develop a price index for the inputs of the nonferrous metal products sector.

[c] Derived by dividing the current dollar value-added estimate taken from Urquhart (1985) into my constant dollar value-added estimates. See appendix.

Table 9d (continued)

[d] Derived by dividing the total current dollar estimates for gross output, inputs, value added respectively into their corresponding total constant dollar values. The constant dollar values referred to here are derived using the price indexes discussed in notes (1) and (2) above.
[e] This is simply the DBS's general wholesale price index (Asimakopulos 1965) brought to a base of the year 1913.
[f] Derived by dividing the current dollar value for total gross output into my estimate for total current dollar gross output. The latter estimate is derived by deflating the gross output of each commodity category by the appropriate price index number provided by the DBS. My index numbers for food and beverages, tobacco and products, leather products, and petroleum and coal products are replaced by appropriate DBS index numbers.
Sources The appendix, notes and table: Bolton (1916) for data on the 1890–1913 period: Michell (1931) for data on the 1870–89 period: Barnett (1963) for data on the 1870–1900 period, the Trade and Navigation Reports for quantity and value data, for the entire 1870–1913 period, from which unit price estimates can be derived: and the censuses for the data on gross output and raw materials from which my weights for the food and beverages sector are constructed. The derivation of the weights are not shown here but are available from the author upon request
Notes Presented here are only the results of a detailed computation procedure. Column 1 is derived by using my value added price index numbers in Tables 10.9A to 10.9D above to deflate, sectorally, the current dollar value added estimates in Urquhart (1985, table 17). This is equivalent to subtracting, sectorally, from my real gross output estimates my real input estimates. Each is derived using a different set of deflators (see Tables 9A to 9D). The real gross output estimates are derived by deflating, sectorally, the current dollar gross output estimates in Bertram (1964, table 3) by DBS index numbers and those constructed by the author (see tables 1 to 3 and notes). The current dollar input estimates are derived from Bertram (1964, table 3) and Urquhart (1985, table 17). For details see Altman (1986, appendix). Column 2 is derived using the gross output deflators (Tables 10.9A to 9D) constructed by the DBS and by the author to deflate, sectorally, the current dollar value added estimates in Urquhart (1985, table 17). For details on the construction of the gross output estimates in table 4, above, see Altman (1986, appendix).
[a] The unbracketed totals assume the percentage of output produced by firms employing more than four workers to be the same in 1990 and 1900 - 81.5% (Bertram 1964, 99 n. 5). This is consistent with Urquhart's estimation technique. The bracketed terms assume this percentage increased at a constant pace over the period 1890-1915, rising to 97.8% by 1900 (Bertram 1964. 99 n. 5). The latter estimate is derived by adjusting downward by 7.3% the current dollar estimates of total output (gross and value added) and inputs, which assumes the percentage of total output produced by small firms remains the same in 1890 and 1900. This percentage is drawn from Bertram, ibid. The difference between these two totals is deflated by the relevant price deflators found in Tables 9A to 9D, above. These constant dollar estimates are then subtracted from the unbracketed constant dollar totals.
[b] For 1890, at a base year of 1880, leather products' inputs are deflated with the gross output price index as opposed to the input price index to avoid a negative value added estimate.
Sources: Altman (1986); Bertram (1964); Urquhart (1985)

Notes

1. Bertram ((1964), p.139): 'The high rates of real gross value of manufacturing output of the 1870s through the 1890s appear to conflict with the generally accepted opinion that these decades had failed to fulfill the promise of economic expansion provided by Confederation.' Moreover Bertram (1965), pp. 172, 184, emphasizes that his estimates demonstrate that there was no sharp break in Canadian manufacturing development from 1900.' Refer also to Skelton ((1914), pp. 191, 252 and Buckley ((1974), pp.3–6).
2. Urquhart's (1985), pp. 60–7 value added estimates are about 82.5% of Bertram's except for 1900. See text below.
3. Bertram (1965), pp. 172, 184 does not deny that the period 1900–1910 was one of vigorous growth, but only that this growth did not mark any significant break with the past. McDougall (1971) makes a similar argument relying entirely upon current dollar output estimates. He also makes very rough 'guesstimates' of manufacturing output per capita. After this manuscript was completed, M.C. Urquhart made available to me a mimeograph by Bamett (1966), whose growth estimates for real manufacturing value added are similar to mine when an 1880 or 1890 base year is used, although our methodologies differ.
4. Urquhart's (1994), p. 47 recently re-estimated current dollar values of gross manufacturing output are almost identical to Bertram's for every decennial year between 1870 and 1910 inclusive, except for 1900, where the difference is marginal. Urquhart does not detail his estimation procedure, but his 1900 gross output estimate ($549,894,000) falls between Bertram's estimate, built upon the assumption that the percentage of total output produced by firms with less than five employees declined at a constant pace from 1890 to 1915 ($534,600,000), and that based upon the assumption that the percentage of total output produced by these firms remained the same in 1890 and 1900 ($575,794,000). See Bertram (1964), pp. 98, 99 notes. The 1900 census provides data only on firms employing five or more employees.
5. It must be noted that the censuses provide data only for decennial years. Urquhart interpolates output figures for the interdecennial years. My growth estimates are based upon the decennial output data alone. Thus, if these are taken from significantly different segments of the trade cycle, my growth rates would distort the 'true' values. Gordon Bertram (1964), p. 136, after an analysis of the cycle literature, concludes that the decennial years of 1870 through 1900 all 'appear to occur in a prosperity phase of the cycle.' Chambers (1964), p. 393 comes to a similar conclusion for the period 1867–1953.

6. These commodity categories comprise 72.8%of total current dollar manufacturing value added in 1870; 71.3% in 1890; 68.9% in 1890; 67.9% in 1900; and 65.1% in 1910.
7. This approach is recommended by David (1966), pp. 419–425. But although this procedure avoids the problems which might now from using value added deflators, it cannot take into account different relevant and relative price movements for inputs and outputs. Arrow (1974) suggests that one should estimate real value added using a production function. But this method possesses certain possible problems, particularly with respect to historical data, but also with respect to determining the price of factor inputs and integrating the extent of technical change in estimating real value added.
8. In 1970 the difference in the two value added estimates amounted to $22,750,000. Wood products contributed $14,833,000 to this total, while food and beverages contributed $4,519,000 and leather products $4,239,000. In 1890 the difference in the two value added estimates came to $21,567,000 of which wood products contributed $9,481,000; food and beverages, $6,054,000; and leather products, $4,850,000.
9. Chambers and Gordon (1966), pp. 319, 327, 328 argue that this relationship cannot be a causal one, since productivity growth is assumed to be given exogenously. However, this is not proven. It is only asserted.
10. Bertram (1965), pp. 181–182 relates to us the relatively high rates of growth of real gross output in the iron and steel products and transportation equipment sectors in the period 1900–10 compared with the period 1870–1890. Bertram attributes little significance to this finding. Rather, he focuses upon the significance of these two sectors in the pre-1900 period.

References

Altman, M. (1984a). *A comparative economic history of Quebec and Ontario, 1870–1910: An analysis of the statistical sources*, vol. 2, (PhD dissertation, Department of Economics, McGill University)

Altman, M. (1984b). *A revision of Canadian manufacturing growth, 1870–1910 and a comparison with the American record*, (Working Paper, Concordia University)

Altman, M. (1986). *New estimates for a revision of Canadian economic growth: 1870–1910 (a challenge to the gradualist interpretation)*, (Working Paper, University of Ottawa)

Arrow, K.J. 1974. "The measurement of real value added." In *Nations and Households in Economic Growth*, ed. P.A. David and M.W. Reder, 3–20. New York and London: Academic Press.

Asimakopulos, A. (1965). "Price indexes," In Urquhart, M.C. and K.A.H. Buckley, eds., *Historical Statistics of Canada*, first ed. (Toronto: Macmillan)

Barnett, R.F.J. (1963). *A study of price movements and the cost of living in Kingston, Ontario for the years 1865 to 1900,* (M.A. dissertation, Department of Economics, Queen's University)

Barnett, R.F.J. (1966). *Canada's manufacturing development and foreign trade*, Mimeograph, (Department of Economics, Bishop's University).

Bertram, G.W. 1964. "Historical statistics on growth and structure of manufacturing in Canada, 1870–1957." In *Conference on Statistics, 1962 and 1963, Papers*, ed. J. Henripin and A. Asimakopulos, 93–152. Toronto: University of Toronto Press.

Bertram, G.W. 1965. "Economic growth in Canadian industry, 1870–1915: The staple model and the take-off hypothesis." *Canadian Journal of Economics and Political Science* 29: 159–184.

Bolton, C.W., ed. 1916. *Wholesale Prices in Canada, 1915.* Ottawa: Department of Labour.

Buckley, K. 1974. *Capital Formation in Canada, 1896–1930.* Toronto: McClelland and Stewart.

The Census of Canada, 1870–1871 (1873–1875) vols. 2 and 3; 1880–1881 (1883) vol. 3; 1890–1891 (1894) (Ottawa), vol. 3; 1900–1901 (1905) (Ottawa), vol. 3; 1911 (1913) vol. 3 (Ottawa: Queen's Printer)

Chambers, E.J. 1964. "Late nineteenth century business cycles in Canada." *Canadian Journal of Economics and Political Science* 30: 391–413.

Chambers, E.J., and D.F. Gordon. 1966. "Primary products and economic growth: An empirical measurement." *Journal of Political Economy* 74: 315–332.

Dales, J. 1963. "Some Historical and Theoretical Comments on Canada's National Policies." *Queens Quarterly* 71: 297–316.

David, P.A. 1962. "The Deflation of Value Added." *Review of Economics and Statistics* 48: 148–155.

David, P.A. 1966. "Measuring Real Net Output: A proposed index." *Review of Economics and Statistics* 48: 419–425.

Davis, L.E., et al. 1972. *American Economic Growth: An Economist's History of the United States.* New York: Harper and Row.

Dominion Bureau of Statistics (1948). *The Standard Industrial Classification Manual* (Ottawa)

Gallman, R. E. (1960). "The United States commodity output, 1839–1899," in *Trends in the American Economy in the Nineteenth Century.* Studies in Income and Wealth, vol. 24 (New York: NBER), pp. 13–72

Gallman, R. E. (1972). "The pace and pattern of American growth," In Lance E. Davis, et al. *American Economic Growth: An Economist's History of the United States* (New York: Harper and Row), pp. 15–60.

Historical Statistics of the United States: colonial times to. 1970. *1975*. Washington: US Department of the Census.

Homer, F.B. 1961. "The meaning of production indexes." *Economic Record* 37: 82–97.

McDougall, D.M. 1971. "Canadian manufacturing commodity output, 1870–1915." *The Canadian Journal of Economics* 4: 21–36.

Michell, H. 1931. *"A survey of prices in Canada from 1848", in Statistical Contributions to Canadian Economic History*, vol. 2. Toronto: Macmillan.

Skelton, O.D. (1914). "General economic history, 1867–1912," In Shortt A. and G. Doughty, eds., *Canada and its Provinces*, vol. 9 (Toronto: McClelland and Stewart)

Trade and Navigation Reports, *Sessional Papers, The Parliament of Canada:* (1871), vol. 2; (1880–1881) vol. 2; (1891) vol. 2; (1901) vol. 4; (1911) vol. 5; (1914) vol. 6 (Ottawa)

Urquhart, M.C. (1984). *New estimates of Gross National Product, Canada, 1870 to 1926: some implications for Canadian development*, Mimeograph, (Department of Economics, Queen's University)

Urquhart, M.C. (1985). *New estimates of Gross National Product, Canada 1870 to 1926: some implications for Canadian development*, Discussion Paper no. 586, (Department of Economics, Queen's University)

Urquhart, M.C., and K.A.H. Buckley, eds. 1965. *Historical Statistics of Canada*, 1st ed. Toronto: Macmillan.

CHAPTER 11

New Historical Canadian Output Estimates: Implications for an Understanding of Canadian Economic Development, 1870–1926

1 Introduction

A new Canadian nominal GNP series has been recently constructed for the 1870–1926 period by M.C. Urquhart (1986) in association with Alan Green, M.C. McInnis, Thomas Rymes, Alasdair Sinclair, and Marion Steel. Urquhart deflates this series largely with a cost of living index to generate a new real GNP series for the 1870–1926 period. These new real GNP estimates mark an important improvement over the earlier estimates developed by Firestone (1958) due to the greater number of data sets which comprise the Urquhart nominal GNP estimates and the more rigorous manner in which they are constructed. This is particularly true of the estimates for the intercensal years (Dales, 1962).[1]

In this article, a new set of real GNP estimates are produced, which build on Urquhart's nominal GNP estimates.[2] Serious deficiencies are found to exist with the price index numbers used by Urquhart to deflate his nominal GNP estimates. This raises some questions as to their capacity to reflect movements and levels in the actual prices of the components of Urquhart's nominal GNP estimates. Therefore, an alternative set of price index numbers, built largely on available wholesale price index numbers, are constructed to deflate nominal GNP.

M. Altman, *Lessons from a Successfully Export-Oriented, Resource-Rich Economy*, https://doi.org/10.1007/978-3-031-03887-7_11

The revised real GNP estimates provide a basis for revisions and additions to Urquhart's growth estimates and to his estimates for the structure of the Canadian economy over the 1870–1926 period. These new estimates shed further light on the much debated question of whether there was a positive break in the Canadian economy which coincided with the Canadian wheat boom, circa 1896–1913. In particular, the revised real GNP estimates indicate more forcefully than do Urquhart's that the period of the wheat boom did indeed represent an important positive break in the economic development of Canada and that the Canadian economy was, by all measures, the fastest growing of all "western" economies in the 1870–1910 period.[3] Also, the revised real GNP estimates yield new implicit price deflators which differ in important ways from Urquhart's. Finally, in the process of constructing the revised real GNP estimates, new real output estimates are provided for many of the important components of Urquhart's nominal GNP series, including the all important manufacturing sector.[4]

2 The Revised Real GNP Estimates

Urquhart deflates his nominal GNP estimates net of gross domestic fixed capital formation (GDCF) using three sets of cost of living price indexes, one each for the 1870–1900, 1900–1913, and 1913–26 periods respectively (Urquhart, 1986, pp. 29, 85–87). Gross domestic capital formation is deflated using a price index for the cost of capital goods. GDCF is estimated, from Urquhart (1986, pp. 33–34), to represent about 15% of nominal GNP, with the significant exception of the 1906–14 period, where it represented, on average, 25.5% of GNP. Therefore, in Urquhart's general GNP deflator, the price index for the cost of capital goods is, in effect, given a weight of about 15% whereas the cost of living price index is given the weight of the residual GNP, about 85%.

The price index numbers used by Urquhart for the years 1870 to 1910 are plagued by serious problems. For the 1870–1900 period the Barnett consumer price index is used. This price index is built on price data from the Kingston, Ontario area alone and contains no data on rents and clothing (Urquhart, 1986, pp. 85–86; Barnett, 1963). For the period 1900 to 1913 the Bertram-Percy consumer price index is used. However, for the years 1901–1904 and 1906–1908, the price index numbers for this series consist of interpolations from expenditure-based weighted wholesale price index numbers for food, fuel and light, rent, and clothing for the years 1900, 1905 and 1909 (Urquhart, 1986, pp. 85–86; Bertram and Percy, 1979). For the period 1913–26 a much more rigorously constructed cost of living index is used. For these years data on rents, food, clothing, fuel and light, and miscellaneous expenses are incorporated. However, the weights assigned to these categories and to the price data within each category are based on the consumption of the relevant commodities in the year 1913 (Urquhart and Buckley, 1965, p. 288), and not on the component distribution of nominal output in Urquhart's nominal GNP series.

Given the many problems with the cost of living index used by Urquhart, in particular the components of his index are not representative of the components of his nominal GNP series, it is fair to ask whether GNP price deflators based upon the prices of the actual components of nominal GNP would yield different real GNP estimates and, thereby, different growth and structural change estimates from those yielded by Urquhart's composite price index numbers.[5] For this reason, price index numbers for manufacturing, transportation, and construction are developed for this article to deflate Urquhart's nominal output estimates for these components of GNP while the Dominion Bureau of Statistics' (DBS) sector wholesale price index numbers for mining, fishing, and forestry are used to deflate Urquhart's nominal estimates for mining, fishing, and forestry. Output estimates for the wholesale and retail trade are deflated using the DBS' sector price index numbers for this sector. Finally, Marvin McInnis' nominal agricultural output estimates (which form part of Urquhart's nominal GNP estimates) plus his price index for agriculture, converted to the appropriate base year, are used to generate real agriculture output estimates (Altman, 1989).

The residual output, which varied at about 30% of nominal GNP for most of the 1870–1926 period, is deflated using Urquhart's composite price index numbers.[6] This deflation procedure yields real GNP estimates and implicit price index numbers which differ from Urquhart's (see Table 1 and Figs. 1 to 4). In effect, the new set of GNP deflators is composed of weighted price index numbers constructed by weighting the different price index numbers used in this article by their respective outputs' contribution to nominal GNP. In contrast, Urquhart deflates the output of each and every component of GNP by the same composite price index numbers.

The manufacturing component of Urquhart's nominal GNP estimates is composed of manufacturing value added estimates which consistently

Table 1 Canadian gross national product and implicit price indexes; 1900 prices ($000)

	Urq GNP	*Revised Real GNP*		*Implicit Price Index*		
	Real	Variant A	Variant B	Urq	New A	New B
1870	369,500	328,053	328,053	1.04	1.17	1.17
1871	385,900	345,454	342,686	1.07	1.20	1.20
1872	382,800	351,573	346,149	1.17	1.29	1.27
1873	419,300	390,046	381,007	1.16	1.28	1.25
1874	427,800	396,132	387,974	1.13	1.25	1.23
1875	417,100	371,745	368,632	1.08	1.22	1.22
1876	391,100	360,928	363,519	1.08	1.16	1.17
1877	416,500	389,488	391,781	1.04	1.11	1.12
1878	402,600	371,636	380,134	1.02	1.08	1.10
1879	441,800	429,138	433,498	1.01	1.03	1.04
1880	462,100	446,193	446,193	1.04	1.08	1.08
1881	527,000	529,788	519,630	1.08	1.09	1.07
1882	547,200	544,068	530,051	1.13	1.17	1.14
1883	545,700	539,886	528,788	1.12	1.16	1.13
1884	592,000	538,087	532,757	0.99	1.10	1.09
1885	556,300	530,337	533,920	1.00	1.04	1.05
1886	559,400	547,721	554,204	1.00	1.01	1.02
1887	579,000	591,093	592,020	1.06	1.03	1.03
1888	616,100	591,733	593,302	1.02	1.06	1.06
1889	620,900	608,135	609,099	1.06	1.08	1.08
1890	657,400	649,102	649,102	1.04	1.06	1.06
1891	679,900	666,670	666,761	1.04	1.06	1.06
1892	676,200	668,567	673,331	1.04	1.04	1.05
1893	666,900	654,175	667,094	1.02	1.02	1.04
1894	700,600	635,553	662,625	0.93	0.98	1.02
1895	698,900	631,326	669,823	0.91	0.95	1.00
1896	680,700	649,313	690,439	0.94	0.93	0.99
1897	757,200	765,363	791,987	0.95	0.90	0.94
1898	786,500	802,687	821,766	0.98	0.93	0.96
1899	857,800	853,015	865,006	0.96	0.95	0.97
1900	907,800	907,000	906,999	1.00	1.00	1.00
1901	984,100	996,284	994,548	1.01	1.00	0.99
1902	1,073,600	1,104,860	1,094,381	1.04	1.02	1.01
1903	1,115,100	1,123,147	1,118,309	1.06	1.05	1.05
1904	1,131,400	1,115,396	1,123,461	1.07	1.07	1.08

(continued)

Table 1 (continued)

	Urq GNP	*Revised Real GNP*		*Implicit Price Index*		
1905	1,248,200	1,270,020	1,268,193	1.09	1.07	1.07
1906	1,380,600	1,395,296	1,384,390	1.11	1.10	1.09
1907	1,456,000	1,533,787	1,510,639	1.19	1.15	1.13
1908	1,383,300	1,410,138	1,422,007	1.20	1.16	1.17
1909	1,520,400	1,575,188	1,579,863	1.21	1.16	1.17
1910	1,655,400	1,715,388	1,715,388	1.22	1.18	1.18
1911	1,770,700	1,849,412	1,846,746	1.26	1.21	1.21
1912	1,905,400	2,049,816	2,039,695	1.28	1.22	1.22
1913	1,979,800	2,138,683	2,140,311	1.34	1.24	1.24
1914	1,835,600	1,889,105	1,965,166	1.33	1.24	1.30
1915	1,964,400	1,948,041	2,026,454	1.37	1.33	1.38
1916	2,182,500	2,202,635	2,236,962	1.49	1.45	1.47
1917	2,273,200	2,252,187	2,236,502	1.76	1.79	1.77
1918	2,141,400	2,103,412	2,098,946	1.99	2.03	2.03
1919	1,994,900	1,985,938	2,006,591	2.19	2.18	2.20
1920	1,992,000	2,001,163	2,001,163	2.54	2.53	2.53
1921	1,800,300	1,804,558	1,898,715	2.26	2.14	2.26
1922	2,060,900	2,182,030	2,273,840	2.05	1.85	1.94
1923	2,194,000	2,415,103	2,477,084	2.08	1.83	1.89
1924	2,210,100	2,410,468	2,485,018	2.04	1.80	1.87
1925	2,450,300	2,619,524	2,648,298	2.04	1.88	1.91
1926	2,611,800	2,848,858	2,848,858	2.05	1.88	1.88
1927	2,851,795	3,124,157	3,124,157	1.95	0.00	1.78
1928	3,118,557	3,418,079	3,418,079	1.94	0.00	1.77
1929	3,132,143	3,429,609	3,429,609	1.96	0.00	1.79
1930	2,994,764	3,268,571	3,268,571	1.91	0.00	1.75

Sources and notes See text

contributed approximately 20% to total nominal GNP throughout the 1870–1926 period. The manufacturing value added consists of the value added of seventeen sectors (Urquhart, 1986, pp. 54–59). I deflate each sector's value added largely using sector-specific wholesale price index data provided by the DBS (Urquhart and Buckley, 1965, series J34-44, pp. 293–294) brought to a 1900 base year, the base year adopted by Urquhart (1986). My annual real manufacturing value added estimates comprise the sum of the sector real value added estimates.[7] Alternatively, one can deflate value added by deflating gross outputs and inputs by separate deflators and, thereafter, subtracting the resulting constant

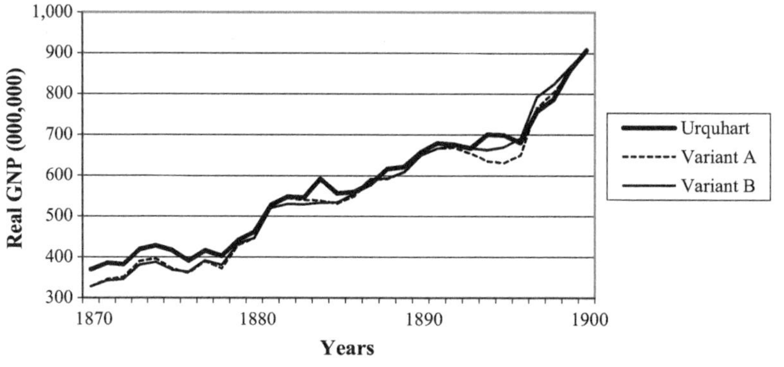

Fig. 1 Real GNP, 1870–1900 (*Source* Table 1)

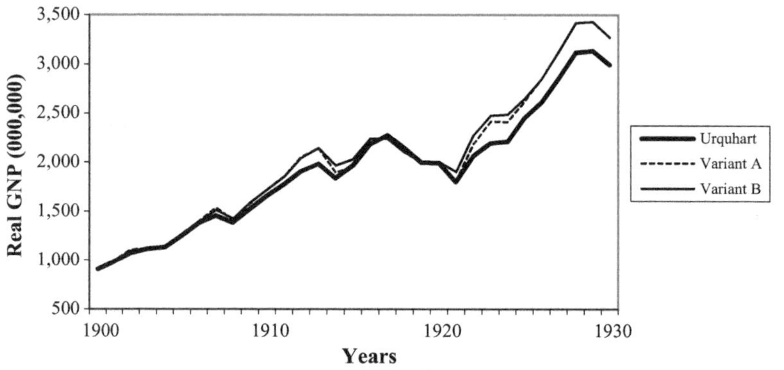

Fig. 2 Real GNP, 1900–1930 (*Source* Table 1)

dollar input estimates from the constant dollar gross output estimates. It remains unclear which approach is more accurate given imperfect price data (Altman, 1987, p. 99). However, presently available price data for the entire 1870–1926 period makes the former deflation procedure the most appropriate.[8]

My real transportation sector output estimates are generated by deflating Urquhart's nominal transportation sector output, which accounts for about 5 to 8% of nominal GNP, using price data for freight and passenger rail transportation (see Table 2). Apparently this sector's

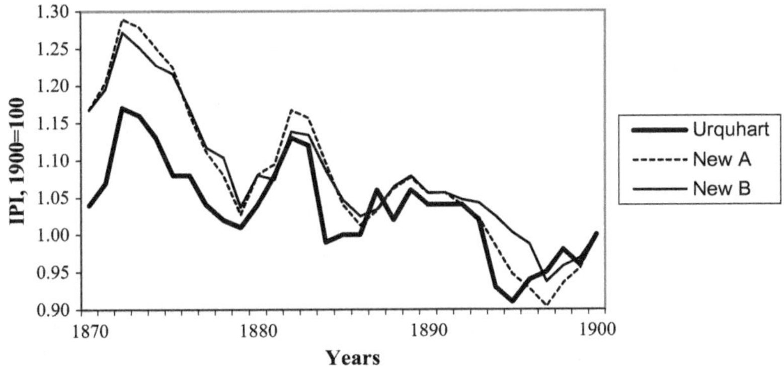

Fig. 3 IPI, 1870–1900 (*Source* Table 1)

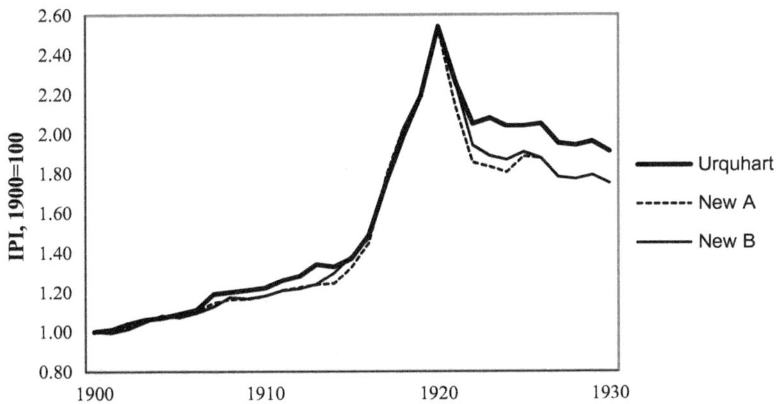

Fig. 4 IPI, 1900–1930 (*Source* Table 1)

output consists entirely of railway output (Urquhart, 1986, p. 66).[9] Thus, the railway sector based deflator is the appropriate one. This deflator is constructed from data on passenger and freight rates per mile produced by Green (1986, p. 81) for the period 1875–1926 and from data on railway revenue derived from freight and passenger services in Urquhart and Buckley (1965, series S53-63, p. 530 and series S129-144, p. 537). The%age distribution of total railway revenue between freight and passenger related services serves as weights for the price data of

Table 2 Components of the Canadian real GNP (Selected Years)

	1871	*1881*	*1891*	*1896*	*1901*	*1911*	*1913*	*1921*	*1925*
Manufacturing									
New	80,421	120,651	172,503	156,859	206,353	418,651	444,750	417,707	512,019
Urquhart	83,557	113,818	165,873	147,607	201,922	372,671	386,411	386,273	467,597
Railroads									
New	9,002	14,337	28,647	39,138	64,317	195,689	283,414	267,099	344,335
Urquhart	21,130	25,860	38,308	46,264	63,162	138,774	184,082	153,977	180,874
Mining									
New	3,860	4,855	14,971	19,625	48,766	61,343	80,558	68,385	88,898
Urquhart	5,004	5,004	14,163	17,553	47,448	45,259	61,122	50,964	64,958
Construction									
New	17,302	21,240	32,796	21,856	41,486	131,149	150,091	69,014	90,922
Urquhart	19,630	20,748	29,989	21,275	40,500	141,454	163,868	77,625	97,162
Forestry									
New	9,651	10,374	11,796	13,749	14,542	16,390	15,450	11,821	26,353
Urquhart	6,505	7,336	10,678	12,938	14,296	19,894	18,165	16,677	32,353
Fishing									
New	3,937	9,546	9,149	9,928	12,340	11,530	10,881	10,362	12,216
Urquhart	3,142	6,461	8,348	10,435	12,035	12,793	11,969	8,459	11,725
Agriculture									
New	111,184	175,912	170,881	168,375	246,703	348,753	388,359	247,992	476,512
Urquhart	135,777	182,427	181,835	167,181	241,004	372,741	386,427	299,931	485,855
Wholesale & retail output									
Nominal	23,389	38,735	54,142	42,853	74,241	222,653	255,926	328,998	480,643
New	17,952	33,385	50,349	47,836	72,726	171,314	191,485	143,162	224,156
Urquhart	21,859	35,866	52,059	45,588	73,506	176,709	190,990	145,574	235,609

	1871	*1881*	*1891*	*1896*	*1901*	*1911*	*1913*	*1921*	*1925*
Community, business & personal service									
Nominal	28,988	44,615	62,170	52,461	90,326	160,763	182,938	231,325	296,768
New	27,091	41,310	59,779	55,809	89,431	127,589	136,521	102,356	145,474

Sources and notes See Text

these two services, generating weighted average prices for freight and passenger services. The resulting series of average prices for the period 1875–1926 is converted to price index numbers with a 1900 base year. These index numbers serve as our deflators of Urquhart's nominal transportation sector output. Since price data are not available for 1870 to 1874, hypothetical price index numbers are constructed for the years 1870 to 1874 inclusive. I regress the transportation price index for the period 1875–1885 on Urquhart's implicit GNP price index for this period and assume that the statistical relationship between these two variables found to exist in this period existed in the 1870–1874 period as well. This yields hypothetical transportation price index numbers for the latter period.[10] This, in turn, yields constant dollar hypothetical transportation output estimates for the 1870–1874 period.

Nominal construction sector output, which contributed less than 5% to nominal GNP for most years in the 1870–1926 period (from Urquhart, 1986, pp. 11–15), is deflated using price index numbers which I construct from estimates for industry-specific construction price index numbers and for industry-specific current dollar nonresidential investment expenditure published by Statistics Canada (1978). Appropriate estimates are available for 27 industries. The price index numbers are weighted in accordance with the%age distribution of nonresidential investment expenditure among the 27 industries. This yields weighted average price index numbers for the construction industry which are converted to a 1900 base year (Altman, 1989). These index numbers are used to generate real construction output estimates (see Table 2).

I deflate the nominal output of the forestry sector (see Table 11.2), which contributed less than 5% to nominal GNP (from Urquhart, 1986, pp. 11–15), using the DBS' wholesale price index numbers for wood, wood products, and paper (Urquhart and Buckley, 1965, series J39, pp. 293–294). Nominal fishing output (see Table 2), which was of even less importance to total nominal GNP, is deflated using Michell's (Urquhart and Buckley, 1965, series J5, p. 291) wholesale price index numbers for fish. With the exception of the late 1890s and the early 1900s, the mining sector (see Table 2) contributed less than 5% to total nominal GNP. I deflate this sector's nominal output using unweighted average price index numbers which I construct from the DBS' wholesale price index numbers for iron and its products, nonferrous metals and their products, and nonmetallic minerals and their products (Urquhart and Buckley, 1965, series J40-41, and J43, pp. 293–294).

Finally, I deflate the wholesale and retail trade's nominal output, which contributed between 7 and 10% to nominal GNP (from Urquhart, 1986, pp. 11–15), using the DBS' wholesale price index numbers for the period 1870–1926 (Urquhart and Buckley, 1965, series J34, pp. 293–294) which are converted to a 1900 base year.[11] However, Urquhart did not publish the nominal output estimates for this sector nor for the community, business, and personal service sector estimates (Urquhart, 1986, pp. 11–15). These are the only sectors for which Urquhart only presents estimates for the census years. One can infer what Urquhart's intercensal output estimates for these two sectors *combined* are by subtracting his published sector output estimates from his nominal GNP estimates. However, to deflate annual estimates for the wholesale and retail trade alone it is necessary to construct nominal estimates for both this sector and the community, business, and personal service sector.

To construct such nominal output estimates, I assume that the%age deviation of "actual" from trend nominal output in these two sectors for the 1870–1926 period, is the same as the%age deviation of "actual" from trend nominal GNP, net of the nominal output in these sectors.[12] The trend values for these two sectors and for net GNP are derived by log-linear interpolation through the bench-mark years. Bench-mark years of 1870, 1880, 1890, 1900, 1910, 1920, and 1926 are chosen since these are the only years for which relatively solid nominal output estimates exist for the wholesale and retail trade sector and for the community, business, and personal service sector. The difference between the log of actual and the log of trend net GNP is the%age deviation of the actual from the trend values. Applying this percentage to the trend values for the wholesale and retail trade sector and for the community, business, and personal service sector for the 1870–1926 period yields intercensal nominal output estimates for these two sectors. These nominal output estimates, when added to Urquhart's intercensal nominal estimates for the other sectors of the economy, yield my adjusted nominal GNP estimates which are little different from Urquhart's nominal GNP at market prices. The differences which exist between these two sets of nominal GNP estimates are a product of my combined estimates for the wholesale and retail trade sector and for the community, business, and personal service sector differing from the estimates for these sectors inferred from Urquhart's published nominal output estimates.[13]

The marginal differences between my adjusted nominal GNP estimates at market prices and Urquhart's nominal GNP estimates yield two different sets of real GNP estimates: Variant A and Variant B. My Variant A estimates differ from my Variant B estimates since, in the Variant A estimates, the residual nominal GNP - the output not deflated by sector-specific deflators and which is therefore deflated by Urquhart's general GNP deflators—incorporates my intercensal estimates for the wholesale and retail trade and for the community, business, and personal services sector (the adjusted nominal GNP), whereas in the Variant B estimates, the residual output equals Urquhart's nominal GNP at market prices net of the nominal output to be deflated by the sector-specific price indexes. In the Variant B estimates, therefore, the Urquhart estimates for the residual components of nominal GNP are either increased or reduced depending on whether the adjusted nominal GNP estimates exceed or fall below Urquhart's nominal GNP estimates. Be this as it may, my two variants of real GNP are almost identical for most of the 1870–1926 period (see Table 1 and Figs. 1 and 2).

The revised real GNP estimates and the two nominal GNP estimates yield two variants of revised implicit GNP deflators. These two variants, like their real GNP counterparts, are almost identical for most of the 1870–1926 period and they both differ from Urquhart's largely in terms of the value of the index numbers for specific periods. Thus, from 1870 to 1896, the new deflators are above Urquhart's except for 1881 and 1887. This gap is widest from 1870 to 1878. From 1907 to 1914 and from 1922 to 1926 the new deflators lie clearly below Urquhart's deflators. This gap is most substantial in the latter period. The movements of these index numbers are similar but for a few years in the periods 1884–89, 1895–99, and 1922–26 (see Table 1 and Figs. 3 and 4). Moreover, the measured volatility of the new and Urquhart price deflators is not much different. Volatility is measured by the standard deviation of deviations (SDDT). My SDDTs reveal that the new series is more volatile than Urquhart's for the entire 1870–1928 period, but by only 11%. However, the new series is less volatile than Urquhart's during the 1870–1908 subperiod by 25%. From 1908 to 1928 the new series is 21% more volatile than the Urquhart series.[14]

3 The Revised Real GPN and Economic Growth

Both variants of the revised real GNP estimates yield growth rates which differ from those generated by Urquhart's real GNP estimates. I focus on the Variant A estimates and, like Urquhart (1986, p. 36; 1988,

p. 51), I compute extensive GNP growth rates from three year averages of real GNP centred on the bench-mark years 1871, 1881, 1891, 1901, 1911, 1921, 1925. Unlike Urquhart (1988, p. 52) who uses only population estimates for the above bench-mark years to compute per capita or intensive growth rates, I construct the population growth rates from population estimates for the above three year averages so as to be more consistent with the output growth rates. The population estimates are those of Urquhart (1986, pp. 30–31). This difference in procedure has some marginal effects on the per capita growth rates.[15] To estimate growth rates of labour productivity I rely largely on Urquhart's (1988, pp. 14a-14b, Table 3) estimates of labour employment for the above bench-mark or census years. Growth rates are computed using the Urquhart, the revised, and the Firestone real GNP estimates (see Table 3).

The revised and Urquhart extensive growth rates differ substantially from Firestone's for most periods examined. However, for both the 1871–1925 and 1871–1911 periods the Urquhart growth rates exceed Firestone's by only 5 and 2% respectively while the revised growth rates exceed Firestone's by 15 and 12% respectively. An important distinction between both the revised and Urquhart, and the Firestone growth rates is that for the latter two estimates, especially for the revised estimates, the 1910s and the 1920s stand out as the periods of the most rapid growth whereas, according to the Firestone GNP estimates, the growth experience of the early twentieth century had little by which to distinguish itself. Finally, in stark contrast to both the revised and Urquhart GNP estimates, the Firestone estimates suggest that the 1880s, which follows the implementation of Canada's National Policy of relatively high tariffs and of government sponsored transcontinental railway construction, was characterized by an inconsequential growth rate. This story changes but little when one refers to either the per capita growth or to the labour productivity growth rates; only now the differences between both the revised and Urquhart growth rates, and the Firestone growth rates become accentuated.

An important distinction between the revised and the Urquhart extensive growth rates is that the revised growth rates exceed Urquhart's for all periods examined but for the 1880s when the two growth rates are about the same and for the 1910s when Urquhart's growth rate exceeds the revised one by 31%. The revised growth rates exceed Urquhart's by the widest margin in the 1870s and in the 1920–25 period, by 32

Table 3 Measures of economic growth

	% p.a. growth rate			*% p.a. growth rate per capita*			*% p.a. growth rate per worker*			*Population % p.a. growth rate*	*Employees % p.a. growth rate*
	Urquhart	Revised	Firestone	Urquhart	Revised	Firestone	Urquhart	Revised	Firestone		
1871–1925	3.49	3.85	3.34	1.77	2.12	1.61	1.42	1.78	1.27	1.73	2.07
1871–1901	3.24	3.65	3.50	1.97	2.38	2.23	1.66	2.07	1.92	1.27	1.58
1871–1911	3.94	4.34	3.87	2.25	2.66	2.18	1.73	2.13	1.66	1.68	2.21
1901–1925	3.81	4.09	3.15	1.51	1.80	0.85	1.11	1.40	0.45	2.30	2.70
1871–1881	3.04	4.02	4.41	1.46	2.43	2.83	1.15	2.13	2.52	1.59	1.89
1881–1891	2.74	2.70	0.73	1.61	1.57	-0.39	1.16	1.12	-0.84	1.13	1.58
1891–1901	3.95	4.25	5.40	2.85	3.15	4.30	2.68	2.98	4.13	1.10	1.27
1901–1911	6.04	6.44	4.99	3.11	3.51	2.06	1.91	2.31	0.86	2.93	4.13
1911–1921	0.94	0.65	1.21	-1.04	-1.34	-0.77	-0.50	-0.79	-0.23	1.98	1.44
1921–1925	5.58	7.10	3.46	4.06	5.59	1.95	3.28	4.81	1.17	1.51	2.30
1871–1891	2.89	3.36		1.54	2.00		1.16	1.62		1.36	1.74
1871–1896	2.55	2.80		1.27	1.52		1.19	1.44		1.28	1.36
1891–1896	1.20	0.61		0.21	-0.37		1.32	0.74		0.98	-0.13
1896–1913	5.96	6.61		3.54	4.18		2.52	3.17		2.43	3.44
1913–1928	3.34	3.56		1.63	1.85		1.33	1.55		1.71	2.01

Sources and notes See Text

and 27% respectively. These differences in growth rates are accentuated in terms of the growth of output per capita and the growth of labour productivity. The revised per capita and labour productivity growth rates exceed Urquhart's by 67 and 84% and by 38 and 46% in the 1870s and in the 1921–25 period respectively. During the 1900–1910 period the revised extensive, intensive, and labour productivity growth rate exceeds Urquhart's by 7, 13, and 21% respectively. Over the entire 1871–1925 period the revised extensive, intensive, and labour productivity growth rates exceed Urquhart's by 10, 20, and 25% respectively. However, for both the revised and the Urquhart GNP estimates the break between the 1901–1911 period and the previous decade is not as dramatic for intensive as for extensive growth. This is due to the surge in population growth which took place in the 1900–1910 period. Population grew by 2.93% per annum in this last decade compared to only 1.10% in the 1890s. Moreover, in terms of labour productivity growth both sets of estimates suggest that the 1901–1911 period, the 1890s and the 1921–25 period were characterized by higher growth rates than the 1901–1911 period. Therefore, the labour productivity estimates suggest that labour productivity growth cannot be correlated in any significant way with the wheat boom. This is contrary to what I find here for both extensive and intensive growth and to what I have found elsewhere for the labour productivity growth in the manufacturing sector (Altman, 1987, 102–103).

However, since these labour productivity estimates are computed for census years alone, one is not truly estimating labour productivity growth during the long upswing in the Canadian economy which begins in 1896 and ends in 1913 (see Figs. 1 and 2). This sustained period of expansion coincides with a period of significant increases in wheat and flour exports from Canada.[16] Using the new real GNP estimates for 1896 and 1913, in addition to new employment estimates for 1896 and 1913, it is possible to estimate labour productivity growth for the 1896–1913 period as well as for the 1871–96 and 1913–28 periods; periods which correspond to different peak to peak phases of extensive economic growth (see Figures One and Two). In this way the period of the wheat boom can be placed in the context of the growth experiences of those years which came before and after it.

This procedure requires the estimation of employment for interdecal years. Urquhart adjusts the census data on the number of gainfully employed individuals to generate estimates for labour employment for the census years which are used to construct the above labour productivity estimates.[17] For 1896 and 1913 there are no estimates for the number of gainfully employed from which to construct employment estimates. However, such estimates can be constructed by regressing the index numbers for the readily available annual employment estimates for the years 1921 to 1928 on the index numbers of my revised estimates for real GNP for these years. All index numbers are to a base year of 1921. This yields the following:

$$\text{Labour Employment} = 0.73927 + 0.249497^{*}(\text{Real GNP}).$$

These results are used to generate index numbers for labour employment for the years 1891–1896 and 1911–13 which are, in turn, used to construct employment estimates for 1896 and 1913 of 1,584,000 and 2,817,000 respectively.[18]

Both the revised and Urquhart labour productivity growth estimates identify the 1896–1913 period as the one with the highest rate of labour productivity growth of all periods examined. Both growth estimates for this period are about twice that for the 1871–96 and 1913–26 periods, with the revised growth rates exceeding those derived using Urquhart's GNP estimates by 34,39, and 17% in the 1871–96, 1896–1913, and 1913–26 periods respectively. The wheat boom clearly coincides with a sharp rise in labour productivity growth. These tentative labour productivity growth estimates, therefore, lend some support to the hypothesis that the wheat boom positively affected the growth of Canadian labour productivity. Finally, the extensive and intensive growth estimates for these periods also suggest that the 1896–1913 period stands alone in the 1870–1928 era as the leading period of sustained economic growth.[19]

4 Conclusion

The revised real GNP estimates presented here are built upon the important nominal estimates constructed by Urquhart and upon a more consistent and representative set of price index series than those used by Urquhart to generate his real GNP series. In effect, the revised real GNP series is derived by deflating the various nominal components of GNP by sector-specific deflators. In the process of constructing the revised GNP series, real output estimates for the most important sectors of the economy are generated. These estimates provide scholars with an additional source of information with which to examine many much discussed and debated questions in Canadian economic history. The revised real GNP estimates differ most significantly from Urquhart's in terms of the level of output. The same is true of the new implicit price index which is a by-product of the construction of the revised GNP estimates.

The revised GNP estimates also generate higher annual extensive, intensive, and labour productivity growth rates than do the Urquhart estimates. In particular, although the revised estimates affirm the pattern of growth suggested by the Urquhart estimates, the revised estimates reveal a much more significant break between the pre and post-1900 period. The latter finding is reinforced by the growth estimates constructed for interdecal periods. This finding which suggests an important statistical relationship between the wheat boom and significant growth in the Canadian economy, is reaffirmed by the new estimates constructed for structural change in the Canadian economy. Therefore, the revised real GNP estimates furnish a basis for estimates which provide strong evidence suggesting that the era of the wheat boom was a unique period of very high economic growth in the sixty-odd years spanning Confederation to the Great Depression.[20]

Finally, the new growth estimates indicate that the Canadian economy was the fastest growing (extensively or intensively) of all the advanced industrial economies of the time, including the United States, the United Kingdom, Germany, and France (Maddison, 1989, pp. 44–45). In particular, for the 1870–1910 period, only the growth performance of the American economy approached Canada's. The U.S. experienced an annual growth rate of real GNP of only 3.9% compared to the 4.3% experienced in Canada while the per capita growth rate for the U.S. and Canada was 1.8 and 2.7% respectively. Nevertheless, American extensive growth lagged behind Canadian extensive growth only during the 1900–1910 subperiod when the U.S. witnessed a 3.5% growth rate compared to the 6.4% growth rate in Canada. In this period American per capita growth also lagged behind the Canadian: 1.6% compared to 3.5%. It was, therefore, Canada's exceptional growth during the Canadian wheat boom which was responsible for Canada's superior growth performance over the entire 1870–1910 period.[21]

Notes

1. Urquhart (1986) is not clear as to how his nominal estimates differ from Firestone's. However, it is clear from Firestone (1958, pp. 277–280), that his real GNP estimates, particularly from 1870 to 1910 are spurious, being based on backward interpolations from his 1910 real GNP estimate. The 1870–1910 series is derived from a weighted series for the volume of wheat, fish, potatoes, coal, tea, coffee, sugar, raw wool, and tobacco produced net of exports minus imports, plus the number of passengers carried by steam railways. Also used are estimates of government expenditures, exports and imports, and estimates of the apparent consumption of construction material. In effect, Firestone produces no nominal GNP estimates for the 1870–1910 period. His estimates for the later period are based on adjusted estimates of other scholars. Finally, detailed estimates upon which Firestone's aggregate real GNP estimates are based remain unpublished and are apparently lost. These factors have precluded any serious use of the Firestone series over the years. In contrast, important components of the Urquhart series have been published (Urquhart, 1986; Green, 1986; McInnis, 1986). Also, Urquhart's interpolators for intercensal years appear to be more extensive than those used by Firestone (1986, pp. 69–71) and, many of these are published. As with Firestone, the most rigorous estimates of the Urquhart series are for the census years, 1870–71, 1880–81, 1890–91, 1900–01, 1910–11, 1920–21. For some insight into the basis of the differences between the Urquhart and the Firestone GNP series see McInnis, (1986, pp. 738–741).
2. Table 1 presents the new real annual GNP estimates as well as the new annual implicit price index for the 1870–1926 period. The 1927–1930 series is taken from Urquhart (1988, pp. 9–11), which is, in turn, taken from Statistics Canada files. Urquhart's real GNP estimates are from (Urquhart, 1986, pp. 30–31). Urquhart's nominal GNP estimates are presented in Urquhart (1986, pp. 11–15).
3. See Pomfret (1993) and Altman (1987) for a discussion of some of the debates surrounding the question of the significance of the wheat boom to Canadian economic growth. See Maddison (1989, pp. 44–45), for comparative growth estimates of what are today's advanced industrial economies.
4. Space limitations preclude all but a presentation of new real component output estimates and the price index numbers used in their construction for sample years only (see Table 2). The years chosen are largely census years which form the basis of most of my growth estimates (see Table 3). For the complete series see Altman (1989).
5. In Altman (1987), a similar question is posed with respect to Bertram's (1964) deflation of nominal manufacturing output estimates. Bertram

(1964) deflates these nominal estimates using sector specific output deflators unweighted for each sector's contribution to total output. When these deflators are appropriately weighted and then applied to deflate the nominal output estimates, the real output estimates generated thereby differ considerably from Bertram's.

6. The share of the residual in nominal GNP is derived from Urquhart (1988, Table 2.1).
7. I also use Michell's hides and leather price index numbers (Urquhart and Buckley, 1965, series J8, p. 291) to deflate leather sector value added. Food and beverage value added is deflated by weighted averages of the DBS's vegetable products and animals and their products price index numbers (Urquhart and Buckley, 1965, series J36 and J37, pp. 293–294). The weights assigned to each set of index numbers are derived from my census data estimates of the percentage contribution of vegetable products and animal related products to food and beverages value added. The weights are: 6.9 and 93.1%, 1871; 8.9 and 91.1%, 1881; 15.1 and 84.9%, 1891; 26.8 and 73.2%, 1901; 24.9 and 75.1%, 1911; and 41.1 and 58.9%, 1921, respectively. The 1921 weights are applied to the 1926 estimates. These weights are used to interpolate weights for the intercensal years. See Altman (1989) for detailed annual sector price deflators and real value added estimates. See also, Altman (1987).
8. Elsewhere (ibid.), both deflation techniques are used since the construction of constant dollar output estimates is restricted to the census years 1871, 1881, 1891, 1901, 1911 only.
9. Urquhart's (1986, Table 2) estimates for transportation output deviate only marginally from Green's (1986, p. 791) estimates for income plus gross fixed capital formation in the railway sector.
10. The following equation is applied: [Transportation price index = constant + *b*(Urquhart price index)].

    The constant equals 1.5483 and b equals 0.5219. One could have used the DBS' (Urquhart and Buckley, 1965, series J34-44, p. 294) unweighted general wholesale price index as an independent variable as opposed to Urquhart's price index. The resulting hypothetical real transportation output estimates are similar to those presented here.
11. See Urquhart and Buckley (1965, pp. 281–283), for a discussion of the construction of these price index numbers.
12. Urquhart (1986, p. 10) does not specify the method by which he constructs the nominal estimates for these two sectors. He only points out that no satisfactory annual interpolators exist for these sectors. The approach adopted in this study to estimate the intercensal nominal output for these sectors yields numbers which, when added to Urquhart's other sector-specific annual estimates, generate Urquhart's GNP at market prices.

13. My adjusted nominal GNP series is not presented in this article, but it can be easily derived by multiplying my Variant A real GNP estimates by their corresponding Variant A implicit price index numbers (see Table 11.1).
14. I use the same method for calculating volatility as that used by Romer (1989), Balke and Gordon (1989), and Altman (1992) to measure the volatility of GNP. Critical to this exercise is the detrending of the price index series and therefore the choice of bench-mark years. Log-linear trend lines through logarithms of the price index numbers for selected bench-mark years are constructed. Bench-mark years approximate "points of mid-expansion in the business cycle" (Romer, 1989, p.18; Altman, 1992). The bench-mark years for both the new (Variant A) and Urquhart series are: 1871, 1880, 1892, 1900, 1914, 1922, 1928. The SDDTs for the 1870–1928 period are 8.16% for the new series (Variant A) and 7.37% for Urquhart's. The SDDTs are 3.50 and 4.67% for these two series respectively in the 1870–1908 period and 12.83 and 10.59% respectively in the 1908–1928 period. Elsewhere (Altman, 1992), I find that the SDDT (5.66%) for the revised real GNP (Variant A) for the 1870–1928 period is 98% of the SDDT (5.79%) for the Urquhart real GNP estimates.
15. Compare Urquhart (1986, p. 32, Table 2.10) to Table 3 below.
16. The Canadian exports of wheat and flour averaged only 3,722,000 bushels in the 1886–1891 period (in 1891 it was only 940,000 bushels). During the years 1892–1895 wheat and flour exports averaged 10,644,000 bushels, an increase of 1.86 times from the previous period. Canada exported an average of 15,854,000 bushels by the period 1896–1900 and by 1901–1905 an average of 25,828,000 bushels were exported. During the 1906–1910 period Canadian wheat and flour exports averaged 53,163,000 bushels. By 1911–1915, an average of 99,616,000 bushels of wheat and flour were exported from Canada. In the 1921–1930 period even more wheat and flour was exported: an average of 271,586,000 bushels (calculated from Urquhart and Buckley (1965), series L139-146, pp. 363–364).
17. Urquhart's 1871 employment estimate is taken from Firestone (1958, p. 184, Table 65). The Firestone (1958, pp. 318–319) estimate for 1871 is based on educated guesswork which has as its.

    basis data contained in the 1881 and later censuses. Urquhart's estimates for gainful employment for the census years in the 1881–1911 period, upon which his employment estimates are based, are the estimates in Urquhart and Buckley (1965, p. 59, Series 2) adjusted for McInnis's upward (1986, pp. 753–756) revisions of the estimates for gainfully employed in agriculture. These adjustments revise upward the Urquhart and Buckley gainfully employed series for all occupations by less than one% for all years except for 1901 (2.93%) and 1911 (1.00%). The 1921 employment estimate is from Urquhart and Buckley (1965, series 51,

p. 61) as are the 1925 and the 1928 employment estimates used in this article. Urquhart assumes that the percentage of the gainfully employed who were working in 1881, 1891, 1901, and 1911 was 98.5%, the same as in 1921, the earliest year for which such an estimate can be made. The employment estimates for these years in thousands of people are: 1,130 (1871), 1,363 (1881), 1,594 (1891), 1,808 (1901), 2,710 (1911), 3,126 (1921), 3,423 (1925), and 3,796 (1928).

18. The index numbers for labour employment for 1896 and 1913 are converted to base years of 1891 and 1911 respectively yielding index numbers of 0.99343 and 1.039343 for 1896 and 1913 respectively. The index numbers for 1896 and 1913 are multiplied by the employment estimates for 1891 (1,594,000) and 1911 (2,710,000) to generate the employment estimates for 1896 and 1913.
19. One can construct estimates for the output structure of the Canadian economy and the manufacturing sector in terms of the percentage distribution of the major components of Gross Domestic Product and of the manufacturing sector. Such estimates are best constructed for census years, years for which the data are the most reliable. Urquhart (1986, pp. 42, 60) presents such estimates for nominal output. These estimates would be no different if constructed for Urquhart's real GNP or real manufacturing output since every component's nominal output would be deflated by the same composite price index numbers. Revised estimates for the structure of GDP, based on the new real GNP estimates, provide the basis for re-examining the extent of structural change in the Canadian economy from one census year to the next over the 1870–1920 period. To measure the extent of structural change, I estimate the Duncan Index of Dissimilarity for both the structure of GDP and of manufacturing. This index is constructed by subtracting the percentage share of each sector in the base year from their respective share in the target year. The absolute values of these differences are summed and divided by two. Zero indicates no structural change. One hundred indicates complete structural change. The Duncan Index for the revised and Urquhart GDP series respectively is: 3.6 and 3.8, 1871–81; 9.7 and 8.6, 1881–91; 8.1 and 6.9, 1891–1901; 12.3 and 8.7, 1901–11; and 9 and 5.6, 1911–2 1. Both GDP series reveal that the 1880s and the 1901–1911 periods were the most significant periods of structural change, with the revised GDP estimates indicating much more significant structural change than the Urquhart series. More specifically, (see Altman, 1989 for details) only the revised estimates suggest that transportation sector's share in real GDP increased by 58% in the 1880s, and by another 58% from 1900 to 1910, after its share had risen by 57% during the 1890s. The revised estimates also suggest an increase in the share of the transportation sector by 50% during the 1910s as

compared to an increase of only 6% for the Urquhart estimates. Since the transportation sector was dominated by the railway, and the railway was driven by efforts to open up the Canadian West to settlement where wheat production would be of great importance, the revised estimates suggest the importance of Canada's wheat economy to this important sector of the Canadian economy (see also Altman, 1988). For manufacturing the Duncan Index for the revised and Urquhart series respectively is: 8.1 and 8.7, 1871–81; 12.4 and 6.9, 1881–91; 10.0 and 7.1, 1891–1901; 16.4 and 8.9, 1901–1911; and 12.8 and 13.2, 1911- 1921. Only the Duncan Index for the revised estimates suggests that structural change of any relative importance took place during the 1880s and the 1901–1911 period. In particular, the revised constant dollar estimates indicate that the period 1900–1910, the period embodying the Canadian wheat boom, coincides with a "rise to prominence of key sectors" (Altman, 1987, pp. 104–107).

20. Inwood and Stengos (1991), using Urquhart's real GNP estimates and measures of extensive economic growth plus estimates for investment, find that the wheat boom (the "shock" which it provided to the Canadian economy in 1896) positively affected the growth process in the 1870–1939 era.
21. The extensive growth rates of real American GNP are derived from, Balke and Gordon (1989, pp. 84–85). To construct intensive growth rates, the population estimates for the U.S. in, U.S. Department of Commerce (1975, series A6-8, p. 8), are used. One should note that per capita growth was greater in Canada than in the U.S. from 1900 to 1910 in spite of Canada's population growing at an annual rate of 2.9% as compared to the 1.9% growth rate experienced in the U.S. From 1870 to 1900 the American economy grew extensively at a faster pace than the Canadian: 4.0 compared to 3.7%. However, the much faster rate of population growth in the U.S. of 2.17% as compared to Canada's 1.27%, resulted in the per capita growth in America for this period being less than in Canada: 1.9 as compared to 2.4% respectively.ss.

References

Altman, M. 1987. "A Revision of Canadian Economic Growth: 1870–1910 (a challenge to the gradualist interpretation)." *Canadian Journal of Economics* 20: 86–113.

Altman, M. 1988. "Railways as an Engine of Economic Growth? Who Benefited from the Canadian Railway Boom, 1870–1910?" *Histoire Sociale-Social History* 21: 269–281.

Altman, M. (1989). *Revised Estimates of Real Canadian GNP and Growth and the Pre and Post World War Two Volatility of the Canadian Business Cycle with Some Comparison to the American Record,* (Discussion Paper No. 89–06, University of Saskatchewan, Saskatoon, Saskatchewan)

Altman, M. 1992. "Business Cycle Volatility in Developed Market Economics, 1870–1986: Revisions and Conjectures." *Eastern Economic Journal* 18: 259–275.

Balke, N.S., and Gordon, R.J. 1989. "The Estimation of Prewar National Product: Methodology and New Evidence." *Journal of Political Economy* 97: 38–92.

Barnett, R.F.J. 1963. *A Study of Price Movements and the Cost of Living in Kingston, Ontario for the Years 1865–1900, (MA Thesis.* Kingston, Ontario): Queen's University.

Bertram, G.W. 1964. "Historical Statistics on Growth and Structure of Manufacturing in Canada, 1870–1957." In *Conference on Statistics, 1962 and 1963, Papers*, ed. J. Henripin and A. Asimakopulos, 93–146. Toronto: Toronto Univ. Press.

Bertram, G.W., and Percy, M.B. 1979. "Real Wage Trends in Canada 1900–26: Some Provisional Estimates." *Canadian Journal of Economics/revue Canadienne D'economique* 12: 299–312.

Dales, J. 1962. Comment. In *Long Term Factors in American Economic Growth*, ed. S.L. Engerman and R.E. Gallman, 89–93. Chicago: Chicago University Press.

Dominion Bureau of Statistics 1948. *The Standard Industrial Classification Manual*, (Ottawa)

Engerman, S.L. and Gallman, R.E. eds. 1986. *Long-term Factors in American Economic Growth, Studies in Income and Wealth*, Vol. 51, NBER, (Chicago: University of Chicago Press)

Firestone, O.J. 1958. *Canada's Economic Development, 1867–1953, With Special Reference to Changes in the Country's National Product and National Wealth.* London: Bowes and Bowes.

Green, Alan G. 1986. "Growth and Productivity Change in the Canadian Railway Sector, 1871–1926." In *Long-Term Factors in American Economic Growth*, ed. S.L. Engennan and R.E. Gallmann, 779–817. Chicago: University of Chicago Press.

Inwood, K., and Stengos, T. 1991. "Discontinuities in Canadian Economic Growth, 1870–1985." *Explorations in Economic History* 28: 274–286.

McInnis, R.M. 1986. "Output and Productivity in Canadian Agriculture, 1870–71 to 1926–27." In *Long-Term Factors in American Economic Growth*, ed. S.L. Engerman and R.E. Gallman, 737–778. Chicago: University of Chicago Press.

Maddison, A. 1989. *Phases of Capitalist Development*. Oxford: Oxford University Press.

Pomfret, R. 1993. *The Economic Development of Canada*, 2nd ed. Scarborough, Ontario: Nelson Canada.

Romer, C.D. 1989. "The Prewar Business Cycle Reconsidered: New Estimates of Gross National Product, 1869–1908." *Journal of Political Economy* 97 (1): 1–37.

Statistics Canada. 1978. *Fixed Capital Flows, 1926–1978*. Ottawa: Minister of Industry, Trade and Commerce.

Urquhart, M.C. 1986. "New Estimates of Gross National Product, Canada, 1870–1926: Some Implications for Canadian Development." In *Long-Term Factors in American Economic Growth*, ed. S.L. Engerman and R.E. Gallman, 9–94. Chicago: Chicago University Press.

Urquhart, M.C. (1988). *Canadian Economic Growth 1870–1980*, (Discussion Paper No. 734, Queen's University, Kingston, Ontario)

United States Department of Commerce. (1975), *Historical Statistics of the United States: Colonial Times to 1970*, Part 1, (Washington, D.C.: Bureau of the Census)

Urquhart, M.C., and K.A.H. Buckley, eds. (1965). *Historical Statistics of Canada*, first ed. Toronto: Macmillan.

CHAPTER 12

How Long Did Canadian Workers Actually Work? The Struggle for a Shorter Work Week and Workers' Standards of Living Before the Great Depression

1 Introduction

There has been a resurgence in the discussion and analysis of the length of the workday in America at the turn of the century (Atack and Bateman 1992; Shells 1990; Whaples 1990). However, the Canadian case is both little known and little discussed, and for good reason. Not much is known about the evolution or extent of hours worked per week or day in Canada from Confederation (1867) to 1930. This is in sharp contrast to the U.S. where careful estimates for hours worked were constructed long ago by Paul Douglas (1930) for the entire 1890–1926 time frame. His estimates are for manufacturing, construction, transportation, mining, unskilled workers, and government employees. More recently his estimates have been extended back to 1880 (Atack and Bateman 1992).

In Canada, reference is typically made to census year weekly hours of work estimates quoted in Sylvia Ostry's and Mahmood Zaidi's textbook, *Labour Economics in Canada* (1975, pp. 60–61). However, this provides estimates for the manufacturing sector alone and for only five years of the entire 1870–1930 period: 64 hours (1870), 59 hours (1901), 57 hours (1911), 55 hours (1921), and 55 hours (1926). Worst still, one is left with little idea as to how most of these estimates were constructed. In fact, their 1901–1931 estimates are from an unpublished and undated paper

M. Altman, *Lessons from a Successfully Export-Oriented, Resource-Rich Economy*, https://doi.org/10.1007/978-3-031-03887-7_12

of George Sanders and Syed M. A. Hameed, which cannot be located. Another series by O. J. Firestone for weekly hours worked in manufacturing exists (1958, pp. 207, 322) for the years 1870, 1890, 1901, 1911, and 1931 of 64, 59, 57, and 53 hours respectively. The 1870 estimate in Ostry and Zaidi is from Firestone, and the latter estimate is no more than an educated guess. For 1890 Firestone relies on testimony by workers to the Royal Commission on Capital and Labour for the year of 1889 reported in 1896. His 1901 estimate is the average number of hours per week reported in the 1901 census and his 1911 estimate is drawn from a sample of manufacturing industries employing 5,000 or more employees. Firestone (1958, p. 322) concludes that "...no direct record of hours worked per week is available for any other year (apart from 1901) in the 1871–1910 period." Firestone's 1931 estimate is based on the average hours of work estimates for 1928 and 1932 in the *General Review of the Manufacturing Industries of Canada*. Apart for Firestone's 1901 and 1911 average estimates for Canada as a whole, the first reliable hours of work estimates for Canada are available only from 1926 (Urquhart and Buckley 1965, pp. 79, 105).

In this article, I present time series estimates for Canadian annual hours worked per week for the 1880s and for the 1901–1926 period. These estimates are for workers in the manufacturing and construction census occupational categories. My estimates, which are also presented on a regional basis, confirm the picture presented by the hours worked estimates found in manufacturing presented in Ostry and Zaidi, namely that hours worked per week fell by about 15% from the beginning of this century to the mid-twenties. This is true for both manufacturing and construction workers. On the other hand, no decline in hours worked took place in the late nineteenth century (Tables 1, 2, 3 and 4). This is in stark contrast to what is suggested by Firestone's guesstimates for the nineteenth century.

In addition to the estimates for hours worked, estimates for real income earned per week in manufacturing and construction are developed. These estimates suggest that although individuals worked fewer hours from one year to another real weekly income did not fall by much, if at all, in the first years of the twentieth century. By the 1920s, workers experienced a significant increase in real weekly income although weekly hours worked had fallen far below what they were in the pre-World War One period. Both my hours worked and real weekly income estimates are consistent with results found for the U.S. Moreover, they are consistent with the long-standing demands of Canadian workers for a shorter workday with no cut in real income. By the mid-1920s, the workweek had fallen to 51 hours in manufacturing and to 47 hours in construction. After decades of agitation by labour, the workweek finally approached workers' preferences until, of course, workers' preferences shifted towards an even shorter workday.

The reduction of hours worked in Canada took place in the context of dramatic increases in real GNP, manufacturing output, labour productivity, employment growth and structural change (Altman 1986, 1992a, 1994, 2000).[1] This is especially true of the 1896–1914 period, which experienced a wheat export boom. It was this export boom that triggered an investment boom in various sectors of the economy which, in turn, helped fuel the process of Canadian economic growth. During this time Canada's real per capita growth was the fastest of all advanced economies, including Britain, Germany, and the U.S.[2] However, hours worked fell substantially only after the outbreak of World War One, once Canadian economic growth moderated. The next trend decrease in hours worked in Canada began in the mid-forties. By the end of the 1950s, the forty-hour week was a reality for most Canadian workers (Urquhart and Buckley 1965, pp. 102, 105).

2 The Derivation of New Hours Worked Estimates

Estimates for hours worked per week are constructed from scratch from a variety of sources on a regional and national basis. The most consistent series for hours worked are produced from data in the *Labour Gazette* and in the *Canada Year Book*.[3] These data were collected by the Department of Labour from 1900. However, these data, collected on the basis of surveys sent to selected employees, are for union labour alone, whose share of the non-agricultural labour force increased from about 8% in 1910–1911 to 14% in 1920–1921, falling back to just over 11% by 1930–1931 (Urquhart and Buckley 1965, pp. 59, 105). These sources nevertheless permit the construction of hours-worked series for the 1901–1926 period.[4] The data are for standard hours worked (hours worked which did not require the payment of overtime) and are consistent with hours worked estimates made for the 1930s and 1940s in Canada as well as with historical hours worked estimates produced for the United States. Relevant data are available for Halifax, St. John, Quebec City,

Montreal, Ottawa, Toronto, Hamilton, Winnipeg, Regina, Edmonton, Calgary, Vancouver, and Victoria for what the producers of these data sets consider to be a representative sample of workers in the building, metal products, and printing trades. The metals and printing trades data yield what I refer to as the basic manufacturing series. And, these occupations represent, together, close to 20% of manufacturing workers. Data are also available for common or unskilled manufacturing labour. This series is constructed both for Canada as a whole and on a regional basis. The building trades data yield my construction industry series (Table 3). Building trades data are available for bricklayers, carpenters, electrical workers, painters, plumbers, stonecutters, and common labour.[5] All in all, manufacturing workers net of common or unskilled labourers comprised over 28% of all non-agricultural workers in 1901, 21% in 1911, 20% in 1921, and 18% by 1931. In addition, construction or building trade workers net of common labourers constituted 8.4% of all non-agricultural workers in 1901 and 1911, 7.8% in 1921, and 7.3% in 1931. Common labourers comprise 12% of non-agricultural workers in 1901, 18% in 1911, 14% in 1921, and 15 in 1931. These occupational categories encompass 49% of the non-agricultural Canadian workforce in 1901, falling to 40% in 1931. We lack reliable hours worked data on the large component of white collar workers (clerical, finance and trade, and service workers) who comprised 37% of non-agricultural workers in 1901, rising to 44% by 1931 (derived from Urquhart and Buckley 1965, p. 59).

Data from the *Labour Gazette* and the *Canada Year Book* are also used to construct, what I refer to as a supplementary series of hours worked in manufacturing for the 1911–1926 period, consisting of data on cottons, furniture, carriage manufacturing, harness and saddlery, boots and shoes, tobacco, meat packing, pulp and paper, and sawmill labour. These data are largely for Quebec and Ontario and incorporate non-union labour. These two provinces contributed 63% to Canada's population in 1900 and 61% by 1930. This series is brought back to 1901 using data published by Board of Inquiry into the Cost of Living (Coats 1915), which also incorporates non-union labour, for textiles, furniture, carriage manufacturing, boots and shoes, and sawmill labour. These occupational categories incorporate over 20% of manufacturing workers. Finally, the above three sources are used to construct a series for hours worked per week by unskilled or common labour in manufacturing. Unskilled workers comprised over 20% of workers in manufacturing in the 1900–1930 period. Unlike the supplementary series, a consistent time series for common labourers can be constructed on both a regional and national basis. All told, the three occupational sub-categories in manufacturing for which we have representative sample data comprise about 65% of manufacturing workers. Although these series are derived from different sources and are, therefore, not strictly comparable, they provide the most comprehensive estimates for weekly hours worked in manufacturing. Moreover, these estimates are presented in a most transparent manner so that the reader can clearly delineate the differences in hours worked between the series. It is evident that hours worked were consistently greater in the union labour based basic series compared to the non-union labour based supplementary and common labour series, albeit trend changes in hours worked are the same for all series (Table 2). These differences were invariably a product of unionization or the different occupations of the workers in question, or some combination of the two. The determination of these differences is a question that needs be addressed, although it lies outside the scope of this paper.

The basic and common labourer series are spliced together to yield one variant (Average II) of an average hours-worked series for Canadian manufacturing. Another variant (Average I) is produced by splicing the basic, common labourer, and supplementary series together (Table 2). These series are weighted averages based on their components' percentage contribution to the manufacturing occupations covered by the sample. The average weight given to the basic series is 29%; to the supplementary series, 39%; to the common labourer series, 33%. In addition, each of the component series is a weighted average, based on the percentage contribution of their constituent components' contribution to the manufacturing occupations in the basic and supplementary series respectively. For example, in the basic series the weight assigned to metals is 80% and to printing, 20%. It is important to note that the weighted series' averages differ from the unweighted series' averages to any significant extent only for Average II, where the average difference in hours worked per week is just over 3% in favour of the weighted average, with the difference diminishing from about 4 to 1% from the first decade of the century to the 1920s. In effect, the weighted average series suggests a greater decline in hours worked from 1901 to 1926 of about 1 hour per week than does the unweighted series. The construction hours worked series is constructed by splicing the common construction labourer series with the series developed from data on the relatively skilled construction workers. The two series are combined by assigning a weight to each series based on each series' average contribution to construction occupations. Common labour is assigned a weight of 33% (Table 3). One should note that common construction labour worked similar, albeit slightly more, hours per week than their relatively more skilled counterparts until 1917. Thereafter, the gap between these two categories of construction workers widened. My final hours worked series is produced by splicing the manufacturing basic hour worked series with the construction series to generate an hours of work time series for an even wider spectrum of Canadian workers, representing about 40% of Canada's non-agricultural labour force by the 1920s. This series is produced for both Canada and its regions and is weighted by each occupational category's contribution to the manufacturing and construction labour force (Table 4).

In addition to the weights assigned to the occupational components of the various series, each of the national series for hours worked are also weighted for each province's contribution to the relevant occupational group. The provincial series are then grouped by region: Eastern Canada (Prince Edward Island, New Brunswick, Nova Scotia), Central Canada (Quebec and Ontario), the West (Manitoba, Saskatchewan, Alberta), and British Columbia.[6] Each provincial series is assigned a weight consistent with its labour force's contribution to the relevant occupational group. This yields a weighted average regional series for hours worked. The weights are derived from the Censuses for the years 1910–1911, 1920–1921, and, 1930–1941. The weights for these census years are applied to the 1901–1910, 1911–1920, and, 1921–1926 segments of my different hours worked series respectively. The final step in my calculations is to convert the hours worked time series to index numbers with a 1901 base year so as to ascertain and compare the extent of change in hours worked amongst the different regions and occupational categories.[7] Finally, estimates are constructed for hours worked in the 1884–1889 period (Table 1). These estimates are produced from data found in various annual reports to Ontario's Bureau of Industries.[8] Data, for up to nine of the occupations used in this article, were previously presented by Douglas Hartle in Urquhart and Buckley (1965, pp. 93, 96). These occupations are butchers, carpenters, cotton mill employees, labourers, machinists, millwrights, paper mill machine tenders, plumbers, and printers. The annual reports provide data for more than 400 occupations. The data

Table 1 Manufacturing: hours worked per week in Ontario in the 1880s

	All occupations Basic series unweighted	*Manufacturing Basic series weighted*	*Manufacturing & Construction Basic series weighted*	*Hartle 1 Unweighted*	*Hartle 2 Unweighted*
1884	60.2	59.7	59.6	59.1	58.8
1885	59.1	59.7	59.3	59.7	58.3
1886	57.5	58.5	57.6	59.3	58.2
1887	56.7	59.0	58.4	59.5	60.0
1888	57.7	58.8	57.2	59.7	57.9
1889	58.8	59.4	58.6	60.0	59.2
Average	58.3	59.2	58.5	59.6	58.7

Source My estimates are drawn from returns to questionnaires by both employers and employees. Hartle 1 is based on the returns from both employers and employees whereas Hartle 2 is derived from returns by employees alone. For further details see the text

used in this article are drawn from thousands of responses to questionnaires provided to both employees and employers. It is not possible to tell whether the sampling procedures adopted by the Ontario bureau was biased or not. Nevertheless, these data provide a more appropriate basis to construct hours of work estimates than the testimony before a Royal Commission utilized by Firestone. I construct three series for hours worked from these data for the 1884–1889 period. Moreover, I use the estimates provided by Hartle to construct two sets of hours of work estimates for the same period. One set (Hartle 1) is based on responses from employees and employers while the other set (Hartle 2) is based on responses from employees alone. My first set of estimates is simply the unweighted average for all occupations. This set also contains the most all inclusive hours of work estimates provided in Table 1. The other set of estimates is a weighted average for the manufacturing occupations also incorporated in my 1901–1926 series. The third series is a weighted average for the manufacturing and construction sectors. These five sets of estimates yield similar results. Obviously, increasing the sample size does not significantly affect the value of the estimates. In fact, there is little difference in hours worked per week between most occupations. Indeed, the percentage variation about the average hours worked is about 3% for all years and for all series, or about 1.8 hours. In all five series, there is no tendency for weekly hours worked to diminish in the 1880s.

Moreover, average weekly hours worked vary between 58 and 60 hours (see Table 1).

3 The Results

Hours worked per week differed amongst the different broad occupational grouping presented in this article. As already mentioned, common labourers as well as workers in the supplementary occupations worked consistently more hours than individuals in basic manufacturing. They also worked more hours than the relatively more skilled workers in construction. Moreover, they worked longer hours than common labourers in construction until the 1920s, when these three categories of workers laboured approximately the same number of hours per week. Workers in metal products and printing, on the other hand, worked more hours than both the relatively more skilled and common construction workers, at least until 1920 when they only worked more hours than the relatively more skilled construction workers. For Canada as a whole, hours worked per week ranged from about 56 hours in construction and metal products and printing to over 58 hours for the other occupations in 1901. By 1926, hours worked per week ranged from about 46 hours for the relatively skilled construction workers to about 52 hours for the common labour in general and workers in the supplementary manufacturing occupations. This suggests that by 1926 an eight-hour day prevailed in those occupations covered by the available sources, given the prevalence of the 6-day week. In manufacturing, the majority of the decline took place in the closing years and immediately following World War One. In construction, the majority of the decline took place prior to the outbreak of World War One (Tables 2 and 3). Splicing the manufacturing and construction hours worked series also yields a clear trend decline in hours worked (Table 4). All in all, hours worked fell by about 13% from 1901 to 1926 in manufacturing and by 16% in construction (Tables 2 and 3). Finally, in the 1880s hours worked per week in manufacturing was about 59 hours (Table 1). This implies that manufacturing workers as well as workers in other occupations typically worked about 10 hours per day given the dominance of the six-day week at the time. This matches the 10-hour day estimated for U.S. manufacturing workers for 1880 (Atack and Bateman 1992). Thus, at least from Confederation in 1867 to the beginnings of Canada's wheat export boom in 1896, there is no clear evidence of a decline in hours worked.

The regional hours of work series for manufacturing suggests some variation in hours worked in the basic manufacturing series or metal products and printing (Table 2 and Fig. 1). What stands out most is that in British Columbia workers worked fewer hours than did workers in other parts of the country, except for at the very beginning of the twentieth century. Also of interest is that workers in the Prairies laboured more hours than did workers anywhere else in the country from 1901 to outbreak of World War One. In the building trades a similar regional pattern emerges (Table 3). However in construction, British Columbia workers laboured more hours per week throughout the period under examination without exception and workers in the East registered more hours than construction workers elsewhere in Canada throughout most of the first two decades of the century. Still, all regions experienced a trend decline in hours worked per week, with British Columbia experiencing its entire reduction in hours worked in the first decade of the century.

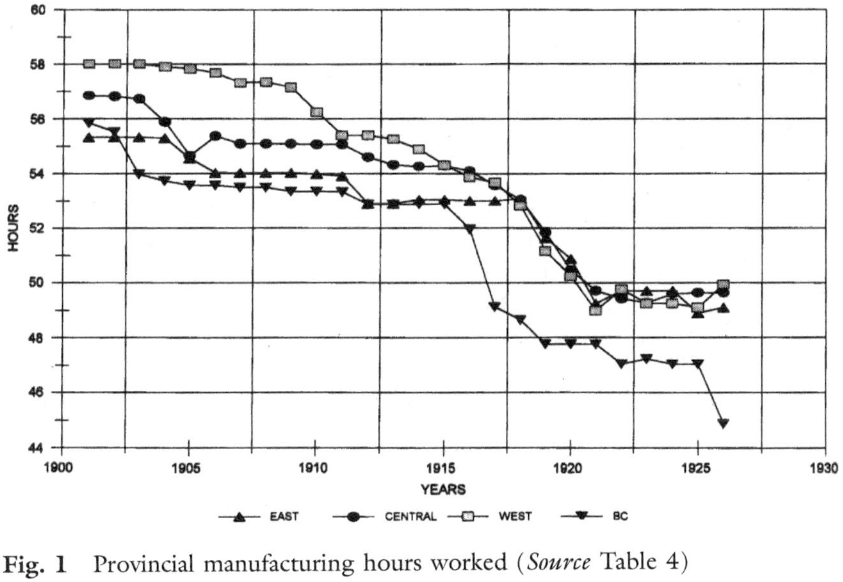

Fig. 1 Provincial manufacturing hours worked (*Source* Table 4)

4 Hours Worked and Real Weekly Income

The new annual estimates of hours worked per week can serve to shed some light on questions related to changes in workers' standard of well-being over the 1901–1926 period. Douglas (1930) initially carried out a similar exercise for the U.S. First, one can compare movements in hours worked in manufacturing and in real wages per hour. There are a variety of real wage per hour series for Canada. I exploit the Bertram and Percy (1979) series (B-P) and the Chambers (1985) series. Of the two series, only the B-P index covers the entire 1901–1926 period. Chambers covers only the 1901–1914 period and focuses on Toronto.[9] It is clear that as hours worked declined there was no trend decline in real wages per hour according to any of the indexes (Table 5). And according to the B-P index there was a trend increase over the 1901–1926 period. In fact, there was a very high negative correlation between hours worked and real hourly wages for both the Canadian (about −0.90) and U.S. series (between −0.80 for union labour and −0.90 for non-union labour). Real hourly wages only dropped in the 1914–1917 period so that by 1917 real wages fell below their 1901 level. However, this was a period when Canada experienced an extraordinary increase in prices. From 1901 to 1914 the general price level rose by about 25% or 1.5% per annum. However, from 1914 to 1917, the general price level jumped by over 44% or 13% per annum (Altman 1992a). During this time of falling real wages there was little movement in hours worked per week. Indeed, hours worked did not fall at all in construction and fell by no more than one hour or by 2% in manufacturing. The major reduction in hours worked took place only when real hourly wages witnessed a persistent trend increase, commencing with the increase from 1917 to 1918. It was from 1917 and, more particularly from 1918 to 1921, that hours worked declined most dramatically in manufacturing, falling by about 4 hours to about 50 hours per week, where it was to remain for the remainder of the decade. By 1921 real hourly wages recovered all losses suffered during the great inflation of the war years so that by 1921 real hourly wages exceeded the 1901 average by 36% (Tables 2, 3, 4 and 5).

The hours worked estimates allow us to estimate the implied changes in real weekly income given the combined movements in hours worked and real hourly wages. I construct such estimates for manufacturing and construction (Table 5). These estimates reveal the extent to which real weekly income increased or decreased, on average, as hours of work and

Table 2 Manufacturing: hours worked per week and index numbers, 1901–1926

	Hours per week									*Index numbers; 1901 = 100*			
	Canada					*Provincial basic & common series*				*Canada*			
	Average I	*Average II*	*Basic*	*Common*	*Suppl.*	*East*	*Central*	*West*	*BC*	*Average I*	*Basic*	*Common*	*Suppl.*
1901	58.4	57.8	55.6	59.6	59.5	55.3	56.8	58.0	55.8	100	100	100	100
1902	58.4	57.7	55.5	59.6	59.5	55.3	56.8	58.0	55.5	100	99.8	100	100
1903	58.3	57.5	55.1	59.6	59.5	55.3	56.7	58.0	54.0	99.8	99.1	100	100
1904	57.9	56.9	53.7	59.6	59.5	55.3	55.9	57.9	53.7	99.1	96.5	100	100
1905	57.7	56.6	53.3	59.5	59.5	54.6	54.7	57.9	53.6	98.8	95.8	99.8	100
1906	58.0	57.1	54.3	59.5	59.5	54.0	55.4	57.7	53.6	99.3	97.6	99.8	100
1907	57.6	56.8	53.8	59.5	58.9	54.0	55.1	57.3	53.5	98.6	96.7	99.8	99.0
1908	57.4	56.8	53.8	59.5	58.4	54.0	55.1	57.3	53.5	98.3	96.7	99.8	98.2
1909	56.7	56.8	53.7	59.5	56.5	54.0	55.1	57.1	53.4	97.1	96.6	99.8	94.9
1910	56.7	56.7	53.7	59.3	56.5	54.0	55.1	56.3	53.4	97.0	96.5	99.6	94.9
1911	57.4	56.7	53.5	59.3	58.7	53.9	55.1	55.4	53.3	98.3	96.2	99.6	98.6
1912	56.6	55.7	53.2	57.9	58.0	52.9	54.6	55.4	52.9	96.9	95.7	97.1	97.5
1913	56.3	55.4	52.8	57.6	57.8	52.9	54.3	55.3	52.9	96.4	95.0	96.7	97.2
1914	56.3	55.4	52.6	57.9	57.8	53.1	54.3	54.9	52.9	96.4	94.6	97.1	97.2
1915	56.3	55.4	52.5	57.8	57.8	53.1	54.3	54.3	52.9	96.4	94.5	97.0	97.2
1916	56.1	55.2	52.3	57.8	57.6	53.0	54.1	53.9	52.0	96.1	94.0	96.9	96.9
1917	55.6	54.5	51.7	56.9	57.4	53.0	53.6	53.7	49.1	95.1	93.0	95.4	96.4
1918	54.9	54.2	50.5	57.3	56.1	53.1	53.0	52.8	48.7	94.0	90.8	96.1	94.3
1919	52.9	52.7	49.2	55.7	53.3	51.6	51.8	51.2	47.8	90.5	88.5	93.4	89.5
1920	51.8	51.3	48.8	53.5	52.5	50.9	50.5	50.2	47.8	88.7	87.7	89.8	88.3
1921	50.6	50.2	47.5	52.4	51.4	49.2	49.7	49.0	47.8	86.7	85.4	88.0	86.4
1922	50.7	49.8	48.2	51.2	52.0	49.7	49.4	49.8	47.0	86.7	86.7	85.9	87.4

(continued)

Table 2 (continued)

	Hours per week									*Index numbers; 1901 = 100*			
	Canada					*Provincial basic & common series*				*Canada*			
	Average I	*Average II*	*Basic*	*Common*	*Suppl.*	*East*	*Central*	*West*	*BC*	*Average I*	*Basic*	*Common*	*Suppl.*
1923	50.4	49.7	47.9	51.1	51.6	49.7	49.3	49.3	47.2	86.3	86.2	85.8	86.8
1924	50.5	49.9	47.8	51.7	51.5	49.7	49.6	49.3	47.0	86.5	86.0	86.7	86.5
1925	50.8	49.9	47.8	51.6	52.4	48.9	49.6	49.1	47.0	87.0	86.0	86.6	88.0
1926	50.6	49.8	47.9	51.4	52.0	49.1	49.6	49.9	44.9	86.6	86.2	86.2	87.3

Source See text. Average I is based on the three manufacturing hours worked series and Average II is derived using the Basic and Common manufacturing hours worked series. These averages are weighted according to their components' contribution to the index in the 1901–1926 period. The basic series has an average weight of 29%, the common labourer series, 33%, and the supplementary series, 39%

Table 3 Construction: hours worked per week and index numbers, 1901–1926

	Hours per week							*Index numbers 1901 = 100*		
			All occupations							
	Canada net of labourers	*Canada labourers only*	*Canada*	*East*	*Central*	*West*	*BC*	*All occupations*	*Net of labourers*	*Labourers only*
1901	55.6	55.8	55.7	55.0	54.7	58.9	52.3	100.0	100.0	100.0
1902	54.9	55.8	55.2	54.8	54.2	58.6	51.6	99.2	98.8	100.0
1903	53.6	54.7	54.0	54.8	53.3	56.8	48.2	97.0	96.4	98.0
1904	52.8	54.7	53.4	54.8	52.6	56.7	47.0	96.0	95.0	98.0
1905	52.4	54.0	52.9	54.5	52.5	55.4	46.0	95.1	94.3	96.7
1906	51.9	54.0	52.6	54.5	52.2	54.3	46.0	94.5	93.4	96.7
1907	51.7	53.1	52.1	54.5	51.6	53.8	46.0	93.7	93.0	95.2
1908	51.5	53.1	52.0	54.3	51.6	53.6	45.6	93.5	92.7	95.2
1909	51.1	52.9	51.7	54.0	51.3	53.4	44.4	92.9	91.9	94.9
1910	50.6	52.1	51.1	53.8	50.4	53.3	44.2	91.8	90.9	93.4
1911	49.3	51.1	49.9	53.7	49.5	50.8	44.0	89.7	88.7	91.7
1912	49.0	50.4	49.5	53.6	49.1	50.0	44.0	88.9	88.2	90.3
1913	48.7	50.4	49.3	52.2	48.8	51.1	44.0	88.6	87.7	90.3
1914	48.6	50.4	49.2	52.2	48.8	50.3	44.0	88.4	87.4	90.3
1915	48.4	50.4	49.1	52.0	48.8	49.5	44.0	88.2	87.1	90.3
1916	48.2	50.4	48.9	51.0	48.7	49.4	44.0	87.9	86.7	90.3
1917	48.3	50.4	49.0	51.0	48.7	49.9	44.0	88.0	86.9	90.3
1918	47.7	50.3	48.6	51.0	48.2	49.8	44.0	87.3	85.8	90.2
1919	46.7	49.5	47.7	49.5	47.5	47.4	44.0	85.7	84.1	88.8
1920	45.2	48.5	46.3	48.2	45.8	46.7	44.0	83.2	81.2	87.0
1921	46.0	51.8	47.9	48.4	48.5	47.7	44.0	86.1	82.7	92.9
1922	45.7	53.0	48.1	47.8	48.7	47.7	45.0	86.5	82.2	95.0

(continued)

Table 3 (continued)

	Hours per week							*Index numbers 1901 = 100*		
			All occupations							
	Canada net of labourers	*Canada labourers only*	*Canada*	*East*	*Central*	*West*	*BC*	*All occupations*	*Net of labourers*	*Labourers only*
1923	45.6	52.7	47.9	46.7	48.7	47.7	44.0	86.2	82.0	94.4
1924	45.6	52.7	47.9	46.7	48.7	47.7	44.0	86.2	82.0	94.4
1925	45.5	52.7	47.9	46.7	48.7	47.7	43.6	86.0	81.8	94.4
1926	45.5	52.5	47.8	45.7	48.7	47.7	43.6	85.9	81.8	94.0

Source See text

Table 4 Basic + common manufacturing and construction: hours of work and index numbers, 1901–1926

	Hours per week					*Index numbers 1901 = 100*
	Canada average	*East*	*Central*	*West*	*BC*	*Canada*
1901	57.1	55.2	56.2	58.3	54.8	100
1902	57.0	55.2	56.1	58.2	54.4	99.7
1903	56.5	55.2	55.7	57.6	52.3	98.9
1904	55.9	55.2	54.9	57.6	51.8	97.8
1905	55.5	54.5	54.0	57.1	51.4	97.2
1906	55.8	54.2	54.5	56.7	51.4	97.6
1907	55.5	54.2	54.1	56.3	51.3	97.1
1908	55.5	54.1	54.1	56.3	51.2	97.0
1909	55.3	54.0	54.0	56.1	50.8	96.8
1910	55.1	53.9	53.7	55.4	50.7	96.4
1911	54.7	53.9	53.5	54.1	50.6	95.7
1912	53.9	53.1	53.0	53.8	50.3	94.3
1913	53.6	52.7	52.7	54.0	50.3	93.9
1914	53.6	52.8	52.7	53.6	50.3	93.8
1915	53.5	52.8	52.7	52.9	50.3	93.7
1916	53.4	52.4	52.6	52.6	49.6	93.4
1917	52.9	52.4	52.2	52.6	47.6	92.6
1918	52.5	52.5	51.6	51.9	47.3	91.9
1919	51.2	51.0	50.6	50.1	46.7	89.6
1920	49.9	50.1	49.1	49.2	46.7	87.3
1921	49.5	49.0	49.4	48.6	46.7	86.6
1922	49.3	49.1	49.2	49.2	46.4	86.3
1923	49.2	48.8	49.1	48.8	46.3	86.0
1924	49.3	48.8	49.3	48.8	46.2	86.4
1925	49.3	48.3	49.4	48.7	46.0	86.2
1926	49.2	48.1	49.4	49.3	44.5	86.1

Source and notes Tables 2 and 3. The above series are produced by weighting period. The manufacturing series is given a weight of 71% and construction, 29%

real hourly wages typically moved in opposite directions over the 1901–1926 period. For real weekly income to at least remain constant in face of declining hours worked, real hourly wages must, at a minimum, rise sufficiently to compensate for the decline in hours worked. This required, hypothetical, real hourly wage increase is also estimated. For real income to increase, actual real hourly wages must increase by more than the estimated hypothetical real hourly wage increase. According to my estimates,

Table 5 Real wage and real income index, 1901–1926; 1901 = 100

	Real wages		*Hyp wages for constant weekly income given hours of work*		*Implied changes in real weekly income*			
	Chambers	*B&P*	*Mfg*	*Construction*	*Chambers mfg*	*B&P*	*Chambers construction*	*B&P*
1901	100	100	100	100	100	100	100	100
1902	101.7	101.4	100.0	101	102	101	101	101
1903	99.5	102.9	100.2	103	99	103	96	100
1904	100.5	104.3	101.0	104	100	103	96	100
1905	100.7	105.8	101.2	105	99	105	96	101
1906	100.2	101.8	100.7	106	99	101	95	96
1907	98.1	103.6	101.4	107	97	102	92	97
1908	99.8	105.5	101.7	107	98	104	93	99
1909	102.3	107.3	103.0	108	99	104	95	100
1910	105.3	109.1	103.1	109	102	106	97	100
1911	108.8	111.0	101.8	111	107	109	98	100
1912	101.1	108.8	103.2	112	98	105	90	97
1913	103.9	111.4	103.7	113	100	107	92	99
1914	105.1	115.9	103.7	113	101	112	93	102
1915		113.0	103.8	113		109		100
1916		101.9	104.1	114		98		90
1917		95.2	105.1	114		91		84
1918		101.2	106.4	115		95		88
1919		112.3	110.4	117		102		96
1920		122.7	112.8	120		109		102
1921		135.8	115.4	116		118		117
1922		133.9	115.3	116		116		116
1923		136.8	115.9	116		118		118
1924		138.2	115.7	116		120		119
1925		134.1	115.0	116		117		115
1926		138.8	115.4	116		120		119

Sources and notes See text and Tables 2 and 3. The estimates for a constant real weekly income are derived by dividing the hours worked index number for 1901 by the index numbers for the following years. The estimates for the implied change in real income, which incorporates the changes in real wages and hours worked, are derived by dividing the index numbers for the change in the real wage by the corresponding index numbers for the hypothetical real wage required to generate a constant weekly income the B-P real hourly wage series generates no persistent decline in real income in manufacturing from 1901 to 1915 as hours of work fall. Real income per week in 1914 actually rose to 12% above its 1901 level. Only during the 1916–1918 period did real income drop below its 1901 level and this was by 2% in, 1916, 9% in 1917, and 5% in 1918. In this period, Canada underwent a serious recession, experiencing a declining GNP from 1916 to 1921 (Altman 1992a). Nevertheless, by 1926 real weekly income was more than 20% greater than it was in 1901 in spite of hours worked falling by about 16%. In the construction industry a different situation might have prevailed since there was a more dramatic fall in hours worked here than in manufacturing. We can only venture an educated guess since we have no real hourly wage data for this important sector. Be this as it may, the B-P real hourly wage series suggests that construction workers experienced no trend increase in real weekly income until the 1920s. However, neither did construction workers suffer a decline in real income in the 1901–1920 period, apart from the highly inflationary period following the beginning of World War One.

Chambers' index tells a different tale. His real hourly wage index suggests that real weekly income remains below its 1901 level for most of the period covered by this index, although only marginally so. Only in 1902, 1910–1911 and 1914 was real income greater than what it was in 1901. For construction workers, Chambers' real hourly wage index suggests that real income was somewhat lower than what is suggested by the B-P real hourly wage index. On average, for the 1901–1914 period, his real hourly wage index suggests that weekly real income was only 2% below its 1901 level. However, during the 1901–1914 period hours worked fell by about 12%. The real hourly wage indexes of Bertram and Percy and of Chambers suggest that, at worst, reduced hours of work in manufacturing was purchased with a small loss of weekly income. The cost to construction workers was greater, at least before World War One, according to the Chambers index.

5 Hours Worked and Real Income in Canada and the US

Paul Douglas' (1930) series for weekly hours worked in manufacturing can be compared to my estimates for the average in Canadian manufacturing and common labour (Tables 2, 6 and Fig. 2). Both of my variants

Table 6 American weekly hours, real wage and real income index, 1901–1926; 1901 = 100

	Hours worked			*Real wages*		*Hyp. Wages for constant weekly income given hours worked*	*Implied changes in real weekly income*	
	All Mfg	*Mfg (Union)*	*Mfg (Payroll)*	*Rees*	*Douglas*		*Rees*	*Douglas*
1901	100	100	100	100	100	100	100	100
1902	99.3	98.9	99.4	103.6	101.0	100.7	102.9	100.3
1903	98.6	98.1	98.9	104.8	100.0	101.4	103.3	98.6
1904	98.3	97.5	98.7	102.4	101.0	101.7	100.6	99.3
1905	98.3	97.5	98.7	104.8	103.1	101.7	103.0	101.3
1906	97.6	97.3	98.1	110.7	103.1	102.4	108.1	100.6
1907	97.6	96.9	97.9	109.5	101.0	102.4	106.9	98.6
1908	96.8	96.2	97.4	108.3	102.0	103.3	104.8	98.7
1909	96.8	96.0	97.3	109.5	103.1	103.3	106.0	99.7
1910	96.4	95.6	96.6	113.1	100.0	103.7	109.0	96.4
1911	96.1	95.0	96.3	114.3	98.0	104.1	109.8	94.1
1912	95.4	94.5	95.8	115.5	102.0	104.8	110.2	97.3
1913	94.5	93.9	95.0	121.4	103.1	105.8	114.8	97.4
1914	94.0	93.1	94.2	119.0	102.0	106.3	111.9	96.0
1915	93.7	92.7	94.0		104.1	106.7		97.5
1916	93.5	91.6	94.0		107.1	106.9		100.2
1917	93.0	90.8	93.5		101.0	107.5		94.0
1918	91.3	90.1	91.4		104.1	109.5		95.0
1919	89.1	88.2	89.0		109.2	112.2		97.3
1920	86.9	87.2	86.4		113.3	115.1		98.4
1921	86.4	88.0	85.1		122.4	115.8		105.8
1922	87.2	88.2	86.3		124.5	114.6		108.6
1923	86.9	88.4	85.6		131.6	115.1		114.4
1924	85.9	88.0	84.2		133.7	116.5		114.8
1925	85.7	87.6	84.3		133.7	116.7		114.5
1926	85.7	87.6	84.3		132.7	116.7		113.7

Source Derived from Rees (1961) and Douglas (1930). See also, Table 5

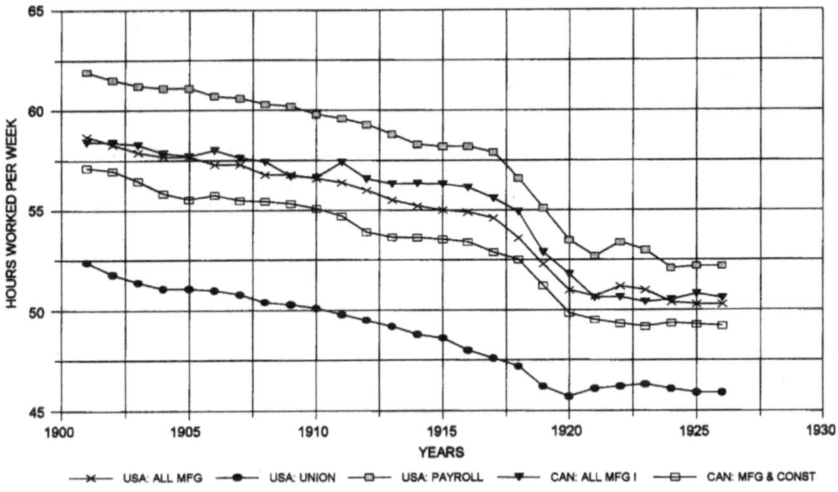

Fig. 2 Manufacturing hours worked in Canada and the US (*Source* Tables 5 and 6)

for average manufacturing hours worked per week are just about identical to Douglas' series for all manufacturing. This is especially true for my Average I. In addition, the correlation coefficient for the relationship between Douglas' series and my Average I is 0.98 and between his series and my average for manufacturing and construction workers combined is 0.99. In contrast, my hours worked series sits above Douglas' series for unionized workers in manufacturing while his hours worked series derived from payroll data sits above all the other hours worked series for both the U.S. and Canada. Nevertheless, all series experience a trend decline in hours worked.

Finally, I compare the implied changes in real income for Canada and the U.S. as a product of the combined movements in real wages and hours worked (Tables 5 and 6). For the U.S., I use the real wage per hour estimates of Douglas (1930) and the more recent and more accurate series of Rees (1961). Rees' estimates extend to 1914 only. Over this period, if one uses Rees' real hourly wage estimates, U.S. workers in manufacturing achieved shorter hours whilst realizing persistent increases in real income. However, Douglas' real hourly wage series spins a tale for the

U.S. similar to the one emanating from Chambers' real hourly wage estimates for Canada. Real weekly income remains below its 1901 level from 1902 to 1919, but never by very much. By 1926, real weekly income in the U.S. rose to 14% above its 1901 level. As in Canada, U.S. manufacturing workers purchased a reduction in hours worked as real hourly wages increased at no or little cost in terms of real weekly income. It is important to note that the real hourly wage series for the U.S. and Canada are highly correlated (Fig. 2). The similarity of hours worked in both countries as well as in trend movements in hours worked plus the similarity in trend changes in real hourly wages raises questions as to the similarity of market conditions and of union activity in Canada and the U.S. at this time.

6 Conclusion

The hours worked estimates for Canada developed here clearly show that there was a trend decrease in hours worked per week in Canada in the first part of the twentieth century. This is true for all of the hours-worked series developed in this article. It is also apparent from the historical literature that workers in both Canada and the U.S. desired to work fewer hours. They demanded a shorter work week at, in the very least, the same level of real income (they attributed a positive utility to working less at a given level of real income).[10] For this objective to be realized, real hourly wages would have to be increased sufficiently; thus the opposition of so many employers to the shorter work day and work week. Employers feared increasing unit costs and reduced profits or, in the very least, the investment in time, effort and money that would make more costly labour more productive. The available evidence suggests that workers were realizing their objectives by the early twentieth century. It is also arguable that the level of wellbeing of the typical worker probably increased for much of the period under study, especially after World War One when both real weekly income increased and hours worked decreased. Workers' level of well-being must have increased during the pre-War period as well if workers attached some value to more leisure time or to the acquisition of more time to engage in non-market activity while experiencing only insignificant, if any, decline in real income. In fact, measuring changes in workers' well-being simply in terms of changes in real income is inappropriate when workers value both higher real income and a shorter work week.

The historical record suggests that, on average, Canadian workers, not unlike their U.S. counterparts, appear to have established *a target* number of weekly hours and *a minimum target* weekly income which were inconsistent with the actual combination of hours worked and real hourly wages by the end of the nineteenth century. The number of hours worked was too many, but a shorter work week at prevailing real hourly wage rates would have resulted in real income falling below the minimum target income. To realize their objective of reducing hours worked while maintaining real income required that real hourly wages rise. Under these conditions, increasing real wages would be devoted towards reducing hours worked per week. Leisure or non-market activities in general would be purchased with higher real wages. The struggle by workers for a shorter work week went hand in hand with their demands for a higher real hourly wage. Without higher real hourly wages workers would have been unable to purchase a reduced work week. Indeed, when real hourly wages and real weekly income diminished with the great inflation of the war period, workers took action. Union membership soared, rising from 166,000 in 1914 to 205,000 in 1917 and to 378,000 in 1919, the year of Canada's great general strike. The number of strikes also increased from 44 in 1914 to 148 in 1917, peaking at 298 in 1919. These strikes affected only 8,600 workers in 1914. By, 1917, 48,000 were involved, peaking at 139,000 by 1919.[11] In short shrift workers were, on average, able to purchase a reduced work week when real hourly wages began to increase once again.

On the supply-side of the labour market, a shorter work week combined with a higher real hourly wage rate could generate higher unit costs and lower profits, *ceteris paribus*. The struggle for a shorter work week, therefore, might very well have contributed towards the search by employers for more efficient and effective ways of employing labour at the turn of the century which would have made the combination of a shorter work week and higher real hourly wages compatible with the competitive position of the firm.[12] Keep in mind that it was this period of time which also just happens to be one which was characterized by rapid growth in labour productivity in Canada's manufacturing sector as well as in the economy in general (Altman, 1986, 1992a, 1994).

In the absence of workers' struggle for a shorter work day, it is quite possible that labour productivity in Canada would not have risen as rapidly as it did at the turn of the century. On the other hand, without the vibrant productivity increases which took place in the Canadian economy in the pre-Great Depression years, a shorter work week at no cost in real income to workers would have been difficult to manage in the face of competitive pressures on the product market. But the evidence in hand allows us to speculate that an important aspect of Canada's success in productivity growth was indeed causally and positively related to Canadian workers' struggle for a shorter work week. This struggle served to endogenize Canada's productivity growth process.

Notes

1. Altman (1992a, and ch.11 in this book) real GNP series are built upon Urquhart's (1986) nominal GNP estimates so as to correct for problems in the methodology adopted by Urquhart to deflate his nominal GNP estimates. The Altman estimates are derived by deflating Urquhart's nominal GNP using a set representatively weighted price index numbers. Urquhart's deflators are unweighted and for most years not representative of the components of GNP being deflated. For a discussion of these problems see Van Ark (1994) and Altman (1992a, 2000). See Urquhart (1994) for a critique of Altman's estimates and Urquhart (1986) for Urquhart's real GNP series.
2. For a classic statement on the indirect impact of the export wheat boom of Canadian growth, see Buckley (1974) and Mackintosh (1978). Wheat exports grew by 3.3% per year from 1871 to 1896 and by 15.5% from 1896 to 1913. Moreover, wheat exports as a percentage of total wheat output increased from 21 to 51% from 1896 to 1913. Thereafter, the rate of growth in wheat exports decelerated. For example, from 1913 to 1925 wheat exports grew at a rate of 8% per year (Altman 2000, Table 9). Moreover, annual per capita real GDP growth in Canada in the 1896–1913 period was 4.7% compared to 1.3% from 1870 to 1896 and 0.05% from 1913 to 1925 (Altman 1992a). In comparison, for example, in the U.S., the annual per capita GDP growth rate for the 1896–1913 period was 2.5%. In Germany this growth rate was 1.6%, in France 1.5%, in the U.K. 1.1%, and in Australia 2% (from Maddison 1995, Tables D1-a and D1-d). Some of the most current literature links Canada's impressive and superior growth performance in the 1896–1913 period with both the direct and indirect effects of its export wheat boom (Altman 1986, 1992a, 2000; Green and Urquhart 1994; Inwood and Stengos 1991; Urquhart 1986).
3. These data are found in, Department of Labour, *Wages and Hours of Labour in Canada, 1901–20,* Report No. 1 Supplement to the *Labour Gazette*, March, 1921, pp. 449–479; Dominion Bureau of Statistics. *The Canada Year Book, 1921*, pp. 634–639; Dominion Bureau of Statistics,

The Canada Year Book, 1922–23, pp. 634–638; Dominion Bureau of Statistics, *The Canada Year Book, 1925*, pp. 722–729; Dominion Bureau of Statistics, *The Canada Year Book, 1926*, pp. 713–721; Dominion Bureau of Statistics, *The Canada Year Book, 1927–28*, pp. 772–773; Dominion Bureau of Statistics, *The Canada Year Book, 1929*, pp. 365–367; Dominion Bureau of Statistics, *The Canada Year Book, 1942*, pp. 385–389.

4. For a detailed discussion on the collection of historical hours of work data see Hartle (1965, pp. 67–68).
5. Buckley and Urquhart (1965, p. 88), report some of the data used in this article. However, this is only for the years. 1905, 1910, 1915, 1920, and 1925 and only for carpenters, electricians, plumbers, and labourers in Halifax, Montreal, Toronto, Winnipeg, and Vancouver.
6. Since no hours worked data are available for Prince Edward Island, the occupational weight of this province is equally divided between the other two eastern provinces.
7. In this article only index numbers for the various national series are presented. The regional index numbers are easily calculated from the hours of work series presented.
8. See, Bureau of Industries for the Province of Ontario, Second Annual Report, 1883, Sessional Papers of the Province of Ontario, No. 55, Tables 23, 24; Bureau of Industries for the Province of Ontario, Third Annual Report, 1884, Sessional Papers of the Province of Ontario, No. 84, Table 24, 25; Bureau of Industries for the Province of Ontario, Seventh Annual Report, 1888, Part IV, Wages and Cost of Living, Sessional Papers of the Province of Ontario, No. 80, p. 25 and Tables I and 2; and Bureau of Industries for the Province of Ontario, Eighth Annual Report, 1889, Part IV, Wages and Cost of Living, Sessional Papers of the Province of Ontario, No. 80, Tables 3, 7, 9.
9. See also, Piva (1979, pp. 27–59), for a discussion of real wages in the Toronto area. Mackinnon (1996), presents nominal and real wage series (using the B-P deflator) for employees in the Mechanical Department of the Canadian Pacific Railway for the 1900–1930 period. She finds a similar trend real wage increase as do Bertram and Percy (1979) in their multi-sector study for the 1901–1926 period, although the railway workers apparently experienced a much greater rate of increase than did other manufacturing workers in Canada.
10. See, for example, Lipton (1973, pp. 29–36, 72–73, 230). In 1872 unionized workers were demanding a 55 hour work week and in 1887–1888 they were demanding a 48 hour work week. By 1919 they were calling for a legal work week of 44 hours. For the U.S. see Cahill (1968) and Whaples (1990).

11. Dominion Bureau of Statistics, The *Canada Year Book, 1927–28*, Ch. 8, Tables 2, 11 and 18.
12. Efficiency wage theory clearly suggests that there is a very powerful relationship between movements in wage rates and labour productivity (Akerlof and Yellen 1986). In behavioural economics the argument is made that higher wages serve to pressure firms into becoming more technically efficient (X-efficient) and into adopting and developing more cost efficient technologies and forms of firm organization. Without such pressures it can be expected that productivity would be less than it could otherwise be (Altman 1990, 1992b, 1996). Surprised that you don't reference Altman (1988 and 1995) or ch.7 of this book at this point.

References

Akerlof, G.A., and J.L. Yellen. 1986. Introduction. In *Efficiency Wage Models of the Labor Market*, ed. G.A. Akerlof and J.L. Yellen, 1–21. Cambridge, England and New York: Cambridge University Press.

Altman, M. 1986. A Revision of Canadian Economic Growth: 1870–1910 (A Challenge to the Revisionist Interpretation). *Canadian Journal of Economics* 12: 86–113.

Altman, M. 1990. Interfirm, Interregional, and International Differences in Labor Productivity: Variations in Levels of "X-Efficiency" as a Function of Differential Labor Costs. In *X-Efficiency Examined and Extolled*, ed. K. Weirmair and M. Perlman, 163–192. Ann Arbor: University of Michigan Press.

Altman, M. 1992a. Revised Real Canadian GNP Estimates and Canadian Economic Growth, 1870–1926. *Review of Income and Wealth* 38: 455–473.

Altman, M. 1992b. The Economics of Exogenous Increases in Wage Rates in a Behavioral/X-Efficiency Theory of the Firm. *Review of Social Economy* 50: 163–192.

Altman, M. 1994. The Evolution of Plant Size in Canadian Manufacturing, 1870–1910. *Canadian Historical Review* 75: 557–585.

Altman, M. 1996. *Human Agency and Material Welfare: Revisions in Microeconomics and their Implications for Public Policy.* Boston, Dordrecht, and London: Kluwer Academic.

Altman, M. 2000. Quantitative Aspects of Canadian Growth and Development, 1850–1926. In *Canada, Confederation to Present*, ed. C. Hackett and B. Hesketh. Edmonton: Chinook Multimedia Inc.

Atack, J., and F. Bateman. 1992. How Long Was the Workday in 1880. *Journal of Economic History* 5: 129–155.

Bertram, G.W., and M.B. Percy. 1979. Real Wage Trends in Canada 1900–26: Some Provisional Estimates. *Canadian Journal of Economics/Revue Canadienne d'Economique* 12: 299–312.

Buckley, K. 1974. *Capital Formation in Canada, 1890–1930*. Toronto: University of Toronto Press, 1955; reprint, Toronto: McClelland and Stewart.

Bureau of Industries for the Province of Ontario, Second Annual Report, 1883. 1884. Sessional Papers of the Province of Ontario, No. 55, 1884. Toronto: Grip Printing and Publishing.

Bureau of Industries for the Province of Ontario, Third Annual Report, 1884. 1885. Sessional Papers of the Province of Ontario, No. 84, 1885. Toronto: Grip Printing and Publishing.

Bureau of Industries for the Province of Ontario, Seventh Annual Report, 1888. 1889. Part IV, Wages and Cost of Living, Sessional Papers of the Province of Ontario, No. 80, 1889. Toronto: Warwick and Sons.

Bureau of Industries for the Province of Ontario, Eighth Annual Report, 1889. 1891. Part IV, Wages and Cost of Living, Sessional Papers of the Province of Ontario, No. 80, 1889, Toronto: Warwick and Sons.

Cahill, M.C. 1968. *Shorter Hours: A Study of the Movement Since the Civil War*. New York: AMS Press.

Census of Canada, 1911, Vol. V, *Occupations of the People*. Ottawa: J. de L. Tache, 1915.

Census of Canada, 1921, Vol. IV, *Occupations*. Ottawa: F.A. Aclund, 1929.

Census of Canada, 1931, Vol. VI, *Unemployment*. Ottawa: J.O. Patenaude, 1934.

Chambers, E.J. 1985. New Evidence on the Living Standards of Toronto Blue Collar Workers in the Pre 1914 Era. *Histoire Sociale-Social History* 18: 285–314.

Coats, R.H. 1915. *The Rise in Prices and the Cost of Living in Canada, 1900–14: A Statistical Examination of Economic Causes*, Board of Inquiry into Cost of Living, Vol. 2. Ottawa: J. de L. Tache.

Department of Labour. 1921. *Wages and Hours of Labour In Canada, 1901–20*, Report No. I, Supplement to the *Labour Gazette*, March, 449–479.

Department of Labour. 1929. *Wages and Hours of Labour in Canada, 1920–28*, Report No. 12. Ottawa: F.A. Acland.

Dominion Bureau of Statistics. 1922. *The Canada Year Book, 1921*, 634–639. Ottawa: F.A. Acland.

Dominion Bureau of Statistics. 1924. *The Canada Year Book, 1922–23*, 634–638. Ottawa: F.A. Acland.

Dominion Bureau of Statistics. 1926. *The Canada Year Book, 1925*, 722–729. Ottawa: F.A. Acland.

Dominion Bureau of Statistics. 1927. *The Canada Year Book, 1926*, 713–721. Ottawa: F.A. Acland.

Dominion Bureau of Statistics. 1928. *The Canada Year Book, 1927–28*, 772–773. Ottawa: F.A. Acland.
Dominion Bureau of Statistics. 1929. *The Canada Year Book, 1929*, 365–367. Ottawa: F.A. Acland.
Dominion Bureau of Statistics. 1942. *The Canada Year Book, 1942*, 385–389. Ottawa: Edmond Cloutier.
Douglas, P.H. 1966. *Real Wages in the United States, 1890–1926*. New York: Augustus M. Kelley (First published, 1930).
Dymond, W.R., and G. Saunders. 1965. Hours of Work in Canada. In *Hours of Work*, ed. C.E. Dankert, F.C. Mann, and H.R. Northrup, 54–75. New York: Harper & Row.
Firestone, O.J. 1958. *Canada's Economic Development, 1867–1953, With Special Reference to Changes in the Country's National Product and National Wealth*. London: Bowes and Bowes.
Green, A.G., and M.C. Urquhart. 1994. New Estimates of Output Growth in Canada: Measurement and Interpretation. In *Perspectives on Canadian Economic History*, ed. D. McCalla and M. Huberman, 158–175. Mississauga, ON: Copp Clark Longman.
Hartle, D.C. 1965. Section D: Wages and Working Conditions. In *Historical Statistics of Canada*, ed. M.C. Urquhart and K.A.H. Buckley, 67–83. Toronto: Macmillan Company of Canada.
Inwood, K., and T. Stengos. 1991. Discontinuities in Canadian Economic Growth, 1870–1985. *Explorations in Economic History* 28: 274–286.
Lebergott, S. 1993. *Pursuing Happiness: American Consumers in the Twentieth Century*. Princeton: Princeton University Press.
Lipton, C. 1973. *The Trade Union Movement in Canada, 1827–1959*. Toronto: NC Press.
Mackinnon, M. 1996. New Evidence on Canadian Wage Rates, 1900–30. *Canadian Journal of Economics* 24: 114–131.
Mackintosh, W.A. 1978. *The Economic Background of Dominion-Provincial Relations*. Ottawa: King's Printer, 1939; reprint, Toronto: Macmillan, 1978.
Maddison, A. 1995. *Monitoring the World Economy, 1820–1992*. Paris: OECD.
Ostry, S., and M.A. Zaidi. 1975. *Labour Economics in Canada*, 2nd ed. Toronto: Macmillan of Canada.
Piva, M.J. 1979. *The Condition of the Working Class in Toronto, 1900–21*. Ottawa: University of Ottawa Press.
Rees, A. 1961. *Real Wages in Manufacturing, 1890–1914*. Princeton: Princeton University Press.
Schor, J.B. 1991. *The Overworked American: The Unexpected Decline of Leisure*. New York: Basic Books.

Shells, M.E. 1990. Collective Choice of Working Conditions: Hours in British and U.S. Iron and Steel, 1890–1919. *Journal of Economic History* 50: 379–392.

Urquhart, M.C. 1986. New Estimates of Gross National Product, Canada, 1870–1926: Some Implications for Canadian Development. In *Long-Term Factors in American Economic Growth*, Studies in Income and Wealth, ed. S.L. Engerman and R.E. Gallman, Vol. 51, NBER, 9–94. Chicago: University of Chicago Press.

Urquhart, M.C. 1994. Gross National Product, Canada, 1870–1926: A Note. *Review of Income and Wealth* 40: 223–226.

Urquhart, M.C., and K.A.H. Buckley, eds. 1965. *Historical Statistics of Canada*. Toronto: Macmillan Company of Canada.

Van Ark, B. 1994. Book Review of, Malcolm C. Urquhart, *Gross National Product of Canada, 1870–1926. The Derivation of the Estimates*. McGill-Queen's University Press, Kingston/London/Buffalo, 1983. *Journal of Economic Literature* 32: 1927–1928.

Whaples, R. 1990. Winning the Eight Hour Day, 1909–19. *Journal of Economic History* 50: 393–406.

CHAPTER 13

Gender Pay Inequality and Occupational Change in Canada, in the Early Twentieth Century (with Louise Lamontagne)

1 Introduction

From 1960 to the 1980s women employed full-time in Canada earned about 60% of what their male counterparts earned.[1] Clearly, with regards to this particular aspect of Canadian women's employment, little has changed over the last three decades. The case of Canadian women has not differed all that much from their American counterparts where the earnings gap remained roughly constant over the same period. Women in other similarly developed economies, on the other hand, as in Australia, Britain, France and Germany, fared somewhat better, witnessing some reduction in pay inequality from 1960, whereas in Sweden the pay gap virtually disappeared (Gunderson 1989, p. 47; see also Fuchs 1988). Significant and persistent gender pay gaps have deep and complex historical roots. We remain largely ignorant, however, as to the composition and determinants of the pay gap in earlier periods for most countries, including Canada, particularly during the first half of the present century.[2] By examining the most systematic data presently available on women's paid work in Canada, the decennial censuses, this study sheds some light on Canada's gender pay gap. Moreover, the data available for Canada allow us to produce some of the most detailed historical estimates for gender pay inequality produced for any industrialized nation to date.

Using the available census material, we estimate the extent and degree of the female/male earnings gap from 1900 to 1930. Nineteen-hundred

M. Altman, *Lessons from a Successfully Export-Oriented, Resource-Rich Economy*, https://doi.org/10.1007/978-3-031-03887-7_13

is the first year for which sufficient data exist to construct such estimates for Canada as a whole. We construct estimates of pay inequality for all broadly defined occupational sectors in the economy for the years 1900, 1920 and 1930. Similar estimates for all broadly defined industrial sectors, however, are only possible for 1930. Pay inequality estimates are also generated for the years 1900, 1910, 1915, and 1930 for the major manufacturing sectors and occupations. These results, combined with our estimates for the distribution of female and male employment between occupations and sectors, allow us to determine the extent to which the estimated earnings gaps are a function of the differential distribution of male and female labour between the broadly defined sectors or occupations as opposed to their being a product of sector or occupation specific earnings differentials.

Our findings suggest that in 1930, on average, women earned about 53% of what men earned in Canada. The degree of pay inequality, therefore, diminishes somewhat from 1930 to 1960. The degree of pay inequality also lessens over the 1900–1930 period as the female/male pay ratio increases from 46% in 1900 to 53% in 1930. This study further finds that the earnings gap for each year examined is only partially determined by "ghettoization" or "job segmentation," the differential distribution of male and female labour between sectors or occupations at a given point in time.[3] Rather, we find that most of the pay gap at this time was a function of income inequality within broadly defined sectors or occupations. These findings concur with contemporary results for Canada (Ostry 1968, p. 41; Gunderson 1985, pp. 229–232) and the United States (Reskin and Hartmann 1986, p. 11) as well as with those of Claudia Goldin (1990, p. 71) for late nineteenth century United States. However, the data used in these studies, as well as in our own, do not allow for an examination of the hypothesis that pay inequality was affected by the differential distribution of women and men within narrowly defined occupations. In this study, however, our sources allow us to examine the role of occupational segregation in determining pay inequality for 1,621 and 439 occupational categories for 1900 and 1930, respectively, which is a marked improvement over all historical and most contemporary studies on pay inequality.[4] Our results are summarized in Table 1.

As to the causes of the reduction in pay inequality which took place from 1900 to 1930, a substantial fraction of this reduction, particularly from 1900 to 1920, was a product of the changing occupational structure of women. It is important to note that this occurred in the context of

Table 1 Summary estimates of female-male adjusted income differentials, 1900–1930

	Actual			Hypothetical		
	Female/male earnings (%)	*Female earnings*		*Female/male earnings (%)*	*Female earnings*	
Manufacturing						
1900	47.00	\$160	(annual)	55.32	\$187	(annual)
1910	52.00	\$238	(annual)	62.25	\$285	(annual)
1915	55.00	\$7.39	(weekly)	54.67	\$7.32	(weekly)
1930	50.34	\$12.50	(weekly)	56.82	\$14.10	(weekly)
All occupations						
1900	45.79	\$16.86	(monthly)	51.17	\$18.84	(monthly)
1920	52.16	\$11.87	(weekly)	49.23	\$11.20	(weekly)
1930	53.22	\$12.01	(weekly)	47.92	\$10.81	(weekly)
All industries						
1930	53.22	\$12.01		58.16	\$13.12	(weekly)
Services						
1930	41.22	\$10.55		56.95	\$14.57	(weekly)

Sources and notes Tables 2 and 4 and text. The hypothetical estimates assume that the distribution of female employment is identical to that of male employment. Row Two of the hypothetical estimates for All Industries is based on integrating the hypothetical pay estimates for manufacturing and services into the computation

little change in occupational segmentation. Pay inequality was reduced, not by women entering male dominated occupations per se, but rather by women entering occupations which were characterized by relatively high rates of pay for women. Consistent with this finding, our estimates suggest that although the increased percentage of women in service-related jobs contributed to depressing the relative wage of women, women's gradual domination of clerical work from the turn of the century contributed to narrowing the earnings gap and not to increasing the degree of pay inequality in men's favour.

2 The Construction of Estimates

The censuses of manufacturing for the years 1900, 1910, 1915, and 1930 provide detailed data on the number of men and women employed and income earned by gender (see also Denton and Ostry 1967, on the censuses). But these data are not completely compatible across census years since the censuses for 1900 and 1910 only record data for those firms which employed five or more workers while the census for 1915 excludes firms which produced less than $2,500 per annum. Only the census for 1930 records data on all firms. This discrepancy in coverage should not affect our estimates of relative female-male earnings unless the pay gap characterizing the smaller firms was considerably different from what it was in the larger firms. At present it is not possible to determine if this would be the case. Nevertheless, irrespective of this possibility, smaller plants were never of great significance in Canadian manufacturing in the period under study, producing possibly 12% of total output in 1900, 6% in 1910, and less than 3% by 1915 (Bertram 1964, p. 99, notes 5–7).

The original census data on manufacturing, tabulated in terms of industries, are re-categorized in accordance with the 17 major manufacturing sectors of the Dominion Bureau of Statistics' *Standard Industrial Classification Manual*.[5] For each of these sectors, estimates are made for the number of men and women employed as well as for their earnings (Table 2).

An important distinction exists in the type of earnings estimates which can be constructed for manufacturing from the 1900 and 1910 data, as compared to those which can be constructed from the 1915 and 1930 data. For 1900 and 1910, data are available on annual earnings only. On the other hand, for 1915 it is possible to construct estimates for weekly rates of pay. And for 1930, detailed data are available from which one can estimate the weekly rates of pay. In addition, the census for 1930 provides data in terms of both industrial and occupational classifications. Our 1930 estimates are constructed with reference to the industrial classification so as to make them comparable to the estimates for the first three census years. No detailed data for manufacturing on any basis are available for 1920.

Our manufacturing earnings estimates for 1900 can be partially adjusted to take into account the degree to which the annual pay gap is a function of differences in the time worked by men and women. The data available on the number of days worked by men and women in 1900 are categorized into major manufacturing sectors and the ratio of days worked by men relative to women is computed for each sector (Table 3). These ratios are then used to adjust our actual earnings estimates for women (Table 2). For example, on average, we find that men worked 91% as many days as women. In this case the annual earnings of women are adjusted downward, to 91% of their estimated values, so as

Table 2 Gender income and employment ratios for Canadian manufacturing, 1900–1930

	Female/sector total (%)	*Sector share of males employed (%)*	*Sector share of females employed (%)*	*Female/male income (%)*	*Male income*		*Female/sector total (%)*	*Sector share of males employed (%)*	*Sector share of females employed (%)*	*Female/male income (%)*	*Male income (%)*
Food and bever-ages						*Transportation equipment*					
1900	30.1	14.4	21.8	34.1	375	1900	0.8	8.4	0.2	63	404
1910	23.3	11.5	17.6	49.6	14	1910	0.5	11.1	0.3	72	552
1915	19.0	12.1	12.9	48.0	23	1915	0.6	12.1	0.3	63	15
1930	17.0	12.8	11.7	47.9		1930	3.6	10.9	1.8	65	27
Tobacco and products					396	*Nonferrous metal products*					
1900	42.1	1.6	4.1	45.2	467	1900	10.6	0.8	0.3	56	457
1910	40.4	1.3	4.6	58.0	11	1910	8.1	0.9	0.4	66	528
1915	49.7	1.2	5.4	67.0	25	1915	12.2	1.2	0.8	55	14
1930	49.3	0.8	3.3	41.3		1930	6.3	3.1	0.9	56	27
Rubber products					416	*Electrical apparatus and supplies*					
1900	33.2	0.2	0.3	52.6	501	1900	11.6	0.8	0.4	55	470
1910	14.8	0.3	0.2	71.1	13	1910	13.6	1.3	1.0	63	522
1915	24.9	0.7	1.1	68.3	24	1915	10.8	1.9	1.0	60	13
1930	23.4	2.2	2.9	51.9		1930	20.0	3.3	3.7	51	29

(continued)

Table 2 (continued)

	Female/sector total (%)	*Sector share of males employed (%)*	*Sector share of females employed (%)*	*Female/male income (%)*	*Male income*		*Female/sector total (%)*	*Sector share of males employed (%)*	*Sector share of females employed (%)*	*Female/male income (%)*	*Male income (%)*
Leather products					364	*Nonmetallic mineral products*					
1900	27.7	6.4	8.6	54.1	471	1900	4.0	1.8	0.3	48	301
1910	24.5	4.8	7.9	58.2	13	1910	3.2	5.0	0.8	42	449
1915	30.9	4.2	8.6	60.9	20	1915	3.8	4.6	0.8	46	13
1930	27.8	3.5	6.0	53.6		1930	5.6	3.8	1.0	63	25
Textile products					281	*Petroleum and products*					
1900	44.5	5.1	14.3	73.0	435	1900	1.9	0.3	0.0	70	408
1910	46.5	3.4	15.0	62.1	11	1910	0.5	0.5	0.0	64	541
1915	50.0	3.7	16.9	67.9	21	1915	0.4	1.4	0.0	60	15
1930	44.8	6.1	22.1	52.2		1930	7.0	1.9	0.6	65	30
Clothing					425	*Chemical products*					
1900	72.7	3.2	30.0	40.7	524	1900	68.5	1.0	7.3	37	403
1910	60.7	4.6	35.8	49.4	14	1910	35.9	1.6	4.4	51	399
1915	62.8	4.1	31.2	58.8	25	1915	43.2	2.1	7.3	49	14
1930	57.2	3.9	23.5	47.3		1930	19.9	2.4	2.7	49	30
Wood products					253	*Miscellaneous products*					
1900	1.0	31.9	1.2	64.4	357	1900	17.2	1.9	1.4	43	436

	Female/sector total (%)	*Sector share of males employed (%)*	*Sector share of females employed (%)*	*Female/male income (%)*	*Male income*		*Female/sector total (%)*	*Sector share of males employed (%)*	*Sector share of females employed (%)*	*Female/male income (%)*	*Male income (%)*
1910	0.9	27.9	1.2	70.3	11	1910	13.0	1.8	1.3	57	526
1915	1.3	16.3	1.0	61.3	18	1915	24.6	1.3	1.9	55	14
1930	2.9	12.9	1.7	72.0		1930	22.4	1.9	2.4	54	26
Paper products					373	*Other industries*					
1900	26.3	2.8	3.6	42.4	485	1900	33.1	0.9	1.5	40	377
1910	19.9	2.8	3.5	44.3	13	1910	22.5	1.1	1.5	38	497
1915	15.4	4.8	3.9	49.0	27	1915	14.0	1.2	0.9		na
1930	11.1	7.4	4.1	48.9		1930		0.0	0.0		0
Printing and publishing					498	*Total*					
1900	24.0	3.4	3.7	38.4	665	1900	22.17	214,645	61,158	47	338
1910	21.5	2.6	3.5	41.8	17	1910	16.60	363,889	72,412	52	459
1915	22.4	3.4	4.5	43.1	30	1915	18.03	334,122	73,516	55	13
1930	20.7	5.9	6.9	51.1		1930	18.28	486,000	108,700	50	25
Iron and steel products					411						
1900	1.7	15.1	0.9	62.5	558						
1910	1.0	17.5	0.8	70.8	15						
1915	1.4	23.7	1.5	46.6	26						

(continued)

Table 2 (continued)

	Female/sector total (%)	*Sector share of males employed (%)*	*Sector share of females employed (%)*	*Female/male income (%)*	*Male income*	*Female/sector total (%)*	*Sector share of males employed (%)*	*Sector share of females employed (%)*	*Female/male income (%)*	*Male income (%)*
1930	5.6	17.3	4.6	62.2	317					

Sources and notes Census of Canada, 1901, vol. 3 (Ottawa, 1905); Census of Canada, 1911, vol. 3 (Ottawa, 1913); Census of Canada, 1931, vol. 5 (Ottawa, 1935), Table 27; The Postal Census of Manufacturers, 1916 (Ottawa, 1917). The census for 1915 does not provide wage data for men and women separately. However, data are presented on wage groups and on the number of men and women in these wage groups for selected principal industries (Table 4). These data are used to estimate the percentage distribution of men and women amongst the wage groups. These estimates are used along with the data on wages per wage group to construct the weighted average weekly wage per industry. The average wage for all working men and women in manufacturing to compute the weights. The female annual income estimates are adjusted for differences in days worked by men and women manufacturing is, in effect, a weighted average of the estimated industry wage using the census data of all (Table 3). Female wages are adjusted upwards or downwards proportionally to the extent that women worked less than men respectively. Since data on days worked are available for 1900, estimates based on these data are used to adjust our 1910 estimates. The 1915 and 1930 income estimates need not be adjusted since they are constructed in terms of payments per week

Table 3 Days worked per worker per annum in the manufacturing sector, 1900

	Men	*Women*	*Women/men*
Food and beverages	260	204	0.78
Tobacco and products	265	285	1.08
Rubber products	238	260	1.09
Leather products	263	277	1.05
Textile products	266	289	1.09
Clothing	237	276	1.16
Wood products	196	205	1.05
Paper products	258	286	1.11
Printing and publishing	255	271	1.06
Iron and steel products	237	194	0.82
Transportation equipment	270	213	0.79
Nonferrous metal products	286	232	0.81
Electrical apparatus and supplies	287	249	0.87
Nonmetallic mineral products	230	210	0.91
Petroleum and products	245	233	0.95
Chemical products	214	287	1.34
Miscellaneous products	276	248	0.90
Other industries	236	283	1.20
Total	213	234	1.10

Source Constructed from data in The Census of Canada, 1901, vol. 3 (Ottawa, 1905), Table 9

to neutralize the effect their differential contribution to work had upon their annual earnings. The 1900 adjustment ratios are applied to our 1910 earnings estimates. The effect of the latter adjustment, which assumes that the differential contribution of days worked by men and women did not change over the decade, is to reduce the female-male pay ratio in 1910 from 57 to 52%. If the former percentage is closer to the "true" value of the pay ratio (which the data does not permit us to determine), then our adjustment of the 1910 data results in our underestimating the extent of the true reduction of the gender pay gap in manufacturing from 1900 to 1910.

Our broader estimates which incorporate all industries, including manufacturing, as well as all occupations, are derived without any significant adjustments, from the censuses for the years 1900, 1920, and 1930. For 1900 and 1920, it is possible to construct estimates on an occupational basis only. Estimates for 1930 are presented both on an industrial and occupational basis. Therefore, the detailed estimates presented for

1900 and 1920 can only be compared to our occupational estimates for 1930. The 1930 industrial estimates, on the other hand, are the only estimates comparable with the industrial estimates produced for manufacturing. Further details on the construction of these estimates are found in the notes to the tables.

3 Pay Inequality in the Manufacturing Sector

We estimate the ratio of the adjusted earnings of women on wages to that of men on wages for the manufacturing sector (Table 2). We also estimate the percentage distribution of male and female employment across sectors based upon our estimates of their employment across sectors (Table 2). Although it is possible to construct estimates for men and women on salary as well, we do not do so since such estimates cannot accurately reflect comparable male and female earnings per unit of time.[6] Most adults recorded by the censuses as being engaged in manufacturing, it should be noted, are on wages.[7]

In the 1900–1915 period women constitute a diminishing proportion of wage-earners employed by the manufacturing sector's "larger" firms (Table 2). The share of women in manufacturing wage employment falls from 22.2% in 1900 to 16.6% in 1910 as total manufacturing employment increases by 58% from 1900 to 1910. During this period male employment increases by 70% while that of women increases by only 18%. From 1910 to 1915 the share of women in manufacturing employment increases slightly to 18% while total manufacturing employment decreases by 6.6%; male employment decreases by 8.2%. Women's share of manufacturing employment remains at 18% by 1930. Manufacturing employment increases for both sexes by about 46% from 1915 to 1930. Although, on average, women's share of total wage employment in manufacturing remains small throughout the period under examination, it will be shown that women's share of employment in specific sectors is of much greater significance.

Overall, from 1900 to 1915, the pay ratio between women and men narrows. This ratio increases from only 47% in 1900, to 52% in 1910, and to 55% by 1915 (Table 2). This small but gradual improvement in the position of women holds true for all but two sectors in manufacturing in the 1900–1910 period. But only one of these two sectors, the textiles products sector (unlike the nonmetallic mineral products sector) is of any real consequence to female employment. In this sector the pay ratio actually falls from 73 to 62% from 1900–1910 but then partially bounces back to 68% by 1915. Nevertheless, this sector is consistently characterized by one of the smallest pay gaps in manufacturing throughout the 1900–1915 period and, as well, employs between 14 (1900) and 17% (1915) of female workers. Finally, developments in the clothing sector, which employs about 30% of all women in manufacturing in the 1900–1915 period, also differ significantly from the mean changes. But here there is a dramatic improvement in the position of women, with the pay ratio increasing from a very poor 41% in 1900, to 49% in 1910, and to 59% by 1915.

Over the 1910–1915 period the average improvement in the pay ratio for women is the result of an improvement in only 7 of the 17 manufacturing sectors. However, these seven sectors, which include tobacco, leather, textiles, and clothing, employ the majority of female workers. The position of women deteriorates most severely in wood products, iron and steel products, transportation equipment, and nonferrous metal products where, in total, only 3.6% of all women are employed.

It is evident from the estimates presented here that male and female employment is concentrated in different sectors. Whereas clothing and textiles together employ almost 50% of all women in manufacturing, these sectors never employ more than 10% of all men. Nevertheless, men contribute somewhat less than 50% of total wage labour to textiles and between 30 and 40% to clothing. The wood products sector employs 32% of all men in 1900 and 17% in 1915, and only about one% of all women from 1900 to 1915. The iron and steel and transportation equipment sectors are of rowing importance to male employment, encompassing 23% of mates on wages in 1900 and 36% by 1915. By way of contrast, these sectors never employ more than 2% of all women engaged in the manufacturing sector.

The particular structure of female employment in Canada from 1900 to 1915 raises the question as to whether women's average relative earnings would have been substantially improved had women not been concentrated in specific sectors like clothing and textiles. In other words, what would the pay ratio have been had the distribution of female wage labour been identical to that of male wage labour, while retaining the actual values for female wages? Under these assumptions, on average, women's income would have increased by 16.9% in 1900 and by 20.1% in 1910. This, in turn, would have resulted in an increase in the pay ratio to

55 from 47% in 1900, and to 62 from 52% in 1910. However, for 1915 the pay ratio would have been reduced, albeit marginally, to 54.5 from 55% (Tables 1 and 2). Clearly, the differential distribution of female and male labour is not the major cause of pay inequality between the sexes in the 1900–1915 period. Therefore, although the differential in the female and male contribution to individual sectors can explain as much as 15 and 21% of the pay gap for 1900 and 1910, respectively, pay inequality in this period appears to have been largely determined by pay inequality within sectors.

Over the entire 1900–1930 period, the extent of pay inequality within the manufacturing sector fluctuates but does not improve to any great extent. By 1930 the pay ratio in manufacturing is 50%, near its 1900 low of 47% (Table 2). The decline in the pay ratio from 1915 to 1930 is found to be significant especially in those sectors which are the major employers of women, namely in clothing and textiles. These two sectors together employ 46% of all female wage-earners in 1930. Conversely, only 5% of all women are employed in the iron and steel products sector, the one sector where pay inequality decreases significantly. In this sector the pay ratio increases from 47 to 62%.

As in previous census years, women find themselves in 1930, for the most part, concentrated in different sectors than men. And, once again, women are concentrated in clothing and textiles as compared to men who are concentrated in the wood products, iron and steel products, and transportation equipment sectors. Nevertheless, as with 1900 and 1910, had female wage-earners in 1930 been distributed identically to male wage-earners across sectors, the pay ratio would have increased somewhat, from 50 to 56%. But, in 1930 as in 1910, pay inequality is also largely attributable to pay inequality within sectors and not primarily to women being "ghettoized" into particularly low paying industries.

In evaluating the significance of ghettoization to the pay ratio in manufacturing, it is important to establish whether, in fact, women were becoming increasingly segregated from men in the manufacturing sector over the 1900–1930 period. The ghettoization trend is measured by the Duncan index of dissimilarity which is constructed by summing the absolute values of the differences in the percentage distribution of female and male labour across the broadly defined manufacturing sectors and dividing the results by two. An index of 100 is generated by a completely segmented labour market in manufacturing. If the index takes on a value of zero, on the other hand, there is complete gender integration in the labour market. Our index numbers for 1900, 1910, 1915, and 1930 are 56.7, 59.6, 56.7, and 43.5, respectively.[8] Clearly, women are not facing increased ghettoization in the manufacturing sector over the period examined. Moreover, the 1915–1930 period, in which there is a large decrease in job segmentation, coincides with a deterioration in women's earnings relative to those of men. It becomes clear, therefore, that even though women are finding relatively more employment in predominantly male sectors, their economic status does not improve. Finally, we find that the reduction in job segmentation over the 1915–1930 period is principally the result of large reductions in the difference between the female and male distribution of labour in the clothing, wood products, and iron and steel products sectors (Table 2).

The pay ratio when using the aggregate occupational data on wage-earners in manufacturing for 1900, 1920 and 1930 is estimated to be 47, 43, and 44% (I don't see this in Table 4) respectively. Thus when using the occupational data the degree of pay inequality increases from 1900 to 1930 (Table 4). Although the pay ratio computed here for 1900 is similar to what we computed from the industrial data on manufacturing (Table 2), the pay ratio for 1930 using occupational data is lower than the 50% derived from the industrial data. Since clerical workers employed in the manufacturing sector are excluded from the occupational data (all clerical workers are included under a separate occupational category) it seems possible that this omission accounts for the difference in pay ratio between the two types of data for this particular year. While we have no data on the earnings of individuals engaged in clerical work on a sector by sector basis for 1930, and only data on clerical work as a whole exists, we do have manufacturing specific data in both industrial and occupational terms. Thus it becomes possible to test the proposition that, for 1930, the low pay ratio estimated from the occupational data is a result of the exclusion from these data of manufacturing specific clerical workers.

The employment count for men and women in manufacturing for 1930 is greater in the industrial than in the occupational category by 37.7 and 31.5% for men and women, respectively. When we assume that these percentages of male and female workers consist entirely of clerical workers, and that they earn our estimated weekly pay for clerical workers in all sectors inclusive of manufacturing while other workers earn our estimated weekly pay for non-clerical workers in manufacturing (Table 4), we can generate a hypothetical rate of pay for men and women incorporated under the industrial classification of manufacturing. These hypothetical

Table 4 Days worked per worker per annum in the manufacturing sector, 1900–1930

	Sector share of labour employed						*Share of women per sector*		
	1900		*1920*		*1930*		*1900 (%)*	*1920 (%)*	*1930 (%)*
	Men (%)	*Women (%)*	*Men (%)*	*Women (%)*	*Men (%)*	*Women (%)*			
All occupations	100	100	100	100	100	100	18.8	21.1	21.1
Agriculture	10.9	0.1	9.9	0.2	9.7	0.3	0.1	0.5	0.8
Fishing and logging	3.6	0.0	2.9	0.0	2.5	0.0	0.0	0.0	0.1
Mining	3.6	0.0	3.0	0.0	4.1	0.0	0.0	0.0	0.0
Manufacturing	25.6	32.4	17.5	19.6	15.3	14.0	22.6	23.1	19.6
Electrical light and power					1.6				0.0
Construction	8.4	0.0	8.0	0.0	8.1	0.0	0.0	0.0	0.1
Transportation	7.2	3.0	11.3	3.7	11.1	3.1	8.8	8.2	7.1
Trade	8.4	0.7	7.9	10.2	9.1	9.9	1.8	25.6	22.6
Finance	0.5	0.0	1.1	0.1	1.2	0.1	0.4	1.4	1.5
Service	8.8	55.8	9.7	43.6	10.4	48.7	59.5	54.7	55.6
Clerical	6.8	7.7	8.5	22.6	6.2	21.6	20.6	41.5	48.4
Laborers and unspecified	16.2	0.5	20.1	0.1	20.6	2.2	0.7	0.1	2.8

	Sector share of labour employed						Share of women per sector		
	1900		1920		1930		1900 (%)	1920 (%)	1930 (%)
	Men (%)	Women (%)	Men (%)	Women (%)	Men (%)	Women (%)			
Total Employees	664,448	153,478	1,464,364	392,631	1,975,200	528,462			

	Earnings per unit of time						Male–female earnings ratio		
	1900 per month		1920 per week		1930 per week		1900 (%)	1920 (%)	1930 (%)
	Men	Women	Men	Women	Men	Women			
All occupations	$36.8	$16.9	$22.8	$11.9	$22.6	$12.0	45.8	52.2	53.2
Agriculture	$20.8	$15.8	$11.4	$9.2	$7.5	$5.3	76.2	81.2	70.3
Fishing and logging	$31.4		$16.5		$13.0	$5.2			40.4
Mining	$51.3		$25.0		$23.7	$57.1			240.2
Manufacturing	$37.3	$18.1	$25.6	$11.1	$25.6	$11.2	48.6	43.5	43.7
Electrical light and power					$27.2	$70.5			258.8
Construction	$39.5	$23.9	$24.7		$24.2	$12.7	60.4		52.7
Transportation	$45.7	$19.8	$27.0	$13.8	$25.0	$14.4	43.4	51.0	57.4
Trade	$44.8	$21.9	$27.2	$12.3	$28.9	$12.1	48.9	45.1	41.7
Finance	$99.5	$40.6	$44.2	$19.7	$49.8	$25.9	40.8	44.6	52.1
Service	$42.3	$15.0	$25.5	$9.9	$29.8	$9.8	35.4	38.7	33.0
Clerical	$43.1	$23.1	$25.2	$15.9	$24.4	$17.3	53.5	62.9	70.8
Laborers and unspecified	$25.8	$17.0	$17.6	$8.3	$14.8	$9.3	66.1	47.4	62.9

Sources and Notes Census and Statistics: Wage-Earners by Occupations (Ottawa, 1907), Table 2. The census material for 1900 is reorganized to be consistent with the occupational classification of 1920. The Census of Canada, 1931, vol. 5 (Ottawa, 1935), Table 16 is used for the 1920 and Table 28 is used for the 1930

rates of pay are $25.45 and $12.61 for men and women, respectively. These numbers can be compared to their actual rates of pay of $24.83 and $12.50, respectively (Table 2). The hypothetical rates of pay yield a hypothetical pay ratio of 49.5%, a pay ratio which is nearly identical to the actual pay ratio of 50.3% for such workers.

This suggests, therefore, that in all probability the estimates based upon the occupational classification significantly exaggerate the degree of pay inequality between men and women in manufacturing in 1930 by excluding manufacturing specific clerical workers. Our hypothetical estimates also suggest that clerical work contributed positively, and significantly, to improving the average rate of pay of women relative to that of men in Canada's manufacturing sector, at least in 1930.

4 The Distribution of the Gainfully Employed

Using the census material on occupations we construct estimates for the distribution of the entire paid work force (Table 4) and thus place our estimates for the manufacturing sector within a broader context. From 1900 to 1930 the share of women in the paid work force increases from 19 to 21%. All of this relatively small increase takes place from 1900 to 1920 and is a product of the number of female employees growing at a faster pace than their mate counterparts, 4.8 compared to 4% (Table 5). During the 1920s the growth rate for both women and men is about 3%.

Although the share of women in the paid work force does not change significantly from 1900 to 1930, women's share does increase dramatically in clerical work and in trade, from 21 to 48% and from 2 to 23%, respectively. And, as well, most of this increase also occurs from 1900 to 1920. The number of female clerical workers grows by 10.6% per year as compared to 5.2% for men during this period. In trade, the growth rates in the number of workers is 20 and 3.7% for women and men, respectively. The massive increase of women in these two occupations, particularly in clerical work, largely explains the increased share of women in the paid work force in the period under study.

Women were not only of growing importance to clerical work, but this occupation gives employment to an increasing percentage of the women engaged in paid labour, from 8% in 1900 to 21.6% in 1930. By contrast, clerical work provides employment to 8% of male paid labour in 1900 but to only 6% by 1930. The same story can be told for trade. This occupation's contribution to female paid labour jumped from less than 1% in

Table 5 Employment growth per annum

	1900–1920		*1920–1930*	
	Men (%)	*Women (%)*	*Men (%)*	*Women (%)*
All occupations	4.03	4.81	3.04	3.02
Agriculture	3.51	10.62	2.80	8.38
Fishing and logging	2.98		1.62	
Mining	3.15		6.25	
Manufacturing	2.06	2.21	1.70	−0.37
Electrical light and power				
Construction	3.78		3.14	
Transportation	6.38	5.94	2.81	1.21
Trade	3.74	20.10	4.53	2.79
Finance	8.60	15.27	4.11	4.61
Service	4.55	3.53	3.78	4.17
Clerical	5.20	10.63	−0.25	2.56
Laborers and unspecified	5.16	−2.38	3.29	38.76

Source Table 4

1900 to 10% by 1930 whereas its contribution to the male paid work force rose only slightly from 8 to 10%.

The importance of manufacturing to women's employment falls dramatically from 1900 to 1930 from 32 to 14% of female paid labour. This fall, however, also holds true for men. Nevertheless, women's contribution to total employment in this occupation is similar to its average contribution to all occupations for the 1900–1930 period, which ranges from 22.6% in 1900 to almost 20% in 1930. It is the service sector more than any other, however, which dominates female employment and whose employment women, in turn, consistently dominate. Women comprise 59% of this occupation's paid work force in 1900. By 1930 their share falls to 56%. The service sector's share of female employment in 1900 is 56% which then falls to 44% by 1920, and rises back up to 49% by 1930. In contrast, the service sector never contributes more than 10.4% to male employment, and this is only by 1930. Combined with clerical work, the service sector contributes over 60% to female paid labour for all the years examined in this study, with this share rising from 63% in 1900 to 70% by 1930. Male wage-labour, on the other hand, is disproportionately represented in agriculture, fishing and logging, mining, construction, transportation, and finance. Of these occupations, agriculture, construction, and transportation are the most important to male paid employment. And, of these, only in transportation do women have more than a negligible representation.

It is not absolutely clear whether, overall, this changing distribution of female and male employment across occupations causes an increase in labour market segmentation between the sexes. In the hope of answering this question, we construct a Duncan index for occupations for 1900, 1920, and 1930. Our index numbers are 54.60, 52.15, and 54.57 for these years, respectively. Therefore it appears that, from 1900 to 1930, there is no apparent trend increase or decrease in the extent of labour market segmentation.[9]

5 Pay Inequality for All Industrial Sectors, 1930

The 1930 estimates discussed in this section are constructed from data on the number of weeks worked together with those for total earnings using the census data classified on the basis of the industrial classification. We find that the average ratio of female to male earnings per week for 1930 for all industrial sectors inclusive of manufacturing is 53 as compared to 50% for the manufacturing sector alone (Table 6). In the agricultural sector, however, women earn 86% of what men earn; in forestry, fishing, and trapping, 80%; in construction, 77%; and in mining, quarrying, oil, and salt wells, 76%. These sectors are all of little consequence to total female employment, however, and are of much greater importance to total male employment. On the other hand, the service sector, where the weekly earnings of women are only 41% of those of men, contributes over 50% to total female employment while adding less than 14% to total male employment (Table 6).

Once again one might pose the question, whether or not the degree of average pay inequality would have been less severe had the distribution of women amongst the various industrial sectors been identical to that of men while holding women's actual weekly earnings by sector constant. Under these conditions the pay ratio increases to only 58% from its actual 53%. Therefore, for 1930, only 10.6% of the degree of pay inequality can be "explained" away by the distribution of female employment by sector.

The service sector (of the industrial classification) is the most important sector to female employment and serves to pull the average earnings of women down. Given its significance to female employment, therefore,

Table 6 All industries: wage earners, income and pay ratios, 1930

	Sector share of labour			*Earnings per week*		
	Men (%)	*Women (%)*	*Female share per sector (%)*	*Men*	*Women*	*Female-male earnings ratio*
All industries	100	100	21.3	$22.6	$12.0	0.53
Agriculture	9.6	0.3	0.9	$7.3	$6.3	0.86
Forestry, fishing and trapping	2.9	0.1	0.5	$13.9	$11.1	0.80
Mining, quarrying, oil and salt wells	3.5	0.1	0.5	$24.9	$18.8	0.76
Manufacturing	24.9	20.4	18.2	$24.8	$12.5	0.50
Electric light and power	0.9	0.3	7.8	$31.5	$18.5	0.59
Construction	10.8	0.3	0.7	$21.2	$16.4	0.77
Transport and communication	12.9	4.3	8.3	$26.6	$16.4	0.62
Trade	10.2	14.1	27.4	$24.9	$13.6	0.55
– Retail	8.0	12.5	29.8	$22.7	$13.1	0.57
– Wholesale	2.1	1.6	17.1	$32.6	$17.2	0.53
Finance and insurance	2.8	4.6	31.2	$35.3	$17.8	0.51
Service	13.7	54.9	52.1	$25.6	$10.5	0.41
Unspecified	7.9	0.7	2.2	$12.0	$13.5	1.13
Total employees	1,947,957	528,457				

Source The Census of Canada, 1931, vol. 5, Table 27

it is important that we examine this sector's specific composition (Table 7). The sub-sector which dominates female employment in the service sector is personal service. It accounts for 56% of all women employed in the service sector and only 24% of all men. Its pay ratio is 36%. Within this sub-sector, private domestic service contributes 80% to total female employment in personal service, but only 18% to male employment. About 52% of male employment in this sub-sector is concentrated in hotels, restaurants, and taverns while this same category contributes only 15% to female employment and has a pay ratio of 50.5%. The public administration sub-sector is characterized by a pay ratio of 63%. But

Table 7 Services: male and female wage-earners, 10 years of age and over, 1930

	Sector Share of Labour		*Female sector share (%)*	*Earnings/week men (%)*	*Female-male earnings ratio*
	Men (%)	*Women (%)*			
All Services	100	100	52.1	25.6	0.41
Professional service	21.9	34.0	62.8	28.8	0.54
Accountancy, etc.	0.9	0.2	17.6	35.6	0.56
Applied science	1.1	0.2	14.4	35.9	0.53
Art and music	0.7	0.4	35.4	28.8	0.50
Art and trade assns.	0.2	0.1	31.2	49.3	0.39
Education	9.4	19.7	69.4	30.8	0.59
Health	3.7	9.1	73.0	22.4	0.48
Law	0.6	2.1	79.6	33.5	0.50
Literature, journ., and library services	0.1	0.3	76.7	26.8	0.70
Religion	4.4	0.6	12.9	26.0	0.42
Social welfare and charity org	0.8	1.4	66.7	23.5	0.49
Other	0.1	0.0	45.2	33.6	0.62
Public admin.	36.9	5.2	13.2	29.8	0.63
Federal and prov.	19.2	4.2	19.1	31.5	0.60
Municipal	17.6	1.0	5.7	27.5	0.67
Other	0.1	0.0	35.0	58.6	0.38
Custom and repair	11.6	3.5	24.8	19.6	0.56
Auto. repair	4.1	0.1	1.5	20.8	0.69
Blacksmithing	1.4	0.0	0.2	17.6	0.68
Boot and shoe	0.7	0.0	0.6	14.9	0.69
Custom tailoring	1.4	1.3	50.8	20.9	0.51
Dying, cleaning and pressing	1.0	0.4	32.0	20.9	0.60
Electrical	0.5	0.0	4.1	21.9	0.65
Laundries	2.0	1.7	47.6	18.2	0.59
Watch repair	0.1	0.0	3.2	20.2	0.69
Other	0.5	0.03	6.0	18.2	0.51

(continued)

Table 7 (continued)

	Sector Share of Labour		*Female sector share (%)*	*Earnings/week men (%)*	*Female-male earnings ratio*
	Men (%)	*Women (%)*			
Business services	1.3	0.5	29.3	37.0	0.47
Advertising	0.8	0.2	23.5	41.6	0.45
Auctioneering and valuing	0.06	0.01	17.6	28.8	0.52
Employment agencies	0.04	0.02	33.3	32.0	0.58
Other	0.4	0.2	38.8	29.9	0.53
Personal service	24.1	56.0	71.6	17.5	0.36
Barber and hairdressing	2.4	1.1	33.9	18.6	0.70
Hotels, rest. and taverns	12.5	8.2	41.7	17.4	0.51
Lodging and boarding houses	2.4	0.9	29.3	17.9	0.47
Photographers' shops	0.4	0.2	33.2	23.9	0.57
Private domestic service	4.4	44.9	91.8	15.5	0.36
Undertakers	0.3	0.0	6.6	25.0	0.70
Others	1.7	0.6	27.9	18.8	0.52
Recreation	4.2	0.8	16.4	25.4	0.52
Total employees	266,682	289,862			

Source Census of Canada, 1931, vol. 5 (Ottawa, 1935), Table 27

public administration contributes only 5% to female employment, whereas it adds 37% to male employment. The service sector's remaining three sub-sectors have pay ratios in the mid-fifties. The most important of these sub-sectors is professional services. It contributes 34% to female employment and 22% to male employment. With the concentration of women in personal service, the sub-sector with the worst pay ratio and with the lowest earnings for women, it is not surprising that had the percentage distribution of female employment within the service sector been identical to that of men, the pay ratio would have improved dramatically, rising from 41 to 57%. In the case of the service sector, 27% of the degree of pay inequality can be explained away by the different distribution of men and women among the various sub-sectors. Nevertheless, a substantial degree of pay inequality between the sexes remains to be accounted for, even if women had not been as concentrated in the lower paying service sector.

We have already noted that, in the case of the industrial classification, if female employment is distributed identically to male employment in 1930, the pay ratio increases from 53 to 58%. This, however, assumes a constant distribution of female employment within all industrial sectors. If we assume the hypothetical rate of pay for women for manufacturing and services constructed above - two industries which together contribute over 70% to female employment—the hypothetical pay ratio rises to 62% (Table 1). In this case, the structure of employment can be said to be responsible for 19% of the degree of pay inequality between the sexes in 1930 as opposed to only 11% when one assumes a constant distribution of female employment *within* all industrial sectors.

6 Pay Inequality for All Occupations, 1900–1930

Using the census data on occupations for 1900, 1920 and 1930 it is possible to construct pay ratios for all the major occupations listed in the various census reports. The average pay ratio increases rather insignificantly from 1920 to 1930, from 52 to 53%, after having increased from 46% in 1900 (Table 4). From 1900 to 1920 the pay ratio increases in agriculture, transportation and communication, finance, services, and clerical work. Together these occupations contribute 66% to total female employment in 1900 and 70% in 1920, whereas services and clerical work alone contribute 63 and 66% to female employment in 1900 and 1920, respectively. From 1900 to 1920, the pay ratio for clerical work, which by 1920 represents 22% of all female workers, increases by 23%. The service sector experiences an improvement in the pay ratio of 21% over this period, while contributing, by 1920, 43% of total female employment. Over the 1920–1930 period, the pay ratio decreases only in the agricultural, trade, and service occupations. However, this group of occupations employs about 59% of female workers and 29% of the men in 1930. And, in the service sector specifically, which employs 83% of the women in this group and 36% of the men, the pay ratio decreases by 15%.

Amongst clerical workers the pay ratio moves in women's favour by 13% from 1920 to 1930. This category employs 22% of female workers in 1930 and 6% of male workers. Amongst transportation workers, who comprise 3% of all female workers in 1930, and 11% of male workers, the pay ratio increases by 19%. The pay ratio amongst manufacturing workers, who represent 14% of all female workers and 15% of male workers, changed but little. General labourers, however, experience a large increase in their pay ratio of 33%, but as this occupation provides employment to only 2.2% of all women, it is hardly significant. Finally, in electrical light and power, which does not appear in the 1920 census, and in construction, where no women are employed in 1920, the pay ratio is found to be very much in favour of women by 1930. But again these occupations employ only a very, very few, much less than one percent, of female workers, and, the very high pay ratio for 1930 is a result of all the women in these occupations being in management positions. When these women are compared to men in similar sub-occupations, their pay ratio remains high, but it is, nevertheless, still in men's favour. The very high average pay ratios for these sectors are, therefore, statistical illusions, a mere result of the exceptionally differentiated occupational composition in these sectors between men and women (Altman and Lamontagne 1990, Appendix).

It is also possible to determine whether the differential occupational structure between men and women makes a significant contribution to the pay ratios which are generally so unfavourable to women for the three census years under consideration in this study. Had women occupied the same broadly defined occupational structure as men in 1920 and 1930, the average weekly pay of women would have been less than it actually was (Table 1). For 1900, however, the hypothetical rate of pay and, therefore, the hypothetical pay ratio would have been higher than the actual: 51 compared to 46% (Table 1). The fact that female and male labour is distributed quite differently between various occupational categories did little, if anything, to generate any significant degree of the pay inequality found to exist, on average, between women and men.

More details are available on the occupational structure for 1900 and 1930 than for 1920. The 1900 and 1930 census material provides specific information on 1,621 and 439 occupational categories, respectively.[10] Using estimates drawn from these data, we determine the extent to which women's labour, if it were distributed identically to men's across occupations, affects women's rate of pay. We find the effect to be positive, but minuscule for both years, yielding a hypothetical average monthly rate of pay of $17.9 as compared to an actual average of $17.0 in 1900, and a hypothetical weekly rate of pay of $12.1 as compared to the actual average of $12.0 in 1930. However, the hypothetical rates of pay are computed using data on occupations in which both men and women find employment. But since in 1900 and 1930 no women are employed in a number of occupations which employ 37 and 28%, respectively of all male workers, it can be argued that in both of these census years the absence of women from such occupations causes the low pay ratio.

This scenario assumes, of course, that these occupations are relatively very high paying, and that women who might have found employment in these occupations would have received a much higher pay rate than what they could earn in other occupations. We find that the average rate of pay to men in these "excluded" occupations is $42 per month as compared to $33 in other occupations in 1900, and $25 per week as compared to an average rate of pay of $21 in other occupations in 1930. The excluded occupations, therefore, are relatively high paying, with men earning 19% more than they earn in the other sectors by 1930 and 27% more in 1900. In 1900, the pay ratio of actual female earnings to that of men for those occupations in which both sexes are employed is 50%. This compares to a pay ratio of 46% when using the male earnings for all occupations in our computation. Comparable pay ratios for 1930 are 56.3% and 53.3%, respectively.

If we assume that women had been employed in the excluded occupations in the same proportion as men (37 and 28% for 1900 and 1930, respectively), and had earned 50 and 56% of male earnings in these occupations in 1900 and 1930, respectively (the actual female-male pay ratio for these years, respectively), then the female rate of pay in the excluded sectors in 1900 and 1930 would have been $21 per month and $14 per week, respectively. The average rate of pay of women inclusive of excluded occupations, would have been $18.48 and $12.6, respectively. The actual average pay rates in those occupations employing women, on the other hand, are $17 and $12, respectively. Clearly, neither the structure of employment, nor the absence of women from certain occupations, can be argued to be a major source of pay inequality between men and women in either the 1900 or 1930 census years even when the relatively more narrowly defined occupations are examined.

Our estimates based on the occupational data reveal that, although the average pay ratio changes little from 1920 to 1930, a majority of women suffered a deterioration in their pay relative to that of men. Conversely, the position of women did improve somewhat over the 1900–1920 period. Moreover, the major source of pay inequality is found in the inequality within the occupational categories examined in this study. This stands in marked contrast to the idea that this inequality was primarily a product of the ghettoization of women into certain low paying occupations. This result is not inconsistent with our findings using the industrial data for the economy as a whole for 1930 and for manufacturing for 1900, 1910, 1915, and 1930. Moreover, these findings are similar to Claudia Goldin's (1986, pp. 578–579; 1990, ch. 3) for the United States for the years 1890 and 1970.

7 Occupational Change Over Time

Although we find that the differential distribution of female and male labour in a particular year cannot account for much of the pay gap, it is possible that the changing distribution of female and male labour over time is in part responsible for some of the pay inequality found to exist between the sexes. In Table 8, following Claudia Goldin's example (1986, pp. 578–584; 1990, p. 64), we attempt to determine the extent to which changes in occupational distribution, as opposed to changes in relative rates of pay, are responsible for the reduction in pay inequality. One assumes a constant rate of pay for men and women for a particular year down every column in Table 8, and, across every row, one assumes a constant distribution of labour amongst occupations. The first row presents the pay ratios for the actual distributions of labour and rates of

Table 8 Female to male pay ratios for occupations, 1900–1930

Wage distribution	*1900 (%)*	*1920 (%)*	*1930 (%)*
1. Actual	45.8	52.2	53.2
2. FM1900	45.8	48.1	50.4
3. FM1920	49.4	52.2	55.3
4. FM1930	49.6	52.8	53.2
5. F1920 M1900	49.6	52.5	55.5
6. F1930 M1900	49.1	51.6	54.9
7. F1900 M1920	45.6	47.8	50.3
8. F1900 M1930	46.3	48.8	48.8

Source Table 4

pay. In rows 2–4, pay ratios at alternative distributions of labour found for 1900, 1920, and 1930 are presented. In rows 5–8, pay ratios at alternative distributions of female relative to male labour for these years are displayed. So in row 5, for example, the pay ratios are a product of assuming the 1920 female and 1900 male distribution of labour while varying the rates of pay across census years. In columns 1–3, pay ratios at alternative rates of pay found in 1900, 1920, and 1930 are also presented. The results, discussed below, illustrated in Table 8, are summarized in Table 9.

Row 1 of Table 8 reveals that the pay ratio actually increased by 7.4 percentage points from 1900 to 1930, increasing from 45.8 to 52.2%. Moving across row 2 to column 3 (holding the occupational structure of women and men to what it was in 1900), the pay ratio increases by 4.64 percentage points. This is the contribution of women's rate of pay, increasing relative to men's, to the reduction in pay inequality. Moving from rows 2 to row 4 increases the pay ratio from 50.4 to 53.2% or by 2.8 percentage points. This represents the contribution of the changing occupational structure, from 1900 to 1930, to the increase in the pay ratio. Thus, over this 30 year period, occupational change contributed 35% to the reduction of pay inequality. The rest of the increase was due to women's relative rate of pay improving within occupations. One should note, however, that occupational change from 1920 to 1930 (row 3, column 3 to row 4, column 3) served to reduce the increase in the pay ratio, which moved from 52.2 to 53.2%, from what it would have been otherwise. Occupational change in this decade thus reduced the net positive impact which occupational change had on the pay ratio over the entire 1900–1930 period.

From row 1 in Table 8, the pay ratio increased by 6.4 percentage points from 1900 to 1920, rising from 45.8 to 52.2%. Thus, 86% of the improvement of the pay ratio which took place from 1900 to 1930 took place in the first two decades of the twentieth century. Moving across row 2 to the second column yields the contribution which changing women's wage relative to men's wage from 1900 to 1920 made to the increase in pay inequality given the 1900 occupational structure. This contribution amounts to 2.4 percentage points. Moving down to row 3 yields the contribution which the changing occupational structure from 1900 to 1920 made to increasing the pay ratio . Occupational change lent 4.0 percentage points or 63% to the reduction in pay inequality which took place from 1900 to 1920.

Table 9 A partition of the change in the pay ratio between changes in relative male and female pay rates and changes in the occupational structure of women and men

A1	Change in the pay ratio from 1900 to 1930	= 7.4
	The partition (occupations changing simultaneously for both genders):	
	1. $(\alpha FM1900_{W1930}) - (\alpha FM1900_{W1900})$	= 4.64
	2. $(\alpha FM1930_{W1930}) - (\alpha FM1900_{W1930})$	= 2.79
	3. Total	= 7.43
A2	The partition (occupations changing for one gender relative to the other):	
	1. $(\alpha FM1900_{W1930}) - (\alpha FM1900_{W1900})$	= 4.64
	2. $(\alpha F1930) - (\alpha FM1900_{W1930})$	= 4.52
	$M1900_{W1930}$	
	3. $(\alpha F1900) - (\alpha FM1900_{W1930})$	= −1.59
	$M1930_{W1930}$	
	4. (3 + 2)	= 2.93
	5. Total	= 7.6
B1	Change in the pay ratio from 1900 to 1920	= 6.35
	The partition (occupations changing simultaneously for both genders):	
	1. $(\alpha FM1900_{W1920}) - (\alpha FM1900_{W1900})$	= 2.35
	2. $(\alpha FM1920_{W1920}) - (\alpha FM1900_{W1920})$	= 4.02
	3. Total	= 6.37
B2	The partition (occupations changing for one gender relative to the other):	
	1. $(\alpha FM1900_{W1920}) - (\alpha FM1900_{W1900})$	= 2.35
	2. $(\alpha FM1920) - (\alpha FM1900_{W1920})$	= 4.39
	$M1900_{W1920}$	
	3. $(\alpha FM1900) - (\alpha FM1900_{W1920})$	= −0.33
	$M1920_{W1920}$	
	4. (3 + 2)	= 4.06
	5. Total	= 6.41

Sources and notes Table 8 and text. Differences between the totals and the actual percentage points of change in the pay ratio is due to rounding. Row one measures the contribution of changes in the rates of pay over time of women relative to men to changes in the pay ratio. Row two in A1 and B1 and rows two to four in A2 and B2 measure the contribution of occupational change to changes in the pay ratio. α refers to occupational structure. W refers to the rate of pay. F and M refer to females and males respectively. The terms immediately following sigma refer to particular rows in Table 8 whereas the subscript terms refer to particular columns in Table 8

Clearly, the changing occupational structure played a large role in reducing pay inequality from 1900 to 1930, especially in the smaller 1900–1920 period. Thus, occupational change dominates the reduction in pay inequality during the period when the Duncan Index indicates some abatement in labour market segmentation (55–52). In contrast, from 1920 to 1930, just when the Duncan Index indicates an increase in labour market segmentation (52–55), the changing occupational structure makes a negative contribution to changes in income inequality. And improvements in the pay ratio from 1920 to 1930 are entirely due to changes in relative rates of pay. In this case, increasing labour market segmentation is found to be positively related to increasing pay inequality. However, since over the entire 1900–1930 period the Duncan index experienced no trend change, one cannot argue that changes in labour market segmentation is what caused the reduction in pay inequality which took place from 1900 to 1930. Rather, the changing occupational structure which changed in a similar fashion for both men and women (hence no change in the Duncan index), in addition to improvements in the pay ratio of women to men within the same occupations, is what generates the increase in pay equality that transpired in the period under study.

So far we have examined the effect of changing the occupational structure of men and women simultaneously. Rows 5 through 9, in Table 8, deal with the possible impact of changing the occupational structure for women relative to men, thereby allowing for a partitioning of the impact of occupational change on the pay ratio between occupational change amongst women, and men. It is evident from row 6, column 3, that simply changing the female occupational structure to what it was in 1930, while holding the male occupational structure to what it was in 1900, serves to increase the pay ratio significantly by 4.5 percentage points as compared to the pay ratio that emerges when both sexes are characterized by their 1900 occupational distributions and their 1930 incomes. Changing income alone increases the pay ratio by 4.6 percentage points (row 2). On the other hand, changing the male occupational structure to its 1930 distribution, while holding the female occupational structure to its 1900 distribution (row 8, column 3), reduces the pay ratio by 1.59 percentage points. Changing the male occupational distribution, therefore, serves to partially neutralize the positive impact that the changing female occupational distribution has in reducing pay inequality.

Similarly, from rows 5 and 7, it is possible to determine the significance of changes in female and male occupational structure to the decline in pay inequality over the 1900–1920 period. The change in female occupational structure contributes 4.4 percentage points to the reduction in pay inequality given the 1920 rate of pay for women and men. Changing the rates of pay alone from their 1900 to their 1920 levels increases the pay ratio by 2.4 percentage points. The change in the male occupational structure once again serves to increase pay inequality, but the increase in this period is only negligible.

These results are similar to those for the United States. In her work, Goldin (1986, p. 579; 1990, pp. 64, 76–77) finds that for the 1890/1900 to 1930 period, occupational change *over time* explains away about 28% of the increase in the pay ratio. Just as in Canada, in the context of little change in labour market segmentation, occupational change contributes to the reduction in income inequality between the sexes in the United States. However, one difference between the American and the Canadian experience appears to be that occupational change in the United States did not decrease pay inequality as much as in Canada where it contributes 38% to the reduction in pay inequality from 1900 to 1930 and 63% from 1900 to 1920 (from Table 9). Clearly, for both Canada and the United States, although providing women with the male occupational structure in a given point in time would do little to reduce pay inequality, occupational change over time, quite unrelated to a reduction in labour market segmentation, played a critical role in reducing pay inequality between women and men.

8 The Clericalization of Female Employment

We have already discussed the growing importance of clerical work to female employment.[11] We now exploit pay estimates constructed for clerical work to establish if the "clericalization" of female work contributed to the relatively low average rate of female pay over the 1900–1930 period. In 1900, the pay ratio for clerical work in Canada is 53.52%. In this year, clerical work was of similar importance to both female and male employment. By 1920, when clerical work contributes 23% to female employment but only 9% to male employment, the pay ratio for clerical work is 62.9% and women earn a weekly rate of pay of $15.85 in this occupation (Table 4).

It is useful to determine what the average pay ratio in 1920 for all occupations together would have been had the proportional contribution of clerical work to total female employment been identical to that of men. We begin by establishing the average weekly earnings of women for all sectors net of the contribution of clerical work. This equals $10.67 (from Table 4). Thus by our estimates female clerical workers earn about 50% more than women in other sectors. We then assume that only 8.55% of the women are employed in clerical work (the male distribution of employment), and that these women earn $15.85 per week (the female rate of pay). The remaining employed women (91.45%) are assumed to have earned $10.67 per week. This yields a hypothetical rate of pay for women of $11.11 as compared to the actual rate of pay of $11.87. This, in turn, generates a hypothetical average pay ratio of 48.8% as compared to the actual pay ratio for 1920 of 52.2%. Clerical work in 1920, therefore, clearly made a positive, albeit small, contribution to the average rate of pay of women.

A similar scenario can be constructed with the 1930 data. For this year the pay ratio for clerical work is 71%, with women earning an average of $17.26 in this job category. We then assume that only 6.16% of the women are engaged in clerical work (identical to the male percentage) and further assume that these women earn the female income for clerical work. We then assume that women not engaged in clerical work would have earned their actual average rate of pay of $10.50 (from Table 4). In 1930, therefore, female clerical workers were earning 64% more than women in other occupations. Under these assumptions, the average weekly income of all women is $10.91 in contrast to their actual earnings of $12.01. Finally, this hypothetical earnings estimate for women generates a hypothetical pay ratio of 49.5% compared to the actual pay ratio for 1930 of 53.22%.

The disproportionate number of women engaged in clerical work at this time then serves to reduce the degree of income inequality between men and women from what it might otherwise have been. This reduction, however, should not be exaggerated. Nevertheless, what is important here is that women's gradual domination of clerical work, which contributed towards labour market segmentation, did not, thereby, serve to depress female earnings.[12]

Our estimates on clerical work for 1920 and 1930 also show that the share of women in clerical work increased as the number of women employed in this occupation grew by 78% while the number of men employed fell by 2.5% (Table 4). Moreover, the pay ratio for clerical work increased from 63 to 71% from 1920 to 1930. This decrease in pay inequality took place in the context of the nominal rate of pay for female clerical workers increasing by 8.9%, and that of male clerical workers decreasing by 3.3% from 1920 to 1930. Thus, women's increasing presence in clerical work did not take place as a result of the increasing cheapness of female clerical workers relative to that of male clerical workers. Rather, women's successful employment gains in this occupation are consistent with the increasingly expensive nature of female clerical labour. Our findings, therefore, do not support the hypothesis that women's employment gains in this occupation are due to their relative cheapness and that women in this occupation constituted a pool of cheap labour.[13] It was, of course, the movement of women into this relatively well paid female-dominated occupation that, while doing nothing to reduce labour market segmentation, comprised part of the occupational change over time which contributed so much to the reduction of pay inequality.

9 Conclusion

Our estimates for the manufacturing sector show that there was little trend reduction in pay inequality over the 1900–1930 period. Thus, by 1930, women were not much better off, relative to men, than they were in 1900. On the other hand, our estimates for all occupations show that, at least on average, women witness a more substantial improvement in their compensation for market-related work relative to men from 1900 to 1930. This improvement over time, particularly from 1900 to 1920 when the decline in pay inequality is most marked, proves to be due to a large extent to the changing distribution of female employment relative to the male distribution, and this changing distribution of labour coincides with a small reduction in job segmentation from 1900 to 1920. On the other hand, from 1920 to 1930, a slight decrease in pay inequality for all occupations parallels an increase in job segmentation. In the manufacturing sector, a large decrease in job segmentation coincides with an increase in pay inequality from 1915 to 1930. Thus we find that changes in the extent of job segmentation per se did not motivate changes in income inequality.

We also find that an increasing concentration of female labour in clerical work as compared to male labour proved to be advantageous to women in the period under study. Clerical work was relatively well paid by

1920 and 1930, and prevented the degree of pay inequality from being any greater than it already was. Nevertheless, by 1930, women are still far behind men, as the pay ratio only increases from 46 to 53% from 1900 to 1930. The dismal state of employed women in Canada was not much different from that of their American counterparts. In comparison, the American pay ratio for all sectors is only marginally higher at 56% in 1930, increasing from a pay ratio of 46.3% in 1890 (Goldin 1986, p. 581).

Our results cannot indicate the ultimate cause of pay inequality in Canada in the 1900–1930 period. However, our results show unambiguously that pay inequality between the sexes permeated all industries, occupations, and sectors of the Canadian economy. Pay inequality between the sexes is not found to be concentrated in specific industries, occupations, or sectors where female labour was relatively predominant. Occupational segmentation is found to be responsible for, at most, 19% of the pay gap between the sexes in any given year. However, by demonstrating that pay inequality in Canada was not a product of labour market segmentation with respect to the relatively broadly defined industrial and occupational sectors traditionally referred to in the literature, our results in no way refute the hypothesis that pay inequality was to a large extent due to labour market segmentation within those industries and occupations examined in this study. Unfortunately, the occupational and industry-based data examined in this study are not detailed enough to test this important hypothesis.

Notes

1. Estimates for the 1980s are derived from Statistics Canada (1984, pp. 117–118; 1987, pp. 126–127). See Gunderson (1979, p. 481, Table 1) for 1970 and Ostry (1968, p. 40) for 1960. For a summary of estimates of Canadian female/male wage differentials see Gunderson (1985, p. 229).
2. Strong-Boag (1979, pp. 147–149), presents some census estimates on annual and weekly earnings of women for 1920 and 1930. Our estimates, particularly for 1930, are much more detailed.
3. These findings speak against the dominant historiographical school in Canadian women's history which holds that the existence of the wage differential in any particular year can be attributed primarily to "ghettoization" (see Armstrong and Armstrong 1984; Strong-Boag 1979, pp. 137, 139–140; 1988, pp. 21, 42, 51–53, 56, 65; Cohen 1988, pp. 24, 26–27, 135–137, 145, 158; Lowe 1986,1987).

4. See Gunderson (1989, p. 49) for a discussion of the empirical and analytical importance of distinguishing between broadly and narrowly defined occupations when discussing the impact of occupational segmentation on pay inequality.
5. For further details on the framework for reconstructing the census material see Altman (1989).
6. Individuals on wages are distinguished from individuals on salary in that the latter, according to the census definitions, encompass those individuals who are managers, officers and salesmen, and owners and partners of an establishment. Earnings estimates for those on salary would not accurately reflect comparable earnings per unit of time, since individuals on salary encompass both workers and employers. Therefore, it is possible that any significant pay gap between men and women on salary would be a reflection of a larger percentage of men being employers as compared to women. And, any pay gap between women on salary and women on wages could be a product of higher returns to those women on salary who are employers.
7. Men's share of the adult population engaged in manufacturing is 94.3, 91.1, and 89.7% for the years 1900, 1910, and 1915, respectively (Altman and Lamontagne 1990).
8. Goldin (1990, p. 80) finds that the Duncan index for U.S. manufacturing in 1900 and 1960 is 60.8 and 33.3, respectively.
9. The Duncan index in the U.S. for all occupations is apparently 66 in 1900 and appears to remain at that level to 1950 (Goldin 1990, pp. 75–76).
10. For the detailed estimates upon which our computations are based see Altman and Lamontagne (1990, Appendix).
11. Lowe's (1987, p. 49) estimates of female and male clerical workers for the 1890–1970 period also suggest a trend increase in importance of clerical work to women.
12. These findings run contrary to Lowe (1987, pp. 59, 144, 150, 163), who argues that the clericalization of female work served to depress average wages in Canada or that clerical work was characterized by relatively low wages in the period under study. For the United States, Goldin (1990, p. 107) finds, "The ratio of female to male earnings in the clerical sector rose from 0.49 in 1890 to 0.71 by 1930 ... and the increase served to buoy the average ratio of female to male earnings in the economy."
13. Rotella (1981, p. 57) makes this argument with reference to the American case.

References

Altman, M. 1989. A Framework for Organizing the Manufacturing Census Material, 1870–1910. Discussion Paper No. 88-04. Department of Economics, University of Saskatchewan, Saskatoon, Canada.

Altman, M., and L. Lamontagne. 1990. Aspects of Female Employment and Pay Inequality in Canada, 1900–1930. Discussion Paper No. 90-04. Department of Economics, University of Saskatchewan, Saskatoon, Canada.

Armstrong, P., and H. Armstrong. 1984. *The Double Ghetto: Canadian Women and Their Segregated Work*, revised ed. Toronto: McClelland and Stewart.

Bertram, G.W. 1964. Historical Statistics on Growth and Structure of Manufacturing in Canada, 1870–1957. In *Conferences on Statistics, 1962 and 1963*, ed. J. Henripin and A. Asimakopulos, 93–146. Toronto: University of Toronto Press.

Cohen, M.G. 1988. *Women's Work, Markets, Economic Development in Nineteenth-Century Ontario.* Toronto: University of Toronto Press.

Cook, R., and M. Mitchinson, eds. 1976. *The Proper Share, Women's Place in Canadian Society.* Toronto: Oxford University Press.

Denton, F.T., and S. Ostry. 1967. *Historical Estimates of the Canadian Labour Force*, 1961. Census Monograph Programme. Ottawa: Dominion Bureau of Statistics.

Dominion Bureau of Statistics. 1935. *Occupational Trends in Canada*, 1891–1931. Ottawa.

Fuchs, V.R. 1988. *Women's Quest for Economic Equality.* Cambridge, MA and London: Harvard University Press.

Goldin, C. 1986. The Female Labor Force and American Economic Growth, in Long-Term Factors in American Economic Growth. In *National Bureau of Economic Research, Studies in Income and Wealth*, vol. 51, ed. S.L. Engerman and R.E. Gallman, 557–604. Chicago and London: University of Chicago Press.

Goldin, C. 1990. *Understanding the Gender Gap: An Economic History of American Women.* New York and Oxford: Oxford University Press.

Gunderson, M. 1979. Decomposition of the Male/Female Earnings Differential: Canada 1970. *Canadian Journal of Economics/Revue canadienne d'Économique* 12: 479–484.

Gunderson, M. 1985. Discrimination, Equal Pay, and Equal Opportunities in the Labour Market. In *Work and Pay: The Canadian Labour Market*, ed. W.C. Riddell, 219–265. Toronto: University of Toronto Press for the McDonald Commission.

Gunderson, M. 1989. Male-Female Wage Differentials and Policy Responses. *Journal of Economic Literature* 27: 46–72.

Lowe, G. 1986. Women, Work and the Office: The Feminization of Clerical Occupations in Canada, 1901–1931. In *Rethinking Canada, the Promise of*

Women's History, ed. V. Strong-Boag and A.C. Fellman, 107–122. Toronto: Copp Clark Pitman.

Lowe, G. 1987. *Women in the Administrative Revolution*. Toronto: University of Toronto Press.

Ostry, S. 1968. *The Female Worker in Canada*. Ottawa: Queen's Printer.

Reskin, B.E., and H.I. Hartmann, eds. 1986. *Women's Work, Men's Work, Sex Segregation on the Job*. Washington, DC: National Academy Press.

Rotella, E.J. 1981. The Transformation of the American Office: Changes in Employment and Technology. *Journal of Economic History* 41: 51–57.

Statistics Canada. 1984. *Income Distribution by Size in Canada*, 1982. Ottawa.

Statistics Canada. 1987. *Income Distribution by Size in Canada*, 1986. Ottawa.

Strong-Boag, V. 1979. The Girl of the New Day: Canadian Working Women in the 1920s. *Labour/le travailleur* 4: 131–164.

Strong-Boag, V. 1988. *The New Day Recalled: Lives of Girls and Women in English Canada, 1919–1939*. Toronto: Penguin Books Canada.

CHAPTER 14

On the Natural Intelligence of Women: How the Feminization of Clerical Work Contributed to Gender Pay Equality in Early Twentieth Century Canada (With Louise Lamontagne)

1 Introduction

This article examines some of the more pertinent details of the feminization of clerical work in the context of early twentieth century Canada and the impact that this had upon gender pay inequality. More generally, we address the question of the conditions under which labor market segmentation, such as the feminization of clerical work, can be expected to adversely affect the relative pay of women. To this end new labor market and related estimates for Canada are developed. The Canadian economy experienced significant economic change during the first three decades of the twentieth century. Output and population grew at unprecedented rates while agriculture became less important, Canada's urban population surpassed its rural and, as well, new forms of business organization were implemented in both the private and public sectors alike (Altman 2001a). It was during these times of dramatic economic and social change that the structure of Canadian women's market employment was transformed in fundamentally important ways. During the 1900–1930 period clerical work became the occupation of choice for a growing percentage of female

M. Altman, *Lessons from a Successfully Export-Oriented, Resource-Rich Economy*, https://doi.org/10.1007/978-3-031-03887-7_14

labor force participants and, in turn, clerical work became increasingly feminized.

A critical finding of this article is that the movement of women into clerical work in the early part of the twentieth century, and the subsequent 'feminization' of the occupation, did not result in increasing the gender pay gap in Canada. Instead, it reduced this gap as women's pay in clerical work increased sharply relative to men's from 1900 to 1930. Since clerical work was consistently the highest paying occupation for women apart from those occupations employing a minuscule percentage of the female labor force, by moving into clerical work, and thereby 'feminizing' it, women contributed towards reducing the gender pay gap, even as the feminization of clerical work contributed towards increasing labor market segmentation or the differential employment of men and women across occupations. In other words, contrary to what leading scholars have argued, labor market segmentation need not contribute to a deterioration of the gender pay ratio against women. The example of the feminization of clerical work in Canada is a case in point. More and more women were simply finding employment in a well-paid occupation, albeit women were paid less than men here as they were in all major occupations.

In the traditional labor market segmentation models women are forced into low wage occupations—women have no choice in the matter—thereby producing persistent gender pay gaps between women and men.[1] But in economies where women have acquired the legal and social capabilities to seek and choose employment opportunities, as was true of both Canada and the United States and most of Western Europe by the early twentieth century, we argue that women can be expected to seek employment where wages and other pecuniary and non-pecuniary benefits are greatest. Whether or not this results in more or less labor market segmentation critically depends on the distribution of relative benefits between women and men across sectors. Moreover, we argue that the existence or absence of labor market segmentation does not necessarily speak to the existence or absence of labor market discrimination. Discrimination, where it exists, often lurks in the shadows of any particular manifestation of labor market segmentation.

Since women were paid less than men, a literal reading of our estimates might suggest that by employing more and more women, employers were simply hiring the relatively low-priced labor. In the process, therefore, clerical work was transformed from its relatively high wage standing, for men and women combined in 1900, into an average wage occupation by 1930, all the while remaining a high-wage occupation for women. The picture we seek to paint, however, is far more complex. The very nature of clerical work was transformed over the course of the 1900–1930 period. It changed from being a relatively insignificant occupation flush with relatively highly skilled men in 1900 to one of increasing importance to employment in Canadian by 1930. By then clerical work consisted of a whole gamut of new job types characterized by different skill levels and was no longer heavily weighted by elite high paying jobs. Both men and women were being employed in the growing number of clerical positions that, as should be expected, were not at the top of the skill and pay hierarchy. And since most new jobs were not at the top of the pay scale, the relative weight of high paying jobs fell which meant that average pay across the many jobs types that comprised clerical work, was bound to fall. Moreover, it is not at all clear from the evidence that women represented a supply of cheap labor. What is unequivocally clear, however, is that the jobs a large number of women were hired into served to increase their pay relative to what was earned by male clerical workers, on average. In addition, what women earned as clerical workers, lifted them above the average pay rates of a third of all male employees in the Canadian economy.

These findings run contrary to the dominant historiographical school in Canadian women's history which is dominated by the view that labor market segmentation was largely responsible for women's relatively low rates of pay at the turn of the twentieth century and that the feminization of clerical work contributed to the inferior position of women in the labor market.[2] Nevertheless, our results are consistent with the most rigorous empirical work for early twentieth century United States (Goldin 1987) and with comparable results for advanced market economies where countries with the most labor market segmentation, such as Sweden and Norway, are characterized by the least gender pay inequality (Rosenfeld and Kalleberg 1990, pp. 88–89). Thus, evidence of labor market segmentation or increases thereof is no proof, in itself, of the inferior economic status of women. In addition, the most recent research on the subject shows that the female-male gender pay ratio improved in Canada in the first three decades of the twentieth century, increasing from 0.46 to 0.53, in spite of the fact that during this period there was no reduction in the significant amount of labor market segmentation prevalent at the time (Table 1).

Table 1 Gender pay inequality in Canada, 1900–1930

	Female/Male earnings	*Female weekly earnings*	*Duncan Dissimi-larity Index*
	All occupations		
1900	45.80%	$3.80	54.6
1920	52.20%	$11.90	52.2
1930	53.20%	$12.00	54.6

Source Altman and Lamontagne (1996)

The Duncan Index of Dissimilarity, a basic measure of differences in the distribution of labor by group, suggests that by 1930, with a Duncan Index of 55, 55% of women would have had to change occupations for there to have been no labor market segmentation.[3] There was no change in this important measure of labor market segmentation over the course of the 1900–1930 period. In addition, we find that the feminization of clerical work contributed to both reducing pay inequality and increasing labor market segmentation. Had clerical work not been feminized, the labor market would have been less segmented (the Duncan Index would have been lower), but the gender pay gap would not have been reduced to the extent that it was. Over the 1900–1930 period, occupational change played a large role in reducing the pay gap, without affecting the extent of labor market segmentation, as women moved into relatively high wage occupations, such as clerical work, be they female or male dominated.[4] Moveover, Meltz (1965) constructs estimates for the Canadian labor force which reveal that the movement of women into clerical work continued from 1930 to 1960 such that clerical work's share of the female labor force rose from 18 to 29% and women's contribution to this occupation increased from 45 to 62%. Over this period, women's rate of pay compared to men's also remained the highest of all occupations that were of importance to women. In addition, the rate of pay for female clerical workers remained far above the average female rate of pay. Most recent research on the Canadian labor market also finds that labor market segmentation has little effect on gender pay inequality. Rather, at the close of the twentieth century, Canada's gender pay is largely explained by within occupation pay inequality (Baker and Fortin 1999; Fortin and Huberman 2002).

2 Clerical Work in Context

An appreciation of the state of women in the American labor market at the turn of the century helps place the Canadian example in context. In the United States, women's share of clerical work increased dramatically from 1880 to 1890 from 4.4 to 19% and again from 1890 to 1900 to 30%. By 1920, women comprised 49% of clerical workers and by 1930, 53%. Over this entire period clerical work increased its share of the non-agricultural labor force from 1.7 to 9.7%. It is important to note that even as clerical work became ever more important to female employment, women's share of employment changed only by a few percentage points from 1900 to 1930, increasing from 18 to 22%. In 1910 and 1920, their share of employment stood at 21 and 20% respectively. Related to this is the percent of women in the labor force which increased somewhat from 19 to 22% from 1900 to 1930, while the percent of men in the labor force actually decreased from 80 to 76% over this period (Carter et al. 1997, Series 11–25). Therefore, the growing importance of clerical work in the American economy and especially to female workers took place in the context of a relatively stable gender split in the labor force and represented a restructuring of female employment in favor of office work.

With regards to the pay of American clerical workers, Claudia Goldin (1986, p. 581; 1987, p. 107) also finds that the female-male pay ratio in the clerical sector increased from 0.49 to 0.71 from 1890 to 1930, contributing to the overall increase in the American gender pay ratio in this period from 0.46 to 0.56. In the same vein Strom (1992, p. 10) argues, with regards to American clerical work: "Office jobs were the best jobs available to most women between 1900 and 1930. Women understood this and made rational choices for the future by investing in commercial education and taking office jobs...office work despite it gendered limits, could open the door to a wide world." And again (Strom, 1992, p. 205): "Most observers in the teens and twenties agreed that the average wage-earning woman fared better in office work than in other kinds of nonprofessional employment. The hours were shorter, the pay better, and vacations and sick days were usually offered to workers whose tenure on the job was long enough."[5] There appears to be a strong consensus that clerical work was the occupation of choice for women in America who possessed the requisite skills. Yet these scholars also hold that these women represented a supply of cheap labor to firms searching for clerical workers in the United States. Thus, Elyce Rotella (1981) argues that this dramatic transformation of America's female labor force was largely a product of technical change, dominated by the development of the typewriter, which required firm-general skills. This generated a dramatic increase in the demand for the "abundant supply of cheap female labor." Women, on the other hand, sought clerical work because "...wages and working conditions were superior to most other jobs that women could hope to hold."

Women's share of employment increased marginally in Canada from 1900 to 1930 from 19 to 21%, not unlike its American counterpart. In 1920, women's share in employment in Canada was already at 21%. During the 1900–1930 period, the percentage of women in the labor force increased from 16.5 to 22%. Most of this increase took place prior to the First World War. By 1910, women's labor force participation rate stood at 19%, increasing to 20% a decade later.[6] Women's increasing share of employment was due to their employment growing somewhat faster than men's in the first two decades of the twentieth century: 4.8 as compared to 4.0%. In the 1920s, there was no difference between women's and men's employment growth (Table 3). Obviously, the First World War had no large lasting impact on women's contribution to market labor in Canada, just as in the United States, this in spite of the contemporary contre temps about the onslaught of women on the bastions of male employment during the war years (Brown and Cook 1974, pp. 240–241; Lowe 1987, pp. 64–69). Nevertheless, the number of female wage earners more than tripled in the first three decades of the twentieth century in Canada. But, of course, this very large increase in female employment must be placed in the context of a similar almost three-fold increase in the number of male wage earners during this period (Table 2a). By comparison, during this same period, female employment in the United States only doubled.[7]

Although there was no dramatic increase in Canadian women's labor force participation rate or in their share of employment, the structure of female employment in Canada underwent significant change in the 1900–1930 period. Most importantly, there was a dramatic growth in female employment in both the trade and clerical occupations. At the turn of the century, trade employed less than 1% of women and women contributed only 2% to this occupation's overall employment. By 1930 it contributed about 10% to female employment and women made up close to a quarter of the workers in this occupation. In contrast, trade contributed between 8 and 9% to male employment throughout the 1900–1930 period. The movement of women into clerical work was even more dramatic. This line of work, which employed 7% of male wage earners in 1900 and over 6% in 1930, employed 8% of all female wage earners in 1900 and 22% by 1930. In addition, women's share of clerical work increased from 21 to 48% over this thirty year period. Canada's clerical occupational sector was clearly in the process of being feminized. It is important to note that women's share in both of these occupations, especially in clerical work, far exceeded their representation in total employment. This reflected one of the most important aspects of structural change in employment taking place during the 1900–1930 period. Yet in spite of these changes, the service occupation was consistently the most important one for female employment throughout the 1900–1930 period, employing close to 50% of all women in 1930. At the turn of the century the service sector employed 56% of all women. In addition, the majority of workers in service work were women. In contrast, this sector employed no more than 10% of all men. By 1930, the service, trade, and clerical occupational sectors together accounted for 80% of female employment. Another important sector for women was the manufacturing occupational sector, which contributed about 14% to the total, similar to its contribution to male employment. By 1930, however, manufacturing's contribution to both male and female employment had fallen dramatically from its 1900 level. In contrast to the above sectors, women were absent or all but absent in the fishing and logging, mining, electrical light and power, and construction occupational categories, which, together, made noticeable contributions to male employment (Tables 2a, 2b, 3).

Most of these structural changes to female employment took place in the 1900–1920 period, a time of rapid growth in the economy in terms of output, productivity, employment, and population, much of it fueled by Canada's export wheat boom which took off in the late 1890s. Indeed, Canada's per capita growth rate for this period led all of the then industrializing countries, while its employment growth rate approached 3% which was far above the American growth rate of less than 2%. Canada's population also increased at a fast pace, almost doubling in the 1900–1930 period, while its urban population almost tripled from over 2 million to 6.3 million. By 1931 about 54% of its population was urban compared to 37% in 1901 and 20% in 1870, following Confederation (Table 4). The urban population provided the supply to meet the rapidly increasing demand for non-agricultural labor, including clerical workers. Overall, sustained and rapid growth took place in Canada throughout most of the

Table 2a All occupations: number and distribution of wage earners, 1900–1930

	Number employed						*Sector share of labour employed*						*Share of women per sector*		
	1900		*1920*		*1930*		*1900*		*1920*		*1930*				
	Men	*Women*	*Men*	*Women*	*Men*	*Women*	*Men*	*Women*	*Men*	*Women*	*Men*	*Women*	*1900*	*1920*	*1930*
All occupations	664,448	153,478	1,464,364	392,631	1,975,200	528,462	100%	100%	100%	100%	100%	100%	18.80%	21.10%	21.10%
Agriculture	72,696	92	144,957	692	191,100	1548	10.9	0.1	9.9	0.2	9.7	0.3	0.1	0.5	0.8
Fishing & logging	23,808	0	42,823	0	50,300	42	3.6	0	2.9	0	2.6	0.01	0	0	0.1
Mining	23,898	0	44,465	0	81,500	5	3.6	0	3	0	4.1	0	0	0	0.01
Manufacturing	169,965	49,658	255,676	76,813	302,600	73,989	25.6	32.4	17.4	19.6	15.3	14	22.6	23.1	19.7
Electrical, light & power	0	0	0	0	32,000	3	0	0	0	0	1.6	0	0	0	0.01
Construction	56,036	4	117,661	0	160,300	89	8.4	0	8	0	8.1	0.02	0.01	0	0.1
Transportation	48,054	4633	165,624	14,701	218,500	16,587	7.2	3	11.3	3.7	11.1	3.1	8.8	8.2	7.1
Trade	55,525	1024	115,768	39,886	180,300	52,520	8.4	0.7	7.9	10.2	9.1	9.9	1.8	25.6	22.6
finance	3004	13	15,649	223	23,400	350	0.5	0.01	1.1	0.1	1.2	0.1	0.4	1.4	1.5
Service	58,351	85,577	142,004	171,213	205,700	257,517	8.8	55.8	9.7	43.6	10.4	48.7	59.5	54.7	55.6
Clerical	45,323	11,767	124,819	88,664	121,700	114,192	6.8	7.7	8.5	22.6	6.2	21.6	20.6	41.5	48.4
Laborers & unspecified	107,788	710	294,918	439	407,800	11,620	16.2	0.5	20.1	0.1	20.6	2.2	0.7	0.2	2.8

Source Altman and Lamontagne (1996)

Table 2b All occupations: income for men and women and pay ratios, 1900–1930

	Earnings per week									*Female–male earnings ratio*		
	1900			*1920*			*1930*					
	Men	*Women*	*Total*	*Men*	*Women*	*Total*	*Men*	*Women*	*Total*	*1900*	*1920*	*1930*
All occupations	$8.40	$3.80	$7.50	$22.80	$11.90	$20.50	$22.60	$12.00	$20.30	45.80%	52.20%	53.20%
Agriculture	$4.70	$3.60	$4.70	$11.40	$9.20	$11.40	$7.50	$5.30	$7.50	76.20%	81.20%	70.30%
Fishing & logging	$7.10		$7.10	$16.50		$16.50	$13.00	$5.20	$13.00			40.40%
Mining	$8.40	$3.80	$7.50	$25.00		$25.00	$23.70	$57.10	$23.80			240.20%
manufacturing	$11.70		$11.70	$25.60	$11.10	$22.20	$25.60	$11.20	$22.80	48.60%	43.50%	43.70%
Electrical, light & power	$8.50	$4.10	$7.50	$24.70		$24.70	$27.20	$70.50	$27.20			258.80%
Construction	$9.00	$5.40	$9.00	$27.00	$13.80	$25.90	$24.20	$12.70	$24.20	60.40%		52.70%
transportation	$10.40	$4.50	$9.90	$27.20	$12.30	$23.40	$25.00	$14.40	$24.30	43.40%	51.00%	57.40%
Trade	$10.20	$5.00	$10.10	$44.20	$19.70	$43.80	$28.90	$12.10	$25.10	48.90%	45.10%	41.70%
Finance	$22.60	$9.20	$22.60	$25.50	$9.90	$16.90	$49.80	$25.90	$49.50	40.80%	44.60%	52.10%
Service	$9.60	$3.40	$5.90	$25.20	$15.80	$21.30	$29.80	$9.80	$18.70	35.40%	38.70%	33.00%
Clerical	$9.80	$5.20	$8.90	$17.60	$8.30	$17.60	$24.40	$17.30	$20.90	53.50%	62.90%	70.80%
Laborers & unspecified	$5.90	$3.90	$5.80	$24.70		$24.70	$14.80	$9.30	$14.60	66.10%	47.40%	62.90%

Sources and notes Census and Statistics (1907), Table 2. The census material for 1900 is reorganized to be consistent with the occupational classification of 1920. The Census of Canada (1935), Table 16 is used for the 1920 and Table 28 is used for the 1930. Since 1900 income data are available only on a per month basis, they are converted to weekly basis so as to be consistent with the data for 1920 and 1930. This table is based Table 4, Altman and Lamontagne (1996)

Table 3 Per annum growth of employment

	1900 to 1920		*1920–1930*		*1900–1930*	
	Men (%)	*Women (%)*	*Men (%)*	*Women (%)*	*Men (%)*	*Women (%)*
All occupations	4.00	4.80	3.00	3.00	3.70	4.20
Agriculture	3.50	10.60	2.80	8.40	3.30	9.90
Fishing & logging	3.00		1.60		2.50	
Mining	3.20		6.20		4.20	
Manufacturing	2.10	2.20	1.70	−0.40	1.90	1.30
Electrical, light & power						
Construction	3.80		3.10		3.60	10.90
Transportation	6.40	5.90	2.80	1.20	5.20	4.30
Trade	3.70	20.10	4.50	2.80	4.00	14.00
Finance	8.60	15.30	4.10	4.60	7.10	11.60
Service	4.50	3.50	3.80	4.20	4.30	3.70
Clerical	5.20	10.60	−0.30	2.60	3.30	7.90
Laborers & unspecified	5.20	−2.40	3.30	38.80	4.50	9.80

Source Altman and Lamontagne (1996)

Table 4 Urbanisation of the Canadian population

				Population growth		
	Total population	*Urban population*	*% of population urban*	*Years*	*Total*	*Urban*
1871	3,689,257	722,343	19.6	1871–1901	1.46	2.79
1881	4,324,810	1,109,507	25.7	1901–1931	1.93	2.77
1891	4,833,239	1,537,098	31.8			
1901	5,371,315	2,014,222	37.5			
1911	7,206,643	3,272,947	45.4			
1921	8,787,949	4,352,122	49.5			
1931	10,376,786	5,572,058	53.7			
1941	11,506,655	6,252,416	54.3			

Source Derived from Leacy (1999), Series A67–69

1900 to 1929, when the Great Depression struck the Canadian economy hard, as it did other market economies with varying degrees of severity (Altman, 1987, 1992, 1994, 2001a). Nevertheless, the rapid growth and growing importance of clerical work that took place over the 1900–1930 period was not a product of rapid economic growth, although this growth might very well have greased the wheels of the structural changes in employment. There is a consensus amongst scholars that the dramatic changes in the manner in which production was taking place over this period was largely responsible for the growing importance of clerical work both to the economy and to female employment in North America.

The period within which clerical work came into its own coincided with the rise of the large corporation and managerial capitalism in both Canada and the United States. Alfred Chandler (1977, 1980, 1990) provides detailed analyses of this important economic phenomenon and its implications for the structure of the firm and the employment opportunities it afforded, especially in the United States (see also Daems 1980 and Lamontagne 2001). The large corporation and the large administrative structure required for its efficacious functioning became significant organizational forms amongst the relatively developed market economies, including Canada, Great Britain, and Germany (Amatori et al. 1997; Chandler and Daems 1980; Lowe 1987, ch. 2). The traditional firm was relatively small in terms of the number of employees, requiring few individuals to manage, coordinate, and monitor the firm's economic activities. The larger firm, by necessity, substituted the visible hand of administration for many of these activities that were previously performed by the invisible hand of the market. The administrative needs of the new corporate form gave rise to the spectacular increase in the demand for clerical workers in the 1900–1930 period. Clerical workers and the corporate office of which they were part became indispensable components of the large corporation, as vital to its function as the traditional worker. As Strom (1992, p. 2) argues, the office provided services that were, "...indispensable to the managing of government, the dispensing of public utilities, the distribution of retail commodities, the production of manufactured goods, the exchange of money and the insuring of property and life. Its organizational form was increasingly hierarchical and bureaucratic. Its purpose was to integrate and facilitate the management of government and business through efficiency, accountability, and precise recordkeeping." Moreover, writes Strom (1992, p. 3): "...without an expanded army of clerks, managers, and business professionals, modern economic and government organization would have been impossible, and ...an office hierarchy based on class and gender produced the paperwork, bookkeeping, and managerial expertise that propelled the machinery of scientific management and the integration of economic functions." (See also Fine 1990; DeVault 1990; Lowe 1987).

A necessary condition for the surge in the demand for clerical workers was the development of the larger firm. Only the larger firm encountered the complexity of administrative tasks that required a large number of clerical workers and only such a large plant could afford to hire a large number of clerical workers. A growing government administration would only add to this demand. One measure of evidence for the larger firm, was increasing plant size in Canadian manufacturing. Average plant size definitely increased from 1900 to 1930 from 30 to 55 workers. Moreover, by the 1920s over 70% of all workers were employed by firms with more than 49 workers. And, by 1930, over one quarter of all workers were employed by firms with more than 499 workers. Although small plants were in the majority even by 1930, they employed no more than 6% of all workers in the 1920s (Table 5). Additional evidence for increasing firm size is the large number of mergers which took place in Canadian manufacturing during the 1900–1930 period, most of which transpired

Table 5 Plant size in the Canadian manufacturing economy

	Average plant size of >5 workers	*% of workers employed by >5 plants*	*% all plants employing >5 workers*	*% of workers employed by 50–99 plants*	*% of workers employed by 100–199 plants*	*% of workers employed by 200–499 plants*	*% of workers employed by >499 plants*	*% of workers employed by >49 workers*
1900	30							
1910	40							
1922	58	94.3	33.6	14.7	15.5	22.4	19.9	72.4
1925	53.6	95.5	44.8	13.5	15.4	20	23.8	72.7
1930	54.8	96.3	47.5	13.3	15.8	19.2	25.7	74
1936	52.6	95.5	44.6	12.3	15.5	21.3	24.4	73.4
1940	58.9	95.8	48.6	11.4	13.9	20.6	30.2	76.1
1945	67.2	97.3	55.7	10.4	12.2	17.3	39.9	79.8
1950	59.8	97.1	53.5	11.3	13.2	18.3	33.4	76.2

Sources and notes Derived from Altman (1994) and Leacy (1999), Series R812–825

in the 1910s and 1920s. Over 60% of all merger activity in the 1896–1918 period took place from 1909 to 1913, just prior to the outbreak of the First World War. The mergers taking place in the 1920s were even more extensive than those of the 1909–1913 period (Marchildon 1996, Appendix; Weldon 1966). In addition, mergers were taking place in other sectors of the Canadian economy (Weldon 1966). As Lowe (1987, p. 31) writes: "The banking industry grew in leaps and bounds after 1900, yet between 1916 and 1925 the number of banks fell from 30 to 11. Telephones and other key utilities came under the control of giant monopolies such as Bell Telephone Company. And the two national railways emerged as Canada's largest employers: the combined workforces of Canadian National and Canadian Pacific numbered a staggering 129,000 in June 1931." Certainly, firms in Canada were developing in a fashion conducive to and consistent with the employment of large numbers of clerical workers.

In addition to the rise of the larger and more complex firm, government employment increased at a fast clip in the first decades of the twentieth century, as government required a larger more complex organizational form, which included clerical workers, to cope with the increasing demands made upon it by the economy. Between 1911 and 1931 government employment increased by 50%. But while government employment of men increased by about 40%, its employment of women almost quadrupled. Still, government's contribution to female employment was not large even by 1931 when it contributed about 2% to the total increasing from 1% in 1911. However, women's share of government employment increased from 5% in 1911 to 13% in 1931. Moreover, although government's contribution to female employment was well under the economy average in 1911, only 40% of what it was in the economy at large, this percentage increased to almost 80% by 1931. Most importantly government employment contributed about 10% to the total pool of female clerical workers and women's share of government clerical work increased from 11 to 38% from 1911 to 1931. Over this period, government's contribution to male clerical employment collapsed from 34 to 15% (Table 6). Clearly, women's employment opportunities in the rapidly growing government sector were improving. A good many of these opportunities, but certainly not all, were in clerical work, affording more opportunities to women interested in pursuing a career in this occupation.

Table 6 Government and clerical workers, 1911–1971

			Government workers				*Government clerical workers*			*All clerical workers*	
	Government F share/Total F share	*Government F/Total F all occupations*	*Males*	*Females*	*M + F*	*F/Total*	*Males*	*Females*	*F/Total*	*F/Total*	*Government F/Total clerical F*
1911	0.388	1.1	74,157	4086	78,243	5.2	34.1	9	11.4	32.6	34.9
1921	0.835	2.6	84,991	12,583	97,574	12.9	21.4	13.2	30.4	41.5	73.2
1931	0.783	2.3	101,303	15,514	116,817	13.3	14.6	10.7	37.6	48.4	77.7
1941	1.01	3.4	111,634	28,002	139,636	20.1					
1951	0.775	4.7	263,964	54,320	318,284	17.1					
1961	0.671	5.5	432,788	97,180	529,968	18.3					
1971	0.739	6.1	529,665	180,045	709,710	25.4					

Sources Derived from Leacy (1999), Series D8–85 and Table 2 above. The estimates for government clerical workers are derived from Lowe (1987), Table A1

3 What Is Clerical Work

The feminization of clerical work is often associated with the deskilling of this occupation with all of the negative social and economic connotations reflected by such a designation. Specifically, references are made to the type of clerical work associated with the employment of female clerical workers, the relatively low wages paid to female clerical workers, as well as to the relative fall in the wages of male clerical workers over time. Why then would women actually seek employment in such an off-putting occupation? It is important to note that even prior to the surge during the administrative revolution of the early twentieth century clerical workers consisted of employees of various levels of skill types. And Strom (1992, p. 175) concludes: "Many of [the] early clerical jobs [of the nineteenth century] were tedious and repetitive; ledger clerks entered figures and did elementary arithmetic, copyists copied documents all day long. Wages were rarely high enough to put clerks into the middle class. Even job security was out of reach." (See also Attewell, 1987, 1989). But in this early period, when the division of labor amongst clerical workers was not yet dominant and manifest, in many firms clerical workers performed both the managerial and the less skilled clerical tasks. A good number of these composite type clerical positions were filled by men. With the advent of the administrative revolution a division of labor increasingly took place, especially in the larger firms, such that the managerial tasks were separated from the less skilled clerical work (Attewell 1989, pp. 364–365; Diprete 1988). This division of labor did not deskill clerical work. Rather, it created new job opportunities for both women and men at lower levels of skill and responsibility compared to what was required of the manager-supervisor-clerk. And women tended to occupy the lower rungs of the clerical job ladder, often for discriminatory reasons, albeit significant opportunities for upward mobility existed up these steps of the job hierarchy. This included jobs at the supervisory level. By the 1920s clerical workers encompassed general clerks, typists, dictating machine transcribers, stenographers, bookkeepers, computing, billing, and related machine operators, file clerks, secretaries, supervisors, check proofers, card punchers, telephone operators, mail order clerks, cashiers and tellers, correspondents, and messengers (Strom 1992, p. 210). Many of these job types either did not exist or were a rarity in late nineteenth and early twentieth century. For this reason Strom (1992, p. 212) could argue that: "Women did not take over or de-skill men's jobs so much as they took jobs created by the revolution in new methods of communicating, cost accounting, and record keeping." Moreover, the increasing mechanization of clerical work often required higher levels or different sets of skills than what was required by the old set of lower level clerical jobs (Strom 1992, pp. 184–186; Attewell 1989, p. 378).[8]

The clerical jobs that women sought out were, therefore, new job types that were classified as clerical work, not dummied-down versions of what were male clerical jobs. Indeed, given the job market constraints faced by women, Strom (1992, p. 10) argues: "Office jobs were the best jobs available to most women between 1900 and 1930. Women understood this and made rational choices for the future by investing in commercial education and taking office jobs…Office work, despite its gendered limits, could open the door to a wider world. Even though many women languished in boring jobs from which they longed to be freed, they also experimented with downtown amusements, pursued friendships and flirtations, and sought more education. Many others did what they considered to be worthwhile and inventive work, experimented with careers, and moved on to more expansive horizons." With regards to the pay secured by women in the United States Strom (1992, p. 206) finds: "Clerical work had a wide range of salaries, with the possibility of making more money as time went by. Except for the lowest ranks of machine work, filing and typing, clerical work generally paid more money to women than all but the professional occupations. On average, women office workers consistently earned more than other women workers outside the professions, and clerical workers continued to make larger gains in salaries in the twenties than did their nearest counterparts, saleswomen. Unlike many other kinds of women's work—especially in manufacturing or domestic service—years of experience in clerical work did usually lead to somewhat higher salaries and promotions to better positions."

Writing in a similar vein, Rapone (1983, 13) argues that in the United States in the first three decades of the twentieth century, "Women moved so rapidly into clerical work because it offered them more occupational opportunity than they had ever had. Clerical work was better than other jobs for women in terms of wages, working conditions, and status. Furthermore, clerical employment offered two channels for mobility—up through the clerical ranks and as the entrée into nonclerical careers" Clerical work, Rapone adds, also often provided women with more benefits such as paid holidays, vacation and sick leave as well as a shorter work week than could be found in other occupations. Drawing upon her research on the burgeoning economy of Chicago of the pre-Depression era, Fine (1990, p. 42) comes to a similar conclusion, finding that clerical work, be it as bookkeeper, cashier, accountant, clerk and copyist, or stenographer-typists, offered women of different backgrounds, age cohorts, and needs, good job opportunities: "In terms of the hours, wages, and conditions of work, a clerical position was one of the best occupational opportunities for women at that time." It is important to note that clerical work became an attractive option for women, even when compared to teaching since it required less training, but also because pay and benefits were often competitive, stress levels were lower (in part due to less attention being paid to the personal lives and lifestyles of clerical workers) and women could much more easily continue employment after marriage. Unlike teaching no marriage ban existed. Given these conditions, there was even significant mobility from teaching to clerical work (Fine 1990, pp. 44–45; Strom 1992, pp. 331–336). These basic findings are affirmed by Posadas (1997) in her survey of the literature on clerical work in the United States.

Thus the various jobs that comprised clerical work, as it evolved from the 1890s to the 1930s, were jobs that women regarded as attractive given the other opportunities afforded to them, as long as they were able to attain, at a minimum, entry-level skills required for the job. These were not jobs that women were being pushed into. Rather they were job opportunities which women actively sought. To be sure, women were relatively constrained as to where they could seek employment. But these constraints were being substantially relaxed from the late nineteenth century to the 1930s. The rapid employment growth in both Canada and the United States, with the expansion of clerical work playing an important and special role, dramatically widened the scope of choice afforded to women who sought market employment. And, as we shall see below, in Canada, as was also true in the United States, the relative income benefits of clerical work was an important reason for clerical work being such a forceful draw to female job seekers.

4 Clerical Work and Income

Of the three most important occupational sectors to women, only in clerical work did the gender pay ratio move in favor of women, increasing from 53% in 1900 to 63% in 1920 to 71% in 1930. In the all-important service sector, the pay ratio, which was already quite low in 1900, at 35%, fell to 33% by 1930. A key factor explaining the poor pay ratio in this occupation was women's concentration in private domestic work which was characterized by the lowest rate of pay and the worst pay ratio of any sub-sector in services (Altman and Lamontagne 1996). In trade, the pay ratio moved against women over the entire 1900–1930 period, from 50 to 42%. And in manufacturing, as well, the pay ratio moved against women, from 49 to 44%. The pay ratio, nevertheless, moved in women's favor in the transportation occupational sector, rising from 43 to 57% from 1900 to 1930. However, this occupation only employed 3% of all women by 1930. In other occupations characterized by a small wage gap or a pay ratio in women's favor, few women were employed and those who were, were largely employed in managerial positions (Altman and Lamontagne 1996). In fact the only occupation employing significant numbers of women that could have positively affected the gender pay ratio over time was clerical work (Table 2b).

The importance of clerical work in motivating improvements in the overall pay ratio was not simply that it experienced a dramatic drop in its own gender pay gap. Rather, throughout the period under examination, women's pay rate for clerical work was significantly above the average pay rate for women in all occupations: 34% more in 1900 and 44% more by 1930. If the relative pay rate for women in this sector had been low, significant improvements in the pay ratio in clerical work would have had little impact on the overall occupational pay ratio. Moreover, a female clerical worker earned well above what was earned by the relatively unskilled laborer throughout the 1900–1930 period. The same is true for male clerical workers. However, during this time, the pay of male clerical workers fell from 17 to 8% above the average for all occupations. Needless to say, the above average pay that could be secured in clerical work made it an attractive occupation for both women and men, especially for women. In the trade sector, women earned 30% more than average in 1900. However, this relative rate of pay fell to the average by 1930. In transportation, women also earned an above average rate of pay. But this occupation employed, at its height in 1920, no more than 4% of all women. Similarly, in those other occupations where the female pay rate was above average, only a handful of women were employed. In service, where so many women found employment, not only did the female relative pay rate deteriorate over time, throughout the 1900–1930 time-frame women earned a below average pay rate in this occupation. In manufacturing as well, women earned a below average rate of pay (Table 7).

The relative significance of the female pay rate in the clerical sector is further highlighted when the occupational pay rates are ranked, especially for those occupations providing employment to more than a handful of women (Table 8). For the entire 1900–1930 period, clerical work's female pay rate was first amongst female pay rates. In fact, female clerical workers earned more than men employed in agriculture, fishing and logging, and men employed as general laborers, which encompassed between 31 and 33% of all male employees from 1900 to 1930. No more than 2% of women were employed in these occupations (Table 2a). Thus, female clerical workers, fared better than male workers, even in occupations where women were largely absent. Even if women could gain more access to these occupations, if this is what they actually desired, and even

Table 7 Sector income relatives, 1900–1930

	1900			*1920*			*1930*		
	Men	*Women*	*Total*	*Men*	*Women*	*Total*	*Men*	*Women*	*Total*
All occupations	1	1	1	1	1	1	1	1	1
Agriculture	0.56	0.94	0.63	0.5	0.78	0.56	0.33	0.44	0.37
Fishing & logging	0.85		0.95	0.72		0.81	0.58	0.44	0.64
Mining	1.39		1.55	1.1		1.22	1.05	4.75	1.17
Manufacturing	1.01	1.08	1	1.12	0.94	1.09	1.13	0.93	1.12
Electrical light & Power	1.07						1.21	5.87	1.34
Construction	1.24	1.42	1.19	1.08	0	1.21	1.07	1.06	1.19
Transportation	1.22	1.17	1.31	1.19	1.16	1.27	1.11	1.2	1.19
Trade	2.7	1.3	1.34	1.19	1.03	1.14	1.28	1	1.24
Finance	1.15	2.41	3	1.94	1.66	2.14	2.21	2.16	2.43
Service	1.17	0.89	0.79	1.12	0.83	0.83	1.32	0.82	0.92
Clerical	0.7	1.37	1.18	1.11	1.34	1.04	1.08	1.44	1.03
Laborers & unspecified	1.07	1.01	0.78	0.77	0.7	0.86	0.65	0.77	0.72
Clerical to laborers	1.67	1.36	1.52	1.43	1.9	1.21	1.65	1.86	1.43
Clerical to service	1.02	1.54	1.5	0.99	1.61	1.26	0.82	1.76	1.12

Source Table 2a

Table 8 Rankings of sector income relatives, 1900–1930

	All occupations									*Significant female occupations*					
	1900			*1920*			*1930*			*1900*		*1920*		*1930*	
	Men	*Women*	*Total*	*Men*	*Women*	*Total*	*Men*	*Women*	*Total*	*Men*	*Women*	*Men*	*Women*	*Men*	*Women*
Agriculture	11	8	10	11	7	11	12	11	12						
Fishing & logging	9		11	10		10	11	12	11						
Mining	2		9	7		3	9	2	6						
Manufacturing	8	6	6	4	5	6	5	8	7	5	4	3	4	3	4
Electrical light & power	7			12		12	4	1	2						
Construction	3	2	4	8	9	4	8	6	5						
Transportation	4	5	3	3	3	2	6	5	4	1	3	2	2	4	2
Trade	1	4	2	2	4	5	3	7	3	2	2	1	3	2	3
Finance	6	1	1	1	1	1	1	3	1						
Service	5	9	7	5	6	9	2	9	9	4	6	4	5	1	5
Clerical	10	3	5	6	2	7	7	4	8	3	1	5	1	5	1
Laborers & unspecified	7	7	8	9	8	8	10	10	10	6	5	6	6	6	6

Source Table 7

if women were paid the same as their male counterparts in these occupations, women would still, on average, be better off in clerical work. By way of contrast, clerical work's male pay rate ranked relatively low amongst male pay rates throughout the 1900–1930 period. The transportation and trade occupational sector's female pay rates followed the clerical pay rate in rank. Manufacturing's female pay rate ranked fourth, followed by services and general labor. The latter sector provided employment to, at most, 2% of all women.

5 Clerical Work and Pay Inequality

What exactly was the contribution of the feminization of clerical work to the reduction of gender pay inequality? To answer this question, we must determine what the overall pay ratio would have been had women's contribution to clerical work been identical to men's in 1920 and 1930 (Altman and Lamontagne 1996). Women employed outside of the clerical occupational sector are assumed to earn the average overall rate of pay net of the contribution of clerical work's pay rate to this average. In 1920, the hypothetical overall female pay rate is \$11.11 per week compared the actual pay rate of \$11.87. This generates a hypothetical gender pay ratio of 0.49 compared to the actual pay ratio of 0.52. The defeminization of clerical work in 1920 would have reduced the pay ratio. Since the pay ratio increased from 0.46 to 0.52 from 1900 to 1920, the increasing importance of clerical work to female employed contributed 53% of the improvement in the pay ratio. For 1930, the hypothetical female pay rate is \$10.91 per week in contrast to the actual pay rate of \$12.01. Here too, the defeminization of clerical work would have reduced the overall female pay rate. The hypothetical pay estimate for women generates a hypothetical pay ratio of 0.50 compared to the actual pay ratio for 1930 of 0.53. For this reason, the feminization of clerical work contributed about 50% of the increase in the gender pay ratio from 1900 to 1930. Were it not for the influx of women into clerical work which, however, contributed to labor market segmentation, the improvement of women's rate of pay in the first three decades of the twentieth century would have been much less than it actually was since the feminization of clerical work contributed so importantly to whatever gains made by women with regards to gender pay equality. Clearly, clerical work did not represent a low wage ghetto for women which served to depress the overall female pay rate. Moreover, as we have already discussed, there were good reasons for women to prefer clerical work over other occupations. Contrary to the predictions of labor market segmentation theory, the feminization of an occupation need not negatively impact the rate of pay in feminized occupations. Rather, the negative consequences associated with 'ghettoization' can be expected to transpire if women are being coerced into a particular occupation which is either low wage from the get go, or becomes low wage as a result of the process of 'ghettoization'. This definitely was not the case with clerical work in early twentieth century Canada.

The different labor market scenarios portrayed in Table 9 serves to clarify some of these points. In Scenario I, consistent with the traditional labor market segmentation hypothesis, we have a low wage sector that is feminized and a high wage sector employing only men, with women having no capacity to switch sectors, for legal or extra legal reasons. If labor markets are integrated men and women would be employed in both sectors and they would be compensated at the same rate of pay within each sector. Moreover, there would be no restrictions on labor mobility. In this scenario, labor market segmentation yields a lower rate of pay since the feminized sector is the low wage sector and women are devoid of any capacity to search out the most favorable employment opportunities. In Scenario II, in both sectors women are paid less than men. However Sector II remunerates women at a higher rate than does Sector I and the gender pay gap in Sector II is less than in Sector I. Women are segmented into Sector II, the higher paying sector for women. In this scenario, an integrated labor market moves some women to the lower wage (for women) Sector I, resulting in the integrated labor market yielding both a lower average rate of pay for women and increasing the rate of pay inequality. Scenario II fits the reality of the type of labor market segmentation that characterized Canada, as well as the United States, during the first decades of the twentieth century, where women chose, given their acquired skills and related capabilities, to move en masse into clerical work, the occupation with relatively high rates of pay and other pecuniary and non-pecuniary benefits. In this scenario, labor market segmentation is not a product of institutional coercion, but rather of women making the best of the opportunities available to them.

Given that labor market segmentation did take place in Canada, the feminization and overcrowding hypothesis predicts that the female pay rate should have fallen relative to the male pay rate in the feminized sector. This obviously did not occur as the female clerical pay rate was catching-up to the male (Table 2b). To underline this point, it is useful to

Table 9 Segmentation scenarios

	Male	*Female*
	1000 Sector I (Male)	1000 Sector II (Female)
Scenario I		
Wage M	5	2.5
Wage F	5	2.5
M	1000	0
F	0	500
Avg M W all sectors	5	
Avg F W all sectors	2.5	
Avg F/M	0.5	
Zero segmentation		
Wage M	5	2.5
Wage F	5	2.5
M	500	500
F	250	250
Avg M W all sectors	3.75	
Avg F W all sectors	3.75	
Avg F/M	1	
SCENARIO II		
Segmentation		
Wage M	5	5
Wage F	2.5	3.5
M	1000	0
F	0	500
Avg M W all sectors	5	
Avg F W all sectors	3.5	
Avg F/M	0.7	
Zero segmentation		
Wage M	5	5
Wage F	2.5	3.5
M	500	500
F	250	250

(continued)

Table 9 (continued)

	Male	*Female*
Avg M W all sectors	5	
Avg F W all sectors	3	
Avg F/M	0.6	

examine the growth in the nominal pay rates for men and women (Table 10). During the 1900–1930 period, the annual growth in the overall pay rate was greater for women than for men: 3.9 compared to 3.4%. Most of this growth took place in the 1900–1920 period. In fact, during the 1920s, the annual growth in the overall pay rate was slightly negative for men and marginally positive for women. In the 1900–1930 time-frame the growth rate for the female clerical pay rate (4%) also exceeded that for men (3.1%), and it did so in the 1900–1920 and 1920s sub-periods. At 4% it was also the fastest earnings growth rate for all occupations for both men and women. Moreover, in the 1920s, when the rate of growth of the female clerical work pay rate remained positive, the rate of growth of the male clerical work pay rate turned negative. The feminization of clerical work obviously did not have the effect of either depressing the rate of growth of the pay rate for female clerical workers, or of this pay rate relative to that for male clerical workers. In this sense, the increasing demand for female clerical workers was not a product of the cheapening of female clerical workers relative to that of male clerical workers. Indeed, women's successive and significant employment gains in this occupation took place in the context of the increasingly relative expensive nature of female clerical labor. Moreover, the relative increase in female clerical workers' pay rate did not price women out of the market even on the margin. At this point it is important to note that increasing pay rates do not necessarily translate into more costly labor nor need they translate into relatively more expensive labor. The costliness of labor is not simply a product of the wage rate. It also critically depends upon the productivity of labor. Increasing the price of labor does not make it more costly if matched by higher productivity, nor does lower priced labor translate into less costly labor if the lower wages are matched by lower productivity (Altman 1995, 2001b). Thus, that women are paid less than men does not prove that they are cheap labor. Nor does an increase in the relative price of female labor prove that women are becoming a relatively more expensive input into the production process. At this point more research is required to address the important empirical question as to the relative productivity difference between female and male labor both between and within occupational categories.

How was it, then, that the pay rate for female clerical workers did not collapse relative to the male clerical workers' pay rate or relative to the female average pay rate, in the face of the feminization of clerical work and the massive relative increase in the number women in this occupation over time? Even when unions and unionization are unimportant, as they were at this time, in the clerical sector, in terms of simple supply and demand analysis, there is no need for the relative female pay rate in any sector or occupation to decline even in face of a surge in the supply of women to a particular sector or occupation relative to others. Much depends on what happens on the demand side. In other words, economists would predict that if the supply of labor increases in a particular sector relative to others, such as occurred with respect to female clerical work, wages should fall, all other things remaining the same. However, if the demand for this labor increases relative to supply, wages need not fall and they might even rise.

Table 10 Per annum growth of income

	1900		*1920*		*1930*	
	Men (%)	*Women (%)*	*Men (%)*	*Women (%)*	*Men (%)*	*Women (%)*
All occupations	5.10	5.80	−0.10	0.10	3.40	3.90
Agriculture	4.50	4.80	−4.10	−5.50	1.60	1.30
Fishing & logging	4.30		−2.30		2.00	
Mining	3.90	5.10	−0.50	0.10	2.40	3.40
Manufacturing	5.70		0.01		3.80	
Construction	5.20		−0.20		3.40	2.90
Transportation	4.90	5.80	−0.80	0.40	3.00	3.90
Trade	5.00	4.60	0.60	−0.20	3.50	3.00
Finance	3.40	3.90	1.20	2.80	2.70	3.50
Service	5.00	5.50	1.60	−0.02	3.80	3.60
Clerical	4.80	5.70	−0.30	0.90	3.10	4.00
Laborers & unspecified	5.70	3.90	−1.70	1.10	3.10	3.00

Source Table 2b

It is impossible to identify and separate out the particular forces at work on the demand and supply side of clerical work in Canada from 1900 to 1930. Estimates for employment growth in the various occupations are available however (Table 3). It is clear from these estimates that employment grew at a faster pace for women than for men in the 1900–1930 time-frame, 4.2% compared to 3.7% percent per annum, and this coincided with the female pay rate growing at a faster pace than the male pay rate. This differential in gender specific employment growth took place just about entirely in the 1900–1920 period. In this period, the growth of female clerical employment, at 10.6%, was respectable, more than double the growth of male clerical employment. The growth of female clerical employment was also the strongest as compared to any of the occupations where female employment was important except for trade whose employment growth rate (20%) for women easily beat out the growth rate for women and men in all occupations in the 1900–1920 period.

At a more general level, the 1900–1930 period was marked by significant population growth that was fueled by large-scale immigration (Table 11). Canada's population grew by 3% in the first decade of the twentieth century, 2% in the 1910s, and 1.7% in the 1920s. Moreover, the composition of the waves of immigration did not change in a manner that might have reduced the potential supply of labor for clerical work. Most immigrants were English-speaking so that the English-speaking and Canadian-born component of Canada's population remained in excess of the 90% range throughout this period. For this reason, the supply of individuals capable of more easily becoming clerical workers did not grow at a slower pace than did the overall potential supply of labor.[9] These high population growth rates, however, were consistently less than the growth in the demand for labor, especially female labor and, in particular, the demand for female clerical workers (Table 3).

To the extent that population growth represents the potential supply of labor and employment growth represents the demand, the overall growth in the demand for labor exceeded increases in supply throughout the first three decades of the twentieth century. Moreover, the employment growth estimates in conjunction with the estimates on relative pay rates suggest that demand for female clerical workers was consistently strong enough to keep the relative pay rate for female clerical workers from diminishing. Even a persistent flood of women into a particular occupation cannot drive down the female pay rate if demand is sufficiently strong. Overall, the evidence suggests that the particular constellation of

Table 11 Canadian population and immigration ('000)

	Population	*Canadian born*	*English-speaking immigrant*	*Can/Pop*	*Can & Eng Pop*	*English speaking immigrants/Pop*		*Annual growth rates*	
								Population	*Canadian born*
1871	3689	3064		0.83					
1881	4325	3722		0.86			1871–81	1.60%	1.96%
1891	4833	4189		0.87			1881–91	1.12%	1.19%
1901	5371	4672		0.87			1891–1901	1.06%	1.10%
1911	7207	5620	1056	0.78	0.93	0.67	1901–11	2.98%	1.86%
1921	8788	6832	1396	0.78	0.94	0.71	1911–21	2.00%	1.97%
1931	10,377	8069	1407	0.78	0.91	0.61	1921–31	1.68%	1.68%

Source and notes Derived from the data contained in Department of Citizenship and Immigration (1951) and Immigration Statistics (1992: Table G1). English-speaking immigrants consist of Americans and British nationals. The number of immigrants estimated for 1911, 1921, and 1931 are for the 1901–1911, 1911–1921, and 1921–1931 periods, respectively

market forces which characterized the first three decades of the twentieth century favored female as opposed to male clerical workers and female clerical workers as opposed to women employed in other occupations which were of importance to the female labor force. This being said, the material incentives for women to opt for clerical work did not dissipate throughout the 1900–1930 period.

6 Conclusion

From 1900 to 1930, women were increasingly important to clerical work and clerical work became of increasing importance to female employment in Canada. During this period, however, the gender pay gap between women and men in clerical work persistently narrowed and the female pay rate in this occupation remained the highest of all occupations where the employment of women was at all important. Clearly, not only did the clerical sector never become a low wage ghetto for women in the pre-Depression period, the feminization of clerical work also contributed significantly to the reduction of the gender pay gap which took place over the 1900–1930 period. In this case, the very forces that contributed to labor market segmentation improved women's position in the labor market as women chose to seek employment in clerical work, which provided them with benefits and opportunities not often provided in other occupations.

The fact that the feminization of clerical work played a large role in reducing the gender pay gap does not recommend labor market segmentation as a policy prescription for improving the female relative to the male rate of pay. Rather, on a microeconomic level, qualified women can be expected to take advantage of market opportunities available to them, even if this has the macroeconomic effect of increasing or preventing a reduction in labor market segmentation. Of course, such behavior can only take place within an institutional framework where women have significant freedoms to seek employment opportunities. Such a framework was already in place in Canada by the late nineteenth century, although it is also true that the freedoms afforded to women still did not approach those afforded to men.[10] The fact that between occupations labor market segmentation did not negatively impact upon gender pay inequality does not at all suggest that labor market discrimination did not exist in Canada at this time. For example, women had a more difficult time than men in securing employment in particular occupations and this no doubt negatively affected the gender pay gap. In other words, had women had freedom to secure employment in a wider array of occupations, gender pay inequality might have been less than it was in Canada in the first decades of the twentieth century. Moreover, most of the gender pay gap was a product of within occupations pay inequality, irrespective of whether an occupation was dominated by men or women. Such gender pay inequality can be a product of labor market discrimination and also of discrimination within the household wherein women are socialized into engaging in less productive occupations than men, where pay inequality based upon the latter type of social discrimination can persist even in a world of zero labor market discrimination. Moreover, pay inequality can be a product of women having less bargaining power than men. Thus, even where there exists zero labor market and off-market discrimination, women can be paid less than men if, for example, they are less unionized than men.[11]

To reiterate, such gender pay inequality has nothing to do with labor market segmentation and even when labor market segmentation does not contribute to pay inequality these other factors are possible causes of such inequality. This being said, given the constraints which they faced, qualified women took advantage of opportunities afforded to them by clerical work, resulting in many women earning more than many men engaged in other occupations. On the macroeconomic level, demand was strong enough to keep women's relative rate of pay from falling. What the results of this study suggest is that labor market segmentation, per se, when it is largely a product of the constrained choices made by women and men on the labor market, cannot be taken as evidence of a relatively poor market position with respect to women just as a relatively integrated labor market should not be taken as evidence of the absence of discrimination or a superior market position on the part of women as compared to when labor markets are relatively segmented. Labor market segmentation is not the be all and end all of a discourse on the existence and determinants of labor market discrimination and its correlates. Had feminization of clerical work been somehow prevented, it seems likely that this would have reduced the material level of well-being of a considerable number Canadian female workers in the pre-Depression years.

Notes

1. The role that labor market segmentation or ghettoization plays in causing gender pay inequality remains a subject of considerable theoretical and empirical debate amongst scholars. One school of thought holds that labor market segmentation, the differential distribution of female and male labor between sectors and occupations, contributes significantly to gender pay inequality. This assumes that women are forced into particular occupations causing overcrowding. In other words, supply increases relative to demand, forcing female wages down relative to male wages. Women are thereby forced into low-wage female ghettos. Men, on the other hand, are employed in the relatively high wage occupations and sectors of the economy. This causal sequence is, for example, central to Barbara Bergmann's (1971, 1986, 1989) influential 'overcrowding hypothesis'. A related but different take on labor market segmentation yielding gender pay inequality is presented by Strober (1984). Becker (1971a, b), on the contrary, argues that although labor market segmentation can result from discrimination, in the long run wages would be equalized across the discriminated and non-discriminated groups of equal productive capabilities, with the non-discriminating employers employing the discriminated individuals. Whether or not wages would be equalized, however, depends on whether the hiring capacity of non-discriminators matches the demand for jobs by the discriminated group. It is interesting to note that Veblen (1899, p. 514) argued, in another context, that institutional arrangements which build upon the unequal power relationship between men and women—he was referring specifically to the institution of marriage—are not compatible with "the exigencies of a peaceful, industrial mode of life" and are "visibly breaking down in modern civilized communities.".
2. See for example, Strong-Boag (1979, pp. 137, 139–140; 1988: pp. 21, 42, 51–53, 56, 65; and Cohen (1988, pp. 24, 26–27, 126, 136–137, 145, 158) and Armstrong and Armstrong (1984). Lowe (1986, pp. 107–122; 1987, pp. 59, 144, 150, 163), in his detailed discussion of the emergence of a female clerical 'ghetto', argues that the growing importance of clerical work to women helped diminish average female wages in Canada and that the clerical sector constituted a low wage ghetto for women. In contrast, discussing the American case, Elyce Rotella (1981) argues that the feminization of clerical work and the growing importance of clerical work to the female labor force was largely a product of technical change, dominated by the development of the typewriter, which required firm-general skills. This generated a dramatic increase in the demand for the already existing "abundant supply of cheap female labor.".
3. The Duncan Index is an estimate of the percentage of men or women who must change their occupation if gender differences in the distribution of

occupations are to be eliminated. It is derived by summing the absolute differences in the percentage gender distribution for each occupation and dividing the total by 2. An index number of 100 indicates complete labor market segmentation.

4. Occupational change contributed 35% to the reduction of gender pay inequality over the 1900–1930 period. The remainder of the reduction in the pay gap was a product of improvement in the female-male pay ratio within the various occupations (Altman and Lamontagne 1996). These results are similar to those for the United States where occupational change explains, statistically, about 28% of the reduction in the pay gap which took place in the 1890/1900–1930 period in the context of little, if any, change in labor market segmentation (Goldin Goldin, 1986, p. 579; 1987, pp. 75–77).
5. See also Rapone (1983). For a discussion of clerical work in Chicago and Pittsburgh respectively, see Fine (1990, ch. 3) and De Vault (1990, chs 1 and 3).
6. These labor force participation rate estimates are based upon Leacy (1999, Series A78–93 and D107–122). These estimates are derived by dividing the estimated population in the labor force (the employed and unemployed) by the population over 14 years of age.
7. Female employment increased by a factor of two while male employment increased by 1.6 times (derived from Carter et al. 1997, Series 11–25).
8. Many of the managerial positions were no longer classified as clerical work as clerical work was transformed in a period of rapid growth clerical jobs. Thus, any calculation of the average clerical wage prior to the administrative revolution might include the wage of the manager-clerk, whereas with the advent of the increasing division of labor the wage of the higher paid clerk might be excluded.
9. Meltz (1965, p. 63) finds that clerical work was easily learnt (in the 1930–1960 period) requiring a few years of high school or secretarial school training. Immigrants who were English speaking could most easily acquire such skills, which would, in turn, generate relatively high rates of pay if clerical work could be found.
10. See Boserup (1987) for a succinct discussion of the evolution of female labor market power and the institutional context of this evolution.
11. See Altman (1995) for a theoretical discussion of the circumstances under which discrimination can persist over time even in a competitive environment. The notion that discrimination can persist over time runs counter to the conventional wisdom based on the work of Gary Becker (1971a, b), where discriminated labor is in effect cheap labor which, in turn, gives the competitive edge to non-discriminating firms which can be expected to eventually drive the wages of all equally skilled workers to equality. The contrary argument presented in Altman suggests that discriminated labor

need not be cheap labor if discriminated women, for example, respond to their unfair treatment by reducing their effort and, thereby, their productivity. In this case, no competitive edge is provided to non-discriminating firms and discrimination can persist for decades on end. On another note, Baker and Fortin (1999) find, using data for the late twentieth century, that an important degree of gender pay inequality that is correlated to labor market segmentation in the United States (where no such correlation exists in the Canadian case) is a product the lower rate of unionization amongst American women. Further to this point, Blau and Kahn (2003), using data for 22 industrialized economies for the 1985–1994 period, find that an important determinant of gender pay inequality is the rate of unionization and other institutional factors which affect the pay rate of the lowest paid workers relative to other pay cohorts. See also Corcoran et al. (1984) on the relative unimportance of labor market segmentation in the United States as an explanatory variable of gender pay inequality.

References

Altman, M. 1987. A Revision of Canadian Economic Growth, 1870–1910: A Critique of the Gradualist Approach. *Canadian Journal of Economics/Revue Canadienne D'économique* 20: 86–113.

Altman, M. 1992. Revised Real GNP Estimates and Canadian Economic Development. *The Review of Income and Wealth Series,* Series 38: 455–473.

Altman, M. 1994. The Evolution of Plant Size in Canadian Manufacturing, 1870–1910. *Canadian Historical Review* 75: 557–585.

Altman, M. 1995. Labor Market Discrimination, Pay Inequality, and Effort Variability: An Alternative to the Neoclassical Model. *Eastern Economic Journal* 21: 157–169.

Altman, M. 2001a. Quantitative Dimensions of Canadian Economics Growth, 1867–1926. In *Canada, Confederation to Present*, ed. R. Macleod. Edmonton: Chinook Multimedia.

Altman, M. 2001b. *Worker Satisfaction and Economic Performance: Micofoundations of Success and Failure.* Armonk, NY: M.E. Sharpe.

Altman, M., and L. Lamontagne. 1996. Gender Pay Inequality and Occupational Change in Canada, 1900–1930. *Journal of Socio-Economics* 25: 285–309.

Amatori, F., A.D. Chandler, and T. Hikino, eds. 1997. *Big Business and the Wealth of Nations.* Cambridge, England: Cambridge University Press.

Armstrong, P., and H. Armstrong. 1984. *The Double Ghetto: Canadian Women and Their Segregated Work*, revised edition. Toronto: McClelland and Stewart.

Attewell, P. 1987. The Deskilling Controversy. *Work and Occupations* 14: 323–346.

Attewell, P. 1989. The Clerk Deskilled: A Study in False Nostalgia. *Journal of Historical Sociology* 2: 356–388.

Baker, M., and N.M. Fortin. 1999. Women's Wages in Women's Work: A US/Canada Comparison on the Role of Unions and 'Public Goods' Sector Jobs. *American Economic Review, Papers and Proceedings* 89: 198–203.

Becker, G.S. 1971a. *The Economics of Discrimination*, first published, 1957. Chicago: University of Chicago Press.

Becker, G.S. 1971b. The Economic Way of Looking at Life. In *Accounting for Tastes*, ed. G.S. Becker, 139–161. Cambridge, MA: Harvard University Press.

Bergmann, B.R. 1971. The Effect on White Incomes of Discrimination in Employment. *Journal of Political Economy* 79: 294–313.

Bergmann, B.R. 1986. *The Economic Emergence of Women*. New York: Basic Books.

Bergmann, B.R. 1989. Does the Market for Women's Labor Need Fixing? *Journal of Economic Perspectives* 3: 43–52.

Boserup, E. 1987. Inequality Between the Sexes. In *The New Palgrave: A Dictionary of Economics*, ed. J. Eatwell, M. Milgate, and P. Newman Vol. 2, E to J, 824–827. London: Macmillan.

Blau, F.D., and L.M. Kahn. 2003. Understanding International Differences in the Gender Pay Gap. *Labor Economics* 21: 106–144.

Carter S.B. et al. 1997. *U.S. Bureau of the Census: Historical Statistics of the United States on CD-ROM, Colonial Times to 1970—Bicentennial Edition*. Cambridge: Cambridge University Press.

Census and Statistics. 1907. *Wage-Earners by Occupation*. Ottawa.

Census of Canada. 1935. *The Census of Canada, 1931*, Vol. 5. Ottawa.

Chandler, A.D. 1977. *The Visible Hand: The Managerial Revolution in American Business*. Cambridge, Mass.: Belknap Press of Harvard University Press.

Chandler, A.D. 1980. The United States: Seedbed of Managerial Capitalism. In *Managerial Hierarchies: Comparative Perspectives on the Rise of the Modern Industrial Enterprise*, ed. A.D. Chandler and H. Daems, 9–40. Cambridge, MA: Harvard University Press.

Chandler, A.D. 1990. *Scale and Scope: The Dynamics of Industrial Capitalism*. Cambridge, MA: Belknap Press of Harvard University Press.

Chandler, A.D. and H. Daems, eds. 1980. *Managerial Hierarchies: Comparative Perspectives on the Rise of the Modern Industrial Enterprise*. Cambridge, MA: Harvard University Press.

Citizenship and Immigration Canada. 1992. *Immigration Statistics*. Ottawa.

Cohen, M.G. 1988. *Work, Markets, Economic Development in Nineteenth-Century Ontario*. Toronto: University of Toronto Press.

Cook, R., and R.C. Brown. 1974. *Canada 1896–1921: A Nation Transformed*. Toronto: McClelland and Stewart.

Corcoran, M., G.J. Duncan and M. Ponza. 1984. Work Experience, Job Segregation, and Wages. In *Sex Segregation in the Work Place: Trends, Explanations, Remedies*, ed. B.F. Reskin, 171–191. Washington, D.C.: National Academy Press.

Daems, H. 1980. The Rise of the Modern Industrial Enterprise: A New Perspective. In *Managerial Hierarchies: Comparative Perspectives on the Rise of the Modern Industrial Enterprise*, ed. A.D. Chandler and H. Daems, 203–223. Cambridge, MA: Harvard University Press.

Department of Citizenship and Immigration. 1951. *Report of the Department of Citizenship and Immigration*. Ottawa: King's Printer.

DeVault, I.A. 1990. *Sons and Daughters of Labor: Class and Clerical Work in Turn-of-the-Century Pittsburgh*. Ithaca, NY and London: Cornell University Press.

Diprete, T.A. 1988. The Upgrading and Downgrading of Occupations: Status Redifinitions vs. Deskilling as Alternative Theories of Change. *Social Forces* 66: 725–746.

Fine, L.M. 1990. *The Souls of the Skyscraper: Female Clerical Workers in Chicago, 1870–1930*. Philadelphia: Temple University Press.

Fortin, N.M., and M. Huberman. 2002. Occupational Gender Segregation and Women's Wages in Canada: An Historical Perspective. *Canadian Public Policy, Supplement* 28: S11–S39.

Goldin, C. 1986. The Female Labor Force and American Economic Growth. In *Long-Term Factors in American Economic Growth*, National Bureau of Economic Research, Studies in Income and Wealth 51, ed. S.L. Engerman and R.E. Gallman, 557–604. Chicago/London: University of Chicago Press.

Goldin, C. 1987. *Understanding the Gender Gap: An Economic History of American Women*. New York/Oxford: Oxford University Press.

Lamontagne, L. 2001. Chandler, Alfred. In *Reader's Guide to the Social Sciences*, ed. J. Michie, 174–175. London: Fitzroy Dearborn Publishers.

Leacy, F.H., ed. 1999. *Historical Statistics of Canada*. Ottawa: Statistics Canada. http://www.statcan.ca:80/english/freepub/11-516-XIE/free.htm.

Lowe, G. 1986. Women, Work and the Office: The Feminization of Clerical Occupations in Canada, 1901–1931. In *Rethinking Canada, The Promise of Women's History*, ed. V. Strong-Boag, A.C. Fellman, 107–122. Toronto: Copp Clark Pitman.

Lowe, G. 1987. *Women in the Administrative Revolution*. Toronto: University of Toronto Press.

Marchildon, G.P. 1996. *Profits and Politics: Beaverbrook and the Gilded Age of Canadian Finance*. Toronto: University of Toronto Press.

Meltz, N.M. 1965. *Changes in the Occupational Composition of the Canadian Labour Force, 1931–1962*, Occasional Paper, no. 2, Department of Labour, Canada. Ottawa: Queen's Printer.

Posadas, B.M. 1997. Crossing the Line: Working Women at Desks, Switchboards, and Tables. *Journal of Urban History* 23: 777–788.

Rapone, A. 1983. Women's Work: Offices and Opportunities. *AHA Perspectives* 21: 13–15.

Rosenfeld, R.A., and A.L. Kalleberg. 1990. A Cross-national Comparison of the Gender Gap in Income. *American Journal of Sociology* 96: 69–106.

Rotella, E.J. 1981. The Transformation of the American Office: Changes in Employment and Technology. *Journal of Economic History* 41: 51–57.

Strober, M.H. 1984. Toward a General Theory of Occupational Segregation: The Case of Public School Teaching. In *Sex Segregation in the Work Place: Trends, Explanations, Remedies,* ed. B.F. Reskin, 144–156. Washington, D.C.: National Academy Press.

Strom, S.H. 1992. *Beyond the Typewriter: Gender, Class, and the Origins of Modern American Office Work, 1900–1930.* Urbana and Chicago: University of Illinois Press.

Strong-Boag, V. 1979. The Girl of the New Day: Canadian Working Women in the 1920s. *Labour/le Travailleur* 4: 131–164.

Strong-Boag, V. 1988. *The New Day Recalled: Lives of Girls and Women in English Canada, 1919–1939.* Toronto: Penguin Books Canada.

Veblen, T. 1899. The Barbarian Status of Women. *American Journal of Sociology* 4: 503–514.

Weldon, J.C. 1966. Mergers: Consolidations in Canadian Industry, 1900–1948. In *Restrictive Trade Practices in Canada,* ed. L.A. Skeoch, 228–279. Toronto/Montreal: McClelland and Stewart.

Index

M. Altman, *Lessons from a Successfully Export-Oriented, Resource-Rich Economy*, https://doi.org/10.1007/978-3-031-03887-7

Kolibri 360 GmbH
Ferdinand-Jühlke-Straße 7
99095 Erfurt, Deutschland
produktsicherheit@kolibri360.de